WASHINGTON

WASHINGTON

———◆———

A History of Our National City

TOM LEWIS

BASIC BOOKS

A MEMBER OF THE PERSEUS BOOKS GROUP

NEW YORK

Books published by Basic Books are available at special discounts for bulk purchases in the United States by corporations, institutions, and other organizations. For more information, please contact the Special Markets Department at the Perseus Books Group, 2300 Chestnut Street, Suite 200, Philadelphia, PA 19103, or call (800) 810-4145, ext. 5000, or e-mail special.markets@perseusbooks.com.

Designed by Jack Lenzo

Library of Congress Cataloging-in-Publication Data
Lewis, Tom, 1942-
 Washington : a history of our national city / Tom Lewis.
   pages cm
 Includes bibliographical references and index.
  ISBN 978-0-465-03921-0 (hardcover) -- ISBN 978-0-465-06158-7 (e-book) 1. Washington (D.C.)--History. 2. Washington (D.C.)--Politics and government. 3. Washington (D.C.)--Social conditions. 4. Social change--Washington (D.C.)--History. 5. City planning--Washington (D.C.)--History. 6. Political culture--Washington (D.C.)--History. I. Title.
 F194.L488 2015
 975.3--dc23

                       2015022843

10 9 8 7 6 5 4 3 2 1

For
Jill,
the best

and
to the memory of
Thomas J. Condon,
mentor and friend

CONTENTS

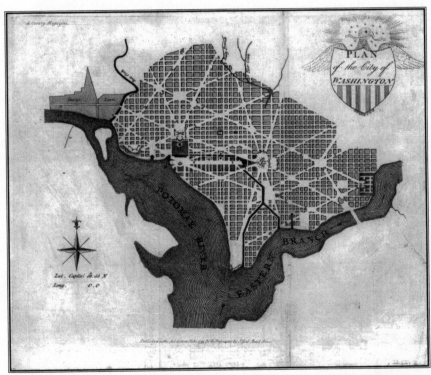

PETER CHARLES L'ENFANT'S 1791 plan, titled in the cartouche, "Plan of
the city intended for the permanent seat of the government of t[he] United
States: projected agreeable to the direction of the President of the United
States, in pursuance of an act of Congress passed the sixteenth day of July,
MDCCXC, establishing the permanent seat on the bank of the Potowmac."
Facsimile created by the US Coast and Geodetic Survey, 1887.

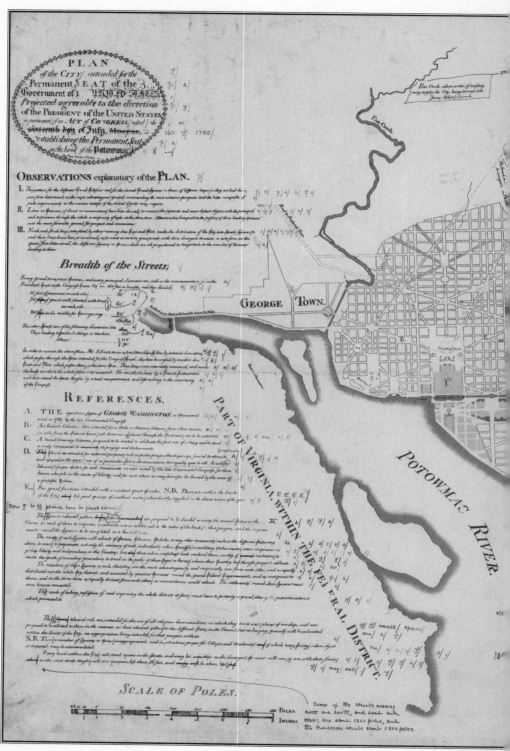

PLAN OF the City of Washington based on Andrew Ellicott's adaptation of Peter Charles L'Enfant's plan. Published in London's *Literary Magazine and British Review*, February 1, 1793.

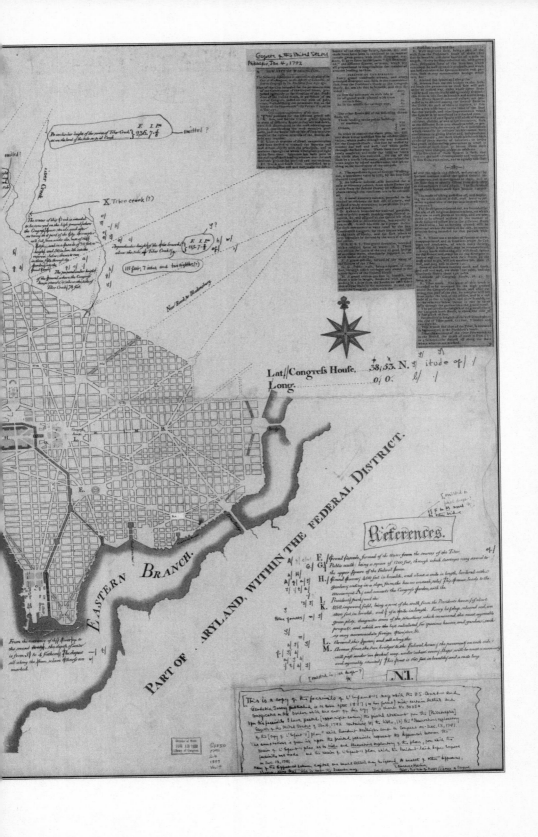

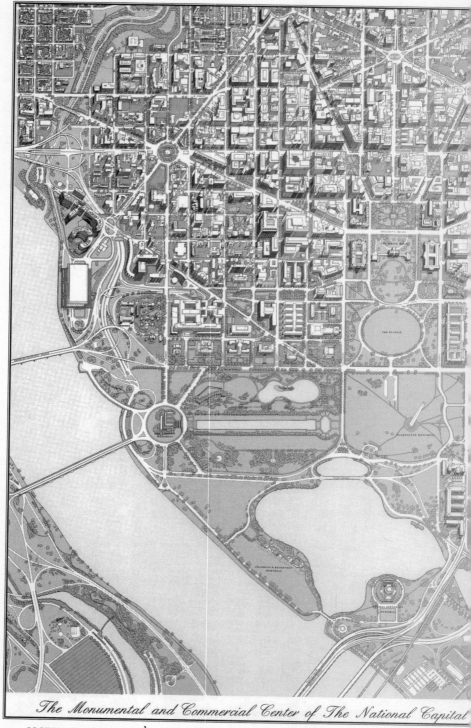

The Monumental and Commercial Center of The National Capital

JOSEPH PASSONNEAU'S 1996 three-dimensional map of central Washington, "The Monumental and Commercial Center of The National Capital and The Surrounding Residential Neighborhoods."

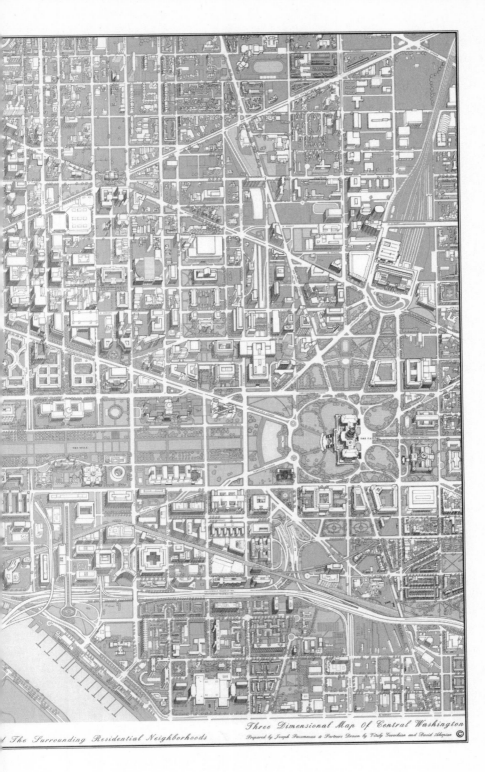

The Surrounding Residential Neighborhoods

Three Dimensional Map Of Central Washington

Prepared by Joseph Passonneau & Partners Drawn by Vitaly Gvozikian and David Akopian ©

INTRODUCTION

The Concerns of the Nation

Whatever concerns the capital concerns the nation.

—Montgomery Schuyler, 1902

I t is an oft-told story. By 1939, many Americans knew of Marian Anderson and were awed by the majestic power of her contralto voice. She had performed in the major concert halls of Europe, Africa, South America, and the Soviet Union; in the previous year she had presented seventy concerts throughout the United States. Enthusiastic Washingtonians, white and black, had filled her annual recitals to benefit Howard University at the Belasco and Rialto theaters and in the auditorium at Armstrong High, the city's vocational school for black students. "Each song seems to be the spontaneous voicing of a mood," wrote a local music critic about an Anderson concert that included works of Handel, Schubert, and Sibelius. "It is this identification of the singer and the song that makes her interpretations a delight." Many others had heard her on WMAL, the city's powerful CBS radio station. Wherever she performed, including at the White House, Marian Anderson confirmed Arturo Toscanini's declaration after her performance at the Salzburg festival: "Yours is a voice such as one hears once in a hundred years."

The impresario Sol Hurok knew he would have no trouble filling Washington's Constitution Hall for an Anderson performance. Built by the Daughters of the American Revolution (DAR) a decade earlier, it ranked as the largest and finest concert hall in the capital and hosted the best classical soloists and orchestras in the world. But it would not host Marian Anderson. "The hall is not available for a concert by Miss Anderson," the hall's manager wrote; the president-general of the DAR added that her organization's contracts for performers restricted the hall to "white artists only." Though segregation was the quiet norm in the capital, and was visible in restaurants, restrooms, hotels, and movie theaters, most in the city were surprised to learn that the color line applied to performers as well as audiences. Many musicians and prominent politicians objected; the violinist Jascha Heifetz took time during his performance at Constitution Hall to attack the DAR's decision, and First Lady Eleanor Roosevelt resigned her membership in the organization.

But the local indignity didn't end with the DAR's refusal. The District of Columbia school board denied Anderson the use of the 2,000-seat auditorium in its white Central High School. After NAACP publicist Walter White skillfully mounted a public and private protest, the school board voted to allow the contralto to sing, so long as the concert was not to be regarded as a precedent. The compromise satisfied no one.

By the end of March, Hurok had devised another plan, and with the help of White, Eleanor Roosevelt, Secretary of the Interior Harold Ickes, and Ickes's assistant, Oscar Chapman, it succeeded: at 5:00 p.m. on Easter Sunday, April 9, Ickes spoke from a temporary stage erected on the steps of the Lincoln Memorial to a crowd of 75,000 that stretched across the Mall to the Washington Monument and to millions more listening across America on the NBC radio network. "In this great auditorium under the sky, all of us are free," the secretary proclaimed. "Genius, like justice, is blind," he continued, "for genius with the tip of her wing has touched this woman . . . a free individual in a free land. Genius draws no color line." And then Marian Anderson stepped to the microphones, looked out upon the crowd and to the Capitol Dome beyond, and filled the Mall with her voice:

> *My country, 'tis of thee,*
> *Sweet land of liberty,*
> *To thee we sing; . . .*

Pointedly, she changed the last line, "Of thee I sing," taking care to emphasize the plural pronoun, *"we."* And just as pointedly, she concluded her program, which included a Donizetti aria and Schubert's "Ave Maria," with a spiritual:

> *Nobody knows the trouble I've seen*
> *Nobody knows my sorrow . . .*

"It was quite a beautiful awakening of blacks in the city," one white witness wrote. "You got this feeling, there she was in front of Lincoln, and what a great step forward this was."

ONE WITNESS of Marian Anderson's concert called it "the most civilized thing that has happened in this country in a long time." A reporter for the *Washington Post* noted "the massive figure of the Emancipator looking down benevolently" as Anderson sang "the great hymn to liberty 'My Country, 'Tis of Thee' . . . as it was never sung before." *Washington Post*, April 12, 1939. CREDIT: Getty Images

THIS BRIEF ACCOUNT of Marian Anderson's concert connects with some of the broad themes that I have threaded into this narrative history of America's national city: the absence of civic governance; the importance of race; and the symbolic significance of everything that happens in the capital to the nation and even the world.

The governance of Washington, DC, has always been an anomaly in American civic life. Most Americans in 1939 could vote for their local officials, their mayor or council member, supervisor or superintendent. They could depend upon them to lead their town or city, township or county, and when necessary to exercise moral or political suasion. But in Washington there were no local officials to perform that role. It fell to the head of the white school board to speak, and then only because he had to. Washington's citizens understood the reason all too well: despite living at the center of American democracy, they had no vote and had little say in their destiny. Since 1871 the capital had functioned without a mayor or city council; since 1874 it had relied upon three presidentially appointed commissioners who often had little experience in managing a city.

In 1939, however, there were just two commissioners, as one of the trio had resigned the previous September. The remaining commissioners left to guide the city of 650,000 were an army engineer, who confined his duties to the city's buildings and infrastructure, and a courtly Virginia gentleman with a bushy white mustache born two years after the Civil War. Though he had to shepherd the capital's budget through Congress, he appears to have devoted most of his time in early 1939 to organizing President Roosevelt's fifty-seventh birthday party on January 30, raising money for the March of Dimes, honoring 250 of the District's safest drivers, and serving on a committee sponsoring a concert held in Constitution Hall to support German refugees.

The 435 congressional representatives and 96 senators of the 76th Congress possessed the constitutional power to control the District's affairs, but for the most part they remained entirely mute. New York's liberal senator, Robert Wagner, criticized the school board's decision about holding Anderson's concert at Central High School, and Representative Joseph A. Gavagan, whose New York district included Harlem, and whose decade in Congress was notable for his many failed attempts to persuade his colleagues to vote for an antilynching bill, said the DAR's action reflected a "Nazi and Fascist philosophy." Conservative southerners who controlled the District's committees in Congress said nothing, and Senator Allen J. Ellender, from Houma, Louisiana, an obstinate and uncompromising opponent of federal civil rights legislation, interrupted a debate on a relief bill to chastise Ickes for allowing the Lincoln Memorial to be used for the concert. It set a "bad precedent," he said; the concert should be held "in some colored theater or hall."

The quiet reaction of members of Congress to a question roiling their city was far from unusual. Over the years they have often been reluctant to speak out about important issues affecting the populace. In the early nineteenth century, members of Congress regarded the capital as a place to be suffered, a place—as William Lowndes, a representative from South Carolina, put it—"to which so many are willing to come . . . and all so anxious to leave." Lowndes defined the problem succinctly: "Every member takes care of the needs of his constituents," he wrote to his wife. But the District's residents were "the constituents of no one." Although in more recent decades an increasing number of senators and representatives have known they would remain in the capital area after their terms expired, they still have used Washington and its residents as scapegoats for all sorts of wrongs and disgraces that are often the result of their own failure to attend to their constitutional duties. More than two centuries of parsimonious funding and despotic governance in the District has not served the city well.

Race has always been of concern in Washington. For its first six decades it stood in the middle of two slaveholding states, Maryland and Virginia, and as the capital, the place where northerners and southerners argued and compromised in their struggle to maintain the Union. From 1861 to 1865 it was the center of our national trauma. After the war, and through much of the twentieth century, Washington once again occupied an uneasy space between segregation and integration. Unlike the South, the city integrated its public transportation—but blacks traveling to Virginia knew they had to move to the back once their bus crossed the Potomac; unlike the North, the District segregated its public accommodations. Before her concert that Easter Sunday, Marian Anderson had to stay at the residence of former Pennsylvania governor Gifford Pinchot. No Washington hotel would have her.

The story of Marian Anderson's concert became an important addition to the centuries-old narrative of Washington's racial history. By 1939, the narrative included accounts of slaves and fugitives, slave pens and auctions, abolitionists and freedmen, Jim Crow laws and segregation. But this moment marked a turning point. "Through the Marian Anderson protest concert," remarked the founder of the National Council of Negro Women and adviser to Eleanor Roosevelt, Mary McLeod Bethune, "we made our triumphant entry into the democratic spirit of American life." Bethune's characterization of the event as a "protest" affirms its political as well as its cultural implications. The concert ranks among the first gatherings at the Memorial to affirm the rich contributions of blacks and their right to participate fully in American life. Since that day, still more Washington stories have been woven into the narrative, and, almost always, they reflect America's troubled heritage of slavery.

From the moment of its conception, Washington has served as a symbol of America's virtues and vices, its aspirations and realities. Those attending the Constitutional Convention in 1787 conceived of the capital as a place where the government might chart the course of the nation free from outside pressure and interference. Its principal designer placed the Capitol—he called it the "People's House"—on the highest hill, connected by a broad avenue to the "President's House," and he imagined a wide greensward stretching from there to the Potomac River. He planned streets and avenues to intersect with circles and squares that would serve as sites for commemorative statues. Designers who followed have built monuments and memorials—the Washington, Lincoln, and Jefferson memorials, among others—with the intention of honoring the republic's greatest heroes.

Washington's symbolic place in America's consciousness has evolved over the centuries. Early visitors derided the nascent capital's grand pretensions; in 1814, the British set fire to the Capitol and the White House, twin emblems of a democracy that was less than four decades old; in 1852, a group of anti-Catholic political dissidents seized the Washington Monument, which was then under construction, in one of the first acts of domestic terrorism in the nation; and the completion of the Capitol dome during the Civil War coincided with the restoration of the Union. In the twentieth century, the Mall, often called "America's front lawn," blossomed with museums and monuments, each intended to be an outward sign of the nation's values.

Of course, Sol Hurok and those working with him to organize the concert understood from the outset the symbolic significance of having

Anderson perform on the steps of the Lincoln Memorial with Daniel Chester French's great statue of the sixteenth president brooding in the background. Walter White proposed the site to Oscar Chapman, who secured the approval of Harold Ickes. The publicist invited members of President Roosevelt's cabinet, the Congress, and the US Supreme Court, along with major performing artists, to lend their names to a "sponsoring committee" for the event. US Secretary of the Treasury Henry Morganthau signed on, as did Chief Justice Charles Evans Hughes and Senator Wagner. Significantly, Justice Hugo Black, a former member of the Ku Klux Klan, joined the sponsoring committee and sat on the platform with his wife. At the same time, Eleanor Roosevelt's resignation from the DAR made newspaper headlines across the nation. And White suggested the words for Ickes's introduction, carefully linking the setting of the Memorial to the cause of civil rights. Rather than the Lincoln who "Saved the Union," as the words over French's sculpture affirm, the concert brought to the foreground his role as the emancipator of the slaves in 1863. Hurok and White understood Washington's symbolic importance to the nation and the world, and they used it.

THROUGH A SELECTION of stories and details, this portrait of Washington, DC, aims to render the history and character of the city, the sum of those distinguishing features that give it a unique identity. Indeed, the idea of "character"—that word the Greeks gave to the engraving instrument they used to make a distinctive mark—is central to this enterprise. Character appears writ large, incised in the very streets and avenues drawn for the city's grand plan of 1791; in the chiseled rock and sculpted bronze of memorials as different as those commemorating Franklin Roosevelt and the war in Vietnam; in the emblematic landscape of the Capitol grounds and the Mall; and in buildings as disparate in architecture and purpose as the Library of Congress and the headquarters of the FBI.

Character appears in unexpected places and at unanticipated moments. We may find it in a pew of St. John's Episcopal Church at Lafayette Square; in a group of tourists riding Segways, or commuters riding the Metro; in the red lights winking in the twilight from the top of the Washington Monument, and the flashing lights and sirens of a phalanx of SUVs escorting a dignitary on an errand of state; in the awed face of a child from Nebraska or the chiseled face of an Afghan cab driver; or even in a photograph of the Ku Klux Klan marching down Constitution Avenue. Such images are part of the narrative and tell us about the city.

Ralph Waldo Emerson's reminder that the force of character is cumulative is apposite to Washington. For more than two centuries, men and women—some transient politicians, others permanent residents—have left their marks on the city. A number of portraits to be found here depict persons of great nobility. George Washington, Margaret Bayard Smith, and Dolley Madison rank chief among them. Other portraits may reveal the innermost characteristics of the sitter that are not always flattering. An otherwise noble man, a Thomas Jefferson or a Woodrow Wilson, may appear less worthy because of his actions with regard to the capital. Still other pictures present the subject in a harsh and altogether unfavorable light. These men, scoundrels or picaros to the core, include James Greenleaf, the avaricious land speculator who promised George Washington millions to build the city but who left behind only a few shells of unfinished houses, and "Johnny Mac" McMillan, the segregationist South Carolina congressman and ruler of the House of Representatives District of Columbia Committee for nearly a quarter century, who treated the city with a contempt that resounds to this day.

This history portrays the interrelated forces that have simultaneously fostered and impeded Washington's growth and development. Like the nation itself, the city has been subject to developments and influences that no one could have anticipated at its inception; and like the nation itself, it has changed, sometimes haltingly, with the realities of the world. Washington is the place where the values of our Declaration of Independence and our Constitution are affirmed or denied. Because the city embodies so much of the essence of America, it is essential to our understanding of ourselves. "It is our national center," wrote Frederick Douglass, one who had shared in the capital's glory and its dishonor. "It belongs to us, and whether it is mean or majestic, whether arrayed in glory or covered in shame, we cannot but share its character and its destiny."

THIS BOOK IS *a history* of Washington, DC, a portrait of the city, but in no way does it purport to be a *definitive* history. Readers will not find a complete study of the capital's founding or construction, the fire of 1814, the city's role in the Civil War, Congress's neglect and meddling, the riots of 1968, or the rise and fall of Marion Barry, to name but a few examples. Although I write about each of these topics, and many others, each merits a volume of its own, and fortunately such volumes exist.

Writing a definitive history would take many books and encompass numerous disciplines, a Herculean task. Early in the twentieth century, Wilhelmus B. Bryan produced two volumes, about 1,400 pages between them, that brought the story up to 1876; in the 1960s, Constance Green produced two wonderful books totaling about 1,000 pages. As fine as these works are, even they did not begin to cover the District's history in full. The complete history lies in the National Archives, the libraries of the Historical Society of Washington, DC, Howard University, George Washington University, the Library of Congress, the New-York Historical Society, in countless libraries and archival collections in Pennsylvania, Ohio, Virginia, and Maryland, among others; and most especially in the marvelous Washingtoniana collection at the Martin Luther King Jr. Memorial Library in the capital. Increasingly, the city's history has also begun to take its place on the Internet in excellent blog sites, list serves, and domains. Washington is fortunate to have an excellent historical society and many gifted university and independent scholars who are actively engaged in studying and writing its history. Better than others they understand the rudeness of forgetting the past. These women and men have enriched our understanding of Washington's history immeasurably, and readers should treat my notes for each chapter as suggestions for more in-depth reading.

I AM SOMETIMES asked—challenged, really—why I have chosen to write about DC's history—after all, I don't even live there. My interest in the city has grown quietly for more than half a century. I used to see the city, its Capitol dome, and its broad streets from the back of a 1946 Studebaker as my family drove between our home in Philadelphia and the places where relatives lived in Virginia. From my father I learned early on—about nine is as close as I can fix my age—that the capital's citizens had no representatives or senators and could not vote. Whenever my numerous research projects and other business took me to Washington, I spent time exploring the city. The usual sights around the Mall and Pennsylvania Avenue captured my attention, of course, but then the streets and neighborhoods beyond—Dupont Circle, Adams Morgan, Shaw, East Capitol Street, Anacostia—began to interest me, too. There I encountered a very different Washington, a city of schools, playgrounds, hospitals, dry cleaners, markets, and theaters that was populated by couples and singles, parents and children, and straights and gays, people of every background and ethnicity. They all lived in a city that has a unique place in the history of the nation, a city where, for more than two centuries, the federal government has expressed—and sometimes thwarted—our collective personality, our aspirations, our failures, and our successes.

My personal fascination eventually led to a more serious investigation. Time and again, I came to appreciate the peculiar circumstances that have made Washington into something of a stepchild of American democracy. I have set out to describe and examine these circumstances in a way that may shed light on our collective history as a nation. The city has much to tell us about ourselves—who we profess to be, who we really are, and what we might become.

PROLOGUE

The "Mutinous Insult"

> Unnecessary changes of the seat of government would be indicative of instability in the national councils, and therefore highly injurious to the interests as well as derogatory to the dignity of the United States.
>
> —Journals of the Continental Congress, 1788

By September 1783, James Madison had had enough—enough of living in the North; enough of the turmoil in his personal life; enough of the political impasse in Congress. The small house on Market Street in Philadelphia where he boarded was a very different place from Montpelier, the wealthiest tobacco plantation on the Piedmont in Virginia. Montpelier's one hundred slaves supported an ordered life; its symmetrical brick Georgian house offered calm; its view took in the thin line of the Blue Ridge Mountains on the western horizon. Life in a city dominated by Quaker merchants who condemned slavery was awkward at best. That spring, Madison's body slave, Billey, had run away. Billey had been captured and returned to his master, but Madison had to sell him, and at a loss, because his mind had been "too thoroughly tainted to be a fit companion for fellow slaves in Virga."

Worse still were Madison's personal trials. That August he had learned from his father that his mother lay gravely ill. And just that month Madison had been spurned in love. Catherine Floyd, the sixteen-year-old daughter of a New York delegate who was boarding at the same lodging house, had accepted Madison's proposal for marriage;

but by August "Miss Kitty" expressed "indifference" for her thirty-one-year-old fiancé and accepted instead the proposal of another boarder, a nineteen-year-old medical student. The Continental Congress, which he had served so faithfully since 1780, was also in trouble. The Articles of Confederation did not empower Congress to impose taxes to pay for the recent war, so Madison and his fellow delegates could only request support from the states, not demand it. The debts mounted.

The issue of money, specifically the payment of troops, had forced Congress to flee Philadelphia. On the afternoon of Saturday, June 21, a group of Pennsylvania soldiers had surrounded the statehouse where the delegates were meeting on the ground floor. Expecting to be furloughed now that the war with the British was drawing to a close, the men demanded their back pay and a settling of their accounts. Although they had come to make their demands not to the Continental Congress, but to the Pennsylvania Executive Council, which was meeting on the floor above, the effect the soldiers had upon Madison and his fellow delegates was clear. Some were drunk, some were cursing, and some pointed their bayoneted muskets at the first-floor windows. "At one moment the Mutineers were penitent and preparing submissions; the next they were meditating more violent measures," Madison recorded in his notes. "Sometimes the Bank was their object; at other times the Seizure of the members of Congress." It was, he said, a "mutinous insult."

Now Madison and his fellow delegates were cramped in the town of Princeton, New Jersey. He had to share a small room "scarcely ten feet square" and a bed with his fellow Virginia delegate Joseph Jones. "I am obliged to write in a position that scarcely admits the use of any of my limbs, he complained to Thomas Jefferson, "and without a single accommodation for writing." It's hard to imagine worse conditions— especially in this time of quill, inkwell, and sand—for the delegate who took copious notes of the proceedings and maintained a voluminous correspondence. Madison's room was small, his bed was narrow, his slave was gone, his mother was ill, his fiancée had flown, his thoughts were bleak.

Madison knew the town of Princeton well. A dozen years earlier he had attended the College of New Jersey, today's Princeton University, and had actually shared a bedroom (about twenty feet square) in the college's Nassau Hall, where Congress was meeting. He dreaded the prospect of spending the winter "in this village where the public business can neither be conveniently done," he told Jefferson, "[nor] the members of Congress decently provided for nor those connected with Congress provided for at all." Yet Madison stayed. Several "measures on foot," as he wrote to Jefferson, demanded he remain. Among the most important was the question of a "permanent seat of Congress." It was an issue that excited sectional interests, challenged the philosophy of many of the founders, and threatened the fragile union of thirteen states.

The divisions were sectional, between North and South; commercial, between city and country; and philosophical, between central government and state sovereignty. The issue traded on the fear that the seat of the democratic government might soon resemble one of the corrupt large European capitals, such as London. A number of delegates believed that a peripatetic Congress continually changing its meeting place from one town or city to another would insulate its members from dishonorable actions and keep their nascent democracy pure. In late November, the delegates moved to Annapolis, Maryland; the following November found them in Trenton, New Jersey; and in early January 1785, they decamped yet again to New York City. By this time the realities of trying to run a sovereign government whose capital was in perpetual motion had cooled the ardor for movement; they would remain at the mouth of the Hudson for four years.

Such was the state of affairs in late May 1787 when fifty-five remarkable men assembled at the Pennsylvania statehouse in Philadelphia to remedy, as Madison put it in his introduction to the Debates on the Constitution, "the defects, the deformities, the diseases and the ominous prospects" of the Articles of Confederation. They debated in secret, and remarkably, given today's customs, there were no pressures from lobbying groups and no leaks to the press. Each delegate's concerns simply reflected his obvious economic and regional interests. Together they hammered out compromise after compromise on questions of taxes and slavery, federal authority and states' rights, popular representation and executive powers. On the afternoon of September 17, four months after they began, the delegates agreed to keep the records of their debates secret lest "a bad use would be made of them," and then affixed their names to the new "Constitution for the United States of America."

Article I, Section 8, Clause 17, which Madison likely wrote, delegated to Congress the authority "to exercise exclusive Legislation in all

Cases whatsoever, over such District (not exceeding ten Miles square) as may, by Cession of particular States, and the acceptance of Congress, become the Seat of the Government of the United States." The debate on the clause was brief, taking up just 4 of the 650 pages of the journals and reports that made up the records of the Constitutional Convention. Several delegates worried that the state that ceded land might gain undue power and influence by placing its own capital in the same city, or that the new federal government might delay erecting its public buildings and use the state's buildings instead.

Madison argued that a bicameral legislature (rather than the single legislative body of the Articles of Confederation) required more members for the new government, many of whom would come "from the interior parts of the States"; and as the Constitution gave the new government greater power, there would be more business to conduct. It was imperative, then, that the seat of government be located in "that position from which [the legislators] could contemplate with the most equal eye, and sympathize most equally with, every part of the nation." After the Constitutional Convention agreed upon the clause, Madison defended it in *The Federalist*. "The indispensable necessity of complete authority at the seat of government, carries its own evidence with it. . . . Without it the public authority might be insulted and its proceedings be interrupted, with impunity," and the members of the government would become beholden to the state "for protection."

The debate in the various state ratification conventions, also brief, reflected Madison's belief that Congress should control the federal district. By focusing on the need to protect the government from "insult," Madison deflected the question of just where the United States might locate its seat of government. After the ratification of the Constitution, he could influence the new Congress to find a place for the new federal district far away from the subterfuges of the North and as close to his native Virginia as possible.

Madison's choice of the word "district" was telling, too. Coming through French from medieval Latin, the word originally denoted a territory under a feudal lord, and over time had come to mean a territory marked for some special administrative purpose. Residents of this district would live subordinate to their masters in the Congress of the United States, who would "exercise exclusive Legislation" over them, always. The peculiar status was likely not an oversight on Madison's part. To suggest that the residents might have rights as voters could raise questions of future statehood and representation in Congress, which in turn might upset his delicate strategy for the adoption of a new governmental compact for the United States. To put the federal government under the aegis of a state would contradict all that federalism might achieve.

In the various state conventions that debated the ratification of the Constitution, only one delegate, Thomas Tredwell, a staunch anti-Federalist from Long Island, New York, spoke of the rights that would be denied to those who would live in the district: "The plan of the federal city, sir, departs from every principle of freedom, as far as the distance of the two polar stars from each other," said Tredwell, "for, subjecting the inhabitants . . . to the exclusive legislation of Congress, in whose appointment they have no share or vote, is laying a foundation on which may be erected as complete a tyranny as can be found in the Eastern world." The proposed district would be an "evil," a "political hive, where all the drones in the society are to be collected to feed on the honey of the land." And he concluded, "How dangerous this city may be, and what its operation on the general liberties of this country, time alone must discover." No one answered him, and on July 26, 1788, New York became the eleventh state to ratify the Constitution.

James Madison and his fellow Federalists had given the thirteen states a new covenant. And just thirty-eight words of that covenant, a single clause that originated in part because of a "mutinous insult" in Philadelphia and a cramped bedroom in Princeton, led to the creation of a city unique in the United States, if not the world.

CHAPTER 1

The General's River and the Federal City

Washington is like no other city in the world. It is a living curiosity, made up of the strangest and most incongruous elements. There is a fairy-tale sense of instability about it. As with the palace of Aladdin which flew away in the night, one feels that this city could easily vanish and that he could wake up some morning to find himself stranded on the empty Potomac Flats.

—Frank G. Carpenter, 1882

George Washington saw the future of the United States in the waters of the Potomac. The river had been a part of his life since birth. He knew it intimately, from its rising in the Allegheny Mountains to its blending with the waters of Chesapeake Bay. He had covered much of its passage on horseback. He understood its currents, its tides, its falls, and its tributaries. He had visited the plantations, villages, and towns that dotted its banks. And George Washington knew most of the important families—proprietors, as they were called—of the land through which the Potomac flowed. Their names included Fairfax and Custis, Mason and Lee, and they had lived and married, and intermarried, for generations. Indeed, Washington considered himself to be a minor proprietor, as he had married a Custis, and his own Mount Vernon estate counted 10 miles of frontage on the river's 383. There was great truth in Thomas Jefferson's playful observation to James Madison: "Gen'l Washington has that of the Potomac much at heart."

The river that held his sentiments begins at the convergence of two small streams in the Alleghenies about 15 miles southeast of Cumberland, Maryland. From there it incises a path though a valley of mostly metamorphic rock, past places with American Indian names like Paw and Great Cacapon and European ones like Hancock and Big Spring. Brooks, streams, runs, and creeks, including Dillons and Tearcoat, Tonoloway and Conococheague, feed its waters along the way until, at Harpers Ferry, the Shenandoah nearly doubles its volume. The river then cuts southeast through a gorge in the Blue Ridge, surges over the rapids of Great Falls and Little Falls, and at Georgetown meets Rock Creek to become the broad waters of the tidal Potomac that ends at the Chesapeake.

No doubt Washington, like every other Virginian, knew of Captain John Smith's exploration of the Chesapeake Bay and the Potomac in 1608. Smith had produced maps that with unusual accuracy had depicted native villages on the river, including the Patawomeke of northern Virginia and the Nacostan, whose name, through a crude Latin transliteration, still designates the place they inhabited, "Anacostia." "The men be fewe," Smith noted. "Their far greater number is of women and children."

It was the abundance of agricultural and hunting opportunities that attracted Paleo-Indians to the Atlantic coastal plain for more than 10,000 years. They hunted beavers and wolves as well as black bears and moose, fished for bass and pike, and left behind fluted spear points dating to 9500 BCE, as well as pottery shards and soapstone vessels, as tokens of their presence.

Traders in search of furs and minerals followed Smith to the region. Etymologists suggest that "Potomac" may in fact mean "trading place." Certainly from the early seventeenth century the natives who dwelled on the river's banks had seen a variety of European explorers, traders, and marauders. By the mid-seventeenth century, Jesuits had established missions there. European settlements began in 1662, when the English crown gave manorial grants along the Potomac for land that became the District of Columbia. George Washington knew the class of manor lords well, for his own 8,000 acres at Mount Vernon made him one of them.

But the Potomac always held far more than sentimental or historical appeal for Washington. He dreamt of building a canal from the falls just west of Georgetown through the Alleghenies to the rising of the

Ohio; it would extend inland navigation to the west and enable the Ohio Valley's settlers to trade with the United States rather than the British or the Spanish who also claimed a presence there. "This is no Utopian Scheme," he wrote from Mount Vernon in November 1784. "Not only the produce of the Ohio & its waters . . . but those of the lakes also . . . may be brought to the Sea Ports of the United States" rather than to the rival ports of Montreal or New Orleans then under British and Spanish control. A southerner at heart, Washington believed that extending the reach of the Potomac to the west would enable Georgetown and nearby Alexandria to rival Philadelphia and New York.

Washington's tour of the western territories only strengthened his conviction that the Potomac must be *the* route to the interior. In March 1785 a group of commissioners, who had been appointed by the legislatures of Maryland and Virginia and were meeting at Mount Vernon, agreed to designate the Potomac "as a common highway for the purpose of navigation and commerce to the citizens of Virginia and Maryland, and of the United States." Once he had the states' cooperation, General Washington organized the Potomac Canal Company and invested in it personally. The directors made him the company's first president.

Eighteenth-century engineering skills would prove to be the Potomac Company's downfall. The task of building a canal through 200 miles of rugged territory between Great Falls and Cumberland, Maryland, with locks to raise and lower boats 600 feet, proved daunting and expensive. By the time George Washington became president of the United States in March 1789, the company was foundering. Still, his dreams for the Potomac River endured.

BY SEPTEMBER 1789, in the first session of the First United States Congress meeting in New York City, James Madison, now a representative from Virginia, knew the question of where to locate the seat of government had to be resolved. It was a perilous subject, which is why he avoided discussing it in the Federalist Papers, for the debate would exacerbate sectional jealousies among the thirteen states. Those jealousies were real, too. Southern representatives feared the North, its wealth, its cities, and its emphasis upon commerce, especially in New York, as well as the movement afoot in many of the northern states to abolish slavery. Already Massachusetts, Pennsylvania, Vermont, and

New Hampshire had done so; Connecticut would follow the next year. (New York and New Jersey would wait until 1799 and 1804, respectively, to enact manumission laws.) Northern representatives disliked the South's primitive roads, which impeded travel; its heat, which some contended led to disease and death; and its agrarian economy, which depended in large part upon the institution of slavery.

Money would also drive the debate. Since June 1783, when the Continental Congress had left Philadelphia for its peripatetic journey through several states, cities, and towns, many citizens had come to realize how important boarding, feeding, and serving the representatives—as well as the accompanying clerks, secretaries, and servants—would be to their economy. Conventional wisdom held that the city selected to become the seat of government would realize as much as $500,000 (about $6,875,000 today) annually. The money was lure enough to bring out bold proposals from those who might benefit from private as well as public gain.

Deciding the location of the capital became one of the first important compromises that the members of the new Congress of the new Constitution had to make. No less than sixteen places in the nation had been put forth as possible locations for the seat of government. Most in Congress that fall, however, believed the choice came down to five: Philadelphia and Trenton on the Delaware, Germantown outside Philadelphia, Columbia or another site on the Susquehanna, and the area of Georgetown on the Potomac. Each had its ardent proponents and detractors. The annals of the 1st Congress, as well as the diary entries of William Maclay, senator from Pennsylvania, tell a story of continual flux and reflux as the tide of sentiment and political trading flowed to favor first one site and then another. To the consternation of the southerners, the prize at times seemed to be within the grasp of Philadelphia. They feared the city's Quakers, who since the seventeenth century had been implacable foes of slavery. As James Madison well knew, southern representatives who had their body slaves accompany them to Philadelphia did so at their peril.

The southerners also feared sites on the east bank of the Susquehanna River, particularly Columbia. A number of Pennsylvania delegates, including Maclay, lobbied hard to lure the representatives to the Quaker hamlet of 320 souls. Such had long been the fervent dream of the town's leading burgher, Samuel Wright, whose family had operated a crude, animal-powered ferry at the spot for decades. Wright had changed the town's name from "Wright's Ferry" to Columbia; he planned streets and private lots and designated other lots for public buildings. Were the federal government to choose Columbia, he and other speculators would profit handsomely. It might have happened. At the end of the first session of Congress, a group of Pennsylvania, New York, and New England representatives voted thirty-one to seventeen to place the seat of government on the Susquehanna in Pennsylvania.

For a time, sectional rancor threatened the future of the Constitution. Even James Madison succumbed at one point in the debate. Fearing that the capital might be in Pennsylvania rather than the South, he declared that if a prophet had foretold the "proceedings of this day . . . Virginia might not have been part of the Union at this moment." Fortunately for his fellow Virginians, Madison was able to exercise his parliamentary skills to delay consideration of the final bill until January 1790, when Congress reconvened, and it would have to pass the legislation again.

By January, pamphleteers and newspaper editors south of Pennsylvania had begun to argue for the Potomac, and especially Georgetown, as the best site for the capital. Located on the Maryland side of the Potomac and the west bank of its tributary Rock Creek, the spot had long been a trading and meeting place of the Piscataway Indian nation. In the eighteenth century, Scots had sought refuge there from turmoil in their own country. By 1790, Georgetown had developed into a thriving port of about 5,000. Millers made it a center for farmers to bring their wheat; tobacco traders Benjamin Stoddert and Robert Peter filled the town's three tobacco warehouses, making it the most important tobacco market in the state, if not the union; and an ambitious gunsmith, John Yoast, produced muskets of exceptional quality that Maryland's soldiers had carried in the recent war. From Georgetown's wharves boats laden with barrels of flour and bales of tobacco leaves sailed for England and the continent. Most of the Virginians, including Washington, Madison, and Jefferson, crossed the Potomac at Georgetown, frequently stopping at Suter's Fountain Inn on their journeys to the Continental Congress or the Constitutional Convention in Philadelphia, or to the temporary capital in New York City.

A small group of proprietors controlled Georgetown and the land east of Rock Creek. They possessed a sense of entitlement that came from holding their property and slaves for many decades, some from the seventeenth century. They included Robert Peter, who owned a large tract that included present-day Washington Circle where Pennsylvania Avenue crosses K Street; Jacob Funk, who in 1770 laid out the streets of "Hamburg," near today's Twenty-second and C streets NW; Daniel Carroll of Duddington, whose land included Jenkins Hill, the site of the Capitol; Notley Young, who with Carroll held the Duddington Pasture, the present-day southwestern part of the city; and David Burnes, whose holdings included much of today's Pennsylvania Avenue and White House grounds. Although their families had tilled the soil for several generations, they were ignorant about crop rotation; by the late eighteenth century, the ravages of tobacco planting had largely exhausted their land's value. City lots in place of spent fields might bring them riches.

Southerners wanted a spot on the Potomac for another reason: the river ran between two states that were home to more than half of the slaves—396,000 men, women, and children—in the nation.

BUT IN THE spring of 1790, as Congress remained deadlocked over the question of where to place the seat of government, it faced another, far graver legislative impasse: Secretary of the Treasury Alexander Hamilton's proposals for the United States to assume the national debt threatened to tear the Union asunder. It was a question recalling tensions that went back to the Revolutionary War, when the states had sold bonds to pay and provision their troops. After the Peace of Paris, the southern states, with the exception of South Carolina, discharged a substantial portion of their debts and paid their soldiers in full; for the most part, the northern states did not. Now, in early 1790, Hamilton, a New Yorker, moved that the United States assume all state debts and pay off the bonds at par value. To do so would restore the nation's credit and place the government on a sound financial foundation, but it also meant that the northern states would slip past their obligations.

From the moment he introduced it, Hamilton's scheme aroused sectional tensions. Many southerners feared that the debt assumption would strengthen the commercial interests of the North, particularly of New York, or that states' rights would be subsumed by the central government. Those in southern states that had retired most of their debts were angry that the proposal would lift the obligation from South Carolina, Massachusetts, and New York. And then there was the matter of speculation in state bonds. When the value of the paper that the states issued plummeted during the war, many sold their bonds to speculators for as little as 10 percent of their value. Hamilton's plan for debt assumption would redeem them at par, thereby making the speculators, a number of whom were the secretary's friends, wealthy. Leading the opponents was James Madison.

At this moment, Thomas Jefferson, the nation's new secretary of state, stepped forward to broker an accord.

THOMAS JEFFERSON HAD always regarded the dinner table as the most suitable place for advancing his own interests, be they social, philosophical, political, or, as was often the case, a combination of the three. While in Paris, he had James Hemings, his light-skinned slave (and half-brother of his deceased wife, Martha Wayles), tutored in the art of French cooking in order to enrich the hospitality he accorded guests. No doubt Hemings prepared the dinner for a small gathering that Jefferson hosted at his house on Maiden Lane on the third Sunday of June 1790.

As Jefferson remembered it, likely with embellishment, the dinner came about because he chanced to meet Hamilton on Broadway in front of the president's house. Hamilton looked "sombre, haggard, & dejected beyond description, even his dress uncouth & neglected," as he discussed the question that had consumed Congress that spring, the assumption of the state debts. Assumption was an "indispensable necessity towards a preservation of the union," he maintained, but the southern legislators had opposed his plan. Feigning that he knew little of the matter or of other matters before the Congress, Jefferson suggested a "conciliation" with James Madison for the next day, "to find some temperament for the present fever."

Although Jefferson had just met Hamilton that spring, he surely knew him by reputation. He had read his contributions (along with those of John Jay and Madison) to the Federalist Papers. He likely recognized that he and Hamilton differed on matters of monetary policy and the role of the president, but as yet such differences were not as sharp as they would become.

Jefferson likely understood, too, how fundamentally opposite they were in matters of lineage, character, and temperament: Hamilton, born illegitimately on the West Indian island of Nevis; he, born of a Virginia planter and surveyor. Hamilton, who married into the privilege of a distinguished Hudson River family; he, who came into the world of privilege naturally through his mother's prominent Old Dominion family. Hamilton, who had pursued a life of military glory as George Washington's secretary and aide-de-camp, had fought beside the general at the Battle of Monmouth, had stood beside him at West Point at the moment of Benedict Arnold's treason, and had become a hero at the decisive Battle of Yorktown in 1781; he, who had sought the quiet life of Monticello after writing the Declaration of Independence, and who, when the British had threatened his mountaintop plantation and his family in 1781, had fled to the west. Hamilton, who believed in the mental equality of slaves and who was a charter member of the New York Society for Promoting the Manumission of Slaves; he, who held that blacks were innately inferior and who depended upon their involuntary servitude to maintain his way of living. Hamilton, who, in disputes, be they personal, physical, or philosophical, believed in and enjoyed direct confrontation; he, who realized the value of, and more often than not practiced, the subtle and serpentine stratagems of courtesy, ambiguity, indirection, and sometimes, even deception.

At his dinner table that Sunday, Jefferson linked debt assumption to the still unresolved question of where to place the federal capital. "I opened the subject to them," he wrote, and "acknowledged that my situation had not permitted me to understand it sufficiently but encouraged them to consider the thing together."

In many ways, James Madison held the key to the compromise. He was steadfast in his opposition to Hamilton's proposal for debt assumption, but he was equally committed to a Potomac site for the capital. Part of his commitment was personal. For years he had dwelled in the North while working to craft and secure the Constitution, but he was far more comfortable in the South. For Madison, the federal district must be below the line that the English astronomers Charles Mason and Jeremiah Dixon had begun surveying in the 1760s to establish the borders between Pennsylvania, Maryland, Delaware, and Virginia, and preferably on the Potomac. Madison knew that while he had outmaneuvered

Maclay and the Susquehanna faction the previous fall, he had not achieved his goal of placing the seat of government in the South.

Although he affected ignorance of the matter, Jefferson also wanted to move the government from New York to the Potomac. That spring and early summer he had tried, albeit quietly, to bring it about. In mid-June Jefferson had suggested to the financier and Pennsylvania senator Robert Morris that the southern states would support a fifteen-year residence of the federal government in Philadelphia if it were followed by a permanent residence in Georgetown. But Pennsylvania's delegates rejected the overture. That initial gambit thwarted, he had recently hosted a dinner with the prominent Philadelphia merchant and Hamilton's assistant secretary of the treasury Tench Coxe to advance his proposal. In the wake of those meetings, Jefferson hoped this dinner with Hamilton and Madison would end with an agreement.

It was a moment of political triage. Though divided by philosophy, temperament, and conviction, each of the guests came with an issue he believed was of the greatest importance to the future of the nation, and, as it turned out, each proved willing to sacrifice long-held convictions to achieve his objective. Hamilton had lobbied to keep the government in New York City, as it had become the financial center of the nation. (Some of his many critics had taken to calling the city "Hamiltonopolis.") But the debt assumption bill weighed more heavily on his mind and had a far greater degree of urgency for the nation. Jefferson and Madison were suspicious of Hamilton's fiscal policies, but they prized having the government of the United States in the South in a location that was at that time the geographic center of the thirteen states. Surely the nation would thrive if its legislators were in their more republican and agrarian world, far from the federalist and commercial orbit of New York. Each man willingly made the sacrifice in order to gain what he most valued.

The strategy for effecting the agreement was remarkably simple: Although he would maintain his opposition, Madison pledged enough southern votes to secure passage of debt assumption; in return, Hamilton promised to secure the votes necessary to place the federal district on the Potomac between the Eastern Branch (today's Anacostia River) and the Conococheague Creek. He also agreed to make Philadelphia the government's temporary residence for ten years while the new seat of government was being prepared.

Over the next few weeks, from June 20 to July 12, Hamilton and Madison worked quietly but diligently, inveigling various members of Congress from Virginia, Maryland, and Massachusetts to make concessions in order for the bill they held most dear to pass. The compromise proved to be a distasteful business for all. One representative from the South said he voted for debt assumption "with considerable revulsions of stomach"; many northerners agreed with Theodore Sedgwick, the staunch Federalist from Stockbridge, Massachusetts, who declared the Potomac to be "unhealthy . . . destructive of northern constitutions," adding that "vast numbers of Eastern adventurers" had gone south, and "all have found their graves there." But in the end enough members compromised in order to achieve their goal. "If the Potomac succeeds," Madison wrote to his friend James Monroe as the bill was before the Senate, "it will have resulted from a fortuitous coincidence of circumstances which might never happen again."

The Residence Act that Congress passed in 1790 was vague in almost every way. It gave George Washington the authority to decide the district's location, and it empowered him to acquire the land and appoint three commissioners who would oversee the surveying, land purchases, and construction of "suitable buildings for the accommodation of Congress, and of the President, and for the public Offices of the government of the United States." The act stipulated that the new capital must be ready by the first Monday of December 1800.

What the act lacked, of course, was any provision for financing the new capital. Congress failed to appropriate any money to build the capital—nothing to pay for land, surveying, architectural designs, construction, or even the commissioners' service. Nor did it approve funds for a long-contemplated memorial to celebrate George Washington and the Revolution. Instead, it "authorized and requested" the president "to accept grants of money" to defray such expenses. No one had any idea of just how much money it might take to build a city.

Vagueness aside, the agreement between Hamilton and Madison ranks among the first, and certainly among the most important, political compromises in US history. Hamilton had the foundation he needed to build the nation's economic system; Madison and Jefferson had their seat of government on the Potomac River. The United States could go forward.

MANY THOUGHT THE venture to create a place for the government—in the South, no less—would be short-lived, the land never surveyed or mapped, the buildings never built. As a writer for the *New-York Journal* put it: "Get the Congress to Philadelphia and farewell for ever to the Potomac."

George Washington believed otherwise. Although the president had remained silent during the debates in Congress over the government's location, no one doubted his desire. He saw the Residence Act as an opportunity to create a magnificent city on the Potomac *and* link the river with the west. Although he had never crossed the Atlantic, he imagined a capital of European scale. It should be graced with great public buildings and institutions, such as a national university, something he had long desired. On the banks of the Potomac, he would link commerce to the heart of the nation's democracy. The capital, so Washington believed, would become "the emporium of the United States."

To achieve this end, he would draw upon his knowledge of surveying, land speculation, and design. Experience had taught him well in each of these subjects; they fit naturally with the current task.

Surveying had come first. From his late father he had inherited the instruments of the art—a compass, parallel ruler, chain, and gunter's rule—and he filled his school copy book with definitions, theorems, and geometry problems, all related to the art of surveying. In 1747, shortly after his fifteenth birthday, he produced a plan of his half-brother Lawrence's turnip field, carefully recording the degrees, minutes, and seconds of its four boundaries. Finishing his drawing with a triumphant flourish, he wrote: "Survey'd by me."

The following year he had received a tract of 550 acres for helping with the survey of Lord Fairfax's land in the Shenandoah Valley. More surveys followed, close to two hundred in all. Washington combined his surveying ability with his knowledge of geometry and triangulation to place order upon the landscape, structure it in space and time, and with the precision of longitude and latitude, make a tangible record of that organization on a map. The surveyor's art appealed to Washington's desire for control and order that he worked so hard to cultivate in his private and public life.

Surveying also whetted Washington's appetite for land speculation. In the vast territories of America—and as the history of Washington,

DC, shows—speculation has always ranked among the chief pursuits of those who take risks in order to gain great financial rewards. Washington speculated in land acquisition with enthusiasm and frequent success. Like all speculators, he tried to buy at a low price, gambling that settlement and development, which he sometimes stimulated with his own money, would increase the land's value. In his twentieth year he purchased 1,459 acres on the Bullskin Creek in Fairfax County, Virginia, which he developed into Bullskin Plantation. After a 1763 visit to the Great Dismal Swamp, the dense marshland that straddles Virginia and North Carolina, he purchased 5,000 acres, which he tried to drain and make into arable land.

More reckless and daring men might place their entire fortunes on the altar of speculation and pray for success, but not Washington. Just as prudence and self-control guided his private life—he eschewed cards and gambling, the perennial pleasures of river gentlemen—he not surprisingly acted with care in land dealings. He incurred debts at times, especially on Mount Vernon, but he never borrowed recklessly, and he certainly never risked financial ruin for great profit. Still, he found prudent risk to be a tonic, and a profitable one. At the time of his death in 1799 he owned more than 52,000 acres in five states and the Ohio Valley, as well as building lots in Alexandria, Virginia, and the federal capital, Washington. Land speculation affirmed his belief in the future of America.

Washington's interest in building design did not equal Thomas Jefferson's, but his accomplishments were considerable nonetheless. He combined his knowledge of surveying, mathematics, and drawing with his reading of pattern books to execute some remarkable designs of his own. They survive in his plans for a delicate, Georgian parish church still standing at Pohick, Virginia, and for Mount Vernon. In 1757 he embarked upon a substantial expansion of his estate, including a new story and additions at each end of the house as well as outbuildings and gardens. Upon completion a decade later, Mount Vernon presented itself as a gentleman's Tidewater plantation and proved he had arrived as a man of property. But he wasn't satisfied. In 1773 he dramatically enlarged the main house by extending its length, topping its roof with a graceful cupola, and adding the piazza overlooking the river.

The Residence Act's ambiguity gave George Washington free rein to mold the new capital according to his vision. His surveyor's eye enabled him to plan the future city in his mind; his designer's sense gave him an understanding of the ways public buildings might express the ideals of the democracy; his speculator's skill offered him a way to unravel the Gordian knot of finance. He would strike a deal with the owners to sell the land for public buildings for a fixed price and create building lots on the remainder of the property needed to make the city. Half the lots would belong to the owners; half to the federal government. An auction of the government's lots would generate the cash he needed for construction. The capital of the United States would become George Washington's greatest speculative venture.

CREATING THE NEW capital was far from George Washington's only task. For the eight years of his presidency he faced unprecedented challenges both at home and abroad as he transformed the vision of a republican government put forth in the Constitution into a tangible reality. He appointed the first Supreme Court, established the idea of a presidential cabinet, and asserted the concept of executive privilege, and through his secretary of the treasury, Alexander Hamilton, he gave the nation fiscal solvency and stability. The nation had just a skeleton army, without a single professional officer, but he managed to muster a militia force of 15,000 men and march for fifteen days from Philadelphia west to Bedford to quell an insurrection of Pennsylvania farmers over a federal tax on whiskey. He had to establish the nation's presence in the world and yet maintain its neutrality after France declared war on Great Britain in 1793; he faced down the meddlesome French ambassador Edmond-Charles Genet, who tried to draw the nation into "war abroad and discord and anarchy at home"; and he had to manage the treaty that his special envoy, John Jay, negotiated with Great Britain, which called for British withdrawal from its forts in the Northwest and America's settlement of its pre–Revolutionary war debts.

All this time he had to contend with the certain knowledge that few in the Washington family survived past the age of fifty. "Washingtons don't live long," he once remarked. He was in his fifty-eighth year when he became president. He wore a full set of dentures carved from hippopotamus ivory. He suffered from the ravages of tumorous carbuncles on his thigh and his cheek. A serious case of pneumonia in early 1790 had brought him close to death.

Seeing him weakened, Jefferson and Madison and their followers sought to take advantage. Innuendo and rumor circulated throughout Philadelphia. The president had assumed the imperious power of a monarch; he was under the sway of Hamilton; his eyes were perpetually teary; he was drifting into senility. Beset by domestic and foreign problems, let down by men like Jefferson and Hamilton, whom he thought he could trust and whom he had long treated as the sons he never had, George Washington still forged ahead.

WITH REGARD TO the new federal district, the president knew his first challenge was to decide the exact place on the Potomac where the buildings for the nation's government would arise. From the outset he preferred the land between the Eastern Branch and Georgetown, a spot that held symbolic, practical, and personal meaning. Located roughly halfway between Massachusetts and Georgia, and close to the population center of the nation, the site suggested the new nation's precarious balance of North and South. One of its wooded hills would be an ideal site on which to erect a house for Congress to emphasize its symbolic importance to the democracy. The port at Georgetown would become a crucial link in trade between the western territories and the world, and the sheltered, deep, and ice-free waters of the Eastern Branch would serve as an anchorage for military vessels should the federal government ever decide to reestablish a navy. Two creeks, the Goose (which came to be called the Tiber) and the James, might be connected by canal to allow for efficient shipping between the Eastern Branch and the Potomac. And for Washington personally, the site was close by his own property on the Potomac. Should he retire in 1793, or even in 1797, he could continue to watch the progress of the government that he had helped to create and nurture from his piazza at Mount Vernon.

But he did not tip his hand. Experienced speculator that he was, he kept all the proprietors anxious lest he choose a site upriver. In mid-October 1790 he arrived on the Potomac "in order," so the *Maryland Journal and Baltimore Advertiser* reported, to locate "the Grand Columbian Federal City." After meeting with and raising the hopes of a number of Georgetown landowners, he rode upriver to examine other locations. At each stop, delegations of citizens welcomed him at their town's edge to lead him on a tour. Later they feted him with a dinner and many toasts.

At "Mr. Beltzhoover's tavern" in Hagerstown, Washington offered a toast of his own that betrayed all his hopes and fears: "May the residence law be perpetuate and Patowmac view the Federal City."

The trip was merely a strategic feint, but it worked. When Washington returned to Georgetown in mid-October, a number of property owners proffered their land, arguing that "no place" between the Eastern Branch and the fall line "offers so many advantages," and that "the hilliness of the Country . . . will at once contribute to the beauty, health, and security of a City intended for the Seat of Empire." The proprietors near the Tiber and Rock Creek made an offer to sell their property to the government for $40 an acre (about $550 today), with the understanding that every third acre would be returned to the seller. The landowners did not realize that Washington wanted all the land between Georgetown and the eastern shore of the Eastern Branch.

Still, Washington said nothing. Instead, he retired to Mount Vernon and awaited the third session of the 1st Congress, which would meet in Philadelphia in December. In his annual message to the representatives and senators, he mentioned the federal district not at all.

At last, on Monday, January 22, 1791, Washington announced his decision in surveyor's terms: there would be four ten-mile "lines of Experiment" denoting the boundaries of the District of Columbia. On a map of the river and its banks, the lines looked like a great diamond, with the apex at Silver Spring, Maryland. From there, two ten-mile lines fanned out, one running southwest to the edge of Falls Church, Virginia, the other southeast to Pleasant, Maryland. From those western and eastern points lines moved southward to converge at the diamond's lowest coordinate, the mouth of Hunting Creek below Alexandria, Virginia. The diamond included all the land Washington wanted: the City of Alexandria, Georgetown, both banks of the Eastern Branch, Carrollsburg, and Hamburgh. In these one hundred square miles, George Washington saw a federal territory that portended a greatness of size and promise for the United States that few others could have imagined.

Now Washington moved swiftly, transmitting his orders through Jefferson, who would initially serve as something of a civilian aide-de-camp. That January he appointed the three commissioners: David Stuart, Daniel Carroll, and Thomas Johnson. In February he named Andrew Ellicott, "a man of uncommon talents," to survey the District's boundary; and in March he had Jefferson send Peter Charles L'Enfant to Georgetown to draw, as Jefferson put it, "the particular grounds most likely to be approved for the site of the Federal town and buildings."

Washington might have made his life easier had he made better commissioner appointments. Instead, he chose friends who possessed no qualifications for the task. Of the three, Stuart and Carroll proved to be somewhat ineffective. Stuart, a doctor who lived on Abingdon Plantation in Alexandria (now the site of the Reagan National Airport), was married to the widow of Martha Washington's son in 1783. He enjoyed the president's complete trust on personal and political matters, and because of his fluency in French, he frequently translated official messages from Paris. But in matters concerning the new capital, Stuart was timid. Carroll, a member of Congress from Rock Creek, Maryland, proved even more so. As a member of one of the preeminent families of Maryland, he could be expected to look after the interests of his cousin Daniel Carroll of Duddington, who owned the land on which the Capitol would rise; and his brother John Carroll, the first Roman Catholic bishop in the United States. But in matters pertaining to the City of Washington, in the Federal District of Columbia, as the commissioners named it in September 1791, Daniel Carroll often seemed to be indifferent.

The third commissioner, Thomas Johnson from Frederick County, Maryland, was by far the most influential of the trio. Short and pugnacious—some called him "the Little Cock"—Johnson often showed himself to be headstrong and fractious. But he held clear opinions, always, and spoke with commanding authority even when he was wrong. A delegate to both Continental Congresses (he had nominated Washington to be commander-in-chief of the army), he had served as the first governor of Maryland, associate justice on the US Supreme Court, and president of the Potomac Company after Washington. He was decisive and strong-willed. As Carroll and Stuart had little appetite for conflict, they were content to let Johnson act alone.

ANDREW ELLICOTT WAS born into a family of Quakers, ardent foes of slavery, but they were industrious and shrewd land speculators. The Ellicotts owned a large wheat farm and a mill on the Patapsco River west of Baltimore at what is now Ellicott City. There, they persuaded neighboring farmers to convert their fields from tobacco to wheat and, for a price, milled their grain into flour. They bought vast tracts of land in today's Howard County between Washington and Baltimore, as well as land in Baltimore City. And they harnessed their aptitude for mechanics and mathematics to become clockmakers. Quaker pacifism notwithstanding, Andrew Ellicott regarded the Revolution as a defensive war and fought in the Maryland militia.

After the war, Ellicott gained renown for the accuracy of his clocks and mathematical instruments, and beginning in 1781, for publishing *The United States Almanack*, an annual filled with facts, weather predictions, verse, recipes, and maxims. He gained the notice of Benjamin Franklin, who proposed him for the American Philosophical Society, and David Rittenhouse, the nation's preeminent astronomer and maker of scientific instruments. In 1784 Rittenhouse invited Ellicott to join him in an expedition to complete Mason and Dixon's survey of the line separating the northern and southern states. (Indian attacks had forced the two Englishmen to abandon their survey in 1767.) More surveys followed in which Ellicott measured the length of the Niagara River and the height of its great falls; recorded the western and northern boundaries for Pennsylvania; charted the islands in the Allegheny and Ohio rivers; and helped bring about a resolution of the boundary dispute between New York and Pennsylvania over access to Lake Erie. Given his scientific and mechanical reputation in Philadelphia and Maryland and his brilliance as a surveyor, it was only natural that George Washington would appoint him to survey the District of Columbia.

Washington's orders to Ellicott, transmitted through Jefferson, were to provide "a true Meridian and the latitude of the place" and complete his survey with "all the accuracy of which your art is susceptible." In the coming months, Ellicott would cut a forty-foot-wide diamond swath through the wilderness, and within it he would translate George Washington's "Lines of Experiment" into an accurate boundary; he also would identify each mile with an eleven-inch-square gray sandstone plinth. Fourteen inches tall with a truncated pyramid at its top, it would be inscribed with the degrees and minutes and the words "JURISDICTION OF THE UNITED STATES."

Rarely a solitary enterprise, a land survey of any magnitude demands assistants, woodsmen to clear the brush and trees, men to run the lines, and especially at that time, someone versed in astronomical clocks, astronomy, and celestial observation. Ellicott often employed as many as twenty men working his surveys. But it was difficult to obtain labor on the Potomac; this time he would have just six.

His most important assistant was Benjamin Banneker. A gifted astronomer and mathematician who farmed a tract near the Ellicotts' land, Banneker lived the solitary life of a bachelor on the edge of the wilderness. Although rumors of his overindulgence in alcohol occasionally circulated through the neighborhood, most regarded him as a quiet, dignified, and contemplative man. He had a full head of white hair and always stood "perfectly upright and correct." Over his sixty years the largely self-taught Banneker had devoured astronomy books, created an accurate clock with gears carved from wood, and calculated the ephemeris—the daily position of the moon, the planets, and the stars—for an almanac that he hoped someday to publish.

It was an extraordinary opportunity. Banneker had never worked on a survey before; he suffered from arthritis, which would surely be aggravated by his exposure to the elements; and he would travel farther from home than he had ever been. But he had an opportunity to assist a talented surveyor, and, more importantly, to use scientific instruments whose sophistication and accuracy would enable him to study the heavens as never before. And no doubt he knew that such an opportunity was unknown to one of his color, for Benjamin Banneker was a free black whose skin was, as he said, "of the deepest dye."

Ellicott and Banneker began by erecting an observatory tent at Jones Point in Alexandria, the southernmost tip of the District's diamond. Their two most important instruments were an astronomical clock, to establish longitude, and a zenith telescope, to verify latitude and true north. For the next two months, the observatory tent was Banneker's home. Daily he maintained the astronomical clock, which was susceptible to even small changes in temperature and humidity. Each night he recorded celestial measurements with the zenith telescope, reputedly the most accurate American-made scientific instrument of the eighteenth century. His work enabled them to determine the meridian center of the District, which extended from Jones Point across the Potomac and up the center of today's Sixteenth Street and intersected the apex of the diamond about a mile west of today's Silver Spring. Banneker kept notes for Ellicott and established the base points that were so important to laying out the lines of the diamond.

Each daybreak, Ellicott, who slept across the Potomac in Georgetown, arrived to review his findings. As the sun rose in the sky, Banneker took yet more measurements to determine the correct longitude.

Banneker appears to have preferred the immutable constancy of the heavens, which he could determine with mathematical precision, over the capricious actions of human beings, which he could never fix. Though a free black, he still felt the sting of Virginia and Maryland law that forbade slaves from learning to read or even possess a Bible, the one book he had as a youth from which he had learned to read. Ellicott often took him along when he met with the commissioners, who each owned slaves, but Banneker likely remained silent, taking the measure of those around him. At meals he sat apart from the engineers and woodsmen. He was happiest when alone making calculations for Ellicott, and whenever time and his energy permitted, gathering celestial information for his own almanac.

While his workmen gradually established the District's boundary, Ellicott grew critical of the land and its inhabitants. "The country thro' which we are now cutting one of the ten-mile lines is very poor," he wrote to his wife from Virginia. "[It] bears no more proportion to the Country about Philadelphia and German-Town, for either wealth or fertility, than a Crane does to a stall-fed Ox."

By April 15, Ellicott and Banneker had completed enough of the survey to permit the dedication of the first perimeter stone at Jones Point. Ellicott, David Stuart, Daniel Carroll, the mayor of Alexandria, members of the Masonic Lodge, and the Reverend James Muir, pastor of the Presbyterian Church, assembled at Wise's Tavern in Alexandria to drink a toast to the "immovable monument of the wisdom and unanimity of North America." From the tavern the party proceeded to Jones Point, where the master of the Masonic Lodge dedicated the boundary marker with an offering of corn (for plenty), wine (for pleasure), and oil (for peace). Afterward the men returned to Wise's, where Rev. Muir offered a toast: "May jealousy, that green-eyed monster, be buried deep under the work which this day we have completed."

At the end of April, his astronomical calculations completed and the boundary stone at Jones Point in place, Benjamin Banneker left Jones Point and the survey to return to his farm. There he could continue his celestial observations and, with the help of the Ellicott family, publish the work he so prized: *Benjamin Banneker's Pennsylvania,*

Delaware, Virginia, and Maryland Almanac and Ephemeris for the Year of Our Lord 1792. Quakers and abolitionist societies promoted the volume as proof that skin color did not determine one's mental abilities.

Before its publication, Benjamin Banneker sent the manuscript of his almanac to Thomas Jefferson. In his letter accompanying the manuscript he told the secretary of state that he was "of the African race," but a free black, not under that state of tyrannical thraldom, and inhuman captivity, to which too many of my brethren are doomed." Recalling the time when "the arms and tyranny of the British crown were exerted with every powerful effort, in order to reduce you to a state of servitude," Banneker turned the Declaration of Independence against its author. "How pitiable is it to reflect, that although you were so fully convinced of the benevolence of the Father of Mankind . . . you should at the same time counteract his mercies, in detaining by fraud and violence so numerous a part of my brethren, under groaning captivity and cruel oppression." Jefferson, so said Banneker, was "guilty of that most criminal act, which you professedly detested in others, with respect to yourselves."

IN FEBRUARY 1791, Washington named the French-born Peter Charles L'Enfant to create "drawings . . . of the federal town and buildings." It was the president's single most important appointment and its consequences endure to this day. L'Enfant possessed exceptional abilities, energy, and vision; but also all-consuming pride, vanity, and arrogance, and also an almost childlike innocence about the realities of late eighteenth-century political life in America. Possibly inspired by a French translation of the Declaration of Independence, L'Enfant had arrived in America in 1777, proudly Anglicized his first name, and joined in the fight for independence as a lieutenant engineer. He fought gallantly in the Battle of Savannah and was captured at the Battle of Charleston in 1780. He was freed in a prisoner exchange of January 1782 as the war neared its end.

It is likely that L'Enfant's appointment unsettled Thomas Jefferson. The secretary of state ranked himself as the grand arbiter of public taste and one of the preeminent designers in America. After all, he had studied the great buildings of antiquity as well as those in European cities; he had absorbed Andrea Palladio's influential treatise *The Four Books of*

Architecture, and was incorporating the principles Palladio had adopted from Roman architecture into the house he was building at Monticello. He had also designed Virginia's neoclassical statehouse at Richmond. Now Washington, who had never lived in Europe, seemed to disregard his wealth of architectural knowledge, planning experience, and taste, entrusting the capital's plan to a different designer.

Given the context of their correspondence about the future capital, Jefferson had good reason to be perturbed by Washington's choice. In response to the president's request for suggestions about the design, Jefferson outlined his own vision in March 1791: about 1,500 acres, with 1,200 to be divided into quarter-acre lots. The remaining 300 acres would do just fine for the public buildings. Jefferson's capital would take in "about 20 good dwelling houses" for those belonging to the government, "about as many lodging houses, and half a dozen taverns." The land adjacent to Georgetown between the Rock and Tiber creeks was the best location for the capital, Jefferson said. He had even offered the president a sketch of where the buildings might be placed.

Jefferson's choice of the word "town," which he used in a March letter to L'Enfant, is telling, for he had a deep-rooted and visceral distrust of cities and those who inhabited them. "The mobs of great cities add just so much to the support of pure government, as sores do to the strength of the human body," he had written in his *Notes on the State of Virginia*. "A degeneracy in these is a canker which soon eats to the heart of its laws and constitution." As he later wrote, he regarded New York, where he had been forced to live in the government's first year, as "a cloacina of all the depravities of human nature." Francophile though he was, he must have lamented the presence of the 525,000 people who populated Paris when he was ambassador. "I view great cities as pestilential to the morals, the health and the liberties of man," he would tell his friend, the physician Benjamin Rush in 1800, the year the government moved to Washington. "True, they nourish some of the elegant arts; but the useful ones can thrive elsewhere, and less perfection in the others, with more health, virtue and freedom, would be my choice."

For Thomas Jefferson, republican virtues thrived best in the fields of small farms. Great tracts of land should be reserved for agriculture. Indeed, his own Monticello, at 5,000 acres, was far larger than the federal town he proposed. "Agriculture," he wrote to Washington in 1787, "is our wisest pursuit, because it will in the end contribute most to real

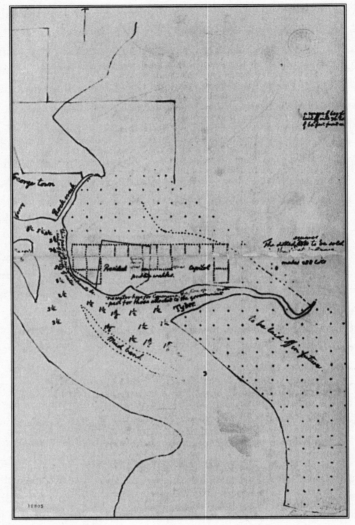

THOMAS JEFFERSON's drawing. CREDIT: George Washington Papers

wealth, good morals and happiness." Farmers were "the chosen people of God," and agriculture the "best preservative of morals."

Washington, however, had good reason for his choice. He had known L'Enfant from the winter at Valley Forge in 1777, when the Marquis de Lafayette had commissioned the young Frenchman, who was also an artist, to paint his portrait. After the war, L'Enfant's career as a designer had blossomed: he had produced panoramas for George Washington of the fortifications at West Point on the Hudson;

elaborate torchlit pavilions in Philadelphia for the French ambassador and his 1,100 guests to celebrate the birth of Louis XVII (including Washington, who was the guest of honor); and an elegant badge
that the general had commissioned for the Society of the Cincinnati,
a group of American and French officers who wished to preserve the
ideals of the Revolution.

Washington's inauguration in New York City in April 1789 revealed
the designer's architectural abilities as well as the extent of his conceit.
L'Enfant produced an elaborate inaugural parade and had transformed
New York's city hall into an august meeting place worthy of the 1st
Congress of the United States. His design for the façade of the building, which featured a grand portico, with a balcony on which Washington would take the Oath of Office, was pure show: four Doric columns
supported a frieze of thirteen stars and a pediment with a great gilt
bald eagle clutching thirteen arrows and an olive branch in its talons,
"surrounded with a glory." The eagle appeared to be, as one newspaper
put it, "bursting from a cloud."

But at the moment of George Washington's inauguration, L'Enfant's arrogance tripped him up, as it would in the months and years
to come. Believing that Congress had snubbed him during the ceremonies, he declined 10 acres of Manhattan land that the city burghers
offered as compensation for his work, though he was quick to accept a
commendation from the mayor and the "freedom of the city," which
gave him the rights of a citizen. Several years later he turned down still
another offer of $750 cash (about $10,000 today). He would have none
of it; presents of money and land might keep impoverishment at bay,
but they could never assuage his wounded pride. He was Peter Charles
L'Enfant, *the* architect of the Federal Hall.

Still, L'Enfant had impressed Washington. In a letter of September
1789, the designer proposed to "share in the undertaking" of creating
the "Federal City which is to become the Capital of this vast Empire."
No nation, he continued, ever had "the opportunity . . . of deliberately
deciding on the spot their Capital City should be fixed." Even though
the United States lacked the means to build a great city at the moment,
"the plan should be drawn on such a scale as to leave room for that
aggrandizement and embellishment which the increase of wealth of the
nation will permit it to pursue." By implication at least, L'Enfant suggested that he was the only choice to be the designer of the city. And

for Washington he was. Here was a man who used words like "Empire" and "wealth," who thought, as he was wont to say, *en grande*—who thought not of the United States as it was, but dreamed of all that it could be. Jefferson had designed an agrarian town. Washington had found the man to design a federal *city*.

No doubt it nettled Jefferson, too, that L'Enfant dismissed out of hand Jefferson's suggestion to place the capital between the Rock and Tiber creeks. The site was not suitable, L'Enfant wrote, "when considering the intended city on that grand scale on which it ought to be planned."

WASHINGTON MET WITH the proprietors of the land he wanted for the capital in March 1791. Having taken care to name only the site for the federal district, not the exact location of the government buildings, he reminded them that their game of resistance was a dangerous one: "whilst they were contending for the shadow," he recorded in his diary, "they might lose the substance"; better now "to surrender for public purposes."

To commissioner Daniel Carroll, Washington likely gave the task of persuading his cousin, Daniel Carroll of Duddington, to yield his land at a reasonable price. He asked Georgetown landowners and merchants Benjamin Stoddert and William Deakins Jr. to act as "agents" and purchase land "in the most perfect secrecy" for £25 (about $111 in the new US currency) an acre for the land that would become government property. Save for property owner David Burnes, the men were successful.

Burnes was another matter. A farmer of Scots descent who had inherited his tobacco fields from his father a quarter century earlier, he could be tough; some thought him a thoroughly unpleasant character, given to truculence, lawsuits, and anger. His buildings included a sturdy one-and-a-half-story planter's house with three dormer windows piercing its roof, a derelict tobacco barn, and a corn shed. The exhausted land was "chiefly cut down, and worn out, very much grubbed and washed," as one adversary in a lawsuit described it. "It will not bring one barrel of corn per acre." Yet Burnes was a shrewd negotiator who owned land essential to the seat of government: 450 acres between today's H Street and Constitution Avenue and Third and Eighteenth streets NW—that is, a good portion of Pennsylvania Avenue leading to today's Capitol,

White House grounds, and Lafayette Square. The Scotsman sensed from the attention being paid to the project that he had a prize to barter, and he bided his time.

The time came in June, when Washington arrived in Georgetown to consummate the government's agreement with proprietors. Only Burnes remained "obstinate," as Washington put it in a letter, but not even he could resist the president. On March 30, 1791, Burnes became the second proprietor to affix his signature to the agreement. The terms of the sale allowed him to continue cultivating his fields even if it meant a delay in constructing Pennsylvania Avenue. At last George Washington had the land he needed for his seat of government.

ON A JUNE afternoon in 1791, George Washington, Andrew Ellicott, and Peter Charles L'Enfant rode east from Georgetown "to take," so Washington recorded in his diary, "a more perfect view of the ground" of the new federal city. From David Burnes's fields they surveyed the prospect of the Potomac River, and then, continuing east across the Tiber Creek, they climbed to the crest of Jenkins Hill. With the confluence of the Eastern Branch and the Potomac, the cities of Alexandria and Georgetown, and the hills of Maryland and Virginia spread majestically before them, the time had come, the president wrote, "to decide finally on the spots on which to place the public buildings."

From their vantage point on Jenkins Hill, L'Enfant presented his vision of a city worthy of the new republic. He began by siting the two principal buildings: the "Congress House," as he called it, would command Jenkins Hill, "a pedestal waiting for a superstructure"; the "President's Palace," L'Enfant's name for today's White House, would rise about a mile away on the land partially belonging to David Burnes. A star of avenues each named for a state would radiate from the center of each house. Pennsylvania Avenue—the name would honor the state's importance in the nation's creation—would connect the two buildings. It would be "a direct and large avenue," 180 feet wide and lined with a double row of trees. These radiating avenues would intersect at circles and squares, to be named for heroes, and they would overlay a grid of streets similar to that of Philadelphia.

There was more, much more. A canal would connect the Eastern Branch with the Potomac; waters from the Tiber Creek would issue "from under the base of the Congress building" in a one-hundred-foot-wide cascade that would tumble forty feet into a broad pool. From the buildings housing the nation's legislative and executive branches of government, the representatives and the president could look across the landscape at flat-bottomed canal boats moving the products of America's agricultural abundance and manufacturing genius to and from the west. From each house, too, future representatives and presidents would take in "a grand equestrian statue," which, though L'Enfant did not say, Congress had proposed to erect in honor of George Washington.

To the designer—and ultimately the president—the plan was a powerful symbol of the potential of the young nation as set forth in its new Constitution. In miniature, the city would embody the rich and various energies of the nation's continental topography and its people; and like the continent itself, in the capital there would be room to grow. L'Enfant's city would begin in a small way, but the distances he had created between the intersection of the various streets allowed for the population, houses, and commerce to spread out in an orderly fashion across the landscape.

L'Enfant was making the best of a difficult site that would have daunted a less competent designer. Aside from the natural terraces, which he wisely used for the Capitol and the President's Palace, there was little else to commend it. The bank along the Potomac River was marsh; beyond it was a small channel and a narrow tidal slough of mire and muck. But L'Enfant envisioned a capital of the future: the riverbanks would be filled; the Tiber would become a canal, and the cascading water descending from the Congress House would evoke the great fountains of Rome.

The president embraced the design with enthusiasm. For George Washington, Peter Charles L'Enfant's plans reflected the nation's bold ideals.

IT IS LIKELY that up to this point Jefferson knew of L'Enfant chiefly by reputation. But it was enough to make him wary. As the American minister to France, Jefferson had had to deal with L'Enfant's creditors—the designer had left Paris without paying his debts, including the bill for the badges of the Society of the Cincinnati. Jefferson had also seen for himself the extravagant embellishments of the Federal Hall, and he knew of the architect's imbroglio over proper recognition for his work.

Where L'Enfant dreamed of a monumental city for the new capital, as grand as any in Europe, Jefferson saw a simple one, as small in scale as the center of Philadelphia. Where L'Enfant pictured the Congress House high above the Potomac on the summit of Jenkins Hill, connected to the President's Palace by a wide avenue, Jefferson saw the Capitol, a word he had drawn from the Temple of Jupiter on Rome's Capitoline Hill, and a President's House on the flat land hard by the Potomac and the Tiber, connected by a short public walk. Where L'Enfant envisioned a city worthy of the empire that he believed America would become, Jefferson saw a town where republican principles might prosper.

L'Enfant, of course, had little understanding of Jefferson's thinking. After the designer presented "preliminary rough drawings" to Washington on his March visit, "the delineation of a grand plan for . . . the city," so L'Enfant called it, he reported breathlessly to Jefferson in his best tortured prose that Washington "has left to me without any restriction soever." He would plan the city in "a new and original way." Jefferson was careful to keep his own thoughts private. "I am happy," he replied in a sentence that L'Enfant carefully underlined in pencil, "that the <u>president has left the planning of the town in such good hands.</u>"

From that meeting in June on Jenkins Hill until his dismissal in late February 1792, Peter Charles L'Enfant thought of George Washington as his king. He would submit to no one else, not to Thomas Jefferson, whom he regarded as little more than his king's secretary, and certainly not to the three commissioners, whom he considered merely as underlings. After all, George Washington had chosen him to lay out the federal city. He had settled on its design and on the location of the federal buildings without discussing them with the commissioners. L'Enfant, so he deluded himself, was a faithful servant to the president alone. But his fealty quickly proved a trial for Washington, who had to employ all his political skill to ensure that the plan to establish the capital on the banks of the Potomac survived.

Three events precipitated L'Enfant's downfall: the designer's reluctance to publish a map of the new city; his demolition of a house; and his absolute and arrogant refusal to submit to anyone other than the president. Taken separately, each offense might have been forgiven, but in the aggregate, especially when used by his adversaries, they would prove his ruin.

The map debacle, which left L'Enfant open to charges of intractability, was a serious issue for the president. Faced with a Congress reluctant to approve funds for government buildings, Washington decided to raise the money by auctioning city lots, setting the first sale for October 17, 1791. It wasn't until August 27 that L'Enfant presented his "Plan of the City intended for Permanent Seat of the Government of the United States" to the president, Madison, and Jefferson. Washington approved it and was anxious to have it printed. But where the president saw a potential for the money he so desperately needed to finance construction, L'Enfant saw confusion, "the beauties of locale reserved for private settlements all being absolutely lost in the chaos of felled timber." Postponing the sale until workers had improved the land, the designer argued, would "rise the property to its proper value." Instead of a sale, he proposed "borrowing a sum on the credit of the property itself." However abhorrent the thought of a loan might be to Washington personally (he had carried debt himself at Mount Vernon), he had seen the nation divide over debt before, and he knew it would be virtually impossible to secure Congress's assent for such a venture. Even broaching the subject might open yet again the nagging question of the location for the permanent seat of government.

His suggestion rebuffed, L'Enfant reluctantly contracted with a small Philadelphia engraver to produce 10,000 copies of the map. But the printing wasn't ready in time for the auction and the sale was a fiasco. The thirty-five lots that did sell realized a paltry $2,000 cash (about $27,500 today). Washington grew indignant. Purchasers naturally would not buy a "pig in a poke." He instructed his secretary to tell L'Enfant "that he must . . . look to the commissioners for directions." But the president still maintained, in a letter to Commissioner David Stuart, that no man "was better qualified" to design the city than Peter L'Enfant.

For a few days after the sale, all went well. The commissioners felt they had acquired enough money to direct L'Enfant to dig clay for bricks and quarry stone at Aquia, Virginia, about twenty miles down the Potomac. Men cleared the land of trees, work they had begun earlier in the summer.

The house demolition in late November 1791, however, demonstrated L'Enfant's imperious resistance to obeying any authority other than the president. The site, on the southeastern slope of Jenkins Hill, where Daniel Carroll of Duddington was building a house, protruded seven feet into the path of L'Enfant's projected New Jersey Avenue. When the designer told him that it would have to be razed, Carroll quickly protested to Washington and rode off to Annapolis for a court order to prevent the demolition. But L'Enfant was faster. When Carroll returned, judge's order in hand, he found his house reduced to a pile of lumber and stone. Washington had warned his architect that he must submit to the demands of others, in this case the commissioners, who had ordered him not to demolish the house. They added this incident to the case they were building to have him dismissed.

The commissioners, particularly Thomas Johnson, had taken a dislike to L'Enfant because the Frenchman contended that he alone was in charge of construction. Shortly after Carroll's house was razed, they arbitrarily ordered the dismissal of the men L'Enfant had hired to quarry stone and dig the foundation for the future Capitol. The foreman refused; his men would follow only L'Enfant's orders. "The conduct of Major L'Enfant and those employed under him, astonishes me beyond measure!" Washington wrote to Jefferson when word of the contretemps reached Philadelphia. He must, the president wrote, "reduce himself."

By January 17, 1792, L'Enfant had grown worried. Addressing a letter and lengthy memorandum to Washington, he proposed a "permanent organization . . . for continuing all future operations." He recognized he was once again going around the commissioners, but to him they were not acting in the best interests of the project. Work had to begin, yet there was no plan, and "the season [is] already far advanced." A loan "must be sought for 1,000,000" to fund four years of work. "The effect of this expenditure," L'Enfant continued, "will enhance the value of Lots to such degree that a more considerable sale may commence."

Another letter followed: the commissioners, he said, presented obstacles "that must Impede the way to a new organization of the whole sistem." He must, he said, "renounce the pursuit unless the power of effecting the work with advantage to the publick, and credit to myself is left me." And still another letter went to Jefferson, whom L'Enfant mistakenly considered to be friendly: the commissioners were guilty of "supercilious conduct and haughty superiority." Washington decided to dismiss his designer. With the president's concurrence, Jefferson curtly replied to L'Enfant, on February 27, "your services must be at an end."

The commissioners prevailed in their struggle with L'Enfant. They now had unquestioned control over the labor and building progress. They could assent to schemes for land speculation and buy and sell property, they hoped, at the most advantageous times. But George Washington had lost the one whose vision of the future American empire was so compatible with his own. His final letter to L'Enfant suggests his regret and the inevitable finality of their formal relationship: "The continuance of your services (as I have often assured you) would have been pleasing to me, could they have been retained on terms compatible with the law. Every mode has been tried to accommodate your wishes on this principle, except changing the commissioners. . . . To change the commissioners cannot be done on ground of propriety, justice or policy." And then he closed "with sincere wishes for your happiness and prosperity."

PETER CHARLES L'ENFANT immediately became a nonperson, one whose very existence as the designer of the capital the commissioners sought to forget. In the month following his termination, the *Universal Asylum and Columbian Magazine* published an article about the new city "illustrated with an accurate engraving." The article glowingly described the "convenience, regularity, elegance of prospect, and free circulation of air" that the plan afforded. It took into account the placement of the buildings, the width of the grand transverse avenues, the footpaths, and the paved ways for carriages. It spoke of the skill of the surveyor Andrew Ellicott, who left "nothing to the uncertainty of the compass." It mentioned L'Enfant not at all.

Nor was the "accurate engraving" L'Enfant's. Even before the designer's dismissal, the commissioners had asked Ellicott to produce a new map. He did so in such short order that the product was flawed in ways that survive to this day. Ellicott's superb talents as a surveyor did not translate agreeably to urban design. Where L'Enfant had conceived subtle shifts of alignment for his avenues that would delight the eye and allow for a reciprocity of views, Ellicott drew straight lines with an engineer's precision that lacked inspiration; where L'Enfant had allowed for rolling hills and grade variations to lend an individuality to the various squares, Ellicott leveled the land; where L'Enfant had designed "five grand fountains" to function as gateways and focus visual attention on public buildings (including the cascade of water from the base of the Capitol), Ellicott saw bare land; where L'Enfant had placed the Capitol back from the western edge of Jenkins Hill, Ellicott moved it forward, adding space on the eastern front. Nevertheless, Washington and the commissioners were satisfied. They had their map at last.

L'Enfant continued his descent from designer to pauper. Despite a letter from Jefferson conveying Washington's belief that L'Enfant should receive between $2,500 and $3,000 (between $34,000 and $41,000 today) as a *"reward for* his past services," the commissioners offered him just $1,500 ($20,000 today) and a city lot. L'Enfant would not stoop to accept it. For a time, Alexander Hamilton hired him to plan the new town of Paterson, New Jersey, and the secretary of war had him design a fort on the Delaware River near Wilmington; but in each case the drawings proved too elaborate. Later L'Enfant would decline the offer of a position as professor of "the Art of Engineering" at West Point proffered by James Monroe.

Soon he was destitute. In December 1800, he moved to the city he had designed. He stalked the corridors of the Capitol, vainly making his case for just compensation. Starting in November 1801, he wrote appeals to Thomas Jefferson, now the president, but met only a cool rebuff. He left a trail of mounting debt as he exhausted his credit in tavern after tavern. Seeing him in 1806, the architect Benjamin Henry Latrobe painted a grim portrait: "Daily through the city stalks the picture of famine L'Enfant and his dog. This singular man, of whom it is not known whether he was ever educated to his profession or not, had the courage to undertake any public work that might be offered to him. He has not succeeded in any, but was always honest, and is now miserably poor. He is too proud to receive any assistance and it is very doubtful in what manner he subsists."

No longer elegant in bearing, L'Enfant drifted into his seventh decade. He suffered "from symptoms of broken shoes, rent pantaloons, [and was] out at elbows," as one observer wrote. Succor would finally come from the Digges family, who gave him lodging first at Warburton Manor, Maryland, now the site of Fort Washington on the Potomac south of the capital, and then at Green Hill, another Digges family plantation at Chillum, near Silver Spring, Maryland. There he would die in June 1825, attended to by the mistress of Green Hill, Eleanor Carroll Digges, daughter of Daniel Carroll of Duddington, whose house L'Enfant had razed in 1791.

IT FELL TO George Washington to cope with the consequences of L'Enfant's dismissal. The president already had a full portion of challenges: France and Great Britain were edging ever closer to a war that might possibly draw in the United States; a monetary collapse in the spring of 1792 threatened the country's financial system; and, most disheartening of all, Jefferson and Hamilton, two men whom Washington had treated as sons, were, as Jefferson later said, "daily pitted in the cabinet like two cocks," locked in a bitter dispute over monetary policy that threatened to rive the slaveholding South and the mercantile North. The enmity between the two men—and their supporters— served to divide the nation's government into factions, Federalists and Republicans. And then added to these challenges was the unbuilt federal capital.

In truth the District of Columbia was but an idea, lines that seemed more imagined than real, drawn upon a map of Maryland and Virginia and their common border of the Potomac. Washington well understood this truth when deciding whether he should accept a second term as president. If he heeded the lure of Mount Vernon and the quiet life of a Cincinnatus tending his fields, a desire he expressed to James Madison that May, the entire enterprise of building a national capital might well fail. "The current in *this* city sets so strongly against the Federal City," the president wrote to Jefferson from Philadelphia in March 1792, "that I believe nothing that <u>can</u> be avoided will ever be accomplished in it." Philadelphians were building a "President's House," with the hope of inducing the government to stay. The public mind was "in an equilibrium" about the location, Washington told his commissioners in March: "The whole success of the federal City depends upon the exertions which may be made in the ensuing season." If the capital of the United States was to be built on the Potomac, George Washington would have to continue as president.

CHAPTER 2

Planners, Speculators, and Slaves

In America, where more than in any other country in
the world, a desire for wealth is the prevailing passion,
there are few schemes which are not made the means
of extensive speculations, and that of erecting the federal city presented irresistible temptations.

—Duc de la Rochefoucauld-Liancourt, 1799

Without Peter Charles L'Enfant, the task of building a capital
city that lay before George Washington became even more
Herculean. Creating a city, even a small one, was almost unheard of in
the eighteenth century. Ideally, it demanded the firm hand of a supervisor, detailed building plans, a renewable stockpile of materials, a large
supply of laborers and artisans, and great reserves of money. Washington had none of these. Instead, he had three commissioners whose
expertise was scant and whose value was limited.

Washington knew he had to show some sign of progress to convince
skeptics in Philadelphia. In the summer of 1792, he visited Rock Creek at
the future K Street, where a handsome arched bridge was rising twenty
feet above the water. No one seems to have told the president that the
structure's piers would force the three-hundred-foot-wide creek into a
channel just sixty feet wide, and that after a hard rain, its waters would
back up, flood the city, and scour the supports. The arch soon collapsed.

More visible than a bridge would be construction on the Capitol
and the President's House, but the buildings had yet to be designed.

Although L'Enfant had begun digging foundations at both sites, he had never revealed his drawings, if indeed there were any. "The plans . . . ought to come forward immediately for consideration," the president wrote to Thomas Jefferson that spring. But as the nation had no design tradition of its own, there were few architects. Indeed, in eighteenth-century America, the word usually meant a master builder, one who combined his knowledge of mathematics with his experience as a carpenter or mason. For inspiration, a master builder usually referred to books like Batty Langley's *The City and Country Builder's and Workman's Treasury of Designs*, or Abraham Swan's *The Carpenters Complete Instructor*, as Washington himself had when building Mount Vernon.

With Washington's concurrence, Jefferson held design competitions for the President's House and the Capitol. In March 1792, newspapers from Boston to Charleston announced "A PREMIUM of five hundred dollars, or a MEDAL of that value" for the winning design of the President's House.

James Hoban took the $500 prize (about $6,875 today). Trained at the Royal Dublin Society's School of Architectural Drawing, Hoban had come to America after the War of Independence to pursue his vocation as a draftsman and carpenter in Charleston, South Carolina. An imposing black-haired Irishman, his florid face, aquiline nose, and calm demeanor inspired confidence in all, including George Washington, who met him in Charleston in 1791. So taken was Washington with Hoban's work that he sought out the architect, discussed his desires for the President's House with him, and commended him to the commissioners.

Hoban's design, which drew its inspiration from the home of the Duke of Leinster in Dublin, conformed to the commissioners' request that the "Central Part" of the house "may be detached and erected for the present," and be "capable of admitting the additional parts" in the future. Its footprint would be about a quarter the size of the foundations L'Enfant had begun. The three stories (later reduced to two, when the basement story was eliminated during construction) featured a center hall at the north entrance, an oval room at the center, whose windows afforded a view of the Potomac, and the great East Room, which would become the setting for receptions. In addition to awarding him the prize for the building, the commissioners hired Hoban for an additional 300 guineas a year (about $19,500 today) to oversee its construction as well as other projects in the capital.

It remained only for the Freemasons to consecrate the President's House with a solemn ritual. That October 13, members of Georgetown's Lodge Number 9 led a parade from Suter's Fountain Inn down a horse path to the southwest corner of the site. After the requisite Masonic formalities, the master mason placed on the cornerstone a brass plate inscribed with the names of the nation's president, the city's three commissioners, the building's master mason, and a closing command: "VIVAT RESPUBLICA." Then another stone was placed atop the first. It was but a few stones in a shallow hole. Yet it marked a beginning.

Choosing an architect for the Capitol did not go as smoothly. The commissioners had called for a brick building, the honest republican material Jefferson favored. It promised to be a huge building, the largest in the United States, dwarfing Independence Hall in Philadelphia, Nassau Hall in Princeton (then the largest in the United States), or L'Enfant's Federal Hall in New York City. The advertisement called for a conference room, room for the representatives "sufficient to accommodate 300 persons each," and a "Senate room of 1200 square feet area," along with lobbies for each and twelve committee rooms. In January 1793, after some delay and much consultation with Washington, who had not been happy with any submission up to the last, the commissioners chose the plans drawn by another recent arrival to the United States, William Thornton. Unfortunately, funds had become so scarce that the commissioners had to borrow the money they had promised for the prize.

Romantic dreamer, Quaker, abolitionist, alphabet reformer, medical doctor, painter, sculptor, poetaster, inventor, horse racer, scientific experimenter, botanist, essayist, and amateur architect, "a little genius at everything," William Thornton possessed all the virtues of a polymath, and many of the vices. Born in 1759 on the island of Tortola in the British West Indies to a wealthy sugar plantation owner, he was sent at the age of five to relatives in Lancashire, England, for his education. After an apprenticeship with a Quaker apothecary and surgeon and medical training at the universities of Edinburgh and Aberdeen, Thornton became a doctor.

Over the years, the bands of Thornton's Quaker precepts tightened on his conscience. He grew increasingly guilty with the knowledge that the seventy to eighty slaves who worked his sugar plantation brought him the income and the freedom to do whatever he wished. The values of America's Declaration of Independence and of abolitionist thinkers in England had only accentuated his pangs of conscience: "I am induced," he wrote to a friend, "to render free all that I am possessed of."

In 1786, the tenth year of American independence, Thornton landed in Philadelphia, where his various interests gained him notice. (He would live at Fifth and Market streets with James Madison and other delegates to the constitutional convention.) Within a few years, Thornton had taken a wife, had been elected to the American Philosophical Society, had joined with John Fitch to help build the first successful steamboat, and had won the competition to design a new building for the Library Company of Philadelphia.

Thornton had so absorbed the ideals of the US Constitution and its bicameral legislature that he was able to translate them into architectural symbols. His Capitol design featured a central neoclassical domed temple and portico flanked by two wings to house the senators and representatives. "Thornton's plan has captivated the eyes and judgment of all," Jefferson wrote to the commissioners. "It is simple, noble, beautiful, excellently distributed, and moderate in size." Washington saw that Thornton had done this and more when he gave his official approval on April 3, 1793. The amateur architect from Tortola had created an allegory of the republic that would be realized in brick and stone.

Thornton's plans, however, were unsound. Delayed at his Tortola sugar plantation, where he was engaged in a futile attempt to free his slaves, he had drawn the designs in haste and submitted them after the July 1792 deadline. He lacked any professional training, a fact he boasted of regularly, and which many found troubling. ("In building an edifice so costly and so important, could they not have brought over one of the more celebrated architects of Europe?" a Polish visitor wondered after meeting with Thornton.) His inexperience exasperated others who had entered the competition, especially Stephen Sulpice Hallet, a French-trained architect who had fled to America in the wake of the Revolution of 1789. Jefferson had encouraged Hallet's submission, going so far as to review several iterations of his plan, and his interest had given the architect the idea that the commission was his. "Some difficulty arises with respect to Mr. Hallet," Washington wrote to his commissioners after Thornton was chosen, "who, you know, was in some degree led into his plans by ideas we all expressed to him." So that his feelings might be "salved and soothed," the commissioners awarded the

AN AMALGAMATION of Georgian architecture that reflected the aesthetics of England and the neoclassical elements that hearkened back to the Roman Pantheon, Thornton's plans captured the intellectual spirit of the new nation. Owing to the designer's want of formal training, however, his design contained many flaws that caused problems for succeeding generations of architects, engineers, and builders. CREDIT: Library of Congress

Frenchman the second-place prize and hired him to "make calculations of the expence and materials" of Thornton's plan.

Hallet perused Thornton's plans with a trained eye. There were some disturbing aspects: many parts of the building, including the Senate, were without adequate light and air; galleries sometimes blocked windows, stairways wanted headroom, and, most troubling of all, "the floor of the central peristyle [was] too wide to support itself." In effect, the building could collapse. Hallet took it upon himself to redesign the west front of the building, reconfigure the placement of windows, and suggest other substantial alterations. Thornton brushed the criticisms aside. The lack of support for the floor was a slight mistake in the plans, he conceded to Jefferson, but any skillful builder would recognize and rectify the problem. Hallet, not he, was the incompetent one, and his motive was jealousy.

Washington himself entered the dispute. He had approved Thornton's design "knowing . . . the anxiety of the public to see both buildings [the Capitol and the President's House] progressing, and supposing the plan to be correct." Now these objections were wasting time at a crucial moment. Eventually, the commissioners would on Washington's orders dismiss Hallet, who slunk back to Philadelphia to practice his art there.

For the moment, Thornton had triumphed. Nevertheless, the good doctor's lack of training would bring him, and the Capitol, considerable difficulty in the future.

Washington decided to make the start of the Capitol's construction a very public and symbolic celebration that would affirm the government's place on the Potomac. He hadn't been present at the dedication of the stone marking the southern tip of the District at Jones Point, or at the laying of the cornerstone at the President's House, but this time he would be there. And since he was a master mason himself, he decided to invest the event with all the symbolic trappings of the Masonic Order.

At 10:00 a.m. on Wednesday, September 18, 1793, the president crossed the Potomac with his brothers from Masonic Lodge Number 22 of Alexandria and members of the Alexandria Volunteer Artillery. After joining with Maryland's Masonic Lodge Number 9, the entourage proceeded up Pennsylvania Avenue in full regalia, stepped gingerly on the fallen tree that served as a bridge across the Tiber, and ascended the hill for the dedication ceremony. The contrast between the marchers, dressed in medieval costumes, and the landscape must have been remarkable to slaves and farmers, and perhaps to David Burnes, across whose land they tramped. The "park," or "President's Square," was an open grassland; Pennsylvania Avenue was no avenue at all but a recently cleared road, still marred by stumps and holes, passing through the wheat and tobacco fields that the prickly Burnes had insisted upon harvesting. Closer to the site of the Capitol, the procession encountered a crowd of several hundred citizens who had come out for the occasion. Still, "the procession marched two abreast," a newspaper reported, "in the greatest solemn dignity, with music playing, drums beating, colors flying, and spectators rejoicing."

As they neared the southeastern corner of the Capitol's north wing (the only part of the building under construction), the procession divided into two columns to allow the "Grand sword bearer," the "Grand Master," and the President of the United States to proceed to the edge of the foundation. Wearing white gloves and the apron of the craft made for him by the Marquis de Lafayette's wife, Washington and his two Masonic brothers descended into the trench. Grand Master Joseph Clark, a skilled mason, handed Washington a silver plate with an inscription that noted it was "the thirteenth year of American

Independence." The president placed the plate on the ground as work-men carefully lowered a three-foot-square cornerstone over it. Clark then followed with the all-significant corn, wine, and oil. Prayers and numerous artillery volleys concluded the ceremony. The entire entou-rage—including onlookers—ended the afternoon in a park east of the Capitol, where they feasted on a five-hundred-pound barbecued ox and celebrated "with every abundance of other recreation."

However imperfect Thornton's plans might be, the Capitol of the United States, one corner at least, had a firm foundation.

EVEN AS GEORGE Washington was dealing with questions about the plans for the Capitol, he had to secure money for the entire project. Maryland had committed $72,000 (about $990,000 today); Virginia, $120,000 (about $1,650,000 today). But he had little else beyond those small sums. The first auction of lots had been an embarrassment, and still Congress had shown no inclination to allocate funds. Prospects were dim.

The situation rendered the president and his commissioners all the more vulnerable to anyone with a scheme to secure funding, no matter how questionable it, or they, might be. As often as not, those who came forth were speculators and swindlers, golden dreamers all, attempt-ing to make or extend their fortunes in buying, selling, and building. Some were competent, others were naïve, and still others were outright frauds. Desperate for money, Washington and his commissioners fre-quently accepted the investors' proposals. It was a moment when men with high ideals and dreams for the nascent republic met adventur-ers who possessed different values. But those values were nonetheless American. Land speculation had helped to develop towns across the American landscape. The new capital offered an opportunity for such speculation on a grand scale; perhaps it might work.

Those who succumbed to the irresistible temptations of speculation were men of varied backgrounds and experience. Several were finan-ciers; some had served in the Revolution; all enjoyed great wealth, or claimed to. For a while they all deceived Washington and his commis-sioners; many deceived their partners also, and some deceived them-selves. In the end they all suffered financial ruin. Four went to debtors' prison; one died there. But far greater than their personal failures were the effects of their dubious financial schemes upon the city, effects that have rippled through Washington's history even to this day.

For the most part the speculators' golden dreams amounted to little more than variations on the theme of buying the building lots at a low price and selling them later at a higher one, on the promise that they would then be close to the federal government buildings and to the workers who would soon arrive. Buildings to accommodate the new citizens would rise, the lots would appreciate, and the owners would sell them at a profit. Unfortunately, the web of lines crisscrossing the maps of the barely planned city proved a trap for the avaricious.

Samuel Blodget was one of the first lured to the web. Typical of many American entrepreneurs, he possessed great ability but was beguiled by a self-assurance that knew no bounds. A failed business venture in Exeter, New Hampshire, had left him and his father (who assumed his debts) in penury, but another speculation in Boston's East India trade brought him a fortune. By 1789, Blodget had moved to Philadelphia, organized one of the nation's first insurance companies, designed the classic marble Bank of the United States, and married the daughter of the provost of the University of Pennsylvania.

Flushed with success, Blodget turned his attention to the new capital. Having purchased five lots in the recent auction, he proposed "purchasing and *building* a whole street in the new City," as Jefferson characterized it to the commissioners. Although that idea failed because Blodget couldn't sell the lots quickly enough, he presented another novel scheme in March 1792: to secure $500,000 (about $6,875,000 today) in loans by selling warrants that would be backed by the collateral of the city lots. With that money in hand, serious construction could begin. Jefferson, Washington, and the commissioners had little choice but to listen carefully. The auction of city lots had yielded little; L'Enfant had been dismissed; a financial panic in New York that spring, the first in the nation's history, had reduced the value of securities by 25 percent in two weeks; and, worst of all, New Yorkers and Pennsylvanians in Congress were caballing to repeal the 1790 Residence Act.

As Washington soon learned, the plan was doomed. "I hope Mr. Blodget does not begin to hesitate concerning the loan?" he wrote to Jefferson on March 21, ending his sentence with the urgency of a question mark. Blodget hadn't hesitated, but he hadn't succeeded, either. On a recent trip to New York and Boston, he had found "a very gloomy aspect" on the Hudson and "a want of Cash" on the Charles. He had promised $50,000 (about $687,500 today) by mid-May and an equal amount by mid-November. But the amount dwindled to just $10,000 (about $137,500 today), money that came from Blodget's personal account.

Neither daunted nor embarrassed, Blodget asked to be named superintendent of construction and cooked up another and bolder scheme for raising cash: a $350,000 (about $4,810,000 today) lottery, the largest ever held in America, with 16,737 prizes, including the grand prize of "1 Superb Hotel, with baths, out-houses, &c. &c. to cost $50,000." As was the practice of the time, syndicates could be depended upon to purchase blocks of outstanding tickets. Advertisements appeared in major newspapers, always headed with the words, in bold type, "**BY THE COMMISSIONERS**." That Washington and the others eagerly embraced Blodget's plan indicates how desperate they were for cash.

The idea of a hotel—the grand prize of Blodget's lottery—was a novel one for the nation, but Blodget believed it would serve the needs of transient members of Congress, merchants, and those with federal business. He enlisted James Hoban to design a three-story Georgian structure graced by a pediment supported by six Doric columns. Along with the Capitol and the President's House, Blodget's hotel would come to dominate the Washington skyline. But months later, when a Philadelphia man, the "fortunate possessor" of ticket 37531, journeyed to Washington to claim the promised "keys of the Hotel," he found little more than a large hole in the ground. Blodget hadn't completed his hotel, and the additional 16,000 winning ticketholders realized just a fraction of their promised winnings. Instead of using the lottery money to build, Blodget had engaged in yet more speculation that yielded little.

By early 1793, Washington, Jefferson, and the commissioners had lost patience. The president had wanted a person of "industry & integrity" to execute his building plans—someone who could always be present in the capital—but his superintendent was busy hustling tickets in Philadelphia, New York, and Boston and was seldom seen in the city. Construction had stalled. A year earlier Washington had called Blodget "<u>certainly</u> a projecting genius," but now he had cause to reconsider: "Speculation," he wrote, "has been his primary object from the beginning." The commissioners dismissed Blodget, but they weren't through with him. His dismissal arrived in May 1793, just as the entrepreneur was advertising a second lottery, this time for $400,000 (about

By the COMMISSIONERS

Appointed to prepare the Public Buildings, &c. within the City of WASHINGTON, for the reception of Congrefs, and for their permanent refidence after the year 1800—

A LOTTERY

FOR THE IMPROVEMENT OF THE

FEDERAL CITY.

50,000 Tickets at 7 dollars, is — — 350,000 dollars.

LIST of PRIZES, viz.

1 Superb Hotel, with baths, out-houfes, &c. &c. to coft					50,000
1 Cafh Prize,	—	—	—	—	25,000
1 ditto,	—	—	—	—	20,000
1 ditto,	—	—	—	—	15,000
1 ditto,	—	—	—	—	10,000
2 ditto,	-	5,000	is	- -	10,000
10 ditto,	-	1,000	is	- -	10,000
20 ditto,	-	500	is	- -	10,000
100 ditto,	-	100	is	- -	10,000
200 ditto,	-	50	is	- -	10,000
400 ditto,	-	25	is	- -	10,000
1,000 ditto,	-	20	is	- -	20,000
15,000 ditto,	-		is	- -	150,000

16,737 PRIZES. DOLLARS 350,000
33,263 BLANKS.

50,000

The fole defign of this Lottery being to facilitate other improvements together with the public Buildings—it is the particular defire of the Commiffioners that thefe may be effected with as few deductions from the Prizes as poffible—how far their endeavours may be anfwered, the Scheme of the Lottery will demonftrate. The keys of the Hotel, when compleat, will be delivered to the fortunate poffeffor of the ticket drawn againft its number. All the other prizes will be paid WITHOUT DEDUCTION, IN ONE MONTH AFTER THE DRAWING, by the City Treafurer at Wafhington, or at fuch Bank or Banks as may be hereafter announced.

The drawing will commence on Monday the 9th of September next, at the City of Wafhington.

Tickets may be had of Col. William Dickens, City Treafurer of Wafhington; of Meffrs. James Weft, and Co. Baltimore; of Mr. Peter Gilman, Bofton; and at fuch other places as will be hereafter publifhed.

N. B. ONE HUNDRED DOLLARS will be given for the beft PLAN of an elegant and convenient HOTEL or INN, with hot and cold Baths, Stables and other out-houfes, *if prefented on or before the 10th of April next*; and a preference will be given to the Artift for a Contract, provided he be duly qualified to complete his plan. The ground on which the Hotel and out-houfes are to be erected, will be a corner lot of about 90 by 200 feet, with a back avenue to the ftables, &c. Sections and eftimates of the expenfe will be expected with the elevations, &c. complete; and 50,000 dollars muft be regarded by the Architect as the utmoft limit in the expenfe intended for this purpofe.

S. BLODGET,

January 19, 1793. Agent for the affairs of the City.

LOTTERY BROADSIDE. CREDIT: The New-York Historical Society

$5,480,000 today) to erect "an elegant specimen of . . . private build-ings." The prizes included six "magnificent dwelling houses" that would never be built. Like the first lottery, the second scheme failed.

Blodget was not finished with Washington, either. He would become the first president of the Bank of Columbia; he would start a fire insurance company; he would take up George Washington's scheme for a national university; and he would go to prison for debt. And it was Samuel Blodget who lured James Greenleaf to the Potomac River.

LIKE SO MANY others who came to Washington, the twenty-six-year-old James Greenleaf had more than one past. Of old New England stock, he possessed a courtly and charming manner and a reckless sense of self-assurance. It was an air that Gilbert Stuart captured in his por-trait: full-cheeked face, powdered hair tied in a queue, ruffled shirt and neckerchief, blue coat and gilt buttons—the very image of a gentleman possessing wealth and confidence. He had made his money through shipping and banking speculation in New York and Holland, and, by appointment of George Washington, had been the American consul in Amsterdam. But other matters of Greenleaf's past were more com-plicated. A Dutch baroness had duped him into marriage by claiming she carried his child; Dutch bankers, from whom he had borrowed a small amount of money, deluded him into thinking he could ask for more. It was this slim promise of ready money that Greenleaf had in his mind when he returned to America in 1793 in search of opportunities for speculation.

Over dinners in Philadelphia in the summer of 1793, Samuel Blodget painted a bright portrait of the new city for James Greenleaf— the capital and the president's mansion, the avenues, the stone and brick "Union Public Hotel," as he sometimes called it, and, especially, the fortune to be had from land speculation. For his part, Greenleaf claimed that a million dollars from Dutch bankers awaited him. He could well be the city's salvation. By August, Blodget and Greenleaf had become partners.

James Greenleaf stepped forward at an opportune time. Another auction of lots had not gone well, and although George Washington had bought four, few joined him. The president and his commissioners determined they had little choice but to sell the lots privately. Greenleaf purchased 3,000 building lots, 5,265 square feet each, for $66.50 apiece (about $900 today), with the promise to make seven annual interest-free payments of $21,000 (about $288,000 today) and build ten houses a year for the next decade. He would also loan the commissioners $2,600 (about $37,750 today) a month, at 6 percent interest. A letter of introduction from George Washington, and the promise of a loan from Amsterdam, helped to convince the commissioners to accept the terms.

That December, two more speculators, Robert Morris and John Nicholson, succumbed to Greenleaf's promise of credit in Amsterdam, joining Greenleaf as partners. Morris's financial acumen was undoubted, and it must have given his friend George Washington heart to know that someone of his sagacity, the one who had carried the financial burden of the Revolution, was now behind the construction. Nicholson, the comptroller general of Pennsylvania, possessed energy, financial skill, and numerous interests. He dabbled in exports, glass and button manufacture, textile production, steamboat promotion on the Delaware, road construction, lead mining, and city development. Eyewitnesses held that he could write a letter with one hand while simultaneously making a copy with the other—and carry on a conversation. Probity sometimes eluded him, however; as comptroller he was forced to resign after cornering the market for Pennsylvania's bonds and lands.

Not content with Greenleaf's original purchase, Morris and Nicholson doubled it to 6,000 lots, about 720 acres of the city. These cost more, so the combined amount of the seven annual payments jumped to $72,000 (about $990,000 today). The money would enable construction of the public buildings in time for the government's move in 1800. But when they began their land speculation, neither Morris nor Nicholson had money. Greenleaf promised them credit, while the lots promised a quick turnover and a profit. Vast tracts of wilderness land had brought them little cash and many debts. Like so many speculators, the pair found flirtation with bankruptcy a test of their nimbleness and wits— an addictive stimulant that made their desire for riches all the more exciting, even sublime.

The partners wanted more. They created the North American Land Company, and under its aegis Morris bought 649 more lots from the original proprietors. Greenleaf inveigled Daniel Carroll of Duddington to give him twenty lots on South Capitol Street "free of charge" with the stipulation that he build a two-story brick house on each within three years. (Carroll's kilns would supply the bricks.) Should Greenleaf not fulfill his part of the bargain, he would forfeit the property and pay a £100 penalty (about $4,400 today) for each lot. With just a year to go in the agreement, Greenleaf quietly sold the lots to Morris and Nicholson. They tried to build the houses in time, but were only able to complete twenty roofless, windowless, empty shells. By this time Carroll was in a financial bind, brought down by the trio's failure to pay him for any of the properties, or even for the bricks he had sold them on credit. After Carroll took back his lots and the buildings, Greenleaf, Morris, and Nicholson had no compunction about suing him for the unlawful seizure of their property.

Initially, however, there were good intentions on all sides, and there was even some progress. If Greenleaf and his partners kept their pledge, there would be public buildings and close to a hundred substantial houses in Washington by the time Congress arrived. Greenleaf hired architects and builders, and he brought William Cranch, a young lawyer who had married his sister, to Washington. Cranch would supervise the operations and act as his legal agent. To further the construction, the speculator brought a builder to the city and found a Philadelphian who had invented a brick-making machine. Greenleaf hoped the device would turn out bricks as fast as slaves could dig the clay for the automated molds. Today, fragments of his work still stand in southwest Washington at what is now the Naval War College and "Greenleaf's Point."

Land acquisition and financing became an elaborate shell game. Having cornered about 40 percent of the choicest private lots in the new federal city, the trio felt free to raise their prices for resale. More importantly, they were able to use their Washington holdings as collateral for still more land that they acquired in Pennsylvania, Georgia, South Carolina, and Virginia. If all worked out as planned, they would sell those lands to European speculators. The commissioners showed their own desperate complicity. Seeing evidence of some construction, and understanding that money from Holland was critical to their success, the commissioners gave Greenleaf clear title to 2,000 of the Washington lots to use as collateral. They knew it was a gamble, for neither Greenleaf nor his partners had made more than a partial payment on their first installment. For Greenleaf there was but the dream of a fortune. In time it would turn to dust.

In the end, Greenleaf would make just one payment of $72,000 (about $990,000 today). George Washington was not happy. Greenleaf "was speculating deeply"; he would make "an immense profit to himself and those with whom he was concerned." Still, Morris maintained that neither he nor Nicholson intended to keep their property, only "to resell [it] when it can be done to our satisfaction." Again George Washington grew angry. Construction of his city was not progressing, and Greenleaf was profiting handsomely. "Why," the president asked, "are speculators to pocket so much money?"

But in the fall of 1794, before the true character of their enterprise had completely emerged, Greenleaf found in Philadelphia Thomas Law, an Englishman who had made a £100,000 (about $6 million today) fortune in Bengal as a collector of taxes for the East India Company. Filled as he was with admiration of America's institutions and a desire to invest in land, Law proved an easy mark for Greenleaf, who spun tales of the brilliant "metropolis" rising at the center of the nation. "There all rays must come to a point," he said, as Law put down $133,000 for 445 lots that he and his partners had purchased in "the New Jerusalem." Never having been to Washington himself, Law let Greenleaf choose the lots. Nine months later, when Law signed the final papers, Greenleaf managed to short the sale by about nine acres.

Finding Law turned out to be one of the few good deeds Greenleaf did for the city. Arriving the following February, Law got to work building houses on his land and promoting the future capital to all. In 1796, at age thirty-nine, he compounded his own fortune by marrying Martha Washington's granddaughter, nineteen-year-old Eliza Custis. He built an elegant house for himself and Eliza on a bluff overlooking the Potomac at Greenleaf's Point. (It survives today at Sixth and N streets SW.) Nearby he erected a sugar refinery in the unrealized hope that he might import cane from the West Indies. Other buildings followed, including a row of ten houses on New Jersey Avenue and a large one near the Capitol on the same avenue at C Street SE. In time, Law would sour on the speculators. Their legal battles would take over two decades to resolve. Throughout the vicissitudes with Greenleaf and his partners, Thomas Law never faltered in his support of the capital. "You may say," he wrote to Greenleaf in 1795, "that I had rather sell my horses or books or anything rather than part with a foot at present of Washington City."

Aside from luring Thomas Law to Washington, the trio of specu-lators had no success. Word came from Amsterdam, where Greenleaf had sent an agent to arrange the fabled loan, that no gilders would be forthcoming. It was only a matter of time before the elaborate confec-tion of air and promises that they had created would implode. Green-leaf had run out of money and ideas for how to raise it.

The speculators employed every subterfuge to wiggle out of pay-ment for anything. It became standard practice to challenge every bill a contractor sent, with the result that many houses remained unfinished and abandoned. Greenleaf went so far as to refuse to pay for a fine set of houses called Wheat Row that Joseph Clark built for him and his part-ners at Greenleaf's Point. They were too small, he claimed; from Bal-timore Clark's wife countered Greenleaf with the stark truth. She and her family were "without money, property, or credit with an helpless husband, whose intellect you have deranged, by your vile treatment."

In September 1796, Morris arrived from Philadelphia to see the city for himself. Although he filled his letters with optimism about the cap-ital's promise of grandeur and beauty, he knew better. Workers were still refusing to complete twenty brick houses he wanted to erect on South Capitol Street unless they were paid; the structures remained roofless and abandoned, a haven for vagrants and squatters who roamed the countryside. Gradually, Morris came to realize that Greenleaf had duped both him and Nicholson. They had made payments to him in good faith and with the understanding that he would transfer the money to the commissioners, but he had not done so. "The return of all Mr. Greenleaf's bills falls heavily upon us," Morris complained. Green-leaf had encouraged his partners with the promise of sure money from Amsterdam, and when he returned to Philadelphia, creditors were waiting. "The blood hounds want food," Morris lamented.

Morris and Nicholson resolved to buy out Greenleaf's shares in the North American Land Company and dissolve their partnership, but this strategy proved near impossible, as they could only pay him with promis-sory notes backed by the company, which faced insolvency. By this time, Nicholson was moving from house to house in order to evade creditors, lawyers, and sheriffs, leaving Morris alone, and afraid to leave his house or let anyone in. Creditors made so many claims on Nicholson's notes that the notary decided to save time by having the appropriate legal forms preprinted. "My difficulties have been brought on by an unfortunate connection," Morris wrote to Amsterdam bankers as he stared at financial ruin. "I was led into speculations too deep and extensive."

Morris had nowhere to turn. "I wish to God I had the same command of money as formerly," he wrote to Gustavus Scott, the commissioner who succeeded Thomas Johnson. "I would make the city of Washington flourish." But from the dunning documents of creditors, Morris could "read Prune Street [Philadelphia's debtors' prison] in every line."

THE SPECTER OF the Prune Street prison was not a happy one for either debtor or creditor, but all three partners would spend time there. Morris called it his "hotel with the gated door," and while there entertained relatives, business associates, and friends, including Hamilton and Washington. Nicholson used his imprisonment to edit a newspaper, *The Supporter, or, Daily Repast.* He wrote voluminously, impressing visitors with his remarkable two-handed dexterity until his death on Christmas Day in 1800. Of the trio, James Greenleaf survived the longest. Released from prison on a technicality, he quietly slipped back into Washington and lived in a house he had built at Greenleaf's Point. There he took solace in his library of over 2,600 volumes, many in French, Latin, Italian, and Dutch. Death came on September 17, 1843. To his brother-in-law William Cranch fell the task of threading a path through the legal labyrinth of legal suits and countersuits that had been filed against him.

The court cases over the mess that Greenleaf, Morris, and Nicholson left in their wake endured long past their deaths. In 1813, Thomas Swann, the federal district attorney for the District of Columbia, filed a suit against Greenleaf for the recovery of six lots near the Capitol. Countersuits followed, succeeded by an endless series of adjournments, continuances, and still more suits of Dickensian proportions. Along the way Swann retired, but the attorneys who succeeded him faithfully kept the suit going; Greenleaf died, but his two daughters and his granddaughter dutifully continued the fight. By midcentury no one really understood what they were contesting. Finally, in 1853, forty-four years after litigation began, the district attorney summarily sold the six lots for $15,000 and distributed the money among the parties.

In 1814, another case in the Greenleaf imbroglio came to an end. Greenleaf, Morris, and Nicholson had sued Daniel Carroll of

Duddington for unlawful seizure of the twenty buildings on South Capitol Street that Morris had not had the money to complete. Two of the plaintiffs were long dead, but Greenleaf lived on like an avenging fury. That July, the circuit court judge for the District of Columbia ruled in his favor, fining Carroll $39,847. The judge was James Greenleaf's brother-in-law and his former property agent, William Cranch.

SUCH PERSONAL DRAMAS and stories of avarice did not advance the construction of the new federal city. Lots did sell, though slowly, to individual purchasers, but Greenleaf's virtual monopoly on their sale meant that cash receipts for sales could not push the building forward swiftly. Virginia and Maryland were not always forthcoming with their payments in a timely manner. Reduced to begging, the commissioners sought to cut costs wherever possible. When a new doctor moved to the District in 1794, they contracted with him to attend to sick and injured workers for £25, a savings of £17 (or $1,530 today) over the doctor they had hired the previous year. Such frugality became the norm.

Compounding the fact of insufficient funds was a labor shortage across the United States. When he began in 1791, L'Enfant had wanted to hire 150 laborers, but he had difficulty finding half that number. In 1792, before the finances became desperate, Jefferson suggested to Thomas Johnson and the other commissioners that they look to Germany for workers, but Johnson replied, "People are on tip toe to come . . . we might probably have 2,000 mechanics and laborers here." They hired Colin Williamson, a Scotsman, as supervisor. Williamson set the foundations for the President's House that summer and would do the same for the Capitol, but he was chronically shorthanded. Contrary to the commissioners' expectations, only a few laborers and mechanics came. By June they grudgingly allowed that workers from Europe would "eventually be useful, perhaps almost necessary," and asked the Dutch to help them secure as many as 100 unmarried German stone masons. That summer they tried to lure workmen from Scotland at 12 shillings a month "to be employed in public work only . . . living as free men," but had no success. In October they sent Williamson to northern ports seeking redemptioners, indentured servants who had to work off the cost of their passage from Europe. When George Walker, a Scottish merchant from Georgetown, returned to Great Britain for a visit, the commissioners asked him to approach Masonic Lodges for men skilled in the craft. When James Greenleaf went to Holland, they asked him to secure "a number of men who have been bred to cutting and laying free stone," including some stone carvers. All these attempts proved to be in vain.

Perhaps in anticipation of failure, the commissioners also turned to enslaved laborers. Although L'Enfant had never hired slaves, even to quarry the stone at Aquia Creek, this practice seemed almost an anomaly in a culture that saw slavery as an essential part of its economic foundation. On the last day of April 1792, the commissioners passed a resolution to hire "good labouring negroes by the year, the masters cloathing them well and finding each a blanket." It was a solution to the labor shortage that came easily to the commissioners, as they themselves were slave owners.

It was a comfortable arrangement for the commissioners and enslavers, at least on the surface. Slave owners could rent out each of their male slaves for about $5 a month (about $70 today). They didn't have to provide them with food and shelter during that time, and only had to supply blankets, although some expenses, such as shoes that had to be replaced, were deducted from the payments the slave owners received. The commissioners got what they needed, too, a cheap supply of workers to dig the foundations of the President's House and the Capitol, quarry stone, make bricks, and clear land. And they got something more, as the relatively low fees paid to masters for their slaves kept wages paid to free laborers low. As the commissioners put it to Thomas Jefferson in January 1793, the use of slaves "proved a very useful check & kept our Affairs Cool."

But using slave labor had considerable drawbacks. The commissioners had to take care of them—feed them, give them shelter, and pay for their doctor when they became sick or injured. The practice became a bookkeeping nightmare because of the necessity of tracking the expenses for each man.

Nor could the commissioners keep affairs as "cool" as they would have liked. Stone cutters from Philadelphia demanded 13 shillings, 6 pence, or about $1.50 a day, for their services. Recoiling at the price, they eventually hired a group of masons to build the basement walls of the Capitol on a piecework basis. However, the work was so shoddy that the walls had to be replaced.

Slaves worked beside freedmen and whites in all the trades—brick making, masonry, and carpentry among them—but they usually had the most menial (and hardest) jobs: quarrying and sawing stone, and felling and sawing trees, were almost exclusively their domain. The great problem the commissioners faced was their lack of experience.

William Thornton, who was by now a commissioner, proposed hiring "intelligent negroes" outright to build the Capitol. He wanted to train them in the necessary skills and let them earn their liberty after five years of labor. His plan was both humanitarian and practical. The slaves would become free, eventually; the commissioners would avoid any interference from the owners, who sometimes took their slaves back to work on their own land; and, most important for Thornton, the Capitol's designer, "it would insure the completion of the building."

The other commissioners preferred to rent workers and came to rely more and more upon slave labor. By 1798, about ninety laborers, nearly half the labor force of two hundred men building the Capitol and the President's House, were slaves.

Outsiders were quick to note the incongruity of slaves building the twin temples of liberty. "*I* have seen them in large numbers," wrote Julian Niemcewicz, a Polish poet and statesman touring America at the end of the century, "and I was glad that these poor unfortunates earned eight to ten dollars per week." But then Niemcewicz learned that the men were not free, that they were hired out by owners who made money on the arrangement. "What humanity! What a country of liberty. If at least they shared the earnings!"

Despite the financial and labor problems, the idea of a capital city and the commerce it would generate began to take hold. The Reverend George Ralph established Christ Episcopal Church on New Jersey Avenue near D Street. He later taught students at the same spot, which was likely the first school in the District. William Prout bought land on the waterfront, built a wharf, and opened a market. In a small frame house at Greenleaf's Point, Robert Bryson from Georgetown established a clothing store to serve the laborers. Richard Forrest, the postmaster of Georgetown, opened a hardware store nearby to supply the builders. Pierce Purcell, an associate of Hoban's, came from Charleston to set up a tavern just east of the President's House. In a slighting reference to Blodget's hole in the ground, he jocularly called it the "Little Hotel," and kept it stocked with porter, rum, brandy, and gin for the thirsty laborers. Purcell soon met with competition from William Prentiss, who opened a tavern at Greenleaf's Point.

Still others were building houses. By regulation the buildings could be no taller than forty feet on streets, but had to be at least thirty-five feet tall on avenues; all had to be parallel to roadways. Rowhouses with common walls, even if they were built individually, became the norm. Some investors bought houses from Greenleaf, Morris, and Nicholson that were already under construction. In 1794–1795, Morris and other investors built a set of Federal-style rowhouses known as the "Seven Buildings," and in 1795, Isaac Polock from Savannah came forward to purchase and complete the "Six Buildings," a project that Greenleaf had begun on Pennsylvania Avenue at Nineteenth Street. (Greenleaf also sold the same contract to Morris and Nicholson.) When the government arrived in 1800, the Six Buildings became the offices of the State Department and the Secretary of the Navy.

The commissioners and the president still had to wrestle with the lack of money. With but $6,864.26 in cash at the beginning of 1795, and projected building expenses for the year of $100,960, they were desperate. As L'Enfant had counseled earlier, now the commissioners, too, recommended to George Washington that they secure a loan. The president assented; the Bank of Columbia gave them a line of credit until May. The president got Congress to guarantee a loan of up to $300,000, certainly not enough to finish construction, but a sufficient amount to continue work. After learning that the banks in Holland had refused a loan, the commissioners had to limp along until the last month of the year, when the Maryland legislature voted to loan the city $100,000.

It should be no surprise that the glacial pace of construction yielded little evidence of progress. When Thomas Twining, a young Englishman whose family was connected to the East India Company and the tea business, decided to pay a visit to Thomas Law in May 1796, he had to endure an eleven-hour coach ride from Baltimore to Georgetown. Unable to secure a stage to the city, he traveled "a very imperfect road," as he later wrote, "made, principally by removing the trees, or rather the upper parts of them." In time he arrived at Pennsylvania Avenue, where the trees had been cut down in a straight line: "I had no doubt but I was now riding along one of the streets of the metropolitan city." Continuing half a mile, he came upon a large clearing "in the centre of which I saw two buildings on an extensive scale, and some men at work on one of them."

John Adams's accession to the presidency in 1797 brought little change to the pace of construction—or relief from the funding question—but Adams did bring about a significant change nonetheless. By 1798, America was finding it difficult to maintain neutrality between the warring nations of Europe. French warships and privateers had taken to harassing anyone trading with Great Britain; by 1797, they had captured close to four hundred American vessels. In response, Congress established a Department of the Navy, and Adams appointed Benjamin Stoddert to be its first secretary. A staunch Federalist, Stoddert had been one of the original proprietors who had worked closely with George Washington to arrange the purchase of land for the capital. Stoddert decided to establish a navy yard at the capital where his men could build and outfit the frigates he needed to protect American ships. In July 1798, Adams approved an act annexing land on M Street between Fifth and Ninth streets and the Eastern Branch, and Stoddert appointed Thomas Tingey to build and operate the naval yard at the site.

British by birth, Tingey had a reputation for valor that appealed to Stoddert and Adams. While commanding a squadron of boats protecting American commerce in the Caribbean for the US Navy, he captured several important French privateers; significantly, he refused to allow the captain of a British frigate, who was searching for British subjects to impress, to board his ship. In the coming years, Tingey would hire scores of skilled laborers to build ships, making the Washington Navy Yard, after Congress, the largest employer in the city.

The slow progress of construction served to increase the reservations of those in Congress about moving the seat of government. Some wanted to modify the plans. John Adams joined with those who suggested building a small house for the president close by the Capitol and reserving the President's House for the Supreme Court and other government offices. Others noted that the Residence Act required the federal government to move to the Potomac, but did not obligate it to stay.

Once George Washington retired to Mount Vernon in March 1797, the commissioners requested a substantial amount from the government to keep the construction going on the public buildings. Ultimately, Congress approved an additional loan of $100,000 to complete the Capitol, which had been Washington's most insistent desire. The commissioners found money to erect a brick building for the US Treasury and to make the President's House habitable, albeit in a crude fashion.

GEORGE WASHINGTON SO liked Edward Savage's painting of "The President and His Family, the full size of life," that he ordered "four stipple engravings" in "handsome, but not costly, gilt frames, with glasses," and hung one of his purchases over the fireplace mantel in the small dining room at Mount Vernon. As the Washington family— George and Martha, and two of Martha's orphaned grandchildren, George Washington ("Washy") and Eleanor ("Nelly") Custis—took their daily repast, Edward Savage's tableau of "The President and His Family" looked down upon them.

It is likely that Washington favored the portrait above many others because of its intimacy and its affirmation of the future. The family gathers about a table at Mount Vernon, George seated at the left, opposite his wife, Martha. Washy, the younger of the two grandchildren, stands in the left foreground, while Nelly stands at the right in the middle ground. Washington rests his right hand upon the boy's shoulder; Washy, in turn, holds a compass in his right hand, which he rests upon a globe, in a stance suggesting that succeeding generations of the family were destined to spread the ideals of liberty and democracy around the world. In the background, framed by large pillars and a swagged curtain, Savage presents a glimpse, as he said in a note, of "a view of thirty miles down the Potomac River."

On the table at the portrait's center rests Andrew Ellicott's map of the new federal seat of government. The family appears to be unrolling the document; Washington holds it flat with his left arm and sword, while Nelly and Martha steady it on the right. With her folded fan, Martha gestures to "the grand avenue," as Savage called it, that connects the Capitol with the White House.

In the right middle ground stands one of the chief contradictions of the new democracy, a nameless black male servant, part of the retinue of more than three hundred slaves the Washingtons depended upon for their comfort, security, and prosperity. Dressed in the colors of Mount Vernon livery, a gray coat over a salmon red waistcoat, he possesses an almost princely quality. His black, combed-back hair frames his dark face with its prominent nose. His unknowable eye impassively takes in the scene. He keeps his left hand enigmatically concealed in his waistcoat; his collar flamboyantly mirrors Washington's across from him. The slave must remain a shadow, unobtrusive, unassuming, unremarkable, almost a part of the frame for the Potomac. Only the slave's destiny seems apart from those gathered about the table examining the plans, yet from the beginning the fates of both slavery and the new city were inextricably intertwined. The nameless man's story, along with the stories of tens of thousands of others, was very much a part of the plot unfolding on the Potomac in the 1790s. The consequences of involuntary servitude would affect *and* effect Washington's development to the present day.

In retirement at Mount Vernon, Washington followed the affairs of the "Federal City," as he called it in his correspondence, and he invested in its future. In the fall of 1798, he purchased two more lots northeast of the future Capitol, contracting to have two brick houses of his own design built upon them. When he was approached to invest in a hotel to be erected near the Capitol, he bought five shares for $250. He followed the efforts of the District's commissioners to secure loans from Maryland and Virginia, and he followed the funding issues in Congress. The money would enable the government to erect a brick building for the Treasury, as well as finish the president's house and the Senate wing of the Capitol.

People still turned to Washington for counsel about the national city rising on the Potomac. By December 1799, however, his patience had grown thin. For nine years he had contended with the myriad questions and disputes that surrounded the nation's boldest project. He had chosen the site, the designer, the surveyor, and the commissioners. He had coped with a Congress reluctant to spend money for the erection of government buildings, and he had selected, sometimes over Thomas Jefferson's quiet intrigues, designs for the city, including the President's House and the Capitol. He had had to contend with labor and material shortages, impractical and unscrupulous speculators, discord among architects and designers, and, unceasingly, the enduring skepticism of Congress, the public, and the press about the entire enterprise. But now a commissioner told him that the attorney general was questioning the legality of yet another loan that Congress had made to complete construction, and he revealed his pique: "By the obstructions continually thrown in its way," he wrote from Mount Vernon on December 8, "by friends or enemies, this city has had to pass through a fiery trial. Yet, I trust will, ultimately escape the ordeal with eclat." Then he added, mourning his own high expectations for the city named in his honor, that "instead of chapter, it would have been more appropriate to have said, it has passed or is on its passage through the ordeal of local interest, destructive jealousies, and inveterate prejudices."

These were the last words George Washington would write about the new city he had done so much to bring into existence. On December 13, 1799, he contracted a chill and sore throat brought about by a hard ride through snow earlier that week. By the time doctors arrived to practice their craft, the general had already ordered an aide to bleed him. The doctors took more blood, and then still more, until at ten o'clock on the evening of December 14, he passed, to borrow Lord Byron's phrase, into "the all-cloudless glory."

ON TUESDAY, JUNE 3, 1800, a group of Georgetown's chief citizens waited on horseback at the District line on the Frederick Road to receive John Adams to the District of Columbia. It was Adams's first trip to the capital—indeed, his first below the Mason Dixon Line. His coach and four had charted a course across the verdant land of Lancaster County, Pennsylvania, before dipping south to Frederick. He found the country "fertile and beautiful." But the new seat of government was most on his mind. He hoped, he told the District's citizens, "that all the reluctance" to move the capital would cease, that "the virtues and talents of the United States may here be displayed forever for the preservation and protection of our country."

The next day, Adams crossed the rebuilt bridge over Rock Creek at K Street. At the future Washington Circle, his carriage turned right onto Pennsylvania Avenue, toward the President's House. Along the way he passed Isaac Polock's Six Buildings, Robert Morris's Seven Buildings, and the cherry orchard at today's Lafayette Square. As the President's House and Treasury Building came into view, Adams saw workers' outbuildings and a shed for brick making. He had ordered the President's House to be finished—at least enough for him and his wife, Abigail, to live there—by fall. He saw also that its exterior, a light brown Aquia sandstone, had been whitewashed, which made it stand out in the barren landscape. After inspecting the building with commissioner Thornton, who no doubt had ordered masons and carpenters to be especially busy that afternoon, he wrote to Abigail: "I . . . shall Sleep, or lie awake next Winter in the president's house."

Adams spent the night at the Washington Capitol Hotel, which had been opened across from the Capitol by an enterprising Englishman, William Tunnicliff. The next day he visited Thornton's still unfinished north wing of the Capitol, the only building that would be ready to accept Congress when it arrived in 1800. Still, Adams congratulated Thornton and the other commissioners "on the blessings which Providence has been pleased to bestow" upon the "permanent seat of government."

Despite the raw landscape, the stark lots without buildings, and the rude paths in the place of streets, Adams remained sanguine. "I like the Seat of Government very well," he wrote Abigail, who had stayed in Braintree, Massachusetts. "The Establishment of the public officers in this place has given it the air of the Seat of Government and all Things seem to go on well." Congress had held its final session in Philadelphia in May, and Adams directed that federal business commence by June 15. Over the summer, the government's furniture and records, along with 131 employees and their families, began to trickle into the city. Most arrived by boat, landing at Lear's Wharf on the Potomac at the foot of G Street. Ill-tempered northerners loath to leave Philadelphia, a city of 41,000, for Washington, 3,210, called the new seat of government "The Capital of Miserable Huts," and "The City of Streets without Houses," but to no avail. The capital of the United States had come to the banks of the Potomac at last.

WHEN ABIGAIL ADAMS arrived in Washington in mid-November, she found an unfinished city. "There are buildings enough, if they were compact and finished," she wrote in a letter to her daughter, "but as they are, and scattered as they are, I see no great comfort for them." Abigail had good reason to complain. She was writing from the unfinished President's House, which was surrounded by mud, several construction shacks, and a brick kiln. Workmen kept blazes burning night and day in the house's thirteen fireplaces to help dry the plaster. Still, she muted her complaints. "The house is made habitable," she continued, "but there is not a single apartment finished." She took to drying her clothes in the great unfinished audience room.

The scene around the Capitol that November was equally bleak. Congress had invested in a walkway of sharp fragments left from shaping the freestone, which cut everyone's shoes in dry weather and covered them with white mortar in wet. The south wing that would house the Senate chamber was still under construction (carpenters were trimming the door jambs and fitting the sash windows); work on the domed rotunda that would connect the two wings and bring harmony to the structure had yet to begin.

Elsewhere development was sparse. On Pennsylvania Avenue, west of the President's House, stood the Six Buildings and the Seven Buildings, offices for the State Department and some members of Congress. William Thornton's unique house for the prominent and wealthy Virginia planter John Tayloe III was rising at what would become New York Avenue and Eighteenth Street. Near Seventeenth Street and the Potomac River, David Burnes's rustic cottage still survived. East of the President's House at Pennsylvania Avenue and Fifteenth Street was the Washington Hotel; nearby at Fifteenth and K streets there was another hotel owned by William Rhodes. Still further east, at Tenth Street, the enormous, unfinished shell of the Union Public Hotel, that monument to Samuel Blodget's failed lottery scheme, awaited completion. On the land bordered by Pennsylvania Avenue, K Street, and Third and Seventh streets (about present-day Judiciary Square), there were dormitories for indentured Irish laborers and barns for hired slaves.

Around the north wing of the unfinished Capitol, development was denser. George Washington's rental houses that he had built on speculation stood on what would become North Capitol Street. Otherwise there were few residences for members of Congress or government workers. For the most part, they would live in boardinghouses or hotels. To the east stood Tunnicliff's Washington Capitol Hotel. On First Street between East Capitol and A streets stood Carroll's Row, three three-story houses, and Pontius Stelle's Hotel. To the south of the Capitol was Daniel Carroll's Duddington. Thomas Law had voluntarily given up his house on New Jersey Avenue at C Street SE for a boardinghouse that served members of Congress. Conrad and McMunn's, as it was known, boasted stables for twenty horses. Across New Jersey Avenue in another Thomas Law building, Robert Peacock established another boardinghouse, the "Congressional mess." Representatives lived there two to a room, but in separate beds.

South of the Capitol on New Jersey Avenue stood a few businesses— a shoemaker, a tailor, a washerwoman, a grocery store, and an oyster shop—and some small houses. According to Albert Gallatin, Thomas Jefferson's secretary of the treasury, the buildings were little more than shanties.

Pennsylvania Avenue, L'Enfant's projected Grand Avenue between the President's House and the Capitol, was mostly still a dream. Although the Washington Hotel stood at Fifteenth Street, the avenue was best known for tree stumps that had not yet been grubbed from the soil and alder bushes crowded on the unpaved, ninety-foot-wide track. After a rainstorm, the avenue became a morass—as the congressmen and senators who listened to John Adams deliver his last State of the Union Address on Saturday, November 22, knew all too well. That evening, Adams hosted a "levée," the name he and his predecessor gave to their formal receptions, at the President's House. But John Cotton Smith, a newly elected representative from Connecticut, found that Pennsylvania Avenue had become impassable: hackney coaches had to take "a road long and circuitous to avoid the swamp . . . and the mud very deep."

Water helped to define the city's limits. To the west was Rock Creek. On Eastern Branch, Thomas Tingey was developing the Navy Yard. The Tiber, that tidal wash that flowed before the President's House, so L'Enfant and George Washington imagined, would serve the nation's commerce as a canal. And to the south flowed the great Potomac. From her window in the President's House, Abigail Adams could look out upon vessels plying the river, many headed for the commercial ports of Alexandria and Georgetown.

Alexandria, five miles from Washington at the southern tip of the District, was the twenty-second largest city in the United States. Because of relatively good roads from the Shenandoah, most of Virginia's wheat, flour, and tobacco production shipped from its wharves on packet boats bound for Europe, the West Indies, and the American seaboard. Georgetown was already an established port. Although the exhausted Maryland soil yielded just a quarter of the tobacco crop of a decade earlier, corn and wheat now accounted for an increasing amount of the town's exports. Georgetown's brick houses and its churches attracted a good number of southern senators and congressmen. They found the amenities of its boardinghouses and taverns outweighed the rutted and muddy three-mile ride they had to make to the Capitol, a trip that regularly took upwards of an hour.

Other government employees lost little time reporting their unfavorable impressions to friends, relatives, or their diaries. On the hot and humid Fourth of July of 1800, Oliver Wolcott Jr., the secretary of the treasury, wrote a disagreeable letter to his wife in Litchfield, Connecticut. New England bred and Yale educated, Wolcott wanted nothing to do with the "perfidious Virginians" and Jeffersonian republicans below the Mason Dixon Line. The Capitol stood in the middle of the "immense country here called the city," he noted. The soil was "bad . . . an exceedingly stiff, reddish clay, which becomes dust in dry, and mortar in rainy weather." There was but "one good tavern about forty rods from the Capitol." Members of Congress would have "to live like scholars in a college, or monks in a monastery, crowded ten or twenty in one house, and utterly secluded from society." The houses themselves were "small miserable huts" that looked all the more pathetic in comparison with the Capitol and President's House. Only those in Georgetown, "three miles distant, over as bad a road, in winter, as the clay grounds near Hartford," offered comfortable lodging.

Of the inhabitants and their living conditions, Wolcott was even more dyspeptic: "The people are poor, and as far as I can judge, they live like fishes, by eating each other." The properties were "unfenced"; the gardens "in bad order." There were "brick kilns and temporary huts for laborers." Although Wolcott conceded that there were exceptions, such as Thomas Law, "most of the inhabitants are low people, whose appearance indicates vice and intemperance, or negroes."

William Thornton assured everyone who would listen that the population would soon number 160,000, but Wolcott was far from convinced. He could think only of the 109 brick structures and the 263 wooden ones that dotted the 5,000 acres. "No stranger can be here a day and converse with the proprietors, without conceiving himself in the company of crazy people," he wrote to his wife that July. "Their ignorance of the rest of the world, and their delusions with respect to their own prospects, are without parallel."

President John Adams took a very different view. Asserting that Washington was indeed the *permanent* seat of government, he affirmed its future in his final State of the Union Address: "I congratulate the people of the United States on the assembling of Congress at the permanent seat of their Government, and I congratulate you, gentlemen, on the prospect of a residence not to be changed." The president offered a prayer: "May this territory be the residence of virtue and happiness! In this city may that piety and virtue, that wisdom and magnanimity, that constancy and self-government, which adorned the great character whose name it bears be forever held in veneration! Here and throughout our country may simple manners, pure morals, and true religion flourish forever!" And then Adams reminded the legislators that the Constitution gave them the unique power to control the destiny of the District of Columbia. The time was upon them to decide if they should exercise it: "You will consider it as the capital of a great nation advancing with unexampled rapidity in arts, in commerce, in wealth, and in population, and possessing within itself those energies and resources which, if not thrown away or lamentably misdirected, will secure to it a long course of prosperity and self-government."

The Constitution gave to Congress alone the power to make the city flourish or fail. Washington's future was in its hands and would be forever.

CHAPTER 3

"The Most Agreeable Town"

The Americans have traced the outlines of a vast city on the site chosen to be their capital. Today its population is barely larger than that of Pontoise, but they say that some day it will be home to more than a million people. They have already uprooted trees for ten leagues around lest they inconvenience the future citizens of this imaginary metropolis. In the center of the city they have erected a magnificent palace to serve as the seat of Congress and have given it the pompous name "Capitol."

—Alexis de Tocqueville, 1840

For Margaret Bayard, love trumped all. Her Calvinist-believing, Federalist-following parents and brothers had implored her not to marry Samuel Harrison Smith. He was her second cousin, a printer, a Philadelphia newspaper publisher, a firm unbeliever, and perhaps worst of all, a champion of Thomas Jefferson and the Republicans. She, too, feared the Republicans and Jefferson, "the violent democrat, the vulgar demagogue, the bold atheist, the profligate man" who would be president. But Jefferson had induced her cousin to establish a newspaper, the *National Intelligencer*, in the new capital on the Potomac. Margaret knew that to accompany him would mean abandoning her friends and family, and her home in Philadelphia—then the most cosmopolitan city in the nation—for "a land of strangers" in a primitive and isolated town, where, contrary to Pennsylvania practice and her deep-felt moral principles, slavery flourished. Despite such misgivings, Margaret Bayard and Samuel Harrison Smith were married on Monday, September 29, 1800. Four days later, the couple arrived in Washington.

Margaret found herself pleasantly surprised by the city. To be sure, Pennsylvania Avenue between the unfinished President's House and the Capitol was partly a swamp, and Greenleaf's miserable attempts at construction were roofless and crumbling. Their new city had few inhabitants—just 2,500 whites and 750 slaves and free blacks—and lacked the conveniences, comforts, and refinement they had known in Philadelphia. But she and her husband immediately became part of an exclusive group of permanent residents who knew everyone but not all. Their friends included the Thorntons, the Laws, and the Tingeys, families that provided a foundation of the community.

Around the permanent residents, an ever fluid group of presidents, cabinet members, senators, representatives, and foreign diplomats circulated, people prominent by virtue of their position in the government. Many possessed the requisite social graces that Margaret Bayard Smith and her circle valued, but they had no real attachment or loyalty to the nascent city. They arrived, often just for the congressional session, served their time, and returned to their homes. Those who were unmarried usually stayed in boardinghouses. Those with families frequently took a separate or a detached house in a fashionable area, such as Capitol Hill, or, increasingly, on F Street near the President's House. But aside from employing poor whites, freemen, or hired slaves to serve as maids, cooks, gardeners, and coachmen, they contributed little to the quality of the city's life, its streets, its houses, its markets, or its government—or even, as the British attack on the city in August 1814 showed, its defense. For most of the transients, Washington was a place to be endured.

The Smiths and their friends had a greater commitment to the city. Margaret's friends included her in their morning visits, afternoon dinners, and evening entertainments. They played whist together, a favorite for groups of four, and loo, a card game for three or five often involving high stakes. Samuel Harrison Smith felt "mortification," he told his wife when she was visiting her family, at winning two dollars from Mrs. Madison and another lady. Such amusement could be overwhelming. "I have unexpectedly been in a good deal of company, and have been much more than I designed," was typical of the sort of accounts Margaret wrote to her sisters, before telling of two dinners with the president, three with the French chargé d'affaires and his wife, and four with the Tingeys. "I have drank tea three or four times and declined several invitations to balls," she continued, before recounting her morning calls.

The original proprietors of the land welcomed people like the Smiths because their interest in Washington's future complemented their own. Despite the financial reversals brought about by his association with James Greenleaf, Daniel Carroll of Duddington remained committed to Washington and confident that his vast landholdings would one day make him wealthy. He erected a fine group of three-story buildings directly across from the Capitol at First and A streets known as "Carroll's Row." After L'Enfant destroyed his house on New Jersey Avenue, Carroll created a self-sufficient estate with a commanding view of both the Eastern Branch and the Potomac that occupied a full block southeast of the Capitol. Its grounds contained a barn and stables, a springhouse, a bathhouse, and quarters for Carroll's twenty-five slaves. There were elaborate gardens, fields of corn and tobacco, and livestock. Near the center of the property stood a two-story house in the Greek Revival style that matched John Tayloe's for grandeur.

David Burnes died in 1799, leaving his entire estate to his only daughter, Marcia. As his death notice put it, Burnes had been "a very considerable proprietor of lots." He had received close to $7,500 for the property he had sold to the government, and his building lots were worth about $1.5 million. He had spent some of his wealth on Marcia's education, first at the School for Young Ladies in Georgetown, and later at Madame Lacombe's Female Academy in Baltimore. Just seventeen when her father died, she now ranked among the richest people in the capital city.

Wealth was but one part of Marcia Burnes's attractive qualities. She possessed good looks, was an accomplished rider, sang beautifully, and her natural grace made her a fine companion at dinner parties. More important still, she possessed a compassionate nature and a formidable intelligence. It was possibly these last two qualities that attracted John Peter Van Ness. As one observer described him, Van Ness was "well fed, well bred, well read." Born into a prominent Dutch family that settled in the Hudson River Valley in the early seventeenth century, he had taken a degree at Columbia College, read law, and in 1800 was elected as a Jeffersonian Republican to Congress. After Burnes and Van Ness were married in May 1802, they moved into a three-story brick house on Pennsylvania Avenue at Eleventh Street. He soon resigned his seat in Congress to become an unpaid officer in the city's militia, help Marcia to manage her property, and devote himself to good works in what was now his permanent home.

CONGRESSIONAL SESSIONS DETERMINED the social calendar. Ceremony in these early years in the capital never seemed to suffocate, which often made entertainment relatively spontaneous and informal. Most congressmen who arrived in December had left their wives and families at home and were grateful for female companionship. They attended balls hosted by foreign legations and various cabinet secretaries as well as the fortnightly gathering of the Washington Dancing Assembly that the Tingeys and Laws had organized.

Below the social pinnacle lived other permanent residents— tradesmen, innkeepers, boardinghouse keepers, government clerks, and minor commissioners—who enjoyed only the most formal intercourse with members of the genteel aristocracy like the Smiths and Van Nesses. Some were native to the area, but many were from England or other foreign delegations that had come with the arrival of the government.

Pontius Delare Stelle counted himself a member of this class of permanent residents. He arrived from Trenton, New Jersey, in May 1800 with his wife, his three children, and $70,000 to invest in a business venture. Soon Stelle established a hotel, the City Tavern, south of Capitol Square. In addition to providing for Congress when it was in session, Stelle's hotel hosted the Washington Dancing Assembly and weekly concerts presented by the Marine Band. Four years later, Stelle took over William Tunnicliff's hotel, a much larger structure north of the square. Soon he moved again, this time to a fifty-room hotel on Carroll's Row. It became Washington's most fashionable hostelry and a choice meeting place for civic events, including, in March 1809, the city's first inaugural ball, for James Madison. By the end of the decade, Pontius Stelle could count himself one of the city's leading burghers.

But not for long. New hotels were proliferating, and Washington's commercial energy was shifting west from the Capitol down

Pennsylvania Avenue. Stelle's quickly went into decline. By 1812, Stelle, secretary of the city council, Episcopal vestryman, Federal Lodge Mason, and fine citizen, was also a failed entrepreneur. After watching his furniture auctioned off to satisfy his debts, Stelle took a clerk's post in the office of the comptroller in the Treasury Department, a position he held until his death in 1826.

There were places that were open to all residents, though not always together at the same time. These places included the churches, the Capitol, a number of intellectual societies, and the racetrack.

Worship occupied an important place in Washington's social life. As early as 1794, Roman Catholics established St. Patrick's parish and erected a small chapel on F Street, between the future Ninth and Tenth streets, to serve the laborers who were building the President's House and the Capitol. That same year, Episcopalians established Christ Church on New Jersey Avenue near D Street. These were "very small and mean frame buildings," Margaret Bayard Smith remembered. St. Patrick's was "little better than a barn," and the Episcopalians had converted a log tobacco storehouse for their services. (For several years, Thomas Jefferson attended services at Christ Church, contributing $50 annually for its upkeep.) In due time, James Hoban would design a grander church for St. Patrick's, and Robert Alexander, a vestry member and associate of the architect Benjamin Henry Latrobe, eventually designed a Gothic Revival structure for Christ Church. By the end of the capital's first decade, Methodists, Baptists, Presbyterians, and the Society of Friends had places to worship.

The Capitol building itself quickly became the center of many of Washington's amusements. On Sundays, a "gay company" of men and women, Margaret Bayard Smith remembered, ascended the hill to listen to preachers, including women. This was the moment for "youth, beauty, and fashion," a time to see, to be seen, and perhaps to listen. "Smiles, nods, whispers, nay sometimes tittering" among the ladies and their beaux often "beguiled the tedium of the service." For a while, the Marine Band, its members dressed in scarlet uniforms, played marches from the gallery to accompany "the psalm-singing of the congregation." But in time, more refined ears prevailed; the Marines left the chamber and the tittering ceased.

Those who came from more populous cities, such as New York, Philadelphia, or Boston, worked to nurture the capital's intellectual life. Realizing the need for reading material, the Philadelphia printers Daniel Rapine and Michael and John Conrad opened the Washington book store near the Capitol on the corner of New Jersey Avenue and South B Street. Rapine, Conrad Company sold pamphlets about the District and its government as well as "a general assortment of books in every department of literature." Residents could also go to a room in the Capitol that held the Library of Congress. In 1801, with $5,000 that Congress had appropriated, the library acquired 740 books along with three maps from England.

It was natural that the new residents also wished to create their own version of scientific and literary institutions like the American Philosophical Society of Philadelphia, and New York's Society for the Promotion of Agriculture, Arts and Manufactures. In 1816, a group of Washington's intellectual elite, including Samuel Harrison Smith and Thomas Law, established the Columbian Institute for the Promotion of Arts and Sciences. Four years later, Congress deeded five acres at the base of the Capitol for the institute to establish a botanical garden. "The extensive limits of our country afford numerous opportunities for discoveries and improvements, in every branch of natural science," the president of the institute said in an early address. "Every parent within the District of Columbia," he added, "who is desirous of seeing his children possessed of general information, should contribute toward the establishment and support of the garden, museum, and library." The Columbian Institute became the forerunner to the Smithsonian Institution.

Horse racing, the sport of southern planters like John Tayloe—and the undoing of men of limited means like William Thornton—ranked as one of the chief amusements of the fall social season. Races at the Jockey Club that Tayloe and Thornton organized on land north of the city attracted "not only the gentle and the simple," as New York Representative Samuel Latham Mitchill told his wife after enjoying a November day at the course, but also "great folks . . . officers of the government . . . ladies who mostly sat in the carriages which brought them," and "reverend clergy." When the horses were running, Congress regularly adjourned to the racecourse north of the city. Not even discussion of the Louisiana Purchase in November 1803 could keep members from the turf.

NO MATTER THEIR class, all of Washington's whites depended upon black servants to make their lives function in an orderly way. When the federal government arrived, there were 3,244 slaves and 783 free blacks in the District of Columbia, including 623 slaves and 123 free blacks in Washington City. For the most part, the same farmers and plantation owners who had hired out slaves to clear land, quarry stone, and build Washington's public buildings now supplied them to serve white families and work at boardinghouses, taverns, and the federal Navy Yard. The nature of their employment made the blacks a silent but forceful group in the life of the city.

The variety of their tasks gave blacks, enslaved and free, frequent opportunities to meet in ways that ordinarily weren't possible on isolated farms and plantations. Each morning women gathered at one of the few pumps in the squares to draw pails of water (one for each hand, and one to balance on the head). The men brought logs from woodlots to the fireplaces (there were few heating stoves at the time) and tended to horses and carriages. Blacks procured food from the markets, and always, they kept the houses. Those meetings enabled them to glean and exchange news about domestic and national events. Since they served men of power and their families who were charting the destiny of the nation, the information was often valuable.

Greater autonomy among blacks heightened their opportunities and desires. The experience of Charles Ball, who served on a plantation near the Patuxent River, is typical of those who were hired out by their masters. When he was about twenty, his master sent him to be a cook on a frigate moored at the Washington Navy Yard on the Eastern Branch. Ball enjoyed the "profusion of excellent provisions," which he had not known on the plantation, and "strove by all means to please." Some whites gave him cast-off clothes, others small sums of money. On Sunday afternoons he was free to walk about the city, where he saw "the new and splendid buildings" and made "many new acquaintances amongst the slaves." And on July 4, naval officers permitted him to "go up town with them . . . and listen to the fine speeches" in honor of liberty.

It was not unusual for masters and employers in Washington to allow their blacks to sell goods or to hire themselves out to perform a variety of tasks. The arrangement made the enslaved into entrepreneurs. They negotiated their wages with the residents, paid their owners a fixed sum, and kept the profit for themselves. The understanding worked well for all: owners made money on their slaves, residents got their servants, and, in some cases, slaves earned enough money to purchase their manumission.

Alethia Browning Tanner, known as Lethe, her sister Sophia Browning Bell, and their extended families were the beneficiaries of this practice. The enslaved sisters, who were bound to a plantation on the Patuxent River in Prince George's County, Maryland, became their own formidable manumission society. First, Sophia received permission to sell any surplus vegetables she grew on the plantation at a Washington market. Within a short while she amassed $400, enough to purchase freedom for her husband, George, who served the Addison family at the eastern boundary of the District. George, in turn, purchased freedom for her and their two sons.

By 1807 George Bell had joined with two other former slaves, Moses Liverpool and Nicholas Franklin, to create a school for black students. Three years later a white English woman, Mary Billings, did the same in Georgetown.

Lethe Tanner's enterprise was even more remarkable. Shortly after the government moved to Washington in 1800, the childless widow arranged with her mistress to sell extra produce at the market in the President's Park, today's Lafayette Square. Tradition has it that Thomas Jefferson, whose appreciation of vegetables was legendary, frequented her stall. Certainly others did, for in 1810 she was able to purchase her own freedom for $1,400. That was only the beginning of her endeavors. Courageous and foresighted, Tanner went on to purchase eighteen other family members, including her sister, Lurena Browning Cook, and her ten children, as well as seven Cook grandchildren and seven friends. The newly manumitted went on to positions of prominence in Washington's black religious and educational community.

But the reality for blacks in Washington was hardly a happy one. In addition to speaking with other slaves on his Sunday outings, Charles Ball frequently encountered "large numbers of people of my color chained together in long trains, and driven off towards the South." Any slave in the District could be sold by a master, whether it was to satisfy a debt or to make a profit.

It was in the slave's best interest to escape to freedom in the North. Ball decided to do just that after speaking with a free black man from Philadelphia who worked as a hand on a schooner moored in the

Eastern Branch. Unfortunately, his plan to stow away in the schooner's hold was thwarted, and Ball was returned to his master in Maryland. Eventually he was sold, along with fifty-one other slaves, to a trader from Georgia, placed in a neck iron and marched to his new owner in Columbia, South Carolina.

SOON AFTER THEIR arrival, the Smiths moved to New Jersey Avenue between D and E streets. It was a two-story frame structure, part of a row of ten that Thomas Law had built. Margaret used her small dowry to "furnish the house genteely"; her husband opened the offices for the *National Intelligencer* in the building next door. One December morning, a stranger called to arrange for the publication of a manual for Congress. While waiting in their parlor for Samuel to appear, Margaret conversed freely with the man, who slouched his tall frame into a chair and carelessly threw his arm on a nearby table. He spoke with a disarming voice that was "almost femininely soft and gentle," she later recalled. They discussed the capital, their *"new home,"* as he called it, until her husband entered and introduced her to *"Mr. Jefferson."* In an instant Margaret's fear of Republicans in general, and Thomas Jefferson's "coarseness and vulgarity," in particular, vanished. Jefferson's "countenance and voice" had unlocked Margaret's heart; not only was he "great," she decided, but he was "a truly good man!"

Margaret Bayard Smith's account of her first encounter with the third president tells us much about the Republican style he brought to the capital. From the moment at noon on March 4, 1801, when Thomas Jefferson walked about a hundred yards from Conrad and McMunn's boardinghouse to the crowded Senate chamber of the Capitol, he set the tone for his administration and the city. "We are all Republicans, we are all Federalists," he declared in his Inaugural Address, tacitly acknowledging the bitterness of the recent struggle for the presidency that had been decided in his favor by a single vote. Still, the Federalists were in eclipse; Republicans would control the nation for most of the next three decades. After his inauguration Jefferson walked back to Conrad and McMunn's, and that afternoon he supped with the other boarders at the mess.

Two weeks after his inauguration, Jefferson moved into what people had begun to call the White House. Considering it Federalist in character, he set out to make it a simple republican structure welcome to ordinary citizens. He ordered John Adams's coaches, horses, harness, and silver decorations to be sold; this president would ride his own mount. He ended the weekly levées that had punctuated the administrations of Washington and Adams and had proved so popular with the wives of senators and representatives; the levée room (now the state dining room) became his office. He limited public receptions to January 1 and July 4; celebrations of the president's birthday ended. But not all was unadorned. Elaborate and expensive neoclassical cornices, chair rails, and garlands began to grace the walls. And Jefferson directed that the wooden presidential privy beside the house be torn down; henceforth, this Republican president would use one of two water closets he had installed on the second floor.

With its unobstructed view of the Potomac River and Alexandria from its south windows, Jefferson's office became his sanctuary. He lined the walls with "maps, globes, charts, books, &c," Margaret Bayard Smith remembered. In the center stood "a long table with drawers on both sides" in which he placed state papers, "a set of carpenters tools," and some "small garden implements," which he used to tend the plants that stood on stands in the windows. Jefferson's "favorite mocking-bird" often flew about the room, chirping melodiously to provide him with companionship "in his solitary and studious hours."

Nearby, Captain Meriwether Lewis occupied an office and bedroom in what is now the East Room. It was from this office that Lewis, with Jefferson's advice and tutoring in mathematics and natural science, prepared for his expedition to uncharted western lands. By 1806, the entrance hall to the White House had become a museum of sorts, filled with stuffed animals, skeletons, and American Indian artifacts that the captain shipped back from his journey. At the north entrance to the White House, Jefferson placed a cage with two grizzly-bear cubs from the far west.

Jefferson brought Republican attitudes about equality and the gentlemanly code of the Virginia country squire to his new home. It would be open to the people, and he would graciously meet any caller. Graciousness, yes, but not formality. Foreign diplomats quickly learned that Republican values changed the nature of their business in Washington. On this matter, the president could be almost juvenile, especially when it came to the British, whom he disliked. When Anthony Merry,

Britain's envoy extraordinary and minister plenipotentiary, arrived in his full court regalia for his formal presentation to the president in late 1803, he found Jefferson "actually standing in slippers down at the heels, and both pantaloons, coat, and underclothes indicative of utter slovenliness." Merry concluded he had been the victim of a calculated insult. And he was right.

Informality extended to the dinner table. He invited Merry to dinner with the secretary of the French legation, the representative of the very nation with whom Britain was then at war. Mrs. Merry, too, believed that Jefferson had slighted her that evening: he neglected the custom of escorting her to the dinner table and placing her at his right. For the president, seating was to be "pele-mele." Never again would the Merrys deign to sup with Thomas Jefferson.

Jefferson's behavior reflected his Virginia gentleman farmer temperament. At Monticello he counted a small dinner for eight to twelve persons the ideal entertainment. Now in the White House he had small invitations printed with appropriate blank spaces. ("Th Jefferson requests the favor of Mr. and Mrs. Smith to dine with him on Tuesday next (26) at half after three . . . " was typical of those that Margaret Bayard Smith and her husband often received.) "The dinners are neat and plentiful, and no healths are drunk at table," one guest wrote. "You drink as you please, and converse at your ease." For Jefferson, the delights of conversation always took precedence over the punctilious demands of diplomatic protocol.

Jefferson even went so far as to codify his Republican sentiments in a document he martially titled "Cannons of Etiquette." It included the dictum: "When brought together in society, all are perfectly equal, whether foreign or domestic, titled or untitled, in or out of office." But in practice, rationality prevailed; over time Jefferson quietly forgot "pele-mele."

Perhaps no act suggested the new tone in the presidency more than the gargantuan wheel of cheese that the good Republican dairy farmers brought from Cheshire, Massachusetts. Inspired by John Leland, the local Baptist preacher who had proposed the gift from his pulpit, the farmers pooled the curds of milk from nine hundred "Republican" bovines to create a wheel about four feet in diameter and seventeen inches tall. The farmers presented it to the president on New Year's Day, 1802. Proclaiming their gift "the greatest cheese in America for the greatest man in America," Leland declared, "we have attempted to prove our love to our President, not in words alone but in deeds and truth," adding that the cheese was but "a pepper-corn of the esteem which we bear to our chief magistrate." It weighed "upward of twelve hundred pounds," one congressman reported to his wife, "and is as large as a burr millstone!" Federalists derided the cheese, which they said was rancid and maggot infested. They called it "mammoth" after the recent discovery of mastodon bones in upstate New York. But Republicans loved the title and consumed the cheese at White House gatherings for several years.

For much of his presidency, Jefferson thought of his house as a place to educate American citizens about the west. He used the occasion of his July 4, 1803, reception to announce the purchase of the Louisiana Territory from France, 828,000 square miles that pushed the nation's boundaries far beyond the spine of the Alleghenies, doubling its size. He brought members of numerous American Indian tribes—Osage, Pawnee, and Iowa among them—to visit and exchange gifts. At his public reception on New Year's Day, 1805, he excited the guests' "interest and curiosity" by presenting a delegation of "Osage chiefs and their attendant *squaws*" in their native dress. The Osages, Margaret Bayard Smith remembered, "were noble specimens of the human race. . . . [T]all, erect, finely proportioned and majestic in their appearance . . . they seemed to be nature's own nobility." Augustus John Foster, an often acerbic Englishman who also attended the president's reception that day, noted of the Indians that Jefferson "paid them infinitely more attention than he ever vouchsafed to show a foreign minister."

IT WAS IN Washington's architecture that Thomas Jefferson saw the chance to leave his mark on the capital, especially its public buildings. Under the Federalists, circumstances had forced him to cede most of the design to Peter Charles L'Enfant and George Washington. He had wanted the capital to be a small city with government buildings closer together; he had wanted the Capitol and the President's House to be built in democratic brick rather than Augustan stone. And he had been ignored. Now president, Jefferson could affect the designs and the construction.

His first act in June 1802 was to have Congress dissolve the Board of Commissioners that had supervised the city's development since 1791.

He was especially happy to be rid of the old Federalist William Thornton, whose cantankerousness over the subject of the Capitol's engineering was matched only by his ignorance of the subject. Perhaps to assuage Thornton's unhappiness at losing his position—or to divert his attention—Secretary of State James Madison appointed him to superintend the issuance of patents, and ultimately to organize the US Patent Office. Jefferson's second act was to appoint Benjamin Henry Latrobe as "Surveyor of the public buildings." Thornton would continue to rail at those whom he considered rivals, but at last the Federal District had in Latrobe a professional architect who could stand up to his bluster.

Raised in England, where he began a brilliant civil engineering and architectural career, Latrobe had emigrated to the United States after a series of reversals, including design prospects that failed to materialize, the death of his wife, and the threat of bankruptcy. His first significant public work in America, a panopticon prison for the state of Virginia, brought him notice, as did several house designs. Commissions in Philadelphia soon followed, including the Bank of Pennsylvania and the Schuylkill Water Works, which pumped water from the Schuylkill River to the city's center. Because of these and other public projects, Jefferson sought out Latrobe to draw up the specifications for the "closets of convenience" that replaced the outdoor privy at the White House, and then to design a huge (but never built) dry dock for Washington's Navy Yard. Latrobe proved himself to be both genial and professional, and Thomas Jefferson knew he had found an architect with whom he could collaborate as he advanced his own vision for the capital's public buildings.

Charles Wilson Peale's 1804 head and shoulder portrait of Latrobe depicts a pleasant-faced forty-year-old man with florid cheeks, a cupid-bow mouth, and an intense stare. Spectacles perch high atop his black, curly hair, whose locks threaten to descend upon his forehead; a deep grey coat with a turned-up collar covers his shoulders, and a white linen cravat wraps his throat. His agreeable demeanor suggests a slight amusement and a gracious air. Latrobe would need these qualities in the coming years, if only to tamp down an arrogance he sometimes felt as he surveyed the amateur engineers and architects around him. From the start he disliked Hoban's design for the President's House, regarded Thornton as an ignorant amateur, and characterized Jefferson as fishing for his architectural ideals from "the old French books." But Latrobe was wise enough to understand the limitations of his power: Hoban, he knew he could dismiss; Thornton, whom he privately characterized as a "stupid genius," he knew he had to tolerate, because of his enormous popularity and political power in the capital—that is, until his actions became intolerable; and Jefferson, he knew he had to "humour," because of, as he wrote to a friend, his "personal attachment."

Latrobe's appointment came none too soon for the two principal buildings in the capital. Although the permanent home of the government was just in its third year, the White House and the Capitol were in terrible shape.

At the White House, the slate roof was leaking, and its weight was causing the walls to bow. Latrobe replaced the slate and installed tie rods to pull the walls into place. The exterior lacked the portico we see on the north side today, and had only a rude wooden staircase leading to the entrance; the half-ring of Ionic columns that frame today's porches on the south side were awaiting erection. The interior had changed little since Abigail Adams had hung her linens to dry in the unfinished audience room. Few rooms were complete, and the main staircase had yet to be built. Even the well that provided the water for the house needed attention. It was contaminated.

In Jefferson's second term, Latrobe adapted the president's designs to effect some modest improvements, adding east and west wings for the domestic household that included a meat-house, a wine cellar, storage for coal and wood, and additional privies, plus stone steps at the north entrance in place of the wooden ones. The president replaced the wooden fence that surrounded the property with a stone wall. The south grounds looking toward the Tiber and the Potomac were to be gardens; a driveway from Pennsylvania Avenue would lead to the north entrance, which was the one open to the public.

As primitive as conditions were in the White House, they were worse in each of the three sections of the Capitol. In a fifty-six-page report he sent to the president in April 1803, Latrobe documented his concerns. The north wing showed evidence of Thornton's faulty design and inherent structural problems: poor air circulation in the cellar had caused the timbers supporting the first floor to rot; leaks from the broken skylights were rotting the roof timbers, and still more roof leaks, caused by bad gutters, were destroying plaster and ceilings (the ceiling in the Senate chamber collapsed later that fall); an inadequate heating system had made the Senate chamber impossibly cold in winter. "The building now leaks so much," wrote William Plumer, a Federalist senator from New Hampshire, "that every storm . . . renders it damp and unhealthy." Thornton deserved, so Plumer thought, "censure for his gross inattention." The south wing, a temporary elliptical brick structure designed by Hoban for the House of Representatives, was so hot and airless that congressmen had taken to calling it the "Bake Oven." Latrobe found that the building's inferior workmanship placed it in danger of immediate collapse. Even more frightening were Thornton's plans for the future House chamber, which featured an enormous dome resting on thin walls that would soon collapse under its own weight. The yet to be built center section of the Capitol that would connect the two wings was but a hazy design for a round colonnade. Its crude foundations bore little resemblance to any plan.

It was clear that the needs of the Capitol were more pressing than those of the White House. Repairs began in May 1804. In the cellar of the north wing, beneath the Senate chamber, Latrobe directed workmen to install a furnace, remove the rubbish that had accumulated over the years, repair and replace the rotting timbers, and cut air vents into the walls. In the south wing, he had the walls of the Bake Oven braced with wooden timbers, and most of Thornton's foundations rebuilt to support new outside walls. By October, when Congress convened, the walls rose to half the height of the Bake Oven.

What would go inside those walls was still an open question. Latrobe continued to insist that Thornton's plan for an elliptical chamber was dangerous and expensive to execute, but Jefferson was loath to abandon it, especially the skylights in the roof, which he frequently compared with the long, tapering glass panels he had seen in the great dome of the Paris grain market, La Halle aux Blés. He suggested a meeting between Thornton and Latrobe, but that led only to an exchange of insults. When Thornton declared that "no difficulties existed in his plan but such as were made by those who were too ignorant to remove them," Latrobe considered resigning, but instead he wrote the president, "My wish to avoid vexation, trouble, and enmities is weak compared to my desire to be placed among those whom you regard in approbation and friendship." Jefferson made it clear that the colonnade and dome should stay and resorted to flattery to keep them: "It is to overcome difficulties that we employ men of genius." In the end, the cajoling and compliment worked. Latrobe's design retained the idea of an elliptical chamber, but with sturdy columns that supported a wooden roof with narrow glass skylights. The architect was able to raise the room to the second level of the building and put offices on the first.

For the rest of Jefferson's time in office, Latrobe executed his plans for both wings, but not without disagreements, delays, and even tragedy. He continued to advocate lighting the House of Representatives with a circular lantern in the ceiling, especially when the shipment from Europe of the glass for the skylights was late in arriving, but Jefferson, who had the final authority, continued to advocate for his dome. A shortage of qualified labor, excessive expenses, and broken promises further strained Latrobe's relationships with many congressmen and senators, who used debates on funding the project to attack him. The tragedy occurred when an arch in the north wing collapsed, taking the life of Latrobe's chief building superintendent.

Construction would continue into Madison's term, until Congress, dissatisfied in part because the skylights Jefferson had insisted upon installing were leaking, declined to approve funds to complete the building.

Throughout it all, the acrimony between Latrobe and Thornton continued. A contemporary admirer of the polymath Thornton described him as "full of talent and eccentricity"; now his eccentricities manifested themselves as never before. Thornton challenged Latrobe to a duel, or so he claimed in the press, but the cowardly Latrobe had failed to appear. Latrobe instituted a suit for libelous defamation of his character, to which Thornton responded with reams of juvenile doggerel. "Judges & Jury of the Court," he wrote in one couplet, "I pray that you'll excuse my sport." They didn't; after five years of delays they found Thornton guilty. Latrobe took a measure of pity on his adversary, however. Knowing of Thornton's straitened financial circumstances, he instructed his lawyer not to seek damages, and received just a symbolic penny. Latrobe got all that he wanted from the errant architect: silence.

But in the end, after the delays, the leaks, and the libel, the Capitol, though still unfinished, began to reveal the beauty of its design. In place of the acanthus leaves that topped classical Corinthian columns, Latrobe had called for sculpted ears of corn. His masonry vaulting system in the north wing lent the structure both grace and strength. Jefferson had secured the services of two Italian sculptors, "republicans at heart," he was told, to create beautiful sculptural decorations for the building, including a majestic eagle for the House chamber. Most importantly, Latrobe had presented a completed vision of the unified Capitol building that showed a center portico (suggested by Jefferson) flanked by columns. Although it would be years before Americans would see the wholeness, harmony, and grace Latrobe had planned for the Capitol, at least there was a refined and workable vision in place.

FOREIGN VISITORS CAME to see this curiosity of America's unique government on the banks of the Potomac River, but apart from the Capitol and the President's House, the twin symbols of the democracy, they found little more than wilderness and mud. Most who stayed but a few hours or days left in shock at the rudeness and pretense of it

THE DRAWING by an unknown artist of the north and south wings of the yet-to-be-completed Capitol (the Senate and House of Representatives, respectively) shows the building as the invading British would have seen it in 1814. Congress had yet to approve funds for the center portion of the building. CREDIT: Library of Congress

all. For the Irish poet Thomas Moore, who visited the slighted diplomat Anthony Merry, Washington was ruled by tribunes foolish enough to think it a second Rome. He noted that the capital's planners had even renamed the trickling waters of Goose Creek for Rome's glorious Tiber. "This capital is the strangest place ever seen," he complained to his mother. "Nothing but dogs and negroes and the few ladies who pass for white are the most unlovely pieces of crockery I have ever seen." He expressed his distaste publicly in a poem:

> This embryo Capital, where fancy sees
> Squares in morasses, obelisks in trees
> Which second-sighted seers, even now adorn
> With shrines unbuilt and heroes yet unborn
> Though naught but woods and Jefferson they see,
> Where streets should run and sages ought to be.

Notwithstanding its primitiveness and pretensions, many who stayed in Washington longer found the day-to-day life in the city to be remarkably pleasant. Augustus Foster, the minor English diplomat who lived there during parts of Jefferson's and Madison's administrations, and who frequently made invidious comparisons between British and American society, found the city to be a "Backwoods Metropolis," adding, "Never was so magnificent a design for the capital so wretchedly executed." Few "private gentlemen" had houses; foreign ministers had "great difficulty in getting suitably lodged"; there were "no paved streets"; and "no public garden whatever." Yet, Foster concluded, despite "its inconveniences and its desolate appearance," despite its failure to measure up to the refinements and amusements of a European city, Washington did not disappoint. He urged writers to "pass one season at least at the Federal City, to get acquainted with its Ministers and members of Congress" and obtain "correct ideas with regard to the whole country." They would find Washington "the most agreeable town to reside in for any length of time."

DELEGATES TO THE Constitutional Convention of 1787 had adopted a clause giving Congress "exclusive legislation" over the future capital without any substantive discussion. But by December 1800

Washington's citizens had begun to understand their disenfranchisement: the Constitution denied them a representative or senator; it would not allow them to vote for the electors of the president or vice president; and without sufferance of Congress, it gave them no voice in their local government. The sovereign power over their destiny rested not with the people, but with Congress. The Constitution had stripped residents of the District of Columbia of many of the rights for which the nation's founders had fought and which all other citizens in the new republic enjoyed.

One of the first to recognize the unhappy truth of disenfranchisement was Augustus Brevoort Woodward, one of the earliest and oddest men to settle in Washington. Woodward arrived from New York in 1797 armed with a bachelor's degree from Columbia College, an interest in law, and a bequest from a late uncle of £150. Well over six feet tall, as thin and ungainly as Ichabod Crane, Woodward, dressed for effect in a dirty, ruffled linen shirt and baggy pantaloons, cut an eccentric swath through his adopted city. However slovenly his appearance, he took Washington and his place in it seriously. He used his modest legacy wisely, acquiring ten parcels of land, including one at Pennsylvania Avenue and Tenth Street, where he built a house for himself and his sister and became one of the first attorneys to be admitted to the District bar.

And in the *National Intelligencer*, Woodward (who wrote under the pen name "Epaminondas," a Theban general who revolted against the Spartans) took on the inherent injustice in the District's civil laws. "This body of people is as much entitled to political freedom, as much entitled to the enjoyments of the rights of citizenship, as any other part of the people of the United States," he wrote. "They are entitled to a domestic government, free and energetic; a government . . . capable of regulating *all* their concerns, without waiting the leisure" of Congress, which was "ignorant of their local affairs, . . . liable to deception," and "engrossed by other subjects." If democracy continued to deny basic liberty at the very heart of its government, Woodward declared, "then has our country become retrograde in the path of political wisdom." It would belong "at the rear of the nations of the civilized world."

In all, Woodward wrote eight essays for Samuel Harrison Smith's *National Intelligencer*, which were later published as a pamphlet. But to little avail. The thinking of congressmen like John Dennis from

Maryland instead prevailed. While conceding that the people of Washington "might not be represented in the national body," Dennis argued that their voice, "if a ready communication was desirable," would be heard because they lived so close to representatives from the rest of the country. In its waning days, the lame-duck Federalist Congress of 1800–1801 decided that the laws of Virginia pertained to those residents living south of the Potomac; the laws of Maryland to those living to the north. Those laws, of course, included slavery, whose presence in the District was never questioned. In 1802 Congress gave the city limited home rule. It incorporated the city and gave its white male property owners the right to elect a council presided over by a mayor appointed by the president. Washington would wait until 1812 for Congress to give the council the right to select the mayor, and until 1820 before the mayor was elected by popular election.

Of course, the citizens of Washington had no part in making these laws, but Congress believed it had discharged its constitutional duty and settled the city's affairs; it then turned to more pressing national business, including the Louisiana Purchase, the impeachment of Supreme Court justice and staunch Federalist Samuel Chase, relations with Great Britain and France, and the treason trial of Aaron Burr (for supposedly plotting to create a western empire). To be sure, from time to time it bestowed some money on the city, including $3,000 in 1807 to improve the mud slough of Pennsylvania Avenue that many called "The Great Serbonian Bog." But as it wouldn't establish a standing committee for the District until 1808, it freely ignored the affairs of the federal capital.

ROBERT BRENT, THE man whom Jefferson appointed mayor in 1802, boasted a pedigree that reached deep into the Carroll and Young families. Traveling effortlessly through Washington society, he commanded the city's fortunes for a full decade. Brent and his council established the Center Market on the swampy south side of Pennsylvania Avenue between Seventh and Ninth streets, bought the city's first fire engine, required building owners to supply one leather fire bucket for each story, called for property owners to drain stagnant water from their land, appointed the first police superintendent to attend to nuisances— including garbage, waste from slaughterhouses, and unlicensed peddlers—and presided at the opening of the first Potomac bridge at

Fourteenth Street, which connected the city with Alexandria, Virginia (it came to be known as the "Long Bridge"). The mayor also championed various manufacturing schemes, including one to make the city into a center for cotton weaving. And in 1808, the year the Constitution forbade the importation of slaves, a clearly fearful Robert Brent and his council enacted the city's first Black Codes.

The codes forbade a "black person or person of color" from walking about after 10 p.m. or from "dancing, tippling, quarreling, or in playing at any game of hazard or ball." It charged the city's police officers—there were now two—with enforcement, including whippings. The penalty was a $5 fine; slaves whose masters refused to pay were to be whipped. Growing ever more fearful of Washington's lure for free blacks, and fearing a slave uprising should the British menace the area in the coming war, Brent and his council decided in 1812 to make the penalties more severe. Free blacks had to register with the city and carry proof of their freedom, and the council raised the fine for code violations to $20 or six months jail. Slaves who broke the codes now also risked forty lashes.

And there were still more laws, some enacted in Maryland at the beginning of the eighteenth century: A slave could not give testimony against a white person, but could against another slave. Slaves who perjured themselves were liable to thirty-nine lashes and having their ears cut off; those who were caught after running away were branded with an "R." The laws were equally harsh upon blacks who had purchased their freedom, who had been manumitted, or who had arrived in the District from a free northern state. Their freedom extended only to being allowed to buy a license to drive a cart or a carriage. As the code made clear, they had to carry papers that established their freedom.

Slavery in Washington stood out as the great incongruity at the center of democracy. Thomas Moore noted the irony in a poem that he wrote from "beside the proud Potomac's stream." Columbia's "bloom is poison'd and her heart decays," Moore declared. Slavery was the cause of her corruption:

> *Who can, with patience, for a moment see*
> *The medly mass of pride and misery,*
> *Of whips and charters, manacles and rights,*
> *Of slaving blacks and democratic whites,*

> *And all the piebald polity that reigns*
> *In free confusion o'er Columbia's plains?*
> *To think that man, thou just and gentle God!*
> *Should stand before Thee, with a tyrant's rod*
> *O'er creatures like himself, with souls from Thee,*
> *Yet dare to boast of perfect liberty.*

To Moore, Washington was the place "where bastard freedom waves / Her fustian flag in mockery over slaves." He even attacked Thomas Jefferson, whose dalliances with slaves were long the quiet stuff of rumor:

> *The patriot, fresh from Freedom's councils come,*
> *Now pleased retires to lash his slaves at home;*
> *Or woo, perhaps, some black Aspasia's charms,*
> *And dream of freedom in his bondsmaid's arms.*

Despite the glaring anomaly, few in the capital or the Congress wanted to abolish slavery in Washington. One exception was James Sloan, a representative from New Jersey. In January 1805, Sloan introduced a resolution proposing to free "all blacks and people of color, that shall be born within the District of Columbia, or whose mother shall be the property of any person residing within said District" on July 4, 1805. The motion failed 65 to 47; the nay votes included 11 representatives from New York and New England.

IT WAS IN Thomas Jefferson's administration that international events began to have an impact upon the mechanical and carpentry trades in the capital. Jefferson arrived in office in 1801 as an advocate of peace, but for the navy he had different plans. He retired obsolete ships and ordered construction of the nation's great frigates, including the *United States*, the *Constitution*, and the *Congress*, to be built in an expanded Washington Navy Yard.

Jefferson's reasons for strengthening the navy stemmed in part from a 1785 meeting he and John Adams had in London with Ambassador Sidi Haji Abdrahaman from Tripoli. Pirates from Tripoli were harrying American ships in the Mediterranean, but to the American protest that the United States had done Tripoli no harm, the ambassador replied, "It was written in their Koran that all nations who should not have acknowledged their authority were sinners, that it was their right and duty to make war upon them wherever they could be found . . . and that every Musselman who should be slain in battle was sure to go to Paradise." To pacify the pirates, the United States had regularly paid an annual tribute of about $1 million (the entire annual federal budget in 1800 was $11 million), but Jefferson would have none of it. In February 1802 Tripoli declared war; Jefferson ordered the frigates at the Navy Yard readied for battle, commissioned Latrobe to design buildings and docks, and ordered the construction of two gunboats. The US Navy prevailed, and peace with Tripoli came in June 1805; nevertheless, the president ordered 50 gunboats to defend America's coastal shipping, and in 1808, another 175.

The Tripolitan War enhanced the Navy Yard's importance as one of the city's leading employers and manufacturers. In 1805 alone, the yard hired 108 new workmen to bring its total number of laborers—rope makers, blacksmiths, painters, plumbers, brass founders, coopers, sail makers, caulkers, joiners, and ordnance makers among them—to well over 200. To hasten the pace of their work, Admiral Tingey purchased 100-barrel lots of liquor to distribute to the thirsty men. Many of the workers, immigrants and new arrivals to the capital, moved with their families to Navy Yard Hill; it became a thriving settlement of homes and merchants, which some said resembled more an English village, with a commons and a public well, than an American city.

IN 1804, SAMUEL Harrison Smith and his wife followed the pattern of many fashionable Washingtonians by acquiring a second house outside the city. Theirs was "Sidney," a country estate with a yellow brick house atop a high hill on the Bladensburg Road just northeast of the city line. His triweekly *National Intelligencer* was thriving as the court newspaper for Republicans; Republican patronage brought him printing orders for government stationery, the *Annals of Congress*, *The Register of Debates*, and *The American State Papers*. But Smith had developed a deep distaste for publishing the *Intelligencer* three times a week, fighting with the postal authorities to have it delivered on time, and transcribing the speeches in the Capitol. He found himself engulfed by Washington, including from his two terms on the District's council. The attacks upon Jefferson, for whom his admiration bordered on idolatry, had made him bitter and ill. On several occasions he had been forced to suspend publication until he recovered. He and his wife enjoyed life outside the city, where they could raise their four children. From their country house they could see the Capitol and the Potomac River. They screwed down their abolitionist principles enough to hire slaves from other owners, and even purchased one whom they paid liberally. Samuel took up gardening, dreamt of retiring, and in 1807 offered to sell the *National Intelligencer* "to a person of sound republican principles." Three years later, he sold it to his stenographer, Joseph Gales Jr. Free of his papers at last, he became president of the Bank of Washington.

BY 1810, A new generation of politicians had taken control of the Congress. Their leaders were Henry Clay from Kentucky and John C. Calhoun from South Carolina, men who had come of age after the Revolution and were well acquainted with all of the war's glories and honors, but who knew nothing of its miseries and hardships. Knowing little of the larger war then raging between England and France, they focused on British "outrages," such as impressment on the high seas. Swayed by the mindless cant of patriotism, they also dreamed of western and northern expansion. "The conquest of Canada is in your power," the thirty-two-year-old Henry Clay declaimed in his maiden speech in the Senate. "The militia of Kentucky are alone competent to place Montreal and Upper Canada [Ontario] at your feet." Emboldened by such rhetoric and keen to assert US sovereignty, Congress declared war on June 18, 1812. The following day, James Madison, who had succeeded Thomas Jefferson as president in 1809, issued a proclamation of war with Great Britain.

Few at the time could imagine the changes that war would bring to Washington. At the heady beginning of the conflict, residents enjoyed the renewed activity at the Navy Yard, where men were kept busy building and repairing vessels. The city's social life—the Jockey Club races in October, the dancing assemblies, the New Year's Day reception at the White House, and the Inaugural Parade down Pennsylvania Avenue celebrating the start of James Madison's second term—went on undisturbed. But in April 1813, a small squadron of British vessels and about five hundred sailors, under Rear Admiral George Cockburn, blockaded Chesapeake Bay. They conducted a series of raids and skirmishes, procuring food and supplies ("much flour, a large quantity of army clothing, . . . equipments for cavalry, etc," Cockburn reported), burning and plundering small communities such as Frenchtown and Havre de Grace in Maryland near the mouth of the Susquehanna. "Until the late alarm I have never been able to realize our being in a state of war," Margaret Bayard Smith wrote to her sister that July. "But now . . . I not only believe in but feel the unhappy *state* of our country."

Washington's residents grew increasingly uneasy. Except for the nearly derelict Fort Washington (also called Fort Warburton) south of the city on the Maryland shore of the Potomac, the capital was utterly without protection. John Peter Van Ness, the major general in charge of the District of Columbia militia, asked Madison's secretary of war, General John Armstrong Jr., for two brigades, only to be rebuffed. When British marines joined Cockburn's squadron in the Chesapeake, Van Ness again approached Armstrong. With indifference bordering on criminality, the secretary replied: "O yes! by God, they would not come with such a fleet without meaning to strike somewhere, but they certainly will not come here," adding, "Baltimore is the place, sir; that is of so much more consequence." Van Ness resigned his commission.

Admiral Cockburn had other plans. An April 1813 attack by the United States upon York (today's Toronto), the capital of Upper Canada, left the legislative buildings and the governor's house in ashes. Another raid the following month on the tiny village of Long Point, Ontario, on the shore of Lake Erie, left houses, a flour mill, and distilleries in flames. By August 1814 vengeance was in the air. From London the orders went out to inflict "that measure of retaliation which shall deter the enemy from a repetition of similar outrages." The US capital, symbolic center of the nation, with a large naval yard but without adequate defense, proved a perfect target.

On Friday, August 19, Cockburn and Major General Robert Ross, who had arrived from Bermuda with 4,000 troops from Wellington's army, landed at Benedict on the Patuxent River and marched east to Bladensburg. The pace of their progress was slow, perhaps because of the intense heat and humidity. By this time, Armstrong had awakened from his delusional torpor long enough to allow American forces to build defensive works at Bladensburg. By Tuesday, August 23, as the

British moved inexorably closer, chaos reigned in the federal city. Government clerks hastily loaded official papers into carts; many citizens took whatever they could carry in a wagon or on a horse and left.

The following day saw the "Bladensburg Races," as one bitter wag called the spectacle of token resistance mounted by the US troops and their hasty retreat over eight miles to the city. Their thought was to mount a defense at the Navy Yard bridge that crossed the Eastern Branch. But Cockburn and Ross decided to bypass the bridge altogether, choosing instead to approach with their silent columns of troops from the north.

As the British were advancing on Washington, Dolley Madison was packing. On Tuesday, the president had learned of the imminent danger and gone out to assay the strength of the British forces and the American resistance. Left to supervise the removal of valuables, Dolley "pressed as many Cabinet papers into trunks as to fill one carriage," she wrote to her sister Lucy. "Our private property must be sacrificed," she added, "as it is impossible to procure wagons for its transportation." She spent much of Wednesday the 24th scanning the city with a spyglass, searching in vain for a sign of her husband's return. Dolley was careful to keep up a cheerful front; she ordered the dining table set and sufficient ale, wine, and cider brought from the cellar for forty guests, though she knew none were expected. At 3:00 that afternoon, James Smith, a free black man who served the Madisons, "galloped up to the house, waving his hat, and cried out, 'Clear out, clear out! General Armstrong has ordered a retreat!'"

"All then was confusion," Paul Jennings, James Madison's body slave, remembered. Dolley hastily filled another cart "with plate and the most valuable portable articles, belonging to the house." An anxious friend arrived to hasten her departure, but, as the story has come down through generations, embellished by Dolley herself in a letter she supposedly wrote to her sister, the president's wife demanded that Gilbert Stuart's iconic Lansdowne portrait of George Washington renouncing a third term as president—an eight-by-five-foot painting—be removed and packed in the cart. By 3:30, she was ready to depart for Georgetown. "And now, dear sister, I must leave this house, or the retreating army will make me a prisoner in it by filling up the road I am directed to take. When I shall again write to you, or where I shall be to-morrow, I cannot tell!!" Dolley Madison was among the last to abandon the city;

future generations would mark her departure as one of the few displays of courage in this moment of national humiliation.

When the British entered Washington that evening, Thomas Tingey was ready. Earlier he had ordered his men to prepare the Navy Yard's buildings, stores, and vessels to be fired lest they fall into the hands of the enemy. At twenty minutes past eight, the last possible moment, he gave the command to destroy his labor of fourteen years. From the deck of a vessel in the Eastern Branch, Tingey watched as the flames followed the lines of powder upward to sails and spars, and made their way to the sawmill and warehouses, the new steam engine building, and his own commodore's house, until with a great explosion that rocked the city, they arrived at the powder magazine.

There were still important buildings left for British torches. After overcoming minor resistance from one of the houses on the northeast corner of Capitol Square (a single gunman shot General Ross's horse from under him), the troops entered the House chamber, "an unfinished but beautifully arranged building," remembered James Scott, Admiral Cockburn's aide-de-camp, "somewhat infected with an unseemly bias for monarchical splendor." Stacking the desks into a "funereal pile," the men covered it with rocket powder and set it ablaze. As the flames flickered on the gilt eagle on the chamber's ceiling, the clock beneath it "told the hour of ten."

Cockburn and Ross then descended Capitol Hill with about 150 men and headed for the White House. "We found the cloth laid. . . . [A] large store of super-excellent Madeira and other costly wines stood cooling in ice." Scott and the men filled their glasses, toasted Madison, and drank liberally. "I absolutely blessed them for their erring providence. Never was nectar more grateful to the palates of the gods, than the crystal goblet of Madeira and water I quaffed off at Mr. Madison's expense," said Scott. Next he went to the president's dressing room and appropriated "a snowy clean linen" shirt. Others helped themselves to Madison's personal effects, including his medicine chest.

Once they had satisfied their desire for food, drink, and mementos, the British set fire to the house and then moved on to the Treasury, the War Department, the Patent Office, and the offices of the *National Intelligencer*, which had been relocated to Pennsylvania Avenue midway between Sixth and Seventh streets. The last two they spared. Tradition holds that William Thornton implored Cockburn's men to pass by his Patent Office because of what the loss would mean to civilization. Joseph Gales, the publisher of the newspaper, and his partner William W. Seaton had fled, but ladies in adjoining buildings persuaded Admiral Cockburn that if he were to set fire to the newspaper, the conflagration would consume their houses. Instead, his men pulled the walls of the *Intelligencer* down, smashed the presses, and wrecked the type. "Be sure that all the C's are destroyed," the admiral is reputed to have said, "so that the rascals cannot any longer abuse my name."

It took an act of God, indeed two acts, to check the British destruction. That night, rain from a violent thunderstorm drenched the city, quite possibly cracking the hot stones of the Capitol and White House. The next day, as British troops were firing a few buildings in the Navy Yard that remained standing, a violent tornado uprooted trees, destroyed houses, and toppled chimneys. The troops survived only by lying flat upon the ground; once the violence passed, they beat a quick retreat to Benedict, Maryland. Although Cockburn's men had spared the Patent Office the night before, nature proved not so sympathetic. The tornado ripped off a major section of the roof.

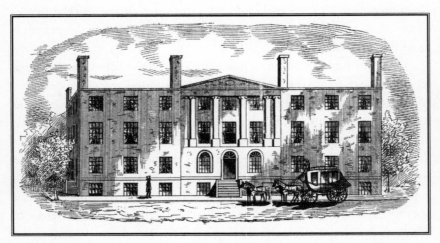

BLODGET'S HOTEL, which occupied a full block bounded by today's E and F and Seventh and Eighth streets, was designed by James Hoban. Lack of funds delayed its completion until 1810, the year the federal government acquired it to house the Post Office and the Patent Office. Tradition holds that William Thornton persuaded the British to spare the building and its patents in August 1814, but it was destroyed by fire in December 1836. CREDIT: Library of Congress

LESS THAN two months after the burning of the capital, a London publisher printed this woodcut of the event. CREDIT: Library of Congress

The burning of Washington proved to be the high point of the careers of Major General Robert Ross and Admiral George Cockburn. Ross would die in the attack upon Baltimore the following month. In 1851, at the end of his career, Cockburn struck a conventional pose for his naval portrait, standing four square in his admiral's uniform, his right hand on his sword, his left on his hip. In the background was a panorama that the admiral ordered: a view of Washington with billowing black smoke and bright orange flames rising from the Capitol and the White House.

"Oh my dear sister how gloomy is the scene," Margaret Bayard Smith wrote on the evening after the attack. Smith and her family had fled from Sidney to Brookville, Maryland, about twenty miles to the north. Like many others, she believed the attack of August 1814 meant the end of the capital on the Potomac. "I do not suppose Government will ever return to Washington. All those whose property was invested in that place, will be reduced to poverty. . . . The consternation about us is general. The despondency still greater." But less than a week later, she recovered enough to write, "But we will retrieve, yes I trust we will retrieve our character and restore our capital." Then she remembered that Rome had suffered a similar fate at the hands of the Goths, but its citizens had refused to leave. "May a Roman spirit animate our people, and the Roman example be followed by the Americans."

CHAPTER 4

Rebuilding and Growing

Even at Washington the new public buildings were pressed forward so rapidly that the effects of the fire were no longer seen. The Capitol began to rise from its ruins.

—Henry Adams, 1891

Tuesday, October 12, 1824. After more than four decades, the hero whose personal valor, integrity, and idealism had become the abiding symbol of the goodwill and spiritual solidarity of America and France, Marie-Joseph Paul Yves Roch Gilbert du Motier de Lafayette, the Marquis de Lafayette, arrived in the capital of the nation whose democracy he had labored so valiantly to secure. All Washington had been preparing for the visit of the French general ever since he had landed in New York Harbor the previous August. After New York, he had already visited Boston, Philadelphia, and Baltimore; now he was coming to a place wholly new, and much smaller. "Neither our population nor resources enabled us to approach the splendor of the Eastern Cities," a reporter for the *Washington Gazette* wrote with some sense of inferiority, but they "endeavored to do their best."

Members of Congress and the mayor awaited at the Capitol to welcome Lafayette as he passed beneath a triumphal arch inscribed "Hail, Friend of Freedom," at Capitol Square. The general seemed especially pleased, too, when twenty-five young ladies dressed in white, their number representing each of the twenty-four states and the District of

Columbia, bowed before him. One of them, Miss Sarah M. Watterston, daughter of the first Librarian of Congress, stepped forward with a greeting: "The young and the old, virgins and matrons alike, welcome thee," said Miss Watterston. "Our youthful bosoms heave with emotions of gratitude."

On his thirteen-month visit, Lafayette spent more time in Washington than any other place in America. The capital became the base for his extended excursions to the south and west. His days in the capital were always full: he enjoyed breakfasts and dinners with President James Monroe and, later, President John Quincy Adams; visits to the completely rebuilt and thriving Navy Yard, still commanded by the spry seventy-three-year-old Commodore Tingey; plays at the Washington Theatre, including a melodrama about his imprisonment, *Lafayette, or, the Fortress of Olmutz*; visits to schools and colleges; meetings with foreign envoys; and, always, receptions and banquets. Everyone wanted the company of General Lafayette.

The city that General Lafayette toasted so warmly had enjoyed a phoenix-like ascension from the ashes of 1814. Once the British frigates had cleared the mouth of the Potomac, the president, his cabinet, and government workers returned to the husks of public buildings with a determination and solidarity that had so often eluded them in the past. James and Dolley Madison took up residence at John Tayloe's Octagon House on New York Avenue. (It was in the house's second-floor parlor that, on February 17, 1815, the president signed the Treaty of Ghent, ending the war and restoring the boundary between Canada and the United States.) Joseph Gales and William W. Seaton gathered up the type at the *National Intelligencer* and resumed publication, and in the fall, Congress convened in the Patent Office.

One of the first questions the representatives had considered, a bill for the "temporary removal of the Seat of Government," underscored the fragility of the Residence Act of 1790. More than once since 1800 had Congress voted down motions to move the capital; this time the bill proposed decamping to Baltimore. Many thought that Margaret Bayard Smith's fears would be realized, that the District of Columbia would not survive.

Washington's citizens refused to let the move happen. The conflagration and the bill for removal had galvanized the capital's permanent residents to take their city seriously. Earlier in the century, authorities had divided the city into six sections, or wards; now residents of each ward pledged money and labor to rebuild Fort Washington on the Potomac. John Peter Van Ness, Thomas Law, and Daniel Carroll of Duddington led a group of citizens to promise $25,000 to build temporary quarters for Congress at First Street and Maryland Avenue NE, adjacent to the shell of its former home. The "Brick Capitol," as it came to be called, was ready by 1815. The Supreme Court, which had previously convened in the burned-out Capitol, met in one of Daniel Carroll's houses at Independence and New Jersey avenues. The City Council built a network of gravel sidewalks to connect the Court and the Brick Capitol with the boardinghouses and hotels. And Washington's banks, led by Van Ness's newly chartered Bank of the Metropolis, offered to loan the government half a million dollars to rebuild.

When Congress considered the bill, it was clear that the sentiment for removal wasn't there. As one representative from Maryland put it, even a temporary move from Washington to a northern city would be a "violation of the public faith" and would "injure public credit more than it would strengthen it." The vote in favor of remaining was substantial: 9 of the 33 Federalists left in Congress voted against moving; 74 of the 104 Republicans joined them. Some, including Daniel Webster, wanted to move the Capitol closer to Georgetown, but this motion, too, met defeat. On February 16, 1815, just 176 days after the British destroyed Washington, the Senate passed a measure to appropriate money, to be financed by loans, "for repairing or rebuilding the public buildings within the city." The nation's seat of government would remain on the Potomac.

In April 1815, once Congress reaffirmed the location, James Madison appointed three commissioners to supervise reconstruction. Benjamin Henry Latrobe would oversee rebuilding the Capitol, and James Hoban the White House. Fortunately for Latrobe, who had unhappy memories of his previous years in Washington, William Thornton would not be interfering with the reconstruction. (Although the aging polymath had urged the commissioners to follow his original plans for the House chamber, they ignored him.) But he would soon face other opponents.

The architect got to work immediately. In just over two and a half years, he removed the damaged stone and timbers and designed a new plan for the south and north wings, the rotunda, and the congressional library wing to the west. He acquired the materials and supervised the laborers. Although the building still looked singularly curious—the north and south wings for the Senate and House of Representatives dwarfed a covered wooden loggia, the site of the still-to-be-built rotunda, that ran between them—Latrobe had achieved a great deal in a short time. But it was not enough to satisfy the meddling demands of the capital's politicians.

The commissioners sometimes spoke with three separate voices, at times complaining about the laborers' salaries and limiting their working hours; at other times bemoaning the lack of progress in construction; and still at others complaining about Latrobe's failure to communicate. Madison cut the number to a single commissioner, but the interference continued. Senators, too, added to the delays, deciding they needed more space just as Latrobe was completing his designs for their wing. The commissioner believed the architect's replies to the politicians' many conflicting demands were impudent; on November 20, 1817, the new president, James Monroe, forced Latrobe's resignation.

Charles Bulfinch, Latrobe's replacement, blended his talents as an architect with his mastery of politics. His architectural study had begun at Harvard with courses in mathematics, linear perspective, and drawing, and continued on an eighteen-month grand tour of Europe, where he took in the works of Christopher Wren, Robert Adam, and John Soane in England, discussed design with Thomas Jefferson in France, and visited the great classical buildings of Italy. Returning to Boston in 1787, he put his knowledge to use in his design for the Massachusetts State House; and with his election as a selectman in Boston in 1791, he began his career in politics. By the end of the decade, he was the chair of the selectmen, superintendent of public schools, superintendent of police, and, in practice, superintendent of the city's streets, drains, sidewalks, and lighting. At the same time he took commissions to design or redesign the Massachusetts State Prison, Boylston Market, Boston Common, Faneuil Hall, a hall for Harvard, and several churches and private houses.

Bulfinch proved a wise choice. He was sensible enough to understand Latrobe's greatness—he modified his plans for the center rotunda as little as possible—shrewd enough to get what he wanted, and wise enough to know when he must yield. When a mean-spirited commissioner cut his salary by $500, Bulfinch quietly asked his Boston friend and then US secretary of state John Quincy Adams to intervene; the salary was reinstated. Yet when Monroe and his cabinet demanded that the central dome over the rotunda be raised in height, Bulfinch yielded. "Architects expect criticism," he later wrote, "and must learn to bear it patiently."

The East Portico of the Capitol and the rotunda interior were still under construction when Lafayette arrived in 1824. By 1827, workmen had completed the rotunda and installed John Trumbull's four giant canvasses depicting great moments in the history of the Revolution—the signing of the Declaration of Independence, the surrender of the British general John Burgoyne at Saratoga, the victory at Yorktown, and George Washington resigning his commission at Annapolis. Construction was well into the fourth decade and had taken more than $3 million, but much remained to be done. Finish work continued, which afforded every member of Congress the opportunity to become an authority on building and expenses: providing stables for members' horses, some said, would lead to paying for the animals' feed; guard rails to protect Trumbull's paintings were unnecessary, even though a vandal had used a penknife to cut the foot off a general depicted in the painting of Burgoyne's surrender; the rotunda should not be heated, "lest it become a haven for loungers and idlers." Bulfinch quietly persevered, slowly whittling through the list of items needed for completion, which he determined would take until the end of September 1829. But not even the skillful Boston politician could master all the machinations of the capital. On June 25, 1829, the commissioner of public buildings told Bulfinch that the project was near completion and no longer required an architect; he should vacate his office in five days.

Despite the dismissal, the architect's accomplishments were extraordinary. Where L'Enfant, Thornton, Hallet, and Latrobe had been denied, Charles Bulfinch succeeded. For a while, at least, the Capitol of the United States was complete.

LIKE THE CAPITOL that Lafayette saw, the rest of Washington was very much a work in progress. Conceived as it was on a gigantic scale, so Lafayette's private secretary perceptively noted, the city would not "be filled out for a century." In some sections, the buildings were spread so far apart that it took "more than 20 minutes . . . to go from one dwelling to another." Many of the lots resembled construction sites. Projected streets were mere muddy slashes across the fields; the felled trees that

Jefferson and others had long decried, and that might have afforded shade in the summer, lent a desolate and derelict appearance to the landscape. But on Pennsylvania Avenue, where Jefferson had planted two rows of Lombardy poplars down each side to make a formal allée of the sort he had seen in Europe, there was "the look of a town."

Washington was growing as never before. The Long Bridge, which had been burned during the British attack upon the city, reopened in 1818, helping to reestablish ties with Virginia and the South. In 1810, Congress had chartered the Seventh Street Turnpike leading north from the Center Market on Pennsylvania Avenue to Boundary Street (now Florida Avenue), and further north to Rockville, Maryland. Its completion in 1822 gave the city a commercial thoroughfare that opened vast tracts of land above Massachusetts Avenue to development. Houses, mostly simple wood structures of two and three stories with flat roofs, began to dot the landscape. Merchants opened a new market, the Northern Liberty, at the intersection of New York and Massachusetts avenues (today's Mount Vernon Square). Seeing Seventh Street as an easy route for entering and leaving the capital, wealthy men would build summer "cottages" on large tracts in Maryland.

Although Washington City was raw and still relatively small, with 9,600 whites, 1,950 slaves, and 1,700 "free colored"—far fewer people than, for example, the 550,000 living in Paris—it still ranked as the ninth largest city in the United States. In July 1822, Washington printer and civic booster Judah Delano thought the "population wealth, and importance of the metropolis," merited a city directory. The 148-page volume listed the members of the 17th Congress and the boardinghouses where they lived, the names and occupations of residents, the names of the foreign legations (from Britain, France, Sweden, and Mexico), and many of the city's institutions.

Delano's directory listed 176 men as carpenters, bricklayers, or plasterers, and two dozen more as painters, millwrights, or cabinetmakers. At the Capitol there were 27 stone carvers and stonecutters. To support them all, there were 46 grocers, 19 butchers, 5 brickmakers, and 6 lumber dealers, plus 42 cobblers, 4 seamstresses, and 21 tailors.

The city government now had a Board of Guardians of the Poor and a Board of Health; a police constable for each ward as well as "Commissioners for Draining Low Grounds"; a collector of taxes and a Board of Appeal; a commissioner of burial grounds and a surveyor;

seven managers of city lotteries, along with sixteen trustees of the public schools that the lotteries supported; inspectors of tobacco and flour; and wood corders (8), coal measurers (6), chimney sweeps (3), hay weighers (4), and "scavengers" (5), who were supposed to "remove nuisances and all offensive substances."

The council licensed and taxed wherever it could. There were licenses for tavern keepers ($60 per annum), auctioneers ($100), and even billiard tables ($100). There were taxes on conveyances, including coaches, chariots, phaetons, hacks, wagons, and carts; taxes on dogs (females, $5 per annum; males, $1), and taxes on slaves (males between fifteen and forty-five, $2; females, $1).

Delano began the section of his book on "Literary and Benevolent Institutions" with descriptions of the city's colleges, Georgetown and Columbian. As if to affirm his belief in the future of the democracy, Lafayette visited them on the days immediately following his arrival. Begun by Bishop John Carroll in 1787 as a Jesuit academy to train boys "in piety and in the discipline of the *literae humaniores*," and he hoped, the priesthood, Georgetown quickly evolved into a college. By 1815, when it received its charter from Congress, the college was receiving, besides Catholics, "members of every other religious denomination," provided that they "respectfully assist at public duties of religion with their companions." Students lived, took classes, and prayed in an imposing four-story brick building modeled on Nassau Hall in Princeton. In Washington it was rivaled only by the Capitol in size and eminence. When Lafayette visited Georgetown in October 1824, he found ten professors who taught mathematics, natural philosophy, moral philosophy, and rhetoric, and two who served as "Prefects of Morals."

The Columbian College, rising on "College Hill," a promontory between Fourteenth and Fifteenth streets, came close to matching the vision George Washington had cherished for a national university. Washington had long regarded the then common practice of training of America's youth in foreign countries—"before their minds were formed"—with "serious regret." Educating boys at home rather than in monarchical and antirepublican Europe would prepare them for national civic affairs and scientific pursuits that would accrue to the nation's greatness. As president, he had twice recommended to Congress that a university be established in the Federal District, even going so far as to suggest a site on the bank of the Potomac between

Twenty-third and Twenty-fifth streets, and wondered if a botanical garden might be placed there as well. To this end he left his fifty shares of stock in the Potomac Company "towards the endowment of a UNI-VERSITY to be established within the limits of the District of Columbia, under the auspices of the General Government, if that government should incline to extend a fostering hand towards it." The government was not so inclined, but in 1821, when the Baptist Convention proposed a university in the District that would be nominally nonsectarian, Congress issued a charter. By that time, Washington's shares of Potomac Company stock were worthless.

Lafayette found an institution with great ambition and few resources. Columbian had six professors and four tutors, about fifty students, two houses for professors, and a single five-story brick building that housed the classical and theological departments. A medical department on Tenth Street NW, near D Street, would open within a year. Two months later, Lafayette joined President Monroe, John Quincy Adams, and Andrew Jackson at Columbian's first commencement.

FOR ALL THE building and energy that Lafayette saw, there were signs of serious problems. Perhaps none was greater or more visible than the Washington City Canal, the sprawling ditch that crossed the city from the Potomac at the mouth of the Tiber to the Eastern Branch below the Navy Yard. L'Enfant had believed the canal would help to make the city self-sufficient, especially when the waterway connected with the canal George Washington's Potomac Company was building into the west.

Like so many other enterprises in the capital, the inspiration for the canal was grand but the execution poor. L'Enfant's design was brilliant: the Tiber Creek flowing down from the north would issue from the base of the Capitol in a waterfall forty feet high and about a hundred feet wide. The waters would splash into a pool, producing "a most happy effect," the designer wrote, before flowing into the canal. The route of the canal was ambitious. From Seventeenth Street, it cut its way gradually east and south until it arrived at South Capitol and E streets. Near that point the waters followed two paths, one cutting eastward to the Eastern Branch, and the other south to Greenleaf's Point and the Potomac. (Today's Constitution Avenue to about Seventh

Street was once part of the canal, as was the center of the Capitol Mall.) It would be grand. From the western entrance to the Capitol and from the White House, America's leaders could look out upon the commerce of the nation floating by.

Implementing L'Enfant's plan turned into a muddle. As was the case with the rest of the city, funding became the great problem. In 1795, Maryland's legislators authorized two lotteries to pay for its construction, but they produced little. Congress chartered a private company to build the canal in 1802, but other than setting its dimensions at eighty feet wide and three feet deep, little happened. Meanwhile, residents like Daniel Carroll, Thomas Tingey, and Thomas Law, who would benefit directly from the commerce the waterway would bring to their part of the city, lobbied hard. In 1809, Congress chartered a second company, with Carroll and Law among its managers, and authorized it to raise $100,000. The following spring, James Madison turned the first spade of earth to start the trench. The company managed to accumulate about $50,000 in stock sales, enough to keep gangs of Irish laborers working for a year. It then raised about $30,000 through two more lotteries ("THE GRAND NATIONAL CANAL LOTTERY . . . 20,000 tickets **More Prizes than Blanks**"), enough money to complete construction in late 1815.

The Washington City Canal, as it was called, was hardly an unalloyed commercial success. True, it did carry whiskey, flour, and firewood close to the Center Market on Pennsylvania Avenue, and stone to the base of the Capitol, but the waterway suffered from a serious engineering flaw. Designers had failed to follow L'Enfant's plans for a large pool at the base of the Capitol that would compensate for the fluctuation of the Potomac's tides. Low tides rendered the canal impassable. Worse still, it soon became filled with silt, debris, and trash. By 1820, the Washington City Canal was an open sewer.

Disregarding the waterway's obvious faults, the City Council decided to take over the enterprise, hoping to at last connect Washington's canal to the Chesapeake and Ohio Canal, fulfilling George Washington's dream. Arguing that the canal was important not only to the city but also to the nation, Mayor John Van Ness persuaded Congress in 1834 to appropriate money for dredging, funded by charging slave traders a $400 license fee. The money helped, but it was not enough. The enterprise had long passed its year of greatest operating profit: $182.10 in 1823.

THE SMALL CIRCLE of early residents—the Thorntons, Carrolls, Laws, Van Nesses, and Smiths—who had been so important to the capital in its beginnings remained at the center of power through the 1820s. Age and circumstance, however, were taking their toll, and for some their earlier presence had been rendered into shadow.

William Thornton was sixty-five when Lafayette arrived. Over the years he had watched his money and influence ebb as he satisfied his passion for thoroughbred horses, indulged his fondness for litigation, and succumbed to his general irresponsibility and fecklessness in business matters. Beginning in 1820, the city had to put tax liens on his house and slaves, even his carriage. Though he still headed the Patent Office, his fights with architects and inventors, which brought him into court numerous times, had diminished his authority. "Oh, how my heart aches when I think of the variety of trouble in which my poor husband was involved," wrote his widow, Anna Maria, shortly after her husband's death in 1828. His passing was the occasion for great ceremony: John Quincy Adams led his cabinet to the obsequies; Congress, the city government, and a generous outpouring of friends and citizens followed. The body of the architect of the Capitol was accorded a place of honor in the Congressional Cemetery beneath a monument designed by his nemesis Benjamin Henry Latrobe.

In 1820, Daniel Carroll of Duddington, too, slipped into bankruptcy. His assumption that the city would develop east and south of the Capitol on lands he owned ignored the realities of L'Enfant's plan, which showed the Capitol looking westward alongside the broad Potomac waters to the mountains of Virginia and Maryland in the distance; it also ignored Thornton's plans for the Capitol, which showed a grand entrance on the west front and just a small ground-floor entrance on the east; and, most especially, Carroll ignored President Washington's last directive, issued on March 3, 1797, which placed the buildings of executive departments close by the President's House. Notwithstanding frequent springtime floods, Pennsylvania Avenue had become the natural axis for development. Aside from buildings he had constructed near the Capitol, and the scars left by incomplete attempts at development by Greenleaf, Morris, and Nicholson, most of Carroll's lots lay bare. But the taxes on them, developed or not, continued to be levied. Small amounts individually, these amounted to a small fortune collectively. At the same time, Greenleaf pursued him in the courts for money; wealthy relatives refused to advance him money; and the city put liens on his lots. At his death in 1849, Carroll was a widower with two unmarried daughters; he was near financial failure, and barely clinging to Duddington itself. "He was a friend to the poor and dispensed much private charity from his own abundant stores," wrote the author of his obituary in the *Daily National Intelligencer.* "But alas, the mutability of fortune deprived him of late years of the means of giving to the poor."

Thomas Law endured the financial sting of his foundering real estate and commercial ventures as well, but his chief pain was his failed marriage to Eliza Parke Custis, which collapsed in 1804. Eliza was rumored to have conducted several affairs, something that Law denied vehemently, saying their parting had been caused by "a disagreement in disposition." The issue of slavery might have accounted for some of the failure: Law was antislavery; Eliza was pro. Her father had left her about eighty slaves; George and Martha Washington had given a young female slave to the bride and groom as a wedding gift; and Martha, her grandmother, had left her forty more when she died in 1802. But there were other issues as well. "He is one of the strangest I have ever met," Margaret Bayard Smith wrote shortly after her arrival in Washington. Law wrote reams of tedious verses for every social occasion, and often chose the most inopportune time to read them. As his biographer put it with admirable succinctness, "he was a poet and loved retirement and males." At the "Retreat," the name Law gave to a farm that he kept in Maryland, he entertained large parties of Washington gentlemen, including James Monroe and John Quincy Adams, with fine punch, lavish dinners, poetry, and song. He died in 1834, "troubled by disease," his biographer reported, and "overclouded by his domestic privation."

For a while, John and Marcia Van Ness survived best of all. Though land rich, they were often cash poor, but they managed to avoid the creditors' lawsuits that so plagued men like Thornton and Carroll. They were the consummate Washington couple, who for three decades exercised their power judiciously for the success of civic enterprise.

Despite his anger at the military ineptitude of the secretary of war in the loss of the capital to the British, Van Ness remained a steadfast supporter of the city. He had been one of the first to subscribe $5,000 to build the Brick Capitol. Of course, it was in his best interest to do so; if the capital were moved, the value of the enormous landholdings that had come to him through his wife's inheritance would plunge. But the allegiance went far deeper than mere self-interest. From the beginning, John and Marcia Van Ness devoted much of their time and energy to improving the city. In 1804 they gave the land at Eleventh and C streets for Washington's first theater and headed a group of subscribers who pledged $50 each for a building. (The theater opened in late 1804 and remained on the site until fire destroyed it in 1820.) They donated building lots for churches—Episcopal, Lutheran, and Catholic—and the Freeman's Vigilant Total Abstinence Society.

The Van Nesses set a tone of refined elegance for the capital. Befitting their wealth and station, they contracted in 1813 with Benjamin Latrobe to design an elegant Greek Revival mansion at Seventeenth Street facing the Washington City Canal and the Potomac. Set on six acres of David Burnes's land, and adjacent to his farmhouse as well as the White House, it was easily the most fashionable private residence in the city: two stories above a raised basement for servants, a

JOHN AND Marcia Van Ness hired Benjamin Henry Latrobe to design their house on land adjacent to the White House. Completed in 1816, it was the most fashionable private address in the capital and the center of Washington's society. After John Van Ness's death in 1846, it served as a beer garden, storehouse for the city's street cleaners, and athletic club until it was sold to the federal government in 1907 to be the location of the Pan American Union building. CREDIT: Library of Congress

Doric-columned porte cochere on the north side, and a giant glass conservatory overlooking the Potomac on the south. The three first-floor rooms overlooking the river—a library, a salon, and a dining room—had generous doorways between them that proved especially hospitable for large social events. The second floor had six bedrooms, dressing rooms, and a small dining room. From the moment workmen completed the structure in 1816, it was open to gatherings of senators and representatives, diplomats and presidents. Every year the couple hosted a party for members of Congress; every visiting dignitary, including Lafayette in 1824, received an invitation to a reception at the Van Ness mansion.

Marcia Van Ness served as an equal partner in a number of business endeavors and charitable ventures, and she promoted one of her own, the Washington Female Orphan Asylum. In October 1815, she gathered Margaret Bayard Smith and the wives of the city's Baptist minister, mayor, and clerk of the Supreme Court to create a shelter for "destitute female orphans." She persuaded Dolley Madison to take the honorific post of "First Directress," saving the Second Directress post, that of overseeing the asylum's operation, for herself. She and her friends made green frocks and beige shawls for the girls and raised money for their care. Most importantly, Marcia and her husband donated a Burnes lot at Ninth and H streets for an orphanage. In 1828, she persuaded Charles Bulfinch to design a new brick building for the site. As it had now enough space to admit boys, she changed the name to the Washington City Orphan Asylum.

The couple was not without tragedy. In 1823, their only daughter, Ann, died in childbirth. The parents erected a mausoleum for her remains on H Street near the orphan asylum, a beautiful columned classical shrine modeled on Rome's Temple of Vestia. Marcia turned inward. She had her father's farmhouse restored and often retired to it for "solemn meditation." And she redoubled her efforts at the orphan asylum, carefully tending to every detail of its operation. When the Asiatic cholera pandemic reached Washington in August 1832, she spent many hours nursing the sick in the city's emergency shelters. She herself fell ill, too, not with cholera, but with fatigue and a high fever. She succumbed on September 9. The following day, members of Congress and the city government joined scores of Marcia Van Ness's friends at her funeral in St. John's Church, which had been built on land she and her husband had donated. Among the mourners were the girls from the

Washington City Orphan Asylum wearing their green frocks and beige shawls. As the coffin approached the Van Ness mausoleum, each girl placed upon the lid her tribute of a single weeping willow branch.

John Peter Van Ness had always believed in Washington's cultural and commercial future. Years earlier, he had joined with Robert Brent in a cotton-weaving venture at Greenleaf's Point. He also had acquired "The Glebe," five hundred acres of fields in Alexandria, where he attempted to cultivate mulberry trees and silk worms. Both projects failed. Still, he remained active in civic affairs until his death on March 7, 1846, tending to his numerous properties and the Bank of the Metropolis.

Margaret Bayard Smith remained ever interested in the national scene and excited about the new leaders. Andrew Jackson's inaugural on March 4, 1829, was "a majestic spectacle and to a reflective mind one of moral sublimity." She understood better than many the significance of the event, the first amassing of thousands of citizens "without distinction of rank" to witness a president taking the Oath of Office. They gathered at the East Portico of the Capitol. After being sworn in, the Tennessean bowed to the people—"Yes, to the people in all their majesty," Smith told her daughter. Only after the ceremony did a "rabble mob" press into the reception at the White House, where only "ladies and gentlemen" had been admitted before. But it was, Smith concluded, "the People's day, and the People's President and the People would rule."

Even before the inauguration, she had been wary of what was to come during the Jackson administration. John Eaton, a widower friend of Jackson's, and soon to be his secretary of war, was marrying the beautiful Washington widow Margaret O'Neal Timberlake. Daughter of a hearty Irish tavern keeper (where Jackson himself had boarded) and a woman with certainly more than one past, she posed a challenge for all of Margaret's friends. "She has never been admitted into good society," she wrote her daughter, meaning, of course, the close society she and her friends kept. Rachel, Andrew Jackson's wife, had died in January, thus depriving Washington society of the opportunity of having to deal with a First Lady who smoked a pipe, but the imbroglio over Peg Eaton continued. Wives of cabinet members scorned the woman. Jackson was outraged; his own Rachel, too, had been subject to whispers about her past. "Mrs. Eaton is as chaste as those who slander her," he declared. But the rumors continued. The president's support was, said Smith, "a noble stand."

Simply put, the Jacksonians smelled too much of the people for Margaret Bayard Smith's taste. They were very different from those who had supported Thomas Jefferson's revolution in 1800. Republican farmers from Cheshire, Massachusetts, had presented Jefferson with a 1,200-pound cheese, which the president served over time at receptions—but now, when a farmer from Oswego, New York, presented Jackson with a 1,400-pound cheese, Jackson rolled it into the White House on Washington's birthday in 1837 and invited a ravenous mob to eat it. In two hours it was gone. Smith was not among them.

But other than her family and friends, few paid attention to Margaret Bayard Smith anymore. She had come to Washington with the Jeffersonian Republicans. Through the Jefferson, Madison, and Monroe administrations, she and her husband had floated in the highest sphere of capital society. She had written about it in two novels, including one with the almost anti-Jacksonian title *What Is Gentility?* that proved such refinement was "independent of birth, wealth, or condition," and derived from "that cultivation of mind which imparts elevation to sentiment and refinement to manners in whatever situation of life they may be found." Jackson's inauguration on March 4, 1829, marked the end of an era for Margaret Bayard Smith. She would continue her writing and observations for another fifteen years, until her death in 1844; Samuel Harrison Smith's death would follow a year later.

George Washington Parke Custis was just nineteen when the government moved to the Potomac. "Washy" had been something of a trial to his step-grandfather George Washington, never quite living up to the high ideals and expectations set for him. He studied classics at Princeton and later at St. John's College in Annapolis, but left before earning a degree. After Martha Washington's death in 1802, he used his legacy to build a Greek Revival house on an 8,000-acre tract on a hill in Arlington, Virginia, across the Potomac from the capital. For the rest of his life he delivered orations and wrote plays and newspaper articles.

Custis filled his plays with history, romance, and scenic spectacles celebrating the nation and George Washington. (He based *The Indian Prophecy; or, Visions of Glory* on the speech that a Delaware chief purportedly made about Washington in the French and Indian War: "See ye not that the Great Spirit protects that Chief; he cannot die in battle.") Custis wrote a column for the *National Intelligencer* in which he frequently related stories about his adoptive father. Indeed, his connection to George Washington consumed his life. Taken with the fact that he was the last link to the first president, he devoted about half his house at Arlington to relics from Mount Vernon and affected knee breeches long after they went out of fashion. Visitors would come from near and far to hear his stories, which he gladly told until he died in 1857. Eight of his oldest slaves placed him in a grave on the grounds, next to his wife. The property fell to their surviving daughter, Mary, the wife of a promising young army colonel, Robert E. Lee.

OVER TIME, THE capital became a destination for those who wanted to study the way a democracy might work—and perhaps to gain support for their own causes. Washington naturally drew men like Louis Kossuth, the father of Hungarian democracy, who arrived to great fanfare in 1851. He took up residence at Brown's Hotel on Pennsylvania Avenue, was feted by Congress at a fundraising dinner, and met with President Millard Fillmore in the White House. But the beribboned military uniform that covered his slight body, and his oversized sword that scraped the ground, seemed odd to the American public; in time, his continual hectoring for financial assistance for Hungary wore thin.

Ever fascinated by Americans and their democracy, the English came to look and write. Their observations were almost always lively, and often astute. Sensitive to any criticism from foreigners, though they dispensed plenty themselves, Americans frequently found British visitors infuriating.

Frances Trollope was among the first to upset Washington's citizens. In an effort to recover from her husband's disastrous investment schemes, she arrived in 1832 to write a book about the new republic. The result, *Domestic Manners of the Americans*, showed her gift for observing the vulgarity of Americans and rendering it in scenes filled with wit and severity. The city of Washington did not escape. Trollope found that senators and congressmen wore their hats in their chambers, they chewed and expectorated tobacco incessantly, and the city's theater was "astonishingly dirty." (She witnessed one man "seized with a violent fit of vomiting, which appeared not in the least to annoy or surprise his neighbors.")

Yet Trollope was careful to make a distinction between the manners of the capital's inhabitants and the beauty of its buildings. The Capitol was "magnificent," she wrote, adding that she was "delighted with the whole aspect of Washington: light, cheerful, and airy." Acknowledging that foreigners had laughed at it because of its scale, she found "nothing in the least degree ridiculous about it; the original design, which was as beautiful as it was extensive, has been in no way departed from, and all that has been done has been done well." Pennsylvania Avenue was "a street of most magnificent width, planted on each side with trees, and ornamented by many splendid shops." Washington, Frances Trollope concluded, was "a spectacle of high historic interest."

Among the most famous observers was Charles Dickens. Everyone from President John Tyler down wanted to spend time with the famous author of *Oliver Twist* when he visited in 1842. The president brought him to the White House; senators and congressmen welcomed him to the Capitol. George Watterston, the Librarian of Congress, gave him a copy of his guidebook to the city, *A Picture of Washington*, which included a map, a detailed description of public buildings, and explanations of the city's government. Dickens was invariably amiable and courteous to all, and then returned their many kindnesses by devoting a chapter to the city in his scathing *American Notes*. "Take the worst parts of the City Road and Pentonville . . . the straggling outskirts of Paris," began his indictment, then burn it down and "build it up again in wood and plaster . . . plough up all the roads . . . erect three handsome buildings in stone and marble . . . and that's Washington." What Peter Charles L'Enfant called "the city of magnificent distances," Charles Dickens called the "City of Magnificent Intentions."

Dickens did like some of the new government buildings, however. All were Greek Revival in design and massive in scale. A new and expanded Treasury Building rose on the site of the old one that had burned down in 1833. The structure jutted into Pennsylvania Avenue, blocking the view from the White House to the Capitol. (Andrew Jackson, so legend has it, determined the location by driving his cane into the middle of the avenue.) At Seventh and E streets, a new Post Office rose on the site of the old building that had also housed the Patent Office. And one block north, at Seventh and F streets, stood a new Patent Office inspired by the Parthenon.

But Dickens despised Washington's other buildings. From the front window at Fuller's Hotel on Pennsylvania Avenue, he looked south to "a long, straggling row of houses, one story high, terminating . . . in a melancholy piece of waste ground with frowzy grass, which looks like a small piece of country that has taken to drinking, and has quite lost itself." From the back window he saw "a common yard" with a line of drying clothes, dogs, a triangle [for summoning help], female slaves, black waiters, and "a pig . . . turning up his stomach to the sun."

At the Capitol, which he visited every day, Dickens saw the place where the ideals of the nation, meant to "correct some of the falsehood and vices" of the Old World, had become a gathering place for the venal and greedy. Here and there were those who represented "the true, honest, and patriotic heart of America," but these few "scarcely colored the stream of desperate adventurers which sets that way for profit and for pay."

Dickens found that Washington was also the capital of tobacco chewing. Looking down from the galleries, he frequently saw an honorable member, his face swelled with tobacco, whittling a new plug with his penknife, "and when it was quite ready for use, shooting the old one from his mouth, as from a pop-gun, and clapping the new one in its place." In the case of this filthy public custom of chewing and spitting, the novelist was absolutely on the mark. From the time of the American Indians until the early twentieth century, chewing was the most common way to consume tobacco, and in Washington one was never far from a spittoon. They were in hotels, offices, hospitals, and, of course, the Congress, where every representative and senator had one beside his desk. Tobacco companies frequently flavored the leaves with molasses, which gave them a sweet taste and a rich brown color, and yielded a juice that stained the teeth and edges of the mouth. The parabolic arcs of yellow and brown spit issued continually from men's mouths, but it seemed from the condition of rugs that only a few hit their target of the spittoon. As women's skirts became more voluminous, they, too, suffered from the shower.

ONE NINETEENTH-CENTURY ENGLISHMAN who never visited Washington had a far greater influence upon the future of the capital, and indeed the United States, than any of the commentators. James Smithson, one of the First Duke of Northumberland's four bastard children, grew up knowing he was the son of one of the richest men in the realm, but he understood he had no legal right even to his father's name. The boy showed promise, took a degree at Pembroke College, Oxford, in

1786, was elected to the Royal Society the following year, and published twenty-seven scientific papers on mineralogy. Other than his penchant for *Rouge et Noir*, a French version of blackjack that he frequently played at Parisian gaming tables, his personal life remains an enigma.

But James Smithson had inherited money from his mother, a member of England's Seymour family, invested it well, and counted himself a wealthy man. After his death in 1829, his will revealed that he had left his money to his nephew; but should that heir die without issue, the whole of his estate would go "to the United States of America, to found at Washington, under the name of the Smithsonian Institution, an Establishment for the increase & diffusion of Knowledge among men." In 1835, the nephew died without issue. The money, about £100,000 ($500,000 in US currency then, the equivalent of about $50 million today), could now pass to the United States.

But would the nation accept it? Andrew Jackson left it to Congress to decide the matter. Some members were suspicious of foreign money and the thought of lending immortality to the name of an Englishman in the heart of the capital. John C. Calhoun saw the bequest as an expansion of the federal government's role in the Union—it was beneath the dignity of the United States to accept Smithson's money. Fortunately, the question landed in a committee headed by the former president John Quincy Adams, now a representative from Massachusetts, who managed to assuage patriotic and isolationist fears by citing Smithson's noble lineage (without mentioning he was a bastard). It took two years for Richard Rush, the special envoy sent by the president, to steer Smithson's will through London's Chancery Courts, defending America's claim against all comers and overcoming all legal impediments. Finally, in 1838, a packet boat sailed into New York Harbor carrying Rush, Smithson's papers and mineral collection, and 105 sacks of gold.

The time was propitious for Smithson's bequest. Despite the opposition of Calhoun and his colleagues, practical demands were moving the United States beyond its provincial attitudes toward empirical knowledge. In the 1830s, Congress revived the United States Coast Survey to produce accurate navigation charts, funded exploration of the American West, reorganized the Patent Office, and allowed the US Navy to build an observatory on the Capitol grounds to aid in the accuracy of its chronometers. As Rush arrived with Smithson's gold, naval captain Charles Wilkes was embarking on a four-year, 87,000-mile expedition to gather information about the South Seas. Accompanying Wilkes were naturalists, zoologists, botanists, and other civilian scientists.

Now Smithson's will forced Congress to decide the meaning of the words "increase & diffusion of Knowledge." There was no shortage of ideas: endow the national university that George Washington had wanted for the capital; create a large library; fund a museum for the many specimens that men like Wilkes were gathering from around the globe; revive the city's Columbian Institute for the Promotion of Arts and Sciences; provide for agricultural experiments; build a normal school for the education of science teachers; and build an observatory. Ever consistent, John Calhoun wanted to return the money to England.

Soon there wasn't much money to give back. In a remarkably short time President Martin Van Buren's secretary of the treasury squandered most of the gold in bonds issued by Arkansas, a state dominated by shady political and financial deals. Fortunately, after Arkansas defaulted, John Quincy Adams came to the rescue. The money had passed through the "gauntlet of rapacious and piratical adventure," he told Congress. It would bring dishonor to the nation to surrender it to "a rattlesnake's fang." Although it was unwilling to look too closely at who had profited from the sale of the original bonds, Congress was still shamed enough to order the Treasury to restore the principal of Smithson's legacy *with* interest.

In the end, compromise ruled. There would be a library, and also a museum. The key provision was the creation of a governing board of regents with a broad mandate to control the destiny of the Smithsonian. In June 1846, ten years after it had learned of the curious bequest by the mysterious Englishman, and five years after it had secured the gold, Congress created the Smithsonian Institution.

The regents named James Renwick to design a building to house the institution, and Joseph Henry to be the Smithsonian's first secretary. More than any other scientist in America, Henry could claim the mantle of Benjamin Franklin. His background included some schooling at Albany Academy, a failed apprenticeship as a watchmaker, and a flair for play writing and acting. As he recollected, a chance reading of a book about experimental philosophy when he was sixteen brought about a Pauline conversion. He gave up acting for scientific study. At Albany Academy, where he returned as professor of mathematics and natural philosophy, Henry made discoveries in electromagnetism that are fundamental to every electric motor and the telegraph. From Albany he went to a professorship at the College of New Jersey, the post he held when the regents appointed him to head the Smithsonian.

Believing that only scientific inquiry would increase knowledge that would benefit all, Henry withstood all pressure to change the nature of the Smithsonian. Under Henry, research would dominate the Smithsonian's mission; the museum, library, and gallery of art would exist only on the margins. In the years that followed, many congressmen either attacked this position or tried to commandeer the money for their own projects. Illinois senator Stephen Douglas would push for agriculture; President Andrew Johnson wanted to rename it "Washington University for the benefit of indigent children of the District of Columbia." But to Joseph Henry, Smithson's money was given "in behalf of the general family of mankind, for the benefit of men of all countries and of all times . . . for the extension of the boundaries of thought." Henry resisted as much as he could, and whenever necessary reached uneasy compromises. He would survive as secretary for more than three decades, until his death in 1878.

Henry hated the building the regents pressed upon him, sneeringly referring to it as the "Norman Castle." Indeed, Renwick's Medieval and Romanesque revival work, the castle Smithson could never attain in England, contained the museum and libraries that the scientist believed drew from the true purpose of the institution. Whenever he could, he delayed construction in order to husband more of the money for scientific study.

The building served the Washington community in a wholly new way. Through Henry's efforts it became a center for the exchange of intellectual ideas. Early on, he instituted a lecture series that would offer "instruction rather than amusement." The Smithsonian joined with numerous institutions across America that were offering lectures to citizens eager to understand the changes and discoveries that were occurring all around them. Among the subjects were "A Recent Naval Expedition to the Artic," "Phases of the Atmosphere," "Recent Progress in Astronomy," "the Foundation of Symetry in the Animal Kingdom," and geology. As Henry put it in an annual report, "the influence the Institution is having on the character and reputation of the city of Washington is by no means small." For Washingtonians, Henry had made the Smithsonian castle into a house of intellect.

TRAINED AS an engineer, James Renwick was twenty-nine years old in 1847 when the design competition was held for the new Smithsonian Institution building. Renwick intended for his medieval and Romanesque Revival structure to reflect the tenor of the great universities of Europe that were founded in the Middle Ages. He expected that the Smithsonian would be home to some of the great minds of the New World, as those institutions had been to the old. CREDIT: Library of Congress

BETWEEN 1822 AND 1859, John Sessford, a Scotsman who worked as a printer for the *National Intelligencer* and the Treasury Department, meticulously recorded the quiet but steady growth of his adopted city. Sessford reported every material change he could: the number of feet of sidewalks and pavement added each year, the number of houses, the number and types of deaths. Ward by ward, he recorded all that he saw: a bell for the steeple of St. John's Church (1822); a keel for a frigate laid at the Navy Yard (1825); an addition to the National Hotel (1827). Sessford recorded the construction of sixty-nine houses in 1824, the year of Lafayette's visit, which increased the number of dwellings to 2,464. Extrapolating from the 1820 census, which found an average of 6⅓ people living in each dwelling, he estimated Washington's population to be 16,600. One hundred and thirty-three adults and 157 children died that year; cholera and consumption led the list of causes. By the time Andrew Jackson took office on March 4, 1829, Sessford could report that there were 91,665 running feet of brick sidewalk. Five stage coaches left the city for Baltimore each day; others went to Fredericktown, Alexandria, Annapolis, and Piscataway. Two steamboats departed daily for Alexandria; others went to Norfolk and Baltimore. In the second ward, "upwards of 1,000 feet of pipe for the conveyance of water" had been added, and a reservoir had been built at D Street and Indiana Avenue;

in addition, a "handsome bridge" had been built over the canal at Seventh Street. Sessford counted 2,900 dwellings that year, about equally divided between brick and wood. Over the next eight years of the Jackson administration, builders would erect about 700 more houses.

In 1835 Sessford reported that the Long Bridge over the Potomac had been rebuilt, after a storm four years earlier had destroyed the previous structure. The National Theater opened at E Street and Pennsylvania Avenue; the avenue itself had curbs and a pavement of crushed Gneiss stone from the White House to the Capitol. Most importantly, in August, the Baltimore and Ohio Railroad inaugurated its Washington Branch depot at Second Street and Pennsylvania Avenue, a moment that George Washington Parke Custis celebrated in an insipid operetta:

> *Of each wonderful plan*
> *E'er invented by man,*
> *That which nearest perfection approaches*
> *Is a road made of iron,*
> *Which horses ne'er tire on,*
> *And traveled by steam, in steam coaches.*

At times, when he could not issue a positive report, Sessford didn't hesitate to criticize the lack of planning. "The Canal through the city has not been prosecuted with either spirit or judgment," he wrote in his summation of the year 1833, "and the execution has been greatly increased by injudicious commencement of middle sections, preventing a proper drainage." So steep was the ascent of the bridge over the canal at Twelfth Street that it appeared to be "on stilts" and was "almost impassable." Sessford took on Congress for its seeming lack of interest in the city: "During the year, but little has been done," he wrote of 1837, the year the nation faced financial panic, "beyond the casual repair of streets, except the filling up of lots by direction of the Board of Health, which were covered with water, and considered injurious to the health of the inhabitants."

Despite such jeremiads, Sessford could usually make a positive report. For 1850, the year the District's population reached 40,000 for the first time (29,730 whites, 8,158 free blacks, and 2,113 slaves), he wrote: "The general improvement of the city has been great." Iron bridges had been erected across the canal at Seventh and Twelfth streets; the south face of Washington's City Hall, begun in the 1820s on D Street between Fourth and Fifth streets NW, was finally finished; the arsenal at Greenleaf's Point in the southwest had been improved; a new foundry was in "full operation"; and the Chesapeake and Ohio Canal was now complete to Cumberland. And, ever the counter, Sessford found 225,217 running feet of pavement. Washington had risen from the conflagration of 1814 to become a serious city.

CHAPTER 5

The Bifurcated Southern National City

From the western front of this Capitol, from the piazza that opens out from your Congressional library, as you cast your eye along the horizon and over the conspicuous objects of the landscape,—the President's mansion, the Smithsonian Institution, and the site of the Monument, you cannot fail to see the horrid and black receptacles where human beings are penned like cattle, and kept like cattle, that they may be sold like cattle,—as strictly and literally so as oxen and swine are kept and sold at Smithfield shambles in London, or at the cattle fair in Brighton.

—Horace Mann, 1849

For the first six decades of the nineteenth century, all who crossed into the District of Columbia entered a distinctly southern town. Representatives and senators from below the Mason Dixon Line considered Washington to be their own preserve, and through positions on congressional committees they maintained as firm a grip on its significant civic affairs as they could. Practices that were quickly fading in the North remained the norm in the capital. But because there were numerous northern representatives and senators present, at least when Congress was in session, Washington was an irreconcilably bifurcated city. Over the decades, the divisions in the nation between North and South widened and political disputes intensified. Aside from the common cause of the Mexican War, unity on any issue—slavery, states' rights, immigration, trade and tariffs, among others—was nearly impossible to attain. Then, as always, Americans were testing the strength of the fragile cords that bound the states in union and questioning what should be the proper balance between federalism and republicanism. The representatives of so many disparate interests naturally found themselves at an impasse.

EVEN THE SIMPLE matter of creating a suitable honor for America's most famous founder brought conflict among the nation's competing interests. The idea of commemorating Washington had its roots in a resolution voted unanimously by the Second Continental Congress in Princeton, New Jersey, in 1783 to commission a bronze statue of the general "in Roman dress" riding upon his steed. A marble pedestal would depict the principal battles of the war *"in basso relievo."* Once it passed, most in Congress forgot the proposal, but it is likely that Peter Charles L'Enfant did not. His design for the capital included an equestrian statue at the approximate location of the present monument, making it the focal point for both the Capitol and the President's House. L'Enfant's idea pleased Washington (who no doubt had not forgotten either), but it was not a priority; the press of preparing for the government's arrival in 1800 occupied everyone's energy.

Washington's death brought the matter to the forefront once again, but by 1799 the very idea of a monument to a Federalist president raised questions in many republicans' minds about the meaning and intent of America's democracy. Some senators and representatives spoke of erecting an equestrian statue on the Capitol grounds as well as a crypt for his remains beneath the rotunda, but old antagonisms prevented Congress from taking any definitive actions. Elsewhere in the nation, people had no hesitation to honor their first president. Eleven of the original thirteen states contained counties, towns, or townships named for Washington; the city of Baltimore held six successful lotteries to raise funds for its own Washington Monument, a slender Doric column crowned by a statue of the general.

The approaching centennial of Washington's birth in 1832 finally shamed members of Congress to act. Although they failed to convince the first president's heirs to reinter his remains in the crypt, they gave the American sculptor Horatio Greenough $5,000 to produce a statue for the rotunda. The classically trained Greenough proved a terrible choice; when the statue arrived nine years later, Americans laughed. They could not contemplate an American version of the Greek sculptor Phidias's lost chryselephantine statue of Zeus: a naked Washington, save for sandals and a chiton draped strategically across his lap, sitting on a marble throne. Greenough's god prepares to relinquish the sword of power that is raised in his left hand as he makes a gesture for constitutional government with his right. Such ideas passed over the heads of the senators, representatives, and public, who saw little more than a nearly naked man striking a silly pose. The fact that its twelve tons cracked the floor of the rotunda and threatened to send the entire mass into the basement gave Congress an excuse to move it to the Capitol grounds, where it became a convenient resting place for pigeons. It would not find shelter from the elements until the Smithsonian Institution gave it a home in 1908.

CONGRESS NEVER knew quite what to do with Horatio Greenough's massive statue of the first president in the guise of a demigod that it commissioned for the Capitol rotunda. Greenough intended it to be a paean to the ideals of freedom, but most of the public saw only a naked man. In 1843, after two years in the rotunda, it began a peripatetic journey to the East Lawn of the Capitol, the Patent Office, the Smithsonian Castle, and finally, to the National Museum of American History, where it stands today. CREDIT: Library of Congress

Meanwhile, the spot L'Enfant reserved on the Mall remained bare. Frustrated by Congress's repeated failures to honor its promise, the federal city's leaders decided to shoulder the effort themselves. In September 1833, they established the Washington National Monument Society with Chief Justice John Marshall president and John Peter Van Ness vice president. The society believed that all Americans would want to contribute. It would build a monument costing no less than $1 million, but, in one of the worst decisions in the history of philanthropy, it decided not to accept more than a dollar from any citizen.

In 1836, the society selected Robert Mills's design for the monument—an Egyptian obelisk rising some 700 feet from the center of a circular colonnaded Greek pantheon. Mills had studied architecture with James Hoban, Thomas Jefferson, and Benjamin Henry Latrobe, absorbing lessons from each, especially their emphasis on classicism. In addition to the monument in Baltimore, he had designed a number of public buildings in his native Charleston, South Carolina, and had recently received commissions for the capital's new Treasury Building and the Patent Office.

Raising money was the rub. Agents for the society crisscrossed the country in search of $1 donations; they brought in just $20,000 in the first three years. Other gambits, too, met with only minor success: the society offered a lithograph of Mills's design with the autographs of public figures, including five presidents: Franklin Pierce, Millard Fillmore, Zachary Taylor, James K. Polk, and John Quincy Adams; US consuls sought contributions from Americans living abroad; members of the army and navy were asked to give, as were members of Masonic Lodges; and enumerators for the 1840 census took up donations as they gathered their data. "The nation mourned for Washington all it knew how with their hearts," Mark Twain said, "but you couldn't get its pocket to shed a tear." It took the society until 1847, a dozen years, to raise $87,000, but it was enough to break ground.

Many inside and outside of Congress disliked Mills's design. One critic called it an "ill-assorted blend of Greek, Babylonian, and Egyptian architecture." In 1844, the House Committee on Public Buildings recommended, instead of an obelisk, "a temple form" that would rise 150 feet and be crowned with a statue of Washington. More than a monument commemorating a single man, the committee's building would be "capable of containing the busts and statues of the Presidents of the

MILLS'S DESIGN for the Washington Monument. CREDIT: Library of Congress

United States, and other illustrious men." In the end, the criticisms and alternate plans did not stop the society, but the cost did; it decided to build only the obelisk. Washington's birthday in 1848 seemed a fitting moment to lay the cornerstone; unfortunately, Congress did not approve the site in time.

At last, on July 4, all was set. At sunrise, as church bells pealed and cannons fired, a great parade assembled at the Capitol. President Polk and the members of his cabinet led the distinguished procession, which included the Georgetown and Washington Freemasons in full regalia;

military companies and militias from Maryland, Massachusetts, and Virginia; heroes of the Mexican War; members of Congress, such as Daniel Webster, Henry Clay, and John Calhoun, and an obscure Whig from Illinois, Abraham Lincoln; fire departments, with their engines; temperance societies; and, at the rear, groups of schoolchildren. Two aged widows, Dolley Madison and Elizabeth Schuyler Hamilton, awaited the marchers at the speaker's platform. Matthew Emery, master mason of the Washington Lodge, wearing the apron that once belonged to the first president, helped ease the 24,500-pound block of marble into place and presided over the appropriate Masonic ceremonies. The orator for the day, Speaker of the House Robert C. Winthrop, delivered a ninety-minute discourse on Washington's life and character, as well as the character of the nation since his passing. The democracy was a locomotive that "gathers strength" as it pulls America into the future, Winthrop asserted. But he warned that engine might leave the ideals of Washington's republic behind. "This wide-spread Republic is the true monument to Washington," Winthrop concluded. "Maintain its Independence. Uphold its Constitution. Preserve its Union. Defend its Liberty."

"Independence," "Constitution," and "Liberty" were the very concepts under contention, of course, but for the Washington National Monument Society, money was the supreme concern. To drum up support, the society invited states, Indian tribes, local fraternal societies, businesses, and foreign countries to send memorial stones for the interior of the shaft. Florida presented a suitably inscribed block of limestone; California's inscription proclaimed "The Youngest Sister to the Union"; the American Medical Association sent a stone; The Masterton & Smith quarry in Westchester County, New York, chiseled its name in marble; New Bedford, Massachusetts, sent a relief of a whale in granite; and foreign countries—Greece, France, China, and England—each contributed a stone.

And then, as the tower reached 154 feet, Pope Pius IX sent a stone from Rome. Unfortunately, it arrived at a moment when the anti-Catholic, antiforeign Know-Nothing Party was ascendant. On the night of Sunday, March 5, 1854, a group of Know-Nothings—who were convinced that the papacy threatened the republic—overcame a night watchman at the monument, broke up the stone, and dumped the shards into the Potomac. In February 1855, just as a reluctant Congress was about to vote $200,000 to aid the construction, the Know-Nothings seized control of the Monument Society's governing board. The next month, members of the new board took control of the building site. Too many foreign-born papist laborers were building an American monument; they would raise the money from *American* donors and finish the obelisk with *American* laborers. Over the next three years they added four courses of inferior stone that the previous builders had rejected. They had raised a mere $285.09 for completion. The stump continued to scar the land west of the Capitol, but Congress did nothing.

Support for the Know-Nothings dwindled in 1857 after some Washington members of the party, reinforced by comrades from Baltimore, rioted at the Northern Liberty Market to disrupt the city's municipal elections. In a rare moment of fortitude, President James Buchanan called out the Marines to quell the violence, which left six dead and several score injured. The following year the Know-Nothings quietly slipped away, leaving the monument site in chaos.

Internal divisions and sectional antagonisms over the issue of slavery swiftly extinguished the meteoric blaze of the Know-Nothing Party from the American firmament; by the end of the decade it was a memory. Only the product of the Know-Nothing's mischief remained, the unfinished marble stump of a monument, an "ungainly old chimney," as Mark Twain would call it, in the middle of the marshy field that some hoped would become the Washington Mall.

BY 1850, THE Capitol that Charles Bulfinch had transformed so well just two decades earlier was now overcrowded. The building had to accommodate a nation that had grown from 13 states on the Atlantic coastal plain to 31 states spanning the continent, which meant that instead of 26 senators and 65 representatives, it was filled when Congress was in session with 62 senators and 232 representatives. So crammed were the legislators that some briefly considered removing their desks and standing. Instead, that September they passed legislation authorizing a competition for an extension of the Capitol; the president would select the winning proposal, and the architect would receive "a premium of $500." Unable to select a winner from the thirteen entries, they decided to split the prize among five architects and directed that a composite drawing be made of the best features from each. Fortunately, President Millard Fillmore asserted his role as the final arbiter, and on June 10, 1851, he selected Thomas Ustick Walter to be architect of the Capitol extension.

The choice of Walter proved to be brilliant. In 1819, at the age of fifteen, Walter had served as an apprentice to his father, a bricklayer and master mason in Philadelphia. Father and son worked together on the Second Bank of the United States, the solid Greek Revival temple to money then rising on Chestnut Street. In the evenings he studied architecture under William Strickland, the bank's designer, and took courses in mechanical drawing that the city's Franklin Institute offered for tradesmen. By 1830, he had become an architect, and soon he was the city's most successful designer, creating houses for Philadelphia's prominent families. He designed several institutions, including a prison—and his triumph, a splendid Greek Revival building for Stephen Girard's school for "poor white orphan boys." The American Philosophical Society elected him to membership, and the Franklin Institute made him a director.

In his winning design for the Capitol, Walter more than doubled the length of the Bulfinch building, with two massive wings that included committee rooms, offices, and new chambers for the House and Senate. To complement the increased mass of the greatly enlarged building, he added a tall dome over the rotunda. For the broad expanse of the ceilings for the legislative chambers and the dome, Walter employed the Industrial Revolution's contribution to architecture and engineering, structural cast-iron.

Walter would serve as architect of the Capitol for fourteen years under the presidential administrations of Fillmore, Franklin Pierce, James Buchanan, Abraham Lincoln, and finally Andrew Johnson. As was the experience of the Capitol's previous architects, especially Latrobe and Bulfinch, he had to navigate perilous waters that were continually roiled by senators and representatives as well as presidents and their cabinet officers. The first test began shortly after his appointment, and the testing didn't end until he resigned in 1865.

On occasion, Congress would allow the funding for the construction of the Capitol to run out, which meant that workers were idled. Votes to appropriate money offered legislators the opportunity to deride the project: Walter's foundations were so unsound that the building would fall, said many, though the Army Corp of Engineers found them to be perfectly sound; no money should be expended as the entire capital would be moving shortly to the geographic center of the country; the building was too long and too low and would be an architectural embarrassment. One senator, whose thirst for contumely would not be assuaged, convinced Washington's commissioner of public buildings to slander Walter and those who worked for him with charges of fraud or malfeasance. Walter, who seemed to have an intrinsic calmness about him, was content to counter slander with facts and kept on working. Once their fury was spent, the legislators voted to continue construction, the laborers took up their tools once again, and the great wings took form.

Presidents and their cabinet secretaries posed a different sort of problem for Walter. First there was the challenge of Captain Montgomery Cunningham Meigs. Oversight of the Capitol had long been under the aegis of the Department of Interior, but President Pierce decided to transfer those duties to his longtime political ally Jefferson Davis, the new secretary of war. Davis, in turn, appointed the thirty-six-year-old Meigs from the Army Corps of Engineers, giving him "general supervision and control of the whole work."

Although it didn't happen immediately, Walter and Meigs were bound to clash. A consummate engineer, Meigs possessed unbounded energy, extraordinary organizational abilities, and an abiding belief in science and technology. At the time he was also supervising the design and construction of Washington's great aqueduct to carry fresh water twelve miles from a reservoir at Great Falls on the Potomac to the city. Also unbounded was his ego. Meigs was determined to put his stamp on the building. He redesigned its interior rooms and corridors; added stairways and embellishments; changed the heating and ventilation system; oversaw the brick laying (53,000 a day); traveled far and wide to procure the proper materials; and hired the Italian fresco artist Constantino Brumidi to decorate the walls and ceilings.

It was inevitable that Meigs's ego would bring about a rupture. It occurred over the great cast-iron dome, Walter's greatest achievement. The captain had made refinements to the engineering of the structure; now, so he reasoned, he should be able to claim it and the entire Capitol expansion as his own. It became an obsession. Meigs took to calling himself the designer of the Capitol extension, demanded that Walter hand over all the plans, and even had a stack of copper plates engraved that he placed beneath the building's marble columns:

CAPT. MONTGOMERY C. MEIGS. U.S. ENGINEERS
IN CHARGE OF
U.S. CAPITOL EXTENSION
EXTENSION OF GENERAL POST OFFICE
NEW DOME OF THE CAPITOL AND
WASHINGTON AQUEDUCT
A.D. 1858

Though Meigs complained bitterly about Walter to Buchanan's notoriously corrupt secretary of war, John B. Floyd, it was ultimately the captain's own honesty and arrogance that brought him down. Floyd considered the Capitol project an opportunity to give contracts to friends in his home state of Virginia. (He once proposed to Meigs that he remove all the building's marble and replace it with Virginia granite.) Meigs's probity was beyond reproach; he refused all such schemes, even rejecting Floyd's orders. Thwarted by such high-minded virtue, Floyd banished the captain in November 1859 as far from Washington as he could, to a fort in the Dry Tortugas at the extreme end of the Florida Keys. A year later, Floyd resigned in scandal after it was discovered that, in anticipation of secession, he was shipping arms to the South. Meigs was able to return and make life difficult for Walter once again. This time he fired the architect and posted a guard to prevent him from entering his office. But by that time the Buchanan administration was in its twilight; the Union was breaking up; Meigs's champion, Jefferson Davis, had left for Mississippi and the Confederacy; and the new president, Abraham Lincoln, having better use for the War Department than overseeing the Capitol's construction, returned its oversight to the secretary of interior.

SLAVERY DID MORE than define Washington as a southern city; its presence in the nation's capital helped to make the inhumanity and injustice of the practice real to legislators from the North. In the relatively small space of the District, northerners could experience the institution and its effects firsthand. They saw it in Washington's homes and public buildings, in slave auctions, and in hotels with slave pens. They saw it in coffles, chained groups of black men and women forced to march through the streets past the Capitol as they made their way to

THIS VIEW of slaves being marched on Pennsylvania Avenue before the Capitol presents a different image from the more picturesque one shown earlier. Created by an unknown hand before the burning of Washington in 1814, the image often appeared in abolitionist tracts prior to the Civil War. CREDIT: Library of Congress

slave ships moored on the Potomac and an auction block in New Orleans. They saw slavery as a part of Washington's daily life.

Foreign visitors saw the institution and its effects as well. Lafayette considered it the one element in the new republic that he could not abide, and wherever he was, he made no attempt to disguise his abhorrence. While on a visit to James Madison at Montpelier, his plantation estate in Orange, Virginia, the general, so his secretary Auguste Levesseur reported, advocated "the speedy emancipation of the Blacks" to Madison and his friends, defending "the rights that *all men without exception* have to liberty."

For Levasseur, too, there could be no practical justification for slavery. From the Greek-styled portico of George Washington Parke Custis's house at Arlington, he and Lafayette took in "the majestic course of the Potomac" and "the rising City of Washington." It took three hundred slaves to maintain the land and house. Levasseur noted in his diary the idleness and slothfulness that involuntary servitude had bred into the servants: "If Mr. Custis employed only a dozen well-paid free workers, instead of a large number of indolent slaves who ate up his produce and left his roads in bad repair, I am sure that he would not have been long in tripling his revenues and in having one of the most charming properties, not only in the District of Columbia, also in all of Virginia."

Lafayette and Levasseur were not alone in their assessment of the complications of slavery. Many slaveholders—though Custis wasn't among them—were finding it an increasingly impractical and ineffi-cient way of getting work done. When slaves escaped, masters had to post rewards and pay bounties for their capture and return. After one of his more intractable servants, French's Will, slipped away to Maryland one night, George Washington doubted if it was worthwhile "to be at *much* trouble, or at *any* expence over a trifle to hunt him up." They were thought to pilfer goods, including food stores (to supplement their usual diet of corn, cornmeal, and pork), cloth for clothes, lumber, bricks, and nails. Washington once wondered why it took 6,000 hand-wrought nails to build a corn house.

By the 1820s, the spread of Eli Whitney's cotton gin had increased the demand for slaves in states such as Alabama, Mississippi, and Lou-isiana. With Whitney's gin, a single slave could increase cotton produc-tion from one to fifty pounds a day. Between 1790 and 1810, the total production of raw cotton in America rose from 3,000 to 177,000 bales per year, and would reach nearly 4 million bales by 1860. This was par-ticularly good news for plantation owners in Maryland and Virginia, especially those farmers whose tobacco fields were exhausted. Now they could sell their slaves to owners in the Deep South and use their land for other crops.

The first slave auction in Washington took place in 1794—coinci-dentally, the year Whitney received the patent for his gin. The slave dealer Edward Burrows advertised an auction near Blodget's hotel of "three males aged ten, thirteen, and nineteen; a mother with son and daughter; and three females aged twelve, fifteen, and seventeen." In the ensuing years, especially after 1808, when the federal act prohibiting the importation of slaves took effect, the number of slave auctions grew almost exponentially. First itinerant traders came, then more serious ones. Lafayette's view from the heights of Arlington took in one of the premier slave marts in the nation.

Blacks were caught in a large economic web whose strands extended far beyond the limits of the District of Columbia, reaching across the continent, and indeed across the Atlantic Ocean. Bankers in New York City funded plantation owners in the South. Millions of bales of cotton fibers left the ports of Charleston, Savannah, and New Orleans for New York, and thence to the giant looms of Manchester, England, the cottonopolis of the world. The fibers returned to America as cloth for the needles of seamstresses and dressmakers. The abundance of cotton brought about a change in fashion. Between 1800 and 1855, the number of yards of material needed to make a woman's dress increased from five to twenty, while the yardage required for her underclothes jumped from seven and a half to sixty-three.

Still, the number of free blacks in the District—those who purchased their freedom or were manumitted—increased with each decade, too. The 1830 census for Washington City found that over the decade the number had risen from 2,330 to 3,129, a 34 percent increase. Some owners manumitted their slaves upon their death; others allowed them to follow the path of Alethia Browning Tanner, the slave who had purchased freedom for herself and her family earlier in the century.

Most white residents in the capital were never completely at ease with either slaves or free blacks. While they understood they needed them to support their way of life, they could not escape the injustice of slavery or the constant reminders of the institution. In 1816, three of the most prominent southern men in Washington—Senator Henry Clay from Kentucky, Representative John Randolph from Virginia, and lawyer Francis Scott Key from Maryland (author of the "Star Spangled Banner")—helped to found the American Colonization Society with the intention of returning, or "repatriating" as they delicately put it, slaves to Africa. Bushrod Washington, nephew of George Washington and associate justice of the Supreme Court, became the society's first president. Each of the men owned slaves. (In 1822, Bushrod Washington sold fifty-four of his to a plantation in Louisiana for $10,000.) With $100,000 from the US government, the society established the West African colony of Liberia. The first vessel, with eighty-eight former slaves, arrived on Africa's shores in 1822.

But the colonization movement never became popular, especially in the capital. By the end of the nineteenth century, fewer than 16,000 blacks had emigrated. Washington's free blacks were self-sufficient. They began their own churches. They created the Resolute Beneficial Society to provide health and burial insurance and a free school for their children. And they were able to gain a foothold in the economic structure of the city. Patrick Leigh Wormley and his son, James, for example, operated a hackney carriage business; another free black, Beverly Snow, managed his own restaurant, the Epicurean Eating House, at Sixth Street and Pennsylvania Avenue, which was "much frequented by good society." Countless others cleaned and cooked in private homes or hired themselves out as laborers.

However, an event in 1831 in "Cross Keys," a rural hamlet on the southeastern border of Virginia, caused the lines between owners and slaves to harden. That summer, the gifted, brooding, and deeply religious slave Nat Turner had a vision in which "a loud noise in the heavens" told him he must lead a "fight against the Serpent" of slavery by killing all whites. The bloodbath that followed—over two days in August, fifty-six white men, women, and children died at the hands of the blacks—filled every white owner in the south with fear of their slaves. "A Nat Turner might be in every family," said a member of the Virginia House of Delegates. "The same bloody deed could be acted over at any time in any place."

No doubt that thought was in the mind of William Thornton's widow, Anna Maria, and those around her in August 1835. As Mrs. Thornton lay sleeping in her house at 246 F Street near Fourteenth, her slave Arthur Bowen slipped into the room and attacked her with an axe. Fortunately, Bowen was so drunk that the sixty-year-old Anna Maria was able to fend him off until other slaves came to her rescue. As word of the assault spread through the District, many said that Arthur had attended gatherings where white abolitionist speakers had told the slaves they depended upon the goodwill of their owners, who might at any time sell them to a hard life on a cotton plantation in the Deep South. Mrs. Thornton had always been known for her kindness to slaves, said the white slaveholders. If she was treated this way, what might other citizens expect?

Arthur Bowen's attack combined with other events to spark Washington's first race riot. Abolitionist pamphlets were already abroad in the city; copies of William Lloyd Garrison's *Liberator* and the British-inspired *Anti-Slavery Reporter* seemed to be everywhere. On Capitol Hill, the American Anti-Slavery Society was flooding Congress with petitions to end the institution.

On the Saturday morning after the attack on Mrs. Thornton, Washington's citizens learned that her assailant was being held in the city jail. That evening, crowds of angry laborers from the Navy Yard gathered in Judiciary Square, vowing to tear down the jail and hang the slave. Most of the men were from Dublin, with a few from Germany and Scotland; alcohol flowed freely—the Navy Yard still served it to its workers daily—and many were probably drunk. They were angry, too, because slaves like Arthur Bowen took their jobs. They needed to look no further than the White House for evidence of this: when Andrew Jackson had arrived in 1829, he had brought his own slaves and dismissed the white servants. As the city's police force numbered just ten constables, the Navy Yard had to send a contingent of Marines to keep order.

Into this charged atmosphere rushed Francis Scott Key, whom Andrew Jackson had appointed US attorney for the District of Columbia in 1833. Key was a deeply religious man, a pillar of the Episcopal Church who twice daily led his wife and ten children in prayer. As his involvement with the American Colonization Society suggested, he believed slavery to be a profound injustice. But he had little time for abolitionists. In the case of Arthur Bowen, Key said it was the seditious literature of abolition, not alcohol, that had incited the slave to attack his mistress with an axe. At the time the District of Columbia regarded the circulation of seditious materials that led to rebellion as a capital crime; Key vowed he would make someone hang. In Reuben Crandall, a white twenty-nine-year-old doctor from Connecticut who had recently arrived in Georgetown to practice medicine and collect botanical specimens, Key found the most unlikely person to serve as an example. Still, federal marshals had found abolitionist publications when they raided the doctor's lodgings, so they took him off to Judiciary Square.

Now the mob, estimated at "300 or 400," turned to rioting, not at Judiciary Square, but at Beverly Snow's Epicurean Eating House. Mechanics from the Navy Yard claimed Snow had spoken "in disrespectful terms about their wives and daughters." In two nights of rioting, the mob drank Snow's wine, destroyed the restaurant's furniture, burned some free black tenements nearby, and moved on to ransack John F. Cook's house and school at Fourteenth and H streets. But Beverly Snow, the one they wanted to lynch, had slipped away to the protection of a jail cell in Fredericksburg, Virginia.

John Cook made an excellent target for the mob's wrath. He was the extraordinary nephew of the remarkable Alethia Tanner, who purchased his freedom when Cook was sixteen and sent him to the Columbia Institute (later named the Union Seminary), a school for free blacks. He did so well that he returned in 1834 to be the headmaster. With an ascetic, solemn personality, he took no drink, read his Bible, studied Presbyterianism, opposed slavery, and considered education to be essential for his race to succeed. By dawn on August 12, 1835, Cook's house and one-room school were in ashes. Cook fled to safety in Pennsylvania.

It was in this tense atmosphere that District Attorney Francis Scott Key prosecuted his cases. In late November he secured a guilty verdict against Arthur Bowen; the slave was sentenced to be hanged. With Reuben Crandall, however, the prosecutor met his match. In court, the doctor's two skillful lawyers produced a succession of witnesses who testified that he had no interest in the antislavery cause. They even put Key's own attitude toward slavery on trial, quoting a speech that the district attorney had once delivered about the institution's evils. The jury of white Washingtonians found Reuben Crandall not guilty. (Nevertheless, the tuberculosis that Crandall contracted in prison condemned him in 1838 to an early death on the island of Jamaica, where he had gone to restore his health.)

Nor did Francis Scott Key's difficulties end with Crandall's acquittal. At Bowen's trial, Anna Maria Thornton had testified in her slave's defense. She had great affection for Arthur, who some said possessed the same stubborn personality as her late husband. (Some wondered if Bowen might even be William Thornton's son.) Anna Maria persuaded thirty-four of her friends to sign a petition for Arthur's release; she pleaded Arthur's case with her friend and neighbor, Vice President Martin Van Buren; and she wrote a seventeen-page letter to President Andrew Jackson in which she suggested that the emotions of the riots had influenced people to seek an unjust verdict. Jackson postponed the execution twice before writing, "Let the Negro boy John Arthur Bowen be pardoned." He was set free on July 4, 1836. Shortly afterward, Anna

Maria sold him to a steamship owner who needed an attendant. She made $750 in the sale, less than the $800 she had wanted.

There was a backstory about Anna Maria Thornton's father, which few in Washington knew, that might have provided another reason for her to fight so hard to save Arthur's life. Her father, an English clergyman, had been hanged for committing forgery.

BY THE 1830S, cotton plantations in the Deep South were dictating the economics of slavery in the District of Columbia, which made the plight of slaves living there far more dire. The conditions in the fields were harsh. A slave in a cotton field was expected to pick 200 pounds of cotton a day and work for about 3,000 hours a year. Except when cotton prices declined briefly in the early 1840s, the price for an average slave in New Orleans rose steadily over the years. By the outbreak of the Civil War in 1861 a male fetched an average of $1,381. A female in her prime went for less, but light-skinned women in New Orleans sold at a premium because they could serve as concubines.

These economic realities made it very tempting for slave owners in Washington to sell their property to the numerous slave traders who looked to the District to make up a coffle for the South. Owners of failing plantations and farms in Maryland and Virginia found it easier to sell their slaves than to hire them out. "The price is monstrous high," said John Armfield, who with his uncle, Isaac Franklin, operated the largest and most successful slave-trading business in the District of Columbia. "And that, in fact," he added, "is the very reason so many are willing to sell." With help from Franklin and Armfield, owners could pay off their debts, redeem a bankruptcy, and even have money to spare. It was clear to all that any slave living in Washington faced a very real chance of being sold for profit.

One resident in desperate need of money was James Madison's widow, Dolley, who since 1837 had lived in reduced circumstances in a house on the east side of Lafayette Square. At Montpelier, her husband's plantation, the gracious and good-hearted former First Lady had had a reputation for kindness to her servants. She nursed them through illnesses, worried about their children, and generally treated them as "her people," as she called them. But on the subject of selling slaves, Dolley lacked all compassion. They were property, nothing more, nothing less; and she needed to sell property to save her ne'er-do-well son from debtors' prison. In late 1847, when Ellen Stewart, Dolley's fifteen-year-old slave girl, saw a dealer well known to slaves arrive at the Madison house, she knew all too well the intention of the visit. She fled immediately. Still desperate, Dolley sold Ellen's mother instead.

Free blacks also moved about the capital at their peril. "The present high price of negroes is presenting a great temptation to unprincipled men to attempt to sell such as are free," wrote Ethan Allen Andrews. In 1836, the Yale-educated Andrews published a series of letters documenting the separation of slave families and their fears about being sold. Like every visitor from the North, he was shocked to see slave traders operating within the shadow of the Capitol. Andrews found that the demand for slaves in New Orleans increased the temptation for traders to resort to kidnapping and imprisoning free blacks under the pretense that they were runaways. The speculators in human flesh had the law on their side, as it presumed that any black without manumission papers was a runaway. Those who eventually proved their freedom still had to pay for the food they ate in prison or risk being sold into slavery by the District's presidentially appointed federal marshal. According to the New England Anti-Slavery Society, several thousand men and women in the District of Columbia and other areas of the South suffered this fate. William Cranch, chief judge of the Circuit Court for the District of Columbia, concurred, writing, "I believe there have been few, if any *legal* commitments of persons as runaways."

Solomon Northup's kidnapping was one of the most famous. Born in New York, Northup was a black man with free papers who in 1841 left his home in Saratoga Springs to join the circus in Washington. While lodging at Gadsby's, Northup was drugged and then imprisoned in the infamous Yellow House slave pen on the Mall. There he was beaten and sold as a runaway slave from Georgia; eventually he was shipped to a plantation in New Orleans. He was fortunate, however. New York had a law that obligated the governor to take whatever measures he deemed necessary "to procure any citizen so wrongfully held in slavery, to be restored to his liberty and returned to this State." After a dozen years in bondage, Solomon Northup became a free man once again.

Others were not so lucky. In January 1848, Joshua Reed Giddings, an abolitionist congressman from Ohio, returned to his boardinghouse, located on Carroll's Row directly opposite the Capitol Park (the site of today's Library of Congress), to find that a black waiter who worked at the house had been carried away in shackles to the Georgia slave pen at Seventh Street and Maryland Avenue. For half a century the pen stood across from the Capitol. It was, wrote Giddings's fellow boarder Abraham Lincoln, "a sort of negro-livery stable, where droves of negroes were collected, temporarily kept, and finally taken to Southern markets, precisely like droves of horses."

Ann G. Sprigg, a Virginia widow who ran the house where Giddings and Lincoln lived, was not a slaveholder, but she had hired the waiter who was buying his freedom from his master. At the time of his abduction, he had earned about $245 of the $300 price for his liberty. It was all too common an event. Owners gave their slaves an opportunity to purchase their freedom only to renege on the agreement at the last possible moment. Keeping the money their slaves had paid toward their purchase as well as the profits from slave traders, owners had a chance to double the return on their investment.

Giddings rushed to the Georgia slave pen, but he was too late. Probably sensing they had stolen a slave from under the gaze of abolitionists, the jailers immediately shipped their quarry off to a boat bound for the Lower South. The next day, Giddings introduced a bill calling upon Congress to investigate the matter, adding, as he often did, a call to abolish slave trading in the District. He expected his bill would be defeated, and in this he was not disappointed.

About this same time, a slave girl of nineteen slipped past her jailer at the Georgia slave pen. Her freedom lasted but a few hours, until she was stopped on the Long Bridge. Instead of capture, she chose drowning and jumped to her death. So singular was the event that it became the occasion for poetry. In "The Leap from the Long Bridge," the nineteenth-century poet Sarah Jane Lippincott likened the fleeing girl to "a wild bird escaped from the snare." The escaped girl's object was the woods of Virginia and eventually freedom, and she chose death over slavery. Lippincott closed her poem with a taunt:

> *Now back, Jailor, back to they dungeons, again . . .*
> *The form thou would'st fetter—returned to its God . . .*
> *Joy! The hunted slave is free!*

William Wells Brown, a former slave who escaped to his own freedom, incorporated the girl's flight in his description of the death of Clotel, the heroine of his eponymous 1853 novel. In Brown's work, Clotel is Thomas Jefferson's daughter by his slave Sally Hemings, and the woodland she seeks is none other than Arlington, "occupied by that distinguished relative and descendant of the immortal Washington, Mr. George W. Custis." The men who block her way to freedom are "true to their Virginian instincts." And the "appalling tragedy," Wells is careful to tell us, takes place "within plain sight of the President's house and the capital of the Union." The message is clear to all that the signs of liberty are everywhere: Arlington, Custis's shrine to Washington looking down on the capital; the President's House, once the home of Thomas Jefferson, author of the Declaration of Independence. If these men so valued liberty, why shouldn't one of their daughters?

That slave trading went on in the shadow of the Capitol and with at least the tacit approval of a majority of those who legislated there angered the abolitionists. "By authority of Congress," Representative Horace Mann declared in a speech to the House, "the City of Washington is the Congo of America." On a December day in 1845, the Quaker abolitionist John Greenleaf Whittier wrote a poem about a coffle he had witnessed being driven before the "grave men" laboring beneath the Capitol dome. But then Whittier's eye takes in "a broader, sadder range," as the prison gates swing open and the procession of slaves begins:

> *Pitying God!—Is that a Woman*
> *On whose wrist the shackles clash?*
> *Is that shriek she utters human,*
> *Underneath the stinging lash?*
> *Are they Men whose eyes of madness from that sad procession flash?*
> *Still the dance goes gayly onward!*
> *What is it to Wealth and Pride,*
> *That without the stars are looking*
> *On a scene which earth should hide?*
> *That the Slave-ship lies in waiting, rocking on*
> *Potomac's tide!*

It is likely that the slaves Whittier saw were bound for the *Tribune* or the *Uncas*, Isaac Franklin and John Armfield's two brigs, which made regular trips to the Gulf states, each with about 180 men, women, and children.

For the most part, especially after the Missouri Compromise of 1820 (which balanced the number of slave and free states at twelve, and prohibited slavery north of Missouri's southern border), southern members of Congress were successful in stifling any proposed legislation to stop the slave trade and slavery in the District. Time and again a member would have the temerity to propose gradual abolition only to precipitate a "warm discussion," as the records called it, and be rebuffed. Time and again representatives and abolitionist groups from the North presented antislavery petitions to Congress only to have them turned away. At best, such proposals went to the congressional committee for the District of Columbia, which was in the firm clutches of proslavery representatives, where they were ignored. In 1836, the slave block succeeded in having Congress refuse all such petitions.

Throughout the 1840s, as the plight of slaves and free blacks in the District of Columbia grew ever more desperate, Congress became even more craven. In 1846, it retroceded Alexandria to Virginia, thereby cutting the District's area by a third and affording slave traders there protection from the more vocal abolitionists who descended on Washington. At the end of the Mexican War in 1848, Congress considered the long-delayed question of whether the newly acquired land of Texas (above the Rio Grande), California, and New Mexico would be slave or free. Representatives from the North, spurred on by committed abolitionists like Joshua Reed Giddings from Ohio, became increasingly vocal. Famous men in Congress—Clay, Calhoun, and Webster foremost among them—entered into the great debate. Slaves and free blacks, their ears attuned to hearing conversations in parlors, at dining tables, and in coaches, gleaned information daily and exchanged it among themselves. They well understood that the outcome of the debate would decide whether their future would be one of servitude or freedom. They were the pawns, hostages to an outcome over which they had no control.

A single event in early 1848 highlighted for the nation the desperation of Washington's slaves. On Saturday evening, April 15, seventy-six black men, women, and children slipped from their masters' houses and headed to an isolated wharf about a mile from Pennsylvania Avenue. There they joined several runaways who had left their hiding places about the city and boarded the *Pearl*, a schooner hired by northern abolitionists to take them to Frenchtown, New Jersey, and freedom. Many weeks in the planning, it promised to be the largest and most daring escape of slaves anywhere in America, and it would have succeeded had Daniel Drayton, the schooner's captain, better understood the fundamentals of tides and wind. On Sunday morning, members of a number of important Washington families awoke to find their kitchens bare and their fires banked. On learning from a black hackman, so tradition has it, that the slaves had left by ship, a group of white slave owners commandeered a steamboat and went off in pursuit. The owners found the *Pearl* lying becalmed in a harbor just above Point Lookout in Chesapeake Bay.

An angry mob awaited the owners and their quarry on their return. The men attempted to lynch Drayton, the schooner's owner, and the ship's cook, but settled for smashing the doors of the municipal police station and attacking the printing office of the recently established antislavery newspaper *National Era*.

Many slaves who attempted to escape on the *Pearl* suffered the fate they all had feared. On the following Friday evening, Hope Hull Slatter, a notorious Baltimore slave trader, purchased about fifty of the escapees and was preparing to ship them by train to Baltimore, and then by boat to auction blocks in the Lower South. John Slingerland, a Whig congressman from Albany County, New York, was at the B&O railroad depot on the Mall at Second Street and Pennsylvania Avenue when he "saw a large number of colored people gathered round one of the cars"; they were looking into the railway car's windows at their families and friends, who were peering out. Slatter had one man, who claimed his wife was free, beaten back from the car.

Then Slingerland saw the Reverend Henry Slicer, the Methodist chaplain of the US Senate, enter the car to greet the trader. It seemed that Slatter was a fellow Methodist: though he sometimes sundered Christian families, he read his Bible daily—and carefully. The chaplain preached against alcohol and dueling, but ignored the fact of slavery and slave trading in front of him. Slingerland watched as the Methodist pastor took in the "scene before him with as little concern as we would look upon cattle!"

Among those bought by a Baltimore trader and shipped to the Lower South was Ellen Stewart, Dolley Madison's fifteen-year-old slave girl, who had been captured on the *Pearl*. Once the president's widow had recovered her property, after the girl's "6 months dissipation," as she called it, Dolley promptly sold her. The price she received for Ellen Stewart was $400.

AS THE 1840S folded into the 1850s and America's destiny passed through the lackluster administrations of Taylor, Fillmore, Pierce, and Buchanan, Washington seemed more than ever a bifurcated city divided between northern abolitionists and southern slaveholders. Over the Capitol, the Treasury, the War Department, and the White House gathered the clouds of sectional dispute and violence. The Compromise of 1850 hammered out by Henry Clay brought the Fugitive Slave Law to every state, slave or free. Now those who captured runaways did so with the assistance of the federal government. It also brought, at last, the prohibition of slave trading to the District of Columbia.

The artist Eastman Johnson found striking evidence of the irreconcilable bifurcation in Washington's geography. In October 1855, he cut his art studies short in Europe to help his recently widowed father, who lived in the family's fashionable house on F Street near Thirteenth. As a young man, Johnson had made a name for himself as a painter of such Washington figures as John Quincy Adams and Dolley Madison (commissions that his father, an official in the Navy Department, had helped him to secure), as well as such prominent Bostonians as Ralph Waldo Emerson, Henry Wadsworth Longfellow, Charles Sumner, and Nathaniel Hawthorne. Johnson might not have immediately realized that his father lived in the neighborhood of many of the capital's ardent champions of slavery, including senators Clement Claiborne Clay of Alabama, Judah Benjamin of Louisiana, and Robert Toombs of Georgia, as well as the secretary of war, Jefferson Davis of Mississippi. All would later declare themselves for the Confederacy and leave the Union. Though there may not have been slave or free black servants in the Johnson household, there were many on F Street, often living in houses beside their masters. The artist had only to look across the rear yard of his family's house to find the setting for the 1859 painting that ranks with his best works, *Negro Life at the Old South*.

At first glance it appears as though Johnson's narrative reflects the sentimental and mythic idyll that southern sympathizers in the city saw in their mind's eye: carefree blacks of all ages enjoying their lives and their music. A black mammy, her arms clutching a baby, peers from a second-story window; a young man, leaning against a bench, holds a courting conversation with a young maid; a small boy listens as an older man, plug hat upon his head, strums a banjo. While an older woman teaches a child to dance to the tune, a furry mongrel watches the scene, its hind legs ready to spring into play. And at the right, a white mistress in a full-skirted dress, accompanied by her lady's maid, steps into the scene through a doorway in a fence separating the yards.

On reflection, though, the stereotypically benign becomes darkly malign. Johnson is rendering his narrative scene as a decaying stage set: the slave house's clapboards and shutters are askew; its window mullions on the second story are broken, as are several panes of glass. The gabled rear wall of the wooden house would probably collapse save for the massive brick chimney; the rear wall of the shed roof has long since tumbled down, leaving only a hint of a foundation, splintered beams, roof trusses, and moss-covered shingles perching precariously above. A discarded axe lies on the ground, and the fireplace at the base of the chimney seems long abandoned. Even the three-story house to the right that glows in the warm afternoon sunlight shares its shed roof with the crumbling wall of the blacks' quarters, and the doorway through which the white woman emerges is made of crude boards. Johnson has revealed a private space of decay behind the genteel façade of F Street, a space restricted to those with secret knowledge of a world unknown to many outside the capital and willfully ignored by most within.

Yet Johnson won't allow his viewers to ignore the imbalance of the structures and the lives within. Through his rendering of the white woman and her ordered house beside the black slaves and their disordered hovel, he forces us to contemplate the disparity of wealth and control. The white woman's entrance seems especially startling to the two young black girls who are the first to see her—after all, she is violating *their* communal space and their moments of amusement. Her stepping through the fence reinforces our understanding that white masters and mistresses control all, even their servants' private lives. Surely Johnson presents no better acknowledgment of white dominion than in his rendering of the young maid leaning against the bench. Her light skin tells us she is likely the product of a master's exploitation of his property. With the woman's entrance, the supposedly carefree blacks on Johnson's stage are reminded that their white owners command their house, their yard, and their lives.

DESPITE THE GROWING divisions, Washington's matrons seemed determined to preserve their gaiety. Wives of cabinet members still received visitors each Thursday morning whenever Congress was in session. Everyone greeted the great Victorian novelist William Makepeace Thackeray when he came to lecture in February 1853. President Fillmore gave a dinner in Thackeray's honor at the White House, and he and President-elect Pierce attended his lecture the following evening. Prominent families listened to the Reverend Smith Pine deliver sermons at St. John's Episcopal Church on Lafayette Square. They stopped at Gautier's restaurant on Pennsylvania Avenue, which always featured oysters and partridges. They turned to their favorite dentist, Dr. Edward Maynard, when they had toothaches. A frustrated military man (poor health had forced him to leave West Point), Maynard had turned to dentistry and invented dental instruments—but his real passion was inventing military arms. His dental parlor resembled a small arsenal; it included strips of percussion caps and a breech-loading rifle whose patent he sold to the army.

Elizabeth Lindsay Lomax, daughter of a wealthy Norfolk Virginia plantation owner and widow of Major Mann Page Lomax, began recording much of the social scene soon after her arrival in Washington early in 1854 with her son and six daughters. She lived on her late husband's government pension as well as money she earned from giving harp lessons and copying documents for the State and War Departments and the Patent Office. And she lived very well indeed. A legacy from her father enabled her to build a fashionable house at Nineteenth and G streets, complete with gas lighting and, when it became available in 1857, running water and a bathroom. "God is very good when he permits us to lead a full life," Elizabeth mused on her situation in 1854. "Mine still goes on in memories of the past, happiness in the present, and hopes for the future."

Part of Elizabeth's hopes lay in her children, who attracted numerous friends and beaux to their house. As her son, Lindsay Lunsford Lomax, was attending West Point, many who called were in the military. Robert E. Lee paid a visit, along with his nephew, Fitzhugh.

Colonels George Brinton McClellan and John Bankhead Magruder stopped by often, as did Commander David Farragut, whenever he was in Washington. Often in the evenings the guests would join her daughters to create "delightful music." Elizabeth recorded all the events in her diary, as well as her children's amusements. On Valentine's Day 1854, the Tayloe family, which now ranked as one of the oldest in the capital, hosted a "fancy ball" at their Octagon House. One of her daughters dressed as "a demure little Quaker maid," and another as "Pocohontas . . . with a black Indian wig, her fair skin transformed to a dusky brown." Their beaux went as "the Missouri Compromise" and a "California Cowboy." George McClellan also attended; he dressed as "a colonial general."

Along with many other Washington residents Elizabeth and her daughters regularly attended concerts on the lawn at the White House; they also turned out to hear Edward Everett, the former president of Harvard College and a Massachusetts senator, lecture on the subject of "charity," after which the Marine Band gave a serenade. On Ash Wednesday, February 22, 1860, in the northwest where Pennsylvania and New Hampshire avenues cross K Street and Twenty-third, the city's leaders gathered at the newly created Washington Circle to dedicate the sculptor Clark Mills's colossal equestrian statue of the first president. It would complement the other Mills equestrian statue, of Andrew Jackson, that the sculptor had created for Lafayette Square seven years earlier.

Yet despite the patina of social decorum, an undercurrent of violence to settle questions of honor prevailed in the capital. In March 1856, Andrew Dixon White arrived in the city fresh from Yale to consider a career in politics. On his first night at the National Hotel on Pennsylvania Avenue, White witnessed "a curious occurrence" that showed him "the difference between Northern and Southern civilization." A dispute in the bar cleared the room, as everyone assumed that "revolvers might be drawn at any moment." White soon left for the North to take up a more sedentary life as a professor of history and literature at the University of Michigan. It was not an isolated incident that he witnessed in the capital, however. At Willard's Hotel on May 8 that year, Representative Philemon Thomas Herbert from California shot an Irish waiter dead because he hadn't received his breakfast on time. A native of Pine Apple, Alabama, Herbert declared himself a southern gentleman who was only upholding his honor.

On May 22, the code of honor led to violence in the Capitol when Representative Preston Smith Brooks of South Carolina beat Senator Charles Sumner of Massachusetts with a cane. Southerners regarded the practice of soundly beating a man about the head and shoulders with a stout hickory cane as the assertion of superior rank over another. Certainly Brooks considered the Republican Sumner to be his inferior. On the subject of slavery, the single-minded senator possessed a "Puritan character," as one observer put it, and a "dogmatic intensity." (When once asked to see the other side of the slavery issue, Sumner replied, "There is no other side.") It was no surprise when on May 19, 1856, Sumner delivered a fiery oration condemning the South, slavery, and especially Senator Andrew Pickens Butler from South Carolina. Brooks regarded the speech as an attack on the southern code of chivalry, and most especially upon Butler, his cousin, who, Sumner said, "believes himself a chivalrous knight," but who had chosen "a mistress . . . who, though ugly to others, is always lovely to him, [and] though polluted in the sight of the world, is chaste in his sight: I mean the harlot Slavery."

Several days after the oration, Brooks entered the Senate chamber, ordered the galleries cleared of ladies, and took a gutta-percha cane to Sumner's head and shoulders. It was an unmerciful beating. As his Senate desk was affixed to the floor with screws, the tall Sumner could not extract his legs and escape. Finally, as Brooks's cane snapped over his head one final time, Sumner ripped the desk from the floor and crawled away. It would take the better part of three years before Sumner would be able to return to the Senate. When news of the beating reached South Carolina, the state's citizens sent Brooks canes by the score. For the moment, "chivalry" had triumphed, and "honor" had been upheld. But the division between the North and South grew ever wider.

Elizabeth Lomax remained silent on the Brooks affair, but on Sunday, February 27, 1859, she took up her journal to record "a most shocking occurrence." That afternoon, Daniel Sickles, a New York congressman, had shot Philip Barton Key to death. Key was a US attorney for the District of Columbia, son of Francis Scott Key, and a widower who was having an affair with Sickles's "pretty, but frail young wife—the cause of the dreadful deed," as Elizabeth put it delicately. At his trial, Sickles would plead temporary insanity, one of the first times anyone had employed such a defense. The jury agreed.

No matter how hard they tried, Elizabeth and everyone else in the capital could not escape the national news of violence. In mid-October 1859, Elizabeth wrote in her diary, "Reported insurrection of the blacks at Harpers Ferry—instigated by Western and Northern abolitionists." The reports were startling. December 2, she noted, was "the unhappy day Brown, the conspirator, is to be hanged—God have mercy on his soul." John Brown quickly became a symbol for the North of one who had died for a hallowed cause, and who, in Ralph Waldo Emerson's words, had "made the Gallows as venerable as the Cross!"

Elizabeth found her sentiments divided by the growing conflict. She was no stranger to slavery and abolition. Her father had kept slaves on his plantation, but for many years she and her husband had lived among abolitionists at the federal arsenal at Watertown, Massachusetts. She regarded slavery as "a condition that many of us deplore," but she believed whites held intellectual supremacy, and she was quick to repeat the oft-stated argument that those slaves bound to "families who are kind to them . . . are happier and better off than those who are free, but do not seem to know how to rule their own lives."

"The Presidential election takes place next month," Elizabeth wrote on October 30. "God grant it may be *favorable to the Union and peace*." Several days later she reflected that a gathering of nine guests at her house had not been "very merry," as "everyone is subconsciously conscious of a dark cloud upon the horizon—the appalling war cloud growing darker and darker each day."

On November 9, Elizabeth recorded in her diary what the telegraph wires had sung. "Mr. Lincoln elected President of the United States." Then she added, ominously, "The papers speak of the dissolution of the Union as an accomplished fact—God spare us from such a disaster."

The disaster would be a personal one for Elizabeth. Although her son, Lindsay, would be part of the phalanx guarding Abraham Lincoln's carriage on its way to the Capitol for his inauguration on March 4, 1861, he crossed the Potomac to Virginia after the state seceded from the Union. Her daughter Vic refused all communication with her ardent suitor, "Chandler," after he announced he would join the Union. The attack on Fort Sumter left Elizabeth feeling "wretched." By mid-May she realized that she, too, would have to declare. She and her daughters would join her relatives in Charlottesville, Virginia. On May 12, Elizabeth Lindsay Lomax packed as many of her belongings as she could, locked her house on G Street, and left for the Confederacy. "Perhaps," she wrote in her diary, "forever."

CHAPTER 6

Union National City

Washington . . . is but a ragged, unfinished collection
of unbuilt, broad streets, as to the completion of which
here can now, I imagine, be but little hope. Of all
places that I know it is the most ungainly and the most
unsatisfactory. I fear I must also say the most presump-
tuous in its pretensions.

—Anthony Trollope, 1862

"Forward to Richmond! Forward to Richmond!" clamored Horace
Greeley's *New York Tribune* in a bold headline that the paper ran
repeatedly on its front page in the months of June and July 1861. "The
Rebel Congress must not be allowed to meet there on the 20th of July!
By that date the place must be held by the National Army." It was easy
for editors in New York City to call for war; it was less so for Abraham
Lincoln, who could look from the second-floor window of the White
House across the Potomac River into the heart of the Confederacy.
Washington's location would place it at the center of the war; its geog-
raphy, as the country had learned in 1814, made it vulnerable to attack.
And what a prize it would be for the Confederates to capture the capi-
tal of the United States.

From the start Lincoln understood the tenuous position of the city,
surrounded as it was by two slaveholding states. Virginia had seceded
in April. That state had 491,000 slaves—more than any other; the port
of Alexandria continued to thrive on human trafficking. Marylanders,

including the state's governor, owned 87,000 slaves. In the presidential election of 1860 they had cast more than 42,000 ballots for the southern, proslavery Democrat John C. Breckinridge; they cast barely 2,000 for Abraham Lincoln.

That February, Lincoln had even encountered difficulty entering Washington for his inauguration. He had boarded a railroad car in Springfield, Illinois, for a serpentine progress that took him past large and enthusiastic crowds in big cities—Indianapolis, Cincinnati, Pittsburgh, Columbus, Cleveland, Buffalo, Syracuse, and Albany—as well as small villages, mere dots on the landscape—Tolono, Illinois; Thornton, Indiana; Willoughby, Ohio; and Westfield, New York.

When Lincoln and his entourage arrived in Philadelphia, however, telegraph wires from the South were humming with ominous reports that secessionist gangs in Baltimore were plotting his murder. As the tracks from the North did not connect directly with those to the South, railroad cars had to be disconnected from their engine at one depot and pulled by horses through Baltimore's streets to the next. Lincoln's friend and self-appointed bodyguard Ward Hill Lamon determined that the danger was too great for him to publish the time of his trip through the city. Disguised as a physician attending a sick man, Lamon boarded the 10:50 evening train at Philadelphia with Lincoln wearing a slouch hat and a shawl about his shoulders. As dawn broke on the morning of Saturday, February 23, 1861, the president-elect stepped onto the platform at Washington's B&O station at Sixth Street and New Jersey Avenue.

Although Washington's population had increased by 50 percent, to 60,000, since Lincoln's one term in Congress ended in 1849, many aspects of capital life remained the same. The narrow ditch of the Washington Canal that cut between the Potomac and the Eastern Branch had become an open sewer, especially where it doglegged on the marshy land in front of the Capitol. The aqueduct system that Montgomery Meigs had designed to bring fresh water from Great Falls on the Potomac was not yet finished. Gas jets lit the Capitol, the White House, and a number of buildings on Pennsylvania Avenue between them, but little else. To save money, Congress continued the practice of lighting the avenue's lamps only when it was in session. (In 1856, the Washington Gas Light Company could count just 1,700 customers, many of them commercial establishments.) Unlike Baltimore, Boston, Brooklyn, Pittsburgh, Chicago, Cincinnati, New Orleans, and

Philadelphia, Washington didn't have a horsecar line because Congress resisted granting any company a charter.

Henry Adams—great grandson of America's second president and grandson of the sixth, and future journalist, historian, and novelist—was in the city when Lincoln arrived. Adams was serving as secretary to his father, a member of Congress from Massachusetts, and would accompany him to the Court of St. James after Lincoln made him ambassador to England. Henry had been absent since 1850, about the same time as the new president, but as he remembered in his famous autobiography, *The Education of Henry Adams*, little had changed. In 1850 he had been taken with the "thick odor of the catalpa trees" that hung heavy in the air as he followed the wheel tracks in the dirt road meandering "from the colonnade of the Treasury . . . to the white marble columns and fronts of the Post Office and Patent Office." These he likened to "white Greek temples in abandoned gravel-pits of a deserted Syrian city." Low wooden houses scattered along the streets reminded him of a southern village. And he had wandered down to the "unfinished square marble shaft" of the Washington Monument. Now, a decade later, he saw that "the same rude colony was camped in the same forest, with the same unfinished Greek temples for work rooms, and sloughs for roads."

The condition of Washington's roads always evoked comment. "Simply disgusting," said Henry Villard, who arrived in the city that February to report on national events for the *New York Herald*. Villard was appalled by what he saw. Washington was "a great straggling encampment of brick and mortar, spread over an infinite deal of space." Excluding the public buildings, there were "half a dozen government palaces, all in a highly aggravating and inconvenient state of incompleteness." Just two tiers of Thomas U. Walter's wedding-cake dome over the rotunda of the Capitol were complete; the cast iron for its vaulted crown lay on the ground. The Washington Monument, a stump at 154 feet, stood as a stark reminder of all that had to be accomplished in the city and the nation. Villard quickly found the three fashionable hotels—the Willard, Brown's, and the National—all on Pennsylvania Avenue, and numerous saloons, but not "a single decent restaurant." Like so many visitors from the North, he couldn't refrain from making an invidious comparison with the South. The city had, he said, "a distinctly Southern air of indolence and sloth." To many, Washington was, like the nation itself, an unfinished union dominated by the South, and far from realizing its ideals.

IN ADDITION to illustrating Thomas U. Walter's dome, and the derrick crane and structural work needed to erect it, this photograph, taken in May 1861, also presents a view of the central portico and the Capitol grounds. CREDIT: Library of Congress

WINFIELD SCOTT, GENERAL-IN-CHIEF of the army, was among the first Washingtonians to meet Lincoln. Long past his prime, Scott was now in his seventy-fifth year, older than the Constitution itself, and his own living memorial. His military victories and political ambitions had passed. Victory and glory had come early for him on the battlefields in the War of 1812 and the Mexican War, but defeat came hard in the presidential election of 1852, when as a Whig candidate he had taken just four states to Franklin Pierce's twenty-seven. Even his nickname, "Old Fuss and Feathers," given because of his vanity and military bearing, no longer seemed to suit the general, who was plagued by numerous ailments—dropsy, gout, rheumatism, and vertigo among them. His three hundred pounds made it impossible for him to mount a horse and difficult for him to climb the stairs at the White House. Still, Winfield Scott held the rank of lieutenant general, the only general since George Washington to do so. He had served under thirteen presidents; now he was ready to serve his fourteenth.

Scott was "the only military figure that looked equal to the crisis," Henry Adams observed. The general had done more than many realized to make the capital safe for his new president. Recognizing that Lincoln's election might well mean disunion and possibly war, he had ordered Charles Pomeroy Stone, a West Point graduate, civil engineer, and veteran of the Mexican War, to take charge of the city's defenses.

Many within the Buchanan administration had helped to transform Washington into a city of divided loyalties. John Floyd had used his power as secretary of war to abolish the laws regulating the District of Columbia militia, thereby ensuring that there were fewer than five hundred regular federal troops to protect the city from attack. Worse still, Floyd and his subordinates had placed Washington's defenses in the hands of four local militias. More social clubs than disciplined military organizations, these militias counted secessionists in their ranks. One, the National Volunteers, was in the hands of an outspoken secessionist; it enjoyed the open support of the city's famously inept police force of twenty-seven daytime and forty nighttime officers, plus the tacit assent of Washington's mayor, James G. Berret, who maintained that the militia was preparing to thwart an invasion from the North. Floyd had given this militia a substantial arsenal of sabers, rifles, and pistols along with two mountain howitzers especially suited for assaulting buildings at close range.

Years of encouragement from federal officials with both words and arms had led secessionist sympathizers and their militias to consider seriously an armed resistance to the change in government. Charles Stone challenged them with his every act. He assigned detectives to watch over the National Volunteers and other Confederate-leaning volunteers, ordered the howitzers and other unsuitable armaments to be returned to the federal arsenal at Greenleaf's Point, and installed loyal militia units at three key points in the city: the Capitol, Lafayette Square, and City Hall. From those positions the men held a commanding view of the Patent Office and the Post Office as well. Most significantly, Stone demanded that the militiamen swear allegiance to the Union. The winnowing worked; he separated from the militia about 500 men, who crossed the river to fight for the Confederacy, but he was left with about 6,500 who remained loyal and ready to fight for the Union.

Such precautions helped to ensure that the inauguration on March 4 went off without bloodshed. As was the custom at the time, the outgoing president, James Buchanan, arrived at noon in his open barouche at the Willard Hotel to escort the president-elect to the Capitol, where he would take the Oath of Office. But other matters were far from customary. From windows and rooftops of buildings lining Pennsylvania Avenue and the Capitol Square, sharpshooters stood at the ready. Cavalry blocked the side streets and rode in two columns flanking the presidential carriage. Thirty thousand people had packed themselves into Capitol Square to witness the ceremony, though, as one onlooker remembered a half century later, "comparatively few" of the city's older residents were there. Some had already left the city to join relatives in the South; others stayed home. The ceremony ended quietly and without violence. "God be praised," said General Scott, who saw the peaceful conclusion of the ceremony from a carriage on Capitol Square. "God in His goodness be praised."

Lincoln's immediate challenge was to keep Maryland out of secessionist hands. Six states had already left the Union; the president of the convention organizing a government for the new Confederate States of America had recently proclaimed the separation to be "perfect, complete, and perpetual." Texans had voted to secede on the Saturday Lincoln arrived in Washington; most expected that Virginia would soon follow. Should Maryland secede, too, Washington would become an isolated Union outpost surrounded by rebels.

Indeed, for five days that April the capital was an isolated outpost. The fall of Fort Sumter, at the entrance to Charleston Harbor in South Carolina, in mid-April electrified secessionists in Baltimore. On Federal Hill, where in 1789 jubilant Marylanders had gathered to celebrate the state's ratification of the Constitution, a rebellious crowd now raised a Confederate flag. On April 19, hoodlums murdered four soldiers of the Sixth Massachusetts Regiment who were en route to the capital. Others cut telegraph lines, destroyed the rail bridge crossing the Susquehanna at Havre de Grace, and tore up the tracks leading to Washington. The newspaper correspondent Henry Villard was returning to the capital from a brief visit with his editor at the *New York Herald* when he was caught in the conflict. He resorted to rowboats, a horse and buggy, and finally a saddle horse to complete his trek across the state to the District line. When he arrived, he found the capital gripped in fear. "It was as though the government . . . had been suddenly removed to an island in mid-ocean, in a state of entire isolation." Cassius Marcellus Clay, the ardent abolitionist from Kentucky, drilled his militia company in the ballroom at the Willard Hotel. James H. Lane, who had just arrived from Kansas to take his seat in the Senate, stationed another group of militiamen in the East Room of the White House. Still others stood guard at the Treasury and War Departments. The Willard, Brown's, and the National, along with Washington's other hotels and shops, had closed. Residents who harbored southern sympathies had shuttered their houses and crossed the Potomac; others sullenly remained, believing their city would shortly be in Confederate hands.

Lincoln remained outwardly steadfast. When a committee of twenty "highly respectable citizens of Baltimore" arrived on April 22 to ask the president to cease sending Union troops through Maryland, Lincoln replied with indignation, a touch of humor, and finally resolution. The indignation: "You . . . come here to . . . ask for peace on any terms, and yet have no word of condemnation for those who are making war on us. You express great horror of bloodshed, and yet would not lay a straw in the way of those who are organizing in Virginia and elsewhere to capture this city. . . . Your citizens attack troops sent to the defense of the Government, and the lives and property in Washington." The humor: "I must have troops to defend this Capital. Geographically it lies surrounded by the soil of Maryland; and mathematically the necessity exists that they should come over her territory. Our men are not moles, and can't dig under the earth; they are not birds, and can't fly through the air. There is no way but to march across, and that they must do." And the resolution: "Keep your rowdies in Baltimore, and there will be no bloodshed. Go home and tell your people that if they will not attack us, we will not attack them; but if they do attack us, we will return it, and that severely."

It was an anxious moment. Without mail, telegraph, or rail communication, supporters of the Union could only pray for northern regiments to arrive. Even Abraham Lincoln despaired: "I begin to believe there is no North. . . . The Seventh New York [Regiment] is a myth."

After five days, the somewhat battered gentleman of the Seventh New York, along with the Eighth Massachusetts, arrived from Annapolis. The New Yorkers favored bespoke gray uniforms, velvet-covered camp stools, and provisions put up by Delmonico's restaurant, though their trek by foot and rail from Maryland's capital had forced them to abandon their stools and eat food foraged from farms.

Although there would be many anxious events during the next four years, Washington's ties with the North would not be severed again for the duration of the war. Within a few days, 7,000 more troops poured into the capital from the North by rail (through Annapolis rather than Baltimore) and steamship. The soldiers marched down Pennsylvania Avenue from the Capitol to the reviewing stand in front of the White House. Never mind that, as Winfield Scott well knew, despite the show the men were undisciplined and untried. Across the capital, rumors spread that they would fight soon, urged on by an impatient Congress, which realized that many of the troops had enlisted for just ninety days, and insistent members of the press, who thought the war would be a walkover. "Forward to Richmond!" became the catchphrase of the day.

THE CRY FROM Greeley's *New York Tribune* and other northern papers helped propel the unprepared men of the Union Army to a devastating defeat that imperiled the capital. In the still and sultry first light of the oppressively hot third Sunday of July 1861, senators, representatives, their ladies, and their friends packed their parasols, field glasses, and picnic baskets into carriages for an excursion to Centreville, Virginia, where they confidently expected to see the 37,000 Union soldiers under the command of General Irwin McDowell whip the Confederates. Their object was to destroy the railroad at Manassas, capture Richmond about 95 miles south, and end the rebellion.

By noon, the battle was unfolding as the Union expected. "On the hill beside me there was a crowd of civilians on horseback and in all sorts of vehicles, with a few of the fairer, if not gentler, sex," the Englishman William Howard Russell reported for the *London Times*. "[One] who was near me was quite beside herself when an unusually heavy discharge roused the current of her blood: 'That is splendid! Oh, my! Is not that first-rate? I guess we will be in Richmond this time tomorrow.'" But by late afternoon reinforcements led by Thomas Jonathan Jackson, an eccentric instructor of both "natural and experimental philosophy" and artillery from Virginia Military Institute, arrived to save the southern cause. The Union defeat was total; the retreat, disgraceful. "All sense of manhood seemed to be forgotten," wrote a correspondent for the *New York Tribune*. "Every impediment to flight was cast aside. Rifles, bayonets, pistols, haversacks, cartridge-boxes, canteens, blankets, belts, and overcoats lined the road."

Bull Run, as the battle came to be called in the North, brought the war to the streets of the capital. From midnight Sunday through the rainy Monday that followed, thousands of disillusioned soldiers, a continuous stream of broken men, straggled back into the city. "Rich and poor . . . high and low . . . opened their doors and dealt out food and refreshments to the footsore, haggard, and half-starved men," Lincoln's secretary wrote in his journal, "so unexpectedly reduced to tramps and fugitives." Then came the carriages and wagons filled with the bloody consequences of battle. For the first time Washington's citizens understood in a serious way that their city lay at the vulnerable center of what promised to be a fierce struggle over the future of the Union. The time for hurrahing had passed; Bull Run made war real.

BY THE FALL of 1861 the city had settled down to the grim task of prosecuting a war. It was a time of skirmishes, testing, and preparation. At Ball's Bluff on the Potomac that October, the federals lost again. Rebel batteries at the mouth of the river harried Union boats attempting to ascend to the capital; Congress voted to fund an army of half a million men; former vice president John C. Breckenridge left the Senate to become a general in the Confederate States Army; and a thirty-four-year-old Union general, George B. McClellan, took up the task of organizing and training the Army of the Potomac.

That fall Julia Ward Howe visited the capital from her home in Boston for the first time since the beginning of the war. A poet and writer known for her ardor—and what her friend and later Supreme Court Justice Oliver Wendell Holmes called "tropical flashes of passion," Howe wrote lines that asked,

> *Leav'st thou the maiden rose*
> *Drooping and blushing,*
> *Or rend'st its bosom with*
> *Kissing and crushing?*

She was also an ardent abolitionist, who with husband, Samuel Gridley Howe, took up the abolitionist cause with men like Charles Sumner and John Brown.

On her approach to the bleak city, Howe passed small groups of soldiers guarding the railroad tracks against attack. Once there she saw the Army of the Potomac drilling close by the stub of the Washington Monument. From her window at the Willard, as she remembered in 1899, Howe "saw the office of the *New York Herald*, and near it the ghastly advertisement of an agency for embalming and forwarding the bodies of those who had fallen in the fight or who had perished by fever." She visited camps and hospitals and the troops of the First Massachusetts Heavy Artillery. With the governor of Massachusetts, she met with Abraham Lincoln, who sat beneath Gilbert Stuart's portrait of Washington, his "sad expression" and "deep blue eyes" appearing in stark contrast to the countenance of the first president.

In mid-November Howe and a small party crossed the Potomac for a picnic at Bailey's Crossroads, about eight miles from the city. They were to be the guests of George McClellan, who promised to review 1,800 of his cavalry. All went well at the picnic; the parade of the soldiers was grand—until the Confederates attacking from Falls Church threw the soldiers and civilians into confusion. "We returned to the city very slowly," Howe remembered, "for troops nearly filled the road." To pass the time during the "tedious drive," she and her companions sang "John Brown's Body," the favorite song of the federal troops. A companion suggested that she write some words more elevated and moving to accompany the tune.

Early the next morning, in the dim light of her bedroom at the Willard, one of her "attacks of versification" visited Julia Ward Howe. She arose from bed, hastily wrote out the stanzas to the "Battle Hymn of the Republic," and then went back to sleep.

In her hymn, Howe drew from those she had encountered while living with her husband in south Boston. She had entertained Senator Charles Sumner often and had walked with John Brown in her garden; she knew and had read Ralph Waldo Emerson; she had read the fiery abolitionist tracts that William Lloyd Garrison published in the *Liberator*; and each week she listened to the strident sermons that Theodore Parker delivered from his pulpit at the Congregational Society of

Boston. Now she mixed those ideas with thoughts of the events taking place in the capital, the Massachusetts boys whose camps she had visited, the sight of the wounded men whom she had seen in hospitals, and the soldiers and politicians who filled the lobby of the Willard Hotel. She combined her abolitionist sentiments with the strident verses of the Old Testament. Wrath, bloody and violent though it may be, was sometimes a necessity if people were to do God's will. For the opening image of her hymn, she turned to the words of Isaiah: "I have trodden the winepress alone. . . . I will tread them in mine anger, and trample them in my fury. . . . For the day of vengeance is in mine heart." The words of the prophet sanctified the great cause of the Union and united every federal action with God's purpose for his people:

> *Mine eyes have seen the glory of the coming of the Lord:*
> *He is trampling out the vintage where the grapes of wrath are stored;*
> *He hath loosed the fateful lightning of His terrible swift sword:*
> *His truth is marching on.*

Howe's experiences in Washington had changed her engagement with the war. The men she saw daily, those who manned the batteries defending the city, were doing God's work:

> *I have seen Him in the watch-fires of a hundred circling camps,*
> *They have builded Him an altar in the evening dews and damps;*
> *I can read His righteous sentence by the dim and flaring lamps . . .*

Her lines connected God's retribution to the inherent evil of the Confederate cause. Only by crushing the serpent that had beguiled Eve can we hope to restore the Edenic state. It is a "fiery gospel, writ in burnished rows of steel," but a necessary one:

> *As ye deal with my contemners, so with you my grace shall deal;*
> *Let the Hero, born of woman, crush the serpent with his heel . . .*

And make no mistake, Christians must answer God's call: "Oh, be swift, my soul, to answer Him! be jubilant, my feet!" Just as Jesus accepted his destiny "in the beauty of the lilies" of Gethsemane, so must we:

> *As He died to make men holy, let us die to make men free,*
> *While God is marching on.*

As macabre as the advertisement for "embalming and forwarding" the dead might be, it was, Howe came to understand, a part of a divine cause. Her trip to Washington had transformed the speeches of Garrison, the preachings of Parker, and the high thoughts of Emerson into the fierce reality of action.

FOR A WHILE, William Wilson Corcoran, the wealthiest man in Washington, did not join the southern exodus in the wake of Lincoln's election and inauguration. Now in his sixty-third year, Corcoran had grown up with the capital. He had witnessed its burning in 1814 and its rebirth following the war. After running a dry goods store with his brothers, he went into banking, and in 1840 he had joined with George Washington Riggs to form Corcoran & Riggs, a banking house that bought and sold US Treasury notes.

In 1845 Corcoran & Riggs moved into the former Second Bank of the United States on Pennsylvania Avenue at Fifteenth Street across from the Treasury Department. From his "little White House," as he called it, Corcoran maintained a close relationship with members of Congress and the various secretaries of the treasury from the administrations of Jackson through Buchanan. The Senate, the House of Representatives, the Smithsonian Institution, and the most important politicians transferred their money to his bank. James K. Polk regarded him as both a financial and personal adviser, asking his counsel on his own investments as well as on redecorating the White House. Private loans that Corcoran (his partner always remained in the background) made to politicians and their constituents in every state of the Union paid off handsomely. In time, the firm's financial tentacles extended far beyond the District of Columbia to help secure other ventures, including railroads and newspapers. Across the land it seemed that almost everyone who held any position of power owed a favor to the bold and calculating gentleman from Washington.

In 1846 Corcoran enhanced his stature as a banker, as well as his purse, when his firm undertook the sale of $14 million in bonds to finance the Mexican-American War. Yet his profit of $250,000 paled in comparison when, a year later, he undertook to sell another war loan of $14 million. This time, he became an American agent for the Treasury and sailed to Europe to promote the bonds on the Continent. He was taking a great risk, too great for the more cautious Riggs, who decided to step back from the gamble. But Corcoran prevailed, restored confidence in America's credit among Europeans, and in 1851 returned to Washington a multimillionaire.

Back in the capital, Corcoran devoted his energies to spending his vast fortune. His pursuits after his retirement from the daily business of banking in 1854 placed him at the center of Washington's social and cultural life. He hired James Renwick, the designer of the Smithsonian Castle, to expand his house on Lafayette Square, making it Washington's premier mansion. (He had acquired the property from his friend—and debtor—Daniel Webster.) His weekly dinner parties attracted Washington politicians, financiers, writers, and important visitors—people such as Jefferson Davis and James Buchanan, the Astors and Rothschilds, Washington Irving, the historian and secretary of the navy George Bancroft, and the Swedish nightingale, Jenny Lind. The Corcoran ball became the highlight of each congressional session. As a man of means, Corcoran had to have a country estate, so on two hundred acres just north of the District line he created "Harewood," complete with an iron fence around its perimeter and a palatial, Renwick-designed hunting lodge for its grounds. Before there was a Gilded Age, there was William Wilson Corcoran.

Corcoran's greatest satisfaction came from investing his enormous wealth in Washington's business and culture. On the 1500 block of I Street, he had Renwick (who was now his personal architect) design a handsome row of six houses, which he quickly rented to the State and War Departments. He made the initial purchase of land for Oak Hill Cemetery, just across Rock Creek in Georgetown, and again had Renwick design a simple, English-inspired chapel for the site. Although he was not an especially religious man, he gave liberally to Washington's Catholic and Protestant churches; and although he was a moderate drinker, he supported Theobold Mathew when the Irish priest brought his Bible-thumping message of abstinence to the capital. Every winter Corcoran had firewood distributed to the poor; every Christmas he supplied turkey dinners; and every year he gave liberally to the late Marcia Van Ness's Washington City Orphan Asylum. In his spare hours he served as the first president of the Washington Horticultural Society.

But William Corcoran's greatest passion—and the one that one day would benefit Washington's life in the most enduring way—was collecting art. Business trips to Europe had brought him into contact with collectors and artists. Back in the United States, Corcoran devoted a wing of his house to French and German paintings, and in 1851 he opened his collection to the public two days a week. One work that drew visitors by the score was a copy of *The Greek Slave*, Hiram Powers's marble statue of the shy and naked Greek female captured by the Turks in the recent Greek War of Independence, her hands bound in chains, awaiting her fate to be decided by her captors. Corcoran recognized the potential of American artists, too. Soon American landscapes by such artists as Thomas Cole and Asher B. Durand, Thomas Kensett and Jasper Cropsey, appeared on the walls at his Lafayette Square home.

After a trip to the Crystal Palace in London and the Louvre in Paris, Corcoran decided he needed even more space to display his art. Renwick produced designs for a three-story, Second Empire–style gallery for the public at Seventeenth Street and Pennsylvania Avenue. It would be an American Louvre, with rooms for portraits of the nation's heroes and space for an art school. Statues of great artists from antiquity to the present would grace eleven exterior niches to inspire the public. All who entered would pass under Corcoran's initials, "WWC," carved into the Aquia Creek limestone, and the motto proclaiming the Corcoran Gallery's mission: "DEDICATED TO ART." Washington would lead the nation's cultural life, and WWC would be the self-appointed arbiter of American taste.

But other cultural forces—slavery and abolition among them—proved to be of far greater consequence. The election of 1860 confirmed Corcoran's worst fears for the fate of the country and his native city. He realized that the issue of slavery was sundering the nation, yet it had been quietly receding in the District of Columbia, where there were 11,000 free blacks and just 3,200 enslaved. He himself had little use for the institution and had freed his own slaves in 1856.

Still, Corcoran's heart had always been with the South. He had been a widower for two decades, so the marriage of the only surviving child of that union, his beloved daughter, Louise, to a Louisiana congressman only served to seal his determination to lend his tacit support to the burgeoning Confederacy. "What is to become of us?" he asked plaintively in a letter as Fort Sumter was falling. "The South should have her rights in peace." The close relationships he had enjoyed with presidents and their cabinets for more than three decades were fast becoming a memory.

The Union defeat at Bull Run changed Washington and diminished its tolerance for men like Corcoran with Confederate sympathies. The war that some said would last but ninety days was turning into a protracted horror. That August, Corcoran watched helplessly as the federal government commandeered his nearly completed gallery for the Army's Quarter Master General's Corps; soon the rooms intended for paintings and sculptures became offices and a warehouse for Union blankets, boots, and uniforms. On suspicion of his harboring southern sympathies, Secretary of War Edwin Stanton had Corcoran arrested, briefly, before cooler heads in Lincoln's cabinet prevailed. Cocoran's city had become an armed camp filled with troops, military reviews, and martial airs.

That November, a Union naval vessel captured and briefly detained the British mail packet *Trent* that was carrying a party of Confederate diplomats and attachés, including Corcoran's daughter and her husband, to London. Once the "*Trent* affair," as it came to be known, was settled, and the Confederate party was allowed to proceed to England, the financier decided that he, too, would leave for Europe. After quietly converting some of his stocks and real-estate holdings to silver and gold and shipping it to the Continent, William Wilson Corcoran abandoned his capital to wait out the war in Paris.

DESPITE THE HUMILIATING defeat at Bull Run Washington society quickly recovered enough to resume its gay pleasures. People of wealth, many of them contractors doing business with the government, took the place of those who had gone south. First Lady Mary Todd Lincoln refused to allow the war and Union failures on the battlefield to curtail her ambitious social schedule. She prepared her wardrobe for the season and, to the consternation of her husband, refitted the White House. On Christmas and New Year's Day, fashionable ladies opened their houses to callers. On Mondays the ladies observed "cabinet calling," visiting all the cabinet wives as well as Ellen Marcy McClellan, wife of Lincoln's new general.

"Washington is perfectly thronged with strangers," Caroline Kasson wrote to newspaper readers in Des Moines at the end of October 1861. "Every nook and corner is occupied with officers and their families, and with lookers-on at this swiftly moving Panorama of life in the Capital." Kasson had recently arrived with her husband, who had led the Republicans in Iowa and helped to write the party's platform in 1860, services that earned him the reward of being named first assistant postmaster general.

Though a newcomer to the city, Kasson understood that Washington was changing in ways that made life difficult for others not of her class. "The city is now a huge crowd," she wrote, describing "the strivings and pushings for houses and rooms." From the capital's beginning, as workers erecting the federal buildings knew all too well, government employment had never been a sure thing, and was always subject to the whims of Congress, which could, and often did, suddenly cut off funding for projects. But for now, employment was more certain than ever. Hotels were crowded throughout the year. The population surge combined with wartime inflation to strain the community in every way. Between 1860 and 1865, prices of eleven necessities, including room and board, woolens, and cotton, rose 130 percent.

However, pay for government workers did not rise. The case of department clerks was telling. Well before the war, Congress established four grades, with annual salaries beginning at $1,200 for the first and rising in $200 increments to $1,800 for the fourth. Yet wartime inflation dictated that these salaries diminished. By 1865, the salary of the grade-one clerk had effectively declined to $579. At the same time the government increased the number of clerks from 1,000 to 6,000 men, which put pressure on housing prices. The annual rent for a house sufficient to shelter a clerk and his family rose from $100 to $500. So expensive was it to live in Washington that several hundred clerks decided to move to Baltimore and commute by railroad. As bad as these conditions were for men, they were far worse for women who worked in the Treasury Department and the Printing Office. Their yearly salaries were just $500.

Even with the high cost of living, the social scene continued unabated. In her letters Caroline Kasson looked at it with a mix of pleasure and midwestern sternness, never quite accepting the city's lighthearted ways in the perilous time. "Houses are being fitted for winter gayeties," Kasson reported in October 1861. "As in the days of the Decameron, there will always be found a merry circle to drown care in bright jest and dance." Three months later she would write: "The wheels of society roll on. The President stands gaunt and care-worn, receiving his friends in the gilded departments of the White House. The crimson and gold tapestry . . . painfully contrast with the worn look of the discontented grumbler, or the disloyal agitator."

But gaiety could not transcend all the dread that was attendant to the death of the Lincolns' eleven-year-old son, Willie. Two days before Washington's birthday in 1862, the first family's youngest child succumbed to a fever, most likely typhoid, very possibly contracted from contaminated drinking water that was piped to the White House. A few days earlier, Mary Lincoln had been the glittering hostess of a party for five hundred invited cabinet members, representatives, senators, distinguished local citizens, members of the diplomatic corps, and their families. While the Marine Band played and guests dined on a rich feast catered by the famous New York restaurateur Henri Maillard, Mary and the president quietly slipped upstairs to their boy's bedside. But what doctors had assured them was a cold turned into a mortal fever whose end brought the parents paroxysms of grief. Willie's death immediately curtailed the capital's social activities for the balance of the season, and indeed for the rest of the war. The Lincolns never held another party of the magnitude of Mary's triumph that February night. Mary dressed in mourning, including a brooch and matching earrings of diamonds set in gold and trimmed in black enamel; the president pinned mourning crepe to his hat and dreamed of the dead boy "again and again."

NOTWITHSTANDING THE EXODUS of many to the Confederacy, disloyal sympathizers and collaborators seemed to be everywhere. "One of the novel sensations is to attempt to return a lady's call," wrote Kasson, "and to find a guard stationed before the door of the fair Secessionist." That was precisely the case of Washington's most notorious spy, the clever, beguiling, and well-connected widow Rose O'Neal Greenhow. Those who called at Greenhow's house on Lafayette Square on the morning of August 26, 1861, found two guards at the door. Greenhow and her young daughter, also named Rose, were under house arrest.

She was the perfect spy for the southern cause. A flirtatious wit, with black hair, dark eyes, olive complexion, full breasts, and a wasp waist, Rose O'Neal quickly softened the hard edges of the southern congressmen and senators whom she met as a teenager while boarding with her aunt in the Brick Capitol, now called the Old Capitol Building. She came to regard John C. Calhoun as "the best and wisest man of this century," and she listened intently as Calhoun in full stentorian voice declared to his fellow senators that "instead of an evil," slavery was "a good—a positive good."

While Calhoun was instructing Rose O'Neal in Washington's political world, her neighbor Dolley Madison tutored her in the mysteries of the capital's manners. It was with Dolley's encouragement that Rose married Robert Greenhow, Virginia gentleman, medical doctor, and librarian at the State Department. Widowed in 1854, she devoted her life to entertainment and intrigue. She sought to advance Franklin Pierce's attempt to annex slaveholding Cuba and thereby bolster the South's interests; and she cultivated her friendship with James Buchanan. When Buchanan was elected president in 1857, Rose Greenhow and Washington's southerners were ascendant. When the aged chief justice Roger Taney delivered the Supreme Court's *Dred Scott v. Sandford* decision two days after Buchanan's inauguration, they reached the apex of their power.

Lincoln's election turned Greenhow to espionage. By May 1861 she had contracted with a Confederate agent to collect information from her contacts in the government, including senators and young and newly minted officers eager to preen their importance before women. Massachusetts senator Henry Wilson, chairman of the Committee on Military Affairs, who purportedly signed a series of letters to Greenhow "Love, H," proved particularly valuable. The idea of a woman using her charm and capacity for gossip to wheedle secrets from her male companions was unthought of in the early days of the war, but Greenhow made it into a high art. She mastered a Confederate cypher and recruited other young women with southern sympathies to carry her reports of cabinet meetings and intimate gleanings to the Confederate general Pierre Gustave Toutant-Beauregard in Richmond. Because of Rose Greenhow, the general knew the number of Union forces that would engage the Confederates at Bull Run, the route they would take, and their arms.

Like William Wilson Corcoran, Greenhow was caught up in the panic following the Union defeat she had helped to engineer, and was placed under house arrest. The government grew suspicious of other women in the city, and they, too, were sent to Greenhow's house. The women were clearly infra dig—"generally of the lowest class," she said—a Miss Poole, who seemed to have fainting fits that the guards readily indulged, and who was "allowed unlimited range of the house at all hours of the day or night"; and a divorcee, Mrs. Baxley, who "raved from early morn till late at night, in language more vehement than delicate." Still, Greenhow managed to smuggle a considerable number of letters from her house to the outside world. One, written to Secretary of State William Henry Seward outlining the indignities of her incarceration, she managed to have printed in a Richmond newspaper. Guards sealed her windows and removed all writing implements, but still she managed to send messages. In exasperation, federal authorities moved Greenhow and her fellow inmates to the decaying Old Capitol, which they hastily converted into a prison. Three decades after she had arrived in Washington, Rose O'Neal Greenhow returned to the place where her life in the capital had begun.

The walls of the Old Capitol enclosed filth and chaos. Rats and mice shared the chambers with the inmates; lice and other bugs, the mattresses. The smell from privies and cooking was overpowering. And the fare of rice and beans usually came floating in grease. Every two days, Greenhow and her daughter were allowed a half-hour of exercise in the prison yard. "We walk up and down, picking our way as best we can through mud and negroes, followed by soldiers and corporals with bayonet in hand," Greenhow reported to her niece. Some prisoners paid for special privileges—cleaner bedding, better food, and fresh water for washing—and the guards allowed some to have visitors who brought gifts of food. Greenhow never stooped to pay for such perquisites. She preferred instead to compare herself with Marie Antoinette, taunting her guards and any Yankee official who encountered her. She complained, endlessly, about the appalling conditions; and when her daughter became ill, she ordered the guards to summon her own physician instead of the prison doctor, whom she had named "Cyclops." With her keen instinct for publicity, Greenhow made a Confederate flag on her sewing machine that she had a guard fetch from her house, and unfurled it through the slats of her boarded-up window. It attracted

ROSE GREENHOW and her daughter, 1861. CREDIT: Library of Congress

reporters and Confederate supporters who came to glimpse the woman federal officials had branded a "dangerous skillful spy."

From his studio, the National Photographic Art Gallery at 350–352 Pennsylvania Avenue, Mathew Brady sent his best photographer, Alexander Gardner, to the Old Capitol to capture Greenhow's image. Including her daughter, also named Rose, in the portrait ensured that it would evoke compassion. The tone is funereal. The pair appear against a dirty whitewashed wall in the prison yard. Behind their heads is a window partially covered with wooden slats. Rose sits in a straight-backed chair, her right arm about the waist of her daughter, who leans her face close to hers. The child wears a gray muslin and crinoline dress with white pantalettes that fall just below her knee; her mother, a silk mourning costume with black gauze sleeves. All is sepulchral, even the dark brooch at the base of the dress's V neck and the black snood that holds her neatly parted hair. Her face suggests a deep-set melancholy. To be sure, the portrait did make for good propaganda, but it also suggested the truth.

It was clear that Greenhow and the embarrassed federal government had had enough. Since she was a woman, the authorities could not hang her as they would an ordinary spy. Yet she remained a major

irritant to the War Department. It must have been with some measure
of relief when the city's military governor read her petition in March
1862: "I am now eight months a prisoner, and cannot regard any useless
prolongation of that period but as a wanton act of cruelty; and I would
not willingly believe that you will lend yourself to it. . . . I most respectfully and earnestly urge you, Sir, to perform the condition of sending
me South without further delay."

But there was a further delay while the two sides arranged for the
exchange. On June 1, a carriage called for Greenhow and her daughter
to begin their journey to Richmond. It must have vexed her that she
was exchanged along with two others whom she held in contempt, "the
woman Baxley, and the one calling herself Mrs. Morris." From Richmond she and her daughter went to England and France, had audiences
with Queen Victoria and Napoleon III, lobbied for the Confederate
cause, visited with William Wilson Corcoran, and wrote a memoir of
her incarceration that became a best-seller. She decided to leave her
daughter at a convent school in England and return to the Confederacy
with the royalties from the sale of her memoir. But on October 1, 1864,
the boat carrying her ran aground in a gale off North Carolina. Rescu-
ers found Rose Greenhow's body in shallow water, weighed down by
her heavy black silk dress and a bag of gold sovereigns tied to her neck.

THE WAR CREATED a vast new population of wounded in Washington. As the capital was less than a day's travel from the sites where many
of the great battles were fought—Carlisle, Chambersburg, and Gettysburg in Pennsylvania; Antietam in Maryland; Richmond, Chancellorsville, Fredericksburg, and Spotsylvania Courthouse in Virginia, among
others—more often than not the casualties were sent there. In May and
June 1861 there had been only a trickle of wounded who were cared for
by their regiments or in private infirmaries, but after the Battle of Bull
Run in July, the flow increased to a torrent. By 1863 about 50,000 men
lay in the capital's hospitals, a greater number than the entire population of the city a decade earlier. As much as the Capitol, the White
House, and the Treasury Building had in the past, hospitals now came
to define the topography of Washington at war.

In effect, the hospitals were jerry-built small villages scattered about
the District. Typical was the one the army established at William Wilson

Corcoran's country retreat, Harewood, where 2,000 patients were treated in fifteen hastily erected sanitary ward buildings. The hospital conformed to the latest thinking in medical practice: whitewash covered the wooden walls inside and out to promote sanitation, and numerous vents and windows allowed for generous air circulation. The buildings were an immense "V" formation. Surrounding the wards were kitchens, dining rooms, barracks, stables, nurses' quarters, an administration building, and a morgue, or as it was generally known, "dead house."

There were many others: Lincoln General, east of the Capitol, had 2,075 beds in twenty ward buildings, and twenty-five tents arranged in a "V" similar to the buildings at Harewood; Armory Square, one of the best, located west of the Capitol on the site of today's National Air and Space Museum, had 1,000 beds in twelve pavilions; Finley, on the Bladensburg Road north of Boundry Street, had 1,061 beds; Campbell, on Seventh Street, 900 beds; and Carver and Mount Pleasant on Meridian Hill, 1,300 and 1,618 beds, respectively. There were fifty-three hospitals in all, not including the numerous churches, mansions, hotels, and, early in the war, the Capitol itself, that were also commandeered to house the sick and injured.

As the war ground on and the shattered survivors of battle slipped back to the city to convalesce, a grim solemnity gradually took hold that even the most ardent social maven could not fail to ignore. Many responded with sympathy and care. In December 1862, Caroline Kasson told her readers in Des Moines of plans she and her lady friends had made to provide Christmas dinner to "twenty thousand homesick soldiers." Each lady would take charge of a hospital. The dinners ("No cold-bit look about them") went off well, especially as "Old Abe" visited, "first to one hospital then the other," offering, she reported, "unvarnished words of kindness."

THE POET WALT Whitman and novelist Louisa May Alcott joined hundreds of other civilians who came to Washington to help nurse the sick. Whitman arrived in December 1862 to assist his wounded brother. On his approach to the city, he was struck by the new topography of hospitals. They were "clusters . . . dotting the landscape and environs. That little town, as you might suppose it, off there on the brow of a hill, is indeed a town, but of wounds, sickness, and death."

Shortly after he settled into "a werry little bedroom" at Fourteenth and L streets, Whitman found that his real calling was with "the great army of the wounded." "How your heart would ache to go through the rows of wounded young men," he wrote to his sister after one of his first visits to the Campbell Hospital. One man, John Holmes from Massachusetts, became "a specimen" that he included in an article he wrote for the *New York Times*. Downed at the Battle of Fredericksburg—not by a shot but by diarrhea, the scourge of both armies—Holmes received "little or no attention" and no food before an ambulance took him to the Campbell Hospital. There Whitman found him "with death getting a closer and surer grip upon him." After several weeks of visiting, the poet could report that the soldier would recover.

Daily, the imposing—nearly six-foot-tall—bearded figure with green eyes and broad face moved through the wards at Armory Square and the Patent Office. From the pockets of his blue flannel coat and vest, as well as his gray, baggy trousers, tumbled gifts for the boys— newspapers, books, writing paper and stamped envelopes, fruit ("oranges, apples, sweet crackers, figs, &c"), tobacco, and small sums of money. "I give him a large handsome apple," he wrote of his gift to one man. To another, who had a great hankering for pickles, "something pungent," he brought horseradish, some apples, and a book. When called upon, he wrote letters, "including love letters, very tender ones." More important than gifts, the poet thought, was "the simple matter of personal presence . . . cheer and magnetism." He maintained that his visits often helped the patients more than "medical nursing, or delicacies, or gifts of money, or anything else." His presence fostered the manly camaraderie that the men needed most of all.

Whitman's movements were systematic: "went pretty thoroughly through wards F, G, H, and I; some fifty cases in each ward," he wrote on January 21, 1863, about his trip to Armory Square. "Evening, same day, went to see [wards] D. F. R." He found the wards in the Patent Office, which served as a hospital from October 1861 to March 1863, to be unique: the large rooms were filled with rows of "high and ponderous glass cases, crowded with [patent] models," and between the cases sick, wounded, and dying soldiers lay crowded close together. "It was, indeed, a curious scene, especially at night when lit up. The glass cases, the beds, the forms lying there, the gallery above, and the marble pavement under foot—the suffering . . . sometimes a poor fellow dying, with emaciated face and glassy eye, the nurse by his side, the doctor also there, but no friend." Such moments were seared into his memory and found voice in his poetry: "Come sweet death! be persuaded O beautiful death! / In mercy come quickly."

The poet became a friend, indeed the last friend, to some of the men. For Oscar F. Wilbur, Company G, 154th New York, who asked him to read from the New Testament, Whitman chose "the latter hours of Christ, and the scenes at the crucifixion." But then Wilbur, who knew his wounds made his own death near, asked to hear the account of Christ's resurrection. As the shadows gathered, "he behaved very manly and affectionate," Whitman reported. "The kiss I gave him . . . he returned fourfold."

The scene, so familiar to the poet—and so charged with eroticism—was never far from the surface of his experience or his writing.

> *Thus in silence in dreams' projections,*
> *Returning, resuming, I thread my way through the hospitals,*
> *The hurt and wounded I pacify with soothing hand,*
> *I sit by the restless all the dark night, some are so young,*
> *Some suffer so much, I recall the experience sweet and sad,*
> *(Many a soldier's loving arms about this neck have cross'd*
>   *and rested,*
> *Many a soldier's kiss dwells on these bearded lips.)*

Whitman regarded these soldiers as the common man, Adamic Americans, "nearly all young men, and far more American than is generally supposed," he wrote. He had written of them so eloquently in *Leaves of Grass*; now they were expressing their humanity and virtue through their valor as they cleansed America.

Louisa May Alcott arrived in Washington at almost the same time as Walt Whitman. Alcott had responded to a call from Dorothea Dix, superintendent of army nurses, for women between the ages of thirty-five and fifty to serve as nurses. The pay was meager—a bed, rations, and forty cents a day—but the idea of service appealed to the ardent abolitionist and feminist Alcott. A tall and imposing woman with deep-set eyes, Alcott wanted the excitement, and, indeed, the peril, that she could not experience picking lint and sewing bandages in a circle of Concord, Massachusetts, ladies. Now women like Dix and

THIS VIEW from the west side of the Capitol takes in much of the city as it appeared during the Civil War. Maryland Avenue and B Street SW (now Independence Avenue) appear to the left; Maine Avenue and Third, Fourth (known as 4½ Street), and Sixth streets SW are at the center. The perspective includes the Washington Armory, the Armory Square Hospital, the Smithsonian Castle, the Botanic Garden, the Washington Canal, the unfinished Washington Monument, and the Potomac River. CREDIT: Library of Congress

Florence Nightingale, whose *Notes on Nursing: What Nursing Is, What Nursing Is Not* had recently been published in America, offered Alcott an opportunity to step beyond the narrow boundaries that society, even the more open-minded Transcendentalists, had assigned to her. For Louisa, nursing was a step closer to what she really wanted to be and to do—she wanted to be a man and fight for the Union.

The hospital Alcott was assigned to, the Union Hotel on Bridge and Washington streets just a few blocks from Rock Creek, had undergone many changes since the end of the last century when George Washington had stopped there when deciding upon the exact location of the capital. Most were for the worse. It was "a perfect pestilence box," Alcott said, "cold, damp, dirty, full of vile odors from wounds, kitchens, wash rooms, & stables." The United States Sanitary Commission, the agency that functioned much like today's Red Cross, reported that the hotel had "no provisions for bathing, the water closets and sinks are insufficient and defective, and there is no dead house."

Alcott kept a journal and wrote vigorous letters to Concord describing her experiences. From these emerged a Dickensian portrait of Washington in the Civil War, the hospitals and women's place in them, and the survival and death of the soldiers she nursed. She had but three day's training when, in the crisp mid-December dawn, ambulances clattered down Bridge Street bearing "their sad freight" of wounded from the disastrous Battle of Fredericksburg. Alcott's task was to superintend a ward of forty beds that had been set up in the hotel's ballroom, "a *ball-room*," she wrote, "if gun-shot wounds could christen it." Amidst "the vilest odors that ever assaulted the human nose," she tended to men, "ragged, gaunt and pale, mud to the knees, with bloody bandages untouched since put on days before." The "legless, armless, or desperately wounded" occupied every bed. Quickly she divided the ballroom into three sections, a "duty room," a "pleasure room," and a "pathetic room." In the duty room she washed her patients, applied dressings, and administered their medicines; in the pleasure room she brought "books, flowers, games, and gossip"; and in the pathetic room, "teapots, lullabies, consolation, and sometimes a shroud." The last proved most distressing. "I laid the sheet over the quiet sleeper, whom no noise could now disturb," she wrote of one who died when she went off to fetch him a cup of water.

Taking an evening shift at the hospital allowed Alcott the liberty to explore the city with her critical eye by day. The spaciousness of the capital "quite took my breath away," she reported on her arrival. The bronze statue of Andrew Jackson astride his horse in Lafayette Square "stood like an opera dancer, on one leg." At the Senate chamber in the Capitol, she sat in her friend Charles Sumner's chair, "cudgeled an imaginary [Preston] Brooks within an inch of his life . . . and pocketed a castaway autograph or two." Outside, she saw the Liberty statue, which was destined to stand atop the Capitol dome, "flat in the mud." On the streets, she took delight in watching roaming pigs, Washington's "porcine citizens," who "appeared to enjoy a larger liberty than many of its human ones." And wistfully, she reported finding the "long, clean, warm, and airy wards" of the Armory Hospital to be a model of sanitation.

It was likely the decided lack of sanitation at the Union Hotel Hospital that curtailed Alcott's nursing work. About three weeks after her arrival, she contracted typhoid fever, one of the principal scourges of

Civil War hospitals, this one likely brought about by ingesting water and food contaminated with the feces of the infected patients. The "cure" of mercurous chloride, or calomel, administered by a misguided doctor proved as debilitating as the illness. For several weeks she suffered in a cold garret room at the top of the hotel before her father arrived to take her home.

MOST INTERESTING TO the abolitionist Alcott were her "colored brothers and sisters" whom she saw on the streets of Washington. In this way she differed from Whitman, who, believing nature had created "an impassable seal" to block the amalgamation of whites and blacks in America, considered abolitionists to be fanatics. Alcott was far more forward-thinking. She recognized that these former slaves were "so unlike the respectable members of society I'd known in moral Boston." Many of those blacks had been educated at Harvard and had dined with her prominent abolitionist friends. These recently emancipated men and women were "the sort of creatures generations of slavery have made them: obsequious, trickish, lazy and ignorant, yet kind-hearted, merry-tempered, quick to feel and accept the least token of the brotherly love which is slowly teaching the white hand to grasp the black, in this great struggle for the liberty of both the races." Her affinity for them was so great that she avowed she would have liked nothing better than "to leave nursing white bodies, and take some care for these black souls." Unlike other nurses who were decidedly cold to the "darkies," Alcott liked them "and found that any show of interest or friendliness brought out the better traits which live in the most degraded and forsaken of us all." In a city where "secesh principles" of the Confederacy "flourished even under Father Abraham [Lincoln]," where people regularly swore at black servants, and added a second "g" when saying "negro," Alcott chose an approach of grace, good humor, and kindness.

On New Year's Day 1863, Alcott heard the singing and shouts in the street as the former slaves greeted the arrival of the Emancipation Proclamation. They had enjoyed freedom since the previous spring, when Congress passed a law emancipating all blacks in the District of Columbia. Many of Washington's white residents objected, arguing that a change in the law would turn their city into "an asylum for free negroes," but the abolitionists in Congress prevailed. The new law, which took effect on April 16, 1862, compensated owners up to $300 for each slave. (A dealer from Baltimore fixed the price.) Many of Washington's household slaves, who had long lived and worked alongside free blacks, simply became paid servants for their former masters, but they now enjoyed the opportunity to find other jobs in the city or elsewhere in the northern states. Though the law also offered the newly emancipated an opportunity for colonization, most resented the proposal. They wanted to partake of liberty on American soil. "We can point to our Capitol," wrote the euphoric editor of the *Weekly Anglo-African*, "and say to all nations, 'IT IS FREE!'"

Emancipation in the District, and later in the nation, brought ever more escaped slaves from Maryland and the Confederate states to Washington. Many slipped across the District line from Prince George's County in Maryland, or formed quiet processions of men, women, and children carrying satchels filled with all their possessions as they trundled across the Long Bridge toward the capital and the promise of freedom. Many were field hands, untutored in city life, and far different from the enslaved house servants, stablehands, and workers who had resided in the capital for decades. By some estimates, as many as 10,000 had arrived by 1863. What to call these fugitives from Maryland and the Confederate states? What was their status? Led by Secretary of State William Seward, the government borrowed a Spanish word for smuggled or forbidden property and declared them to be "contrabands."

The designation was something of a legal fiction that had little to do with reality. Runaways escaping their masters had long been slipping into the District of Columbia from slave states, but after the war began they came in throngs. Washington knew not what to do. Though by 1861 federal law had prohibited the slave trade for more than a decade, slavery and the Fugitive Slave Law in the District remained the rule, and legally the new arrivals remained government property until they were emancipated in 1862. Abetted by the District marshal, who followed the law like a martinet, including the Black Codes, enterprising slave catchers roamed the streets looking for blacks to sell into the South. More often than not they took their quarry to the Old Capitol prison, where a shockingly corrupt superintendent who hated all blacks held them for money, and had them beaten with a flat board upon their backs and buttocks in a practice known as "cobbing."

Fortunately, in March 1862 a new military governor, General James S. Wadsworth, an abolitionist from Geneseo, New York, took charge. Wadsworth kept the fugitives in a group of houses adjacent to the prison known as Duff Green's Row, now the site of the Folger Library, and though a few still fell into the hands of slavers and were whisked back to the Confederacy, the general did much to ensure their safety. He created a contraband department to find a more lasting solution, naming the Reverend Danforth B. Nichols to head it. In the same month, a group of Washington's citizens formed a District of Columbia chapter of the Freedmen's Relief Association to support the new arrivals with "contributions of . . . clothing suitable for men and boys[,] . . . calicoes, shirtings, flannels, and garments for women, girls, and infants."

At first, Nichols and the Freedmen's Relief Association were able to ensure that those under their care had adequate clothing, a food ration, an unskilled job (furnished by the federal government at forty cents a day), rudimentary schooling (for the children), and shelter in Duff Green's Row, and later at Camp Barker, north of R Street between Twelfth and Thirteenth. In 1863 Nichols set up camps on abandoned farms in Alexandria and a "Freedmen's Village" on the grounds of the Custis Lee mansion at Arlington. (The property had belonged to Robert E. Lee, who acquired it through marriage to George Washington Custis's daughter Mary, but in one of the many paradoxes of the war, it was confiscated by the federal government in 1861.) That July the superintendent was able to report that he had provided "fresh air and pure water, and work on the soil to employ the people."

But as the tide of freedmen rose steadily, to about 40,000 by 1865, the government, the Freedmen's Association, and Rev. Nichols were overwhelmed. By the end of the war many of the former slaves were living in wretched conditions. Murder Bay—a marshy area that formed a right triangle with Fifteenth Street as a short side, B Street as a long one, and coming to a narrow point at Sixth Street—was typical: B Street (now Constitution Avenue) on the edge of the Washington Canal perpetually stank of sewage, and Fifteenth Street bordered the grounds of the White House. "Here crime, filth, and poverty seem to vie with each other in a career of degradation and death," the superintendent of Washington's Metropolitan Police reported at the end of the war. "Whole families, consisting of fathers, mothers, children, uncles, aunts . . . are crowded into mere apologies for shanties." The land on which the squalid buildings rested was so marshy that river freshets raised the water above the floorboards. Most of the rooms, the superintendent reported, were between six and eight feet square, with only a door to admit light. The rents for a room, however, were steep, "from five to eight dollars per month." Still, most freedmen clung to land within sight of the Capitol and the White House, believing, almost mystically, that those buildings alone guaranteed their freedom.

The increase in the black population and the changes that came to Washington's economic life brought out the worst in some whites. Unprovoked attacks became all too common events. For a while, until Congress threatened to revoke the charter, conductors on the new Washington and Georgetown Street Railroad line—the first in the capital to pull passenger cars on metal wheels over metal rails—refused to allow blacks to ride with white passengers. Of the $25,000 allotted for schools in 1864–1865, Washington's City Council gave black schools $628. But many white residents regarded the "problem" of freedmen in the capital as a national matter, and they resented paying even a small tax to ameliorate their condition.

Real anger among the white population erupted early in 1863 when the council, unable to fill its draft quotas with white men, decided it had no other recourse than to raise black regiments. Some worried that the freedmen might not be loyal; others that they would be "uppity." Prudently, training for the new recruits went forward on Analostan (now Roosevelt) Island, where they could drill knowing that the Potomac's waters separated them from gratuitous attacks. A year later, draft brokers began offering as much as $150 to have a "colored" recruit take a white's place. By April 1865, 3,269 black men from the District of Columbia had served the Union cause.

DURING HIS STAY in Washington, Walt Whitman developed a profound and mystical connection with Abraham Lincoln. "I see the President almost every day, as I happen to live where he passes to or from his lodgings out of town," he wrote. Usually riding on horseback, dressed in black ("somewhat rusty and dusty," said Whitman) with his silk plug hat atop his head, Lincoln took Vermont Avenue to and from the Soldiers' Home, his respite from Washington's heat, about three miles north of the White House. "I see very plainly ABRAHAM LINCOLN'S dark brown face, with the deep cut lines, the eyes, &c., always to me with a deep latent sadness in the expression," wrote the poet. "We have got so that we always exchange bows, and very cordial ones." The expression caught Whitman's imagination. Earlier in the summer, when Lincoln and his wife passed in a barouche, he wrote: "I saw the President in the face fully, as they were moving slow, and his look, though abstracted, happen'd to be directed steadily in my eye. He bow'd and smiled, but far beneath his smile I noticed well the expression I have alluded to. None of the artists or pictures have caught the deep, though subtle and indirect expression of this man's face. There is something else there. One of the great portrait painters of two or three centuries ago is needed."

But it was more than a mere exchange of greetings that connected Lincoln with Whitman. Each in his own way embodied the broad potential he saw for America in the nineteenth century. Lincoln, who saved the Union and bound it with iron; Whitman, who chanted as a poet and prophet:

> *Lo, soul! seest thou not God's purpose from the first?*
> *The earth to be spann'd, connected by network,*
> *The races, neighbors, to marry and be given in marriage,*
> *The oceans to be cross'd, the distant brought near,*
> *The lands to be welded together.*

ON A MID-AUGUST evening in 1864, Private John W. Nichols, Company K, 105th Pennsylvania Volunteers, was standing guard outside the Soldiers' Home when he heard the report of a rifle, which was followed a few moments later by the arrival of Abraham Lincoln without his hat. A shot had spooked his horse, the president said, and so had "jerked his hat" from his head. Thinking "the affair rather strange," Nichols remembered several decades later, he and a corporal went to investigate. "At the intersection of the driveway and the main road," said Nichols, "we found the president's hat—a plain silk one—and . . . discovered a bullet hole through the crown." When Nichols returned the hat to the president the next day, Lincoln said he "wanted the matter kept quiet."

Threats of violence swirled about Lincoln throughout his presidency, especially toward the close of the war in 1864; indeed, the imminent defeat of the Confederacy only stiffened the bitterness of Confederate sympathizers in the capital, especially the Copperheads, the nickname given to northern congressmen opposed to the Civil War and Lincoln. About a month after the attempt that destroyed his hat, another Confederate group hatched a plan to kidnap Lincoln as he arrived at the Soldiers' Home, and hold him for ransom in Richmond. Before spiriting him off to Richmond, the men thought they might hide him in the cellar of John Van Ness's house. It now belonged to a man who had used it as a slave pen before the war. On the appointed night, however, the plotters found their quarry surrounded by a military guard.

A steady flow of letters with threats and warnings arrived at the White House almost daily, but Lincoln ordered his secretaries to throw most of them away, secreting just a few in a pigeonhole of his desk. To be isolated behind a wall of saber-armed guards was the way of emperors, not presidents, Lincoln believed. Such threats were the price of leading a democratic republic.

The president remained willfully and serenely oblivious to danger. He strolled alone about the White House grounds late at night, walked unaccompanied between his office and the War Department, and frequently went to plays with Mary Lincoln and their friends, but hardly ever with a guard. When Jubal Early's Confederate troops made a last, vain effort to capture the Capitol in July 1864, Lincoln looked directly across at the enemy from the parapet of Fort Stevens. A surgeon standing beside him fell to Confederate fire, but the president remained unmoved. Oliver Wendell Holmes, a young captain from Massachusetts who was the son of one of Lincoln's favorite poets, and who would one day be a justice on the Supreme Court, reportedly shouted, "Get down, you fool!" But it took the commanding officer's threat to "remove him forcibly" before Lincoln grudgingly agreed to a "compromise" of "sitting behind the parapet instead of standing upon it."

Still, dreams affrighted him. If we are to believe Ward Hill Lamon, the president's bodyguard, in the spring of 1865 Lincoln recalled a recent dream he had had after a late night awaiting dispatches from the front. He remembered hearing "subdued sobs, as if a number of people were weeping," and wandering through the White House, where "every object was familiar to me." On entering the East Room, he "met with a sickening surprise, . . . a catafalque, on which rested a corpse wrapped in funeral vestments." "Who is dead in the White House?" he asked. "The President," was the reply. "He was killed by an assassin." Lincoln awoke and slept no more that night.

At 9:30 on Tuesday morning, April 18, 1865, thousands of mourners began passing through the East Room of the White House. They mounted the step of the catafalque and stared for approximately one second each into the open walnut coffin that held the remains of Abraham Lincoln.

THROUGHOUT THE CIVIL War, architect Thomas U. Walter stuck to the business of erecting the cast-iron dome over the Capitol. Although the country was out of money and could not pay the laborers, the company erecting the dome felt it had no choice but to continue. Walter had no salary, but he never stopped. Congress didn't approve more funds until mid-April 1862. The following year, as the exterior of the dome neared completion, Constantino Brumidi began the gigantic fresco of the apotheosis of George Washington for its interior. On December 3, as the head and cap of the cast-iron Statue of Freedom was bolted into place, a battery of artillery fired thirty-five rounds (one for each state) to celebrate the dome's completion.

Walter stayed on to oversee the work that remained and produced designs to extend the east front of the building. (Construction of that addition would wait for nearly a century.) The death of Abraham Lincoln brought a new president, Andrew Johnson of Tennessee, and a new secretary of the interior, James Harlan. Harlan promptly declared he would "weed out the needless and worthless material," and so, regarding the office of architect of the Capitol as unnecessary, he transferred all public works to the commissioner of public buildings, a man with no training in architecture but great pretensions. At noon on June 1, 1865, Thomas U. Walter boarded a train for Philadelphia. But his legacy, the brilliantly transformed US Capitol, remained.

ABRAHAM LINCOLN LAY in a public tomb at Oak Ridge Cemetery in Springfield, Illinois; John Wilkes Booth lay in a secret hole hastily dug in the subbasement beneath the arsenal on Greenleaf's Point; Jefferson Davis lay shackled in a damp cell at Fort Monroe on the Chesapeake.

By the end of May, after four years of fratricidal conflict and fiery trial, the end of the war was at hand.

In Washington, the funeral bunting came down from the White House. A large covered stage capable of holding Andrew Johnson, General Ulysses S. Grant, cabinet members, and scores of other dignitaries stood before the mansion's North Portico. On Pennsylvania Avenue, workers had erected stands to accommodate the members of Congress, the Supreme Court, various state delegations, and disabled soldiers. For days trains had brought thousands from the North to witness the last and greatest event of the Civil War, a two-day parade from the Capitol down Pennsylvania Avenue and past the White House. The Grand Army of the Potomac that had defended Washington and laid siege to Virginia would march on the first day; General William Tecumseh Sherman's Army of the West that had captured the Mississippi and stormed its way east to the sea would march on the second.

One who came from Boston for the spectacle was twenty-two-year-old Marian Hooper. Known as "Clover," she had devoted much of her time during the war preparing bandages for the Sanitary Commission. Her cousins had fought in the war; one of them was Robert Gould Shaw, who had died at Fort Wagner in South Carolina with the all-black regiment he had raised. She was also well connected with Washington, as her uncle was a representative from Massachusetts and the father-in-law of Charles Sumner. When Clover learned of the grand march, she vowed to attend.

At daybreak on Tuesday, May 23, "the most perfect day I ever saw," wrote Clover, all was ready. On East Capitol Street, Maryland Avenue, and New Jersey Avenue, the Grand Army troops mustered by the thousands for one last time before filing onto Pennsylvania Avenue. Endless rows of men in blue uniforms and flat-topped kepis, 80,000 in all, marched sixty abreast, curb to curb, down the avenue. Crowds filled the sidewalks and every window and roof, cheering and tossing garlands of spring flowers upon the men. They roared when General George Armstrong Custer passed, hatless, with, as Clover Hooper reported, "long golden curls . . . streaming in the wind." The soldiers waved battle-scarred flags while the bands played tunes that had carried them through the fight. Spectators by the thousands joined to sing the chorus of "The Battle Cry of Freedom," the soldiers' favorite song, and the one that carried Lincoln through his reelection campaign of 1864:

The Union forever, Hurrah! boys, hurrah!
Down with the traitors, Up with the stars;
While we rally round the flag, boys,
Rally once again, Shouting the battle cry of Freedom.

These were the men who had defended the capital, who had tended "the watch-fires of a hundred circling camps" bearing patriotic names such as Slocum and Meigs, Bunker Hill and Saratoga, Washington and Lincoln. Some of the soldiers' fiercest battles had taken place less than a hundred miles from where they now marched. They had lost 12,000 brothers on a single September day at Antietam, and another 17,000 on three sweltering July days at Gettysburg; they had endured humiliations at Bull Run and Ball's Bluff; and that spring they had stood with Grant in triumph at Appomattox Court House.

On they streamed for six hours, the "lines eighteen or twenty miles long," Clover Hooper estimated, "their colors telling their sad history. Some regiments with nothing but a bare pole, a little bit of rag only, hanging a few inches, to show where their flag had been. Others had been Stars and Stripes, with one or two stripes hanging, all the rest shot away. It was a strange feeling to be so intensely happy and triumphant, and yet to feel like crying."

The following day was Sherman's moment. The scourge of Georgia and South Carolina, accompanied by Oliver Otis Howard, commander of the Army of the Tennessee, Sherman led the parade with thousands of men and boys carrying battle flags inscribed with the names of victories—Donelson and Shiloh, Vicksburg and Chickamauga, Atlanta and Savannah. Their bands played a new tune inspired by their leader's great victory, each verse punctuated with its stirring chorus:

Hurrah! Hurrah! we bring the jubilee!
Hurrah! Hurrah! the flag that makes you free!
So we sang the chorus from Atlanta to the sea
While we were marching through Georgia.

These were America's frontiersmen, who had lived their lives aggressively taming the land beyond the Alleghenies, "who in physique and marching, surpass decidedly the Potomac Army," Hooper noted. They favored billowing shirts and loose-fitting pants instead of heavy uniforms. On this their last march they took the same long strides that had carried them across half the continent. And they brought the jubilee, too—emancipated slaves with picks and shovels on their shoulders, who followed Sherman and his men after he had set them free, and followed him still. They made "a very queer sight to see" for the easterners, one observer wrote. "The horses mules and jacks were ridden by men and boys of all sizes, colors, and complexions." Despised in Georgia and South Carolina, these men and their jubilee marched as heroes in Washington.

In a few days, most of the men would return to farms, villages, and cities across the land to take up their lives with their sweethearts, wives, and children, the families they had not seen in months or years. The war, as Oliver Wendell Holmes later said, had touched their hearts with fire. But the conflict touched them in another way, too. They had learned that the nation was something more than a collection of states—"a sentiment," as Henry Adams observed. Now the states had joined into a singular union, *the* United States, with a national capital, Washington, DC.

CHAPTER 7

The Making of an Undemocratic City

The people of the United States owe a peculiar duty to Washington and to the people of Washington. They are bound to give the capital a good government, because they have taken away from it the right to govern itself.

—Judson Welliver, 1908

The idea proved to be fleeting, but it took hold shortly after the Civil War, and by the end of the 1860s it had grown ever more insistent. Washington was beyond saving. A fresh start west of the Alleghenies would signify the change from, in the words of one editorial writer, the "Old Government" that was confined to "the narrow slope of the Atlantic." The nation was now the "New Republic" blooming in the "great field of the west." Unencumbered by restraints of the past, representatives and senators would be better able to lead the "new" America to unrivaled greatness and prosperity. "I fancy," wrote a reporter for Horace Greeley's *New York Tribune* in 1867, "it will not be many generations before the National Capital will be removed beyond the Mississippi."

Logan Uriah Reavis, a newspaper editor, was certainly the most insistent of those advocating the relocation of the capital, but he was hardly alone. Greeley, who advised Civil War veterans to "go West and grow up with the country," wanted the capital to do the same, as did the editor of the *Chicago Tribune*. Reavis even held a "national" convention in St. Louis to champion his city. Nor did these proponents of change confine their proposal merely to a new venue for the capital. The White House, the Treasury, the Capitol—every stone, timber, and brick—could be dismantled and reassembled near St. Louis on a bluff overlooking "the great Father of Waters," the Mississippi, Reavis said.

The conditions of Washington itself strengthened the case to move the capital. Though never a major battleground, Washington was very much a war-torn city. It suffered the ravages of the hundreds of thousands of federal troops who encamped in hastily built shelters; patronized its gambling dens, saloons, and bawdy houses; and filled more than 50,000 hospital beds. The tens of thousands of newly freed and escaped former slaves who turned to the capital as a refuge only added to the city's troubles. And the exodus of many of its residents for the South and Europe left an even greater vacuum of civic leadership.

After April, 1865, the city seemed to slip further into economic and physical decline. Hotels, boardinghouses, and restaurants no longer could rely upon the steady stream of visitors, financiers, manufacturers, and military men. Many of the workers who had packed the Navy Yard, military depots, and government offices had left with the departing soldiers. Merchants and suppliers who had become used to their bounty found themselves facing economic collapse. The prices of many goods and housing were exorbitant; crime and disorder increased, especially as military patrols left the city; many freedmen, as blacks were still called, continued to live in squalor, on the fringe of society, and without jobs; and services that city dwellers in the North took for granted—paved and lighted streets, running water, sewers, and some attention to public health—remained primitive. As one dyspeptic visitor during the war noted, Washington "was built for a city of the future, and the future has not yet been realized." In the war's aftermath the future seemed further off than ever.

Many of the reasons for Washington's crude and unfinished state lay in more than six decades of congressional inaction and neglect. Over the years, most members of Congress had been loath to spend money for streets, transportation, lighting, and sewers, much less for schools and police, for a city they regarded as their encampment for the fall and winter months. For them the very idea of a capital occupying neutral ground on the banks of the Potomac was something of an anomaly, a curiosity of the Constitution to be tolerated during the months the houses were in session and to be forgotten when they were in recess. As a general rule, the presidents who had succeeded George Washington had taken little interest in the city, and, as in the case of Andrew Jackson's decision to locate the Treasury Building in the middle of Pennsylvania Avenue, had paid little or no attention to the original plan.

But merely broaching the subject of removal helped to galvanize Washington's leaders into action. Not since the British burned the city in 1814 had they been so fearful that the federal government might leave the Potomac. Residents who had lived in the city for at least two decades formed the Oldest Inhabitants Association, many clinging to the hope of perpetuating their past heritage and reviving their antebellum society. Businessmen hastily created the city's first board of trade. Led by George Riggs, the group returned to George Washington's original dream of making the capital a commercial center. They negotiated with the Baltimore and Potomac Railroad for favorable passenger and shipping rates and to improve connections between the city and the South. Although they would regret the agreement before the end of the century—it called for tracks to bisect the Mall at Sixth Street, and a huge, Victorian-Gothic station on the site of the present-day National Gallery of Art—at the time city leaders believed it would bring economic prosperity.

After March 4, 1869, the capital's staunchest ally, Ulysses S. Grant, lived in the White House. When he first visited the city in 1852, Grant had reported to his wife his disappointment "in the appearance of things. . . . The place seems small and scattering and the character of the buildings poor." Most stood in stark contrast to the public ones, which were "ornamental" and stood on lots that were "highly improved." The intervening eighteen years and the war had brought few improvements. Although Grant had lived in St. Louis before the Civil War, he had no thought of moving the seat of government there, or to any other place in the Midwest. In 1870, when his former officer, Representative John A. Logan from Illinois, proposed his home state as the best place for the government, Grant suggested he would veto any bill for removal. "It has been my desire," the president told a group of visiting firemen in 1870, "to see this great national capital built up in a manner worthy of a great and growing republic like ours." A letter to Grant from Reavis insisting "that the immediate removal of the National Capital is demanded" went unanswered.

Grant understood perhaps better than most that the Civil War and its aftermath had changed the city in ways that even Congress could not ignore. In just four years the federal government had garnered more power than ever before. For better or worse, Washington had become the true seat of empire. Nowhere was this more evident than in the Department of Agriculture. Before the war, southerners had maintained that there was no need for such a department, and that individual states could best look after their own interests. Lincoln and the Republican-controlled Congress thought otherwise and in 1862 established what the president called the "the people's department." The Agriculture Department grew steadily during the war, and dramatically afterward. A cadre of botanists, entomologists, chemists—proto bureaucrats all—now worked in the department's Washington offices promoting the cultivation of silk and cotton, tobacco and sugar, even tea. The commissioner, a close friend of the Lincolns, whom many thought a corrupt and foolish man, established an experimental farm on the Mall.

President Grant pushed for more public buildings. "The business of the government required several new department structures," a group of Washington's leaders reported after meeting with the president in January 1870, as "many of the structures now rented and occupied by the government were unsuitable." A year later Congress voted to erect a huge new building adjacent to the White House for the Departments of State, War, and Navy. Designed by Alfred B. Mullett, the federal government's supervising architect, it was a baroque, Second Empire–inspired mass of granite, slate, and cast iron spread over four floors and fifteen acres, with eight enormous staircases and two miles of black and white marble corridors. Its cost: $10 million, but when completed in 1888, it was the largest office building in the capital. Its presence underscored the fact that the seat of government would remain where it had been since December 1800.

ITS PLACE ON the Potomac secure, Washington would become the political center of the "Gilded Age," the name Mark Twain and Charles Dudley Warner gave to the tide of corruption that was sweeping through the nation's financial, political, and social life. It was an "era of incredible rottenness," Twain wrote a friend, "not Democratic, . . . not Republican, it is *national*."

The rottenness that flourished after the Civil War made Americans cynical about their democracy. They watched as a few amassed vast fortunes—often illegally—and spent their new wealth in extravagant and vulgar ways, as the attempt to control the price of gold by financial buccaneers Jay Gould and Jim Fisk caused a financial panic that ruined many small merchants. They learned that the votes of many senators and representatives could be bought; that Massachusetts Congressman Oakes Ames bribed his colleagues with virtually free stock in the Union Pacific Railroad that he also ran; that federal officials and President Grant's private secretary had conspired with whiskey distillers in the Midwest to defraud the government of millions of dollars. And Americans' cynicism grew even deeper when, in the presidential election of 1876, Congress ignored the popular vote for Democrat Samuel J. Tilden in favor of the Republican Rutherford B. Hayes, who had pledged to end Reconstruction and federal control of the states of the former Confederacy, and to appoint a southerner to his cabinet. Americans took to calling him "Rutherfraud."

Aside from the fact that many of these national scandals were born in Washington's executive offices and legislative chambers, the city itself shared with the nation the turbulence of Reconstruction and its aftermath. The capital had its own share of fiscal schemers, some of whom profited handsomely from the liberal amounts of money that were spread throughout the city. But there was more to Washington than rich arrivistes and venal maneuverers. There were unwavering Radical Republicans who wished to continue harsh reconstruction policies in the South and to expand civil rights for blacks; returning Confederate sympathizers; newly manumitted freemen; and ordinary citizens. Each group influenced the shaping of the capital in the years after the Civil War.

AT WEST POINT, his fellow cadets called him "The Christian Soldier." He joined a Bible class, which earned him ridicule from northerners; he declared himself for abolition, which brought him contempt from southerners; and he renounced strong drink and profanity, which made him the mockery of all. Still, Oliver Otis Howard graduated fourth in the class of 1854 and continued to read his Bible every night. Like so many New Englanders of the second quarter of the nineteenth century whose characters were formed in the crucible of Christianity and abolitionism, Howard believed in the power of God to reveal and support a just cause. "He was always taken up with Sunday Schools and the temperance cause," said fellow Union general Fighting Joe Hooker, whose capacity for drinking, swearing, and loose women was so great that wags in the Civil War named the fifty saloons and one hundred bawdy houses of Washington's Murder Bay that he frequented with his men "Hooker's Division." "If he was not born in petticoats," Hooker said of Howard, "he ought to have been, and ought to wear them."

Petticoats, temperance, the Bible, and his sanctimonious priggishness notwithstanding, Howard attended to his duties as an officer, followed the orders of his superiors, and, always, showed loyalty to the nation. In the Civil War he fought gallantly, if not always successfully, at the major battles—Bull Run, Chancellorsville, and Gettysburg among them. He lost his right arm to a Minié ball at the Battle of Seven Pines, and he commanded the Army of the Tennessee on General Sherman's March to the Sea. It was on Sherman's devastating march that General Howard asserted his moral authority among his men, imploring them not to visit even more suffering upon the vanquished civilians by committing assault or plunder. Howard's record as a commander and his reputation as "The Christian Soldier" commended him to Abraham Lincoln. Just before Lincoln was assassinated, he told his secretary of war that Howard should head the newly created Bureau of Refugees, Freedmen, and Abandoned Lands, popularly called the "Freedmen's Bureau," whose task was to assimilate the nation's 4 million newly freed blacks into American life.

Sherman warned Howard that he was undertaking "Hercules' task." The job was made all the harder by President Andrew Johnson's steady efforts to undermine the Freedmen's Bureau and his repeated attempts to eviscerate Reconstruction. In 1866, Congress overrode his veto of legislation continuing the bureau, as well as his veto of the Civil Rights Act that awarded blacks full citizenship in the United States. (The president was opposed to the Fourteenth Amendment to the Constitution, but was powerless to stop it from becoming law.) Each of the states that Johnson restored to the Union instituted harsh Black Codes that served to return the freed slaves to social servility and economic bondage. "This is a country for white men," he wrote to the governor of Missouri shortly after entering the White House, "and by God, as long as I am President, it shall be a government for white men." Despite the warning from his friend Sherman, and Johnson's opposition to any advancement of freedmen, Howard remained optimistic.

The city of Washington, where 40,000 freedmen lived, offered Howard a chance to translate his ideals into action. The new arrivals sought a safe refuge and a place where they might lead a decent life. He realized that to survive and thrive in their newfound world of freedom, these new arrivals would need shelter, jobs, and education. Only then would they become self-sufficient. Few were prepared for the challenges that came with their liberation, so their welfare fell largely upon his shoulders. A fellow general remembered Howard telling him that "the Creator had placed him on earth to be the Moses to the Negro."

Adequate shelter and sufficient jobs proved difficult to come by in the District of Columbia. Howard found the newly freed fearful that any change might mean a return to servitude. Although one Freedmen's Bureau agent found jobs for 7,000 blacks tilling fields on farms in the North, Howard had difficulty persuading them to move to a colder climate farther from the security of friends and family. Some even refused to move across the District line. They preferred to huddle in shockingly overcrowded and squalid areas of the city like the infamous Murder Bay, or the group of hovels dubbed "Adams shanties" east of the Capitol, or, increasingly, in the service alleys that snaked behind many of the city's streets. The few jobs that the army had provided contrabands in the wartime capital disappeared. It was a human catastrophe in the making; one estimate placed the death toll of freedmen between January 1862 and January 1866 at 33 percent.

A farm across the Eastern Branch in the southeast portion of the District of Columbia (the east side of George Washington's original diamond), generally known today as Anacostia, gave Howard an opportunity to realize one of his cherished hopes of making blacks landowners. He believed that owning property would make blacks truly free, and he thought that the law establishing the Freedmen's Bureau gave him the power to "set apart" lands confiscated from the Confederates "for the use of loyal refugees and freedmen." But Andrew Johnson pardoned the southern landowners, restored their properties, and ordered the bureau to return the land. Thwarted though he was in the former Confederacy, Howard saw a way of realizing his dream in 1867 across the Eastern Branch.

Some creative accounting on the bureau's part helped him to succeed. With $52,000 of the bureau's funds that he channeled through three freedmen's schools in the District, he purchased the entire 375 acres of the Barry Farm, one of the largest tracts in the southeast. After army surveyors mapped the land, and paid free blacks $1.25 a day to cut down the trees and build roads, Howard then sold one-acre lots on credit for $125 or $300, each with enough wood to build a house. Men and women, many with children, purchased the land, which came with a two-year mortgage. A number of the men clearing the land and building the roads had fifty cents of each day's wages placed in a savings account to put toward their own purchase. Enough lots had sold by the end of the decade for Howard to return the modest profits from his venture to the freedmen's schools.

Howard had created an industrious and close-knit black community. Many residents worked at a job in the city by day and built their house long into the night. The men translated the skills they had acquired in slavery into jobs as farmworkers, blacksmiths, cooks, and carpenters. Some worked nearby at St. Elizabeth's Hospital, or across the river at the Navy Yard. The women took in laundry, worked as seamstresses, and grew flowers and produce to sell at the city's markets. Among the first to locate at Barry Farm was a black minister, who established a Baptist church. The Freedmen's Bureau and the residents created the Good Hope School in Anacostia and retained a minister from Bangor, Maine, to be the teacher-principal. By the end of the year, forty-nine students were struggling to learn in a twelve-by-fourteen-foot room. The number increased the next year to fifty-two, of whom thirteen were learning the alphabet while the rest were reading and spelling. In 1867, the bureau established another school at Barry Farm and named it after Howard. Soon the principal could report that the classes were filled. In addition, the bureau established night schools for adults, while blacks themselves opened their own schools and filled them with teachers recommended by the bureau. Barry Farm succeeded because it demonstrated that with modest assistance, freedmen could own and maintain land, acquire an education, and participate in the larger community of Washington.

Providing a university primarily for blacks proved a greater and more enduring triumph for Howard. At the time, many whites, both South and North, viewed freedmen as ineducable; the idea of providing them with training in the humanities as well as the professions of law, medicine, teaching, and theology seemed a fool's errand. Yet Howard and some fellow members of Washington's First Congregational Church understood that black education must take place at all levels. In March 1867 they received a charter from Congress to establish "a college for the instruction of youth in the liberal arts and sciences." As was the case in the recently created federal land-grant universities, women were to be as welcome as men. Though it was not specifically stated, most understood that the college was created primarily for the instruction of blacks. At the insistence of the incorporators, and over the objections of the commissioner of the Freedmen's Bureau, the new institution would be named Howard University.

Charter in hand, Oliver Otis Howard drew upon all of the available resources of the Freedmen's Bureau for funding. Bold moves and more creative financing through an exceedingly liberal interpretation of the law were the standard. That spring he purchased a 150-acre farm on land between Seventh and Fourth streets NW for about $150,000, and made the $30,000 down payment with money he drew from a refugees and freedmen's fund that he controlled within the bureau. Freedmen's Bureau funds covered the costs of the university's first buildings—the main academic building, with thirty-two classrooms and a library; a one-hundred-room dormitory for women, a medical building, and a hospital. For a time, Howard even moved the Freedmen's Bureau into the main academic building and had the government pay rent to the university. The board of the university financed the rest of its payment for the farm through sales of building lots. With $1,000 of his own money, Howard purchased a lot overlooking the fledging campus and built a handsome three-story house with a graceful porch, fashionable mansard roof, and dormer windows, and topped at the corner by a modest tower. Other faculty and black families moved to houses just south of the university's campus in an area that came to be known as Howard Town.

It was clear that Howard had a deeper commitment to the welfare of blacks than most in Congress. Even those in the Congregational Church, for whom abolition was no longer a proposition but a reality, worried about the prospect of commingling with blacks. Howard harbored no such anxieties. His position as an army general and commissioner of the Freedmen's Bureau fitted him well for the presidency of the university.

Howard's work as president of the university was tireless. With $25,000 that he raised from a Hartford philanthropist, he built a dormitory for male students. He also raised money for what he hoped would be a $300,000 endowment, pledging $10,000 of his own money to create a professorship of law. He even asked Queen Victoria and Fighting Joe Hooker to endow professorships. They declined.

His interest in students was paternal. No doubt harkening back to his days at West Point, and to instill discipline among the males in the dormitory, the general awakened them with reveille, marched them to classes, and instituted the practice of saluting professors whenever they were encountered. Everyone attended morning chapel, which Howard led, followed by an hour of Bible recitation. To help his students meet their tuition bills, he set out to employ them in any way possible. No doubt with thoughts of Barry Farm, he hired some to grade the land and build roads for the new campus; others he put to work raising crops and selling the produce. No scheme seemed too outlandish. For a while he even employed students to manufacture a contraption called a "convertible lounge bed," and planned to build a shoe factory and a paper mill. Fortunately these schemes came to nothing.

While he would do almost anything to enable his students to learn, Howard resisted all calls to lower the standards. This meant that in the beginning the collegiate department was small, but the preparatory department, where professors taught the requisite Greek and Latin courses necessary for college work, was much larger. And Howard took great pride in the impressive achievements of his students, displaying their accomplishments to all visitors. Each success helped to prove the capabilities of blacks—as he put it, "the dark color of skin does not of itself unfavorably affect the intellect."

Howard's enthusiasm for the university and the welfare of its students sometimes blinded him to the impracticality and even the look of impropriety of some of his ventures. When a New York inventor offered the university exclusive rights to use his patented machinery that made building blocks of lime and sand, Howard thought the proposal a positive boon. Students would manufacture the blocks for his house and other buildings on the campus, and after they were finished, the university might sell the blocks to other builders in Washington. He made an enthusiastic $10,000 investment of his own money in the scheme, encouraged others in the Freedmen's Bureau to do the same, and allowed his name to be linked to the company's. But the American Building Block Company, as it was called, proved to be deficient, something Howard and others learned when two walls of the university's new hospital collapsed.

It was the American Building Block Company and similar schemes, his sleight of hand with the Freedmen's Bureau's finances, and the simpatico relationship between the bureau and the university that left Oliver Otis Howard vulnerable to attack. Charges of his malfeasance were continual, and congressional investigations of his purported misconduct frequent. These would continue far past the shuttering of the Freedmen's Bureau in 1872, when Howard managed to transfer about $525,000 to the university. Democrats and Copperheads in Congress, smarting over the defeat of the Confederacy and the harshness of Reconstruction, forced a Court of Inquiry, but after forty days of deliberations it concluded that under Howard's leadership, "the Freedmen's Bureau has triumphed; civilization has received a new impulse, and friends of humanity may well rejoice." The secretary of war brought the general before a military court, but the judges exonerated him fully, and Congress later impeached the secretary for taking bribes. Private parties with one complaint or another filed civil suits against Howard. It was not until 1880 that the last trial ended. None found him guilty.

By then, Howard was long gone from the university he had helped to found and had then led until Christmas Day 1874. Throughout his time in Washington he had maintained his ideals and commitment to the welfare of blacks. "He was sympathetic and humane, and tried with endless application and desperate sacrifice to do a hard, thankless duty," wrote W. E. B. Du Bois. To be sure, Oliver Otis Howard was flawed, "neither a great administrator nor a great man," but, Du Bois concluded, "he was a good man."

MANY MEMBERS OF Congress, especially its Radicals, saw the District, over which it exercised full control, as the place where they might impose their vision of a new society in which racial equality prevailed. They had done so in 1862, when they enacted the emancipation proclamation for the District nine months before Lincoln's became the law for the nation. Now they thought that by extending suffrage to black males in the capital they would set the standard for the states to follow. But proposals for suffrage for blacks in the District raised the ire of white Washingtonians. When the wives of Republican legislators sought a hall where they could have Frederick Douglass deliver a speech on the subject, no one would rent them one. (Ultimately, they found a venue at the First Presbyterian Church.) The City Council passed a resolution that claimed the superiority of the white race, adding that "not . . . one in a hundred [blacks] can read or write," that granting suffrage to women was surely preferable, and that working men were hostile because blacks were vying for scarce jobs. A council-sponsored referendum on the question found just 35 voters were in favor of granting blacks the right to vote and 6,591 opposed. Ignoring the objections of white citizens, Congress maintained that the District of Columbia was the "seat of the government" of the United States, and in December 1866 passed a bill granting manhood suffrage without a literacy requirement. Andrew Johnson objected, but the legislators quickly overrode his veto to make suffrage for the District's black men the law.

In 1868, Washington's blacks and whites elected, by a whisper-thin margin, Sayles J. Bowen to be their mayor. Bowen espoused suffrage, desegregation of the school system, and a public works program that would create fifteen miles of new sidewalks and four miles of sewers. He lasted until 1870, when he was voted out by white residents who charged that he had increased the city's indebtedness by a third, all the while favoring ignorant blacks for public works projects that achieved little. Bowen's successor, Matthew Gault Emery, was a master stonemason who had worked on many of the city's public buildings, including the Capitol, the White House, and the Treasury; in 1848, he had dressed and laid the cornerstone for the as yet unfinished Washington Monument. But in the eyes of many citizens, as well as members of Congress who complained of the city's conditions, Emery proved to be inept.

In the postbellum period, Washingtonians and members of Congress began to rethink the way the District of Columbia was governed. Their concerns were long overdue, for since 1800, the spasmodic development of municipal structures had produced a continual muddle. In the waning hours of John Adams's administration, the Federalist-controlled Congress divided the District into Washington County for the land on the Maryland side of the Potomac that wasn't a part of Washington City or Georgetown, and Alexandria County for the land on the Virginia side. Although Congress gave the city a charter for limited home rule in 1802, the District always had been subject to its whims. One such impulse resulted in the retrocession of Alexandria in 1846. After the Civil War, however, as Congress had to address ever more complex issues in the nation, it had little time for the affairs of the District. "There are so many public measures pressing upon the attention of Senators and Representatives," admitted the head of the Senate's committee on the District, Hannibal Hamlin of Maine, "that they are utterly incompetent or do not have the time to devote the attention to the affairs of the District of Columbia which the District requires and demands."

In 1871, Congress decided to make the District of Columbia into a territory, as it had done with so much of the land in the nation's western expansion. It was usual for residents of the territories to elect a governor and representatives to a bicameral legislature, as well as a single nonvoting delegate to Congress, and such was the proposed bill for the District. But in a sausage-like approval process, legislators decided to strip Washington's residents of the limited self-government they had enjoyed since 1802. The resulting Organic Act, as it was called, gave the president the power to appoint a governor, a seventeen-member council, a Board of Health, and a Board of Public Works; the citizens still enjoyed universal suffrage, but could elect only a house of delegates and a nonvoting delegate to the House of Representatives. The boards would help Washington become a modern city, or so Congress hoped, but the legislation left the question of payment for improvements unresolved.

Still, the new territory did unite Georgetown, Washington City, and Washington County, which was cause for celebration. When President Ulysses Grant signed the bill on February 21, 1871, all Washington celebrated with a three-day carnival on the newly paved Pennsylvania Avenue. Schoolchildren enjoyed a holiday; foot, horse, carriage, and dog-cart races took place by day; fireworks blazed in the evenings; and, as Shrove Tuesday fell in the middle of the celebration, the revelers held an elaborate masquerade. They also approved the District's new corporate seal depicting Lady Columbia placing a wreath at a statue of George Washington; above the pair was the motto, "Justitia Omnibus." Surely a new and more prosperous era was dawning for the capital.

Soon a local plumber-turned-politician would transform the city and in the process stretch the meaning of "Justice for All." Alexander Robey Shepherd understood the capital's customs, manners, and idiosyncrasies, and he used his great store of energy and connections to change the face of Washington into that of a modern city. A civic booster to the core, Shepherd believed he could make Washington into the city L'Enfant had intended; to do so he would place the end above the means whenever necessary to achieve his goals. Business had been his forte ever since his father, a slaveholding lumber dealer of moderate means, had died in 1845, leaving a widow and seven children. To help support his mother and six younger siblings, Shepherd had apprenticed himself with Washington's leading gas and plumbing contractor, who, even in a city with primitive water, sewage, and gas systems, had a thriving business.

By the onset of the Civil War, Shepherd was flourishing. Six feet four inches, 225 pounds, possessed of titanic strength, he cut an imposing figure in the early defense of the city after Lincoln's inauguration. After his three-month enlistment with the federal militia in 1861, which conveniently ended before the first Battle of Bull Run, Shepherd turned his attention to business, to his new wife, and to politics. He helped finance construction of the Raleigh Hotel on Pennsylvania Avenue and invested in the Metropolitan Railroad Company, the city's second horsecar enterprise; he bought a country house, and fathered ten children. In 1861 he made his formal entry into Washington's politics, serving first on Washington's Board of Aldermen and then, at the age of twenty-six, as president of its City Council. His business ventures in the capital were numerous: real estate, especially land along train lines; paving and stone companies; insurance; and bank directorships. By 1870 Shepherd had emerged as the leader of an energetic fresh wave of young Republicans who promised a new order for the city.

Shepherd and his associates set out to break the firm grip that the older, southern-oriented, socially conservative, and far wealthier generation had exercised over the city until the Civil War. In response to Shepherd and the newcomers, these deep-rooted residents formed a Citizens Executive Committee, boasted of their wealth and tax support, and advocated maintaining the status quo. To them, the new group was simply a board of interlopers out for their own gain, men who had no lasting interest in the capital.

For their part Shepherd and his followers pointed to the basic conditions of the city as the primary reason for change. The Civil War might have made Washington the capital of a newly united nation, but four years of military occupation had rent its physical fabric and assaulted its spirit. Washington's population had whipsawed from 60,000 in 1860 to as many as 140,000 in 1865, before leveling off at 100,000 at the end of the decade. Its citizens had witnessed legions of escaped slaves, and later freedmen, living in squalid shanties and hovels and taxing the city's meager resources. They had seen the city's canal, which an earlier generation heralded as the key to its commercial success, become ever more clogged with trash, sewage, and dead animals. Each time citizens pumped water, they were reminded that much of their water system was still incomplete. Each time they ventured from their houses, they were reminded that their streets and avenues, assaulted over the war years by countless thousands of horses' hooves, ambulances, and army wagons, remained rutted and unpaved. With every shower of rain they saw scores of young black men carrying boards to place in the muddy streets so that pedestrians, "for a consideration," might cross; and with every spring freshet they saw the lowlands south of Pennsylvania Avenue begin to flood. And daily they looked from their houses to see goats, chickens, pigs, dogs, and cows roaming the landscape. More than ever, Peter Charles L'Enfant's proposal for a "Federal City which is to become the Capital of this vast Empire" seemed a distant and half-forgotten dream.

Over the complaints of the entrenched conservatives, President Grant appointed Shepherd to the Board of Public Works in 1871. Within weeks, the new board member produced a plan to rebuild the capital that confirmed the conservatives' greatest fears. Shepherd intended to level the streets to a consistent grade and pave them, build an extensive system of sidewalks and street lamps, and reorganize and improve the city's markets. And, most ambitious of all, he intended to pave over the Washington Canal and make it into a proper sewer. The cost would be $6 million—$2 million would come from taxes, and $4 million from a loan to be repaid later. In November, the territory's voters elected the House of Delegates and approved the loan by an overwhelming margin. Curiously, the financing scheme didn't obligate the federal government to pay anything.

Though appointed, not elected, the Board of Public Works now ruled Washington; and Alexander Shepherd, its vice president, ruled the board. He became known to all as the "Boss."

And the Boss got results. Almost instinctively he mastered the council, which held nominal power, and the elected House of Delegates, and he created a series of alliances with stone quarriers, real-estate barons, and the bankers who ruled the new territory. By the end of 1874 the city had gained more than a hundred miles of newly paved streets, two hundred miles of sidewalks, thirty miles of water mains, and seventy miles of sewers. More than 3,000 gas lamps now glowed throughout the city. Shepherd's workers had completed filling in the Washington Canal and paved what is now Constitution Avenue above it. They also planted 60,000 trees, which served to lend a third dimension to the streets that L'Enfant had projected in his plan. The improvements helped to define Massachusetts and Connecticut avenues, which, north of the city center, had gradually dwindled to rutted tracks; Shepherd had them paved for several miles toward the Kalorama neighborhood in the northwest, and he built the squares, circles, and intersections that L'Enfant and Andrew Ellicott had envisioned. (Congress would name them after such heroes of the Civil War as generals George Henry Thomas, Winfield Scott, and James B. McPherson.) However, the grading of streets, which heretofore had followed the hill-and-dale contours of the land, often caused great consternation. When Vermont senator George Franklin Edmunds returned to the city for a new session of Congress, he found his house and barn perched high above Seventh Street, accessible from the newly paved road only by a crude ladder.

As he so often proved, Shepherd shared a character trait of reckless impetuosity with the city's designer, L'Enfant, who eight decades earlier had ordered the demolition of Daniel Carroll's house because it intruded into the path of New Jersey Avenue. In the twilight of Tuesday evening, September 3, 1872, about two hundred workmen, armed with shovels, sledgehammers, and axes, marched to the Northern Liberty Market, a 400,000-square-foot collection of ramshackle brick and wood buildings on Mount Vernon Square. There were good reasons to demolish the market. The market had started in 1843 with several brick buildings near the Seventh Street side of the square, to meet the needs of the city's expansion northward above H Street, but over the years it had grown in a jumbled and chaotic way. By 1857, when the Marines battled the Know-Nothings at the Market, leaving six dead and a score injured, flimsy wooden stalls covered the site. Long before the end of the Civil War it had become a disgrace. Civic change in Washington customarily moved at a glacial pace, so few paid attention when it was announced that the Northern Liberty Market would soon be demolished.

The wreckers took the merchants by surprise. They could do little to protest as their businesses fell into debris and dust and thousands of rats and mice scampered away in search of new shelter. By morning, there was little left other than huge piles of wood and bricks. In the night, a large wooden sign fell on John Widmayer, a butcher trying to save his property, killing him instantly. Millard Fillmore Bates, a boy who was on the scene to test his terrier's prowess at catching rats, also died, when a heavy section of roof struck him on the head. The stalls where James Lavender and Sons had sold dried fruit, and where William Oliver Shreeve had sold strawberries; where merchants had done a brisk trade in Dr. Bates' Celebrated Tonic Beer and Jester's Celebrated Pawnee Medicine Root; and where about a hundred other markets offered fish and meat, vegetables, and slices of "Washington pie"—these and more were all reduced to a memory.

The merchants did try to procure an injunction to halt the demolition, but their efforts were in vain. That evening, the District judge who could have stopped it happened to be five miles away, attending a lavish party at "Bleak House," Shepherd's large country estate five miles outside the city, named after Charles Dickens's novel about an interminable legal case that exhausted and consumed all litigants. In his drive to improve Washington, Alexander Shepherd had no time for the niceties of the law, and he never allowed litigants to block his way. "The damned old shed was so hideous that it had to come down," he said later. Entertaining the judge that September evening was the surest way to carry out his plans and keep the law at bay.

One night two months later, and with a different work crew of two hundred men, Shepherd had the Baltimore and Ohio railroad tracks at the foot of Capitol Hill torn up. The tracks served only as a holding yard for freight and passenger cars, and they were at the wrong grade level for Maryland Avenue. By daybreak the tracks were gone and the avenue was at the proper grade. An incensed president of the B&O demanded that Shepherd explain himself; the Boss did, and so skillfully that the president offered him a job with the railroad.

Shepherd's changes would eventually help Washington look like a capital city, but at the moment it looked more like a battleground. The Boss's incautious presumption of his own right in all matters concerning construction would ultimately help bring about his downfall and contribute to the dissolution of the territory of the District of

Columbia. He had made many enemies among the entrenched parties of Washington, who claimed that he was part of a ring skimming money from the various construction projects. Chief among them was William Wilson Corcoran, who had slipped back into the city after his protracted sojourn in Europe. Corcoran retained his civic spirit despite the abuse of his property. The federal government kept Harewood, his former country estate and site of the Civil War hospital, and joined the property with the Soldiers' Home to create a large city park. But Corcoran was able to wrest control of his still unfinished and much abused art gallery at Seventeenth Street and Pennsylvania Avenue from the Army's Quartermaster Corps. After completing construction according to James Renwick's original plans, Corcoran opened it to the public on George Washington's birthday 1872, with a grand ball to raise money for the completion of the Washington Monument.

Such generous acts and his considerable wealth helped restore Corcoran to civic power. Shepherd earned his enmity, especially after sewer workers damaged the building of his chief charity, a home for "destitute but refined and educated gentlewomen who have known brighter days and fairer prospects," named in memory of his deceased wife and their daughter, Louise. With Corcoran's voice among those who were opposed to Shepherd's work, Congress could no longer ignore their complaints.

By 1873 it was clear that the territory was running out of money and resorting to financial gimmicks to pay its bills; even a federal infusion of $3.5 million could not stave off bankruptcy. The financial panic on September 18 of that year that swept the city and the country into a five-year economic depression, the scandals in the Grant administration, and widespread cynicism about government and finance sealed Shepherd's and Washington's fate.

As the dictator of change in the capital, Shepherd naturally became the scapegoat for all the territory's financial problems. He had already endured an investigation in 1872 that largely exonerated him, praised the Board of Public Works, and called for "generous appropriations from Congress." But a second investigation that followed in 1874 demonstrated his casual approach to finances and failure to attend to detail. The law had limited him to borrowing $10 million, yet Shepherd had created a Gordian knot of contracts that obligated the city to pay more than $20 million, and had expected that Congress would pay the balance.

The revelations spelled the end of the territorial government and the Board of Public Works. Almost immediately after the release of the report in 1874, Congress abolished the post of governor, the legislature, and of course the board. It imposed new real-estate taxes to meet expenses, and created a plan to handle the enormous debt. And it directed the president to appoint three commissioners who henceforth would govern the city. The Organic Act of 1878 codified the directive into law and specified that, henceforth, the cost of operating Washington would be divided equally between the federal government and local tax revenues. Thus ended the District of Columbia's three-year experiment with territorial government.

For the better part of the next century, residents living at the center of the greatest democratic experiment in human history would have no say in their destiny. Gone was the elected (but nonvoting) representative to the Congress; gone, too, was the limited suffrage accorded to white and black men. Washington's citizens were made wards of an all-too-often capricious and undependable guardian.

DESPITE THE FINANCIAL debacle, Alexander Robey Shepherd helped to rescue the capital's residents from decades of congressional indifference. However devious his methods, however slippery the building contracts, and however short lived some of his improvements turned out to be, the changes to Washington that he brought about were swift and tangible. And fortunately, the transformation largely hewed to L'Enfant's and Ellicott's baroque plan for the capital. More than anyone else, Shepherd ensured that the seat of empire would be worthy of the great republic that the United States was fast becoming. Largely because of the radical improvements Shepherd brought to the city's fabric, Washington showed new and unusual signs of vitality and spirit. Over the next three decades, the city's population would rise steadily, reaching 279,000 at the turn of the century, an increase making the capital larger than any city in the South save New Orleans.

Building and expansion of the city had begun in the years following the war. In 1867, workers enlarged the Smithsonian, which had been damaged by a serious fire two years earlier. That year a new YMCA opened, and the Masons completed their temple on Ninth Street. New houses emerged on Meridian Hill. And in 1869, at Thirteenth and

K streets, workers completed the huge and innovative Franklin School, which was designed by the city's most fashionable architect, Adolf Cluss. Other schools followed, including Cluss's Sumner School at Seventeenth and M streets. Cluss's designs called for classrooms with large windows and ventilating shafts to increase light and air circulation. So innovative were his plans that in 1873, judges at the Vienna International Exposition awarded Washington a Medal of Progress.

Religion felt the expansion, too. The new buildings included Cluss's superb, red brick Cavalry Baptist Church for members who took the Union side in the Civil War, at Eighth and H streets. In 1876, Ulysses Grant and his vice president, Henry Wilson, attended the dedication of the new conservative synagogue Adas Israel, at Sixth and G streets NW. A decade later the red brick and granite Gothic Revival–style African Methodist Episcopal Church opened at Fifteenth and M streets NW; it would serve the largest black congregation in the country.

On a large plot above Boundary Road in the capital's northeast, the campus of today's Gallaudet University was taking shape. Begun in 1856 as a school for twelve deaf and six blind children, and originally called the Columbia Institution for the Deaf and Dumb and Blind, Gallaudet was unique in American education when Congress chartered it as a college in 1864. (By then Gallaudet had changed its mission to focus on deaf students; the blind went to a school in Baltimore.) After the Civil War, its president, Edward M. Gallaudet, hired Frederick Law Olmsted and Calvert Vaux to create a master plan for the campus, which already included a gasworks, a carriage house, a stable and a large classroom building. A chapel and a huge dormitory, executed in the High Victorian Gothic style, as well as houses for faculty and the president, followed in the 1870s.

Congress began to take responsibility for the Mall. By the 1870s, just about everyone agreed with the *New York Herald* that the white stump of the monument intended to honor the memory of the nation's first president was "a disgrace to our people." Nothing had been done to complete the obelisk since the Know-Nothings had abandoned their project in 1857, and no one really knew much about its condition. In July 1876, in the full flush of the nation's centennial and after much procrastination, and studies of the soundness of the footings and the condition of its masonry, Congress unanimously adopted a joint resolution stating that it would "assume and direct the completion of the Washington Monument." At last the federal government was taking over the land and the stone shaft from the society that had begun construction with high hopes in 1848. Congress approved $200,000 for construction and created a Joint Commission to oversee the building. The president headed the commission, which included the chief of the Army Corps of Engineers and the head of the old monument society, William Wilson Corcoran.

Just the thought of resuming construction led to angry debate and delays. The debate centered on American aesthetics, which had moved beyond the clean lines of classic revival structures and the unadorned simplicity of republican political virtues. Critics with a Victorian vision, very possibly influenced by the ornate 176-foot-tall Albert Memorial that had recently been completed in London, declared the plain, white, symmetrical shaft to be monotonous and lacking in the ornamentation and variation that they so admired. To satisfy their passion for irregular surfaces and complex details, ideally expressed in several varieties of stone and brick, they advocated abandoning Robert Mills's obelisk altogether. "No person interested in our reputation as a civilized people," wrote one critic, "can contemplate this completion without pain." Architects flooded the Joint Commission with elaborate substitute schemes, each embellished with statuary. The sculptor William Wetmore Story proposed encasing the present stump with a marble "envelope" that would emulate in High Victorian fashion the Campanile of Giotto in Florence. Montgomery Meigs looked to Venice in his plan for a large viewing platform capped by a tall metal spire. Still others wished to place terraces and steps about the lower part of the stump, and a statue of Washington at the top.

Fortunately for all, Colonel Thomas Lincoln Casey, an uncompromising—and incorruptible—civil engineer, cut through the thicket of words and proposals to impose his strong will on congressional and architectural critics and forge a plan for completion. The son of a general, Casey had been born in the army garrison at Sackett's Harbor, New York, in 1831, and raised in the military tradition. He had graduated first in his class from West Point in 1852, and had then spent the Civil War years building coastal fortifications in New England. After he became chief of the Office of Public Buildings and Grounds in the capital in 1877, the task of completing the monument fell to him.

Casey regarded the project as "the football of quacks." Still, he brought the attitude of a consummate military professional to his task. He had little time for the political intrigue that gripped the most prominent civilian member of the Joint Commission, William Corcoran. Corcoran favored Story's design, as did many in Congress. But there were so many proposals that the legislators reluctantly acquiesced in Casey's plan to finish the obelisk.

While disagreement raged over the monument's design, Casey was shoring up the foundation for the stark spire, because he found that it rested in loose soil rather than on bedrock. His task was to spread the weight over a much broader area by widening the existing foundation twenty-three feet on each side while increasing its depth by thirteen and a half feet. In addition, he would build a series of buttresses to reinforce the sides. As the job demanded skilled workmen who were used to digging tunnels, he looked as far as Nevada for miners who were working the Comstock Lode. He knew, too, that success was far from a sure thing, that he might have made mistakes in his calculations, that the tunnels might collapse, that the soil still might not hold the more than 80,000 tons of the obelisk, and that, ultimately, the Washington Monument would rest on sand.

"Perhaps it may fail after all," he wrote his father in 1880, after he had completed the shoring and was preparing to complete the marble shaft. Casey had spent months getting ready for this moment. An elaborate steel crane and platform for the workers that could move upward with the courses of stone stood in place of the crude roof and rotting wooden derrick that had been exposed to the elements since 1855. He ordered new lapidary sheds to be built on the site, and he took special pains to obtain the finest marble—"white, strong, sound, and free from flint, shakes, powder cracks, or seams"—that would also be compatible with the texture and color of the courses already in place. (At the same time, he ordered the three courses of marble that the Know-Nothings had set removed.)

At 11:00 a.m. on Saturday, August 7, 1880, a new safety elevator—a device that Elisha Otis had yet to invent when construction of the monument began in 1848—lifted President Rutherford B. Hayes, Casey, and two members of the Joint Commission 150 feet to the top of the shaft. After the president produced a small coin on which he had inscribed his name and date, and placed it on the bed of mortar, workmen lowered the first block of marble into place. Hayes had made the project's completion his special cause. The monument, he determined, "should overtop all other structures." For Hayes and Casey, the morning marked a visible new beginning for all Washingtonians, and for the nation.

It was Hayes's ambassador to Italy, the antiquarian and philologist George Perkins Marsh, who helped determine the exact proportions of the obelisk. A study of obelisks had led Marsh to conclude that its height should be ten times its width at the base. Following Marsh's calculations, Casey fixed the height at 555 feet, including the 55 feet of the pyramidal apex, the angled point at the top.

With the ceremonial laying of the stone, the debate over a substitute monument or a group of sculptures adorning its base largely evaporated, though sculptors still dreamed of snaring a rich commission. It needed sculptures, one critic argued, "to relieve its stern structural simplicity," and to "humanize the shaft." Casey dashed all their hopes, quietly ignoring orders to produce drawings to depict such a sculpture. Through an assistant, he put out the word that there would be no "fancy work" at the base.

As course after course of white marble rose above the city, Washingtonians became transfixed by the spectacle of masons laying down mortar at untold heights. By the end of 1882, the monument eclipsed the height of the Brooklyn Bridge then nearing completion in New York. Early in 1884 the Brush-Swan Company demonstrated the power of electric lighting by illuminating the shaft with ten brilliant arc lamps. On December 7, 1884, thousands cheered and soldiers fired cannon in salute as Casey lowered the 3,000-pound capstone into place. Some of the spectators wore necklaces and brooches purchased at Karr's Jewelry Store on Pennsylvania Avenue and made from "genuine chips" of the monument's marble. At the very top, the chief engineer placed the 5½ by 9½-inch tip upon the obelisk. Known as a "pyramidion," it was of cast aluminum, a metal that would resist corrosion and act as a lightning rod, and so novel that Tiffany's had put it on display in New York.

Casey had triumphed. Some still wanted sculptural reliefs around the monument's base, but as he probably anticipated, Congress quietly ignored the requests. Once the scaffolding had come down and the formal dedication had taken place, on Washington's birthday in 1885, the complaints vanished. It became a commonplace to say that the

TROWEL IN hand, Thomas Lincoln Casey directs his masons at the top of the Washington Monument. CREDIT: Library of Congress

monument stood as stoic and severe as the Father of the Country himself. Twentieth-century critics have praised the minimalist modernity of the building's four white faces and sharp corners, which continually reflect the changes of light and atmosphere. In completing Robert Mills's vision of purity, Thomas Lincoln Casey had created a timeless symbol for the capital and the country.

In part because of the monument, Washington's citizens began to speak of their city as beautiful, daring at times to mention it in the same breath as London or Paris. "Like a giant refreshed with new wine," wrote an effusive city reporter, "Washington has risen out of the dust and mire and clay which formerly was its abiding place and stands today in new and becoming attire infused with new life."

ALEXANDER ROBEY SHEPHERD did not see Colonel Casey top off the monument. He had remained in Washington after Congress dissolved the territory, but by late 1876, his extensive debts had forced him to declare bankruptcy. Grateful Washington businessmen kept him afloat until 1880, when friends from New York City asked him to run a seemingly exhausted silver mine in Chihuahua, Mexico. In just a few years he had consolidated all the mines in the area and found new veins, including one that yielded a 4,900-pound nugget. When he returned to his native city in October 1887, all Washington feted him with a parade down Pennsylvania Avenue, a key to the city, and fireworks. Though he kept Bleak House as his residence, he spent most of his time in Chihuahua; it was there that death came from peritonitis in 1902. Seven years later, Washington's citizens gathered on the small plaza before their new District Building to watch Master Alexander Robey Shepherd unveil a nine-foot-tall bronze statue of his grandfather. "The rugged lines of face and head," said one of the many speakers at the dedication, "portrayed . . . the man of power, of abnormal strength and energy, of elemental dominating force." The fiscal scandal that Shepherd had left in his wake had receded from the memories of all but the bitterest of critics. Although he spent with "a lavish hand," as one observer put it, his works showed Washington's citizens and Congress what the capital of the United States might become.

CHAPTER 8

Gilded Neighbors, Progressive City

> In 1868, Washington stood outside the social pale. No
> Bostonian had ever gone there. One announced one's
> self as an adventurer and an office-seeker, a person of
> deplorably bad judgment, and the charges were true.
>
> —Henry Adams, 1918

By the election of 1876, Washington had become an attractive city for new millionaires searching for a suitable place to flaunt their wealth and for those who wished to settle close to the radiance of federal power. For families like the Cabots of Boston, the Biddles of Philadelphia, and the Coopers of New York, the capital would remain beyond the pale. But the new arrivals, who would be counted parvenus if they tried to scale the very highest peaks of American society in the old cities of the Northeast, found Washington to be a place where they might make an indelible mark upon the world as entrepreneurs or members of Congress, and where they might gain influence with those at the center of the nation's political power. No matter that many had more than one past, and some had made their millions in questionable ways. They brought new energy to the capital and ushered in its Gilded Age.

The civic improvements undertaken by Alexander Robey Shepherd, President Grant's energetic governor of the District of Columbia, made it possible for entrepreneurs to create new neighborhoods for the capital's increasing population. Before the Civil War, most of Washington's prominent citizens had lived in Georgetown, on Capitol Hill and in the southwest, on Seventh Street around Pennsylvania Avenue, and in the few blocks west of the White House. Beyond those areas and even within them, the city was, as one reporter said, a "Slough of Despond"; Shepherd had turned it into "one of the finest cities in the world." Just in time for the nation's centennial in 1876, workers tore up the wooden blocks on Pennsylvania Avenue from the Capitol to the Treasury and replaced them with the latest—and smoothest—road surface, asphalt. As the capital became more attractive, senators, congressmen, and cabinet members decided to bring their families to the city. Boardinghouses and group messes yielded to imposing houses and large apartments.

Many of those arriving looked to the northwest, out Vermont Avenue to Thomas Circle (named after General George Henry Thomas, who saved the Union Army at the Battle of Chickamauga), or out Connecticut Avenue to the as yet unnamed Dupont Circle at the intersection of Massachusetts and New Hampshire avenues. Edward Weston of New York City and Yonkers saw an opportunity to invest in Thomas Circle. Having made his fortune in banking and railroads, the "retired capitalist," as a story in the *Washington Post* called him, built a five-story brick townhouse at Fourteenth and K streets NW shortly after his arrival in 1878. Two years later he hired Adolf Cluss to design "Portland Flats," a six-story apartment house, one of Washington's first, on the pie-shaped intersection on the south side of Thomas Circle. The Portland's large, balconied viewing tower facing onto the circle reminded many of the large steam-powered ocean liners now cruising the Atlantic. Its thirty-nine apartments included rich wood carvings, ebony mantels over the fireplaces, and an abundance of marble. Even though the rents were exorbitant—$150 a month for the largest apartments, about $3,000 today—they attracted wealthy members of Congress and government leaders along with other newcomers of means.

William Morris Stewart was among the first to arrive at Dupont Circle. His was a typical nouveau riche story: a native of western New York, he had combined his nimble intelligence with brash self-assurance to make a fortune in the California gold rush. Soon he had acquired enough money to abandon his pick and shovel for a career as a mining lawyer. He quickly became district attorney in Nevada City, and briefly served as attorney general for the state of California. By 1859 he had moved to Virginia City, Nevada, the center of the newly discovered Comstock Lode. Litigation on behalf of large mining corporations

THIS EARLY twentieth-century photograph reveals much about the city. At the center and framed between Fourteenth Street and Vermont Avenue is the ship-like High Victorian Gothic Luther Place Memorial Church. (Martin Luther's statue can be seen in front of the church.) Note the gaslights, the formal gardens surrounding General Thomas's statue, the baby pram, the street cleaner, and the horse-drawn car line leading to the north. CREDIT: Library of Congress

brought him even more wealth, and the nickname "the Silver King," though his enemies—including Mark Twain, who skewered him in two bitter sketches—maintained that he frequently cheated on stocks and bribed judges to get his way.

Stewart's rise to power and his championing of mineral exploitation with a minimum of government supervision endeared him to politicians. When Nevada gained statehood in 1864, the governor appointed him to be its first senator. A moderate Republican, he blocked some of the more pitiless and cruel measures of his radical reconstruction colleagues. However, he helped to draft the Fifteenth Amendment to the Constitution, which gave black American men the right to vote.

Stewart's forte always lay in speculation, and Washington offered him abundant opportunities. After the war, he and a group of gold and silver millionaires formed "The Honest Miner's Camp," a syndicate that purchased land around Dupont Circle for ten cents per square foot. That much of the vast acreage was swampy, and drained by Slash Run, a creek that generations of misuse had turned into an open sewer, accounted for the price. Most likely the syndicate stretched the meaning of "honest," as the members were well connected with Alexander Shepherd, and knew he intended to turn the creek into a covered sewer, and to build a new bridge to Georgetown at P Street. They knew, too, that the Metropolitan Railroad Company, of which Shepherd was president, was laying track for a horsecar line up Connecticut Avenue; Shepherd had built his own house at the corner of K Street and Connecticut Avenue. A park at the circle built by the Army Corps of Engineers completed the transformation. And recognizing the importance of the money The Honest Miner's Camp had brought, the Corps of Engineers named the area "Pacific Circle."

The cleared land only awaited the builders. William Morris Stewart was the first with an extravagant brick and mansard roof pile at the intersection of Connecticut and Massachusetts avenues that his architect topped with a five-story circular tower in the French Victorian style. Charges that funds for the house came from a mining swindle— "The House you have built and furnished is with my money, and you know it," wrote one man, who charged that Stewart had cheated him of half a million dollars—meant little to the senator, or to the many visitors who rode out Connecticut Avenue to see the extravagant structure. The senator thought that Stewart's castle, as it was called, was just the house for his Mississippi-born wife and three daughters.

In the 1880s and 1890s, others equaled Stewart's excess with opulent mansions of their own: James G. Blaine, Republican congressman and senator from Maine whose wealth was tainted with railroad and land scandals, placed his mansion just off the circle at Twentieth and Massachusetts in 1882. George Hearst, another Comstock Lode millionaire, enlarged an already considerable mansion on New Hampshire Avenue for his family. (Although the nearly illiterate Hearst had a reputation for crudeness of language and behavior, his wife, Phoebe, became a civic leader. She helped to establish the Parent Teachers Association and kindergartens across the city, and gave away more than $20 million to cultural institutions and charities.) Levi Leiter, a real-estate and dry-goods tycoon from Chicago, built a three-story white-brick mansion with fifty-five rooms for his wife and three marriageable daughters on New Hampshire Avenue north of the circle. (Two daughters would wed British nobility; the third, a British major.) By the turn of the century, more than a hundred fashionable houses lined the avenues and surrounded the circle, which in 1884 was renamed in honor of the Civil War admiral Samuel Francis Du Pont.

OVER THE YEARS, George Washington's vision of a capital that was a gateway to the West and a center of manufacturing gradually receded in the minds of Washingtonians. Most traces of the Washington Canal had vanished entirely. The Chesapeake and Ohio Canal that terminated at Georgetown had never become the major commercial artery that its creators dreamt of when they began it in 1828. Floods frequently disrupted shipping, and a devastating deluge in 1889 forced the company to declare bankruptcy. (The company would limp along into the first quarter of the twentieth century, until another flood in 1924 forced it to cease altogether.) Nor had the city become a national manufacturing center, as the schemes of early residents like John Peter Van Ness had once promised.

But there were successful local businesses that grew up to supply the needs of the transient population of elected officials, diplomats from foreign nations, and permanent residents, including government workers, immigrants, and blacks. Over two decades between 1870 and 1890, Washington's population grew from 109,000 to 230,000. A number of them had come to Washington because they saw an opportunity to prosper.

Samuel Walter Woodward and Alvin Mason Lothrop arrived from New England in 1880 to open the Boston Dry Goods Store at Seventh Street and Pennsylvania Avenue; by the turn of the century the Woodward and Lothrop Department Store commanded an entire block on Tenth and Eleventh between F and G streets, with over a thousand employees and a fleet of delivery wagons. Fashioning their enterprise on the merchant prince John Wanamaker's Philadelphia emporium, Woodward and Lothrop stocked a little bit of everything, imported Paris fashions (after the World's Fair of 1893) to the capital, and made shopping a pleasure for their customers, especially for ladies, who could rest in the store's reception room on the mezzanine. The store was among the first to anticipate the seasons; customers in July could peer through "highly polished French plate glass" windows at the latest winter coats, and in January at summer frocks. The merchants allowed returns and exchanges of merchandise and established a "one price" policy that freed customers from the task of bargaining over every purchase.

Woodward, who was also the president of the enterprise, appeared to be the model of rectitude—slightly priggish in his tightly buttoned coat, wing-tip collar, and tie, his pince-nez, and his carefully trimmed handlebar mustache, goatee, and sideburns. He headed the Board of Trade, served as president of the YMCA and vice president of the National Metropolitan Bank, and prayed regularly at the Calvary Baptist Church. *Men of Mark in America*, a puff volume of the time dedicated to "biographies of eminent living Americans" that illustrated the "ideals of American life," said that Woodward's employees felt "the bracing effect of [his] strict but kind oversight." In their memories, however, employees had a somewhat different definition of bracing and kind. They told of a man quick to anger who regularly threw pens across the office whenever the nib gave out; who mercilessly cross-examined buyers when they returned from trips; who ordered the windows curtained on Sundays; and who, presumably because they promoted loose morals, forbade the sale of playing cards.

Soon, Woodies, as it was known throughout the city, had imitators. Kann's opened in 1893, Hecht's three years later, and Garfinckel's in 1905. To meet their new competition, older dry-goods stores, including Lansburgh's—which had supplied the mourning crepe for Lincoln's funeral—and the Palais Royal expanded their offerings.

Christian Heurich arrived from Germany by way of Baltimore in 1872 and purchased one of Washington's five small breweries at Twentieth Street and M; by the turn of the century, the Christian Heurich Brewing Company was operating from a new four-story, fireproof building on the Potomac in Foggy Bottom (at the site of today's Kennedy Center for the Performing Arts). It had the capacity to produce half a million barrels of beer annually. Across the city, even in the White House, Washingtonians were drinking Heurich's Senate Lager, so much lager that Christian Heurich could count himself a millionaire.

Heurich capitalized on the fact that Gilded Age Washington needed a large group of working- and middle-class artisans and merchants to support its ostentation, and that these workers, too, thirsted for entertainment. While the "cave dwellers" (as the earliest inhabitants were known), diplomats, and members of Congress took their whiskey and wine in townhouse parlors on Connecticut Avenue and the halls of the Capitol, government clerks, store owners, and immigrants working on Alexander Shepherd's municipal projects drank their beer in saloons and beer gardens. Even before the creation of the District of Columbia, small enclaves of Germans had lived in the area, especially in Jacob Funk's Hamburg; but emigration from Germany rose significantly in the second half of the nineteenth century. There were about 5,000 German Americans in Washington when Heurich arrived. They read two German-language newspapers. They had a gymnastics club and two shooting clubs, and at the Capital Saengerbund they sang traditional German songs. These were the consumers Heurich sought to please; neighborhood saloons across the city, including one attached to the brewery, became social centers, the places where a man might go after a day's labor for the company of friends and, in Heurich's terms, "good German lager."

The city's burghers were just as quick to weave the successful German immigrant into their elite social fabric as they were millionaires from the West. Heurich's decision to invest much of the profit from his brewery in Washington real estate and rental buildings made him even more welcome. He became a member of the Chamber of Commerce and a charter member of the Washington Board of Trade; and he joined the boards of such German American philanthropies as the Eleanor Ruppert Home for Aged Indigent Residents and the German Orphan Asylum. Like many men of means, he kept a farm nearby in Maryland. On New Hampshire Avenue and Twentieth Street, he erected a grand and modern fireproof mansion in the Romanesque Richardson style. Elaborate cabinetry and iron work executed by immigrant German craftsmen, furniture handcrafted in Germany, and a bierstube in the basement complete with carved drinking mottoes reminded Heurich whence he came and signaled to others all he had achieved.

IN 1868, AMZI Lorenzo Barber moved from Ohio to Washington, DC, to do good. The son of a Congregationalist minister, Barber's upbringing and education at Oberlin College was egalitarian and abolitionist. Upon his arrival, he took a position in the Normal Department at

Howard University and a seat on the board of trustees. Just a year later, he married, resigned his university position, and joined his brother-in-law Andrew Langdon to take advantage of the capital's growing need for real estate. From that moment on, Amzi Lorenzo Barber did well.

For their first speculation Barber and Langdon purchased land from the university to build a suburban residential community beyond the boundary of Washington City. The fifty-five-acre triangular plot was wedged between present-day Florida and Rhode Island avenues on the south, and the university property and group of modest dwellings called "Howard Town" on the north. To honor the first name of their father and father-in-law, the partners named their new community LeDroit Park.

By design, LeDroit Park had the romantic air of an exclusive rural setting within the city. The plantings would be lush, the streets (though off the axis of L'Enfant's plan) would be quiet, and no fences or walls would separate the properties. Barber and Langdon hired the enterprising architect and contractor James H. McGill to design and build the houses and oversee the grading of streets, the installation of gas, water, and sewer lines, and the laying of brick sidewalks. McGill freely adapted plans and ideas he found in *Cottage Residences* and *Villas and Cottages*, books by two of America's most influential architects of the time, Andrew Jackson Downing and Calvert Vaux. He especially favored those in the Gothic and Italianate style. The contractor built and appointed the houses and publicized them in a book with the capacious title *James H. McGill's Architectural Advertiser: A Collection of Designs for Suburban Houses, Interspersed with Advertisements of Dealers in Building Supplies.* By 1876, LeDroit Park counted, one newspaper reported, "forty-one superior residences . . . no two being alike either in size, shape or style of finish, or in the color of exterior." McGill and his family lived in one of his houses, 1945 Harewood Avenue (present-day Third Street).

LeDroit Park would attract middle-class Washingtonians—white doctors, teachers, lawyers, and other professional men who relished their isolation, yet needed to have easy access by the horsecar line on Seventh Street to downtown two miles away. Congressman and later commissioner of patents Benjamin Butterworth chose LeDroit, as did the geographer who is often called the "father of government mapmaking," Henry Gannett, and the former Civil War general and lawyer William Birney. The developers intended LeDroit Park to be segregated and gated. To make certain that blacks other than servants would not walk down the streets of their community, Barber and Langdon erected a wooden and cast-iron fence around the site, placed gates at the southern entrance, and hired a guard to keep watch at night. No one could enter from the north.

But the fence did not last. By 1887, groups of angry residents of Howard Town—who had to walk around the property to get to their jobs downtown—began to tear it down. A legal opéra bouffe ensued, with the antagonists alternately tearing down and boarding up the street entrances; installing and snipping though barbed wire; and filing suits and countersuits. In March 1891, the *Washington Post* reported that the fence "suddenly disappeared," and no one seemed to know who had spirited it away. In August a judge ended the comedy with a ruling that the fence must be permanently removed.

Racial barriers in LeDroit Park also began to crumble, though not without hostility. When Octavius Augustus Williams, a barber who cut hair at the Capitol, moved into 338 U Street, someone fired a bullet through the window as his family was eating dinner. Robert and Mary Church Terrell had to resort to subterfuge to purchase a home there. Though Robert had graduated from Groton School and Harvard and held a law degree from Howard University, and Mary had a degree in classics from Oberlin and taught Latin at the city's new "Preparatory High School for Colored Youth" on M Street, the owner of the house at 326 T Street refused to sell it to them. To work around that resistance a white businessman purchased the property and immediately resold it to the Terrells. Middle-class black families like the Williamses and the Terrells gradually and steadily moved into the neighborhood. The result, however, was not an integrated community. The white middle-class families moved to other suburbs made ever more accessible by streetcar lines.

In October 1897, the black poet and novelist Paul Laurence Dunbar and his wife moved into a LeDroit Park house. Dunbar's lyrics often contained lines about the plight of blacks:

> *We wear the mask that grins and lies,*
> *It hides our cheeks and shades our eyes,—*
> *This debt we pay to human guile;*
> *With torn and bleeding hearts we smile,*
> *And mouth with myriad subtleties.*

Such poems earned Dunbar national and even international popularity, but he still had to take menial jobs in Ohio to support himself and his mother. When a sympathetic Ohio congressman heard of Dunbar's position, he arranged for him to become an assistant in the reading room at the Library of Congress for $750 a year. But long hours in the library and the dust from the books diminished Dunbar's already frail health; after being diagnosed with tuberculosis in 1898, the poet went to Colorado. Although his residence in the capital was brief, Washingtonians were eager to recognize him. In 1916, the city's school board named its new segregated high school after Dunbar, "whose name is a household word," an editorial in the *Washington Bee* said, "in the home of every American negro."

BY 1881, AMZI Lorenzo Barber had moved on to his next great venture, another housing project, with John Sherman, the secretary of the treasury. Sherman acquired a large tract of land north of Boundary Street (today's Florida Avenue) between Tenth and Sixteenth, and Barber set out to market it as the newest and best suburban development. As much of the land had belonged to the small and struggling Columbian College, he named it "Columbia Heights." "Under the rapid growth of Washington," read the advertisement in the 1882 edition of Boyd's *City Directory*, "this property will soon become the most desirable and fashionable part of the City." Columbia Heights would appeal to the "Creme de la Creme."

Barber saved ten acres of the choicest land for himself. There he built "Belmont," a granite mansion executed in the Romanesque and chateau styles and graced at its corner with a slender, round, four-story Queen Anne tower topped by a narrow conical roof. From the dormer windows of Belmont's tower, which dwarfed William Morris Stewart's castle at Dupont Circle, Barber could take in downtown Washington and the Potomac. And he could see the city's streets—seventy miles of them by 1890—that he had paved with the best material available, Trinidad asphalt.

In part, the new pavements were a response to a craze that began to overtake the nation in 1878, when Union Army veteran Albert Augustus Pope of Boston introduced the Columbia bicycle. To promote his bicycles and smooth roads, the former colonel formed the League of

American Wheelmen in 1880, which lobbied for highway improvements. At the time, there were about 175 wheelmen in the District, who rode their "iron horses" over forty-five miles of paved roads. By 1895 there were at least five bicycle stores doing a brisk business in the capital, with about 12,000 bicyclists in the city. A number of the cyclists formed the Capital Bicycle Club, which held annual races around Iowa (now Logan) Circle with rival bicycle clubs from Baltimore and Arlington as well as distance races in Maryland and Virginia.

Recognizing the American desire for mobility, speed, and good roads, as well as the success of the recently paved Pennsylvania Avenue, Barber decided in 1878 that his future wealth lay in asphalt paving. In the coming years he would demonstrate his prescience, business acumen, and ruthlessness to control the entire industry. He gained a near monopoly on the source of bitumen, or pitch, the key ingredient of asphalt, improved paving machinery, rapaciously bought out smaller competitors, and tied up other challengers with lawsuits that stopped or at least impeded their progress. Believing that the automobile would supplant the bicycle and increase the demand for paved roads, he also helped found the Locomobile car company in 1899. By the end of the century he could boast that the Barber Asphalt Company had paved the streets in one hundred cities and half the paved roads in America. Amzi Lorenzo Barber was "The Asphalt King."

But early in the new century, the kingdom collapsed. Barber failed in his attempt to buy up all the competing asphalt companies. He died in greatly reduced circumstances in 1904. Belmont remained in the family until 1915, when a syndicate of Washington real-estate investors purchased the property and razed the mansion for a new residential development, the Clifton apartment houses.

HENRY ADAMS BELIEVED to his core that his family had been put upon the earth to serve the public good. The Adamses held a hereditary claim upon Washington, the nation's government, even the White House. His great grandfather, John Adams, had served in the Continental Congress; had helped to draft the Declaration of Independence, and later to negotiate the Treaty of Paris; and was the first president to live in the executive mansion. His grandfather, John Quincy Adams, had learned diplomacy as secretary to his father in Europe and had served as secretary of state under James Madison; he had become the sixth president, and after his defeat for reelection in 1828, had served nine terms in the House of Representatives. His father, Charles Francis Adams, had served as the US ambassador to Great Britain during the Civil War, had twice run unsuccessfully for vice president, and had wished to follow his father to the White House.

Clearly, by the fall of 1868, Henry thought the mantle of his family's public service had come to rest upon his shoulders. Just as John Quincy had served as diplomatic secretary to his father, so Henry had attended his father in London during the Civil War. However, his would be a different kind of public service. To Charles Francis Adams's distress, his thirty-year-old Harvard-educated son would be a reformer: he would "join the press," as Henry put it, and in Washington, not Boston. The decision was in part a mild rebellion against his New England roots, but Henry had felt a strange affinity for the capital from the time of his first visit to his grandparents' house on F Street in 1850. Although Bostonians might consider Washington "outside the social pale," Henry Adams found it to be "the drollest place in Christian lands." He took a house on G Street—suitably removed from Lafayette Square—with views of the Potomac and Georgetown. The government buildings remained "unfinished Greek temples," the roads were "sloughs," and "a thin veil of varnish" covered "some very rough material"; but, as he wrote to an English friend, from the window of his house he could "see for miles down the Potomac," and he knew "of no other capital in the world which stands on so wide and splendid a river."

It was a bold step, a "leap into the unknown," Adams later acknowledged in his famous *Autobiography*, but he scarcely realized how hard his landing would be. He would not be a "regular reporter" for a daily paper, but one who would present longer and more considered articles that placed current events in a historical context. For Adams, reform meant steering the government away from the false appeals of the Jacksonian common man and returning it to the noble ideals of the founders. "We want a national set of young men like ourselves," he wrote his brother—men who would "exert an influence" upon America's politics, literature, law, and "the whole social organism." But his arrival in Washington coincided with Grant's election to the presidency. After the confusion of Andrew Johnson's stormy tenure, Adams, along with most Americans, looked forward to the general reestablishing "moral and mechanical order" in the land, as he put it in his autobiography; instead, moral and mechanical chaos prevailed. Grant filled his cabinet with knaves and frauds beholden to the interests of a small group of business oligarchs. Henry protested Congress's imposition of high tariffs ("Capital accumulates rapidly, but . . . in fewer hands, and the range of separation between the wealthy and the poor becomes continuously wider"), Jay Gould and Jim Fisk's brazen attempt to corner the gold market in 1869, and countless venal acts of Washington officials. Rail though he might, however, his articles counted for little. He was a relic of the eighteenth century, he said, but America, "more eighteenth century than himself," had "reverted to the stone age."

The old world of public men, as Henry Adams called them, often Harvard-educated and patrician men like Charles Sumner and John Hay, Abraham Lincoln's private secretary, seemed to Adams to be in eclipse. In their place came men from recently minted states of the West, with pockets filled with bullion. "Slowly a certain society had built itself up about the government," he remembered later. "Houses had been opened, and there was much dining; much calling; much leaving of cards; but a solitary man counted for less than in 1868."

To escape his melancholy, which had been brought on by Grant's ineptness and his own family's declining influence at the center of the republic, Adams became a solitary traveler worthy of William Wordsworth. His Lake District was "the dogwood and the judas tree, the azalea and the laurel" of the unspoiled Maryland countryside. The "Potomac and its tributaries squandered beauty," he wrote, and "Rock Creek was as wild as the Rocky Mountains." But he could not escape the realities of "vulgar corruption" that he saw about him. "The progress of evolution from President Washington to President Grant," Adams wrote in discouragement, "was alone evidence enough to upset Darwin." He had hoped to write of "a new Washington," but now he saw only a capital that bred "endless corruption." After two years of witnessing political decay and the devolution of American culture, he left the capital to tour Europe and take a professorship of history at Harvard.

Yet Adams's heart lay not on the Charles but rather on the banks of the Potomac; so in 1877 he decided to retire from Harvard and return. To be sure, signs of the firm grip exerted by amoral mediocrities upon all branches of the government were everywhere: in the Supreme Court, peopled by justices who resolutely affirmed the power of business; in the Congress, controlled by mendacious frauds; and in the executive branch, headed by one mediocre president after another. Although his political future as a reforming journalist may have been thwarted in 1869, Adams realized that his strong suit lay in writing. He would mine the documents in the State Department and the Library of Congress for a chronicle of the Jefferson and Madison administrations, a time before America's moral ideals had been sullied by political corruption.

Adams returned to Washington with a wife, Marian "Clover" Hooper, the same young Boston woman who had been in Washington in May 1865, at the grand military parade marking the end of the Civil War. Her father, a wealthy Boston doctor, and her mother, the Transcendentalist poet Ellen Sturgis Hooper, had ensured that their daughter received the best education of the time, at a school for women run by the family of Louis Agassiz, where the great Harvard professor occasionally lectured on "physical geography, natural history, and botany." Henry considered his wife to be "not handsome; nor would she be called quite plain," as he wrote to an intimate English friend; but, he said, "She knows her own mind uncommonly well. . . . She talks garrulously, but on the whole pretty sensibly." She was tractable, too, he believed, "open to instruction." And, he added in his best masculine temper, "*We* shall improve her." It didn't hurt, either, that Clover had "enough money to be quite independent." His income and hers, and often a generous check from Dr. Hooper, enabled the couple to live as they wished.

Henry and Clover's wish was to make their refined mark on society. They rented a mansion from William Corcoran at 1607 H Street at the north end of Lafayette Square for $2,400 a year, and in late 1880, after extensive refurbishing, moved into it with fifteen wagonloads of furniture and *objets d'art* gleaned from their travels around the globe, and a staff of six servants. From the front windows, they could look past the statue of the Adams family nemesis, Andrew Jackson, to the White House. Although Henry had called the present occupant of the White House, Hayes, a "third rate nonentity," and other detractors called Hayes's prohibitionist wife "Lemonade Lucy," the president and Lucy Hayes proved to be most cordial neighbors. Lucy sent Clover "a quantity of cut flowers" to welcome the Adamses to H Street, and more than once she invited the Adamses to dine with them. Henry was careful to confine most of his political thoughts to patronizing comments he wrote in letters to American and English friends.

The couple prized the richness of elegant, intellectual social intercourse. Soon Henry and Clover opened their doors for teas, discreet dinner parties, and worldly gossip. Theirs was a select circle of guests whom they found intelligent and amusing. More than a house with a pleasant reception room, 1607 H Street became a salon of quiet refinement in the midst of the noisome political world, a place where intelligent conversation prevailed over crude talk of power. In a private but very public way, the Adamses served as arbiters of all that society should value. "Money plays no part whatever in Society," Henry wrote to his English friend, "but cleverness counts for a good deal, and social capacity for more."

Many scientists and diplomats were welcome, but most senators and congressmen, along with Mark Twain, all infra dig, were not. The writer Henry James, who had known both Clover and Henry before their marriage, was welcome, always. James, who had a warm relationship with Clover, likely drew upon her when he limned his portraits of Daisy Miller and Isabel Archer, and he always enjoyed the "perennial afternoon teas" that she hosted. Yet when the novelist asked if he might bring along an Anglo-Irish writer of his acquaintance who was in Washington as part of his lecture tour in America, Clover flatly refused. Oscar Wilde, whose reputation had preceded him, was not welcome at 1607 H Street.

It was not the ever-present political intrigue that kept the Adamses in Washington so much as the city itself. "One of these days this will be a very great city if nothing happens to it," Henry had once written to a friend. For him, it was steadily approaching the ideal. With every season, Washington took on more of the character of a national capital. As Civil War heroes died, Congress commissioned statues; by 1880, four new ones (commemorating McPherson, Thomas, Scott, and Ulysses Grant's aide and confidant, John Rawlins) were already in place. In front of the Capitol stood the great white marble Peace Monument dedicated to sailors who had lost their lives in the Civil War. The federal presence was conspicuous across the city: in the Surgeon General's office, which had taken over Ford's Theater, where Booth had assassinated Lincoln; in the twenty-six-inch refractor telescope, then the largest in the United States, that had been built at the Naval Observatory on the bank of the Potomac, near today's Lincoln Memorial; and on the roof of the Army Signal Corps headquarters at 1719 G Street NW, where the War Department had installed a weather station.

This was the Washington that lured Henry Adams and his wife. He and Clover spent their time researching the Jefferson and Madison papers in the State Department for his life of Albert Gallatin, Thomas Jefferson's secretary of the treasury and minister to France and the United Kingdom, and his multivolume history of the Jefferson and Madison administrations. "As I am intimate with many of the people in power and out of power," he told his English friend, "I am readily allowed or aided to do all the historical work I please." He and Clover indulged their passion for horseback riding almost daily in the Virginia countryside, in the Rock Creek Valley, or on the grounds of Harewood and the Soldiers' Home. By 1882, Henry could report that he was writing for five hours a day, riding for two, and saving his remaining waking hours for "Society."

For Henry and Clover, "Society" was synonymous with culture and intelligence. The Adamses' guests reflected the intellectual and scientific ferment that was abroad throughout the capital. America's expansion across the West, the Smithsonian under the leadership of Joseph Henry, and the Civil War had attracted numerous scientists to the capital. In 1871, Henry organized the Philosophical Society of Washington, where they might discuss "all subjects of interest to intelligent men." Seven years later, in the year that Joseph Henry died, a number of distinguished men in science created the Cosmos Club, "to bind the scientific men of Washington by a social tie," but the club also included men of literature and the arts like Henry Adams, who served on its Committee on Admissions. Like the Philosophical Society, the Cosmos Club offered scientists an opportunity to present papers. Major John Wesley Powell served as its first president. He was well known for having lost his right arm at the Battle of Shiloh in the Civil War, but his scientific eminence came from his work as a geologist, anthropologist, and explorer. It was Powell who, in 1869, led an expedition of ten men down the Colorado River and through the Grand Canyon. Those who spoke at the Cosmos Club ranked with the finest scientific minds in the nation, and many were guests at H Street. John Wesley Powell came often, as did Simon Newcomb, the mathematician and astronomer at the Naval Observatory who produced mathematical tables and formulae to show the movement of the planets and stars, and Francis Amasa Walker, the preeminent statistician who in 1880 supervised the tenth Census of the United States.

The scientist who visited most often was the director of the United States Geological Survey, Clarence King. A short, puckish man with a Vandyke beard and bright blue eyes, King regarded geology as scientific history, a perspective that fit well with the view of Henry Adams, who considered himself to be a scientific historian. Their friendship had begun by chance in 1871 in Wyoming, where Adams had been a visiting a member of the Geological Survey, and it intensified after Henry and Clover moved to the capital.

King joined John Hay and his wife, Clara, at 1607 H Street so often that the five became intense companions. By 1882 they were calling themselves the "Five of Hearts." They had stationery embossed with a playing card and five red hearts, and King gave Clover a tea service with a pot and bowls in the shape of hearts. The friendships were warm and intensely homosocial. King was a confirmed bachelor who had sworn off marriage (though it was later revealed that when in New York City he lived under an assumed name with a black common-law wife). Adams and Hay frequently began their letters with salutations like: "My Beloved," "Apple of Mine Eye," or "Light of Mine optics." Clara and Clover often appeared removed from the center of discussion about scientific and literary subjects, and yet always at the ready to serve in a social role.

Clover's letters to her father paint a picture of a frenetic life of social, intellectual, and political amusements. Typical is one she wrote on March 27, 1881, in which the names of guests at three evening dinners flows from her pen: Clarence King; Francis Amasa Walker; the retired Civil War general and now Rhode Island senator Ambrose Burnside; secretary of the Swedish legation de Bildt; Attorney General Wayne MacVeagh; Secretary of War Robert Todd Lincoln (twice); and John Hay (twice). On another evening, Clover reports that Henry went to dine with the historian George Bancroft and his wife; she begged off on account of a cold, but Walker and MacVeagh stopped by "to cheer my solitude." Their dear friends ("intimates") Hay and King had left Washington, Hay to join his wife at Fort Monroe, King to search for gold in Mexico. Gossip overflows: about scheming to have John Wesley Powell succeed King as head of the Geological Survey; about President

James Garfield's fractious new cabinet; and about the new assistant secretary of state—"rich, but socially of little use." She had begun reading Gibbon ("a bone that will take months to gnaw"), and Henry was hard at work on his history of the republic. That week, the Adamses had to decline four dinner invitations—"even Lent does not stop society in this social town," Clover remarked.

Despite the heady scientific and literary discussions that took place at Sixteenth and H streets, Henry Adams knew he wielded little political power. The intellectual and cultured presence at the Adams house on the north end of Lafayette Square was hardly a counterweight to the crude political intrigues hatched in the White House at the south end. A decade earlier, he had failed to effect any practical reform of the government and had vowed to leave the political world. But the political world could never quite leave Henry Adams. If he couldn't exert a practical influence upon the political course of the nation, at least he could show his scorn for the ethical decline of the democracy in a satirical novel; and better still, he could do it anonymously, keeping everyone in the capital guessing as to who the author might be. He would publish it on April Fool's Day, 1880. Even its title would reflect his disgust at the devolution of the noble ideals that had so motivated his forebears in the beginning of the republic: *Democracy*.

The plot would be simple: an innocent young lady is attracted to and courted by a man of corrupt moral character, only to be rescued from committing herself to marriage by one who reveals awful truths about him. The innocent was Madeline Lightfoot Lee, a naïve but curious New York widow, with $20,000 a year, who decides to pass the winter in Washington with her sister. They would observe life in the capital, the place where "the interests of forty millions of people" were guided "by men of ordinary mould," men who wielded the great forces of power. She would read reports of Congress and sit in the galleries listening to the great political orators, and she would entertain them at the house she leased at the epicenter of power, Lafayette Square. Madeline Lee would be witness to a great play, Adams suggests, reaching for a metaphor; she would see "how . . . [it] was acted and the stage effects were produced; how the great tragedians mouthed, and the stage-manager swore."

The man of corrupt moral character, Senator Silas P. Ratcliffe from Illinois, takes the stage in Chapter 2. Called by newspaper writers "the

Prairie Giant of Peonia," Ratcliffe possesses a six-foot frame, a large head, a silver tongue, and an unslakable thirst for power and the presidency. He is the new political man, the one who places his own interests above the ideals of the founders. Ratcliffe is drawn to Madeline, who possesses the refinement and culture he lacks, and who will serve him well when he attains the White House.

To the refined conversation of assorted diplomats, former Confederates, and minor nobility who frequent Madeline's house, Ratcliffe brings the corruption of the capital. Living up to the *nomen est omen* of his surname, Ratcliffe speaks of power and political plots, scheming to embarrass, even unseat, the president. On an excursion to Mount Vernon with Ratcliffe, Madeline listens as the senator contends that George Washington's virtues could not cope with the political realities of the present-day republic: "If virtue won't answer our purpose, we must use vice." Madeline believes "the associations with Mount Vernon, indeed, everything Washington touched [were] purified." Ratcliffe was soiling all that was sacred to democracy.

"Is a respectable government impossible in a democracy?" Madeline asks early in her stay in the capital. Though drawn to Ratcliffe, the great lodestone of power in Washington's affairs, she comes to realize that men like the senator who dominate Washington no longer act for the public good. Recognizing that she is "not fitted for politics," she refuses marriage. Her education complete, Madeline Lee returns to New York.

The models for the characters in *Democracy* were all around in Washington. James G. Blaine, the congressman, senator, and Republican contender for the presidential nomination in 1876, who had been implicated in a colossal railroad bribery scheme, bore a striking resemblance to Ratcliffe. Clover and Henry's sensibilities and circumstances mirror those of Madeline. Madeline's natural grace and virtue enable her to resist the vulgar in all its guises. Henry had once shared Madeline's belief that the politicians in Washington acted with a common understanding of right and wrong and conducted their affairs in an ethical and honest way. And like Madeline, his disillusionment had driven him from the capital to seek diversions in foreign lands. But Henry Adams's sensibilities resided in other minor characters, too: in the rectitude of a former Confederate who uncovers Ratcliffe's sale of his vote for $100,000; in the desire of a young New England congressman "to purify the public tone"; and in the speech of a foreign minister who declaims, at one of Madeline's parties, "I have found no society which has had elements of corruption like the United States."

Viewing the world through the lens of literature, as he increasingly did, gave Adams the luxury of withdrawing from Washington's political life. In July 1881, when a crazed Charles Guiteau shot James Garfield as the president was boarding a train at the Baltimore and Potomac Station for a seaside vacation in New Jersey, Adams wrote a friend that Thackeray or Balzac could not have invented so "lurid" a tale as "Garfield, Guiteau, and Blaine." Several months later he and Clover attended Guiteau's trial for a day; they even visited the assassin in the city's jail and asylum at Nineteenth Street and Independence Avenue SE. Clover regarded him as "the accursed beast," while Henry used the occasion as an opportunity to express his disgust with politicians who played to public sentiment and wanted only for Guiteau to hang. "To say that any sane man would do this," he wrote, "is a piece of, not insanity, but of idiocy, in the District Attorney." But public sentiment prevailed, as Adams knew it would. Guiteau went to the scaffold singing, "I am going to the Lordy, I am so glad."

Satirize the newly minted money and manners of Washington's Gilded Age though they might, all was not well within the circle of the Five of Hearts, most especially in Clover and Henry's marriage. Henry proved to be cut from the cloth of an upper-class, late nineteenth-century American male, at times distant, at times critical, and always controlling. His marriage to Clover was barren. By the fall of 1885, Clover Adams was slipping into a deep depression from which she would never recover. On the first Sunday in December, Marian Hooper Adams took her life. The shock of her violent passing left Henry silent. He had her buried in an unmarked grave at Rock Creek Cemetery, near the valley where he and Clover had often ridden. He destroyed Clover's correspondence and her journals, and never again allowed her name to pass his lips. "I can endure," Henry wrote to a friend two days after his wife's death. "But I cannot talk, unless I must."

Travel—to Japan, to Samoa, and to Europe, among other places—offered Adams little respite from his pain. On his return to Washington in February 1892, Henry went directly to the grave at Rock Creek Cemetery to view the memorial he had commissioned from the Beaux-Arts sculptor Augustus Saint-Gaudens. There Adams beheld a seated figure, cloaked in coarse drapery, whose face, eyes shut, seems to peer into the mysteries of life and death, contemplating forever a world beyond human comprehension.

Adams returned to his wife's grave again and again. He considered the work in "every change of light and shade . . . to see what the figure had to tell him that was new," he wrote in his *Autobiography*. "But," he added, "in all that it had to say, he never once thought of questioning what it meant." Not so for others, who speculated about its meaning and gave it titles such as "Sadness" or "Grief." He knew better. "The interest of the figure was not in its meaning," he wrote, "but in the response of the observer." In his unutterable suffering, Henry Adams had given his favorite city a work of haunting and sublime grace.

ALTHOUGH HE DID not swim in the same refined and intellectual waters of his neighbor Henry Adams, Charles Carroll Glover, who lived in a three-story house at 20 Jackson Place on Lafayette Square,

THE ADAMS Memorial as it appeared c. 1935. Adams had Augustus Saint-Gaudens design the statue. Saint-Gaudens turned to his friend Stanford White to design the granite plinth and stele beneath and behind the bronze sculpture as well as the hexagonal plaza and benches. CREDIT: Library of Congress

also enjoyed rambles in the wilderness of the Rock Creek Valley. Like Henry and Clover, he frequently followed the paths beside the creek north to Oak Hill Cemetery and the rugged terrain beyond. He, too, saw the broad fields of wildflowers blooming through spring, summer, and into fall, the small and silent dells surrounded by gray barked beeches and oaks, and the tangles of wild honeysuckle. There were small streams to ford; red and gray foxes, flying squirrels, whitetail deer, coyotes, turtles, and northern water snakes were plentiful. On Thanksgiving Day 1888, Glover led a party of two lawyers and the assistant engineer for the District of Columbia on just such a horseback ride. The men knew that developers were fast pushing north from the Potomac to create suburban communities. Much of the landscape they were viewing might soon be prime real estate. To preserve the land, they would have to convince the federal government to make it a national park.

Glover had all the proper connections to get his way: his roots were in old Washington, and he counted his ancestors among the District's original landholders; he was president of the Riggs Bank on Fifteenth Street and Pennsylvania Avenue, across from the Treasury, which held the money of presidents, senators, congressmen, generals, admirals, and foreign legations; and he moved with ease between the offices of the Capitol and the White House. His companions that Thanksgiving were also well connected: two, Calderon Carlisle and James M. Johnston, were lawyers from old Washington families; the third, Thomas W. Symons, an assistant engineer in charge of the city's water and sewage, had graduated first in his class at West Point, had been a member of the US Geological Survey in the West, and had the respect of the District commissioners. In a meeting at Jackson Place after Thanksgiving, Crosby S. Noyes, editor of the *Washington Evening Star* and consummate city promoter, pledged his paper's full support. In mid-January 1889, the men decided upon a plan: Congress was to vote on the creation of a National Zoological Park. To this bill a sympathetic member of Congress introduced an amendment drafted by Carlisle and Johnston, authorizing the purchase of 2,000 acres of land for Rock Creek Park. District residents would pay half the cost of $1.5 million.

The very idea of the United States paying any of the costs of a park for the city raised all the old animosities that congressmen had long harbored about the District of Columbia. Representative Judson Claudius Clements of Georgia declared that the capital's open squares meant that Washingtonians had more park land than residents of other cities; a representative of Texas voiced the sentiments of many of his colleagues when he said that, if the city's residents wanted a park, they should pay for it themselves. Another Georgia congressman, James Henderson Blount, argued that the Soldiers' Home had ample lands for a park. Such bluster swayed the debate; the amendment to the bill lost by ten votes.

But Glover was not discouraged. Congress's approval of the bill to purchase land in Rock Creek for the National Zoo, over the strenuous opposition of a cadre of southern Democratic representatives who opposed most public expenditures for the District, augured well. The vote for the zoo was timely, too, for thousands were coming daily to see exotic animals from across the continent and the world that the Smithsonian was housing in temporary pits and cages, including panthers and lynx, eagles and vultures, venomous snakes and lizards, and three different kinds of bears. (Animals were arriving with such frequency that Smithsonian officials hastily erected an ugly barn on the Mall to house a bull and cow, four deer, and a pair of buffalo.) Security was lax; wild dogs had already attacked a Rocky Mountain goat that was tied to a tree on the Mall, and would kill an antelope that Senator Leland Stanford had shipped from California.

Neither Glover's optimism nor his commitment faltered. He turned his energy to convincing Congress of the park's importance and took wavering representatives on tours of the land, all the while reminding them of the growing importance of Washington in the world. Like L'Enfant before him, Glover thought of the capital as a grand stage on which all the ideals of the republic would be seen by all the world. His persistence paid off. On the last Saturday of September in 1890, after the usual delays and speeches about the corruption and rapacious greed of Washington's citizens, members of the 51st Congress approved a bill creating a "pleasuring ground" in the Rock Creek Valley. In 1892, the government acquired 1,600 acres on both sides of the winding creek above the National Zoo.

Rock Creek was not the only land in the capital that held Charles Carroll Glover's interest. He had long wanted to reclaim the marshes in southwest Washington that citizens called the "Potomac Flats." When L'Enfant had surveyed the site for his seat of government in 1791, the waters of the Potomac had covered the marshes between the

White House and the river; the high tide of two feet served to keep the marshes passably fresh, and heavy rains often brought flooding, which sometimes extended inland as far as Pennsylvania Avenue. Over time, the city's growth had changed the ecology even more. The Long Bridge of 1809, along with its earthen approach across the marsh, altered the river's currents and tides; still John Quincy Adams thought the waters of the Potomac were clean enough to swim in when he was president. But the addition of sewers and a great discharge pipe at Seventeenth Street dumped the human waste of thousands directly into the river. Every summer the sewage created what one newspaper reporter called "a hellbroth" in the Potomac and a "miasma" in the air.

Most Washingtonians who could do so fled the city in the months of July and August. That had been James Garfield's intent in July 1881, when he met Charles Guiteau. Instead the president spent the summer in the White House as doctors probed his body with dirty fingers and unsterilized instruments in their vain search for the bullet fragments that were slowly poisoning him. To cool the dying Garfield, military engineers rigged up fans in his bedroom that blew air over blocks of ice. The fans lowered the temperature but also drew in the putrescent stench from the Potomac Flats. It was in part the "evil effect of this poisonous atmosphere" that brought the question of reclamation of the flats to the fore.

That fall, Glover organized a group of citizens, including Crosby S. Noyes of the *Washington Evening Star*, to champion reclamation. Knowing Congress as Glover did, and knowing the opposition of many to any expenditure on the city, he moved in incremental steps. By 1882, Congress had approved enough funding, $400,000, to begin dredging a deeper channel in the Potomac. Silt from the river bottom served as fill to reclaim the marshes, and eventually army engineers erected a flood wall. By 1886, about 350 acres had been added to the Potomac waterfront, but a dispute over ownership of land near what is now the Lincoln Memorial, and the opposition of many in Congress, made progress for the next decade painfully slow.

And what was to be done with the new land? Some in Congress wanted to sell it for building lots. The railroads saw it as a great opportunity to build a huge siding, where roads from the North could meet those from the South. Glover thought otherwise. Working quietly with his friends in Congress, he promoted the idea of a great park. Congress defeated a park bill in 1895, but in late February 1897 it established the Potomac Park. Glover now used his easy entrée to the White House to lobby Grover Cleveland. On March 3, 1897, his last day in office, the president signed the bill.

CITIZENS WITH MEANS and influence like Charles Carroll Glover could effect change in Washington. They were welcome at the homes of representatives, senators, cabinet members, even the White House. Many of them believed that life under three presidentially appointed commissioners was better than when the District was a territory. They remembered the brief time when those without property, including blacks, had enjoyed suffrage, and some had flirted with the notion of desegregating the schools. They were happy that the federal government and the District shared the city's expenses equally. But as Washington and the government that dominated it grew in numbers and complexity, the impotence of the general populace became ever more apparent. District residents could not elect local representatives to tend to their interests in fundamental matters like streets, sanitation, or transportation; they could not elect someone to represent their interests in Congress; and they could not vote for presidential electors.

Over time, associations took the place of true representation. The first, the East Washington Citizens' Association, formed in 1870 because, as its history noted, the city's post–Civil War development was "leaning towards its western borders, and even the nurturing wave of Governmental care and appropriations seemed to be receding from the eastern half." Membership was open to "any reputable citizen or taxpayer" who paid a fee of fifty cents. Nearly a score of similar associations followed, each advancing its own parochial interests to the commissioners, and on some occasions joining with others for the commonweal of the city.

Washington's businessmen had created a Board of Trade in November 1889. Its membership grew quickly, reaching 655 by 1900. Prominent Jewish merchants belonged, as did James Wormley, who had succeeded his father as head of the Wormley House Hotel. (Starting in 1895, the board opened its membership to women.) In the absence of a municipal governmental structure, the bankers, realtors, lawyers, and department store owners who made up its board of directors formed the nucleus of the capital's civic power structure. In its annual report for 1892, the Board of Trade proudly proclaimed itself "practically a state legislature, city council and chamber of commerce combined into one."

Boards of trade, common in cities across America, were usually filled with proto-Babbit boosters. Washington's board certainly had that role; it extolled the virtues of business in the capital and sent speakers into schools on patriotic days, such as Washington's birthday. But from its inception, Washington's board played a unique role, helping to supplement the insufficient and ineffective efforts of the three presidentially appointed commissioners and a largerly uninterested and overwhelmed Congress. Who would educate Congress about the inadequate fire department? About the need to improve the sewage system, and to fill in the abandoned canal in the southwest that had become such a pestilential sewer? About the importance of education and the value of a free public library?

The Board of Trade had a busy agenda. It set up committees to study numerous matters of importance to the District, including public safety, water purification, charities, and streets and avenues, among others. It advocated the removal of the B&O tracks and train station from the eastern edge of the Mall, and it fought the proposal from a Virginia railroad company that wished to lay tracks on the land being reclaimed at the Mall's western end. Its aim, an early secretary said, was to make Washington the equal to Paris in beauty and attractions, to Rome in art, and to Berlin in education.

Theodore Williams Noyes, the son of Crosby and editor of the *Washington Evening Star* after his father's death in 1908, disliked the present commission form of government. But he dismissed the idea of an elected limited municipal government that some proposed as a "sham"; without full representation, he said, Washington was shut out "from the bodies which make its laws and impose taxes upon it." Starting in 1888, when he was associate editor, he frequently used the pages of the *Star* to advocate a constitutional amendment that would give the citizens the right to elect representatives to Congress as well as presidential electors. Few heeded Noyes's call; Congress utterly ignored it. For decades, the issue of how to accord representation to the District's citizens would continue to smolder beneath the scant platform of the city's meager governmental structure—though, from time to time, a citizens group, a well-intentioned senator, or Noyes himself would attempt to coax the embers into flame.

SINCE MUCH OF its business was government, Washington appeared relatively isolated from the consequences of financial panics and depressions that sometimes beset the nation. However, one jobless man, Jacob Selcher Coxey, a populist from Massilon, Ohio, brought the depression of 1893 to the capital. Coxey organized an "army" to march east to the nation's capital, where the men would demand that the government create a relief program that would pay them $1.50 for a day's labor. On the last day of April in 1894, about four hundred men arrived at the Capitol steps, where guards promptly arrested Coxey for trespassing. The men quietly dispersed. Insignificant as the protest was, it augured a future role for the capital as the destination of choice for those who wanted to effect social change.

Throughout the 1890s, Washington's white citizens remained generally cheerful and confident about their nation and their city. In 1900, William McKinley was reelected president with the largest margins ever in both the electoral college and the popular vote. Catching the wave of patriotic and religious fervor that came with the nation's victory in the Spanish-American War, and taking credit for ending the economic depression of 1893, he rode on a platform of prosperity and the slogan "A Full Dinner Pail." That December, the secretary of the treasury reported that the government had a surplus of $79 million. (An excise tax on telephone service had financed the war in Spain as well as the continuing fighting in the Philippines.) The American flag flying over the Capitol now had forty-five stars. In the wake of the war with Spain, Americans believed they had a "divine mission," as Albert Jeremiah Beveridge, a young senator from Indiana, had put it. God had made Americans "the master organizers of the world to establish system where chaos reigns." The decennial census showed that the population of the United States had reached 76.2 million. One of every thirteen families owned a telephone; one of every seven had indoor plumbing. America's future was brighter than ever.

Washingtonians, too, embraced the nationalistic fervor. A regiment of volunteers had served gallantly in Cuba in the recent war.

Its citizens had welcomed the hero of Manila Bay, Admiral George Dewey, in a grand ceremony when he returned home. Although they had been disenfranchised by Congress, had no control over their civic affairs, and no representatives in the federal government, they took an intense interest in politics and the presidential election. On the evening of November 6, the *Washington Post* had used lantern slides to show the results on a large screen outside its building; men with megaphones shouted out the latest news.

Washington's white citizens were enjoying great prosperity. Real-estate prices and sales, already robust for the year, were experiencing a postelection surge; brokers reported they were "dickering with capitalists from Chicago, New York and other places" for choice properties; builders were busy erecting houses in the northwest, where building lots in Cleveland Park were trading for fifty cents per square foot; and Rhode Island Avenue, on the edge of LeDroit Park, was fast becoming a thoroughfare to the growing suburban tracts of Eckington and Edgewood in the northeast.

That December marked the opening of Washington's season, which would extend through the winter months. "GAYETY IN FULL SWING," proclaimed a typical headline in the *Post*. "Society Busy with Debutantes, Dinners and Receptions." With the assistance of the wives of cabinet members, Mrs. McKinley and her husband had a reception for the ladies of the Women's Christian Temperance Union (WCTU), which was holding its convention in the capital. (Although the WCTU ladies were unhappy that the president hadn't banned serving liquor in army canteens, they appreciated his wife Ida's firm stand against alcohol.) On Thursday the 13th, the city's first automobile show at the convention hall culminated with a parade of electric, gas, and steam-powered cars, each bedecked with flowers, circling the hall. Washington's theaters had a full complement of offerings, including the "Great Lafayette's" vaudeville act at the New Grand; acrobats, pantomimists, and "a bevy of pretty girls" at the Columbia; and at the New National, Lottie Blair Parker's melodrama *Way Down East*, which had just finished a year's run in New York. On Friday evening, December 14, a former war correspondent, British army officer, and recently elected member of parliament lectured on the Boer War at the New National Theater. "[He] is not an orator," wrote the reviewer for the next day's paper. "He appeared embarrassed when he began, and throughout the lecture his words came out in a jerky halting way." But in the peroration, Winston Churchill laid aside his embarrassment "and rose to the heights of eloquence."

Surely the most important events that December for every one of the city's 278,000 citizens, white or black, were the ceremonies marking Washington's one-hundredth anniversary as the capital of the United States. They celebrated on Wednesday the 12th—a date chosen by the president—with an elaborate parade. The sky was bright and blue, the temperature was "balmy," as the *Evening Times* described the day; all Washington was a "wilderness of flags and bunting." Following McKinley and members of his cabinet up Pennsylvania Avenue to the Capitol were the nation's forty-five governors (including Rhode Island's, who rode with his staff in open automobiles), nine marching bands, and thousands of soldiers and sailors. That evening, after enduring three hours of speeches at the Capital and a reception at the Corcoran Gallery, Washingtonians saw their city aglow with light, including an American flag of red, white, and blue bulbs suspended over Pennsylvania Avenue at Seventeenth Street that "alternately brightened and paled," to give the appearance of waving in the breeze.

One group of Washingtonians, those who lived in Murder Bay and the alley dwellings, had but a marginal relationship with the centennial festivities. Alley dwellings, and those who lived in them, occupied a netherworld behind the houses that generally fronted on the lettered and numbered streets, and beneath the powerful who occupied them. (Eastman Johnson's *Negro Life at the Old South* hints at their existence.) They were an unintended consequence of L'Enfant's plan, which had created large square blocks that allowed developers to erect multiple houses. The division of streets made for neat blocks, but they allowed for a narrow passage to lead from the street into a dark, crowded interior, and frequently the passage ended in a blind. Typical of this time was Blagdon Alley. In 1890, about eighty houses occupied the square block bounded by M, N, Ninth, and Tenth streets. Narrow paths leading from each side of the block led to Blagdon, and no less than twenty alley dwellings, sheds really, with no running water and but the most primitive of privies.

Blagdon was but one of about two hundred alleys in the city, some with as many as five hundred dwellers. Some white immigrants lived in alley dwellings, but at the turn of the century blacks counted for

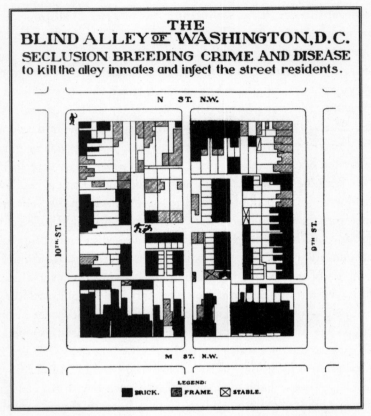

THE
BLIND ALLEY OF WASHINGTON, D.C.
SECLUSION BREEDING CRIME AND DISEASE
to kill the alley inmates and infect the street residents.

N ST. N.W.

10TH ST.

9TH ST.

M ST. N.W.

LEGEND:
BRICK. FRAME. STABLE.

HOME TO thousands of immigrants and blacks, the capital's alleys seemed forbidding places to white middle-class Washingtonians. By placing the outline of a billy-club wielding policeman outside the alley and the fighters inside, the artist of this 1912 drawing is emphasizing the dangers of the lawlessness within. But the real danger was to the public health of the alley dwellers. CREDIT: Private collection

most of the alley population. Many dwellers were the sons and daughters of freedmen who had migrated to the capital from the South. The conditions were horrendous. Tuberculosis flourished, as did outbreaks of cholera. Yet Congress refused to allow any District health officer to condemn the structures, and only in 1892 did District law begin to prevent the construction of new alley dwellings without running water and sewers. The law made no provision for the thousands already living there without such necessities. The alleys would continue.

Still, despite the setbacks they experienced with the collapse of Reconstruction, as well as the discrimination they faced daily,

Washington's black citizens, especially its educated class, managed to retain a measure of pride against indignities and insults. The faculty at Howard University was almost entirely white, and of course the institution was led by a white man. McKinley had failed to appoint many blacks to civil service positions; political equality in a city that disenfranchised everyone was out of the question. Most indicative of the blacks' treatment was their experience in the District of Columbia Militia. Since the 1870s, men and boys had marched in segregated battalions, drilling monthly and taking part in competitive military reviews. Only a protest to President Benjamin Harrison by the prominent black lawyer Robert Terrell, Frederick Douglass's son Lewis, among others, prevented the commanding general from disbanding the black battalions altogether in 1891. A greater indignity followed in 1898, when another virulently anti-black commanding general forbade the "colored battalion" to fight in Cuba. Nevertheless, the black militiamen were able to circumvent the general's orders and serve in Cuba as members of "immune companies," soldiers whose skin color, it was erroneously thought, made them resistant to the ravages of yellow fever.

In the face of such obstacles, blacks still looked to education, self-discipline, and good works as the best way to advance. Representative George Henry White from North Carolina spoke to audiences at Washington's black cultural societies, such as the Second Baptist Lyceum, of the "wonderful progress" that proved his race's "capacity for development." But those words marked the triumph of hope over the grim realities that surrounded him. White's state, along with the rest of the South, had rewritten its constitution in 1900 to disenfranchise blacks. When he made his remarks, the congressman was in the final days of his term, a remnant of the late nineteenth century, the last black person from the South to serve in Congress until 1972.

But the troubles of black Washingtonians were of little matter to the city's or the nation's leaders. They were more concerned with the safety of the president. That same December, the papers carried reports of deranged men who had wanted to see McKinley. Guards apprehended one of them on the White House grounds after he said he wished to talk with the president about a $3 million pension that he claimed the government owed him. Another man, a tailor from Baltimore, declared that he was coming to a state dinner "in celebration of the reelection of the President."

THE ANNUAL Easter Egg Roll on the South Lawn of the White House
has been a tradition since the time of the Hayes administration. CREDIT:
Library of Congress

Both men were clearly insane, but then so was Charles Guiteau,
who had murdered Garfield two decades earlier. Along with the insane,
and perhaps Spanish Cubans, whom some feared would strike the president, there were now anarchists. It was rumored that the latter had
drawn up a list of world leaders they would assassinate, and evidence
from Europe substantiated just that. In April 1900, two shots from an
anarchist's gun had missed the prince of Wales; and in July an anarchist
who had recently worked in Paterson, New Jersey, had murdered King
Umberto I of Italy. Particularly worried for the president's safety was
his manager and sometime confidant Senator Mark Hanna from Ohio,
who regarded Vice President Theodore Roosevelt as nothing more than
a cowboy, once exclaiming, "Don't any of you realize that there's only
one life between that madman and the Presidency?"

"THERE IS ONLY one National Capital. . . . There is only one incom-
parable residence city in the United States," the Washington Board of
Trade proclaimed in a pamphlet it published at the turn of the century.

Washington was the best place on earth. Three commissioners operated the city, "completely devoid of dishonesty's taint," a system far better than the usual practice of "Board of Aldermen and a Common Council," who regard "taxpayer's contributions . . . as legitimate spoils." The capital's population was now approaching 300,000; its death rate was 19.32 per 1,000 souls (15.53 for whites and 27.51 for blacks). "Shallow wells have been filled up, marshes drained and streets cleaned, water-supply increased, milk carefully inspected, food adulterations sought and located, drainage stopped and sanitation taught." The assessed value of new buildings in the previous year was nearly $2 million. New subdivisions were growing beyond the boundary set by L'Enfant, which afforded developers opportunities for profitable investment. Trains and steamboats linked the capital with Virginia and Maryland, and "all prominent suburbs" were "electrically connected to the city."

As an educational center, the city offered the Library of Congress, the Smithsonian Institution, a chance to study "the government of the great republic"—and, the pamphlet noted, "one of every five-hundred inhabitants is a scientist of more than local repute." With an "excellent" fire department and a police force that strove for "physical and mental fitness," it said, "a mob in Washington is almost an impossibility." Sports of all sorts were present in the capital: sailing, rowing, golf, and "an estimated fifty thousand bicycles" that could be "propelled over the smoothest of streets." Even Washington's weather came in for commendation. The city attracted many invalids in the fall who remained until they took to the mountains or seashore in the spring. Nevertheless, "in the summer it is much cooler than are many cities to the north of it. . . . The local record of sunstrokes and heat prostrations shows almost entire immunity from fatal cases." Hyperbole aside, one truth was irrefutable: the thriving city of Washington had earned its place as the capital of the nation.

CHAPTER 9

L'Enfant Redivivus

> I have just returned from Washington after three most interesting days with Burnham and Olmsted over the District of Columbia problem. If half of what is talked about can be carried through it will make the Capital City one of the most beautiful centers in the world.
>
> —Charles Follen McKim, 1901

Over the course of Washington's first century, Peter Charles L'Enfant's vision for the city had gradually faded from the minds of planners and architects. Their changes, to Pennsylvania Avenue, the Capitol grounds, and the Mall, made largely in ignorance, amounted to nothing less than benign acts of civic vandalism. Pennsylvania Avenue—L'Enfant's "Grand Avenue"—suffered the most. The avenue had lost L'Enfant's intent to create a "reciprocity of sight." Andrew Jackson's supposed placing of the Treasury Building in the middle of Pennsylvania Avenue in 1836, and Alfred Mullett's locating the State, War, and Navy Building for the middle of New York Avenue in 1871, destroyed views of the White House from the east and west.

Congress's siting of its library on the east corner of Independence Avenue and First Street SE illustrates just how far L'Enfant's plan had receded in the minds of architects and designers, as well as that of the Librarian of Congress, Ainsworth Rand Spofford. Spofford especially wanted the library's monumental façade and interior to celebrate American contributions to knowledge and culture. A bust of Benjamin Franklin occupies the center of nine circular windows in the portico above the building's entrance; busts of Demosthenes, Ralph Waldo Emerson, Washington Irving, Goethe, British historian Thomas Macaulay, Nathaniel Hawthorne, Sir Walter Scott, and Dante flank him. Inside, visitors pass paintings and sculptures of such subjects as the Oral Tradition, Imagination, Memory, Intellect, Research, and Truth before arriving at the library's great reading room, an immense octagonal rotunda crowned by an interior dome and oculus. The room's shape reflects Spofford's desire to organize knowledge into eight classes: religion, philosophy, law, science, commerce, history, literature, and art. "The library . . . is a national possession," America's foremost architecture critic, Montgomery Schuyler, wrote in *Scribner's Magazine* in 1897, "an example of a great public building monumentally conceived, faithfully built and worthily adorned."

Yet as imposing and monumental as the Library of Congress is, its placement desecrated L'Enfant's design for the city as much as, if not more than, Andrew Jackson's siting of the Treasury Building in the middle of Pennsylvania Avenue. The building's chief engineer, Thomas Lincoln Casey, brought the same uncompromising approach to the new library as he had to the Washington Monument, but this time the results were far from felicitous. The new building forces its way into Pennsylvania Avenue to obscure the view of the Capitol from the southeast, and its roof and lantern oculus compete with Thomas Walter's Capitol dome. Architecturally impressive, to be sure, the library is nevertheless a planning blunder of monumental proportions.

The siting of its library was not the first misstep of Congress. In 1792 it had allowed Andrew Ellicott to move the location of the Capitol itself to the western edge of Jenkins Hill. The unhappy result was a narrow earthen terrace of little use and a building that seemed to turn its back on the White House, L'Enfant's Mall, the Washington Monument, and the western half of the city. Now, with the protrusion of the library building into Pennsylvania Avenue, the Capitol Park on the eastern side seemed cramped and out of scale with the surrounding landscape. Fortunately, Congress hired Frederick Law Olmsted in 1873 to reconfigure the Capitol grounds.

Olmsted regarded his commission as an opportunity to bring order and unity to the buildings between the Capitol and the White House. "As it is," he wrote to the chair of the Senate's Committee for Public

OLMSTED'S DESIGN for the Capitol Park. SOURCE: William C. Allen, *History of the United States Capitol: A Chronicle of Design, Construction, and Politics* (Washington, DC: US Government Printing Office, 2001).

Grounds in early 1874, "the effect produced is admitted to be a broken, confused and unsatisfactory one often alluded to as a standing reproach against the system of government. . . . In short the Capitol of the Union manifests nothing so much as disunity," and without a "coordinating purpose." To Olmsted, the need for coherent design in the landscape reflected the need for a coherent purpose in the popular democracy. "What is wanting," he concluded, "is a federal bond."

Olmsted set about to create a visual bond on the landscape so that "the observer can hold [the Capitol and its grounds] all in fair perspective." The result was a visual sleight of hand that compensated for and masked the irregular development of the buildings and the land over eight decades.

OLMSTED'S SUMMERHOUSE. SOURCE: William C. Allen, *History of the United States Capitol: A Chronicle of Design, Construction, and Politics* (Washington, DC: US Government Printing Office, 2001).

To give the Capitol's western side definition, Olmsted created a broad marble terrace that integrated it with the Mall, the Washington Monument, the Potomac, and the Arlington Heights beyond. "As the building cannot be moved back, the only remedy possible is to be found in bringing it simply and boldly forward." Two broad marble staircases would connect the upper level of the Capitol building and the Mall below, lending unity to the entire prospect. When his plan was executed fifteen years later, he added a massive octagonal stone fountain between the stairs.

For the Capitol Park on the eastern side (at the top of the drawing), Olmsted created two enormous tear-drop grass ovals, each extending five hundred feet in length by four hundred feet in width and embellished with clusters of trees. These afforded a broad and verdant transition from the severe angularity of the numerous streets and avenues leading to the square. He softened the approach of East Capitol Street, which terminates at the Capitol's center, with an allée of tulip poplars. Bronze ornamental lights, stone fountains, benches, and walls, many with subtle variations of texture and color, accented these larger elements of the design.

Close by the Capitol, Olmsted planned for two hexagonal brick summerhouses. These would be subtle structures, grottos with streams and fountains and stone benches for the rest and reflection of visitors. Over time, Congress executed almost all of Olmsted's plans. The Capitol Park came first, finished in 1879; the first summerhouse followed in 1881; and the terrace and stairs in 1893. After some members objected to the construction of the first summerhouse, Congress decided to omit the second, thereby destroying the harmony of the original design, and leaving visitors to the grounds with just one opportunity for repose.

The Mall demonstrated, too, how planners had ignored L'Enfant's designs. Olmsted had wanted to expand the scope of his commission to include that land, but Congress would have none of it. Yet, over time, as the view from the west front of the Capitol affirmed, the Mall had devolved into a hodgepodge of misplaced buildings, odd structures, and meandering garden paths, all constructed without regard for the designer's intentions. The Smithsonian's red sandstone castle, teeming with crenellations and turrets, obtruded into the space that L'Enfant had dreamed of as a greensward with an allée of trees. The Washington Monument stood tall, but off axis with the Capitol and the White House, thereby destroying the symmetry its designer had intended. The verdant footpaths that the romantic landscape designer Andrew Jackson Downing had created seemed more suitable for a woodland glen than the public lawn of the national capital. The three-story, red-brick Second Empire Agriculture Department building, which was topped with a mansard roof and wrought-iron crestings and finials, continued the discordant note of the Smithsonian on the east. Greenhouses flanked the building, and gardens stretched across the Mall to B Street, today's Constitution Avenue. In their midst between Twelfth and Thirteenth streets stood the General Noble Redwood Treehouse. Fifty feet tall, and topped by a peaked roof (with redwood shingles) and two dormer windows, the "treehouse" was actually a hollowed out stump of a giant redwood that had been part of the US exhibit at the 1893 World's Columbian Exposition in Chicago. It now served as a gardener's shed.

By far the boldest intrusion into L'Enfant's plan was the overcrowded and inadequate Baltimore and Potomac Railroad Station at Sixth and B streets. Wonderful High Victorian Gothic concoction though it was, the station was in the wrong place. The train shed at its rear crossed about half the Mall and detracted from the view east from the Washington Monument, as did the engines belching black smoke that shuttled across the tracks to Sixth Street and Maryland Avenue. But the prospects for removing this blemish to the Mall were not good. Indeed, Congress had recently passed a bill that allowed the railroad to lay more tracks and build an even bigger station on fourteen acres between Sixth and Seventh streets.

Although Congress and the army's engineers entrusted with the city's design had forgotten Peter L'Enfant, the nation's most important architects had not. City planning always involves weighing groups with competing interests and egos; in the case of the capital, they were especially powerful and well connected. The most formidable were the Army Corps of Engineers, which had been filling in the tidal flats west of the Washington Monument, and the War Department's Office of Buildings and Grounds, which controlled the Mall and the siting of public buildings. The head of Buildings and Grounds, Colonel Theodore Bingham, had his own portfolio of plans that would leave his imprint on the city: two giant wings for the White House in a style that borrowed heavily from the architecture of the Library of Congress; new public buildings along Pennsylvania Avenue; and a wide "Centennial Avenue" that would bisect the Mall and cross a bridge to Arlington. The army produced accomplished engineers, but none of them had been trained in the profession of architecture, or in the emerging profession of city planning. The credentials of those in Congress were no better, though its members had an abundance of ideas and schemes. The Senate and the House of Representatives were divided on the best action to take. But as the events between December 1900 and January 1902 proved, there was one senator who understood the capital and its potential better than most.

At first glance, Senator James McMillan from Michigan was an unlikely arbiter of aesthetics. A Gilded Age plutocrat from Detroit, he had made his fortune through controlling interests in foundries, steam forges, engine and iron works, the Michigan Railroad Car Company, street railroads, banks, and prime blocks of the city's commercial real estate. His interests lay in the development of his state, investing in Detroit's Ferry Seed Company, constructing a railroad into the state's Upper Peninsula, building ships for the Great Lakes, and, in 1881, financing the Michigan Bell Telephone Company. McMillan's creed was laissez-faire capitalism and limited government; his religion was the Michigan Republican Party, which he bankrolled liberally, running its state committee like a well-oiled machine in one of his factories. He despised reformers, social and political, and championed self-reliant men who through hard work alone determined their destiny. For pleasure he read biographies of Napoleon.

It was only natural that the grateful Republican state legislators who owed him their seats sent their patron to the US Senate in March 1889. Once in Washington, however, he demonstrated that his interests went far beyond accruing benefits for his party or increasing the thickness of his wallet. His gold-rimmed glasses, silver hair neatly parted down the center, full mustache, and goatee lent him a careful and sober demeanor and an air of gravitas. Leaving the practice of florid oratory and stentorian bluster to others, McMillan preferred a quiet conversation in the Senate cloakroom or in the front parlor of the mansion he and his wife had erected on Thomas Circle. When placed on the Senate's District of Columbia Committee, which some of his venal colleagues regarded as an opportunity to profit from advance knowledge of local land developments, McMillan approached his assignment with unmatched thoroughness and unusual probity. His job brought him into contact with those who mattered in Washington, he said, and a chance to improve the capital. When Republicans gained control of the Senate in 1891, they elected him to head the committee. Even when the chairmanship passed to the Democrats for a term in 1893, his opinions about the District held the most authority. Many of his colleagues jocularly called James McMillan Washington's mayor.

The senator owed much of his stature to Charles Moore. Born in Michigan and educated at Andover and Harvard, Moore had worked as a journalist in Ypsilanti and as an assistant to McMillan before accompanying him to Washington as his senior aide. Ever tactful and loyal, he performed his many duties—press secretary, speech writer, and, under the nom-de-plume "Seymour," author of columns about the senator's services and good deeds for Michigan's newspapers—with remarkable ease. Over time he mastered the subtle art of circumventing obstructionists in the House of Representatives. Should the House vote down legislation passed in the Senate, Moore knew just how and when to slip it back as an amendment in the conference report.

As his boss became more absorbed in the affairs of the capital, so did Moore, quietly learning the history of the city and its unique governance, the nature of its current affairs, and the tensions between its citizens and the federal government. His urbane manner, no doubt honed at Andover and Harvard, enabled him to move among journalists, businessmen, government officials, and Washington's society with ease. By 1900 he had established a web of powerful connections among every white person of importance in the capital. Despite his work and his continual need to attend to his web and its often diverse strands, he still found time to make frequent visits to the Cosmos Club and to earn a PhD in history at Columbian University. His thesis was on the American Northwest in the seventeenth and eighteenth centuries.

Among Moore's connections were members of the American Institute of Architects (AIA), especially its executive secretary, Glenn Brown. Formed in 1857 "to promote the artistic, scientific, and practical efficiency of the profession," the organization quickly evolved into a lobbying group for architects. To better influence Congress's decisions on the design of public buildings—the dozens of post offices, customhouses, and courthouses that were proliferating in cities and towns across the country—the institute had recently moved its headquarters from New York to William Thornton's Octagon House at Eighteenth Street in the capital. Brown himself was especially unhappy with what he saw around him in Washington, including the Second Empire State, War, and Navy Building, the Romanesque revival of the Old Post Office, and Adolf Cluss's polychrome and red brick Arts and Industries Building adjacent to the Smithsonian Castle. With calculation, he scheduled the annual AIA convention to coincide with the capital's centennial celebration. The AIA's theme was "The Grouping of Government Buildings, Landscape, and Statuary."

Brown's timing proved to be brilliant. Had the AIA not moved swiftly, the proposals of Colonel Bingham and the Army Corps of Engineers to enlarge the White House and redesign the Mall, or other schemes that were afoot—including a proposal to move the president's residence to Meridian Hill north of Florida Avenue—might well have prevailed. Over the four-day convention at the Arlington Hotel, speakers reviewed the architectural and planning blunders of the past; they excoriated Bingham's plans for the White House as an architectural desecration; and they repeatedly argued for a return to L'Enfant's plan.

Moore used the occasion to forge an alliance between the architects and James McMillan. The senator's heart lay with commerce and the railroads, which meant eliminating level grade crossings in the city, enlarging the Baltimore and Potomac station, and building more tracks across the Mall. Indeed, he and his committee had proposed a plan for the capital that included an ill-conceived boulevard from the Capitol to a memorial bridge across the Potomac to Arlington, Virginia. Still, he recognized the importance of aesthetics and respected intelligent urban planning. In Detroit, he had hired Frederick Law Olmsted to design Belle Isle Park, and had made a major donation to begin the city's Institute of Art. With Moore's subtle guidance, the senator and architects developed a compromise: the AIA would accept the fact of a railroad terminal on the Mall, and McMillan would secure money from Congress for a commission to recommend a plan for the capital's parks, including the Mall. When senators and representatives, usually skeptical of aesthetics and suspicious of experts, objected to McMillan's proposal, Moore devised a strategy to save it. An executive session of the Senate, held after the House of Representatives had adjourned its session, passed a resolution to "secure the services of experts" to prepare "plans for the development and improvement of the entire Park system of the District of Columbia." So on March 8, 1901, when most congressmen had left the city they controlled, but so often failed to appreciate, James McMillan got his wish: the Senate Park Commission was born.

INITIALLY, MCMILLAN, MOORE, and the AIA settled on three commissioners, arguably the most important designers of public buildings and spaces in the country: Daniel Hudson Burnham, Charles Follen McKim, and Frederick Law Olmsted Jr. Burnham, who chaired the commission, had recently presided over the design and the phalanx of architects who had transformed the muddy shore of Lake Michigan into the Court of Honor, or "White City," of the 1893 World's Columbian Exposition in Chicago. In Burnham's mind, the Exposition's buildings augured the future, the "City Beautiful," as he often called it. The purity of the Exposition's white stucco buildings—"Thine alabaster cities gleam," in the words of Katharine Lee Bates's poem "America the Beautiful"—glowed at night in the refulgence of George Westinghouse's 200,000 electric lamps.

Burnham's attention to urban planning and his return to classical form, as demonstrated at the World's Exposition, set an agreeable standard for most Americans. Planning by trained architects and urban planners could bring order to the chaos of overcrowded cities. Now, as chairman of the Senate Park Commission, he could apply his progressive aesthetic to the nation's most important public space; Washington would serve as a shining example for the rest of the Union. McKim, of the firm McKim, Mead, and White, the court architects for New York society, had designed the Agricultural Building for the Chicago Exposition, worked with Burnham in the planning of the White City, and helped to create its uniform plan. Frederick Law Olmsted Jr., who had joined his famous father in landscape architecture and assisted him in the design of the Emerald Necklace of parks encircling Boston, had already studied the problems of Washington's park system. On McKim's suggestion, a fourth expert, the sculptor Augustus Saint-Gaudens, joined the group later in the spring. He would help them site the sculptures for Lincoln and Grant. And always, accompanying the commissioners was the unassuming presence of Charles Moore.

Implicit in the Senate resolution was the need to put the design of Washington's public spaces back on course. For the commissioners that meant returning to L'Enfant's plan for the seat of government and adapting it to the changes that for good and ill had taken place over the past century. Their task, as Burnham put it, was "to make the very finest plans their minds could conceive." They had a limited budget—about $15,000—and the pressure to produce their designs by the end of the year. And the commissioners served without pay.

Prophetically, the commissioners gathered at "the Obelisk-Capitol axis" on Friday, April 5, 1901, to begin their work. Just as it had been for L'Enfant, the axis would be the backbone of their plans. Their task in part would be to restore the impression of balance and baroque order that the French designer had so prized.

Burnham announced on the day the trio surveyed the monument and the Capitol axis that they must visit tidewater plantations and Williamsburg, the former capital of Virginia, to consider the planning that George Washington knew. Even more significantly, he announced that they would tour Europe to study the public buildings and capitals that had inspired Jefferson, and especially L'Enfant. "Surely," as Burnham wrote to McKim later that month, "the Government, and especially our great uncle George, has the right to expect of us the very best we can give."

Although the excursion, including passage across the Atlantic, lasted seven weeks and suggested a Cook's Tour of Europe, it was anything but an opulent, government-paid junket. It gave the four men an opportunity to focus on nothing else but Washington. Burnham proved himself an unflagging taskmaster. The moment their boat cleared New York Harbor, he ordered the commissioners to his stateroom to study Washington maps, which Olmsted always carried in a tin tube, and discuss the dimensions of the project. At 3:30 on the morning after their late-night arrival in Paris, Burnham had them come to his hotel room so they could take in the sunrise over the Tuileries.

Every city they visited—London, Paris, Rome, Venice, Vienna—inspired their designs for the capital. They usually stayed together except to sleep. Conversation at meals always centered on what they had seen and what they might propose. Paris and Rome held special significance: Paris had been the font of inspiration for L'Enfant, and so it would be for the party, especially McKim. They carefully studied the axis of the Place de la Concorde between the Louvre and the Arc de Triomphe, which became the organizing principle for the city. In place of the Louvre, Washington would have the Capitol; in place of the Arc de Triomphe, a new memorial to Abraham Lincoln. Indeed, that axis would extend beyond the memorial to the Custis Lee mansion on the hill above the river. Rome had inspired Burnham's career, and it would continue to be in his design for the new railroad station. There they gathered ideas for public buildings and their placement, especially at the Villa Borghese, where they also agreed on the best location for the bridge to Arlington.

Olmsted served as the de facto recorder of the group. Never without his notebook, tape measure, tin tube of Washington maps, camera, tripod, and lenses, he recorded all that he saw and much that the group considered; he photographed chateaux and palaces, gardens and greenswards, fountains and large water basins; he measured the distances between trees and the widths of paths. His enterprise gave the commissioners a permanent record of all they saw, which they could consult in the future.

One of the most significant moments of the European tour was not a building or a landscape, but a meeting that changed the course of the commission's plans. On July 18, Burnham joined Alexander Johnston Cassatt, president of the Pennsylvania Railroad, to discuss the siting of the new railroad station. In addition to his solid training in engineering, which he acquired at Rensselaer Polytechnic Institute, and his practical experience building rail lines, Cassatt brought modern vision to the enterprise. By 1901 he was beginning ambitious plans to modernize and consolidate his railroad, including new stations, a tunnel under the Hudson River to bring the Pennsylvania into Manhattan, double and even quadruple tracking, and electrification. Cassatt matched his business acumen with a deeply rooted civic sense. His railroad must make money, of course, but must serve the public, too, and its stations must ennoble the human spirit.

As part of the consolidation plans, the Pennsylvania had just acquired a substantial interest in the Baltimore and Ohio railroad; Cassatt would be willing to build a new station for the combined lines north of the Capitol, provided that James McMillan would secure $1.5 million from Congress for a railroad tunnel under Capitol Hill. The tunnel would divert the tracks connecting the South from the Mall. The commissioners welcomed the plan. No longer did they have to consider the presence of trains, tracks, stations, and sidings that had insinuated themselves into their plans. The area known as Swampoodle, a wretched lowland north of the Capitol (so named for the swamps and pools that remained whenever the Tiber Creek overflowed) where the new station would be built, became an integral part of their proposal. For Daniel Hudson Burnham, moving the station offered him the opportunity to create a monumental entrance to the city.

Back in the United States in August, the commissioners dispersed to their long-neglected practices: McKim to New York, where he continued to design the Mall and its surrounding public buildings; Olmsted to Brookline, Massachusetts, where he produced plans for the Washington park system and general landscape design; and Burnham to Chicago, to design a new railroad station that would complement, but not challenge, the Capitol. Charles Moore remained in Washington to write the commission's report; supervise the cartographers who were creating maps of the Mall, White House grounds, and Capitol; and quietly arrange for meetings later that fall between the commissioners and important members of Congress.

On Wednesday, January 15, 1902, all was ready for a public unveiling. At noon McMillan submitted the report—172 pages, 107 illustrations, and 11 maps—to the full Senate. That afternoon the commissioners opened an exhibition of their proposals in three rooms at the Corcoran Gallery. McKim, who had taken charge of the show and the publicity surrounding it, demonstrated his shrewd sense of public relations. In order to whet the public's interest, that fall he had released selective nuggets of the plan to reporters and commissioned writers to seed magazines with positive articles about the coming report. He supervised the construction of two large and detailed models—one depicting the downtown core as it existed in 1901, the other showing that core with the commission's proposed changes. He hired six magazine illustrators to draw some of the design features and principal buildings, including views of the Mall and the transformation of Murder Bay into today's Federal Triangle.

Theodore Roosevelt and members of his cabinet arrived to see the exhibition at 2:30 p.m. Roosevelt had been president just four months. Two bullets fired by an anarchist point-blank into the chest of William McKinley had brought reality to Mark Hanna's worst fears. The change in Washington was startling. TR, as he came to be called, his wife, and six children transformed the White House with a new liveliness largely absent from the Gilded Age administrations. In place of a single telephone line to the White House, telephones sprouted in all the executive offices; in place of a single secretary, teams of stenotypists took dictation. And not since Abraham Lincoln's boys had there been such a wild ruckus as the Roosevelt children made playing hide-and-seek in the attic, popping out of large palm vases in the East Room, sliding down the stairs on trays commandeered from the kitchen, and bursting into official meetings. Their father was a man of unsettling impetuosity and thundering decisiveness. ("You must always remember that the president is about six," the British ambassador once remarked to a friend.) Roosevelt had already declared that the president's residence would remain on Pennsylvania Avenue (thereby scuttling discussion of moving it to Meridian Hill), and that "The White House," rather than "The Executive Mansion," would be its official name. That afternoon, Charles Moore reported that the president's reaction to the exhibition was "interested, curious, and at first critical and then, as the great consistent scheme dawned on him, highly appreciative."

The commission's report and models were at once a blueprint for the future of the capital and an early twentieth-century primer for enlightened urban planning. It returned to and extended L'Enfant's plans for the Capitol, White House, and Mall between them. Nineteenth-century romantics had strayed from L'Enfant's designs when they had considered the White House and Capitol separately, and the land between them simply as a place of recreation and rustication for city dwellers. Instead, the Senate commissioners regarded the Mall as the nation's front lawn, a symbolic sinew that tied together Congress and the presidency, the twin forces of the democracy. For the areas surrounding the lawn, they projected building monuments of democracy's achievements in the arts and sciences.

A bird's-eye view of what came to be called the McMillan Plan for the monumental core shows a Latin cross two and a half miles long and one mile wide. On the east, at the foot of the cross, is the Capitol, surrounded by a square of buildings, including the Library of Congress, a site for the Supreme Court (directly north), and offices for the members of the Senate and House. Water cascading from fountains and basins down the western slope to a "great central pool" would ease the transition to the 1,600-foot-wide Mall.

The Mall itself revealed the brilliance of the commission's landscape design to subtly trick the eye into seeing an axial relationship between the Capitol and the Washington Monument that in fact doesn't exist. The allée of elms leading west veers just slightly toward the south, and the space for the public buildings on Constitution Avenue is wider than the one on the Independence Avenue side.

Proposals to erect buildings for the executive branch on Lafayette Square north of the White House were less successful and abandoned. More interesting were the plans to make the space south of the Washington Monument "a place of recreation," with baseball diamonds, tennis courts, and swings for children. The Tidal Basin would have bathhouses, a beach, and boats. For the south side of the basin, and on an axis with the White House, the commission suggested a "great memorial." That would come in the New Deal and would be dedicated to Thomas Jefferson.

Most important to the Mall was the proposed Lincoln Memorial, situated forty feet above the river at the end of the reclaimed flats. Not only would it be a memorial, but also "a gate of approach to the park system." Drives along the bank of the Potomac would lead southeast to Potomac Park, or northwest by Riverside Drive to Rock Creek Park.

Behind the memorial, a low bridge would lead directly across the river to the Custis-Lee house and the cemetery at Arlington.

McKim's public relations strategy worked. Elihu Root, secretary of war, and John Hay, secretary of state, the two most important men in Roosevelt's cabinet, were enthusiastic; the models and drawings brought crowds of citizens to the Corcoran; the newspapers wrote extensive and positive reviews of the report; and in the *Architectural Record*, Montgomery Schuyler praised the "magnificent scheme" of the commissioners: "Their part in the making of a beautiful city has been so well done that they already deserve to be ranked with L'Enfant in the gratitude of Washingtonians and of all Americans who wish to be justified of their pride in the Capital."

Perhaps. But not for the moment. Bypassing the House of Representatives raised the ire of a number of its members, including Joseph Cannon, the cantankerous, small-minded, and ruthless head of the House Appropriations Committee, who had made criticism of big government the hallmark of his career. At every opportunity, the congressman from Illinois vowed to block whatever elements of the proposal he could, especially the Lincoln Memorial, which, he said, would be in a swamp. For years, he succeeded.

DANIEL BURNHAM GOT his railroad station, and, for Washington, with remarkable speed. As was the case elsewhere in the city, the demands of the federal capital trumped all else, even if they meant obliterating a neighborhood. Swampoodle, the area marked for destruction, was home to thousands of impoverished and sometimes violent Irish American laborers and their families. No matter that many of them had worked in the building trades for half a century; they had no voice and were expendable. By the time the first trains arrived in 1907, four years after start of construction, about 300 houses had been razed; some 1,700 people had been displaced to make way for the railroad's thirty-four tracks and a building whose size rivaled the Capitol's.

More than a mere depot for trains, Burnham's Union Station serves as a grand entry to the city and a Beaux-Arts tribute to the genius of American enterprise and culture. The architect took his inspiration from Rome—especially from the Baths of Diocletian, for the immense coffered and barrel-vaulted ceiling of the waiting room, which is supported by Ionic columns and graced with allegorical figures; and from the Roman triumphal arches that greeted ancient travelers to the city for his own trinity of arches welcoming American travelers to their capital. Standing before the great arches are six Ionic columns, each topped with an entablature and statue intended to symbolize the primary elements of a powerful nation: Fire, Electricity, Freedom, Imagination, Agriculture, and Mechanics. Burnham sheathed the entire building—panels, entablatures, and walls, as well as the columns—with white Vermont granite, lending the entire work a sense of integrity, honesty, and purity. His choice of materials and design set the standard for many of the federal capital structures that followed over the next four decades. At the entrance, an elliptical, D-shaped plaza, with a grand fountain in tribute to Columbus, provides a smooth transition between the station and the streets and avenues that radiate to the rest of the city. And perhaps those arriving or departing the station might look upward to the words about traveling that Harvard president Charles William Eliot selected to be inscribed in the central panels between the entablatures, including one from Homer's *Odyssey*: WELCOME THE COMING, SPEED THE PARTING GUEST.

Burnham's influence could be seen in other monumental buildings rising in the city. Just west of the station was the Beaux-Arts Post Office, completed two years after the architect's death in 1914 by the design firm that succeeded him. Its similar Ionic columns, Vermont granite, and inscribed entablatures (this time with postal paeans, such as SERVANT OF PARTED FRIENDS, CONSOLER OF THE LONELY, BOND OF THE SCATTERED FAMILY) complemented the station. Its location was practical, too, as mail could be transferred across a bridge connecting the two buildings to waiting trains.

Other buildings across the city reflected Burnham's philosophy and conformed at least in spirit to the McMillan Plan. Mount Vernon Square, where the Know-Nothings had their battle in 1857, and where Alexander Shepherd had razed the Northern Liberty Market in 1874, now saw a new Carnegie Library. On Capitol Hill, two office buildings for the Senate and House stood at opposite sides of Frederick Law Olmsted's Capitol Park. Pennsylvania Avenue at Fourteenth Street saw a new five-story building for the District commissioners. And on the Mall, the federal government erected the first two buildings conforming to the commission's plans: the National Museum of Natural History, on the north side opposite the Smithsonian Castle, and the two massive wings of a contemplated Department of Agriculture building, west of the Castle on the south side. (The building's center section would be built in the Hoover administration.) Owing to cost constraints, neither was as graceful or distinguished as it might have been, but at least each held to the commission's central tenet that new buildings should border the Mall. Even this concession was hard won. The inflexible and intractable secretary of agriculture actually laid the cornerstone and had begun the foundations for his building in the middle of the Mall before Theodore Roosevelt ordered construction halted and the building moved to its present location.

The remarkable change to the city's fabric brought about by the McMillan Commission drew the attention of those outside the capital. "He who visits Washington now after ten years," Montgomery Schuyler wrote in *Scribner's Magazine* in 1912, "finds so great a transformation that he is fain to take his bearings anew from the ancient landmarks and is relieved to find the Capitol and the Monument still predominant." Congress had loosened the federal purse-strings to create new quarters for an enlarged government; following Burnham, architects were creating an "official style" for the public buildings that would be the standard in the capital for decades. True, the architectural style, derivative of classical models, was not to everyone's taste then or now; nor was it adaptable to modern demands. Some critics considered it a vulgarization of the Greek and Roman, but it was solid and reassuring. A republic with brash ideas of originality, and scorn for Europe and its monarchies, found comfort in the aesthetic stability in the Western past.

One building begun in this period that was not in the Beaux-Arts style, but reassuring nonetheless, was the Gothic Revival Cathedral of St. Peter and St. Paul, often called the Washington National Cathedral. In 1893 Charles Glover and a group of prominent Episcopalian friends received a charter from Congress to create "a cathedral and institutions of learning for the promotion of religion and education and charity." By 1907 the bishop of the diocese had acquired a large tract of land at the summit of Mount St. Albans, 400 feet above the Potomac in northwest Washington. On September 29, Theodore Roosevelt spoke at the laying of the cornerstone—a rock from Bethlehem—and then left for a bear hunt in Louisiana. From the time of its first services in 1912, many have come to regard the cathedral as a national spiritual space, an almost nonsectarian gathering place for state funerals and memorial services, speeches by important ministers, and concerts.

BY 1910, WASHINGTON'S population had grown to 331,000, not the 700,000 envisioned by L'Enfant, yet an increase of 53,000 over the decade. The number was especially impressive because the capital had not become the commercial and manufacturing center that L'Enfant and Washington had envisioned. Commerce had long since gone to Baltimore, among other cities, and a flood in 1889 on the Chesapeake and Ohio Canal, which linked the city to the west, had forced the canal company into receivership. Although some occasionally called for Washington to take advantage of its abundant water and proximity to the coal fields of West Virginia, and replicate the great factories that were coming to dominate the American landscape, especially in the North and Midwest, most agreed that such development would be incompatible with the McMillan Commission's vision. Since December 1800, and especially since the Civil War, Washington's largest enterprise had been government. Its second largest was accommodating visitors who came to see the capital, do business with the government, or, increasingly, attend a convention. Washington was particularly popular in the spring and fall, when lodges, civic groups, and various business associations wanted to visit the city; 1910 saw groups as various as the Sons of Veterans and the Socialist Party; the National Institute of Dental Pedagogics and the American Clan Gregor; the Association of Life Insurance Presidents and the Daughters of 1812. After President William Howard Taft's wife, Helen, and the wife of the Japanese ambassador planted the first of 3,000 cherry trees at the Potomac Tidal Basin in March 1912, the capital became even more popular in the spring.

Washington's economy and the livelihoods of many of its residents increasingly depended upon serving the needs of the government and visitors. The city directory for 1910 provides a snapshot of the sorts of enterprises that flourished in the capital: nearly 200 boardinghouses and more than 800 restaurants and dining rooms; 33 banks and savings institutions, ranging from the Penny and Nickel on Fourteenth Street NW to the Riggs at Fifteenth Street and Pennsylvania Avenue (which had a desk at the Treasury Department next door, so that it might get the jump on monetary changes); 179 offices of newspapers from other cities; and 11 cigar wholesalers and 181 cigar dealers, including 23 along Pennsylvania Avenue between the Capitol and the White House.

Visitors had their choice of about 125 hotels: the Shoreham at Fifteenth and I streets and the New Willard at Fourteenth Street and Pennsylvania Avenue offered the best accommodations; the National catered to southern politicians; the Johnson at Fourth and Thirteenth drew mostly men; and the Dolley Madison House, at Fourteenth Street and Massachusetts Avenue—"Mrs. A McDonough, Prop . . . Just the place for ladies traveling unaccompanied"—catered to women. For $1, "The Seeing Washington Automobile Company" at Fifteenth and G streets opposite the Treasury Department advertised "a personally conducted tour through the interior of the Government Buildings." The company's primitive buses carried thirty sightseers, fifteen inside on seats arranged lengthwise, fifteen above on seats arranged "side-wise." A tour of Georgetown and Arlington, including the cemetery and the Custis-Lee mansion, cost $1.50. On summer afternoons, visitors and residents could sit on the White House lawn to listen to a concert by the Marine Band. If the weather was hot, as it almost always was in the summer, they could bathe in the Potomac Tidal Basin.

THE AIMS OF Washington's Board of Trade coincided with the McMillan Commission's. The board had advocated the removal of the Baltimore and Ohio from the Mall, and the elimination of railroad grade crossings throughout the city. And it consistently emphasized public improvements that were essential for the success of the commission's recommendations. "Sewers and sewage are not pleasant things to think of or see," the board said in its annual report of 1902, "but the city beautiful cannot be without these modern improvements."

More and more, Washington's residents—and even the commissioners and Congress—looked to the Board of Trade for guidance. In 1910, after the board joined the American Institute of Architects to advocate the appointment of a group of architects and artists to pass judgment on the numerous projects proposed for the capital, President Taft established the Commission on Fine Arts. The board championed improvements to the parks, the advancement of the city's colleges and universities, the dredging of the Anacostia River and the use of the clay and sediments to raise the flats on its edge, and presciently, in 1910, the creation of an "aviation field."

The Board of Trade always made it a point to cultivate its relationships with commissioners and congressmen. Annual dinners and excursions down the Potomac that culminated in a shad bake became a springtime ritual. The liaisons its members formed over speeches, alcohol, boat trips, and planked shad proved invaluable when the board produced reports on vital issues. Since they had neither the time nor the resources—nor, sometimes, the inclination—to gather the information, the commissioners and members of Congress began to rely upon the board's work. As one president of the board observed early in the century, if a recommendation came from Washington's Board of Trade, citizens took it seriously. The board had woven itself into the fabric of Washington's civic life.

AT THE TURN of the century, higher education in Washington, which had lagged behind that in northern cities, underwent a massive transformation. Throughout the nineteenth century, the capital's colleges and universities had been slow to develop for a variety of reasons, but the chief one was that the capital lacked the educational zeal of New York, Philadelphia, Boston, and many other New England communities. Washington did not lack for fine minds—men such as George Bancroft and Henry Adams, Simon Newcomb and John Hay among them—but their roots and education were elsewhere.

The city also suffered from a fantasy that one day, if only Congress would provide the money, it would have a great national university. The thought had proven to be a mental impediment, as it remained an unrealized, but nonetheless diverting, hope that never seemed to die or become a reality. Many, including George Washington, had shared the same dream. In the 1790s, Samuel Blodget, the creator of the 1793 hotel lottery, had promoted a university scheme before his entanglements with James Greenleaf brought him into bankruptcy; a fanciful 1802 map of the city showed its imaginary building west of the White House (where Washington himself had once thought it should be located). Benjamin Henry Latrobe had produced designs for it in 1816, and some in Congress suggested using James Smithson's legacy to fund it. The idea resurfaced again in 1872, when Senator George Franklin

Edward Savage, *The Washington Family*. Despite the spiritless expressions and lack of eye contact among the five subjects, the heroic composition became a symbol of all George Washington and the nation had achieved in just two decades. Savage's engravings of the seven by nine and a quarter foot canvas proved so popular that Savage could boast to the president, "There is Every Probability at present of its producing me at Least ten thousand Dollars in one twelvemonth." CREDIT: National Gallery of Art

William Birch, *The Capitol in 1800*. An English-born artist, Birch emigrated to Philadelphia in 1794, where he produced miniatures of important figures such as George Washington and engravings of Philadelphia. On a visit to the new seat of government in 1800 he produced a watercolor of the primitive Capitol on Jenkins Hill. CREDIT: Library of Congress

John James Halls, *George Cockburn*. Halls's 1817 portrait presents an imperious and arrogant Cockburn in full naval dress before the flaming buildings of the capital. CREDIT: Getty Images

George Munger, *The Capitol following the Burning by the British in 1814*. The heat from the fire in the Capitol on August 24, 1814, was so intense that it melted the glass in the building's skylights. The flames also consumed most of the furniture, manuscripts, and books in the Library of Congress. CREDIT: Library of Congress

Robert Cruikshank, *President's Levée, or All Creation Going to the White-house*. Andrew Jackson's inauguration on March 4, 1829, marked the beginning of a new presidential era that did not sit well with some of Washington's first residents. "What a scene did we witness!" wrote Margaret Bayard Smith. "The *Majesty of the People* had disappeared, and a rabble, a mob, of boys, negros, women, children, scrambling, fighting, romping. What a pity what a pity!" CREDIT: Library of Congress

Eastman Johnson, *Negro Life at the Old South*. In 1859 Eastman Johnson did not have to look far from his father's house on F Street for the subject of his painting. His attention to the condition of the two structures, the white mistress's entrance into the black world, and the intimation of miscegenation reveals some of the disparities present in Washington's ante-bellum society. CREDIT: The New-York Historical Society

Contrabands with Union Soldiers. This stereograph of three young black "Contrabands" with three members of the Rhode Island Volunteers was taken at Fort Stevens, possibly before the Confederate attack and Abraham Lincoln's visit in July 1864. CREDIT: Library of Congress

E Sachse & Co., *View of Washington City, 1871.* The popular lithography company E Sachse produced a number of "bird's-eye" views of southern cities including Washington. This somewhat fanciful one from the perspective of the Capitol, takes in the Mall, including the as yet uncompleted Washington Monument. CREDIT: Library of Congress

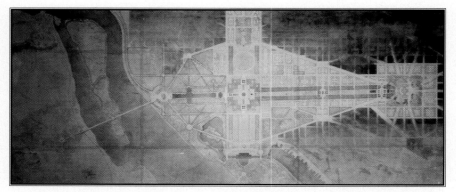

The Senate Park Commission Plan for the Mall. Shaped like a giant kite, the plan extended the east-west axis of L'Enfant's plan from the Capitol to the site of the future Lincoln Memorial and created a major north-south axis from the White House through the Washington Monument to the site of the future Jefferson Memorial. CREDIT: Senate Park Commission

Women's Suffrage Parade, March 3, 1913. Mounted the day before the inauguration of Woodrow Wilson, the Women's Suffrage Parade was the beginning of Alice Paul's fight for the Nineteenth Amendment to the Constitution, affirming the right of women to vote. Because of the often militant efforts of the suffragettes, Wilson ultimately supported ratification of the amendment. CREDIT: Library of Congress

Construction of Dupont Circle Station, 1975. After its opening in 1977, the Dupont Circle station helped to stimulate the energetic mix of residences and businesses that sustain the area. CREDIT: Washington Metropolitan Area Transit Authority

Duke Ellington Mural on the True Reform Building. It is fitting that the Ellington mural should be on the site of the True Reform Building (or True Reformers Hall) as each embodies the spirit of the Shaw neighborhood and its importance in contemporary Washington. CREDIT: Getty Images

L'Enfant's Grave. It wasn't until 1910 that the remains of Peter Charles L'Enfant were interred at a site directly in front of the Custis Lee mansion at Arlington Cemetery. CREDIT: Corbis

Jorge Pérez-Rubio, *Aerial Construction of Washington, DC, 2005.* "Lines are much more important to me than colors," Jorge Pérez-Rubio has written of work that emphasizes Peter Charles L'Enfant's bold geometric plan for the city. "Color fades, lines carry meaning . . . like words." CREDIT: Private collection

Edmunds from Vermont proposed that Congress charter and finance a national university to be staffed by faculty from America's other leading universities. Students and faculty, so the thinking went, would draw upon the capital's resources to enrich instruction and research. But this time, Harvard's Charles William Eliot scuttled the plan, in fear that the federal government would have a role in university education, or perhaps that the new institution would rival his in Cambridge.

One institution in the capital actually called itself *The* National University, despite the fact that its faculty and most of its students were part time. It began as a law and medical school in 1870 with great aspirations and even greater pretensions. Cabinet members, generals, admirals, and diplomats were always in attendance at graduation, as was the president of the United States, who served as ex-officio head of the board of trustees. In the 1880s, John Philip Sousa's Marine Band regularly played marches at the university's ceremonies. Aside from its questionable credentials, National had the dubious distinction of having tried to withhold a diploma from the person who become its most illustrious graduate. Though Belva Lockwood had done well in her courses and completed the requirements, her professors and fellow students in the class of 1873 objected to her graduation because they did not wish to share the stage with a woman. Only after she appealed to President Ulysses S. Grant did Lockwood receive her diploma. She became the first woman to establish a law practice in the capital; the first woman to ride a penny-farthing from her law office to the courts (because, she said, the primitive bicycles saved time, and male lawyers, who used them regularly, were moving ahead of her); the first woman, in 1879, to argue a case before the Supreme Court; and, in 1884, Belva Lockwood became the first woman to appear on the ballot for president of the United States.

Columbian College had followed a rocky path through the nineteenth century and into the twentieth. It suffered from the feeling among many that it had inherited the mantle of "national university" when it was chartered by Congress in 1821 and received George Washington's worthless legacy of Potomac Company stock. A charter was one thing; congressional support was quite another. In 1873, the trustees sold the college's land on Meridian Hill, moved the campus downtown to H Street between Fifteenth and Sixteenth, established a School of Graduate Studies, and, with a sizable endowment from William W. Corcoran in hand, changed its name to Columbian University. Although Columbian had been nonsectarian since 1821, when Congress had demanded that it loosen its ties to the Baptist Church as a condition for granting it a charter, the trustees later yielded to the temptation of a large donation from a prominent Baptist to return to the fold. But as the gift never came and other donations evaporated, Columbian had to return to its nonsectarian status. Weighed down by an overly ambitious president who expanded the university's programs with the delusional promise of rich financial returns, the university spent down Corcoran's endowment, dismissed revered professors in an effort to economize, and by the first decade of the new century drifted into insolvency.

By that time, Columbian had acquired a new name, George Washington University, and in 1912, a new campus at 2023 G Street, the tract of land where 140 years earlier Jacob Funk had created his town of Hamburg. Finally, a new university president, an admiral, brought order and stability to the foundering institution. By reorganizing the various schools and departments, instituting retrenchments, and practicing extraordinary frugality—the admiral took no salary—he soon balanced George Washington's budget. By its centennial year, 1921, the university was stable enough to celebrate, knowing that if it hewed to fiscal prudence and an intelligent educational philosophy, it would thrive in the expanding capital.

While George Washington University was struggling to control its finances and find its direction, another new institution was striving to take its place as the national university. In 1889, Methodist bishop John Fletcher Hurst acquired a farm near Tenleytown in the city's northwest that had served as Fort Gaines in the Civil War, one of the "hundred circling camps" Julia Ward Howe had mentioned in her "Battle Hymn of the Republic" that the Union Army built to protect the capital. But Bishop Hurst was more taken with the legend that George Washington himself had once stopped at the farm; surely, the purported connection of the first president with the land prophesied that this was the very place to build *the* national university. Never mind that the American University, as Hurst had to call it, since there already was a National University, would be a Methodist institution; the nation had entered a period of robust Christianity, and few in power doubted that the United States had a mission to Christianize the world. Hurst was careful to court as many influential people as he could: President William

McKinley (a Methodist who believed it was the country's duty to spread Christianity) served as a trustee, and Senator James McMillan signed on as one of the thirteen incorporators. McMillan helped secure the extension of Massachusetts Avenue above Wisconsin Avenue to Ward Circle and American's campus.

Infatuated with the buildings of Chicago's World's Columbian Exposition, Hurst asked Frederick Law Olmsted to design the campus grounds. But when Olmsted created a romantic plan that would maintain the former farm's hills and rugged landscape, Hurst would have none of it. American University would be classical in design, with white marble buildings (significantly, he called it the "White City"), and it would sit upon an acropolis overlooking the city of Washington, a beacon of truth for all. Development did not proceed as swiftly as Hurst had planned, however. By the end of 1903, the university's chief backers—McKinley, McMillan, and Hurst himself—had died. It wasn't until 1914 that American University held its first classes. There were twenty-eight students.

Of all the capital's educational institutions, those run by the Catholic Church made the greatest strides in the closing years of the century. Georgetown University, the oldest university in the District, and the oldest Catholic University in the country, had suffered setbacks in the Civil War, when Union troops had commandeered the campus on the palisades of the Potomac for the city's defense, and its classrooms for a hospital. But a new law school in 1870 and the vigorous leadership of a new president restored Georgetown's fortunes and laid the foundations for a modern university.

Georgetown University's president, the Reverend Patrick Francis Healy, SJ, a black, was an unusual choice for Washington, DC, and for the time. Born in Georgia to a wealthy Irish plantation owner and his common-law wife of African descent, Healy was deemed a slave by the laws that governed the South. In the North, however, where he had been schooled, his light skin enabled him to pass as an Irish American. After he took orders while studying at the College of the Holy Cross in Worcester, Massachusetts, the Jesuits prudently sent him to Belgium during the Civil War to take a doctorate at the University of Leuven. He returned to Georgetown after the war to teach philosophy, until in 1874 he became its twenty-ninth president. From the start, Healy stated that his goal was to make Georgetown University "equal to any in the country."

Healy created a nonclassical program for those interested in science, mathematics, and history; emphasized instruction in public speaking and disputation; increased the standards of the university's medical school and new law school; and, in 1877, laid the cornerstone for an immense five-story building to house laboratories, classrooms, a library, an assembly hall, and offices. The granite and sandstone Romanesque structure, capped by a steep, polychromed roof with dormers and a tall spire, would not be completed until the new century. But unlike other buildings on the Georgetown campus, Healy Hall faced the city rather than the Potomac, signaling the university's intention to become an important part of the life of the capital.

In recognition of Washington's growing importance as the political center of the United States, the Catholic Church chose Brookland in the city's northeast as the site for its graduate theology school. Shortly after its founding in 1887, The Catholic University of America, as it was known, included graduate instruction in the sciences and philosophy, and early in the twentieth-century added an undergraduate curriculum.

WASHINGTON'S CENTRAL CORE, the area clustered near the White House, had long proven inadequate for holding all the city's residents. Early forays after the Civil War had been to new neighborhood developments, such as those at Dupont Circle, LeDroit Park, and Meridian Hill. Old Washington families, the "cave dwellers," still tended to populate the core, but new neighborhoods, developed by syndicates of real-estate speculators, and made accessible by electric trolley lines and the Baltimore and Ohio's Metropolitan Railway, lured wealthy families to rural tracts beyond the original boundary lines that L'Enfant had laid out for Washington City. The new developments might all have been haphazard, with streets that went "nowhere" and connected with "nothing," but vigorous pressure from the Board of Trade and the District commissioners pushed Congress to enact the Highway Act of 1893, which called for extending L'Enfant's street plan in an orderly fashion. Although the act was later amended to allow the streets and houses that had been planned before 1893 to remain, the new developments largely hewed to L'Enfant's design of a century earlier.

The money that real-estate investors made in the latter years of the nineteenth century speculating on future developments was often impressive. Once the trolleys and trains made the land accessible from downtown Washington, the building began. Kalorama, beyond Dupont Circle in the capital's northwest, experienced a suburban transformation. There had been many owners of the land since Lord Baltimore had controlled it in the seventeenth century, including Joel Barlow, pamphleteer of the revolution, minor poet, and diplomat. (It was Barlow who found the view of the Potomac and Rock Creek from his house so pleasing that he adapted the Greek words for "beautiful view" to call the land "Kalorama.")

Barlow was long dead when an Illinois regiment in the Civil War pitched its tents on the estate and turned the house into a smallpox hospital. After Appomattox, and especially after 1871, speculators feasted on the land, selling and reselling parcels (often doubling their profits) and subdividing it. Some of the streets had been laid out before Congress passed the Highway Act, so Kalorama's developers were particularly vocal in pushing through amendments that would accommodate houses that had already been built and roads that did not conform to the extension of L'Enfant's street plan. They had good cause to exert pressure, too, as the last group of parcels had sold in 1887 for close to $6,000 an acre. Extensions of Massachusetts Avenue along Rock Creek Park, and of Connecticut Avenue—including the Taft Bridge across the deep ravine of Rock Creek—completed definition of the land. Two streetcar lines afforded easy access to the city. Along with other speculative developments, Kalorama was helping to make a reality of George Washington's belief that land speculation could build the capital.

The buildings on Massachusetts Avenue leading northwest from Dupont Circle appeared at an especially opportune time in the city's development. At Twenty-third Street, the avenue connected to the circle named in honor of Philip Sheridan, the Civil War general whose Union troops had scorched the Shenandoah Valley seventy-five miles away. On the circumference of Sheridan Circle, newly minted millionaires built lavish homes, including one owned by the general's widow, who from her fourth-floor balcony could look down on her late husband spurring his famous horse Rienzi in his furious ride across the valley to save the Union Army at Winchester, Virginia.

Northeast of Sheridan Circle, apartment houses offered a different sort of accommodation, not to millionaires, but to a growing middle class of high-level government workers. The first, the seven-story

CREATED IN 1908 by Gutzon Borglum (who later designed the four presidential heads on Mount Rushmore), the statue depicting Sheridan on his horse, Rienzi, radiates tension and energy; the circle helps to ease the jog in Massachusetts Avenue as it follows the edge of Rock Creek Park. CREDIT: Library of Congress

Mendota, at Twentieth Street NW and Kalorama Road, housed forty-eight apartments, a drugstore, and a dining room. Everything about the building—its rough-hewn limestone of the first and second stories topped by a terra cotta cornice, its rounded and octagonal bays, and its large, double-hung windows, each crowned with a terra cotta key—suggested a middle-class stability that would appeal to the lawyers, brigadier generals, congressional librarians, and teachers who, along with the occasional representative or senator, came to reside there.

When completed in 1901, the Mendota set a standard for other apartment buildings across the city. Almost immediately, its builders, the Iowa Apartment House Company, began another luxury building at Twenty-first Street. But apartment houses were by no means limited to Kalorama; the year the Mendota opened, others sprang up across the city—at Fourteenth Street and Massachusetts Avenue, at Seventeenth and T, and at Fifteenth and L, among other locations. Some realtors feared the speculators had built what would become a glut of empty buildings, but many were fully rented by the time they were completed.

The apartments reflected a greater change for Washington residents and the nature of their employment. People were making the capital their permanent home, and their incomes were rising. For this burgeoning class of residents, boardinghouses no longer sufficed.

Since the turn of the century, a fresh civic spirit had swept through the capital, breathing new life into the city. "It is more and more the pride of Washingtonians that they live in Washington, the National Capital," the effusive editorial writer of the *Washington Post* proclaimed on Christmas Day 1910. The plan for the capital's monumental core, improvements to its colleges and universities, development of its new neighborhoods—and improvements to older ones—and new business opportunities had given middle-class Washingtonians a new sense of their city's grandeur and importance, and the belief that its prospects were brighter than at any time in the past.

IN APRIL 1909, a small party led by Henry Macfarland, president of the District's commissioners, traveled to the Digges family farm in Chillum, Maryland, to preside at the disinterment of the bones of Major Peter Charles L'Enfant. They transported the scant remains— just two bone fragments and a tooth—in a casket to lie in state in the Capitol rotunda; after speeches by the vice president and the French ambassador, a military escort installed the casket in a fresh grave directly in front of the Custis-Lee mansion at Arlington Cemetery.

Two years later, a memorial for L'Enfant's grave was ready for dedication. A descendant of Daniel Carroll pulled the ribbon that lifted the flag from the flat slab of granite. On the rock was chiseled L'Enfant's great plan. The president made a brief speech. "There are not many," said Taft, "who have to wait 100 years to receive the reward to which they are entitled." L'Enfant's reward lay before everyone gathered that day. From the vantage of the green knoll on which they stood, their eyes could travel across Arlington's fields of graves and the Potomac beyond. They could take in the reclaimed marshes of the Mall, Pennsylvania Avenue, the White House, and the Capitol shining upon Jenkins Hill, the very spot where the French designer had outlined his plans to George Washington. In the expanse that lay before them, those who came to dedicate L'Enfant's grave could see his signature, writ large across the landscape.

CHAPTER 10

Washington Apartheid and
the End of Innocence

The method of exerting . . . influence in Washington
was different. . . . In Washington, where there were no
elective city positions, it was through the power of the
White House.

—Louis Brownlow, 1958

In January 1901, *The Atlantic Monthly* published an article entitled "The Reconstruction of the Southern States." The author, a Princeton University professor of jurisprudence and political economics, justified the Jim Crow laws that enabled the return of white supremacy. Reconstruction, so the professor maintained, had failed because the federal Bureau of Refugees, Freedmen, and Abandoned Lands, or Freedmen's Bureau, had refused to accommodate the defeated Confederacy, preferring to advance the interests of their wards, the emancipated slaves, rather than a "peaceable, wholesome, and healing progress." Sudden emancipation, the professor continued in his indictment, left the South to deal with a landless, homeless and leaderless, lazy, insolent, and aggressive class without prudence or self-control, "a host of dusky children untimely put out of school." The following year, the trustees of Princeton named the professor president of the college; eight years later, the voters of New Jersey elected him their governor; and in 1912, those enfranchised to vote in the United States, which of course did not include women or residents of the District of Columbia, chose Woodrow Wilson to be their president.

A curious blend of progressive ideals and regressive acts, broadminded thoughts and narrow-minded judgments, Wilson, often reluctantly, ushered the nation and its capital into the modern world. The eight years of his administration (1913–1921) saw dramatic transformations: the United States enacted the income tax and reformed the banking system; created Prohibition and gave women the right to vote; entered the first great war of the twentieth century; and limited the freedom of black Americans. Originating in the nation's capital, the changes affected daily life in Washington for the rest of the century, and many continue to do so even today.

DURING HIS CAMPAIGN, Wilson had promised a "New Freedom" for the nation; the words resonated throughout the republic that fall of 1912, though few understood their meaning. Many, including black voters— who cast more ballots for him than for any previous Democratic presidential candidate—believed that the words, especially "freedom," meant something more. Just what that "more" was, however, they could not say. They trusted the assurances Wilson gave, in a campaign letter to a prominent bishop of the African Methodist Episcopal Zion Church, that blacks "may count on me for absolute fair dealing and for everything by which I could assist in advancing the interests of their race."

In the first weeks of his presidency, Wilson revealed a very different conception of the mantra that had helped him to win the White House. The president thought that rather than advancing the interests of blacks, "New Freedom" meant changing the economic policies that concentrated the nation's power into the hands of a few.

Wilson's attitude became clear in the early weeks of his administration. His Georgia-born wife, Ellen, so many believed, became upset when she saw black men and white women working side by side in the same room at the Post Office Department. By April 1913, the postmaster general, himself the reactionary son of a Confederate major from Texas, brought the subject of segregating federal departments to the president's cabinet meeting. The postmaster general had "the highest regard for the negro and wished to help him in every way possible," or so he said, but "segregation was best for the negro and best for the service."

The president, who was said to prefer the role of moderator in cabinet discussions, stated that he wished only to do "Negroes . . . justice," but wanted "the matter adjusted in a way to make the least friction." Soon, segregation became the operative method of dealing with black workers throughout the United States, especially in the capital. Certainly Jim Crow practices had been the norm in many government offices before the Wilson administration, but now, with the president's blessing, the wall of segregation for the "dusky" children and grandchildren of those who were once enslaved became ever more intimidating.

The composition of the leadership in Congress completed the dominance of Dixie in Washington. Champ Clark from Missouri became the Speaker of the House of Representatives. In the Senate, Hoke Smith, Benjamin Tillman, and James Kimble Vardaman, each a virulent white supremacist and former governor of his state, commandeered all discussions of race, stirring up race hatred whenever possible and regularly introducing anti-black legislation. Smith had engineered the disenfranchisement of blacks in Georgia; Tillman, a Confederate veteran, boasted of his murder of blacks in South Carolina; and Vardaman, called "The Great White Chief" for his shoulder-length black hair and affectation for white suits, campaigned on his promise to Mississippi voters to repeal the Fourteenth and Fifteenth Amendments to the Constitution, which forbade states from denying any person "life, liberty or property, without due process of law," or from denying any person "within its jurisdiction the equal protection of the laws," and which gave black men the right to vote. Since he was afraid that southern senators such as these might jeopardize the economic legislation he really cared about—creating the Federal Reserve, establishing the federal income tax, and reforming federal tariffs—and since he had no serious interest in the plight of America's blacks, Wilson was content to allow these members of Congress and his southern segregationist cabinet secretaries to have their way.

The effect of the Wilson administration's policies on Washington's nearly 100,000 blacks was devastating. To be sure, their position in the capital under Roosevelt and Taft had not seen any significant advancement, and civil service positions for blacks had declined since the days of Cleveland, Harrison, and McKinley. Still, before Wilson, blacks could hold jobs as clerks or assistants in federal offices, and take their place among the city's burgeoning black middle class. For them,

Washington was not only the capital of the nation, but also the citadel of black American intellectual and cultural life. By this time Howard University boasted serious dental, medical, architecture, and law
schools. Segregated Dunbar High School, which ranked with the best
white school in the District, sent many students to Howard or the best
eastern colleges. (Williams College in Massachusetts gave a full schol-
arship each year to the Dunbar graduate who ranked first in his class.)
The frequent meetings of the Bethel Literary and Historical Society
featured speakers like Booker T. Washington, W. E. B. Du Bois, and
professors from Howard. Now all who thought education and skills
would yield advancement faced a federal barrier few could clear.

By the summer of 1913, federal departments in the capital were feeling the effects of the president's new policy. Almost all appointments
throughout the city, including those that Republican and Democratic
administrations had traditionally reserved for blacks, were now going to
whites. All applicants for civil service jobs had to submit photographs.
Blacks in the Post Office and Treasury who weren't drummed from
their jobs found themselves working in separate offices, or in offices
with curtained partitions; dining in separate lunchrooms; drinking from
separate water fountains, or, hygiene being what it was, drinking from
separate glasses; and using separate restrooms—in the basement. By
August, even Booker T. Washington, the moderate black leader who
preferred cooperation to confrontation as the best way to advance his
race, reported after a visit to the capital that he "had never seen the colored people so discouraged and bitter as they are at the present time."

Four months into Wilson's presidency, southern racists in the Senate proved their power when they blocked his nomination of Adam
Edward Patterson, a black man, to be registrar of the treasury. Although
the position was a minor one, and a black had held the position on five
previous occasions, Senators Vardaman, Tillman, and Smith would
have none of it. President Wilson was a southerner, and they expected
him to halt any black advancement; they vowed to block confirmation.
Wilson also heard from the Southern Baptist minister and racist novelist Thomas W. Dixon, with whom he had had a casual acquaintance
while they were students at Johns Hopkins. Dixon protested "as a citizen & your friend" the "appointment of a Negro to boss white girls."
Wilson replied: "We are handling the force of colored people who are
now in the departments in just the way which they ought to be handled.

We are trying—and by degrees succeeding—a plan of concentration which will put them all together and will not in any one bureau mix the two races." And then the mild president left it to Patterson to withdraw his name. He had dearly wanted the position, Patterson wrote, but he would "stifle personal ambitions" in the interest of harmony. "I refuse to embarrass your administration, Mr. President, by insisting upon my confirmation, and I also believe it is best for my race that I withdraw my name from further consideration."

The actions of senators and cabinet members, coupled with the inaction of the president, had a pernicious effect upon life in the capital. Anti-black zealots formed the National Democratic Fair Play Association. In addition to challenging the Fourteenth and Fifteenth Amendments, the association declared that its special mission was to block every black presidential appointment and segregate the federal civil service system, which it contended was a "fraud" filled with incompetent blacks. Association meetings featured lurid tales of abuses. "A Woman from the South," as she called herself in a letter that the association's president read before his believers and the credulous white press, complained of the indignity of having to take dictation from a black man who was "drunk most of the time" and "blew his whisky fume in my face." Other women would lose respect for her should she continue to be forced to work under him. Separation of the races was the only solution to this problem. "I believe in segregation," said one prominent member, C. B. Matthews, "but not in discrimination." Such supposedly benign distinctions became the norm for the capital. Wilson's New Freedom had quickly devolved into virulent Jim Crowism.

Violence followed in the wake of Jim Crow. The Ku Klux Klan, which had waned, but had never quite been dormant since its inception shortly after the Civil War, gained new energy in 1915 by attacking blacks and immigrants—and especially Catholics and Jews—and supporting Prohibition. Wilson had unwittingly helped to launch a resurgence of the circle of brothers when he allowed his acquaintance Thomas W. Dixon to show the new film *Birth of a Nation* at the White House. Dixon had collaborated with the filmmaker D. W. Griffith in the adaptation of Dixon's novel *The Clansman*, which depicted the antebellum South as benign, and white supremacy and racial segregation as being in the best interests of blacks. On Thursday evening, February 18, 1915, Wilson gathered with members of his cabinet and the Supreme Court in the East Room of the White House to watch Griffith's preposterously romantic and scurrilously racist presentation of the South during Reconstruction that began with a title card quoting Wilson's *History of the American People*: "The white men were roused by a mere instinct of self-preservation . . . until at last there had sprung into existence a great Ku Klux Klan." When the film ended, the president slipped away without comment, but that didn't prevent Dixon's ears from hearing his approval, something Griffith's lawyers asserted in New York and Boston when protesters attempted to prevent the film's screening. Nor did it prevent Dixon from manufacturing a sound bite, supposedly from Wilson's lips: The *Birth of a Nation* was "like writing history with lightning. And my only regret is that it is all so terribly true."

LIKE THE CITY he now resided in, Wilson possessed many contradictions. Part of him wished for an older, gentler stability; another part relished the twentieth century. Wilson preferred to read by the soft light of a kerosene lamp that he kept on the desk in his White House office; but he also loved to take long rides around Washington in his Pierce Arrow automobile. Certainly the president's actions with regard to the capital's black population, particularly those who worked as clerks for the federal government, set the city back; but his appointments of District commissioners helped to move it forward. Many who counted themselves members of Washington's white establishment weren't especially happy that he did not follow the unwritten laws that other presidents had followed: dividing the two civilian commissioners between a Democrat and a Republican, and seeking recommendations from local business leaders. Without consultation, Wilson named two Democrats in 1913: Frederick Lincoln Siddons, an English-born lawyer, and Oliver Peck Newman, his frequent golfing companion and a reporter for United Press. In 1915, Wilson nominated Siddons to the Supreme Court of the District of Columbia and replaced him with another newspaperman, Louis Brownlow.

Brownlow was well connected in Washington. For many years he had reported news about the capital for papers in Tennessee and Kentucky, and in 1909 he had married the daughter of Tennessee congressman Thetus Sims. Having immersed himself in the life of the District for years, and having served as president of the Monday Evening Club, a group of social workers and civic-minded citizens who gathered regularly to discuss the city's social conditions, he was happy about the prospect of taking on his new duties as commissioner in charge of public welfare in the city—that is, the police, fire, health, and welfare agencies. When he took office in January 1915, he found that city services belonged to the horse and buggy era: the capital's hospital building was over a hundred years old; the police department was antiquated, both in structure and practice; the sewer system was inadequate; and each commissioner had a carriage, coachman, and two dappled grays at his disposal.

Brownlow brought his first reforms to the police department. Some members of the low-paid force protected gambling and houses of prostitution; others collaborated with burglars; still others worked exclusively—though on police pay—guarding the gaudy millionaires Edward "Ned" Beale McLean and his wife, Evalyn, at "Friendship," their seventy-five-acre estate on Wisconsin Avenue in the northwest. Brownlow began by replacing the chief, a man who had been well regarded in the nineteenth century, but had fallen far behind in the twentieth. The new chief, Raymond W. Pullman, a thirty-two-year-old newspaperman who had written for the *Washington Star*, brought women into the force, expanded its size, raised the officers' pay, and increased their training. His strict enforcement of the city's traffic laws, while annoying to the White House chauffeurs, who were unaccustomed to yielding or stopping for anyone, brought order to the city's streets and reduced the number of traffic fatalities.

LOUIS BROWNLOW SET a progressive agenda for reforming the governmental structure and improving social conditions in the District of Columbia. Although his accomplishments were many, he often faced a Congress that was reluctant to approve any funding increases for the capital. And he soon found that national events over which he had little control—including World War I, the influenza epidemic of 1918, the campaign for women's suffrage, and tensions in racial relations—would dominate his tenure as commissioner.

Long before the United States entered the war in April 1917, Washington felt its effects. Brownlow and Pullman arranged for compliant secretaries in the German embassy to pass along sabotage plots. The commissioner and his police chief had the phone lines tapped at the

German military attaché's house on Fourteenth Street near Thomas Circle, and they employed three stenographers to record every conversation. Brownlow also managed to thwart a plot to dig a tunnel into the basement of the British embassy on Connecticut Avenue and N Street. But the pair were unable to prevent a former German instructor at Harvard from destroying the Senate Reception Room on July 2, 1915, with three sticks of dynamite he had smuggled into the Capitol.

While all the espionage and counterespionage was taking place, Washington society seemed, as stories in the *Washington Post* affirmed, caught between concern over the conflict and its desire for normal order. In early 1916, as Brownlow and Pullman were absorbed in reading telephone transcriptions from German operatives, a thousand Masons gathered at a luncheon in the Willard Hotel to hear their grand master and sovereign grand commander. As the ladies auxiliary of the German American 1914–1916 relief committee organized a fair to benefit the widows and orphans of Austrian soldiers, the Association of the Oldest Inhabitants of the capital put on a reception. As Dr. Albert Van Hecke, a professor from the University of Louvain, presented an illustrated talk to "prominent society folk" on the Belgian refugee crisis, Brownlow and Pullman prepared to judge what the *Washington Post* described as a "floral automobile parade" organized by "the colored people of Washington."

But war was coming. In May 1915, a German submarine sank the British liner *Lusitania* with 114 Americans aboard; more attacks on ships with American passengers followed. In 1916, as Wilson traveled across the country on a "preparedness tour," Congress increased the size of the army to 175,000 and the National Guard to 450,000, and appropriated millions of dollars for new weapons, including $12 million to purchase machine guns. Meanwhile, the navy embarked on an emergency plan to build battleships, cruisers, destroyers, submarines, gunboats, and a hospital ship. Early in 1917, Wilson's secretary of war and his top generals moved to institute military conscription, and with the help of Louis Brownlow had 10 million registration forms ready in April, when Congress passed the Selective Service Act. In February and March 1917, German attacks on US merchant ships took the lives of a score of sailors. At the same time, Congress authorized the purchase of the Virgin Islands from Denmark in order to prevent them from becoming a German submarine base, and unlike the District of Columbia, the island was given limited home rule.

THE FLIMSY biplane drawn by a team of horses suggests just how unprepared Americans were for World War I. The placard on the float reads, "THE CURTIS SCOUT / AN AERIAL SENTRY / 100 MILES PER HOUR." CREDIT: Library of Congress

IN THE FALL of 1917, Washingtonians understood just how little control they had over their destiny. On November 1, more than two years before the Eighteenth Amendment to the Constitution prohibiting the production, transport, or sale of alcohol, became law across the United States, Congress exercised its power to decide the affairs of the District of Columbia by prohibiting the sale of alcohol. That Halloween, revelers held closing parties at local bars and saloons; at midnight, Chief Pullman's police officers shuttered the establishments, thereby cutting off the nearly half-million dollars of revenue the District received from licenses, and leaving about 1,500 workers, including many blacks and German Americans, without work. While Washington's elite continued to gather for whiskey and wine in the salons and dining rooms of their private houses, Washington's laborers were prevented from drinking beer in the saloons and social clubs of their neighborhoods.

In fact, the momentum for Prohibition in the capital had been building for decades. The white ribbons signifying the purity pledge of the Women's Christian Temperance Union began to appear in District churches in the 1870s, and the Anti-Saloon League formed a chapter in 1893. Church pastors, especially Methodist, Baptist, and Presbyterian ones, connected the League's work with God's and made sure to open their sanctuaries for meetings. Pressure from the League had already forced the Washington Liquor Excise Board to close down bars in prominent hotels, including the Normandie, the Shoreham, and Wormley's, because they sold liquor within four hundred feet of a school or church; the League succeeded as well in reducing the number of saloon licenses across the city by about half, and in imposing heavy license fees on the establishments that remained.

Congress's imposition of Prohibition for the capital added another difficulty to an already troubled year for Washington's German American residents. The war had made many in the city suspicious of all Germans. Immigrants who had not become naturalized were expelled from the city; many were shipped to the Midwest. Those who remained lived in fear of violence and reprisal. Once proud of their heritage, and usually bilingual, they now spoke English exclusively. Members of the Capital Saengerbund, whose club at 314 C Street NW was already in financial debt because it could no longer sell beer, now performed their songs in English; some members Anglicized their surnames.

Christian Heurich, Washington's most successful German American, who had made his fortune brewing beer, suffered more than most. After President Wilson signed the Prohibition bill for the District, in March, Heurich tried to create a nonalcoholic drink, "Liberty Apple Champagne," but fermentation swiftly converted it into an intoxicating beverage. Only his ice-making plant, a minor sideline of the brewing enterprise, continued. Worse in many ways were the questions Heurich suffered for being German. Rumors of his lack of patriotism circulated through the city. He was using powerful radio equipment to talk with the enemy from his country home in Maryland; he had installed gun emplacements on the property to train on the city when the Germans arrived in the capital; and, as part of a German plot to assassinate the president, Heurich had constructed a tunnel from the basement of his house on New Hampshire Avenue to the nearby home of Edith Galt, Woodrow Wilson's future wife.

"THE WORLD MUST be made safe for democracy," Wilson declared on April 2, as he asked Congress for a declaration of war. In the District of Columbia, preparations that had been in the making for months suddenly became paramount. Brownlow and Congress insisted it was the "supreme duty" of "every man, woman, or child" to plant home gardens. More than a thousand federal workers formed the Home Defense League, which would be directed by the American Red Cross, whose Washington chapter raised millions for assistance and succor.

Woodrow Wilson set out to make his family the paragon of the patriotism that he urged upon the nation. Meatless Mondays and wheatless Wednesdays became standard at 1600 Pennsylvania Avenue, and lights were dimmed and thermostats lowered. The president's new wife, Edith (Ellen, his first, had died in 1914), sponsored war bond rallies with Hollywood stars; his eldest daughter sang at benefit concerts. The president himself decided that a flock of sheep would be just what was needed to save the cost of clipping the grass on the White House lawn. The sheep—sixteen in all, including four lambs—initially had a rough time adjusting to the noise of passing automobiles, but soon they were producing wool and more lambs. To raise funds for the Red Cross, Wilson had them sheered and sent two pounds of the fleece to each state and the District of Columbia with the request that they be auctioned. It fell to Louis Brownlow to run the auction.

Washington's transformation into a capital of international importance was swift and, to longtime residents, crude. In his house on Lafayette Park, Henry Adams, now in his eightieth year and in poor health, heard the drone of airplanes flying overhead. "This little town has returned to its old habits of the Civil War," Adams wrote to a friend shortly before his death in March 1918. It was "crowded with strange people in Khaki in so many English, Italian, and French uniforms that you would not know where you were. The railways are all running wild, every train is six or eight hours late, and every house is crowded beyond all reckoning."

Adams was right. In 1861, the Mall had served as a venue for troops, cattle, abattoirs, and a hospital; now the broad swath of land before the Capitol had again become valuable real estate for the military. Since the State, War, and Navy Building west of the White House could no longer house all the military departments, the administration decided to build "temporary" offices for them on the Mall. The first, a series

SHEEP ON the White House lawn. CREDIT: Library of Congress

of wooden structures on the north side of B Street at Sixth, erected in the summer of 1917, provided 800,000 square feet of office space. But it wasn't enough. The Navy and War Departments contracted to add 1,880,000 square feet of offices on the Mall itself south of B Street between Seventeenth and Twenty-first streets. The buildings of reinforced concrete went up between March and September 1918; so many laborers were needed for construction that the navy built temporary barracks and a commissary for 1,200 men on the Mall. In just a few months, they created what was at the time the largest office building in the world—eight blocks of three stories facing B Street, with nine parallel wings extending 600 feet onto the Mall. Still more "tempos," as they were known, would rise on the land around the Smithsonian and the Washington Monument. The Mall of the McMillan Plan had become an office tenement.

The government was quick to build workspace, but slow to acknowledge that the influx of tens of thousands of new workers would put extraordinary strains on everyday life in Washington. The population increase was alarming: in 1910, the Census Bureau counted 331,000 residents in the District; five years later, it estimated the number had risen to 353,000; by September 1917, it stood at 400,000. (The 1920 census would count 437,500.) With new departments of the burgeoning federal bureaucracy taking over private residences and even entire apartment buildings, decent housing within the District became hard to find. Every city service—police, fire, sanitation, and streets included—suffered under the inundation of people. Ignoring the cries of some indignant congressmen that he was leading the District into "the business of socialism," Brownlow arranged for the city to take over trash collection, after the private contractor declared he could no longer keep up with the mounting waste. Brownlow had to appeal directly to Woodrow Wilson to increase the salaries of the men operating the city sewage station across the Anacostia, as they could no longer afford to live in the city on an annual wage of under $900. The president filled out a requisition for $8,000 in his own hand to keep the pumps operating. Still other problems ensued. Labor shortages caused by conscription meant that streetcars lay idle for want of motormen. Newspapers reported a scarcity of electricity, gas, and telephones, as well as schoolrooms for the children of the new government workers. In December 1917, the *Post* reported that there were not enough coal cars to keep Washington's boilers running, and that delays in food shipments could put the city in danger of a "famine."

DESPITE THE HIGH prices and shortages, newcomers from across the country flocked to "the main war shop," as the *Washington Evening Star* took to calling the capital. Women, many of them single, saw a chance for adventure and an opportunity to break from the traditional family constraints that had kept them close to home for generations. Champions of women's suffrage, traditionally pacifists, believed that helping to win the war was a patriotic act. "Fate has prepared women to share fully in the saving of civilization," wrote Harriot Stanton Blatch in her book *Mobilizing Woman-Power*; no less a hero than Theodore Roosevelt contributed a preface, writing that the nation had entered a "new world" in which "women are to stand on an equal footing with men, in ways and to an extent never hitherto dreamed of." Government, the former president said, "should welcome" their service, and make use of it "to the utmost."

Washington was desperate for workers of either gender. "I believe that all the prettiest girls in this country are now seeking jobs under the government or in the Red Cross," Henry Adams observed, adding,

"They are accomplished besides and do things exactly as though they were in for a profession." Women broke down the resistance of male doctors to serve as physical and occupational therapists at the government's Walter Reed Hospital, though they had to endure "exceedingly ugly" uniforms that one therapist described as "designed by a man who believed that women working in the hospitals were a menace to men patients." They joined the capital's Red Cross Motor Corps and trained in mechanics, first aid, and sanitary home care. Even black women managed to break the shackles of menial work and take jobs in offices such as the Treasury Department's Bureau of Engraving.

Josephine Lehman was typical of the young women who left their home towns for a new life in Washington. She grew up on a farm outside of Ionia, Michigan, and had watched as the young men, including four of her brothers, enlisted in the army. She, too, wanted to serve in what people in Ionia called "the glorious cause of world freedom." Her high school diploma and two years of reporting for the *Ionia Sentinel* enabled her to pass the government's civil service examination with "flying colors." On February 21, 1918, just a few weeks shy of her twentieth birthday, Josephine walked into the tempo building on B Street for her first day as a stenographer with the Ordnance Department, the agency that supplied the military with everything from toothpaste and shoes to grenades and guns. "My hours are from nine to four-thirty with double pay for overtime," Lehman reported in a letter to her family. She advanced quickly. By June, she was being transferred to the high-explosives division to serve as private secretary to a French captain on a confidential mission with the War Department. "I know how to blow up just about anything," she confided to her diary.

As was the case of almost all young women working for the government, Lehman's living conditions were cramped. The government housing office secured a place for her to board with twenty-two other women in a three-story brick and stone private house on Massachusetts Avenue near Thomas Circle. "It just seems like a college dormitory," she wrote to her family, and Mrs. Dudley, who operated the house, seemed like a dorm mother. Although the room and board were expensive, her salary of $1,100 a year ($600 more than she had made in Ionia) helped to cover the additional costs.

It was the social and work opportunities, and especially the sheer energy of the capital in wartime, that captivated young women like

Josephine Lehman. The War Department arranged for trucks to carry them to Saturday night dances at nearby camps—"twenty-five going from our house, accompanied by Mrs. Dudley . . . [to] a farewell party for the boys who are leaving this week." Mrs. Dudley sometimes rolled up her own living-room rug on Saturday evenings, cranked up the Victrola, and invited soldiers and sailors—"nice boys, not objectionable"—in to dance. There were times, however, when Josephine had to deal firmly with the "baser passions" of the men she met; she did not wish to be, as she said in her diary, "a fast piece of furniture." The dress and customs were all new to the farm girl from Michigan, but Josephine adjusted quickly. "I have gotten over being shocked by such a display of arms and necks," she wrote of women's fashions. By the end of June, she looked back on her first five months in the capital with awe: "I wonder what has happened to the innocent unsophisticated child I was last winter," she wrote, but quickly added that she was glad to be in Washington.

JOSEPHINE LEHMAN and friends on an outing at the National Zoo.
CREDIT: Margaret Thomas Buchholz

On April 6, the first anniversary of the United States' entry into the war, Josephine Lehman and a large group of fellow workers left their steno pads and typewriters at the War Department to join the crowds on Pennsylvania Avenue, where the Marine Band led Marie Dressler, Mary Pickford, Charlie Chaplin, and other movie stars on a Liberty Loan parade to the Treasury steps. (And like so many others, Lehman bought a $50 bond.) At Poli's Theater on Fifteenth and E, she took in D. W. Griffith's propaganda film, *Hearts of the World*, which the director hoped would stir up as many mindless passions about heartless German Huns as *Birth of a Nation* had stirred up about brutal American blacks.

In late September and October, along with the rest of Washington and much of the country, Josephine had to contend with the Spanish influenza epidemic. The flu had felled huge numbers of soldiers in the army camps of Virginia and Maryland before claiming its first life in the capital—John W. Clore, age twenty-four, a brakeman on the Pennsylvania Railroad, who lived on Florida Avenue in the northeast. Josephine reported to the *Sentinel* that twenty-one of the twenty-three women who lived with her at Mrs. Dudley's were taken sick, though she herself was spared, and none of the other women in the house died.

The contagion proved a far greater challenge for Louis Brownlow, as overcrowding made Washington an ideal incubator for the virus. The gauze masks many wore seemed to offer little protection, and the "Three C's" touted throughout the city—"CLEAN MOUTH, CLEAN SKIN, CLEAN CLOTHES"—even less. Brownlow ordered theaters, department stores, George Washington University, and schools shut down; streetcars lay idle for want of conductors; churches held services outdoors. As the numbers stricken with influenza increased, the Red Cross created an emergency hospital at Sixth and F streets. But, as one doctor remembered, "the only way we could find room for the sick was to have undertakers waiting at the door ready to remove bodies as fast as the victims died." Death certificates and coffins became dear, and grave diggers dearer still. On one day alone, 92 perished. The War Industry Board, which had been created to ensure the supply of materiel to the military, procured two railroad cars of coffins, and Marines from the base at nearby Quantico arrived to dig the graves. By early November, the scourge had passed, but 3,500 Washingtonians, 10 percent of those stricken, had died.

WOODROW WILSON'S CONCEPT of New Freedom and his ideas about spreading democracy across the globe initially did not extend to women in the United States. Before he became president, he had opposed "universal suffrage," presumably for women as well as blacks, believing that their lack of education made them unable to participate in a democracy. Although his campaign organized a national association of female supporters, and welcomed the influence they might have upon their husbands' votes, Wilson believed in his heart that a woman's rightful place was at the hearth with her family. Early in his presidency he had signed into law a bill making the second Sunday in May "Mother's Day," and asked everyone to "display the flag . . . as a public expression of our love and reverence for the mothers of our country." But Wilson was content to leave the question of women's suffrage in shadow; and so it might have remained, had not Alice Paul come to Washington.

Alice Paul combined her Christian conscience as a Quaker with the military stratagems of a general. After earning degrees at Swarthmore and the University of Pennsylvania, Paul witnessed the ways in which British suffragettes in London employed the power of publicity and radical action to garner public support. Since the deaths of Elizabeth Cady Stanton and Susan B. Anthony earlier in the century, the cause of women's suffrage had lacked forceful leadership in America. Leaders of the National American Woman Suffrage Association chose moderate tactics to pursue their goals, while local branches of the national association, including the one in the District of Columbia, had devolved into social clubs. Into the vacuum stepped Paul. She established a committee in Washington to call for a federal constitutional amendment for women's suffrage, and she publicized the association's commitment to the cause with an elaborate parade down Pennsylvania Avenue on March 3, 1913, the day before Wilson's inauguration.

It was to be a great procession of "beauty," as Paul and the newspapers billed it, complete with floats from state delegations and a tableau on the steps of the Treasury Building of Columbia, Justice, Peace, Liberty, Charity, and Hope. There was a place for all women, except black women, whom Paul excluded for fear of alienating southern white marchers. The great spectacle of about 5,000 nearly precipitated a riot. Hoodlums jeered and attacked the marchers, some of whom had to go to the hospital. The US cavalry came from Fort Myer in Arlington to restore order. Editorial writers across the country condemned the marchers' treatment and blamed the police, who were, the *New York Times* said, "in sympathy with the rioters." But for Paul, the demonstration was a success. She had learned that confrontation and publicity could become powerful weapons in America just as in England. No doubt she was also happy to learn that when Woodrow Wilson arrived on a special train that afternoon, only a small crowd was on hand to greet him; his chauffeur had to take the president-elect on side streets to his suite in the Shoreham Hotel, as the suffrage marchers had blocked Pennsylvania Avenue.

The National American Woman Suffrage Association wasn't happy with Paul's tactics, either. It wanted to pursue a more benign course of persuading legislators in the forty-two states that did not enfranchise women to pass suffrage legislation. Paul created her own suffragette group, the Congressional Union, to pursue her more aggressive agenda for a constitutional amendment. Her headquarters would be Washington.

The Congressional Union's first acts included more parades and public opposition to Democratic congressional candidates in the 1914 and 1916 elections. These efforts failed to arouse much interest. After Wilson's reelection, Paul changed the name of her organization to the National Woman's Party and set up pickets at the White House gates. At first the purple, yellow, and white banners she and her followers carried were benign—"MR PRESIDENT, HOW LONG MUST WOMEN WAIT FOR LIBERTY?"—but after the United States entered the war to preserve democracy, the tone of the protest changed. By July 1917, Raymond Pullman's police force had begun arresting the women for obstructing traffic in front of the White House. A judge sentenced a score of them to sixty days in the District's work house at Occoquan, Virginia. Reportedly "shocked" by the arrests, which he had not condoned, Wilson complained to Louis Brownlow and issued pardons, which the women grudgingly accepted before returning to the picket lines.

The protesters' provocations only escalated. When Paul's suffragettes created a banner that reminded "KAISER WILSON" of his sympathy for "Poor Germans" who had no self-government, and neglect for the 20 million American women in an equally grievous situation, a mob of government workers attacked them while the police stood by.

KAISER WILSON. CREDIT: National Archives and Records Administration

"The suffragettes have been having high old times picketing the White House to ask for the vote," Josephine Lehman wrote to her mother. "The police are arresting them by the hundreds and giving them free rides to the lockup." Inevitably, more riots, arrests, convictions, and incarcerations precipitated hunger strikes, force feedings, and stories of ill treatment.

Of course, Wilson, Brownlow, and the Washington police had fallen headlong into Paul's trap. The women were happy to go to jail for their cause, even though the sentences were for six months. That November, Washington officials compounded the problem by transferring Paul to a psychiatric ward of the prison and denying her an attorney or visitors. Just as Rose O'Neal Greenhow had done in the Civil War, however, Paul smuggled notes filled with descriptions of her ill-treatment to her supporters on the outside.

The issue of women's suffrage could not be evaded. In addition to Paul's relentless harassment, the more moderate and more accepted National American Woman Suffrage Association, under more vigorous leadership, had lobbied state legislatures to pass laws granting women the right to vote. Although President Wilson and his cabinet thought the demonstrations by the National Women's Party were disorderly and unpatriotic acts that weakened the nation in a time of war, the arrest and treatment of Paul and her followers had become an embarrassment. "We must not let this madness touch us," Wilson wrote to a close friend. "It is the sort of strength I pray for all the time." But in early November, he heeded the advice of his private secretary "to seriously consider this matter." Wilson knew that Alice Paul and her followers now controlled the question of suffrage.

Once he concluded that he was in check, Wilson acted with remarkable force and even a measure of grace. In the still of a late November night, if accounts are to be believed, the president's emissaries struck a deal with his tormentors: Paul was freed from her cell in the prison's psychiatric ward, the picketing outside the White House ceased, and the administration supported passage of the vote in Congress to bring the Nineteenth Amendment before state legislatures. The president would have nothing to do with Alice Paul, but he began to support the National American Woman Suffrage Association. On January 8, 1918, Wilson made his announcement: women had proved themselves as munitions workers, Red Cross workers, volunteers, and nurses; their patriotic war effort should be rewarded with suffrage. Though it was a far cry from arguing that women should have the right to participate in the democracy because they are human beings and equal citizens, it still marked a significant change. The following day, Congress approved the amendment. Its fate now lay in the hands of ninety-six senators.

That September, the president proved that his change of heart was genuine. Before the Senate held its vote, he made an impassioned plea: Women's suffrage, he said, was "vitally essential to the successful prosecution of the great war of humanity." The world had entered a "new age"; should the Senate reject suffrage, "women will cease to follow or to trust us." Great Britain had recently promised "justice to women, though they had before refused it," he continued, "the strange revelations of this war having made many things new and plain, to governments as well as to peoples. Are we alone to refuse to learn the lesson?"

By two votes, the Senate decided to refuse. But Wilson would not relent—he even sent a cable to Congress from the Paris Peace Conference supporting the amendment. On June 4, 1919, the bill finally cleared both houses and went to the states for ratification. On August 18, 1920—forty-two years after universal suffrage was first introduced in the Congress—the Nineteenth Amendment became law.

SUFFRAGE FOR WOMEN was one thing, but Woodrow Wilson had no change of heart on the subject of race. It was inevitable that after the war, violence would come to a head in Washington. When the 480 black American soldiers of the capital's separate battalion returned victorious from Europe in the spring of 1919, white Washington greeted them with silence. Never mind that 25 of them wore the French Croix de Guerre and Légion d'honneur for their heroism in the Argonne Forest; bravery and medals brought them no honor in the capital of democracy.

Indeed, the returning black soldiers found Washington to be a more segregated city than the one they had left. Federal departments, which had burgeoned in Wilson's war effort, refused to consider blacks who had scored well on their civil service examinations for work in their segregated offices. The Metropolitan Police Department turned down blacks for positions; the fire department so effectively kept blacks from promotion that the District commissioner in charge of public safety had to create an all-black brigade in an attempt to ensure a modicum of fair treatment. And on Capitol Hill, southern congressmen routinely offered Jim Crow legislation. Although it didn't pass, it satisfied their voters back home. Meanwhile, the representatives rejected bills that would benefit the capital, including one that would address the housing crisis for alley dwellers.

In the heat and humidity of July 1919, the city's white newspapers wrote ominously of the "crime wave" breaking over Washington's streets. Leading the charge was the *Washington Post*, now owned by Ned McLean, who had wrested control of the paper from his father's estate in 1916. More virulent on the subject of race than the capital's other dailies, the *Herald* and the *Evening Star*, the *Post* specialized in incendiary headlines that made whites fear for their safety, especially women. That spring it published lurid accounts of a black attack on a girl of thirteen in Maryland, a brutal lynching and burning in Mississippi for an attempted rape, and a trial in Martinsburg, West Virginia, in which the victim said: "There stands that dirty black negro who tried to kill me in my own house." With headlines like "POSSES KEEP UP HUNT FOR NEGRO"; "HUNT FOR COLORED ASSAILANT"; and "NEGRO FIEND SOUGHT ANEW," the *Post* injected racial trouble into the District of Columbia. It was no wonder that the headline of Saturday, July 19—"NEGROES ATTACK GIRL . . . WHITE MEN VAINLY PURSUE"—triggered a mob that was set upon both avenging the assault on white womanhood and teaching all of the city's blacks a lesson about their place. The skirmishes were the first race riots in a major US city; they began what the novelist, lawyer, and black civil rights activist James Weldon Johnson aptly called the "Red Summer."

Violence filled the weekend. When it was rumored that one of the women who was attacked was the wife of a serviceman, recently furloughed soldiers, sailors, and Marines spilled out from the city's bars seeking revenge. Joined by a gang of unemployed men, mainly from Murder Bay, they began beating blacks indiscriminately. The mob pulled blacks off streetcars, assaulted them with clubs in front of the White House, and terrorized them on Pennsylvania Avenue. All the while, the outnumbered police stood by.

By Monday, Washington's black community, especially its veterans, had had enough. That morning a completely fabricated story in the *Post*, with the ominous subhead "Mobilization for Tonight," reported that "every available service man in or near Washington" had been called out to "a clean up, that will cause the events of the last two evenings to pale into insignificance." For blacks this would be war, not a riot. Hundreds of men bought guns from pawnshops, or dusted off the military rifles they had brought home from Europe, and took their stand in and around Seventh and U streets, the black district in the capital's northwest.

Seventh Street became an armed camp. Black sharpshooters perched on the roof of the Howard Theater, then the tallest building on the street, while others erected crude barricades at the perimeter of the neighborhood. Random killing seemed to be everywhere. The city was engulfed in chaos. Blacks fired on whites from speeding cars; one opened fire on white people in a crowded streetcar; and a seventeen-year-old black girl who had locked herself in a room of her house killed a detective from the Metropolitan Police Department. By dawn on Tuesday, July 22, 10 whites and 5 blacks lay dead. Finally, later that day, Woodrow Wilson called out 2,000 troops. The soldiers' presence and a hard rain that night ended the violence.

Little was done in the wake of the bloodshed. Louis Brownlow attributed the troubles to "white ex-servicemen" who had been "paid to provoke the trouble," and to the inflammatory article in the *Washington Post*. Others related it to "Reds," or Communists. The National Association for the Advancement of Colored People (NAACP) asked Woodrow Wilson's attorney general to prosecute the *Washington Post* for publishing "Mobilization for Tonight," but the attorney general declined to do so. At the behest of the NAACP, some in Congress vowed to hold investigations of the lynchings and riots that were burning through the country, but southern members blocked the inquiries. Although the soldiers had restored order and returned to their barracks, the bitterness of segregation remained at the capital's heart.

THE VIOLENCE OF July 1919—along with the changes brought by the war, and a president preoccupied with world affairs and remote from the capital—dimmed the spirit of Washingtonians. The city's postwar landscape was gray and sullen. Tours of the White House and the annual Easter Egg Roll had stopped. The hastily built tempo buildings diminished the Washington Monument and brought blight to the National Mall. The twin smokestacks of the great power plant in the city's southeast filled the sky with acidic soot. The barren dormitories for government workers that had mushroomed on the land in front of Union Station destroyed the first view of the capital that had greeted visitors in the past. These and other signs troubled the city and had an effect upon the minds of all residents, at least all who were white, and who saw that the life of their comfortable old capital had been changed.

The greatest cause of a weakening of spirit among Washington's residents was the failure of a constitutional amendment to give them representation in the US Congress. It was a cause that the editor of the *Washington Star*, Theodore Williams Noyes, and many private citizens and commercial organizations had championed for decades. In 1917, they had united into the Citizens' Joint Committee on National Representation for the District of Columbia, a ponderously named

THE FEDERAL government had to build dormitories as well as offices for the flood of new workers it hired. The "tempos," as the buildings were known, went up quickly, but remained well after the war. CREDIT: Library of Congress

coalition headed by Noyes, with the purpose of educating Americans, especially those in state legislatures, about the constitutional disenfranchisement that Washington's residents suffered. Their campaign began auspiciously, and many citizens believed they were making progress. The District was "the only slave pen . . . established by the law of the land anywhere on the face of the earth," Representative Sherman Everett Burroughs of New Hampshire said in February 1918, when he called on the 65th Congress to authorize an amendment granting suffrage.

But the measure died in the Judiciary Committee. Noyes and his fellow members of the Citizens' Joint Committee remained hopeful when a new Congress, controlled by Republicans, convened the following year. But rioting on U Street in July, and fear of "Red" agitators, whose presence was beginning to be felt in America, dulled the ardor for representation among Washington's businessmen. The city had flirted with black enfranchisement in the 1870s; perhaps, some reasoned, the more prudent course would be to maintain the present commission form of government. Southern and rural members of Congress, many of whom were wary of cities and fearful of the black migration from the South to the North that had begun during the war, did not favor the change. Once again, distrust of political democracy as the basis of government prevailed, and the opportunity for change passed. Although Kansas senator Arthur Capper, chair of the Senate Committee on the District of Columbia in the 1920s, would regularly introduce a joint resolution on a constitutional amendment, no one took the effort seriously. Governing the District of Columbia as a fiefdom of the federal government would continue, as it had for more than four decades.

BY AUGUST 1920, Louis Brownlow, impoverished by his small salary, was preparing to leave the capital for Petersburg, Virginia, where he took a job as city manager. Raymond Pullman, the city's chief of police, lay in the Congressional Cemetery, a victim of double pneumonia. Woodrow Wilson, ravaged by a stroke he had suffered in October 1919, remained isolated in the White House. In a moment of supreme self-delusion, he had flirted with running for a third term—which, mercifully for him, the nation, and the District of Columbia, Democratic Party leaders deflected. That November 2, 60 percent of the electorate across the forty-eight states chose Republican Warren G. Harding to be the next president.

The following March, Washingtonians seemed especially happy to see Wilson leave the White House. Every president since George Washington had presented some message, even if it was but a sentence or two, expressing interest and support for the capital and recognizing its unique place in the republic. But not Woodrow Wilson. Indeed, the twenty-eighth president had seemed almost contemptuous of his surroundings. So cool was he about his adopted city that some thought it surprising for him to buy a Georgian Revival townhouse on S Street in Kalorama for his retirement. But his wife, Edith, had exercised her formidable will upon her husband, and he did. On Inauguration Day, March 4, 1921, Wilson was moved there with Edith and his black valet. More surprising still was Wilson's burial in Washington's National Cathedral upon his death three years later; he was the first, and is today still the only, president to be interred in the capital.

CHAPTER 11

Normalcy and Neglect

Let it express the soul of America. Whenever an
American is at the seat of his Government, however
traveled and cultured he may be, he ought to find a
city of stately proportion, symmetrically laid out and
adorned with the best that there is in architecture,
which would arouse his imagination and stir his patriotic pride.

—Calvin Coolidge, 1926

After the eight priggish and puritanical years of Woodrow Wilson, of war, shortages, Red scares, and foreign entanglements,
Americans were eager to embrace their new leader, Warren Gamaliel
Harding, when he took the Oath of Office on March 4, 1921. Six feet
tall and manly, white-haired and gray-eyed, Harding looked and acted
like the very model of a modern president, and a polar opposite to the
one he was replacing. In his mellifluous baritone voice, he promised
the nation "normalcy," a word of his own invention, which no one,
least of all Harding himself, understood. Historians today remember
his time in office as something of a joke—for the alcohol-fueled card
games with venal cabinet members, and occasionally reporters; for the
supposed sordid affairs with mistresses; and for a White House that at
times resembled, as one witness said, the back room of a speakeasy. But
those revelations came after his passing in August 1923. For most of his
881 days in office, Americans loved their president.

Though they hadn't been allowed to vote for him, Washingtonians, too, loved Harding. He opened the White House grounds to all; resumed and extended White House tours, and sometimes showed up to chat with visitors; reinstated the annual Easter Egg Roll for 5,000 delighted children; restored the outdoor teas that had been a springtime tradition; revived the president's New Year's Day reception, after an eight-year hiatus; and, to the delight of everyone, brought the first celebrity dog—Laddie Boy, an Airedale terrier—to unofficial and official events. Sporting a hand-wrought collar studded with Alaskan gold nuggets, Laddie took his seat at cabinet meetings in his own specially carved chair. It was rare in those heady first months of the Harding presidency for a Washington newspaper to go a week without publishing a rotogravure of the purebred dog and his consummately handsome master at play. "The Washington atmosphere of to-day is that of Old Home Week or a college class reunion," wrote one journalist in 1921. "It beats all what a change has come over the spirit and manners and disposition of this town since Mr. Harding came in."

Residents were especially pleased on May 30, 1922, when Harding presided over the dedication of the Lincoln Memorial. As had been the case with the saga of the marble monument to the first president, the capital's memorial for the sixteenth was a long time coming, endured just as tortured a history, and concluded with an equally impressive result. As early as 1867, Clark Mills, the sculptor of the capital's equestrian statues of Washington and Jackson, had presented sketches for a huge monument dedicated to Lincoln on the Capitol grounds. In 1871, Vinnie Ream Hoxie created a standing Lincoln holding the Emancipation Proclamation for Statuary Hall, and in 1876, black Americans paid for a sculpture of a twelve-foot-tall Lincoln emancipating a kneeling and suppliant slave. But after the collapse of Reconstruction with the election of Rutherford B. Hayes in 1876, the memory of Lincoln became too contentious for Congress to agree upon a monumental sculpture and memorial.

In the refulgence of time, the Great Emancipator metamorphosed in American memory, from the commander in chief of armies that brought the Confederacy to its knees, to a figure of introspection, benevolence, and sadness who struggled to save the Union, in the hope that a government of the people, by the people, and for the people should not perish from the earth. The change, which coincided with the diminishing number of surviving Confederate veterans, gradually overcame the legacy of bitter sectionalism to allow the new Abraham Lincoln to take his place in the mythic pantheon of America.

In the minds of Americans, this iconic Lincoln was larger than life, as was the president who approved the McMillan Plan for the memorial, Theodore Roosevelt. TR revered the sixteenth president—in the White House, he ordered his portrait hung above his desk. After Congress created a memorial commission in June 1902, many believed that construction would soon begin on the reclaimed land at the western end of the National Mall.

Two decades of acrimony, persistence, and hard labor passed before the great memorial would be finished. The acrimony came over alternate plans: Automobile enthusiasts and supporters of the good-roads movement argued for a majestic memorial road lined with gardens and stately trees connecting the Gettysburg battlefield with Washington, or perhaps even with Richmond. Others, including members of Congress, proposed locating a tribute to Lincoln on the land between the Capitol and Union Station. But the greatest impediment to placing the building on the Mall was the powerful conservative Republican congressman from Lincoln's district in Illinois, Joseph Gurney Cannon. Ever the opponent of Teddy Roosevelt's progressive plans, Cannon regarded the site as "malarial" and vowed to "never let a memorial to Abraham Lincoln be erected in the God damned swamp." Congress allowed the centennial of Lincoln's birth on February 12, 1909, to pass without taking action.

Champions of the McMillan Plan quietly persisted. They met with success in 1910, when insurgents in Congress overthrew Cannon's leadership, and Roosevelt's successor, William Howard Taft, created the Commission of Fine Arts, which would "advise upon the location of statues, fountains, and monuments." Taft appointed only supporters of the McMillan Plan to the commission. A year later, Congress created a Lincoln Memorial Commission, made Taft chairman, and funded the memorial with $2 million. The money brought even more proposals for the best place to locate a memorial. Finally, in 1912, the Fine Arts Commission decided on the Mall site and the memorial's architect, Henry Bacon. Early the following year, the lame-duck Congress hustled to approve another $2 million for construction before the Democrats and Woodrow Wilson took control.

Schooled in the Beaux-Arts tradition by his mentor Charles Follen McKim, and deeply appreciative of classical design, Henry Bacon created "a Greek temple," a place of "reverence and honor" that was still accessible to "the heart and brain of the citizen." He procured flawless white marble from Colorado to enhance the building's austerity and remoteness and to suggest the pure ideals of the republic. And he commissioned his friend Daniel Chester French, with whom he had collaborated on a number of memorials and monuments in the United States and Europe, to produce a twelve-foot-high statue of Lincoln seated on a throne-like chair fit for a Roman proconsul. And the architect had engraved on the walls to the left and right of the president the simple words of Lincoln's Gettysburg Address and Second Inaugural Address.

To execute his plans, Bacon had to navigate a perilous labyrinth of bureaucracy, proposals from other architects, and a recalcitrant Congress. He clashed with Frederick Law Olmsted Jr., the lone surviving member of the Senate Park Commission, who wished to change the elevation of the road encircling the memorial and alter the design of the cruciform reflecting pool. He countered proposals for a standing Lincoln in bronze rather than French's sitting Lincoln in marble, and proposals for more inscriptions to be chiseled into the marble. And to secure additional money to complete the project, he had to wait until the election of 1920, when Warren Harding and the Republicans gained control of Congress from Woodrow Wilson and the Democrats.

In the end, the critics diminished, Congress approved the money, French completed his colossal sculpture, and the great temple gleamed like alabaster over the temporary gray buildings that clustered on the Mall. Even Joseph Cannon, "in hindsight," conceded that the memorial was "where it ought to be."

At last, all was ready for the dedication, which, appropriately enough, took place on Memorial Day 1922. Breaking his vow to steer clear of sitting presidents, Robert Todd Lincoln, the sixteenth president's oldest son, sat on the dais as an honored guest. Robert had come to think of himself as a bad omen for presidents, for a tragedy occurred whenever he was near them. He had been in Washington in 1865 when his father was shot, at the train station in 1881 when James Garfield was shot, and at Buffalo's Pan-American Exposition in 1901 when William McKinley was shot. Robert always cleared his travel plans with the White House so as never to be in the same city as the president. But the invitation to attend from Chief Justice William Howard Taft, who had continued to chair the Lincoln Memorial Commission after his presidential defeat in 1912, had been too enticing.

Robert Todd Lincoln listened as the poet Edwin Markham, famous for celebrating the cause of the laborer, read lines commemorating his father's life. "His words were oaks in acorns," Markam intoned, "and his thoughts / Were roots that firmly gripped the granite truth." He listened as Taft called Lincoln "the Nation's savior," and the memorial "a shrine at which all can worship . . . an altar upon which the grim sacrifice was made in the cause of Liberty . . . a sacred religious refuge in which those who love country and love God can find inspiration and repose." And he heard Warren G. Harding laud the sixteenth president's "heroic patience" in reestablishing the "union and security."

The day's lone black speaker, Robert Russa Moton, the Virginia-born son of former slaves and the president of the Tuskegee Institute, delivered an opening address. Three centuries earlier, Moton began, the *Mayflower* had landed at Plymouth Rock with pilgrims seeking religious freedom, and a Dutch ship had landed at Jamestown with a cargo of enslaved humans. By God's providence, "the black race in America was thrust across the path of the onward-marching white race," Moton said, "to demonstrate not only for America, but for the world[,] whether the principles of freedom were of universal application." Since the arrival of those ships, freedom and bondage had developed side by side. Lincoln's greatness rested on his actions: "In the hour of the nation's utter peril, he put his trust in God and spoke the word that gave freedom to a race, and vindicated the honor of a nation conceived in liberty and dedicated to the proposition that all men are created equal."

Moton had been a late addition to the program, brought in only after the commissioners belatedly realized their failure to include a single black at the dedication. He was a safe choice, for he espoused Booker T. Washington's conservative vision of race relations: that through high morals and hard work, blacks would gradually bring down the barriers of segregation and earn their rightful place in American society. Nevertheless, Taft and the Memorial Commission were clearly worried about what Moton might say. When they vetted his speech two weeks before the dedication, they had asked him to delete about a quarter of his remarks, including a passage in which Moton cited Lincoln's warning that "this nation cannot endure half slave and half free: it will become all one thing or all the other." Moton also agreed to remove, "With equal truth, it can be said today: no more can the nation endure half privileged and half repressed; half educated and half uneducated; half protected and half unprotected; half prosperous and half in poverty; half in health and half in sickness; half content and half in discontent; yes, half free and half yet in bondage."

Partly in response to Moton, Harding said Lincoln "would have compromised with the slavery that existed, if he could have halted its extension," while Chief Justice Taft never uttered the words "slavery" or "emancipation." Although he was far too accommodating to betray his feelings, Moton must have found it an especially discordant moment. He had just published *The Negro of Today: Remarkable Growth of Fifty Years.*

The treatment of blacks on that dedication day laid bare a deep flaw in the nation's character that was apparent to all who cared to see and hear it in the District of Columbia. At the dedication they could see it in the roped-off, segregated "colored" section, reserved for the few blacks who had been invited. They could hear it when a white-gloved Marine reportedly commanded "Niggers over here" to those forced to sit behind the rope. No one had seemed to object when Colonel Clarence O. Sherrill, commissioner of public buildings and parks, and military aide to President Harding, had created the special enclosure for blacks. "The venomous snake of segregation reared its head at the dedication," wrote a reporter for the *Chicago Defender*, adding, "What a change since Appomattox! The conquered have become victorious."

WHEN THE FRAIL Woodrow Wilson moved with his wife and butler to S Street in March 1921, he brought his personal wine collection. For this Congress granted a special dispensation, since the Volstead Act, which it had passed over his veto on October 28, 1919, forbade the transport of alcohol as well as its manufacture and sale. Wilson's successor possessed no such scruples. Though dry in public, Harding and his cronies were wets in private, so wet that Justice Department agents often diverted shipments of liquor they had seized in raids to the White House. Alice Roosevelt, who had remained in Washington after her father left the presidency, remembered "the cabinet member who did not take a drink when it was offered to him was an exception," adding, "It was rather shocking to see the way Harding disregarded the

Constitution he was sworn to uphold." She had firsthand knowledge, too, for her husband, Nicholas Longworth, a hard-drinking Representative from Ohio, was often found at Harding's side.

The Washington couple closest to the president and his wife, Florence, were the flamboyant and sybaritic Evalyn and Ned McLean. The daughter of an immigrant Irish gold miner who moved his family to the capital in the late nineteenth century after striking the motherlode in Colorado, Evalyn became famous for purchasing the cursed Hope Diamond, which had brought disaster to the European potentates who had owned it before her. After their marriage in 1908, the *nouveau riche* couple began to thrust themselves into the circle of Washington's political and embassy elite, while along the way they set about the task of squandering their combined fortune of $100 million. Their lavish, alcohol-fueled parties and profligate spending had become the stuff of legend. By the 1920s, they had become Washington's equivalent of Scott and Zelda, though with far greater wealth and no talent.

Social climbers that they were, Warren and Florence Harding felt a natural gravitational pull into the McLeans' orbit. For the president's delight, Ned hired a Scottish architect to design an eighteen-hole golf course at Friendship, their large estate on Wisconsin Avenue, and turfed it with sod imported from Switzerland. Along with Maryland's Chevy Chase Club, it became a favorite venue for the president on fall and spring afternoons, especially as he and his alcoholic partner could count upon a white-jacketed butler to be waiting at the ninth hole with a silver tray of martinis.

Throughout his first months in office, the president hewed to his line of normalcy, or at least to the illusion of it. Behind the normalcy stood an unsophisticated, naïve, Babbitt-minded man from Ohio, who, despite appearances, had been very ill for many years. Harding's weight topped two hundred pounds, and his high paunch crowded his breast bone. He suffered from shortness of breath; slept on a hill of pillows to prevent apnea and asphyxia; and was so addicted to nicotine that, in addition to cigars and pipes, he chewed tobacco and even ripped cigarettes apart to eat their contents.

Harding's naïveté and his high office made him an attractive mark for unscrupulous friends and members of his cabinet, who took the idea of normalcy to mean theft. As the truth of the ever metastasizing corruption slowly came to light in the early months of 1923, the president's popularity began to wane. It was still ebbing that summer as he headed for the western states to recuperate from a bout of influenza and connect with the people. By the time he reached San Francisco on the first Monday in August, Harding was so exhausted that he succumbed, so his doctors said, to "apoplexy."

An even more dramatic sight than the funeral train that crossed the nation from California to the capital, or the thousands of silent citizens massed along Pennsylvania Avenue, or the obsequies that followed at the White House and Marion, Ohio, was the pyre that burned for days on the lawn of Friendship. Beside the blaze sat Florence Harding with boxes of her late husband's White House papers. She reviewed them quickly, put a few aside, but cast the rest into the flames. It was her vain attempt to obliterate any connection between Warren Gamaliel Harding and revelations of graft, kickbacks, and corruption that would come to characterize his presidency.

VICE PRESIDENT CALVIN Coolidge, who succeeded Harding, combined his midwestern predecessor's desire for normalcy with an authentic rectitude engendered by a spare and spartan upbringing in Plymouth Notch, Vermont. He seemed to be the man that all Americans had in mind when they thought of a New Englander—quiet and pious, thrifty and restrained, simple and temperate. Coolidge's press agent, speechwriter, and secretary emphasized these qualities through photographs, movie-house newsreels, and radio addresses, which they gave to eager reporters. He was "Silent Cal," whose shyness was genuine. Genuine, too, was his integrity, which stood him in good stead as the scandals of the Harding years gradually unfolded before the American populace. But for the most part, Americans seemed to care little for the revelations of malfeasance and theft. (Even the *New York Times* declared the representatives and senators investigating the corruption to be "assassins of character.") As the election of 1924 affirmed, Americans were content to have a president who stood for prosperity, stability, and thrift while they were busy changing morality, speculating financially, and running wild.

Coolidge's New England taciturnity proved a measured counterpoint to his wife Grace's innate charm and outgoing friendliness. He and Grace entertained regularly, with elegance and ease—and without the set who had attended the Hardings' card- and alcohol-fueled gatherings in the private quarters. The Coolidges used the White House and Washington itself to full advantage. Whenever a visiting delegation came to call, be it the American Law Institute or Washington's Association of the Oldest Inhabitants, the president dutifully trotted out to the lawn for a ceremonial photograph. When local soldiers from Walter Reed Army Hospital, still recovering from wounds inflicted in World War I, came for a garden party, Grace made sure to talk with everyone, especially those without limbs and confined to wheelchairs.

The annual Easter Egg Roll became more popular than ever, especially as the First Lady greeted the guests with her two white collies, Rob Roy and Prudence Prim, in tow. Rob Roy, whom Coolidge called "a stately gentleman of great courage and fidelity," regularly accompanied his master to the office. In time, a menagerie of domestic and wild animals began to accumulate, including cats, canaries, more dogs, and Rebecca, Calvin Coolidge's pet raccoon, which occupied a special box in a tree on the South Lawn. Spurred on by his Secret Service bodyguard, Coolidge, who abhorred exercise, went on daily walks, which he said gave him a greater understanding of the city. Some afternoons he met Grace after her weekly appointment with a hairdresser on Pennsylvania Avenue, and walked with her as she shopped. Newspaper pictures showed Washingtonians that the First Lady followed fashion; she kept her hemlines raised and her hair marcelled. She walked daily, sometimes with Rob Roy, and encouraged exercise. An avid baseball fan since her days at the University of Vermont in Burlington, she transferred her allegiance from the Boston Red Sox to the Washington Senators, attended home games frequently, and even got Calvin to watch the Senators' victory over the New York Giants in the 1924 World Series.

Even more than the rest of the nation, Washingtonians seemed to revere the Coolidge family and to feel assured by their presence at 1600 Pennsylvania Avenue. On the surface, at least, the city's residents were happy to take part in the frivolous age that was consuming the rest of the nation. A dancing craze swept the city. Meyer Davis and his dance band played nightly at the restaurant atop the New Willard Hotel; a table d'hôte dinner and dancing could be had at the Arlington Hotel's roof garden for just $1.50. Social mavens and society columnists for all the capital papers followed the activities of the two Coolidge boys with

WASHINGTON'S CHERRY trees have always been a popular subject for artists and photographers. The trees, the curve of the Tidal Basin, and the Washington Monument in the background have attracted thousands to this spot each spring. CREDIT: Library of Congress

avidity, and when the youngest, Calvin, died from a blood infection in the summer of 1924, Washington mourned along with the rest of the nation. Significant news, be it the earthquake that leveled Tokyo and Yokohama, the devastating Mississippi flood of 1927 that inundated ten states, or the elementary school bombing in Bath, Michigan, that killed thirty-eight children, seemed to make only a fleeting impression on the minds of those living in the capital. Like other Americans, Washington's citizens depended upon Calvin Coolidge to handle international and domestic problems in a way that limited the government's role in relieving the distress. And they depended upon him to exercise thrift and balance the budget.

Thrift was the Coolidge mantra, and the president exercised it in the budget for the District of Columbia. But not as much as one might assume. Learning from Treasury Secretary Andrew Mellon that the federal government was spending an exorbitant amount in renting offices for many of its departments, the president approved the Public

Buildings Act, an ambitious federal building program for the nation, but which included billions each year for the District. Work began on the Commerce Department and Internal Revenue Service buildings, the first of the Federal Triangle, the land that begins at Sixth Street where Constitution and Pennsylvania avenues form a "V" and ends south of the White House at Fifteenth Street. Work also finally began on another important part of the McMillan Plan, the bridge connecting the Lincoln Memorial with Arlington Cemetery. When the bridge opened in 1932, a key piece of the capital's transportation network became a reality. Coolidge also took an interest in increasing support for schools, which had been chronically underfunded. He weighed his appointment and reappointment of the District's commissioners carefully.

Although Coolidge and his budget director talked ad nauseam about thrift, he raised the District's budget nearly 50 percent, from $26 million in 1924 to $36 million when he left office in March 1929. The District's budget for Coolidge's last full year in office (the fiscal year ending June 30, 1928) presents a snapshot of where the president's, Congress's, and the commissioners' priorities lay—as well as the social attitudes and civic realities of a city that now numbered 450,000. Older nineteenth-century departments under the commissioners' supervision—including building and plumbing inspection offices; the city assessor's, auditor's, and collector's offices; a register of wills and recorder of deeds; a coroner and a superintendent of weights and measures; and a license bureau that issued metal identification tags for horse-drawn vehicles—had increased the size of their staffs to 486 and their expenditures of $781,546. The District's police and fire departments now consumed about $17.5 million.

Other city departments, born of new technologies as well as a new sense of civic responsibility, took still more money to operate: nearly $200,000 for the sewer department; more than $1.5 million for trash collection; $4,562,546 for the highway department; and nearly $100,000 for traffic lights, which were introduced in 1925 to smooth the flow of cars and trucks along Sixteenth Street. The budget for the city's public library, which now had four branches in addition to the Carnegie building at Mount Vernon Square, had reached $285,600. And there were still more expenditures for items as diverse as St. Elizabeth's Hospital, playgrounds, and the National Zoo. No amount of thrift on Calvin Coolidge's part could ignore the fact that Washington, DC, was, however haltingly, taking its place as a modern city in twentieth-century America.

But the budget that Congress passed did not mean that the federal government would pay for the entire $36 million. Indeed, it wouldn't come close. The Organic Act of 1878 called for the budget expenses to be split 50–50. In 1920, the southern-dominated leadership in the Congress had changed the federal share to 40 percent. But it wasn't enough. Not content with the 10 percent cut, Congress made more reductions and demanded that Washington's citizens tax themselves for the difference. For a while in the heady 1920s, when businesses could not fail, and work and wealth would come to all, civic leaders on the Board of Trade believed it was acceptable, if not entirely agreeable, to acquiesce to Congress; after all, they had no recourse.

SEVERAL ITEMS IN the 1928 budget acknowledged the fact that the formidable barrier of segregation remained strong in Washington. About 26 percent of the city's residents were black, or "colored," as they were referred to in the budget, and they remained on the trailing edge of appropriations. The highway department's list of streets and roads to be repaired or built shows that most were in white neighborhoods. The Columbia Institute for the Deaf would receive $27,000 to educate white children, and the state of Maryland received $5,000 "for the maintenance and tuition of colored deaf mutes of teachable age." The white District Training School received $255,700; the Industrial Home School for Colored Children, $54,250.

Black Washingtonians were used to such treatment. They listened as Harding and Coolidge spoke with a measure of eloquence about them and showed sympathy for their plight in twentieth-century America, but they knew all too well that presidents rarely followed up with deeds. "I believe the Negro citizens of America should be guaranteed the enjoyment of all their rights," Harding declared on accepting the Republican Party nomination for president: "That they have earned the full measure of citizenship bestowed, that their sacrifices in blood on the battlefields of the Republic have entitled them to all of freedom and opportunity, all of sympathy and aid that the American spirit of fairness and justice demands." Once elected, he told a crowd of 100,000 in Birmingham, Alabama, that the time had come to bring "economic equality between the races" and "equal educational opportunity for both." The cautious and restrained Coolidge noted, in his First Annual Message to Congress, that there were "12,000,000 colored people" whose rights were "just as sacred as those of any other citizen." It was incumbent for the federal government "to exercise all its powers of prevention and punishment against the hideous crime of lynching." But neither president did much more than talk; between them, they appointed just six blacks to significant federal posts in the capital; they turned a blind eye to heads of departments in civil service who continued and intensified Wilson's policy of segregating the federal government. Coolidge remained passive as Colonel Clarence O. Sherrill, his commissioner of public buildings and parks, the one who had penned up black citizens at the dedication of the Lincoln Memorial, segregated the picnic areas in Rock Creek Park and forbade blacks from swimming at the public bathing beach at the Tidal Basin directly across the Mall from the White House. The bitter message his inaction sent was clear: fine though these presidential sentiments had been, they were nothing but words for the wind.

DESPITE THE hundreds of tons of raw sewage that were dumped into the Potomac daily, the District's segregated bathing beach on the southeastern side of the Tidal Basin remained a popular place from 8:00 a.m. to sunset, June to October. Run by the District, the beach included a tall diving platform and "Bathing Houses" where patrons could rent suits and lockers. CREDIT: Library of Congress

Inaction and silence encouraged racism. This certainty became distressingly clear for all Washingtonians, and even the nation, when on a hot August afternoon in 1925, 30,000 members of the Ku Klux Klan marched in the capital. After the screening of Griffith's *Birth of a Nation* in the White House and movie theaters across the country, the revived Klan thrived even in northern states—Pennsylvania, Indiana, Illinois, and Michigan, among others—where, especially after World War I, whites felt threatened by the thousands of blacks migrating from the South to take jobs in factories, and to live, or threaten to live, in neighborhoods that the whites considered theirs alone. Anti-Catholic, anti-black, and anti-immigration, the Klan stressed Protestantism, Prohibition, and purity. Its national leader, the "Imperial Wizard," defended the KKK before Congress as a "moral teaching fraternity . . . dedicated to the great Lord of Hosts." The Klan's activities were part fraternal, on the order of Masons or Shriners, and part murderous. Those who joined its secret chapters, or "klaverns," held elaborate ceremonies complete with white robes, hoods, and blazing torches. The revived Klan created klaverns for women and children and adopted the burning cross as a symbol and a menacing threat. For many Americans, especially blacks, the words "Klan" and "lynching" were synonymous. By the 1920s, Washington had a chapter led by a "King Kleagle" (an amalgam of "Klan" and "eagle"), whose job it was to sign up new members. Rumors circulated about the city that men in white robes and hoods had performed secret midnight initiation ceremonies in the Capitol office of a Georgia representative, or in a crypt beneath the Capitol dome, or in the State, War, and Navy Building.

Although the rumors were likely false, the fact that in the spring of 1925 Colonel Sherrill gave the national Ku Klux Klan permission to march down Pennsylvania Avenue could not be denied. Later that spring, the Imperial Wizard moved the Klan's national headquarters to the capital and invited Calvin Coolidge to address his marchers, as the president had done when a Catholic organization had visited the city the year before. Jewish and Catholic groups joined with the National Association for the Advancement of Colored People to protest the planned gathering, especially after the District's King Kleagle predicted it would be a "monster parade" that would draw perhaps 150,000 members of the Hooded Empire from across the nation to the capital. Disregarding the complaints, and denying another group permission to hold a "peaceful anti-Klan gathering" on the same day, Colonel Sherrill outlined the route: up Pennsylvania Avenue from the Peace Monument at First Street to Fifteenth, and from there to the Sylvan amphitheater near the Washington Monument. But, the colonel said, the Klan must not wear their hoods, and they would not be allowed to burn a cross in the District.

By late July, some members of the city's Board of Trade and many black Washingtonians viewed the coming march with alarm. The Grand Kleagle of the District's klavern kept changing the number of marchers he expected; sometimes it was 150,000; other times it was 5,000. How could officials prepare when they had no idea how many would attend? White citizens, some of them members of the Board of Trade, quietly formed a group to settle matters pertaining to accommodations, health, and safety; the District commissioners called for the Marines to guard the Treasury Building; and Colonel Sherrill ordered a double line of ropes along Pennsylvania Avenue to separate the marchers from onlookers. Black Washingtonians, who followed the Klan's activities in the nation's leading black newspapers, the *Chicago Defender*, the *Pittsburgh Courier*, and the *Washington Tribune*, heard from the pulpits of their churches that the best measure they could take would be to stay home and ignore the event altogether.

Early in August, automobiles filled with Klan members from states as far away as Maine and Texas began arriving in the capital for the parade. Men, women, and children set up their tents on a large lot at Fifteenth and H streets that the city had made available, or they crossed the Potomac to camp at Arlington. On the morning of Saturday, August 8, forty-three special Klan trains from Ohio, New York, Pennsylvania, and New Jersey, among others, arrived at Union Station. At 3 p.m., when the temperature hovered at 95 degrees, Pennsylvania Avenue filled with a snowstorm of white robes and conical hats. The men and women, about 30,000 in all, marched twenty-five abreast up the avenue toward the Sylvan amphitheater. As they arrived at the amphitheater in the early evening, an ominous cloud from Virginia filled the sky. "We shall pray," the Grand Kleagle of the District commanded. "Never yet has God poured rain on a Klan assembly." The rain came and the assembled dropped to their knees as the Reverend A. H. Gulledge from Ohio intoned, "Oh God, I pray that the remainder of this service will be conducted without rain." With those words the downpour became a deluge that drove the crowd away.

THE PHOTOGRAPH shows a few of the approximately 30,000 Klan members who marched up Pennsylvania Avenue on a sultry Saturday afternoon in August 1924. The day was a high-water mark for the klaverns, which have never again mustered the numbers who came to Washington that day. The Capitol dome and the Peace Monument are in the background. CREDIT: Library of Congress

The following evening, the Klan rallied across the Potomac at the Arlington horse show grounds. After Rev. Gulledge warmed up the crowd with a full-throated denunciation of Catholics and Jews, blacks, and all "un-Americans," the Klansmen lit an eighty-foot-tall wooden cross. The flames lit up the sky for miles around. And then it was over. Washington had endured the white-robed disruption of its civic life with a measure of self-assurance. No one could have known at the time that this national march would be the last significant event for the Ku Klux Klan, whose national leadership was riven by scandal and dissent.

Although many klaverns would sputter on through the 1930s, the organization would never again command as much attention as it had that summer.

IT IS UNLIKELY that those living in the community called "Uptown" took much notice of the fiery sky that hot Sunday evening in August 1925. Uptown had evolved from a mixed-race area in the late nineteenth century into an almost entirely black community favored by the bourgeoisie. Howard University and LeDroit Park were part of Uptown, as were the commercial areas of U and Seventh streets NW. Unlike the racist threat of 1919, when open, gratuitous, and raw white violence came to Uptown, the Klan march that August seemed almost a cartoon of menace; it was downtown, and did not threaten the community's safety. But the residents of Uptown knew all too well that whites, especially those who occupied the White House, had continually raised their hopes only to dash them. If Coolidge had meant his fine sentiments about race, he would have heeded the resolutions of black civic groups across the nation to stop the march. The president, however, had remained silent.

The residents of Uptown knew that theirs was a Jim Crow world shaped by white indifference and discrimination. The barrier of segregation had only grown taller and stronger since the spring of 1913, when the Wilson administration had begun separating the races in federal departments. Congress had not codified Jim Crow into restrictive laws for the District of Columbia, as state legislatures in the South had, but Washington's residents, both white and black, had codified Jim Crow by custom. Everyone tacitly understood the rules. With the exception of schools, playgrounds, and—after the US Supreme Court made race covenants in property deeds legal in 1926—real estate, laws did not separate black Washingtonians from whites. But all understood that blacks would not be given a seat in a whites-only theater or a bed in a whites-only hotel; that white-owned department stores would serve them only with great reluctance; and that although white-run lunch counters would serve them, they had to eat standing up.

In the 1920s, white Washingtonians attended Broadway-bound plays at the National Theater, or took in movies at Loew's Palace, a 2,400-seat house on F Street with a brilliantly lit marquee, or the Earle, a marble-and-gold-encrusted 1,800-seat palace at Thirteenth and F, or any of about a dozen other whites-only theaters. Meanwhile, blacks could see films at the 1,200-seat Lincoln or the 1,300-seat Republic, two theaters on U Street owned by white companies with black stockholders. By the time the films arrived at U Street, they were often on their second run.

The tacit rules were not laws. Indeed, local ordinances gave blacks the right to education, streetcar seating, and public accommodation. But by the turn of the century those ordinances had largely been forgotten. Whites remained downtown, while middle-class blacks stayed Uptown, apart and silent. Such silence reflected neither acquiescence nor acceptance, but a recognition of the reality of racism inherent in American life.

Yet the physical and spiritual isolation from white Washington only increased the self-esteem of the blacks living Uptown. A number of residents could trace their ancestors in the District to the Civil War, and some to the antebellum period; and a select few had ancestors as old as the capital itself. They lived in tidy Italianate rowhouses. And they knew, too, that they were the elite of the largest black population of any city in the Union.

Left free to pursue their own destiny, Uptown residents developed a self-sufficient community. Many set high standards for themselves as well as high expectations for their children. People were to conduct themselves properly, and always with a measure of dignity. They strove to create a community of disciplined men and women who believed that education, business entrepreneurship, and artistic expression would bring them satisfaction and security. By the 1920s, their intellectual, commercial, and artistic culture was in full flower, and it possessed a vibrancy that equaled, and often exceeded, the culture centered in downtown white Washington just two miles away.

Howard University, the center of black education in Washington as well as the United States, set the intellectual tone for Uptown. Although it suffered through a series of financial crises and the administration of a mediocre and craven white president, James Stanley Durkee, who feared the brightest and most productive members of his faculty, Howard still attracted important erudite professors dedicated to education and learning. The advent of the university's first black president, Mordecai Johnson, in 1926 augured a new era for the university. A Baptist

minister endowed with a commanding presence and a gift for rich oratory, Johnson worked to attract an excellent faculty and to elevate academic standards.

By the end of the decade Johnson had tapped Charles Hamilton
Houston to be dean of the law school, and he encouraged Houston as
he worked with the NAACP to mount challenges to Jim Crow laws
in the federal courts. (Houston also secured the school's accreditation
by the American Bar Association.) Johnson hired the augustly named
Numa Pompilius Garfield Adams to be the first black dean of the
medical school, giving him a mandate and the money to improve the
school's faculty and training of physicians. He recruited Ralph Bunche
to create Howard's political science department, Abram Harris to teach
economics, and the poet and essayist Sterling Brown to teach English,
and he rehired the brilliant Alain Locke, whom Durkee had dismissed,
to develop a first-rate philosophy department. They were joined in
the 1930s by other important scholars, including the sociologist and
authority on race relations E. Franklin Frazier, surgeon and medical
researcher Charles R. Drew, and historian of Reconstruction Rayford
Logan. Each man earned distinction outside the academy; Bunche,
who helped form the United Nations, and received the Nobel Peace
Prize for mediating an accord with the Arabs and Israelis, was probably
the most famous.

Under Johnson, and despite Durkee, literature thrived on the campus in the 1920s. Montgomery Gregory from the English department
joined with Locke to create a reading series consisting of the most
important black poets, novelists, playwrights, and essayists of the time,
including William Stanley Braithwaite, Countee Cullen, Charles W.
Chesnutt, Claude McKay, Willis Richardson, and W. E. B. Du Bois.
The theater department and Gregory established the Howard Players,
so that "the Negro play-wright, musician, actor, dancer, and artist in
concert shall fashion a drama that shall merit the respect and win the
admiration of the world." Out of their collaboration Locke and Gregory
published *Plays of Negro Life: A Source-book of Native America Drama.*

Most important of all for Howard's future, in 1929 Mordecai Johnson persuaded President Herbert Hoover to double the annual federal appropriation for the university to $500,000. By the time of his
retirement in 1950, Johnson had raised the annual federal payment to $7
million.

Uptown's high schools reflected the high aspirations everyone in the neighborhood had for their children. Armstrong Manual Training School on O Street, named for a white Union commander of a black Civil War regiment, offered vocational training in business and the "applied arts" of design, painting, and music. The school became famous for producing jazz musicians of the caliber of Duke Ellington and Billy Eckstine. While Armstrong gained its fame from its superb training of musicians, Dunbar High School on M Street, named for the poet Paul Laurence Dunbar, gained renown for its fine preparation of scholars and leaders. Its high standards and faculty, many of whom held doctorates from the leading universities in the North, made it into the finest high school for blacks in the nation. Test scores of Dunbar students often equaled those of the best white students downtown. Black families from other areas of the country, especially those on the East Coast, sent their children to Washington so that they could get a Dunbar education. And the education paid off, too. Dunbar graduates regularly earned admission to such northern colleges and universities as Amherst and Williams, Columbia and Harvard.

Uptown became the center of new black literary and cultural societies. Such associations had been present in the capital since Emancipation, when a group of government clerks had formed the Lotus Club. The Monday Night Literary Society, the Bethel Literary and Historical Association, and the Musolit Club followed. The most prominent of these groups, the Musolit Club, rented an Uptown house for its meetings. Republican in politics and staid in outlook, it limited its membership, as it said in its literature, to "high-class men, true-hearted men, with whom it is a pleasure and honor to be associated." (Musolit did, however, allow women to join in an auxiliary.) The associations drew many of their members from Howard, Dunbar, and Armstrong, but also attracted prominent black professionals from around the country.

On many Saturday nights, the unofficial literary and cultural center of Uptown could be found at Georgia Douglas Johnson's house at 1461 S Street. Howard mathematician Kelly Miller, Alain Locke, and others called it the "S Street Salon." Johnson was a widow from Georgia. Her husband, a recorder of deeds for the District of Columbia, hadn't been happy when she had started publishing poems and a regular column in the NAACP's magazine *Crisis*, for he feared his wife would neglect their two boys and her household duties. But Johnson persisted, and after her husband's death in 1925, she thrived. She wrote poems and plays, gave readings around the country, and made her home a center for Washington's most promising young black writers and intellectuals, including Jean Toomer, Langston Hughes, and Angelina Grimké, who were integral to what came to be called the Harlem Renaissance.

By 1920, U Street, Uptown's commercial center, had more than three hundred businesses, almost all black-owned. Black entrepreneurs built and owned the buildings that lined the street. They operated restaurants, beauty parlors, barber shops, drugstores, banks, florist shops, clothing stores, and tailor shops on the ground floors, and rented the floors above to lawyers, doctors, and dentists. In the evenings, the lights and marquees of black theaters, clubs, and dance halls came to life. Frequently called the "Great Black Way," in the 1920s U Street affirmed that Uptown's citizens, too, were worthy of the displays of wealth and style that whites enjoyed downtown. As the singer Pearl Bailey remembered, it was the street "where all the fancy people strolled."

Three buildings—the True Reformers Hall, the YMCA, and the Whitelaw Hotel—helped to define Uptown. The five-story True Reformers Hall that towered over U Street at Twelfth became one of the first symbols of what blacks might achieve. Built in 1903 by the Grand United Order of True Reformers, a black fraternal and benevolent organization, the hall was conceived, designed, financed, built, and operated by blacks. John A. Lankford, who had gained much of his training in architecture and mechanical drawing at Tuskegee Institute as well as from a correspondence school, created the red and buff brick Romanesque structure. It featured eighteen-foot-tall windows on the second story and an elaborate pressed tin frieze at the top, along with meeting rooms, a concert hall, offices, and large plate glass windows at street level for commercial establishments—the Gray and Gray Drug Store, Chapman's Tailoring and Designing School, the Silver Slipper Club, and a branch of the True Reformers. "ERECTED BY NEGROES," the headline writer for the *Washington Post* titled an article about the building, somewhat enviously: "White Race Had No Hand in Any Part of Work." President Theodore Roosevelt took note of it in a letter of congratulations: "No one can watch with more interest than I do the progress of the colored race; and with the colored man as with the white man, the first step must be to show his ability to take care of himself and those dependent on him." The singular achievement of the True Reformers Hall brought Lankford so much success that he moved his home and architecture practice from Virginia to 1448 Q Street, several blocks away from the building he designed.

The YMCA on Twelfth Street, between S and T streets, stood as a testament to the neighborhood's growing sense of self-sufficiency. In 1853, two years after the Christian organization began in Boston, Anthony Bowen, an ex-slave who had purchased his freedom in 1826, and now worked in the US Patent Office, founded the first Y in the country "for colored men and boys." Half a century later, it still lacked a permanent home and received no support from the national, segregated YMCA. When Uptown residents took up a subscription to raise $100,000 for the building, John D. Rockefeller of Standard Oil stepped forth with $25,000. At the cornerstone-laying ceremony in November 1908, President Theodore Roosevelt called the building "a monument to the advancement of the city of Washington." Finances remained precarious, and construction even stalled, until Julius Rosenwald, the philanthropist and head of Sears, Roebuck, pledged an additional $25,000 to complete the building in 1912.

William Sidney Pittman spared little in his design for the Twelfth Street Y. Pittman, who received his training at Tuskegee Institute in Alabama and Drexel Institute in Philadelphia, created a Renaissance Revival, four-story brick building with a social room, a reading room, twenty-four bedrooms, and a bowling alley. A large two-story gymnasium with a basketball court and a swimming pool projected from the rear. It quickly became a meeting place for civic organizations like the NAACP and the Negro Medical Society; a magnet for young men, who learned to swim and play basketball; and a haven where black men doing business with the government might find a place to sleep.

The Whitelaw Hotel at U and Thirteenth streets, "the first hotel of its size built for the exclusive use of colored people," as its developer called it, was the inspiration of one of Uptown's most successful entrepreneurs. John Whitelaw Lewis arrived in Washington in 1894 with Coxey's Army and stayed on to take a job as a hod carrier for ninety cents a day. Three years later, he organized the carriers into a union and negotiated a raise to $2.25 a day. Seeing that his fellow workers were spending their earnings recklessly, he pooled $13.50 to create the Industrial Bank at Twelfth and U streets, the first bank for blacks in the District. By the 1920s, the bank had 11,000 depositors and assets of

$800,000. It was a considerable achievement for Lewis, who had grown up on a Virginia farm in the shadow of the Civil War, and who had just three months of schooling.

Lewis wanted his hotel to be an entirely black enterprise. Black stockholders joined him in the $160,000 venture. Isaiah T. Hatton, who had worked as a draftsman for both Lankford and Pittman, designed the five-story building. It had hotel rooms for visitors and one-bedroom apartments for those staying long-term. The hotel attracted black travelers; black entertainers, who came to play at Uptown clubs; and any black diplomat or representative of a foreign government who was refused a room in white Washington. But the chief attractions for the neighborhood were the ballroom, the banquet hall, and a restaurant, which demanded formal dress for seating.

If an Uptown resident had a party or wedding reception at the Whitelaw, or a graduation ceremony at Dunbar High School, or a prom at Howard University, Addison Scurlock was sure to be on hand to take photographs. As Howard University's official photographer for six decades, Scurlock seemed to be present at every football game, dance, and commencement. He photographed almost every important black leader who arrived at the capital for an official visit. For years his pictures ran in black newspapers, including the *Pittsburgh Courier*, the *Amsterdam News*, and the *Washington Tribune*. When he wasn't recording events around Uptown and the capital, Scurlock could be found in his studio at Ninth and U streets, composing sensitive photographs of politicians, musicians, and intellectuals like W. E. B. Du Bois, Mary Church Terrell, Sterling Brown, and John Hope Franklin. It was said in Uptown that if Addison Scurlock didn't take your wedding picture, you weren't married.

Edward Kennedy "Duke" Ellington was one of many Washington-born Uptown musicians whom Scurlock photographed. Ellington grew up in several places in Uptown, including Thirteenth Street, just south of the Whitelaw Hotel, and 1212 T Street NW. From childhood he recognized that models of "black accomplishment" were all around him. His eighth-grade English teacher, Miss English, "spent as much time in preaching race pride as she did in teaching English," he remembered at the age of seventy. "She would explain that everywhere you go . . . your responsibility is to command respect for your race." At home, his parents instilled the same sense of self-worth. His father imparted a sense of style, decorum, and outward bearing that he had likely absorbed from his years as a butler in the households of prominent white families, and occasionally at the White House. His mother protected him, considered him her "jewel," sang and played the piano, and encouraged him to realize his musical talents. Together they tended to his spiritual life at Sunday services rich with hymns and preaching, sometimes at his father's John Wesley African Methodist Episcopal Church, and sometimes at his mother's Nineteenth Street Baptist Church. "From sun to sun," Ellington remembered,

> *Their hearts beat as one*
> *My mother—my father—and love.*

Ellington's formal music training began with private piano lessons, and they ended when he left Armstrong High School in 1917. Undisciplined at the beginning, he often skipped his lessons, and though he learned harmony and notation from his music teacher Hugh Grant, he never completed Armstrong's applied arts course. More informal training came from listening to a host of Uptown's ragtime pianists, including Doc Perry, Washington's most popular black bandleader. Perry, whom Ellington called "my piano parent," taught him to "read notes, not just spell them out." By 1918, Ellington had taken to calling himself "Duke," created the Duke's Serenaders, and commanded obeisance. His advertisement in the city's telephone directory affirmed his confidence.

IRRESISTIBLE JASS
FURNISHED TO OUR SELECT PATRONS
The Duke's Serenaders
COLORED SYNCOPATERS
E. K. ELLINGTON, Mgr.
2728 SHERMAN AVE. N. W. Phone Columbia 7842

Appropriately, the Duke's Serenaders played their first gig at the True Reformers Hall at Twelfth and U streets.

By 1919, the Duke's Serenaders were popular in white Washington and Virginia as well as in Uptown, where the Howard Theater, at 620 T Street NW, became the center of a flourishing musical scene. That scene included the Capital City Clef Club at Ninth and R streets, the Murray Palace Casino near the True Reformers Hall on U Street, and the Lincoln Colonnade in the basement of the Lincoln Theater, among others. Ellington played them all.

On the Wednesday evening before Christmas 1922, Armstrong High School held its "Yuletide Exercises." One of the features of the evening was "Dancing in the gymnasium with music by Duke Ellington." But the event, which appropriately took place in Uptown and at his former school, marked the end of Ellington's beginning. The next year he moved his band to New York City. What he gained from Washington, particularly from his parents and the bourgeois environment of Uptown—refinement, smoothness, tact, and urbanity—remained with him for the rest of his life.

NOT ALL UPTOWN residents were as bourgeois and gentrified as those who lived in the world of Howard University, the Musolit Club, and U Street. Other residents living on and around Seventh Street, many of whom had arrived from the Deep South after World War I, held very different attitudes and aspirations, and this did not escape the moral gaze of the middle class. In *Recreation and Amusement Among Negroes in Washington*, the young Howard sociologist William Henry Jones found that the leisure pursuits of those on Seventh Street weren't the wholesome ones of taking in a football game at Howard University, a baseball game at Griffith Stadium at the end of U Street (where black and white fans mixed freely), a round of golf at the segregated nine-hole course at Potomac Park near the Lincoln Memorial, a game of tennis at the Howard Playground, or a cotillion at the Lincoln Colonnade. Those on Seventh Street enjoyed playing pool, dancing, and attending cabaret shows, and, sometimes, frequenting the area's prostitutes. The pool halls were, Jones said, "headquarters for incipient gangs"; the dance halls were places for "sexual pantomimes . . . publicly arousing human passions in preparation for lascivious orgies"; and cabarets were "dance hall behavior intensified," where one might drink alcohol, mix with "undressed women," and hear "jungle laughter" and "jazz . . . music carried to extremes." And "vice dens, even open solicitation," flourished along Seventh Street, too. Ever class conscious, Jones sometimes allowed his observations to stray into racism.

But Seventh Street was the Uptown area that many artists and writers found more congenial. The Howard Theater at Seventh and T streets, and Frank Holliday's Pool Hall next door, were places where doctors and lawyers mixed freely with Pullman porters and janitors, a mix of classes that attracted Duke Ellington, a host of other musicians, and two of the finest writers of the 1920s, Jean Toomer and Langston Hughes.

In 1923, Toomer made Washington's Uptown the center of his lyrical novel *Cane*. "Seventh Street is a bastard of Prohibition and the War," he wrote with geographic precision, "[a] soft-skinned wedge of nigger life breathing its loafer air, jazz songs and love, thrusting unconscious rhythms, black reddish blood into the white and white-washed wood of Washington. Stale soggy wood of Washington." The street, which cleaves Washington and slices Pennsylvania Avenue between the Capitol and the White House, was a symbol of the racial divide across the nation. Its bastardy came from not playing by the rules of the white order. Lured by the false promise of work in the North, many of its residents were not prepared for urban life; and Prohibition had brought about a thriving culture of bootlegging. Significantly, Toomer begins and closes his meditation on Seventh Street with a bitter quatrain:

> *Money burns the pocket, pocket hurts,*
> *Bootleggers in silken shirts,*
> *Ballooned, zooming Cadillacs,*
> *Whizzing, whizzing down street-car tracks.*

After a peripatetic journey across Africa, France, Italy, Mexico, and most recently New York City, Langston Hughes arrived in Washington in 1925 to live with his relatives in LeDroit Park. His relations were quick to remind him of his grand uncle, John Mercer Langston, who had started the Howard University Law School in 1868, and had served briefly as a representative from Virginia before the state disenfranchised blacks. Through them he met "the best people" of Uptown. Hughes found them pompous and self-satisfied, "descendants of distinguished Negroes," he remembered bitterly several years later, and better, blacks who could "trace their ancestry right on back to George Washington and his colored concubines." But to him, they were "un-Negro," pale or "coffee and cream ladies," "pinks," and "high yellows," members of the leading women's clubs, or "cultured doctors and lawyers and caterers and butlers," who thought more of passing in white theaters than of reading *Cane*, or the many other novels, poems, and plays created by the rising group of black authors.

To the horror of his relatives, Hughes left LeDroit Park for a small apartment at 1749 S Street and eventually landed a job managing the office at the *Journal of Negro History*. Once free, he wrote and published prolifically, establishing himself with the other younger writers at Georgia Douglas Johnson's Saturday night salons.

Seventh Street, what Hughes called "the long, old, dirty street, where the ordinary Negroes hang out," became his haven. For him, it was the true heart of black life in the capital, the place where "they played the blues, ate watermelon, barbecue, and fish sandwiches, shot pool, told tall tales, looked at the dome of the Capitol and laughed out loud." He considered those who lived on U Street to be liars, weavers of "dark garments / To cover the naked body / Of the too white Truth"; on Seventh Street could be found the authentic Truth of his race and its plight in America.

Feeling such alienation, Hughes could not last long in Washington. His most bitter moment came when Uptown's literary ladies invited him and his mother to a formal dinner in celebration of younger writers. But the ladies withdrew the invitation to his mother when they learned she did not have a suitable dress. The truth was inescapable: Washington was not congenial to a poet of his talents and aspirations. In February 1926, he left to attend college at Lincoln University in Pennsylvania. But his experience in Washington toughened and refined his resolve to resist what he later called "this urge within the race toward whiteness, the desire to pour racial individuality into the mold of American standardization, and to be as little Negro and as much American as possible." Langston Hughes's art would affirm the distinction of his race.

HUGHES LEFT THOUSANDS of black Americans who daily were arriving in Washington from states like Georgia, Alabama, Louisiana, and Mississippi with high expectations and dreams of jobs. What they found all too often were menial jobs, life on Seventh Street, sometimes an alley dwelling, and the high wall of middle-class blacks on U Street.

There was little hope of gaining welcome in a society that traced its roots to the city's founding. It was the world that Lead Belly found in the 1930s, when he arrived from Louisiana to record his blues and folk songs at the Library of Congress:

> *Home of the brave, land of the free*
> *I don't wanna be mistreated by no bourgeoisie . . .*
> *Well, them white folks in Washington they know how*
> *To call a colored man a nigger just to see him bow . . .*
> *Gonna spread the news all around*
> *I tell all the colored folks to listen to me*
> *Don't try to find you no home in Washington, DC*
> *'Cause it's a bourgeois town.*

CHAPTER 12

New Deal City

The New Deal was called many things, some not complimentary. But of this it could be said: it made Washington a cosmopolitan Capital. And a powerful one.

—Charles Hurd, 1948

An engineer by temperament and training, Herbert Clark Hoover abhorred waste and inefficiency in all its guises. By applying his principles of orderliness to mining operations in Australia and China, he made millions. He organized relief for Belgians during World War I and relief for Europeans after the conflict—all the while insisting upon proper planning, organization, and productivity. All Europe was grateful. An Austrian astronomer named an asteroid "Hooveria." Back in the United States, where he served as secretary of commerce for presidents Harding and Coolidge, he created regulations for the hitherto unchecked chaos of the new radio industry, increased home ownership and lending for mortgages, attacked government waste, and promoted business prosperity.

In November 1928, America's grateful citizens elected the self-made millionaire, humanitarian, and public servant to the presidency. Again, Hoover insisted upon order and economy. He eliminated the White House stables and the presidential yacht, *Mayflower*, which his predecessors had used frequently. Never mind that the savings supported the president's new, thirteen-building fishing camp in the wilds of the Blue Ridge Mountains of Virginia; or that the Filipino personnel from the *Mayflower* became the domestic staff at the camp; or that the Interior Department kept the Rapidan River stocked with an abundance of trout for the president's lures.

And efficiency would come at last to the White House itself. Within weeks of his inauguration, workers began rebuilding and expanding the West Wing. Following plans that Hoover himself had approved, they tore out walls, built new partitions, and added offices—three with fireplaces—to accommodate his burgeoning staff. By mid-June 1929, when the streamlined office complex was complete, all proclaimed it to be the very ideal of the way the US government should operate. Hoover's personnel performed in their new quarters with the precision of a finely engineered machine until the night of December 24, 1929. As a group of Girl Scouts were serenading presidential guests with Christmas carols in the Blue Room, an electrical short circuit in the West Wing caused a fire that consumed much of the White House, including the Oval Office.

In a very physical way, the conflagration in the West Wing characterized much of Herbert Hoover's administration. Good engineer that he was, the president planned and executed with the best of intentions only to achieve the worst of outcomes. Engineering had given him the "fascination of watching a figment of the imagination emerge through the aid of science to a plan on paper," he wrote in a paean to his profession, and then it is realized "in stone or metal or energy." Engineering, he continued, brings "jobs and homes to men . . . elevates the standards of living, and adds to the comforts of life." But as the stock market crash in October 1929 proved, the talented and accomplished engineer was a naïve and artless politician. Communication had never been his strong suit, but as long as the nation prospered, it did not matter. The economic collapse called for a show of empathy, an emotion the president seemed incapable of conveying. And engineering the financial system didn't work. He proposed lower taxes, instituted work programs, and improved housing, but to the hundreds of thousands across the nation who were without work, Herbert Hoover appeared to be cold, uncaring, and inept.

Rebuilding the West Wing after the Christmas Eve fire brought the employment problem right to the door of the White House. At the time, few in government believed they were witnessing the prelude to an economic collapse, yet even in Washington, where 33 percent of workers held federal jobs, legions of the unemployed and the desperate came to the construction site in search of work. By mid-July 1930, when the economy had only worsened, the president named three new District commissioners and brought them to his Virginia fishing camp for a weekend of discussions about stimulating federal building programs in Washington. They returned with plans to speed the construction of new schools and the renovation of old ones, as well as street-paving and bridge-rehabilitation projects. The government continued with its massive Federal Triangle project, for which Hoover had secured $2.5 million a year for ten years to build the National Archives, Department of Justice, and Commerce Department buildings.

"Well, they're going to elect that superman Hoover, and he's going to have some trouble," Calvin Coolidge had remarked to his bodyguard after he announced that he would not run for reelection. "He's going to have to spend money. But he won't spend enough." Coolidge's words proved prophetic. Although many Washingtonians believed that federal projects would protect the capital from the tough economic times the rest of the nation was enduring, they learned differently in 1932, when lack of funds forced the Smithsonian Institution to halt construction of its new wing. The Smithsonian's troubles proved to be just the forewarning of the arrival of the Great Depression in the capital. That year, federal workers were furloughed without pay; four of the city's banks were shuttered; restaurants closed; and the owners of 28,000 parcels of property who could not pay their taxes saw their land repossessed and put up for auction. As was the case in cities across the country, Washington's relief rolls grew dramatically. By year's end, the number stood at 40,000. The city commissioners asked the military to loan five hundred cots, mattresses, and blankets to the Salvation Army and the Gospel Mission. The bodies of men and women, often nameless and homeless, arrived from the city's streets and alleys at the city's single, antiquated morgue. Dr. Luther H. Reichelderfer, whom Hoover had appointed president of the Board of Commissioners, wrote a plaintive appeal begging Washington residents to hire their unemployed neighbors to perform home improvement chores. "Odd jobs around 5,000 homes would keep 5,000 men at work," Reichelderfer said, adding that they "would work gladly and happily knowing they earn something for their dependents."

The tide of good will and support that Herbert Hoover enjoyed in March 1929 had long since ebbed. Evidence of just how far it had receded appeared in the faces of 13 million men nationwide, one of every four, who were out of work; in the 10,000 banks, about 4 of every 10, that had failed; and in the statistics for industrial production—in which the president had placed so much faith—that showed an 80 percent plunge since his inauguration. By the end of 1932, many Americans were singing a popular new song, "Brother, Can You Spare a Dime?" To them, the president seemed aloof and out of touch.

For many, Herbert Hoover's handling of the Bonus Army stood as a clear symbol of his insensitivity to the plight of the nation. The marchers, a group of World War I veterans, was largely the brainchild of Walter W. Waters, a thirty-four-year-old unemployed ex-sergeant from Portland, Oregon. His money long gone, his wife and two daughters suffering from malnutrition, Waters decided in the spring of 1932 to join a group of veterans who were headed to Washington to lobby for immediate payment of their Adjusted Service Certificate. Nicknamed the "Bonus," or the "Tombstone Bonus," by many, the certificates were Congress's promise—passed over President Calvin Coolidge's veto—to give veterans of World War I a payment of about $1,000 each, but not until 1945, a date when Congress expected many of the men would be dead. The veterans regarded the money as theirs and wanted it right away. They called themselves the "Bonus Expeditionary Force," after the name of the America Expeditionary Force that had fought in the war. But the nation soon knew them as the Bonus Army.

When Waters and convoys of veterans from across America entered the District of Columbia in late May, they brought a titanic problem to the doorsteps of the Capitol and the White House. Congress, the president, and the city's citizens had to deal with a group of essentially homeless men, many with their families, but few with money, lodging, or anything to eat.

Some representatives and senators introduced legislation to pay the bonus. With conviction and a measure of optimism, Waters declared that his men would stay "until the veterans' bill is passed." There had been large gatherings in Washington before—Lincoln's funeral, the Union Army's two-day parade in May 1865, Coxey's Army's march in 1894, the Klan's march in 1925, and quadrennial inaugurations among them—and just a few months earlier, a thousand Communist-inspired "Hunger Marchers" had descended on the city. But this time, 20,000 veterans were singing in protest:

You're going to see a better day
When Mr. Hoover says "OK."
Hinky, dinky, parlez vous.

Initially, Hoover declared the issue of the veterans and their families to be a local rather than a federal problem. The District commissioners, in turn, looked to Washington's new superintendent of police, Pelham D. Glassford, whom they had hired to clean up corruption in the force.

Glassford was ready when Waters and his men entered the District. Despite Congress's refusal to fund emergency housing, he received Hoover's quiet assent to commandeer a group of vacant buildings on lower Pennsylvania Avenue that were to be part of a federal work project. In all, there would be twenty-seven encampments across the city, of which Camp Marks, a dormant army installation on the muddy flatland along the east bank of the Anacostia River, near Washington's dump, was the most substantial. There, Waters and his veterans created a small city complete with streets, large latrines (nicknamed "Hoover Villas"), a police force, a city square with a speakers' platform, a newspaper (the *B.E.F. News*), even a lending library. "The men are sleeping in little leantos built out of old newspapers, cardboard boxes, packing crates, bits of tin or tarpaper roofing," John Dos Passos reported in *The New Republic*: "every kind of cockeyed makeshift shelter from the rain, scraped together out of the city dump." Some veteran builders erected small houses. Money for food poured in from District residents, including Pelham Glassford's contribution of $750 to purchase 3,000 pounds of meat, 500 pounds of sugar, 200 pounds of salt, 4,000 loaves of bread, and 1,000 pounds each of coffee, onions, and potatoes. And unlike the rest of Washington, the encampment was a fully integrated city. Black, American Indian, and white veterans and their families lived together in harmony.

Across the nation, theater newsreels showed thousands of veterans marching to the steps of the Capitol's east front, where Congress was considering a bill to pay the service bonus. As expected, the House of Representatives approved the measure by a wide margin. Then, on the evening of June 17, word spread among the veterans at the Capitol steps that the Senate had resoundingly defeated the bill by a margin of 62 to 18. Few among them were surprised. "We have received a temporary setback," said Waters to his men. "But we are here to stay." The veterans then sang in unison—and loudly—the words to "America."

Evalyn Walsh McLean, all forty-five carats of the great blue Hope Diamond shining like a beacon on her breast, was among those who came to the Capitol that night. She was stirred by the "unshaven, tired faces" of the veterans when they rode by the gates of her house on trucks emblazoned with crude signs, which proclaimed "BONUS ARMY." And she was "horrified to see plain evidence of hunger in their faces; I heard them trying to cadge cigarettes from one another. Some were lying on the sidewalks, unkempt heads pillowed on their arms." After a chance meeting with Glassford, McLean and the police chief walked down Pennsylvania Avenue to the Childs restaurant at Fourteenth Street. He ordered 1,000 cups of coffee; she, 1,000 sandwiches and 1,000 packs of cigarettes.

After the Senate vote, many of the original group of marchers quietly acknowledged defeat and slipped out of their camps for home. But new arrivals from across the country joined the ones who remained. The July heat made living conditions horrific. Reports circulated through the city of veterans drowned while bathing in the gross and stenchy waters of the Anacostia; a thirteen-month-old died from diarrhea; and a four-year-old from measles and pneumonia, worsened by malnutrition. Despite Waters's standing orders that forbade alcohol and weapons, and the efforts of his own appointed police and the Metropolitan Police, some drunken veterans threatened the peace; others were reported to be brandishing guns. Many worried that the disappointed, unemployed men would become prey for Communist agitators, who were reportedly trying to recruit them for more violent acts.

How to get the men and their families to return home when many had little to return to? Glassford proposed that the government give them land to farm in the West, but, like the plan to give forty acres and a mule to the recently emancipated slaves seven decades earlier, it came to naught. Nor did the men want to move. New York governor and presidential candidate Franklin Roosevelt offered the marchers from New York free return to the state, but no one accepted.

The hot and muggy final Thursday of July saw a violent end to the Bonus March. That morning, the *Washington Post* presented the usual fare for its readers: Mrs. Hoover was planning a party for the wives of prominent Republicans at the presidential retreat in the Blue Ridge Mountains; a group of society's wettest matrons were making final preparations for their "Repeal Ball," to be held on the roof garden of the Willard Hotel (although the dry members of the Congressional Country Club had objected to its being held there); the District's commissioners were settling plans to spend nearly $1,750,000 that Congress had voted for building projects to relieve unemployment; the Democratic presidential nominee, Franklin Roosevelt, was in Albany preparing a radio address, which he would deliver to the nation on Saturday night; and President Hoover was planning for a conference on job creation that he would hold in the White House the following Monday. But at the foot of Pennsylvania Avenue, three blocks from the Capitol, where a group of about fifty marchers were staying in abandoned government buildings, Pelham Glassford's Metropolitan Police were not acting in the usual fashion. The buildings were already partially demolished when the veterans took them over in late May, but now President Hoover wanted the demolition work—and employment of the workers who had been hired to do it—to go forth.

Glassford's men moved in to evict the veterans. In the ensuing melee, one officer, who was being beaten with his own club, fired his revolver point-blank into the heart of one of his assailants, William Huska. Huska was a thirty-four-year-old Lithuanian immigrant from Chicago who had sold his butcher shop to enlist in World War I. Another shot mortally wounded Eric Carlson, a veteran from Oakland, California. The deaths changed the dynamic of the veterans' presence in the capital: the Bonus Army had two martyrs, but General Douglas MacArthur, the commander of the army in Washington, now had the authority he had longed for to rid the city of the veterans.

Often valorous and ever vainglorious, MacArthur had long been used to getting what he wanted. Over a career that spanned the Battle of Veracruz and World War I, earning him two Distinguished Service Crosses and seven Silver Stars, MacArthur had shown a flair for the dramatic and the reckless—and for exceeding or disregarding the orders of his superiors. He displayed his assumption of authority and aggressive conceit often, especially as he referred to himself in the third person when describing his exploits. The presence of homeless veterans daily marching "to the Capitol, to the White House, and to all the other sacrosanct federal buildings," he remembered, offended his sense of order. They were pacifists and Communists, thieves, murderers, and rapists, he alleged, a stain on the city of Washington. Now that they had become "a sullen, riotous mob," they offered the general the chance to display federal military might. Disregarding the advice of his young aide, Major Dwight D. Eisenhower, who later remembered that he had thought it unseemly for a general to become involved in "a local street-corner embroilment," MacArthur donned his dress uniform, complete with its fruit salad of battle decorations, and rode forth on his crusade.

MacArthur felt himself beholden to no one. As more than one of his deputies remarked, the general believed that his personal ambitions and those of his superiors were one and the same. The president of the United States had called upon the troops to remove the men from downtown Washington but to halt at the Anacostia River. What did it matter that he would disobey his commander in chief?

That afternoon MacArthur's force of six hundred armed soldiers proceeding down Pennsylvania Avenue from the White House—a battalion of infantry, a squadron of cavalry, a platoon of tanks, and a machine-gun unit—presented a sight never before seen in the capital. Using tear gas, bayonets, and mounted cavalry wielding sabers (the general kept the tanks and machine guns in abeyance), the men made short work of their assault on the veterans and a number of citizens who happened to be nearby. The gas took its toll on many, including two babies who died; sabers inflicted head wounds and cost one man his ear; and horses trampled several of those who tried to flee.

Anxious about the reports of what MacArthur had done, and fearful of what he yet might do, President Hoover dispatched an aide with a second set of orders repeating his demand that the troops halt at the bridge. But MacArthur imperiously replied that he was "too busy and did not want either himself or his staff bothered by people coming down and pretending to give orders."

Once they were across the Anacostia, soldiers surrounded the small city of Camp Marks that the bonus veterans had erected two months earlier. MacArthur gave the veterans an hour to evacuate, which most did. In a final act of defiance, though, they set fire to the tents, shacks, and small houses that had sheltered them. That night, the ragged and ill-fed men, a number of them with wives and children, set forth from the capital—some heading toward home in nearby states; some for Johnstown, Pennsylvania, where the mayor had offered shelter; and some to beg for shelter nearby. A few were fortunate enough to still have an automobile. The flames rising from the encampments outlined

BURNING OF the Bonus Camp, 1932. CREDIT: Getty Images

their silhouettes, while in the haze on the hill across the Anacostia stood another silhouette—that of the Capitol dome beneath a smoke-filled sky.

Walter Waters's Bonus March of 1932 marked a change in the idea of public assembly in Washington. A harbinger of the mass rallies and protests that would so dominate the capital's political life in the years to come, the march was far more significant than Jacob Coxey's workers, or Alice Paul's suffragettes, or the Klan demonstrators of the preceding decades. Newspapers, movie theater newsreels, and radio had broadcast the veterans' plight to millions of Americans who were themselves without work, food, and often, shelter. In the minds of these Americans, Washington became the place where they could assemble to petition their government for change.

The protest bore a striking resemblance to the one that had confronted James Madison and the Continental Congress in 1783, when an angry group of Pennsylvania soldiers had surrounded the statehouse to demand back pay and a settlement of their accounts. That "mutinous insult" had led Madison and the framers of the Constitution to create a separate seat of government, apart from any state, that was endowed with "complete authority" to ensure that the proceedings of government might not be insulted or interrupted. Now, nearly a century and a half later, as Washington faced its first mass protest, the president and Congress, along with the District's citizens, found they were not insulated from the momentous events spreading through the nation. More than ever, as Americans looked to their government for relief and succor, James Madison's dream of isolating legislators from the people they represented seemed unattainable.

IMAGES OF THE Bonus Army veterans—the men and their Washington encampments, their family members, and especially their violent end—flickered on movie theater screens and in the American consciousness in the summer of 1932 and helped to define the presidential election. The ebullient Franklin Delano Roosevelt was a welcome relief after the dour Herbert Hoover. Hoover had refused to meet with the veterans when they were in Washington; Roosevelt would deliver a radio "Invitation to all Veterans for Cooperation" the day after his inauguration as president in March 1933. He recognized their "sacrifice and service" in the past world conflict and linked those words to the condition of the nation. "I invite the support of . . . all men and women who love their country," he said, "who know the meaning of sacrifice and who in every emergency have given splendid and generous service to the Nation."

In the coming months, Roosevelt would mix sacrifice and service with a hearty dose of good cheer. Old Washingtonians and staid members of Congress found themselves caught in a storm of economists, social scientists, city planners, and political scientists, jocularly called the president's "brain trusters," who spoke earnestly and endlessly, and who had little time for the social conventions that had long dominated capital life. At the White House, the calm center of the storm, sat the president, ever radiating a charming confidence. He explained his plans over the radio in terms ordinary people could understand, delivering four "fireside chats" in 1933. In each he sought to explain complex problems and often arcane subjects on banking or currency, always calling for Americans to draw upon their courage and banish their fears.

Among the formidable challenges Roosevelt faced at the beginning of his administration was feeding people and giving them a purpose by putting them to work. By the end of 1933, the District of Columbia had received money for food, including butter and beef from the Federal Relief Administration, and shared in the thousands of jobs hastily created by the Civil Works Administration. CWA workers, more than 17,000 in all, took jobs paving the District's streets, demolishing the piers of the old Aqueduct Bridge, shoveling snow, and painting Roosevelt High School. CWA cooks made meals for undernourished schoolchildren; CWA teachers tended nursery schools and taught adult classes. True, the CWA jobs often emphasized employment and wages over productivity, but the Roosevelt administration believed that work, any work, was far preferable to living on the dole. Engineers and foremen had standing orders to use hand labor rather than machines whenever possible. The wages they earned collectively, as much as $230,000 a week, helped many Washington residents. The money seemed especially timely, too, because the winter of 1933–1934 frequently saw temperatures in the single digits, with the coldest February ever recorded.

CWA jobs eased the circumstances for many, but not all. New Dealers mixed the relief the program brought with hard measures that affected the city's economy. Every federal employee took a 15 percent pay cut, and on July 1, 1933, 17,000 veterans had their pensions reduced or lost them entirely. A stream of desperate men and women flowed into missions across the city for food and shelter, including two on Pennsylvania Avenue within sight of the Capitol—the Volunteers of America Mission at Fourth Street, and the Penny Cafeteria at Sixth. By 1934, the number of relief centers in the city had risen from 5 to 14, each capable of serving 1,000 persons. Many residents had been evicted from the 28,000 homes that the District tax office prepared to sell at auction on Thanksgiving Day. Commissioner George Allen authorized the District police to give emergency supplies of food and fuel to those in need.

A number of those receiving the supplies, including blacks and other minorities, lived in the network of Washington's alleys. Over the years the alleys had evolved from a series of wood shanties to simple brick structures, but insanitary conditions—overcrowding, primitive plumbing, lack of sewers, and polluted drinking water—persisted despite the best intentions. In his 1904 Annual Message to Congress, Theodore Roosevelt decried "the hidden residential alleys." They were "breeding grounds of vice and disease," and the "death rates, especially from preventable diseases, are so unduly high as to suggest that the exceptional wholesomeness of Washington's better sections is offset by bad conditions in her poorer neighborhoods." Woodrow Wilson's first wife, Ellen, visited the alleys and sought to create model housing in their place. After her death in 1914, Congress passed an alley clearance bill in her honor, but failed to fund it.

Eleanor Roosevelt and a group New Deal social reformers tried to effect change. In 1934, Congress created the Alley Dwelling Authority with the goal of eliminating the houses by July 1, 1934. The Authority made modest progress clearing out derelict structures and refurbishing others. But the city's overcrowding, created, in part, by the expanding New Deal programs and World War II, thwarted its larger plans.

Faced with hardship, many of the needy turned to evangelists and storefront churches, some suspect, some sincere, that opened in Washington. Among the suspect was the black evangelist Charles Emanuel Grace, who arrived in 1927 from New Bedford, Massachusetts, where he had sold patent medicines and preached the gospel. Called "Daddy" or "Sweet Daddy" by his followers, Grace proclaimed himself "Boyfriend of the World," established his first United House of Prayer for All People in Washington at Sixth and M streets, and installed himself in a seventeen-room house at Logan Circle. Washington became the

DESPITE THE efforts of various New Deal programs, many of Washington's alleys persisted. CREDIT: Library of Congress

hub for Grace's United House of Prayer churches, which he established along the Atlantic seaboard from Boston to Savannah and later in the Midwest. He preached extemporaneously and fervently in services that included singing, shrieking, weeping, and speaking in tongues on the part of his believers. He reached out to the poor and desperate, and he baptized hundreds at a time with a fire hose.

Grace was also fond of teasing out the idea that he was indeed God. "I never said I was God," he told his believers, "but you cannot prove to me that I am not." Often donning a ten-gallon hat, a pince-nez, a multicolored cutaway coat, and a chartreuse vest, Grace cut a singular figure in the capital. He had bejeweled fingers and wrists, as well as six-inch fingernails that were painted red, white, and blue. It all seemed bizarre to white Washington and discomfiting to many blacks in LeDroit Park. The eminent black anthropologist Arthur Fauset complained of the naked eroticism in Daddy's services. But he offered the less established, many of whom had recently arrived from the South, the sense of community and the structure they so desperately needed. Grace was also a real-estate entrepreneur, and he offered people shelter in his buildings. His church cafeteria served free meals to those in need.

To many in Washington, another preacher, Lightfoot Solomon Michaux, seemed the opposite of Daddy Grace. Often called "Elder Michaux," he opened his church on Georgia Avenue at V Street NW. Cut from the cloth of Booker T. Washington, the stocky Michaux dressed conservatively in a dark suit, white shirt, and tie, and strove to get along with the white community. He formed alliances with the District's commissioners, with presidents Hoover and Roosevelt and their staffs, and with Clark Griffith, owner of the Washington Senators baseball team. Griffith, Major Eisenhower, and the president's press secretary, Steve Early, were among those he named honorary deacons in his Gospel Spreading Association of the Church of God. He matched Sweet Daddy Grace in showmanship, but he was a far more powerful speaker. He preached to thousands in Griffith Stadium, once staging the Second Coming of Christ, who descended from a cloud suspended above left field. His annual baptisms of hundreds in the Potomac River were spectacles made for newspapers, newsreels, and radio broadcasts, as much as for God.

Michaux was among the first to exploit the power of radio for his evangelism. Beginning in 1929, he broadcast his weekly "Happy Am I" program on local station WJSV. The call letters, the evangelist said, stood for "Willingly Jesus Suffered for Victory." His appeal lay in his pithy, aphoristic sermons filled with lines of simple, homely truths that his listeners could remember easily ("God has written His law in your conscience"; "Security is not in money; it is in God"; "If the devil looked like a mouse, more women would be safe"), and in the gospel choir of forty that always sang his signature hymn, "Happy am I with my Redeemer." Whites listened as well as blacks, for he served up what they believed was a good old-fashioned camp meeting. When the CBS network took over WJSV and the program in 1933, Michaux had a national audience who listened on fifty stations spread across the country.

But Michaux was far more than a showman, and unlike Grace, he never relied on his charisma or flirted with the idea that he was divine. Michaux, too, offered his group of mainly black worshipers structure and conservative values. He delivered sermons excoriating the evils of drinking, gambling, smoking, prostitution, jazz, and the theory of evolution. But when Washington, DC, began to feel the effects of the Great Depression, Michaux's Church of God was ready to assist the impoverished. He preached sermons to the veterans at the Bonus Army encampment in Anacostia. He bought a building at Seventh and T streets NW to shelter those evicted from their houses and apartments, and he created an employment agency to help them get jobs. His Happy News Cafe at 1721 Seventh Street served hot meals for a penny to thousands daily and gave work to the unemployed as cooks and waiters. Other church members earned their meals by selling copies of the *Happy News*, a monthly newspaper with a circulation of 8,000 featuring articles and sermons by Michaux.

As the Depression eased, Michaux sought to create permanent and superior housing for Washington's blacks. In 1941, he joined with Albert I. Cassell of Howard University's architecture department to secure a $3 million Federal Housing Administration loan to create Mayfair Mansions, 596 apartments on the site of the racetrack near Benning Road in the northeast. Cassell had long wanted to design a group of garden apartments, but had lacked the political means to achieve his goal. To secure the loan, Michaux turned to a District commissioner, George E. Allen, whom he had made an honorary deacon of the Church of God. Despite construction delays and financial difficulties, the apartments opened 1946.

Reports in the white press of Michaux's various activities reflect a bemused and condescending attitude toward the evangelist. Typical was an article in the *Washington Post* reporting the shock that officials experienced when they received his appeal to use the Lincoln Memorial Reflecting Pool for his annual baptismal rite. After noting that Michaux maintained two chauffeured cars—a Pierce Arrow and a streamlined Ruxton—and lived in an "expensively appointed home," the writer conceded that "Elder Michaux has created a highly organized and effective bureau for lodging and generally aiding many poor and destitute, but worthy families."

FORTUNATELY FOR MICHAUX and the missions, federal programs began to change Washington's economy by 1935. The CWA had been a temporary measure to give the discouraged a productive enterprise and meager income while Roosevelt's New Deal administrators created permanent agencies. The alphabet soup they produced—SSA, NRA, WPA, REA, PWA, FCC, NLRB, among others—proved a positive boon for public and private Washington. The staffing needs of each agency brought hundreds to the capital. In roughly a decade, the number of federal employees grew 160 percent, from 63,000 in 1929 to 93,000 in 1934, 116,000 in 1937, and 166,000 in 1940. By 1937, there were 220,000 telephones in Washington, more per capita than in any other city in the country. Between 1933 and 1936, the number of passengers arriving at Union Station doubled, rising from 20,000 to 40,000. Out-of-towners doing business with the federal government, always a rich source of income, flocked to the city as never before; in 1935 alone, they spent $15 million in the city's 76 hotels.

Construction blossomed across the city as the federal government strove to give offices to the men and women who had been hired to carry out New Deal programs. The Roosevelt administration and Congress temporarily delayed the completion of the Federal Triangle, possibly because it had been the brainchild of the Coolidge and Hoover administrations and the now reviled former secretary of the treasury Andrew Mellon. But construction had begun on all the buildings save the Department of Commerce at the apex of the triangle. Gradually they would all open—offices for the Departments of Justice and Labor and Interstate Commerce in 1934; the National Archives and the Post Office in 1935; and the Internal Revenue Service in 1936.

The construction boom gave free rein to Roosevelt's abiding interest in architecture. As assistant secretary of the navy under Woodrow Wilson, he had investigated redesigning the State, War, and Navy Building with a Greek Revival skin, which he believed would bring it into greater harmony with the Treasury Building and the White House. He also ruefully remembered that he had convinced Woodrow Wilson to erect the Temporary Office Buildings on the Mall. These acts of government vandalism were to have been demolished, but in 1941 they were still defacing the Mall and "the whole plan . . . of the loveliest city in the world." It was, the president said, "a crime for which I should be kept out of heaven."

Now that he was president, Roosevelt intruded himself into the design of federal buildings, vetoing and approving architectural plans, and often sketching counterproposals. Only the most unusual circumstances would prevent him from presiding over a groundbreaking ceremony in the capital; and he brought out George Washington's Masonic trowel for the laying of cornerstones. Better than most, Roosevelt understood that his New Deal buildings would endure long after his social programs had ended. "A social or economic gain made by one Administration may, and often does, evaporate into thin air under the next one," the president reflected in a fireside chat in 1938. But "once you build a house you always have it." The "houses" whose design Roosevelt influenced were often monumental and gargantuan: the Supreme Court on East Capitol Street, on the site of the Old Capitol Prison, in 1936; an additional building for the Interior Department at C and Eighteenth streets, with two miles of corridors and sixteen acres of floor space, in 1936; the Federal Reserve, at Constitution Avenue and Twentieth Street, in 1937; the Jefferson Memorial, at the Tidal Basin, in 1938; and, across the Potomac in Arlington, the world's largest office building, the Pentagon, in 1943.

Roosevelt even contributed to the design of several buildings. He produced sketches for the architect of the reviewing stands for the parades at his first three inaugurations. (There was no parade for his fourth inauguration, which occurred in wartime, in 1945.) For each new term, he drew upon the vocabulary of a different American design—L'Enfant's New York City Hall, Andrew Jackson's Hermitage, and a building that evoked the nation's colonial roots. In 1938 Roosevelt decided that Congress, which had been debating the location for a new airport for a dozen years without reaching a decision, had talked long enough. He announced that it would be on the mudflats of the Potomac at Gravely Point, a site on the Virginia side of the river about four miles below the city. In June 1941, two and a half years and 20 million cubic yards of fill after the president made his decision, National Airport was ready. Its modern terminal featured an eight-columned portico, inspired by the president's design, that drew from the one George Washington had created at Mount Vernon.

The Department of Commerce building was altogether another matter. In his campaign for president, Roosevelt had singled it out as an example of Hoover's "extravagance and improvidence." This "Temple of Fact Finding," as Roosevelt called it in a campaign speech, suffered from guilt by association with Herbert Hoover, who had headed the department under Warren G. Harding, and with Andrew Mellon, for whom New Dealers and FDR had a particular aversion. Perhaps the site might serve better as a memorial for Thomas Jefferson, Roosevelt suggested; perhaps it might be best to leave it vacant. It wasn't until 1937 that the president's uncle, Frederic Delano, chairman of the National Capital Park and Planning Commission, and John Russell Pope, architect of the National Archives building and the future Jefferson Memorial, persuaded Roosevelt to allow the Commerce building's construction. But it would be a chaste and stripped-down version without the confection of curves and colonnades to complement the adjacent National Archives.

WHEN IT CAME to creating the National Gallery of Art, the most magnificent structure built in New Deal Washington, however, Franklin D. Roosevelt could not wield his power over Andrew Mellon. The president's dislike of the plutocrat and his ilk ran deep. Roosevelts had been in America since the seventeenth century, when New York City had been New Amsterdam; the Mellons were parvenus, having only arrived in western Pennsylvania in the nineteenth. Roosevelts, the president's branch at least, had made their money—and a lot of it—in business, but they wore their wealth modestly in the Hudson River Valley. "Extravagance," his father, James Roosevelt, had said, was "the pervading sin among all classes of people." In Pittsburgh, Mellons, Carnegies, and Fricks, nouveau riche, rock-ribbed Republicans, bankers, and big businessmen all, were economic royalists who believed in the primacy of capital over labor, always. They lived, so he believed, profligate, self-indulgent lives, and their prodigality had brought the nation to economic collapse. He would hold them up to public shame and censure, and through legislation, control the system they had so disgracefully and selfishly exploited for their ends.

By 1934, FDR and his attorney general decided to make Andrew Mellon, the secretary of the treasury under Harding, Coolidge, and Hoover, a scapegoat for the sins of reckless Republican profligacy. Their first attempt, a criminal suit for tax evasion, collapsed when the government's special prosecutor failed to persuade a grand jury to indict Mellon. Their second, a civil suit, charged him with evading $3 million in taxes. In the fifteen-month-long trial before the Board of Tax Appeals that followed, the government alleged that Mellon had channeled millions of dollars in works of fine art to the A. W. Mellon Educational and Charitable Trust, which he allegedly had created simply to avoid his tax obligation.

Though not without fault, Mellon was hardly a capitalist buccaneer from the Rockefeller and Gould mold. Since the turn of the century, he had chosen to spend his wealth on great art, especially European old masters. A steady flow of acquisitions crossed the Atlantic by artists such as Durer, Rembrandt, Velázquez, Van Dyck, Botticelli, and Vermeer, including, in 1930, a spectacular purchase of twenty-one paintings from the Hermitage Museum in cash-strapped Soviet Leningrad. These were the works that he had placed in the hands of his trust. The prosecutor planned a complete review of his acquisitions to shame Mellon, and by inference all indolent men of wealth who squandered their money on art while honest families starved.

The plan backfired. True, Mellon had transferred his extensive art collection to the Mellon trust, but he planned that through the trust, he would give the works to the nation. In addition, the trust would pay for a gallery to house the collection in a building large enough to attract the gifts of other wealthy Americans. Newspapers heralded the planned gift, making much of his intentions to build a gallery. The prosecutor chose to follow his strategy of considering the paintings, dismissing the proposed gallery as just another deception from one given to deceit. But as Mellon's attorney brought out the facts about the paintings that his client had acquired, including expert testimony as to their quality and worth, the government's case grew ever weaker. The Roosevelt administration appeared ever more vindictive. Why would "a man planning such benefactions," Mellon's attorney asked, "at the same time be plotting and scheming to defraud his government?" The question could not be answered. "Every time we bring out a bad point," the prosecutor lamented, Mellon's attorney "brings out a picture." By the trial's end, the government's charge of a bogus trust lay in tatters.

Shortly after his nemesis won reelection to the presidency in 1936, the financier turned philanthropist was diagnosed with cancer. It was in a failing condition that he and the architect John Russell Pope completed the plans for the gallery building to house his paintings. Mellon had determined the site on the Mall, and with considerable forethought, the site for an addition that would surely come after his death. With his lawyers he prepared an iron-clad proposal for the A. W. Mellon Educational and Charitable Trust, the same trust that the federal government was contesting in tax court. He would deed the works of art he had acquired to the "people of the United States," along with a gallery to house them and a liberal endowment for further expenses. The endowment would "permit the indefinite growth of the collection" and pay the salaries of the gallery's senior administrators. To ensure against the abusive exercise of raw political power of the sort that had bedeviled him for the past three years, the financier insisted that the gallery would be governed by a self-perpetuating board of trustees accountable neither to Congress nor to the president. And in an act of self-effacement all too rare in the capital, he insisted that the building would not bear his name. It would be the "National Gallery of Art."

This National Gallery would be like none other in the world. At Mellon's insistence, John Russell Pope had kept the building long— thirty-six feet longer than the Capitol—and low, which allowed most of the collection to hang on a single main floor. Its eighty small galleries flanking a central rotunda and two garden courts would lend an intimacy to the viewing not often found in national museums. Its exterior would be simple and without ornamentation, but made distinctive nonetheless by a pale pink Tennessee limestone. The capital, of course, was never short of critics, and some modern architects castigated Pope's plan as an expression of conservative and Republican values. They lobbied for a modern architect, someone like Frank Lloyd Wright, Ludwig Mies van der Rohe, or Le Corbusier, who would produce a building far more democratic in spirit. But Mellon, who controlled the purse, would have none of it.

Roosevelt realized he had little choice but to accept the offer on his adversary's terms, which, as his attorney general said, left little room for "give and take." Accordingly, the president recommended the appropriate legislation to Congress. It was, said Roosevelt, a "magnificent gift."

In his last months, Mellon continued to acquire art for the National Gallery, and he topped off his trust with an additional $9.5 million, raising its value to $22 million. He also purchased American portraits, an interest he developed in his final years, with the farsighted thought that they would someday become the nucleus of a National Portrait Gallery. He offered to give the paintings to the United States if Congress established a gallery within twenty-five years. In 1958, Congress approved the necessary legislation, and a decade later the National Portrait Gallery opened in the old Patent Office.

Early in the summer of 1937, Andrew Mellon was taken to his gallery building site, where the excavation was getting under way. It was his last visit; he would die that August. On December 7, 1937, the tax board dismissed the charge that Mellon had established his trust to defraud the government; instead, it declared that the "transfer . . . of certain paintings in 1931 was a complete and valid gift." At 10:00 p.m. on the evening of March 17, 1941, Roosevelt arrived at the National Gallery of Art to speak at its dedication. Dressed in a dinner jacket with a green carnation in the lapel in honor of St. Patrick's Day (it was also his thirty-sixth wedding anniversary), Roosevelt briefly touched on Mellon's munificence: "The giver of this building has matched the richness of his gift with the modesty of his spirit."

But that evening, Roosevelt, and no doubt many of the foreign diplomats and government officials gathered at the ceremony, had far more than Andrew Mellon and old masters in mind. Uncertainty about the future of the world left everyone anxious. Although English airmen had triumphed in the Battle of Britain, and London had recently withstood fifty-seven straight days of bombing, Adolf Hitler had just declared in a bellicose speech that the Germans would fight on to crush the British forces in the coming year. In Washington, Roosevelt and his aides had long since turned their attention from New Deal programs to arms production. Just that afternoon, rumors had circulated through the city that Nazi submarines were headed for American waters to harry ships bound for Great Britain.

With such thoughts in mind, Roosevelt accepted "the work of German painters such as Holbein and Durer, of Italians like Botticelli and Raphael, of painters of the Low Countries like Van Dyck and Rembrandt, and of famous Frenchmen, [and] famous Spaniards," saying, "to accept this work today for the people of this democratic Nation is to assert the belief . . . in a human spirit which now is everywhere endangered and which, in many countries where it first found form and meaning, has been rooted out and broken and destroyed."

For inspiration, the president looked back to the completion of the Capitol dome in 1863, and Lincoln's reported reply to those who criticized the expenditure of money and the labor of men on a building rather than the war: "If people see the Capitol going on, it is a sign that we intend this Union shall go on." Roosevelt vowed the same: "We too intend the Union shall go on. We intend it shall go on, carrying with it the great tradition of the human spirit which created it."

CHAPTER 13

War City

Washington in wartime has been variously described
in numbers of pungent epigrams, all signifying chaos.

—Dwight D. Eisenhower, 1948

June 8, 1939. Washington's days and nights had been scorching for a
week. Yet despite the heat and humidity, and the forecast that the
temperature would be in the mid-nineties, thousands began to line the
route from Union Station to the White House before dawn to cheer
the arrival of King George VI and Queen Elizabeth of Great Britain.
The size of the crowd had swelled to 750,000, the largest ever to gather
in the city's 140 years, when Franklin and Eleanor Roosevelt arrived in
the station's presidential lounge at 11:00 a.m. to greet the royal entou-
rage. "At last, I greet you," said the president, looking down from his
six-foot-two-inch height upon the slightly built, five-foot-nine-inch
king, who stood resplendent in his gold-trimmed admiral's uniform,
complete with a naval sword.

AFTER A TWENTY-ONE-GUN salute from army cannon outside the
station, the presidential and royal progress began its slow drive to
the White House. A rolling wave of applause greeted them. Throngs
cheered from the plaza in front of the station and along the sidewalks
of Delaware, Constitution, and Pennsylvania avenues; they looked
down from windows and roofs of office buildings or from trees and

pedestals of statues they had climbed for a better view; and, if they were steelworkers, from the girders of the unfinished skeleton of the National Gallery of Art. Close to 1,500 police officers and firemen and 6,000 soldiers kept everyone under control; teams of Red Cross nurses, doctors, stretcher bearers, and ambulances gave succor to the hundreds who collapsed from the heat.

George and Elizabeth were the first British monarchs ever to visit the United States, and certainly the most important English visitors to the White House since August 1814. This time they came at the president's personal invitation. Although Roosevelt first suggested that the monarchs might wish to "avoid the heat in Washington," the British ambassador determined it was imperative that they visit the capital as well as New York. Once the question was settled, the president planned a two-day itinerary that would please the most energetic sightseer: visits to the Lincoln Memorial, the Washington National Cathedral, and Arlington National Cemetery; a drive through Rock Creek Park, and a sail on the presidential yacht *Potomac* to Mount Vernon; a tour of a Civilian Conservation Corps (CCC) camp in Virginia; and tea with cabinet members and federal department heads. Back at the White House, they listened to a recital by Marian Anderson.

They discharged official duties, too: At Arlington, the king laid wreaths at the Tomb of the Unknown Soldier and at the foot of the Canadian Cross; and, in a tacit acknowledgment of his forebears' defeat, he quickly placed a wreath of lilies and iris trimmed with royal colors—red, blue, and gold—at the sarcophagus of George Washington at Mount Vernon. At the British embassy on Massachusetts Avenue, the royal couple hosted a garden party and a dinner for the president. In the Capitol rotunda, they shook hands with more than four hundred members of Congress, including one who greeted his majesty "Hello Cousin George," and who told "Cousin Elizabeth" she was "nearly as pretty as the blue-bonneted girls of Texas."

As in 1814, war was the occasion for the coming of the British, but this time it was the imminent war in Central Europe, which King George VI believed would surely engulf Great Britain. Roosevelt, too, recognized the seriousness of the threat, which had been building since about the time he had become president. By coincidence, his first inauguration in March 1933 had occurred within days of Adolf Hitler's seizure of power in Germany. Although Roosevelt had spent the early years of his administration consumed with the economic crisis and New Deal programs, he had watched with increasing unease as the Third Reich and other totalitarian powers—especially the fascists in Spain and Italy, and the Japanese in China—advanced across the world.

The withdrawal of Germany, Japan, Spain, and Italy from the League of Nations had eviscerated what little influence it had. Austria had succumbed to the Nazis in March 1938; six months later, Czechoslovakia fell into their hands with the Munich Agreement; and that November 9, on the night known as Kristallnacht, Nazi thugs across Germany destroyed everything Jewish that lay in their path. By January 1939, when he wrote to the king to suggest a royal visit to the United States, Roosevelt had become convinced that the partnership of Berlin, Rome, and Tokyo would engulf not only England but also the New World in war. Although at a state dinner in the White House, the king and the president exchanged toasts for "friendship in a world of peace" and a "peaceful world," each understood the coming hostilities. And Roosevelt believed the United States had an obligation to help its closest ally.

For years, many across America had held a different view. Starting in 1935, isolationists in Congress, led by Gerald Prentice Nye—an agrarian North Dakota senator who believed that Wall Street bankers, munitions makers, and US military departments were in collusion to promote armaments and war—passed a series of Neutrality Acts that limited the president's power to come to the aid of any "belligerent" nation. (In early 1938, Congress came close to passing a resolution for a constitutional amendment requiring a national referendum, except in the case of attack, before the United States could declare war.) A cadre of recent Irish immigrants and their children, fascist sympathizers, and the naturally Anglophobic tended to bolster the isolationists' position. Roosevelt held a different view. Should Germany conquer Great Britain, it would control the Atlantic; should Japan, whose naval fleet and aggression were growing steadily, control the Pacific, the United States would be isolated between two hostile powers. Nevertheless, the isolationists were ascendant: the president and his State Department were reduced to issuing muted protests over the events on foreign shores.

Still, public opinion was mixed. In 1937, George Gallup's American Institute of Public Opinion had found that 66 percent of Americans were neutral or had no opinion about the Spanish Civil War; 69 percent believed that Congress should support stricter neutrality laws; and 70 percent believed it was a mistake for the United States to have entered World War I. Six of every ten Americans polled after the Munich Agreement of September 1938 believed that England and France had done the best thing by yielding to Hitler (although news of Nazi-sanctioned atrocities, especially Kristallnacht in November 1938, had begun to change sentiment). Yet in January 1939, the Gallup Poll found that 94 percent of Americans believed that Germany, Italy, or both countries together would start a war with England by the end of the year.

Believing war was inevitable, Franklin Roosevelt knew that Britain would need the support of Congress and American citizens. Part of the reason behind his invitation to "George and Elizabeth"—to the shock of Anglophiles everywhere he addressed them by their names—was to present them to Americans in a sympathetic light. The United States and Great Britain were, after all, the two bastions of democracy, despite the vast ocean separating them, and they were bound by the threads of a common civilization.

All too often, Americans thought of the British as distant, class bound, and patronizing. The British delegation in Washington seemed to affirm the perception. Many, especially those in the press, regarded the ambassador as imperious and arrogant. In the course of their visit, however, the royals would belie these assumptions. Seemingly devoid of pretension or airs, the king and queen possessed a disarming regal grace that gave Americans, who thoroughly loathed the idea of monarchy, a reason to love monarchs. Their majesties asked questions of all whom they encountered. King George quizzed members of the CCC and other New Deal agencies about their programs; Queen Elizabeth met with American newspaper women. When the couple greeted a representative Girl Scout and Boy Scout, the queen discussed the badges her daughter Elizabeth had earned as a Girl Guide, and the king accepted a hand-carved walnut neckerchief ring made from one of George Washington's trees at Mount Vernon. His Royal Highness seemed, so the Eagle Scout reported to the press, "just like a regular American citizen."

Once war began in Europe in September 1939, Roosevelt's popularity jumped dramatically. By the end of October, the Gallup Poll reported that nearly 65 percent of voters approved of his presidency. By mid-1940, as nations were falling across Europe, the "Committee to

Defend America by Aiding the Allies," a pro-British propaganda group, had formed to counter isolationist sentiment. Soon, about 330 chapters of the group opened across the United States, including one in the District of Columbia. The group's affirmation of Roosevelt's foreign policy helped set the tone for his reelection to an unprecedented third term in November. In March 1941, Congress passed the Lend-Lease Act, the imaginative name the president gave to his plan to lend war materiel to Britain (and other allies) at no cost for the duration of the war.

Still, the strident and powerful opposition to Roosevelt's, and consequently Congress's, support of Britain would not be silenced. Shortly after Roosevelt's reelection, the America First Committee demanded that "Congress refrain from war, even if England is on the verge of defeat," and began to disseminate propaganda to whip up isolationist fervor. Its chief spokesman, the aviator Charles Lindbergh, whose solo flight across the Atlantic in 1927 had brought him world fame, took to peppering his addresses with anti-Semitic rants about Jews' "large ownership and influence in our motion pictures, our press, our radio, and our government." Senator Nye led the isolationists in Congress, who regularly delivered their broadsides against Roosevelt's support of Great Britain. If the war comes, Nye said in a speech he honed before crowds across the country in the summer and fall of 1941, it would be known as the "Roosevelt War."

THE FIRST SUNDAY in December 1941 dawned gray in Washington, where typically chilly temperatures in the thirties would edge toward the forties by noon. It being the Christmas season, the *Post* and *Evening Star* were thick with advertisements. Raleigh Haberdasher (Raleigh's to everyone) at Eleventh Street and Pennsylvania Avenue announced a holiday special on men's dress shirts; Hecht's, at Seventh and F, offered winter coats for boys and girls at $10. The recently expanded Lansburgh's department store one block south on E Street offered dramatic savings on Christmas stockings, a Victor record set of Dickens's *Christmas Carol*, and "a gift she'd choose for herself and enjoy all year"—a Hoover vacuum cleaner.

The stories in the *Post* that morning concerned a far more serious matter than vacuum cleaners, coats, and records. The lead story told of President Roosevelt's direct appeal to Japan's Emperor Hirohito "to call a halt to Japanese moves which might precipitate a general war in the Pacific." Other stories that day spoke of the Japanese threats elsewhere in the Pacific and a declaration by the Japanese press "that the moment of supreme crisis is at hand." On the editorial page, the conservative columnist Mark Sullivan declared, "We are extremely close to war with Japan. . . . [W]e face a world war."

But it was December in the capital, the season of parties and football. That morning in Wesley Heights in the city's northwest, Mrs. Thad Brown, widow of a late member of the Federal Communications Commission, was busy preparing her home for a party in honor of her newly married son and his wife. The guests were set to arrive at five; Mrs. Harlan Fiske Stone, wife of the chief justice, would assist at the tea table along with the wives of three senators. As Mrs. Brown's son, a Princeton graduate, was a recently commissioned junior officer in the navy, "the young set . . . from Army and Navy circles," the *Post* said, would be attending. And many, like Brown and his bride, were hastening their nuptials because they feared war would separate them.

At Friendship, her large estate on Wisconsin Avenue, Mrs. Evalyn Walsh McLean was making final preparations for a party in honor of the marriage of her daughter, also named Evalyn, to the stridently isolationist, Anglophobic, pro-Nazi, and virulently anti-Semitic senator Robert Rice Reynolds from North Carolina. ("Our Bob," as he was known to all in his home state and in the corridors of the Capitol, was fifty-seven, his bride and fifth wife, nineteen.) In July, Evalyn McLean had been widowed. Her dipsomaniac husband, Ned, having driven the *Washington Post* to bankruptcy, had died in a Maryland insane asylum, where he had been confined since 1933. But the fabled McLean dinner parties continued. For this evening the bride-to-be's mother had compiled a list of 115 guests that included two ambassadors, two foreign ministers, two Supreme Court justices, thirteen senators, five House representatives, the assistant secretary of war, and three generals.

Meanwhile, the attendants at Griffith Stadium at Georgia Avenue and Fifth Street, were preparing to open the gates to 27,000 lesser folk who were coming to see the Washington Redskins take on the Philadelphia Eagles in the last game of the season.

That afternoon, however, the young men never arrived at Mrs. Brown's tea, and Evalyn McLean's dinner never took place. At Griffith Stadium, the Redskins came from behind in the fourth quarter to beat the Eagles, 20 to 14, but by that time loudspeakers had already paged army captains, colonels and generals, navy admirals, members of the FBI, and cabinet members to report to their posts and offices immediately.

In Pittsburgh, Gerald Nye was speaking to an America First gathering. The senator was in full-throated harangue about the president's treasonous acts and the crime of Lend-Lease when a reporter quietly approached the podium and slipped him a note: "The Japanese Imperial Government at Tokyo today at 4:00 p.m. announced a state of war with the U.S. and Great Britain."

At about the same hour in Washington, a fleet of taxicabs filled with attachés arrived at the entrance of the Japanese embassy on Massachusetts Avenue. They carried metal boxes of papers into the garden and set them aflame. For a while, the Japanese diplomats, secretaries, attachés, and even the housekeeper, who lived in southwestern Washington, were captives in their embassy while the FBI figured out what to do with them. (They eventually were sent to the Homestead resort in Hot Springs, Virginia, where they remained until August 1942, when they were exchanged for American diplomats.)

However, soldiers failed to guard the Japanese cherry trees at the Tidal Basin. They dated from the Taft administration, when the mayor of Tokyo had given more than 3,000 seedlings to the United States in a gesture of friendship. Over the decades they had grown into hearty specimens with ten-inch boles, and their two-week burst of pink and white along the Potomac had brought Washingtonians together to celebrate the coming of spring. On that first Sunday evening of war, December 7, 1941, the night of the Japanese attack upon the United States Pacific Fleet in Pearl Harbor, Hawaii, vandals wielding handsaws leveled four of Washington's Japanese cherries. For the next four years, the National Park Service thought it best to call them "Oriental flowering trees."

IN ALMOST AN instant, December 7 changed Washington into an international symbol of freedom for the world—and a closed city. As the *Post* put it, the "city of white buildings" immediately became "an armed camp." Before December 7, anyone could walk onto the north grounds of the White House without a pass, and in springtime, when the trees were in bloom, could often walk on the South Lawn. People could leave a calling card at the north entrance, and on occasion, during a thunderstorm, motorists in open cars drove under the White House's North Portico to put up their cloth tops. The vice president usually traveled without a body guard, and Eleanor Roosevelt frequently drove her own car about the city alone. Within hours of the attack on Hawaii, Marines with machine guns cordoned off every entrance to the Capitol. Armed guards were now patrolling all government buildings, and thirty-eight soldiers were assigned to protect the Washington aqueduct from sabotage. The Secret Service blocked off Pennsylvania Avenue in front of the White House; guards stood in sentry boxes placed every one hundred feet on the perimeter of the fence, ordering anyone who lingered to "move on." Soldiers manned guns on the roofs of the Post Office and Interior Department and the White House. Agents now rode on the running boards of the presidential limousine and kept pace with Roosevelt wherever he went in the White House. Keepers of the Washington Monument announced that it would close at 4:00 p.m. rather than 6:00, to reduce the possibility that a saboteur might arrive with a bomb under the cover of darkness. By the end of the month, archivists had moved the Declaration of Independence and the Constitution from the Exhibit Hall in the National Archives building on Pennsylvania Avenue to the security of Fort Knox in Kentucky. But for Washingtonians, the most symbolic change occurred on the Monday night following the Japanese attack, when the lights bathing the Capitol dome were extinguished. When the United States entered the Great War in 1917, Woodrow Wilson had ordered the dome lit to inspire patriotic fervor. Now, in a new war, which had begun for the United States with an awesome strike unleashed from the air, the dome would remain in darkness. It was not relit until Germany capitulated in 1945.

Philosophically fatalistic as he was (he had already survived an assassination attempt in February 1933), Roosevelt rejected many of the Secret Service's proposals to increase his safety. Although he allowed blackout curtains to be installed in all the White House rooms, the blackening of skylights, and sentries to patrol the roof, he refused to consider either installing a bomb shelter under the East Wing or covering the building's exterior with camouflage paint, and surrounding the mansion with a fifteen-foot-high wall of sandbags. The Secret Service created a shelter for the president in the basement of the Treasury

THE ARMY installed antiaircraft guns on the roofs of government buildings throughout the capital. On September 3, 1942, a soldier cleaning a gun on the Interior Building roof garden fired it accidentally. He hit the frieze of the Lincoln Memorial. CREDIT: Private collection

Building, accessed through a tunnel connecting the two buildings, but he steadfastly refused to visit it.

The Secret Service was also worried because the president insisted on lighting the National Community Christmas Tree on December 24. The event had been an annual tradition since Calvin Coolidge began it in 1923. The president's bodyguards were cheered somewhat to know that this year the ceremony would move from the Ellipse to the South Lawn behind the White House fence, "my yard," as Roosevelt called it. They expected a crowd of 15,000; at least they could control who would be allowed onto the grounds. They were also reassured that the president and his guest, Prime Minister Winston Churchill, would speak from the South Portico. After Roosevelt pushed the button that lit the red, white, and blue bulbs on the 25-foot-tall Oriental spruce, Churchill addressed the crowd: "Let the children have their night of fun and laughter. . . . But now, by our sacrifice and daring, these same children shall not be robbed of their inheritance or denied their right to live in a free and decent world."

Despite Roosevelt's determination to carry on as usual, Washington changed. No longer would a cabinet member or vice president enjoy a chance encounter with a citizen at the portico. To the consternation of the Secret Service, Eleanor still seemed to go wherever and whenever she wanted—sometimes to New York, where she kept an apartment. The Secret Service gave her a small pistol to carry in her purse, though she vowed she would never use it. She often drove alone or with a single guard; and when she walked, her stride was so swift that the man assigned to protect her had to jog.

Even before the attack on Pearl Harbor, preparations for Washington's defenses had been lurching forward. Shortly after the attack, Colonel Lemuel Lewis Bolles—World War I veteran, former adjutant of the American Legion, and head of the District's Defense Council—declared that "Washington has nothing to worry about at the present time," which was surprising, because in late November he had declared the capital to be "one of the No. 1 targets of the Nation." Whatever Bolles was thinking, his actions betrayed the fact that Washington was unprepared. The plans were grand, but confusion reigned. There would be "policing [on] every corner of the city," Bolles said, but the police were already overextended helping to protect the White House, embassies, and public buildings. There would be air raid drills, but in the first test, conducted in late December, the capital's one siren, a relic from World War I, failed to sound. There would be practice blackouts, but as late as April 1942 the federal government refused to turn off the lights in its buildings. There would be air raid wardens, but no one had a plan for equipping or training them.

BY COINCIDENCE, A nine-page article entitled "Washington: Blight on Democracy" appeared in the December 1941 issue of *Harper's Magazine*. Its author, Alden Stevens, a former employee of the National Park Service, intended to present "Plain talk about our Capital City," which he viewed darkly. He began with unsettling statistics. The metropolitan district, which had counted 621,000 people in 1930, now had more than 1 million, with "more than 5,000 new federal workers . . . pouring into Washington every month." He estimated that an additional 4,000 to 6,000 more family members and employees of private companies arrived with the workers. More employees meant more cash for merchants, who enjoyed more than $400 million a year in trade, and for banks, which recorded $440 million in deposits. That fall the federal government's payroll for its 225,000 workers in the capital had topped $33 million. Hotels were booming, offering rooms to new arrivals as well as some 80,000 visitors, who attended more than 200 conventions. As dramatic as Stevens intended his words to be, they surprised few in the District. By 1941, overcrowding and stress had become the norm for almost all. It was evident in classified advertisements that reflected the fact that median rents of nearly $50 a month for an apartment were the highest in the nation. New workers frequently arrived with their families in tow, which strained school enrollments. Moving around the city became an expedition. Cabs and buses became scarce. Evidence of the dramatic increase in the District's automobile registrations could be seen daily on the city's exhaust-filled streets, which, in the words of one official, had reached the "traffic saturation point." The fact that the federal government issued forty different kinds of license plates for its vehicles only seemed to add to the confusion.

And that was not all. The opening of National Airport in the summer of 1941 choked the bridges over the Potomac. Congestion on Washington's 400,000 telephones, more phones per capita than any other city in the world, prompted the Chesapeake & Potomac Telephone Company to take out half-page newspaper advertisements urging subscribers to limit their conversations to business calls, especially at Thanksgiving and Christmas. Hospitals, already chronically underfunded, understaffed, and wholly inadequate, could not contend with the steady stream of patients. That September 1941, the director of the Health Department, who over the years had made heroic progress reducing the District's infant mortality rate, blamed an outbreak of dysentery at Sibley Children's Hospital, which killed nine babies, on overcrowding and a shortage of nurses. Long lines and short-tempered staff in shops and stores became the standard, especially on government paydays, and even more so after sugar and coffee rationing began in 1942. Many dry cleaners and laundries refused new customers, suggesting instead that newcomers mail their clothes home.

While such statistics described conditions for those living in Washington, they didn't account so much for those traveling *through* the city. The capital's recently opened Art Moderne Greyhound Bus Terminal at Eleventh Street and New York Avenue, and especially the vaulted concourses of the classic Union Station, served as a crossroads for servicemen returning from a brief leave or en route to a new posting. The waiting rooms became makeshift dormitories. The United Service Organization (USO) formed in 1941 to provide recreation and entertainment for soldiers, sailors, and Marines; it opened a "club" with Ping-Pong tables and a canteen at Sixth and E streets.

After the war began, Roosevelt approved the expenditure of funds to convert the Presidential Reception Lounge at Union Station into another USO recreation center. More than four hundred volunteers, including wives of senators, congressional representatives, and a large contingent of female government workers, took it upon themselves to serve the men. They answered questions; provided writing paper, envelopes, and stamps; and, on occasion, secured marriage licenses and corsages. Several accomplished artists stopped by often to sketch portraits, which were then sent to mothers, wives, or girlfriends. Many whom the volunteers served had never been to a city before, much less one as chaotic as the capital.

One January afternoon in 1942, Private Harold R. Chrisman, a military policeman from Syracuse, was in the USO center enduring a long wait for a train that would take him to his post in Cincinnati, when he found himself talking with Eleanor Roosevelt. Would the young man like to walk with her to the White House? Mrs. Roosevelt asked. "She's a fast walker," the private said later, "and I had a time trying to keep up with her." Along the way the First Lady pointed out some of the buildings and monuments, and when they arrived at the White House she invited him to dine—"turkey . . . candied sweet potatoes, diced beets, broccoli, salad and hot rolls." After dinner in the second-floor dining room, Private Chrisman walked back to the station and took the train to Cincinnati.

Chrisman was lucky. Every night, thousands of soldiers slept wherever they could, as there were accommodations for fewer than five hundred at the YMCA at Seventeenth and G streets NW, as well as at two additional YMCAs on Ninth and Tenth streets. At Union Station they slept on benches, in telephone booths, and on the floor. Many pinned wake-up times on their jackets so USO volunteers could rouse them to make their trains.

THROUGHOUT THE CAPITAL area, the government needed offices for its new departments and rooms for its new employees. Well before

Pearl Harbor, federal buildings had spread like mushrooms around the capital. Visitors surveying the National Mall from the top of the Washington Monument took in a crowded landscape of temporary office buildings extending west to the Lincoln Memorial and east toward the Capitol. Woodrow Wilson had confined his "tempos," as they were usually called, to the Constitution Avenue side of the Mall; Franklin Roosevelt had added a story to the original Navy and Munitions Building on Constitution Avenue, and had put up additional buildings on both sides of the Lincoln Memorial Reflecting Pool. (Two bridges supported by stilts allowed workers to cross the water.) Concrete, crowded, and soulless, the tempos were quick to construct and, everyone hoped, would be quick to demolish. It took just thirty-eight days to erect "Temporary R," a three-story, 119,000-square-foot building to house 2,500 employees of the government's Office of Production Management. More tempos quickly arose for 4,000 workers in the capital's southeast near the Army War College, and across the Potomac for Civil Aeronautics Authority workers at the new National Airport. Still another tempo cluster, seven immense and bunker-like concrete structures for a thousand navy workers, took shape immediately adjacent to the National Cemetery in Arlington.

Although Congress accepted Roosevelt's plans for the tempos, it grew angry when in 1941 the president sited—and largely designed—a tempo on Pennsylvania Avenue at Fourteenth Street, just north of the Willard Hotel, to be called the United States Information Center. Headed by Lowell Mellett, the president's aide in charge of the Office of Government Reports, the center's staff would assist government workers needing housing, especially private contractors arriving at the capital daily to conduct business with the government. But construction noise assaulted the ears of the editor in the nearby *Washington Post* building; he denounced the project as a "Great Boondoggle," and wrote headlines about "Mellett's Madhouse." As the very idea of government reports smacked of Roosevelt's manipulation of information for his own ends, many congressmen were quick to take offense. They ordered Mellett before them to testify, raged about Roosevelt's supposed socialist agenda, and demanded that construction halt. Meanwhile, the president defended Mellett's Madhouse as his brainchild, and slyly diverted money from other agency budgets to pay for it. *Washington Post* and congressional fulminations notwithstanding, the carpenters continued to nail together the three-story plywood structure day and night. The information building opened for visitors thirty-six days after construction began.

Yet even the mushrooming tempos could not satisfy the federal government's insatiable appetite for office space. Across the city, federal agencies converted private houses and apartments into jury-rigged offices. Levi Leiter's mansion on New Hampshire Avenue at Dupont Circle became home to the National Advisory Committee for Aeronautics, the agency charged with developing aircraft and rockets.

The military's appetite for land and buildings in and around Washington proved insatiable, even by government standards. The services set their sights on women's educational institutions, far easier targets than the male schools. In Virginia, the Army's Signal Intelligence Service commandeered the Arlington Hall Junior College for Girls for a cryptology laboratory. In Maryland, the Army Medical Corps expropriated the 180 acres and buildings of the National Park College, a school for girls in Forest Glen, for use as a convalescent home in conjunction with the General Walter Reed Hospital. On November 20, 1942, the navy arrived at the Mount Vernon Seminary and Junior College, which had been educating girls since 1875. Without warning, the secretary of the navy commandeered the buildings and declared that Mount Vernon's 35-acre campus on Nebraska Avenue would become a Naval Communications Station on December 15. Unlike Arlington or National Park, which never reopened, Mount Vernon's entire faculty, administration, and 160 students resumed their classes on a floor of Julius Garfinckel's Department Store at Massachusetts Avenue and Forty-ninth Street. Perhaps it was some consolation that the school's buildings would be occupied by Women Accepted for Volunteer Emergency Service, or WAVES, the navy's newest division of volunteers, created to free men for sea duty.

ABOUT 5,000 NEW employees were arriving in the capital every month, so many that apartment owners raised their rents, and homeowners let out their spare rooms for as much as $60 a month with board, $35 without. In addition to scanning newspaper classified advertisements, new arrivals consulted room registries kept by the capital's YWCA, the Jewish Community Center, and the City Housing Association's Washington Room Exchange. In an attempt to set uniform standards, the government's Defense Housing Agency sent volunteers from the Junior League, churches, and other civic organizations across the city to inspect and grade the rooms. They found a number that were dirty, as well as apartment rooms without windows. Accommodations with private baths, or even a landlord willing to allow a roomer a bath, were at a premium. At the end of March, the Census Bureau reported that a family renting in Washington could expect to pay $53 a month, higher than any other place in the United States. That month the Defense Housing Agency assembled a register of rooms for more than 2,000 people, but there was "a dearth" of "one-room bath and kitchenette apartments." And, the agency noted, there was a "marked shortage . . . of accommodations for colored persons."

Boardinghouses became especially popular with young arrivals. Such establishments had been a part of the capital from the beginning, when, with a preponderance of transients and few private houses, almost everyone visiting Washington, from the lowliest of clerks to Thomas Jefferson, had lodged in one. Boardinghouses never faded from city life entirely, and during national emergencies, such as the Civil War and World War I, they flourished. The number in the capital had dipped to about 150 by 1940; but by 1942 it had risen to more than 1,600 by some counts, and to more than 5,000 by others.

Homeowners were converting every spare room, no matter how small, at such a rate that volunteer evaluators couldn't begin to keep up. Large houses, out of date and expensive to maintain, became especially attractive for conversion. One District of Columbia housing official found that an owner of an antiquated gas-lit house had stuffed nineteen women and four men into twelve rooms, two bathrooms, a kitchen in the basement, and a reception room. The men lived in two basement rooms, which were partitioned off with composition board next to an antiquated furnace.

In the past, boarders had often shared a bed, as Josephine Lehman had in 1918. They had taken their meals at a common table and subscribed to the rules set down by a landlady. The practice of bed sharing had largely become a thing of the past by 1941, but the communal meals, the camaraderie, and the watchful eye of an often benevolent landlady and her family continued.

Not all boardinghouses were quick conversions; nor were all landlords out to exploit those in need of shelter. Adolph and Anne Dissin boarded young Jewish men and women in a group of four brownstones at Twentieth Street and Massachusetts Avenue NW. Dissin's, as it was known, kept a kosher kitchen and allowed dancing in the dining room. Adolph and Anne acted more as parents and gentle counselors than as strict chaperones to their boarders. Although the men lived on the lower floors and the women on the upper, and visits between floors were supposedly forbidden, socializing, but no cohabitation, became the norm. As resident Roselyn Dresbold remembered, the tacit disregard of the rule promoted "lifelong friendships . . . and plenty of marriages, too."

Dresbold knew from experience. She arrived in late 1940 from Portsmouth, Virginia, with one suitcase and a letter affirming her passing grade on the civil service examination. Though she had earned a degree from the College of William and Mary, Dresbold had never held a serious job before coming to Washington. Nor had she ever earned a salary close to the $28 a week she received from the government. She married a fellow resident in 1942 and moved with him to an efficiency apartment in Georgetown. She returned to Dissin's a year later when he went to war and hung his picture on her bedroom wall; the bride and groom topper from their wedding cake she kept on her dresser.

In 1943, when the gifted photographer Esther Bubley visited her sister who was living at Dissin's, she found a house full of ready subjects for a documentary that she hoped would land her a job as a photographer for the government's Office of War Information. More than three dozen photographs record the new intimacy of boardinghouse life: three young women, dressed in bathrobes, towels on their arms and carrying soap discontentedly, wait for their turn outside the bathroom door; three women triple up in a bathroom as they wash up and brush their teeth; a woman takes a shower in a narrow stall. In others, men and women sit or rest on beds, sometimes to share drinks or read the paper, or just talk. Bubley's pictures show cramped quarters—narrow passages, separate twin beds and dressers, clothes drying on racks or strung across a narrow room on a clothesline, and shelves holding bottles of liquor, alarm clocks, pictures, books, and radios. Clearly, the arrival of great numbers of young women to Washington had transformed its boardinghouses into heterosexual social spaces, neither entirely public nor exactly private.

ONE OF Esther Bubley's photographs of boardinghouse life. CREDIT: Library of Congress

The spirit of the benevolent landlady and her family dominated life for those lucky enough to live in the decidedly stylish Scott's Club at Twenty-first and P streets NW near Dupont Circle. Begun at the close of World War I by Margaret "Maggie" Scott, a former schoolteacher from Peoria, Illinois, the boardinghouse had expanded over the years. By the beginning of World War II, it took in twenty-three brownstone and brick houses. The six hundred residents, some married, some single, worked for the government. In 1943, Ralph and Harry Scott, who ran the business along with their mother, obtained a loan from the Defense Housing Agency to begin a six-story hotel for 250 government girls at 2131 O Street NW. The cruciform building featured a pipe organ, a laundry room, a ballroom, and separate roof decks for sunbathing, dancing, and Ping-Pong, as well as a party deck with an outdoor fireplace for picnics.

Ralph Scott subjected all the men and women who applied for admission to a vigorous screening process that presumably considered education and family background. Once admitted to the Club, boarders paid a handsome rent of $45 a month for a room with breakfast. (The single women at the hotel paid $28 a month without breakfast.) Scott's Club was well organized; boarders published their own newspaper, *The Wash*, fielded baseball and basketball teams, and held bridge tournaments in the dining room, dances in the living room (until 9:15), outings on the Potomac, and picnics in Rock Creek Park. Scott's even ran a bus service to shuttle its residents about the city. Visiting in rooms was allowed until midnight, and as was the case at Dissin's, propinquity often led to nuptials. About 150 Scott's couples wed during the war— and, always, had their receptions at Scott's.

Early in 1942, construction began at McLean Gardens, the name the government gave to the housing development it built on the grounds of Evelyn Walsh McLean's Friendship property. (The cash-strapped widow sold her estate for $1 million cash, money that came in handy because by then she and her late husband had squandered most of their fortune.) By the end of the year, the mansion, the swimming pool, and the golf course where Ned McLean had played golf with Warren Harding were gone; taking their place were forty-five buildings, including the headquarters of the General Accounting Office; a recreation and community center; housing for 720 families; a model child care center; and dormitories, three for men and six for women. The competition for a coveted apartment proved so intense that the federal government hired Ralph Scott to oversee the application process and manage the entire project.

As government housing sprang up across the landscape, thousands of bricklayers, carpenters, and concrete men worked with the precision of finely tuned machines, producing houses the way automobile and aircraft plants were beginning to turn out tanks and planes. In October 1942, the government announced its intention to build sixty-one separate housing projects in the District and adjacent areas in Maryland and Virginia. These would include tens of thousands of apartments, or, as Washington bureaucrats called them, "dwelling units." The federal government became the capital's major landlord.

MANY OF THE new "dwelling units" were for women who had taken jobs with the government. Mostly in their late teens or early twenties, they had come from across the nation and for reasons that mirrored those of their mothers, aunts, and older cousins in 1917—they wanted to serve the country in the way that many of their brothers were being asked to do, and to partake of the excitement of living at the center of their nation in the midst of war. Many worked in the same tempos on Constitution Avenue and the Mall that had been erected a generation before, as well as in navy buildings in Arlington. Others worked in one of the slew of government offices scattered throughout the District. The work proved a liberating adventure for the women and an asset for the country. A mechanized war that mobilized 13 million men and women to serve across the globe demanded an extraordinary force of civilians to keep track of procurement and supplies, to ensure paychecks, and to record the hundreds of thousands of deaths and casualties.

With a hint of condescension and yet recognition of their importance, Washingtonians and reporters called the women by a term first used in the Civil War, "government girls." "The women—girls mostly, and pretty young girls at that—come from everywhere," one reporter wrote, wondering "how long it will be before each government bureau will have its Dean of Women." Newspapers portrayed the girls as young and single, unsophisticated and white—a "lipstick brigade," as one writer called them—and as more interested in a wedding ring than munitions.

The idea of great numbers of young women living independently in a city proved disquieting to many. At a press conference, Eleanor Roosevelt wondered if women really should be wearing pants to work rather than skirts and dresses. After a seventeen-year-old War Department employee from Chippewa Falls, Wisconsin, was raped and murdered, the First Lady "emphasized the necessity of parents giving their children instructions about how to combat the evils of the world." From their pulpits, ministers decried the crime—especially as newspapers had presented lurid descriptions of the event—and the tragedy of a "girl" having "to give up the relative security of her own home to seek a living in an overcrowded city where one is easily lost in the crowd, and where the normal restraints . . . are practically unknown." In an editorial entitled "Girls on the Loose," a writer at the *Washington Post* railed against the "frightening degree of promiscuity," the rise in venereal disease, illegitimate births, and "attempted abortions," before declaring that "Government agencies have made little or no effort . . . to supervise the conduct in hours off duty of the thousands of young girls who have been removed from the surveillance of parents and restraints of family life and turned loose in a city swarming with soldiers and sailors in search of diversion."

Such paternalism, stereotyping, and fantasy ignored the fact that the women who went to Washington *wanted* to be there. Certainly some women (and men) did run "loose"; certainly many found mates and married while in Washington, too. But the prospect of running loose or a finding a union was not what brought them. They came for the adventure and excitement, for the opportunities—and for some, especially those from the many rural towns that dotted the land, even for the uncertainties that are a part of city life. And most knew they were carrying out a mission crucial to the success of the war. Their eight-hour days were sometimes tedious, and often, in Washington's ever-shifting bureaucratic landscape, chaotic. Many took shifts that began at 4:00 p.m. and ended at midnight. Others worked through the night. Whatever the circumstances, almost all the women understood that their typing and shorthand, their filing and compiling of statistics, made them essential; and they knew they were living at the center of one of the most important moments in America's history.

The labor shortage in wartime Washington benefited women across America. Women drew maps for the Coast and Geodetic Survey, created forecasts in the Weather Bureau, assembled mosaic maps for the Agriculture Department, and mastered the intricacies of the new federal tax code for the Internal Revenue Service.

Nor were women the only ones to benefit from the new jobs: by the end of the war, the federal government had become the largest single employer of those with disabilities. On any given day Washingtonians might encounter an armless telephone operator, a one-armed teletype operator, a chauffeur without legs, or a blind mechanic.

Early in 1943, Mary Herring, who had been trained to read lips and sign at North Carolina's school for black deaf children, took a job with the Navy Department. Profoundly deaf since the age of ten, she left her rural farm for the capital over her family's objections. ("She's got no more business there than a pig has with a Bible," her father said of her intention to work in the capital.) But Mary did have business there, the four to midnight shift at the Navy Annex in Arlington, accounting for the more than 2,000 men on the battleship *North Carolina*. Despite her disability, she found Washington life, its streets, buildings, and customs, easy to master. She learned the streetcar system, knew where to catch the bus for Arlington, and could cash her $72 biweekly paycheck or deposit her earnings in a bank account. At first she lived with an aunt in Uptown, but she soon moved to a room in South Arlington close to the Annex.

Mary was one of thousands of young women from across the country who fell into the rhythm of wartime work: a daily commute from a room, a boardinghouse, or an apartment shared with others, to a job in one of the hundreds of offices; a paycheck every two weeks, the purchase of a $25 war bond once a month; and, often, a check or money order to be sent home to one's family. There were trips to the grocery store and occasionally to department stores, many of which remained open until 9:00 on Thursday nights.

There was the awe of the city. "D.C. was beautiful," Mary Herring wrote of her first spring. "I saw the famous cherry blossoms in bloom for the first time. I passed them all, the Washington Monument, the Lincoln Memorial, and the White House, every day on my way across the river." On her Sundays off, she could visit the Smithsonian's museums, the National Zoo, or Rock Creek Park. And there were parades: everyone knew that the capital was the perfect place for a gaudy demonstration, and the American Legion, veterans groups, and fraternal organizations were always happy to march. But there were other groups, too, organizing parades—Boy Scouts, lodges, even an annual parade of safety patrol officers—10,000 boys and girls from schools across America who in 1940 heard an FBI officer extol their virtues: "You stand for law and order and parade for safety, while the youth of other countries parade for destruction."

Politics and the war added to the significance of Washington's parades. In October 1940, Republicans staged a "No Third Term Parade" before the White House. Three months later, the reelected president used his Inaugural Parade as a chance to show off the nation's military strength and designated Pennsylvania Avenue in front of the White House as the "Court of Free America." As the war ground on, the capital's parades became ever more martial. Eleanor Roosevelt used an Office of Civil Defense march in 1943 to recruit capital citizens. Perhaps no parade was greater than the "Hollywood Bond Cavalcade" of September 1943, staged as a way to launch a cross-country train tour of stars to sell war bonds. Military attendants escorted Lucille Ball, Harpo Marx, James Cagney, Fred Astaire, Judy Garland, Mickey Rooney, and dozens of others down Pennsylvania Avenue in military jeeps to the Washington Monument grounds, where the military had installed a display of tanks and guns called "Back the Attack."

PATRIOTIC DEMONSTRATIONS WERE a staple of Washington life, especially in times of war. Other displays, embarrassing to those in power but no less patriotic, were also a frequent part of the capital's culture. For Woodrow Wilson it was Alice Paul's suffragettes in 1917, who chained themselves to the White House fence; for Herbert Hoover in 1932, it was the Bonus Army that camped on the banks of the Anacostia River. Now for Franklin Roosevelt in 1941, it was 50,000 or perhaps a 100,000 of the nation's increasingly frustrated blacks who threatened to march in protest up Pennsylvania Avenue.

The frustrations were real. While New Deal programs had helped millions of blacks weather the Depression, they had been excluded almost universally from America's preparations for the coming war. White managers and union bosses had barred black employment even in defense plants that were suffering labor shortages. At the same time, the majority leader of the Senate declared that the "international situation and our defense program" made it impossible to pass an antilynching bill. To add to their discontent, blacks faced an army and air corps that were segregated; a navy that allowed blacks to serve only as mess attendants, cooks, and stewards; and a Marine Corps that barred them altogether.

The administration had tried to ignore these issues, but A. Philip Randolph, head of the Brotherhood of Sleeping Car Porters, wouldn't let that happen. Tall, refined, and well educated in English literature, especially Shakespeare, Randolph possessed a natural courtesy that sometimes masked his steely passion for civil rights. His organization of sleeping car porters, men long and shamelessly exploited by the Pullman Company, had earned him a measure of power and respect in the nation. By 1940, Randolph was turning his attention to effecting broader change for America's working blacks. In sympathy with Randolph's desires and in recognition of his growing authority, Eleanor Roosevelt arranged a meeting for her husband with several black leaders, including Randolph and Walter White, head of the NAACP.

When the meeting took place, the exchange was cordial, and Randolph and his group left, so they thought, with the president's assurances that he would move to end discrimination in defense plants and the armed forces. But the president's press secretary, a virulent white supremacist, instead reasserted the War Department's policy "not to intermingle colored and white enlisted personnel in the same regimental organizations." Newspapers across the country reported that the segregation policy had been approved "after Roosevelt met with Walter White and two other negroes."

Randolph cordially upped the stakes. "I think we ought to get 10,000 negroes to march down Pennsylvania Avenue," he wrote to a friend. "It would shake up Washington." Over the winter he formed a committee to stage the march on July 1, 1941. Soon a flyer entitled "CALL TO NEGRO AMERICA" appeared in black neighborhoods of northern cities and in the two hundred black newspapers published across the nation. Invoking "Nat Turner, Crispus Atticus, Harriet Tubman, Denmark Vesy, Gabriel, and Frederick Douglass" in language of sacrifice and martyrdom, the flyer asked for "an 'all-out,' bold and total effort and demonstration of colossal proportions." The enthusiastic response caused Randolph to up his estimate of marchers five and even ten times, to 100,000. To get the president's attention, he sent a copy of the "CALL" to Eleanor Roosevelt and asked if she would write a comment in her newspaper column, "My Day." "I have talked over your letter with the President and I feel very strongly that your group is making a very grave mistake at the present time to allow the march to take place," Eleanor replied. "If any incident occurs, it may engender so much bitterness that it will create in Congress even more solid opposition from certain groups than we have had in the past."

Randolph was not to be deterred, and the White House knew not what to do. Randolph's tactics were far different from Booker T. Washington's or Robert Moton's, who had advised presidents early in the century and advocated black advancement through education. Those leaders had articulated the wants and desires of blacks, but they had never resorted to action of this sort. No one had ever before proposed that blacks march on their segregated capital to achieve the equality they had so long been denied. It had been hard enough to manage 50,000 veterans and their families in 1932: How could the overcrowded city absorb that many black men and women? Where would the marchers eat and sleep? What restrooms would they use? What violence would ensue?

After Eleanor failed again to get Randolph and White to back down, she arranged for them to meet again with her husband. This time, on June 18, they would be joined by the secretaries of war and navy, the head of the National Defense Council, and the head of the National Youth Administration. "You can't bring a hundred thousand Negroes to Washington," Roosevelt is said to have told the group. "Somebody might get killed." And then he asked, "Will you march against the President of the United States?" Randolph replied, "We have no other alternative."

Roosevelt knew he was cornered. He enlisted Randolph and White to work with his staff in writing an Executive Order reaffirming "the policy for the United States that there shall be no discrimination in the employment of workers in defense industries or government because of race, creed, color, or national origin." To reinforce the order, he created the Fair Employment Practices Committee. All the while the order was being drafted, Randolph refused to back down. As late as June 23, he invited Eleanor to speak to the marchers before the Lincoln Memorial. It wasn't until June 25, the day Roosevelt issued the Executive Order, that Randolph called off the march.

Randolph's victory was significant, but it was not complete. Roosevelt's order omitted any mention of segregation in the military, but he tacitly agreed to name one black officer a general and advance others in rank. No one was more relieved than Eleanor. "I am very glad the march has been postponed," she wrote to Randolph. "I hope from this first step we may go on to others." And Franklin Roosevelt had won, too. Had the march gone forth, with even a half or a third of Randolph's anticipated 100,000, it would have likely brought violence to the capital. The president knew that while preparing the nation to fight one war across two oceans to secure world freedom, he could ill afford a conflict at home that would bring into stark relief all the contradictions between America's bright ideals and her dark realities.

TO ROY EMERSON Stryker in the government's Office of War Information fell the job of presenting a benign image of democracy to the world. As the one who had directed the photographers who recorded the devastation of the Depression for the New Deal's Farm Security Administration, Stryker was a natural choice. Since wartime rationing of gas and rubber made extensive travel across the nation more difficult than ever, many of his photographic essays centered on Washington life. Esther Bubley, who had photographed Dissin's, created essays on the Office of Civil Defense march in 1943, young women shopping and fraternizing with servicemen, a Memorial Day remembrance service in Arlington, a band concert at the foot of the Capitol steps, and student and faculty life at Woodrow Wilson High School.

Black Washingtonians also figured as subjects for Stryker's photographers. In 1942, he assigned the visual anthropologist John Collier to create several essays about black subjects. For one of them, Collier photographed students at Howard University. For another, he documented the workday of a clerk at the Library of Congress, Jewel Mazique, who, with her husband, was raising her three nieces. We see Mazique reading papers at her office desk, retrieving books from the library stacks, organizing for her union, eating lunch with her white colleagues, shopping for food in a well-stocked grocery store with her husband, and "lecturing at church on Negro participation in the war effort." This was the portrayal of democracy that the Fair Employment Practices Committee wanted. Jewel Mazique represented the best of American values.

But it was another photographer, the only black one on Stryker's staff, who captured an iconic image of black life in the capital. Gordon Parks arrived in 1942 "with enthusiasm," but with "scant knowledge of the place," he later recalled. He found a city where "racism was busy with its dirty work. Eating houses shooed me to the back door; theaters refused me," and the "scissoring voices of . . . clerks at Julius Garfinckel's prestigious department store riled me with curtness." Parks also found Ella Watson, a charwoman cleaning the floors in the Office of War Information, who though she received just $1,080 a year managed to support herself and her family and put "ten percent of her salary in war bonds." In a quiet conversation, Watson told him of her life of "bigotry and despair"; of her father, who had died at the hands of a lynch mob; of her husband, who had been shot to death; of her stepdaughter;

Ella Watson and Her Grandchildren, by Gordon Parks. CREDIT: Library of
Congress

and of her deceased daughter, who had left behind Watson's grandchildren—one "stricken with paralysis." Parks followed Ella Watson to her
house "within the shadows of the Capitol . . . her storefront church . . .
her small happinesses and daily frustrations." From this came a remarkable set of images, including *Ella Watson and Her Grandchildren*.

In his neatly divided image, Parks has us looking through a doorway into Watson's cramped kitchen. Two small children in the left
foreground, one clutching a doll, sit at a small table with their dishes.
Behind them Watson sits Madonna-like as she gazes with a half-riant
smile upon the infant in her lap. Behind her an assortment of carefully
arranged cans and jars ascends to meet a refrigerator that is perfectly
aligned with a door jamb. Through the door we catch an expansive
glimpse of a tree and sky that contradicts the compressed interior. To
the right we see a dark dresser with a curve-framed mirror standing
against a crazed plaster wall. The mirror captures the smiling face
of Watson's adopted daughter, who appears to be contemplating the
framed formal photograph of Watson's dead parents that sits upon the
dresser top. In this one image, Parks managed to evoke the dignified

American Gothic, Washington, DC, by Gordon Parks. CREDIT: Library of Congress

past of Watson's parents, the noble distress of her present circumstances, and the uncertain future for all.

But it was Parks's first photograph of Watson—and his first professional photograph—that came to symbolize the contradictions of America's democracy. Standing with a broom and mop before an American flag hanging from the ceiling, Watson appears stoically resolute in her polka dot dress. The downward falling stripes of the flag of liberty contrast with the upward thrust of the broom and mop to suggest that she is trapped in a new form of servitude. Titling his portrait after Grant Wood's equally iconic painting, Parks called it *American Gothic, Washington, DC.*

DESPITE THE HEAVY, rain-filled clouds that loomed over the capital on Friday morning, November 10, 1944, many Washingtonians turned out to celebrate Franklin Delano Roosevelt's fourth presidential election victory. Waiting on the platform as the Pullman green private railcar *Ferdinand Magellan* arrived at Union Station from Roosevelt's house at Hyde Park were the present and future vice presidents, Henry Wallace and Harry S. Truman. The rain began in earnest just as Roosevelt, Wallace, and Truman arrived at a cluster of reporters, microphones, and the Packard Twelve convertible that would carry them to the White House. John Russell Young, chairman of the Board of Commissioners, whom Roosevelt had appointed in 1940, offered congratulations and greetings from the city. The president replied that he would "always remember" the "very wonderful welcome home." But then he quickly checked himself: "And when I say welcome home I hope that some of the scribes on the papers won't intimate that I expect to make Washington my permanent residence for the rest of my life." Roosevelt was acknowledging a fact of life for many in the capital—it was not his true home. Although he would have spent nearly a third of his sixty-one years in Washington, "8 in the Navy Department, 12 in the White House—and 4 to come," like so many of those who lived in Washington he regarded himself as a permanent transient.

"The city is very different from the first Washington that I came to in the first Administration of President Cleveland," the president concluded. He was right, of course, and he was in good measure responsible for the differences. In 1889, the last year of Grover Cleveland's first term, about 220,000 people resided in the capital; when Roosevelt became president, there were 495,000; and as he spoke that day in late 1944, there were 890,000, nearly 80 percent more than when he had taken office. Many of the current residents, at least 265,000, worked for the federal government, which had mounted the largest mechanized fighting force in history to fight a war across (and on) two oceans. Franklin Roosevelt's policies had transformed the federal government and the District of Columbia. And they had helped to make Washington the world capital of democracy.

Franklin Roosevelt had always loved motorcades and parades—and riding at the head of them—no matter the weather. Disregarding the rain that morning, he ordered the rag top of the Packard Twelve put down so that he might better see the crowds of federal workers, schoolchildren, and ordinary citizens who lined the route to the White House. But it would be unseemly to have an Inaugural Parade in wartime; a brief swearing-in on the South Portico of the White House, followed by a lunch at the Capitol, would suffice on January 20, 1945.

This Friday morning would mark the last time Franklin Roosevelt would hear the waves of cheers of hundreds of thousands on his way to the White House, and the last time he would see signs of adulation—"BALLOTS SUPPORTED YOUR BULLETS"; "NOW FOR VICTORY"; "NOW LET'S BEAT JAPAN."

Five months and three days later, at 10:00 a.m. on the morning of April 14, 1945, the *Ferdinand Magellan* and another private railroad car, the *Connaught*, arrived at Union Station from the president's "little White House" in Warm Springs, Arkansas. This time, half a million people lined Pennsylvania Avenue, but in silence. Roosevelt was dead.

CHAPTER 14

World Capital, Congressional Town

> The National Capital, the embodiment of the Soul of
> the Nation, is politically outside of the Nation.
>
> —Theodore Williams Noyes, 1946

In New York, 500,000 people crushed into Times Square; in London, crowds massed before Buckingham Palace. But in Washington on the afternoon of Monday, May 7, 1945, when unofficial word came that Germany had surrendered, everyone remained at their desks, grinding out the seemingly endless memoranda and letters, directives, and orders that prosecuted the war. Since rumors of surrender had come and gone that spring, many remained skeptical that the end was really in sight. District commissioner John Russell Young declared that schools would remain open, and although shops were free to close, the District offices would conduct "business as usual." Most in federal offices throughout the city paused to listen to their radios when Harry Truman made the formal announcement from the White House at 9:00 a.m. the following morning, but they continued their work. War had dominated life in the capital for five years, eight months, and seven days, since Hitler had invaded Poland; it would continue to do so until the defeat of Japan.

Newspapers underscored the routine. The morning Truman spoke, readers learned that Aaron Copland had won the Pulitzer Prize for his orchestral suite *Appalachian Spring*; that Mary Chase had won for her play about a giant, anthropomorphic rabbit named Harvey; and that Joe Rosenthal of the Associated Press had won for his photograph of

Marines raising the flag of the United States over Iwo Jima. They still had a chance to catch *God Is My Co-Pilot*, a documentary drama about army air ace Robert Lee Scott shooting down the fictional but deadly Tokyo Joe, playing at the Metropolitan, or *Here Come the Waves*, a celluloid confection starring the singers Betty Hutton and Bing Crosby showing at Loews. They learned that knuckleballer Roger Wolff would pitch for the Senators against the Browns in St. Louis that night, and of the recent easing of rationing: Book Four, stamp 35, was valid for five pounds of sugar through June 2; airplane stamps 1, 2, and 3, in Book Three, were good indefinitely for shoes. And they read the list of men from the District and nearby who had been killed recently, including Captain Olin W. Bales, brother of Mable and Muriel Bales, 1722 Nineteenth Street NW, who had been missing in action over India since the previous August; and Chief Commissary Steward Sylvio Faela, husband of Kathleen Lee Faela of Arlington, Virginia, who lost his life "during a Jap air attack" upon a ship somewhere in the Pacific. Bales was one of 3,029 District men and women who did not return. Before the war was over, the number of men and women from the District of Columbia losing their lives in combat represented 5.05 percent of the city's population, a greater percentage than in any of the forty-eight states.

When Harry Truman announced to a crowd gathered in Lafayette Park on August 14, "This is the day we have been looking for since December 7, 1941," the city seemed to breathe a collective sigh of relief. Lights shone on the Washington Monument, the Lincoln Memorial, and the Capitol dome once again; revelers danced in a conga line in Lafayette Park and tossed streamers on F Street; many threw random kisses at anyone nearby, and some, fueled by alcohol and their general state of excitement, engaged in more overt sexual acts in public.

But the news of the loss of 875 men on the heavy cruiser *Indianapolis* to a Japanese submarine torpedo off Guam seemed to temper the celebration, especially as young navy clerks, such as Mary Herring, had the job of recording the names of the wounded, the missing, and the dead, and the captain of the *Indianapolis*, Charles B. McVay, lived with his wife on Bancroft Place NW in Kalorama. Nevertheless, the intimate connection people in the District of Columbia had with the war was coming to an end. Men and women who had come to their capital to serve in the war were making plans to return home.

CONGA LINE at the White House. CREDIT: Library of Congress

Some residents talked of returning Washington's pace to what they remembered it to have been in the salubrious days before the New Deal and World War II. But it was not to be. The war had changed American life in ways that few understood. By virtue of its victory and the industrial might that had made that triumph possible, the United States had become the most powerful nation in the world. It was an uneasy moment for America's political leaders, who faced global challenges that were altogether new. Just two months after Japan's surrender, George Orwell, writing for the left-wing weekly *Tribune*, coined a term that would dominate America's domestic thinking and international actions for the next five decades: Cold War.

THE EFFECTS OF the Cold War and the expanded government that accompanied it would reverberate throughout the District of Columbia and the surrounding counties of Maryland and Virginia. For the next fifty years, presidential candidates who followed Roosevelt often evoked a simpler time—a time of piety, virtue, McGuffey Readers, and smaller federal government—in their campaign speeches, only to increase government's power once they gained the White House. They had no choice but to meet the challenges and realities of an increasingly complex age. The number of cabinet-level departments increased from eleven to nineteen, agencies multiplied, and the number of federal employees proliferated, rising from 1.4 million in 1946 to roughly 3 million in 1990. As for the White House staff, fewer than 50 had served Franklin Roosevelt in 1933, and more than 600 served Ronald Reagan. Even Nancy Reagan's social staff was larger than Franklin Roosevelt's entire wartime staff had been.

Although wartime agencies such as the War Production Board and the Office of Economic Stabilization ended their work shortly after peace with Japan, other agencies expanded. The War Research Service joined the army's Chemical Research Service, which then changed its name to the Chemical Corps. Still other agencies, including the Petroleum Administration for War, were abolished in 1946, but revived in the Korean War period, sometimes with slightly different names. Roosevelt had dreamt of turning the Pentagon into a giant center for American archives once the war ended. Instead it became the headquarters for the nation's Department of Defense, essentially a reorganized and streamlined War Department with a new name.

The tempos that had blotted the Mall and Constitution Avenue since World War I reflected the government's insatiable demand for space. For three decades after Victory over Japan (V-J) Day, presidents, members of Congress, and bureaucrats vowed to raze the eyesores, but as quickly as one agency moved out of a tempo, another moved in. When the War Production Board vacated Tempos E and R in the Mall's southwestern section in 1946, the Veterans Administration quickly gobbled up the space. When the State Department moved from the Munitions Building to its new offices in Foggy Bottom in 1959, the Defense Department commandeered every square foot. When State vacated its other offices in Tempo S opposite the National Gallery, the new Department of Health, Education, and Welfare settled in, much to the annoyance of the Federal Aviation Agency and the Civil Aeronautics Board, which also wanted them. From time to time an official in the General Services Administration that controls all the government's real estate would announce a two-, three-, or five-year plan to eliminate the tempos, only to admit several months later that the buildings would have to stay. In time, as government buildings were constructed in Maryland and Virginia, or in the District itself, the tempos did come down, but slowly. Sometimes age and nature helped the process along. In 1968, a dramatic crumbling of the foundation forced the evacuation of the Navy and Munitions Buildings on Constitution Avenue. Three years later, the last tempo on the Mall, between Fifth and Seventh streets, fell to make way for the Smithsonian's National Air and Space Museum.

Despite the postwar growth of the Washington metropolitan area, the District of Columbia began to slip into decline. Between 1950 and 2000, its population decreased 29 percent, from 802,000 to 572,000. In the same period, the number of people living in the areas adjacent to the District—Montgomery and Prince George's counties in Maryland, and Arlington and Fairfax counties and the city of Alexandria in Virginia—jumped from 708,000 to 2,962,000. Just like Americans in cities throughout the country, and especially in older cities in the eastern United States, Washingtonians felt the seductive lure of suburban life. They could escape high taxes, which inevitably increased as a consequence of their neighbors leaving the city before them; they could exchange their small apartments for houses with separate bedrooms for their children, and garages for their new cars; and, especially after 1953, they could leave the city's declining schools to the urban poor who remained.

The idea of the suburb was not new, of course. Americans had craved open space from the time of their arrival in the New World. Affluent city dwellers before the age of steam and internal combustion engines often sought another house in the country where they might find respite, especially in the summer, in more salubrious air. William Thornton had owned a house in Maryland, as did Samuel and Margaret Bayard Smith. Lincoln, too, had found refuge three miles from the White House at the Soldiers' Home. In the nineteenth century, horsecar lines—and later, trolleys and buses—had made Mount Pleasant and LeDroit Park, private housing developments outside Washington's core, accessible. In the twentieth, developers such as Harry Boss at Foxhall and the Miller brothers at Wesley Heights had created exclusive Tudor style homes far from downtown in the city's northwest. Across the District line in Chevy Chase and Silver Spring, even more exclusive suburbs accommodated the wealthy.

The migration to cities from America's rural areas brought about a housing crisis that the Roosevelt administration sought to ameliorate through progressive urban planning. With the coming of the New Deal, the larger cities across the country had hired urban planners. Universities, starting with Harvard in 1924, had begun to offer planning courses; and Le Corbusier's radical design to rid Paris of its slums had gained currency. City planners had prophesied that the nation's bright future lay more in new suburbs than in old cities. New suburban communities across the American landscape offered an opportunity to build anew and not repeat urban mistakes of the past.

Imbued with this spirit, New Deal dreamers working for the Farm Resettlement Administration set up their offices in Evalyn Walsh McLean's childhood home on Massachusetts Avenue in 1935 to plan Greenbelt, a model suburban development that would serve as a prototype for others. Located in Prince George's County, Maryland, half an hour from Washington by automobile, Greenbelt would have houses for 885 white families, superbly planned schools, playgrounds, libraries, roads and walkways, and a community center. Eleanor Roosevelt's intense interest in the development ensured that Greenbelt would have a cooperative grocery store, a weekly newspaper, and the New Deal Cafe. The new community became the focus of *The City*, a documentary film the American Institute of Planners produced for the 1939 New York World's Fair. "The age of rebuilding is here," Lewis Mumford declared in the script, which damned the smoke-choked industrial cities and extolled the planned city, where "sweet air and open greens are part of the design." The city of the future, Mumford said, would be organic, "molded to our human wants as planes are shaped for speed."

In early 1937, families began moving into Greenbelt, but the age of rebuilding—and new building—had to wait until the conclusion of the war. After 1945, Federal Housing Administration–insured mortgages fueled the construction of new communities in the counties around the capital. The Urban Land Planning Institute, founded in Washington during the Depression by a group of realtors interested in research and planning for the coming subdivisions, published the *Community Builders Handbook* in 1947. It offered a glowing picture of planned neighborhoods, recommending well-placed houses on at least an acre of land, no more than one mile from shopping, parks, and grade schools, and two and half miles from high schools. There would be long blocks in the suburbs, especially in affluent neighborhoods, and lawns would "roll" to the curb. The planners emphasized that, "except in the highest priced developments," where people could depend upon an automobile for all their needs, "good mass transit facilities will continue to be of distinct importance."

Planning for the suburbs neatly dovetailed with the growing belief that the proliferating government agencies need not be located within the District boundaries. Indeed, after the Soviet Union's detonation of an atomic bomb in August 1949, many believed that the capital was the prime target for the Russians. Fear of a nuclear attack only strengthened planners' resolve to spread the federal government's departments and agencies across the suburbs of Maryland and Virginia. Over the next decade, the relocation included the CIA, the Defense Communications Center, the Office of National Reconnaissance, the FBI Academy, the Patent Office, the Atomic Energy Commission, the National Bureau of Standards, the National Security Agency, and the Naval Ordnance Laboratory. As a matter of course, private companies, especially defense contractors who did business with these agencies, chose to move their offices close by. As often as not, when people spoke of "Washington" or the "capital," they meant the metropolitan area.

In the beginning, few in Washington worried about the economic consequences of the move to the suburbs. In January 1948, the president of the Board of Trade declared that the city was the sixth-largest retail market in the country, and predicted a rise in private employment levels to approximately twice as many as those working for the federal government. Not even the Census Bureau's report that year of a dramatic population spurt in the counties surrounding Washington since 1940 worried many. Noting that the population in those counties had grown by as much as 92 percent, and the District's by just 27 percent, an editorial writer for the *Washington Post* wrote: "We are inclined to view this trend with satisfaction rather than alarm. . . . The general move to the suburbs is a healthy development. . . . This is a big country, and there is good reason why its inhabitants should spread out and enjoy it, instead of cooping themselves within the city walls."

Congress believed that proper planning would ensure that the new suburban developments would become model communities linked to the District by well-designed, interconnected, and limited-access highways. The Federal Bureau of Public Roads had created a prewar prototype in the Mount Vernon Memorial Parkway, which hugged the south bank of the Potomac River from the Arlington Memorial Bridge to the first president's home. By 1950, portions of the Baltimore-Washington Parkway had been opened to traffic. That year the National Capital Park and Planning Commission created a comprehensive plan; it called for still more express highways, which would circumscribe the District with three ring roads, or beltways. Crossing those highways would be radial roads that would reach deep into the surrounding counties. Two of the ring roads would be within the District, the innermost coming within one mile of the White House, and the outer ring between three and six miles. The third ring followed the path of the present Beltway. Congress believed that the roads would serve the capital's transportation needs and provide an easy escape route should the city come under attack. By 1955, civil defense planners were contemplating evacuating Washington's residents to the Maryland countryside, "considerably beyond the District line."

But the District's complacency about its rich future faded steadily during the 1950s and 1960s. The decennial censuses between 1950 and 1970 showed the metropolitan area population growing from 1,510,000 to 2,068,000, and then to 2,860,000, while the District's was declining from 802,000 to 764,000, and then to 757,000. By 1952, Woodward and Lothrop had found that business in its two suburban stores, Chevy Chase and the Pentagon, was exceeding that of its downtown store; Hecht's and Garfinckel's confirmed that their experience was similar. To keep up with the exploding population, these department stores and others would open many more branches in Alexandria and Falls Church, Virginia, and Columbia, Maryland, among other suburbs, as well as in dedicated shopping malls such as Prince George's Plaza, Landover Mall, and the Laurel Shopping Center in Maryland. In 1955, the formerly sanguine editorial board at the *Washington Post* wrote with alarm about "Our Eroding City."

Of course, Washington's plight was far from unique. Other cities in the East and Midwest—industrial centers such as Philadelphia, Baltimore, St. Louis, and Detroit—saw their populations erode as their white middle-class residents fled to the surrounding suburbs. They, too, faced the challenge of a declining tax base, and sometimes wrestled with municipal incompetence or even corruption. But citizens in those cities, as well as those who lived in the capital's suburbs, were enfranchised. They could participate in democracy, could vote for their representatives and their mayors, and usually for their town or city councils or commissioners. They could elect their school boards and local judges. Residents of the District of Columbia could not.

THE GOVERNMENTAL STRUCTURE of the District of Columbia remained just as it had been in 1874, when the city of 110,000 had a primitive water supply, few sewers, and fewer paved roads. At that time, the Washington Monument was still a stub; the Library of Congress and the Supreme Court were still housed in the Capitol; railroad trains shunted across the eastern end of the Mall, and the western end was a tidal marsh. Three commissioners, two appointed by the president, and one "engineer commissioner" chosen by the army, still directed the daily operations of the city. Since 1908 they had worked with a small staff and a few department heads in the District Building at Fourteenth Street and Pennsylvania Avenue. (Outside the building stood the statue of Alexander Robey Shepherd, the man who in some measure was responsible for the post–Civil War civic improvements, and, paradoxically, for their offices.) The commissioners, and all Washington residents, were beholden to a de facto city council of 96 senators and 435 congressional representatives who were residents of places as far away as Cheyenne, Sheridan, and Laramie, Wyoming, a state whose population has never equaled the District of Columbia's. Although few of that de facto council had the time or inclination to immerse themselves in the minutiae of the capital's affairs, when it came to questions about the efficiency of the District's operations, or to the way the government spent the money given by Congress for those operations, many had both time and the inclination for demagoguery.

By the coming of the New Deal, administering the city had become a Gordian knot, intricate and convoluted, tied by members of Congress who resisted all efforts at unraveling it. The agencies Congress appointed to run the District often were given overlapping or contradictory mandates. Although the commissioners had control over some of these, others were independent. The New Deal, which added more agencies, simply snarled the administrative structure all the more. Time and again a Senate or congressional committee, or the Roosevelt administration, would call for another study, report, or proposal that went nowhere. Members of Congress sometimes complained about the burden of running the capital, but in truth, they didn't wish to relinquish their power.

The District of Columbia's finances were a perennial problem. Unlike other cities—Atlanta, Los Angeles, and New York among them—Washington could not resort to annexation of its surrounding suburban areas, not even those parts of Virginia that George Washington had included in the original ten-miles square. The federal government's share of the District's operating costs had changed over the years as well. Since 1925, when Congress capped the federal payment at $9 million, the ever-expanding federal government had removed more property from the tax rolls. To compound the problem, the capital still lived under the prohibition from borrowing that had been set in place in reaction to the debt that Alexander Shepherd had incurred in his building program after the Civil War. Yet whenever congressional committees thought about a version of home rule or representation, which was infrequent and fleeting, they always wanted to maintain their supervision of the purse.

Reacting to congressional inertia, a coalition of 271 community organizations held a plebiscite in April 1938 on the subject of District suffrage. Even the idea of voting was a novelty for the 300,000 adults living in the city, but 95,500 made their way to polls set up in schools to vote 6 to 1 in favor of home rule, and 13 to 1 in favor of having representation in Congress and presidential electors. The House and Senate committees took little notice, and despite the overwhelming vote, William Henry King of Utah, chairman of the Senate District Committee, declared that Washington's residents "shy away from responsibilities."

The District's House and Senate committees in Congress controlled all governmental affairs. In the Gilded Age of the city's expansion, many members had prized a seat on them, as it gave them a chance to profit from advance knowledge of future development. But those days had long passed. Since voters in members' home districts cared little for what took place in Washington, most senators and representatives considered an assignment to a District committee as a political purgatory at best, or as a career graveyard at worst. They knew that expending energy on Washington or acquiring government funds for it brought no thanks from those at home, and might even be looked upon as a waste of their money. Those who did serve often took a patronizing view of their job, or, if they were from the South, looked upon it as a way of maintaining the District's segregated policies.

At times, even finding someone to head a District of Columbia committee could prove difficult. When Chairman William Henry King from Salt Lake City was defeated for reelection to the Senate in 1940, the next senior Democratic senator, Pat McCarran of Nevada, was chosen to replace him. But McCarran refused, because he was holding out to chair the Judiciary Committee. The next three in the Senate's pecking order—Carter Glass from Virginia, Millard Tydings from Maryland, and John Hollis Bankhead II from Alabama—also declined to stand for election for similar reasons. The senators then turned to Robert Rice Reynolds from North Carolina, but when Reynolds was offered a more desirable chairmanship, he, too, turned down the position. Next in line was Theodore Gilman Bilbo, a white supremacist from Mississippi; Bilbo declared he was "a pig for trouble" and wanted the job. But in mid-May 1941—mercifully, before Bilbo could be elected—McCarran learned he would not be chair of the Judiciary Committee and accepted his January election.

To his credit, McCarran worked diligently at his post and guided the city through the war years. He advocated home rule, something which his predecessor had opposed, and pushed for Virginia to return the thirty miles of territory that had been part of the District of Columbia until the retrocession of 1846. (The proposals went nowhere.) His chairmanship lasted until he finally did become head of the Judiciary Committee in 1944.

The composition of the District of Columbia committees was overwhelmingly southern on the Democratic side and, typical of the time, narrow-minded, overtly racist, often anti-urban, and sometimes anti–New Deal. Glass had helped to write his state's poll-tax law "with a view to the elimination of every negro voter who can be gotten rid of, legally, without materially impairing the numerical strength of the white electorate." Tydings, a proponent of segregation and states' rights, had once proposed that blacks who came to Baltimore to work during the war be housed in trailers, "so they can be easily moved out after the war is over." Bankhead consistently opposed repeal of the poll tax and federal antilynching legislation. Reynolds believed that his state, North Carolina, had "the finest, purest racial strain in the union," and his reputation for anti-Semitic, isolationist, and racist remarks was so poisonous that Franklin Roosevelt tried unsuccessfully to have him defeated for reelection in 1938. Bilbo was infamous for his 1938 amendment to a work relief bill to deport all of America's 12 million blacks to Liberia and other countries in West Africa.

Theodore Bilbo took over the chairmanship of the Senate District of Columbia Committee in 1944. Declaring himself "Governor of Washington," he immediately reaffirmed his opposition to suffrage, demanded that all alley dwellers be evicted, and proposed a variation of the theme he regularly made when filibustering antilynching and anti–poll tax bills: send the capital's alley dwellers to Liberia, or to farms outside the District, or keep them penned in a stadium. If blacks were to have the vote, he warned, the "alleys would control the avenues."

Washingtonians spent a harrowing two years enduring Bilbo's demagoguery, which made for good press with the voters in Mississippi but did nothing positive for the District of Columbia. Even the Congress grew weary of Bilbo's bluster and acidulous tongue. Charges that he had intimidated black voters and taken kickbacks from defense contractors in his reelection campaign of 1946 enabled the senators to refuse to seat him when Republicans took control of the 80th Congress in January 1947. By this time Bilbo was suffering from terminal cancer and could only summon enough strength for a weak fight. In the final, malevolent months of his life, he summoned the strength to self-publish a distillation of his credo: *Take Your Choice—Separation or Mongrelization.*

ON JULY 4, 1946, the first peacetime Independence Day holiday in five years, Washington lost one of its most powerful and famous citizens, Theodore Williams Noyes. Born in the city three years before the Civil War, Noyes had attended a District school, received a master's degree from Columbian College at the age of nineteen, and a law degree from Columbian at the age of twenty-two. Except for three years practicing law in the Dakota Territory, he had spent his working life with the *Washington Evening Star*, the newspaper that his father, Crosby, had edited since 1867. Succeeding his father in 1908, Theodore developed the *Star* into the most powerful newspaper in the capital. While the *Post* was recovering from its near-death experience under Ned McLain, the *Star* prospered under the steady leadership of the Noyes family. For generations, Noyes, father and son, had overseen the editorial side of the paper, while their financial partners, the Kauffmann family, oversaw business operations. What the Sulzberger family was to New York and the *Times*, the Noyes family was to Washington and the *Star*. Congressmen, senators, and presidents paid court to the editor of the *Star*; visiting business tycoons, high-ranking diplomats, and foreign potentates all sought an audience with Theodore Noyes.

As his father had before him, Noyes worked with unflagging determination to improve the capital. He used his editorial page as well as his deep list of political connections to effect change. He had a hand in removing the trains and tracks from the Mall and erecting Union Station; in promoting the McMillan Plan and building the Lincoln Memorial; and in founding the city's Board of Trade and establishing the city's free public library.

But Theodore Noyes failed to effect the one change that had obsessed him since he had first written about it in 1888: the District of Columbia's representation in the United States Congress. As the federal government expanded in the twentieth century, the anomaly of Washington, DC, became more striking. Although Washington's residents lacked representation, they, too, were subject to the Sixteenth Amendment to the Constitution, which allowed Congress "to lay and collect taxes on incomes," when it was ratified in 1913. They had no say when the US Congress imposed prohibition in the District on October 31, 1917, two years and three months before it was imposed upon the rest of the nation; nor did they have any say when it was repealed in 1933. And in World War II, Congress accorded soldiers serving abroad the right to vote by absentee ballot in congressional and presidential elections, but not to those soldiers whose home address was Washington, DC.

With the hope of achieving in death the goal that had eluded him in life, Noyes bequeathed $25,000 in trust "to continue in a small way, even after my death, the campaign for District national representation." In addition, he left $12,000 for his two daughters to complete and publish a book that he had drafted on the subject. In 1951, they published *Our National Capital and Its Un-Americanized Americans*.

Noyes's posthumous argument, augmented by his daughters, was straightforward: only a constitutional amendment would grant the capital's residents the full rights of American citizens. Washingtonians suffered from being placed in the "humiliating and vitally hurtful category of aliens politically and less than aliens in access to the federal courts." Washington had a larger population than thirteen states (Rhode Island, Arizona, Utah, New Mexico, South Dakota, North Dakota, Montana, Idaho, New Hampshire, Vermont, Delaware, Wyoming, and Nevada). These states had twenty-six senators and twenty-three representatives among them; the District of Columbia had none. Residents of the District had sent over 100,000 men and women to serve in the recent world war, a greater number than fourteen states. Washingtonians sent more money annually to the Internal Revenue Service than the residents of twenty-five states, yet they had no say in either the levying of federal taxes or the spending of federal revenue. The District of Columbia should enjoy the "distinctive basic right" of representation in Congress, Noyes argued. "Since the Americans in the District pay national taxes, obey national laws and go to war in the Nation's defense, they are entitled on American principles to be represented in the National Government, which makes all laws for them and which sends them to war."

Noyes's final attempt to remedy the fundamental flaw of the Constitution's Article I, Section 8, proved quixotic. Congress and the American public remained deaf to Noyes's argument. Few in Congress wished to confront the incontrovertible fact that more than 800,000 American citizens were disenfranchised by virtue of their place of residence. As had been the law for more than seven decades, two committees of the Congress and three commissioners, appointed by the president and approved by the Congress, continued to control their destiny and their city's. District of Columbia residents, so long beaten down by the nation's lack of interest in the welfare of those in the capital, seemed resigned to their peonage. Little notice was taken of Noyes's book.

The post-Bilbo era of the Senate's committee on the District of Columbia ended the chairman's provocations and race-baiting, but this was not the case in the House of Representatives. Between 1948 and 1966, from the 78th to 89th Congresses, the Senate passed six home-rule bills only to watch them die on the desk of Democratic representative John Lanneau McMillan of South Carolina. Whenever the Democrats controlled Congress, "Johnny Mac," as he was known to his constituents in Florence, South Carolina, chaired the House District of Columbia Committee. He called Washington "the last plantation." Like Senator Bilbo before him, racist but absent of bluster, McMillan thought himself mayor of the District, and acted accordingly. He cut the welfare budget to the bone, passed legislation favorable to Washington's white business establishment and the Board of Trade, and, whenever a bill was introduced to give any autonomy or home rule to Washington, made certain it died in committee before holding hearings. Home rule would never pass while Johnny Mac was in control.

However, neither McMillan nor his confederates in Congress could resist history. Nor could they resist many of the actions of the thirty-fourth president, Dwight Eisenhower. "I believe we should eliminate every vestige of segregation in the District of Columbia," Eisenhower said while campaigning in September 1952, and once he was president, he vowed in his first State of the Union address "to use whatever authority exists in the office of the President to end segregation in the District of Columbia, including the Federal Government, and any segregation in the Armed Forces." Through the newly appointed District commissioner Samuel Spencer, he ended discrimination in the local District government. Moreover, he used his influence with the heads of major Hollywood film studios to achieve the integration of Washington's movie theaters.

In the matter of restaurant accommodations, Eisenhower, again through Samuel Spencer, vigorously argued the case of *District of Columbia v. John R. Thompson Co., Inc.* before the United States Supreme Court. The case began in January 1950, when the tireless octogenarian educator and civil rights advocate Mary Church Terrell tested the validity of the District's "Lost Laws"—antidiscrimination laws enacted in 1872 and 1873, but abandoned after the collapse of Reconstruction. After Thompson's Cafeteria refused to serve Terrell and three other patrons, the District took the restaurant to court. The District's Municipal Court decided that the law had been repealed by "implication." On January 22, 1953, two days after Eisenhower's inauguration, the United States Court of Appeals for the District of Columbia held that the Lost Laws were invalid. On Monday, June 8, Justice William O. Douglas, writing for a unanimous Supreme Court, upheld the laws of 1872 and 1873. Less than a year later, in May 17, 1954, the Supreme Court issued its unanimous school desegregation decision in *Brown v. Board of Education*. Eisenhower vowed to make the District's schools "a model for the nation."

Although southerners in Congress could not block executive actions, or the decisions of the Supreme Court, they did stop

Eisenhower's attempt to increase the number of District commissioners by two, "to broaden," as he said in the State of the Union, "representation of all elements of our local population . . . [as] a first step toward insuring that this Capital provide an honored example to all communities of our Nation." Everyone in Congress knew the president's words were code for appointing a woman and a black man, and they would have nothing of it.

Despite the intransigence of many in Congress, the rising tide of the civil rights movement ultimately engulfed them. It began in 1959, when northern congressmen proposed a constitutional amendment to abolish the poll tax that southern states had used since Reconstruction to keep blacks from the ballot box. Backers of District voting rights quickly grafted language for congressional representation and voting for presidential electors onto the amendment, using Theodore Noyes's bequest of $25,000 to finance a lobbying campaign. But representatives of the southern states managed to strip the abolition of the poll tax from the bill, and the District commissioners, who enjoyed their power in the capital, saw to it that congressional representation was removed. The greatly diminished amendment, which was ratified in 1961, enabled residents of the District of Columbia to vote for electors for the president and vice president. The Twenty-third Amendment was a small step, to be sure, but it meant that in 1964, for the first time in 164 years, Washingtonians could vote in an election for their president.

IT WAS IN the Eisenhower administration that Washington's progressive architects and urban planners put in motion their long-cherished plans for revitalizing the city. Over the years the capital had served as a laboratory for a number of Congress's schemes, some good, some bad. Washington had seen the emancipation of slaves a year before Lincoln had issued his Emancipation Proclamation, and had instituted prohibition two years before the rest of the nation. Now it would be home to one of the nation's great experiments in urban renewal on a cyclopean scale.

In 1950, the term "urban renewal" was relatively new to America's lexicon. A product of planners in the late 1930s, it was a worthy substitute for the term "urban redevelopment," as it summoned up physical and spiritual images of restoration, renovation, taking fresh life—even the biblical injunction "Thou shalt renew the face of the earth." When planners and members of Congress looked from the west terrace of the Capitol to the southwest, they saw crowded streets; blighted, substandard houses; and railroad yards that in no way resembled their own houses and apartments in northwestern DC or suburban Maryland and Virginia. And they were certain in their knowledge that the area offered an excellent opportunity to create a dynamic city. Proper urban planning would enable the US capital to recover from the successive traumas brought on by the expanding federal government and world war. They would renew Washington and make it prosper.

Such progressive thinking gave Washington architects Louis Justement and Chloethiel Woodard Smith the opportunity they had longed for. Educated at Stanford and George Washington University, Justement established a practice in the capital in the 1920s that grew in influence over the decades. His projects reflected his protean aesthetic and ranged from a group of modest, Spanish-style houses in the Chevy Chase section to the large, Art-Deco Valley Vista apartment building in the northwest; from a colonial-style set of apartments called Falkland Chase to an early Federal Housing Administration project in Silver Spring, Maryland; and from a classically influenced, collaborative design for a new House office building on Independence and New Jersey avenues to the Federal District Courthouse on Judiciary Square. He patented his design of an apartment building with "a number of separate entrances giving direct access to individualized apartments" that would, he hoped, eradicate alleys and provide for more green space. Along with his growing practice, Justement acquired more influence in the profession. He served on District committees concerned with building codes, slum clearance, and planning, as well as on committees of the American Institute of Architects that were devoted to urban renewal. In 1950, he became a consultant to the federal government to make plans to disperse its employees to the suburbs as a defense against atomic attack.

Chloethiel Woodard Smith thrived in a profession that at the time was an almost exclusively male enclave. A native of Peoria, Illinois, she arrived in the capital in 1935 with architecture degrees from the University of Oregon and Washington University in St. Louis. After five years as chief of research and planning for the Federal Housing Administration, she began her own practice. By the 1950s, especially after teaching at the Higher University of San Andrés in Bolivia, presenting an exhibition on planning for the city of Montreal, and writing essays for architecture magazines, Smith was beginning to be known for her sensitive, humane, and sensible approach to architecture and design.

As was the case with so many in their profession, Justement and Smith fell under the spell of the French-Swiss architect, designer, and urban planner Le Corbusier, especially his unrealized *Ville Contemporaine* plan of 1922. At once a provocative and influential proposal, Le Corbusier's contemporary city would house 3 million souls in clusters of sixty-story cruciform-shaped buildings that he called *unité d'habitation*, or unified settlement. Like Le Corbusier, Justement and Smith wished to purge the capital of its slums and ameliorate the conditions of those crowded into them. In 1946, Justement proclaimed, in his own polemic, *New Cities for Old*, that "disorder caused by the crazy-quilt pattern of land ownership," that is, intimate streets filled with lively shops, various—and often variegated—houses, and pedestrians engaged in the daily pursuit of living, must be purged from the cityscape to achieve a new, healthier environment. Centering his proposals on the capital, he championed a series of ring roads with conveniently placed parking garages that would enable suburban drivers easy access to the city. Never mind that the new and cooler community that supplanted the old included the pitiless repetition of architectural forms, expressways, and, always, cars. The plans were up to date and would advance Washington to the forefront of urban design.

In 1952, Justement and Smith got a chance to put their ideas into practice. The National Park and Planning Commission had decided that Washington's southwest—the triangle of land bordered by South Capital Street, Independence Avenue, and the Washington Channel—would become a giant urban renewal demonstration project. Viewed from the Capitol's west terrace, the vantage point for members of Congress, the area appeared to be a hodgepodge of overcrowded and often substandard dwellings and commercial buildings, alley dwellings, stables, and shacks that in the pre–Jonas Salk vaccine era offered a fertile breeding ground for polio and other diseases. In one census tract known as "Area B," the city's public health officer found that death from tuberculosis was 136 percent higher than in the rest of Washington, and death from syphilis 489 percent higher. Literally on the other side of the wide swath of railroad tracks that connected the city with the South, residents in Area B were almost wholly separate from the Mall and the more vibrant parts of the city. A renewal proposal by Elbert Peets, a distinguished landscape architect and urban planner, eradicated the alleys and other blighted structures, but called for saving many of the low buildings and tree-lined streets. To many on the commission, as well as the District of Columbia Redevelopment Land Agency, which had been created by Congress in 1946 to clear the city's slums, Peets's ideas for a gradual rehabilitation of the area weren't dramatic enough.

Justement and Smith proposed a radical redevelopment, in many ways as sweeping as Peter L'Enfant's plans of 1791. Change would come "in a purposeful and accelerated fashion" that demanded leveling nearly all structures and trees and starting anew: A wide esplanade leading from the Smithsonian Castle at Tenth Street and the Mall would cross the railroad tracks. It would be "uninterrupted by buildings . . . bordered by parks on the east and a wide planted park on the west," and would lead to "an attractive waterfront drive" beside the Washington Channel. East-west roads would link residential areas populated by a mixture of townhouses and high-rise apartment buildings. Public buildings, including a grand opera house, would provide "welcome breaks in the design and scale" of the residential area.

The proposal put a human face on their massive redevelopment scheme. Although they were proscriptive in their outline of the streets and esplanade, Justement and Smith allowed "scope for the maximum of initiative and imagination" on the part of planners and architects who would follow. Their desire was for Washington to serve as a model for urban renewal in other blighted parts of the city, and, indeed, for the nation.

The Capital District Planning Commission purported to choose the mean between the two ends of Peets's gradual rehabilitation and Justement and Smith's grand redevelopment, but it was merely a simulacrum of compromise. While the commission acknowledged the "historic and sentimental interest" of the area, it did nothing to preserve it. Houses, trees, stores, and shops would all fall, though the structures to replace them would be smaller in scale than Justement and Smith had advocated. The author of the commission's report, Harland Bartholomew, was disposed to favor redevelopment, because it would allow highway planners to have their way on a landscape where all the structures had been removed. As the commission's chief authority on highways for many years, he had advocated ring roads for the capital in its 1950 report.

Of course, Bartholomew had good reasons for his belief in the importance of highways. By the 1950s, motor vehicles were beginning to rule the American landscape and the federal government's consciousness. As a highway and urban planner, Bartholomew believed that the symbiotic compact between the forces for highways and urban renewal would make redevelopment possible and improve the lives of those who lived in cities. He saw that a surfeit of cars and trucks were choking Washington's streets. Although many automobiles came into the city from the suburbs, the city itself was filled to capacity. Just over 114,000 motor vehicles had been registered in the city in 1945; a decade later, the number reached 197,000—which meant 3,228 cars, trucks, buses, and motorcycles for about every 60 square miles. Three of every five residents held a license to drive.

In 1956, when Dwight Eisenhower signed the Interstate and Defense Highways Act into law, Bartholomew saw a way to bring automobile efficiency to the capital. The law committed the federal government to pay 90 percent of the costs for divided highways that would connect every major city in the nation. Now Washington would have a chance to build the roads that the National Capital Park and Planning Commission had proposed in 1950. One of the most important of the contemplated highways, Interstate 95, which followed the East Coast from Florida to Maine, would pass through the southwest, tunnel under the Mall, and head north to Maryland. It would also form part of Bartholomew's cherished beltways, the Inner Belt. With his signature, President Eisenhower had assured that the highway transportation portion of the redevelopment would go forward.

Progress took place in fits and starts. Several residents contested the government's right to eminent domain, a matter that was not settled until October 1954, when Justice Douglas declared for a unanimous Supreme Court: "If those who govern the District of Columbia decide that the Nation's capital should be beautiful as well as sanitary, there is nothing in the Fifth Amendment that stands in the way."

About the time Justice Douglas spoke for the Court, the celebrated real-estate mogul William Zeckendorf arrived in the capital to put a glossy and commercial stamp upon the project. The L'Enfant esplanade changed from a broad allée bordered by parks to a treeless roadway between what the developer called "stately government buildings." At its entrance on Independence Avenue, the Defense Department's James V. Forrestal Building, a squat, concrete structure with windows resembling an enormous waffle, obscured the view from the Smithsonian Castle. At the Washington Channel the road ended at a blank concrete wall supporting the highway above. Mercifully, by 1965 Zeckendorf's empire collapsed in bankruptcy, which left other developers and architects, including Chloethiel Smith, to take over smaller parcels for their own projects. Their projects, Harbor Square, Carrollsburg Square, and River Park among them, are some of the most successful parts of the new community.

Was the redevelopment worth it? Was it truly urban renewal, or a case of urban remuddling? By the end of the decade, the bulldozers had finished, and 560 acres lay barren. The toll included 4,800 structures, 1,500 businesses, 6,000 households, and countless trees, some of which had delighted the eye of Thomas Jefferson. Twenty-three thousand citizens, most of them black, had been moved to other areas in the city, usually without much assistance. In time, 13,000 middle- and upper-middle-class residents, living in 5,800 new homes, would take their place. In a bow to history, however, the redevelopers decided to spare a Baptist and a Roman Catholic Church, and also Wheat Row, the three-story brick houses that James Greenleaf had built in 1794.

WHILE THE SOUTHWEST was undergoing renewal, the District's population was shrinking. More alarming for many whites in the segregated city was the rise in the proportion of black citizens, from 35 to 54 percent; meanwhile, the proportion of whites declined from 64 to 45 percent. Some of the white exodus came as a reaction to the Supreme Court's May 1954 decision ending school segregation and President Eisenhower's efforts to implement it swiftly. The white and black elementary schools merged in time for the start of classes in September, and the high schools followed in 1955. Many white parents chose to move to Virginia, where the governor vowed to resist the court's ruling, or to Prince George's County in Maryland, where the school board president declared that the county's schools would integrate slowly—a process that took nearly two decades. By June 1956, the number of white students enrolled in the District's schools had declined by 6,000. A decade later, 95 percent of Washington's schoolchildren were black.

The effort to desegregate schools helped the cause of civil rights across the nation. Harry Truman and Dwight Eisenhower used persuasion and executive orders to spur on integration, but outside of such token measures as integrated cafeterias and bathrooms in federal facilities, Washington remained a segregated town. Johnny Mac still controlled his last plantation, and the various congressional committees that had a say in the direction of the District were too simpatico with the white power bloc as personified by the Board of Trade. Even the capital's football team, the Washington Redskins, which was owned by an avowed racist, refused to include a black player until the John F. Kennedy administration forced it to do so in 1962. The increasingly black population of the capital, cut off from any role in the city's commerce or government, had little interest in its future. But the black experience in the capital as well as the rest of the nation came to trouble President Kennedy. "We lose them," he told a group of business leaders in June 1963, "I don't think we are going to get them back." "This isn't just a southern matter," he told the governor of Louisiana. "It's Philadelphia and it's going to be Washington, DC."

Such was the mood on August 28, 1963, when twenty-one trains and hundreds of chartered buses began arriving in the District. More than 200,000 strong, they presented the face of America: old and young, black and white, men and women, students and workers, children and grandmothers. And they were joined by their commitment to black equality.

White Washington was on edge. For weeks cautious radio commentators and newspaper columnists warned about the consequences of bringing so many people to the capital for an assemblage that would call attention to deep-rooted injustices in American life. That spring, more militant blacks were predicting that the march would be just the first salvo in a larger struggle. In a June meeting with black leaders at the White House, Kennedy worried that such "a big show on the Capitol" might give Congress an excuse to vote against his proposed civil rights legislation. Among those listening was A. Philip Randolph, who had heard similar words from Franklin Roosevelt in 1941. "The Negroes are already in the streets," Randolph said, interrupting the president. "There will be a march."

MARCH ON Washington, 1963. CREDIT: Library of Congress

Recognizing by mid-July that he could not stop the march, the president announced his support for it. At the same time, he quietly prepared the FBI and military installations around the city for possible action if violence were to erupt. By August, religious groups with largely white memberships, such as the Jewish Community Council for Greater Washington, the Greater Washington Council of Churches, and the Unitarian Church of Arlington, along with numerous Catholic priests and local civic organizations, had announced their intention to march for civil rights. Indeed, the march became a place to show solidarity openly. Fearing trouble from some of the capital's less generous residents, the *Washington Post* reminded its readers on the morning of August 28 that the capital was on stage and "must stand as a symbol of freedom—freedom of speech, freedom of movement, freedom of petition and freedom of the human spirit."

The March went off without any serious incidents. For the most part, people left as peacefully as they came. Although the marchers had hoped to persuade Congress to pass Kennedy's civil rights legislation, which did not happen, the gathering marked the most important moment since emancipation in the movement for equality. And the steps of the Lincoln Memorial served as a national stage for Martin Luther King Jr., who moved into the consciousness of all Americans.

WHEN WALTER WASHINGTON had arrived in the capital from Jamestown, New York, in 1934, he had found that blacks couldn't get a job or even buy a hot dog at a Peoples Drug Store lunch counter. Frustrated, he had joined with the New Negro Alliance, which mounted a "DON'T BUY WHERE YOU CAN'T WORK" campaign. The black press had printed photographs of picketers in front of the Sanitary Grocery Company and Peoples, and an advertisement for the New Negro Alliance inviting blacks to "JOIN NOW! FOR ECONOMIC AND CIVIL EMANCIPATION AND SECURITY." "We had some success," Washington recalled years later. "The A&P stores agreed to employ blacks. But the Peoples Drug wouldn't hire. They gave in a little, you could eat your hot dog at the counter, but they served it on a paper plate."

By 1946, Walter Washington's group and others had prompted a study by the National Committee on Segregation. The committee—which counted people like Eleanor Roosevelt; the young mayor of

Minneapolis, Minnesota, Hubert Humphrey; the Chicago millionaire Marshall Field; and other prominent people as members—reported the steady degradation of the position of blacks from the 1870s, when Reconstruction had ended. "Negroes are denied an equal chance to make a living," the report declared. "A closed door employment policy forces Negroes into the least desirable jobs where they earn less and have the least security. . . . We preach democracy to the world, but we practice it in the capital with segregation." Despite the pervasive segregation, Walter Washington stayed in the capital and prospered. He earned bachelor's and law degrees from Howard University, married into one of the District's elite black families, and worked for the Alley Dwelling Authority. He served as executive director of the National Capital Housing Authority and New York City's housing authority. It was in 1967 while he was in New York that President Lyndon B. Johnson invited Walter Washington to return to the capital for a wholly new job.

Lyndon Johnson had called the capital home for his entire adult life. He arrived in the late 1930s from Texas as a congressional aide, made friends, raised his daughters, put down roots. Though given to making crude racial epithets, he saw the injustice of a majority black city run by white congressmen. In July 1964, he persuaded Congress to pass the Civil Rights Act. In the spring of 1965, after he was elected president with 61 percent of the popular vote, he introduced legislation that would give the District home rule. By then, the city's black residents numbered more than 400,000. Home rule for the District of Columbia was, Johnson believed, a logical extension of the civil rights that all Americans deserved.

Like every previous home-rule initiative, Johnson's bill failed. This time, though, it was because of sabotage. In November, as the bill neared a vote in the Congress, Washington's Board of Trade sent a mass mailing to almost every newspaper across the country, which declared that many Washingtonians, including an overwhelming majority of local and professional business leaders, opposed the legislation. The ruse worked. Constituents swamped their representatives with letters protesting the bill, and newspapers wrote editorials in opposition.

"It was a bitter, bitter defeat," said John W. Hechinger, a prominent District businessman with a reputation for appointing and advancing blacks and women in his hardware and home improvement. Hechinger had worked Johnson to secure the bill's passage. "Here was a man who had devoted so much of his energy to bringing people into the political system through civil rights legislation and the War on Poverty and yet he couldn't manage to bring the basic right of self-determination that all other Americans enjoyed to the nation's capital." Smarting from the sting, but still resolute, Johnson introduced a half measure: let the president appoint a mayor and council for the city; Congress could hold on to control of the budget. After Congress agreed in 1967, Johnson appointed Hechinger to the City Council and put through a call to Walter Washington. The man who had been refused service at the Peoples Drug lunch counter now found himself mayor.

The appointment incensed Congressman Johnny McMillan. When Walter Washington sent his first budget up to Congress for approval, Johnny Mac sent the mayor a truckload of watermelons.

Walter Washington's challenges did not stop with McMillan. At the same time that Johnson appointed Washington to be mayor, power and energy in the black community was passing to a new, more militant generation. People like Stokely Carmichael, leader of the Student Nonviolent Coordinating Committee; Walter Fauntroy of the Southern Christian Leadership Conference; and Julius Hobson, the leader of the District's chapter of the Congress of Racial Equality, were beginning to ignite the attention of black residents with their strident rhetoric. Hobson proved to be a brilliant provocateur. The black Uptown neighborhood, which Washingtonians had taken to calling Shaw, was continually struggling with its rat infestation: Hobson killed two hundred of the rodents and dumped them in Georgetown. "We want to move rats out of black houses into the white houses of Georgetown; even into the White House itself," Hobson declared. The city responded with more rat patrols.

Thus, oddly, the first black mayor of the District found himself challenged not only by the solid segregationists, but also by younger militant voices within the black community. "Great tests awaited me," Walter Washington later remembered. "When I was appointed by President Johnson in 1967, Washington was known as riot proof. The federal government was here; the Secret Service was here; the Pentagon; it was assumed to be riot proof. Detroit, Philadelphia, Los Angeles, New York, and Newark had riots, but Washington did not."

The myth of the riot-proof city ended abruptly at about 6:00 p.m. on Thursday, April 4, 1968, in the wake of Martin Luther King Jr.'s

KING RIOTS, April 1968. CREDIT: Library of Congress

assassination in Memphis, Tennessee. For three days, roving bands of black youths looted businesses, mostly owned by whites, and set nearly a thousand fires. Areas near Seventh and H, Fourteenth and U, and McPherson Square were devastated.

"I had a 2,300-man police force, and 150,000 people in the street," said Walter Washington. "The second day of the riot, I went up to the National Cathedral to a memorial service for Dr. King. President Johnson sat near by me. He said 'I want you to ride back to the White House with me. I hear you have some problems in the streets.' I said, 'Mr. President, this city is in flames.'" Back at the White House, Johnson called up 12,000 troops from the army and National Guard. But the looting and fires continued.

As the newscasts carried live images of young men stepping out of the smashed windows of storefronts with televisions and clothing, members of the District committee in Congress and the Board of Trade told Mayor Washington to shoot the criminals. "The committee wanted to know why I wouldn't shoot. The only response I made was, 'We can replace a suit of clothes or a television, but we cannot replace a human life.' They said: 'Dick Daley is shooting them in Chicago,' and I replied: 'Dick Daley's in Chicago. I'm in Washington. The site of my riot is Fourteenth Street and Georgia Avenue around Howard University, and I'm not going to spill blood in the street in order to protect a suit of clothes or a TV.'"

In the end, about 20,000 people were arrested, including 2,000 women. Most had jobs; many worked for the federal government. Half of the property on Fourteenth Street was destroyed. Twelve people died over the three days—many of them caught in the fires they themselves had set. More than a century and a half earlier, Congress had established a federal city on the banks of the Potomac in order to insulate itself from the threat of violence. Now the domestic problems of the nation had once again come to the capital's doorstep in a way that left America in shock.

CHAPTER 15

Free Fall and After

The question is whether the white majority of this country and the Congress has the grace to grant basic rights to the capital city which has a black majority.

—Representative Gilbert Guide (R–Md.), 1972

With the riots of April 1968, Washington entered the most turbulent period in the history of the city since the Civil War. Events tested the relations between the District and federal governments, between the white and black races, and between the capital and rest of the United States. For the next four decades, the city would experience times of lawlessness and chaos, malfeasance and near bankruptcy, and often the contumely of members of Congress. But Washington would endure these trials and would emerge as a stronger and better capital of the United States, a city that came closer to embodying the ideals of the nation than ever before.

In 1968, the commonweal was in eclipse, and whatever cooperation and consensus had been present among the populace in earlier times was in shadow. More than ever it seemed that Washington was a loose agglomeration of its unassimilated groups—white residents new and old; black residents new and old; a growing number of immigrants speaking foreign tongues; members of Congress, some permanent but many transitory, who controlled the purse; and presidents whose interest in the city waxed and waned with each term, and who were always subject to the political exigencies of domestic and international events.

Sometimes the groups showed coherence and even became united in a common purpose, but many times they remained in separate, disorderly clusters. Each believed that it had the answers to the city's problems and, all too often, each acted independently.

There were also complexities within each of the groups. Neighborhoods frequently vied with each other for government support; different departments of the federal government habitually wrapped programs intended to support the city in a bureaucratic tangle; and members of Congress continued and intensified their traditional divisions of rural and urban, North and South, Republican and Democrat. Racial tensions were at their zenith and showed little sign of abating. As James Reston, a columnist for the *New York Times*, put it, the capital of the United States was "strangled."

Other American cities suffered from serious violence in the wake of Martin Luther King Jr.'s murder. In Baltimore, six died; in Chicago, where Mayor Richard J. Daley ordered police to "shoot to kill," the death toll reached eleven. And other cities, especially older ones in the Northeast, were already suffering from fiscal mismanagement, a declining commercial base, and an eroding population. But Washington's violence seemed unique. Before this, the last serious, racially motivated disturbance in the capital had taken place in the Wilson administration; less than four years earlier, King and his associate Ralph Abernathy had brought several hundred thousand people to the capital in racial harmony. With the federal government in its midst, the District enjoyed a solid and ever-expanding employer; compared to other large cities, such as Harlem and Philadelphia in 1964, Los Angeles in 1965, and Newark and Detroit in 1967, it had seemed safe from the racial disturbances. But violence had come to the capital, and its effects would be felt for decades.

The response among blacks in Washington to the murder in Memphis signaled a suspension of King's message of nonviolence. On the morning of Sunday, March 31, 1968, four days before his death, King had intoned from the pulpit at Washington's National Cathedral that "all too many people find themselves living amid a great period of social change" and must respond with nonviolence. "Anyone who feels, and there are still a lot of people who feel that way, that war can solve the social problems facing mankind is sleeping through a great revolution." King had come to the cathedral as part of his effort to link the civil rights movement with the plight of the impoverished of all races and to assure his listeners that he would lead a Poor People's March on the capital later that spring. Now Stokely Carmichael, the former head of the Student Nonviolent Coordinating Committee, was ascendant. At a Howard University service on the day following King's murder, Carmichael waved a pistol and cried, "Stay off the streets if you don't have a gun, because there's going to be shooting."

Carmichael had not been alone in promoting guns. After the riot, merchants and some members of Congress criticized Mayor Walter Washington for not shooting the looters. Merchants were angry that police and soldiers merely watched as young looters made off with their merchandise—clothes, TVs, and liquor were hot items—and, more often than not, set fire to the building. Democratic senators Robert Byrd of West Virginia, George McClellan of Arkansas, and Russell Long of Louisiana were the harshest critics. Byrd, who had been an Exalted Cyclops of the Ku Klux Klan, and had filibustered against the 1964 Civil Rights Bill, endorsed Mayor Daly's response: "No criminal is afraid of a gun that is not loaded or of a policeman or soldier who is under orders not to shoot"; Long offered that the best way to stop the rioting was to shoot the looters "before you'd let them escape." Not to be outdone, Democratic representative Paul Rogers from West Palm Beach, Florida, a staunch opponent of all civil rights legislation, said Congress should place the capital under army control. But Patrick V. Murphy, the city's first director of public safety, who had been appointed to improve the troubled relations between the police and black residents, said repeatedly that if he was ordered to shoot looters and arsonists, "I'd resign."

THAT SUMMER AND fall, Washingtonians seemed to be in a state of trauma. Stunned by the riots and arsons, frustrated by the expanding war in Vietnam, upset by college student demonstrations, and trembling with fear for the future, they came to question whether they could ever again enjoy the security they had known in the 1950s. That spring, they learned that the crime rate in the year *before* the riots of April had increased by 27 percent, including a 46 percent rise in robberies. Merchants, especially liquor store owners, took to keeping guns near their cash registers, and using them. The unease of Washingtonians matched the malaise of many across the country who began to wonder if the nation could keep what some newspaper writers called its "guns and butter" policy of fighting a costly war in Vietnam and maintaining President Johnson's Great Society social programs. As King had put it in his sermon at the National Cathedral, the country was "spending five hundred thousand dollars" to kill a Vietcong soldier, but "only fifty-three dollars a year" for a US citizen in poverty.

White Washingtonians were particularly wary of the Poor People's March that King had promised later in the year. The organization and tactics were similar to the Bonus March of 1932: groups of the poor would form caravans, nine in all, in various parts of the country, and would wend their way across the landscape, gathering more protesters and the destitute as they went. At the capital, many would live in "Resurrection City," a fifteen-acre assemblage of prefabricated plywood, canvas, and plastic huts to rise on the Mall. Once they arrived, members of the march would lobby Congress to relieve their plight with antipoverty legislation. Even though there would be but a fraction of the people in this encampment, as there had been in 1932, they would have electricity, plumbing, and telephones. King's Southern Christian Leadership Conference, which lived on after his assassination, hoped that the city would be a great symbol of the poverty that could be found across the nation.

As the march would come on the heels of the April riots, southern conservatives in Congress and many Washingtonians feared more violence. The Senate triumvirate of McClellan, Long, and Byrd were the most outspoken. "There is no legitimate reason for the march," Byrd said, adding that it carried "the potential for additional civil disorder." McClellan and Long warned about the presence of communists, or at least communist sympathizers, among the organizers. The *Washington Post*, which seemed quick to publish stories about blacks who opposed the march, called in an editorial for "a moral equivalent to this project." Why not a march *from* the capital rather than to it: "Would it be more dramatic and more effective if the people who make national policy went to the poor instead of waiting for the poor to come to them?"

But the Reverend Ralph Abernathy, who succeeded Martin Luther King as head of the Southern Christian Leadership Conference, vowed that the march would go on. Indeed, the circumstances left him with little choice. In the immediate aftermath of King's murder, the more

DAILY LIFE in Resurrection City before rain turned the encampment into a mire. CREDIT: Jill Freedman

militant black leaders had remained silent, "in personal tribute," as one person put it, "to Dr. King." But now they were growing restless, and Abernathy feared what might happen to his organization if it did *not* act. In early May, caravans in various cities, including New York, Los Angeles, Detroit, and Dallas, began their journeys; by mid-month, Resurrection City was rising with the help of John Wiebenson, a talented young architecture professor from the University of Maryland, and a cadre of volunteers. Wiebenson planned the site to be an ideal "city" of five hundred small temporary houses plus several larger buildings for a "government" and a health clinic. Telephone and electric lines would run underground, and the waste lines for sinks, showers, and toilets would connect with the sewers of the former tempo buildings that had been on the Mall. Volunteers built the houses—canvas stretched over two-by-four A-frames strengthened with plywood panels—at a small Catholic college in Silver Spring, Maryland, and trucked them to the site.

In the beginning, Resurrection City became a destination spot for liberal politicians and black entertainers. Charles Percy, a progressive Republican senator from Illinois, arrived to drive a ceremonial nail at one of the houses; Mayor John Lindsay came from New York City;

Joan Baez and Marlon Brando took a tour. Mainstream performers such as Diana Ross and Muddy Waters gave concerts. At the community's gathering spot, the Many Races Soul Center, Pete Seeger led Resurrection residents in protest songs; Bernice Reagon, in black spirituals; George Crow Flies High in American Indian chants; and Miguel Barragan in Mexican ballads. More often than not these events sparked long and informal conversations about race and poverty among the diverse residents.

But Abernathy and his leadership never really defined what the march and the city were about. Was it connected with the Vietnam War? Were they joining the black civil rights movement with liberal whites, Chicanos, and Indians, and if so, was that desirable? King had seen the civil rights and peace movements as inextricably bound; but for many weeks, Abernathy never quite articulated this point. Although the marchers made the rounds of Congress to protest cuts in various federal antipoverty programs and the early childhood education, health, and nutrition program Head Start, they appeared to reporters to be disorganized and confused.

Reporters generally focused their attention on Resurrection City and its trials. After an initial and short burst of enthusiasm, it quickly devolved into a microcosm of the political and racial divisions and civic disorder then rending Washington, and indeed, much of the nation. The much-acclaimed infrastructure wasn't ready in time for the residents. Young militants, including a security detail recruited from urban gangs, routinely harassed reporters and chanted threatening slogans, pushing the concept of nonviolent confrontation to its limit—and beyond. Press conferences were chaotic, and filled with so many exaggerated claims that the reporters quickly became cynical. Continual rainstorms over nine days mired the city in thick mud and gave reporters an opportunity to emphasize poor planning, disorder, and chaos. They wrote stories about a caravan of Mexican Americans who, on learning that the city was not ready, arranged to board at a private and progressive school on Fifth and I streets SW. Surely, so the narrative went, this was evidence that black separatists had turned Resurrection City into an exclusive and segregated enclave.

Walter Washington was worried, too, especially about health and safety. "It was a mud hole. It rained nineteen out of twenty-three days," he recalled three decades later. "Mayors came from other cities to give the Resurrection City support, and even money. I saw John Lindsay of New York City there, and I told him, 'Give these people money to go home, but don't give them money to stay here.' Do you know what it's like to get sanitary facilities, police protection, and first aid to 5,000 people living in the rain under a stack of plywood?"

"The Poor People's Campaign may be dangerously close to falling apart," William Raspberry wrote at the beginning of his column in the *Washington Post* that June, before recounting the failure of leadership at the city. Indeed, Ralph Abernathy and the other leaders were absent altogether. Rather than live in the city, they opted for the Pitts Motor Hotel at Fourteenth and Belmont in Cleveland Heights. "On at least three or four occasions" during the rainstorm, Raspberry noted, residents from Resurrection City "invaded the motel to demand that Mr. Abernathy come back to the campsite and its ankle deep mud." Nor was Abernathy's cause helped when a *Washington Post* photographer captured him entering a spa in Tacoma Park for a sauna.

Poor planning, failed leadership, and terrible weather were bad enough for morale, but on the morning of Thursday, June 6, the marchers, along with the world, learned that presidential candidate Robert F. Kennedy had been assassinated in Los Angeles after winning the California primary. It was Kennedy who in 1960 had interceded with an Atlanta judge to have Martin Luther King Jr. released from jail, and Kennedy who had said, on learning of King's assassination, "What we need in the United States is . . . love and wisdom, and compassion toward one another, and a feeling of justice toward those who still suffer within our country, whether they be white or whether they be black." The murder was a turning point for the marchers, who believed that Kennedy had understood their circumstances. The following Saturday evening, many in the city stood silently and watched as the hearse carrying the senator's body stopped before the steps of the Lincoln Memorial while the Marine Band played "The Battle Hymn of the Republic."

The end of the Poor People's March was relatively quiet. No doubt crushed by the cumulative pain of King's assassination, the April riots, and Kennedy's murder, the protesters, with the exception of young militants, had little appetite for violence. Nor did Patrick Murphy and his chief of police; even clamorous congressmen tempered their remarks. On Wednesday, June 19, organizers gathered 50,000 protesters for a Solidarity Day march at the Washington Monument and Lincoln

Memorial, but as William Raspberry wrote, "We Shall Overcome," the "credo" of the civil rights march in 1963, had a hollow ring; it was now "just a song."

On June 24, after anxious negotiations on both sides, police carefully arrested 337 people in a demonstration at the Capitol and at Resurrection City. It was far different from the July night in 1932 when General Douglas MacArthur had ordered the shacks of the Bonus Marchers to be torched. Police and the Southern Christian Leadership Conference prudently staged events so that demonstrators could affirm their civil disobedience credibility and officials could proclaim they had kept public order. It was a turning point for the capital. Protest had become theater, a happening to be performed for radio, television, and film; and the National Mall had become a great stage for public dissent.

THROUGHOUT THE FALL of 1968, Republican Richard Nixon made the issue of crime in the cities, and especially in the US capital, one of the cornerstones of his campaign for president. Washington was, in Nixon's words, "the crime capital of the world"; if elected, he would bring about order. Was his opponent, Vice President Hubert Humphrey, "proud of the fact that under his Administration . . . a great section of America's Capital" burned down? "No mob tried to burn down Washington, D.C., while Dwight Eisenhower was in the White House." Skillful politician that he was, Nixon had mastered the art of lying with statistics. Certainly the number of crimes in Washington had risen in the Kennedy and Johnson years, but at the same rate as it had during the Eisenhower administration. Nor was the city the "world capital of crime"; indeed, as FBI reports showed, the crime rate in the capital didn't even lead the nation. Newark, Baltimore, Detroit, Los Angeles, Miami, San Francisco, New York, and Oakland were each ahead of the District of Columbia, whose murder rate was the lowest of any major US city.

Facts were one thing; perception was another. After the April riot, Nixon knew that a majority of Americans equated Washington's crime and lawlessness with its nearly 70 percent black population, and he exploited their belief to his advantage. That spring Americans across the nation watched flickering TV images of black youths setting fires and looting stores; in the summer they saw in the pages of *Time* and *Life* as well as in their newspapers blacks striking defiant and menacing militant poses before the backdrop of Resurrection City, the Lincoln Memorial, and the Washington Monument. Linking crime with the capital and with blacks became a sure way of splitting off the white Democratic voters Nixon needed to win the presidency.

The Gallup Poll confirmed that the subject resonated with a majority of Americans. In late February 1968, *before* the riots, it found "crime and lawlessness (including riots, looting, juvenile delinquency)" to be the number-one domestic problem cited by most Americans, more important than the quality of education, transportation, high taxes, or unemployment. (Few seemed to connect these other problems to the incidence of crime.) Subsequent polls found that significant numbers of Americans, even those living in small cities, were afraid to walk alone at night in their neighborhoods. The gambit worked. On Monday, January 20, 1969, Richard Nixon moved into the White House and in effect became the sheriff of the city he had maligned for the past year. He vowed to make it a model for the nation.

Crime, and worse, the fear of crime, continued to plague the capital as Nixon took office. Newspapers and local TV news programs lost no opportunity to report on the latest robbery, rape, shooting, stabbing, or murder. The day after his inauguration, the *Washington Daily News* declared in a front-page editorial that "fear stalks the streets of Washington." The tabloid regularly published a "Crime Clock" column that identified the time and nature of crimes in the city as well as the races of the perpetrators and victims; not to be outdone, the *Washington Post* started its own "Crime and Justice" column, giving prominent coverage to shootings, stabbings, muggings, and murders. The opportunities to do so were abundant. The January of Nixon's inauguration, the crime sheet included, among others, robberies of nineteen banks; the robbery of the Federal Credit Union at the Department of Health, Education, and Welfare; the murder of two FBI agents; and the murder of the assistant principal of Cardozo High School by three youths who were holding up the school's bank. Before his second day in office was over, Nixon scribbled a note to his attorney general and his chief of staff about the *Washington Daily* editorial: "Let's get going with an announcement . . . of *some* action. It is of highest priority to do something meaningful on D.C. crime *now*."

On the last day of the month, the president outlined his "Actions and Recommendations for the District of Columbia," which addressed the issues of crime, rebuilding, and home rule for Washington's residents. Naturally, the proposals meant to address crime proved the most controversial. Although some of his proposals—an additional 1,000 DC police officers, more district attorneys, a streamlined court and juvenile justice system, expanded prisons, and a "significant" increase in the role of the Bureau of Narcotics and Dangerous Drugs—had been made by a previous crime commission that President Johnson had appointed, Nixon also asked for the authority to hold "hard-core" suspects in "preventive detention" without the possibility of bail. Such a flouting of the long-held legal tenet of presumed innocence until proven guilty naturally stirred controversy in Congress. Senators, representatives, and many editorial commentators charged that such a law would repeal the Bill of Rights. (Democratic senator Sam Ervin of North Carolina, an upholder of Jim Crow and segregation, but a staunch defender of civil liberties, declared the legislation to be "as full of unconstitutional, unjust, and unwise provisions as a mangy hound dog is full of fleas.") But approval of what came to be known as the DC crime bill did come, in July 1970, and along with it the administration had added a "No-Knock" provision giving police in the District the power to enter buildings unannounced and without permission.

Clearly, the new administration had decided that, at least in the District of Columbia, the powers of the federal government transcended those of a free people. The general populace and members of Congress were in agreement, if only because they believed crime was out of control. On the morning of the very day that Nixon announced his plan, a Treasury Department trainee was shot during a holdup attempt outside the Sulgrave Club on Massachusetts Avenue near Dupont Circle. Three senators, a representative, and Nixon's director of communications, who were just leaving the club, came to the rescue.

RICHARD NIXON'S YEARS in the White House marked one of the angriest and most troubled periods in America's twentieth century. Simply put, the old order of the Eisenhower years had passed. Increasingly, blacks were embracing "Black Power" and nationalism, and sometimes, through groups like the Black Panthers, violence; youths were taking psychoactive drugs; young women were taking oral contraceptives; and students on college campuses were questioning the morality of the war in Indochina. Nixon, as well as Vice President Spiro T. Agnew and Nixon's myopic attorney general, John N. Mitchell, viewed these changes as evidence of moral decline, a lawless and unpatriotic challenge to American values. Whenever possible, they responded with the full force of the law.

The administration regarded the demonstrations against the Vietnam War as a serious test of its resolve. On October 15, 1969, tens of thousands gathered in Washington as part of a nationwide protest to end the war. That evening, Martin Luther King Jr.'s widow, Coretta Scott King, gave a short speech at the Sylvan Theater behind the Washington Monument to about 20,000 candle-holding listeners before leading them to the White House gates. Other speakers, including senators, representatives, and pediatrician Benjamin Spock, spoke at smaller rallies around the city. A month later, hundreds of thousands more citizens came on the same mission.

By the spring of 1970, American youth, along with a growing number of older citizens, war veterans, and members of Congress, felt they had been duped by a president who had campaigned on the promise of a secret plan to end the fighting. But Nixon seemed only to expand the war, especially when he announced an allied incursion into Cambodia. On Thursday, April 30, 1970, protests erupted on campuses from Bowdoin College in Maine to Stanford University in California. In truculent fashion, Nixon reacted by calling the protesters "bums." After National Guardsmen killed four demonstrators at Kent State University in Ohio, an equally truculent Agnew said the violence was "predictable and avoidable." The killing, the remarks, and the seeming absence of any sympathy for the Kent State victims or their families were enough to provoke students, faculty, and thousands of distressed citizens to take their frustrations to the capital. In the 90-degree heat of Saturday, May 9, five days after the shootings, more than 100,000 people massed on the Mall and the White House Ellipse.

The event marked a departure for a city that had seen many demonstrations about the war; this time, the crowd was larger, angrier, and more resentful. In addition to the usual banners calling for withdrawal from the war, a number of demonstrators carried signs proclaiming "I'M A BUM FOR PEACE." Though he refused to say so, Nixon, too, was deeply troubled. In the middle of the night before the demonstration, he roused his valet and went to the Lincoln Memorial to meet with the protesters. In an awkward exchange, the president with heavy hand tried to explain his policy, drawing an analogy with former British prime minister Neville Chamberlain's appeasement of Germany before World War II. He tried to connect by talking sports, and he told the students to be peaceful. After about an hour, he left for breakfast at the Mayflower Hotel, then he returned to the White House, which Mayor Walter Washington had ringed with city buses to keep the crowds at bay.

It was inevitable that the fighting abroad and the seeming escalation of the war would bring protests to the capital. In 1970, bombs exploded in seven foreign embassies, though no one was injured. Nor was anyone hurt on March 1, 1971, when a bomb destroyed a Senate reception room at the Capitol; it was the first explosion in the building since 1915, when Woodrow Wilson was president. The FBI and the administration blamed members of the Weather Underground, a violent group of radicals who advocated the overthrow of the government, and vowed to match such actions with force.

A month later, the administration had to back down. Fearing "a situation of potential violence and disorder," the Interior Department denied the petition from a group of antiwar Vietnam veterans for a permit for a five-day encampment at the Capitol end of the Mall. The legal battle that followed ended with Chief Justice Warren Burger upholding the Interior Department's denial, but the veterans came and camped out anyway. For the better part of a week, veterans protested before the Supreme Court and lobbied senators and representatives. On April 23, they threw their medals over a chain-link fence onto the Capitol steps. With the soldiers was Ann Pine, an American Gold Star mother from New Jersey, who carried a sign with a photograph of her soldier son and the words "MY SON DIED IN VAIN."

Administration officials tried to prevent the veterans from marching down Pennsylvania Avenue, but Walter Washington intervened. "These veterans had fought the war for us," Washington later said. "The parade went on." Even the most callous in the administration understood that the federal government, too, was on stage, and that disaster would ensue if it ordered police to evict the veterans. The Justice Department had no choice but to ignore the injunction it had so aggressively sought.

A veterans' protest was one thing, but civil disobedience by May Day Tribe, a group of war resisters set upon anarchy, was quite another. United under the slogan, "If the government won't stop the war, we'll stop the government," 25,000 members of the Tribe arrived in the capital on May 1, 1970, to create a spectacle that they knew would reap national TV coverage. They would close bridges, block intersections, barricade entrances to government buildings, and engage in other tactics to disrupt the city. Since the Tribe unwisely published a manual outlining its plans, 14,000 National Guardsmen, army troops, Marines, and police were ready with tanks, helicopters, guns, nightsticks, mace, and tear gas. It all created a scene that one witness said "seemed more appropriate to Saigon in wartime than Washington in the spring."

Over three days Washington's residents witnessed the exercise of unbridled military and police power, including the powers granted to them in the DC crime bill, as they arrested more than 13,000 people and intimidated thousands more. The dragnet yielded so many victims, most of whom had no connection with the protest, so fast that police had to stuff them into city buses and rental trucks for trips to holding pens at the city jail, Robert F. Kennedy Stadium, and the Washington Coliseum. Criticizing press accounts of the events, a White House spokesperson maintained that Nixon was "totally satisfied" with the way the demonstrations were handled, and the administration had "no evidence of unlawful arrests." The courts, however, were not satisfied. Unable to process the thousands of citizens who had been arrested, judges criticized the police. In the end, the arrests yielded just seventy-nine convictions. And a class-action suit by the American Civil Liberties Union on behalf of those who had been illegally arrested and imprisoned yielded a financial settlement from the federal government in 1974.

Although the president and his administration professed to be sanguine with the gassing, clubbing, and mass arrests, a White House aide described them as "shaken." Washington had devolved from a symbol of democracy—the national capital of a people living under a Constitution that protected freedom of expression and the right to assemble even in protest—into an armed camp without regard for constitutionally ensured rights. As one observer put it, Washington was "listening to sirens luring liberty onto the rocks of safety."

IN ADDITION TO the crime bill that Nixon created in January 1969, the president also promised "a swift start on restoring those areas devastated nearly 10 months ago." The riot areas—Seventh and Fourteenth streets in Shaw, as well as H Street to the east—had been stripped of the vitality of commerce. "Scarcely any of the shops and homes destroyed during the riots of last April have been rebuilt, and very few of those damaged have been made habitable or usable again," Nixon said. "These rotting, boarded-up structures are a rebuke to us all and an oppressive, demoralizing environment for those who live in their shadow." His commitment seemed genuine; even the 1969 inaugural committee, the president reported, had pledged that the net proceeds of the money it raised would be donated for playground equipment and improvements.

On the Friday morning of the last day of January, Nixon made a short but symbolic visit to the startled residents on Shaw's riot-scarred Seventh Street. The man who had used race so effectively in his recent campaign now stood before the burned-out shells of a Waxie Maxie Record Store and three other businesses to announce his rebuilding program. A small "vest-pocket" park would replace the rubble. "This is our capital city," Nixon said as Mayor Walter Washington and his secretary of housing listened beside him. "We want to make it a beautiful city in every way." After a crane with a wrecking ball ceremonially whacked at one of the store's remaining walls, Nixon crossed the street to shake hands with the surprised but friendly crowd, one of whom shouted "Soul Brother" in welcome. In fifteen minutes the visit was over. The president quickly left for the Pentagon to solicit the views of his generals and admirals on the Vietnam War.

A visit to the riot area, fine words, and a photo opportunity were easy to bring off; it was far harder to carry through on the assurances of change. Six years later, after Nixon had resigned, the landscape of greater Shaw still lay ravaged. The park the president had promised that Friday morning hadn't materialized, having fallen victim to "bickering" among community groups, as a *Washington Post* editorial put it, along with different proposals from four competing agencies and commissions, the city council, and "almost anyone else with a plan." Lost in the interagency bickering among bureaucrats was the sight of the shells of decrepit buildings, such as the Peoples Drug Store and Jordan Fine Furniture on Fourteenth, the Standard Drug Store on H Street, and the Safeway supermarket on Seventh, and apartment houses like the once noble Columbia at Fourteenth and Girard. Over the years, these and scores of other structures had devolved into ghostly presences, testaments of an earlier, more decent civilization long abandoned to rats and drug addicts.

NIXON ARTICULATED HIS third proposal—"to give the people of the District of Columbia the voice they legitimately should have in the public policies that affect their lives"—in a long special message he sent to Congress in April. He put the case for self-government clearly, with words he might have copied from Theodore Noyes's *Our National Capital and Its Un-Americanized Americans*: The District government couldn't "be truly responsible," the president said, until it was "made responsible to those . . . under its rule." Its citizens should not have to "pay taxes for a government which they have no part in choosing—or to bear the full burdens of citizenship without the full rights of citizenship." Once again, home rule for the District of Columbia had come to the fore.

Like every other president since Harry Truman, Nixon had to deal with Representative John McMillan, chair of the House Committee on the District of Columbia. McMillan and his fellow southerners might have lost on civil rights in 1964 and on voting rights in 1965, but they still could deny Washingtonians full citizenship and the right to elect voting representatives to Congress. Over the years they had thwarted nine home-rule bills; indeed, only one, Lyndon Johnson's, got to the floor of the House for a vote, where it was defeated. "Washington is a federal city," McMillan declared in one of his committee's reports, "established exclusively for the benefit of, and as a home for, the federal government." Most of those who "swarmed here" were "intruders" and "not vital" to its operation.

By 1970, however, McMillan's ruthless grip on the committee was beginning to weaken. That February, liberal Republicans and Democrats on the committee had defeated him and his conservative confederates when they had attempted to graft an amendment onto Nixon's crime bill that would have given Congress the power to appoint, and thereby control, the District's police commissioner. Those same liberals then forced a vote on Nixon's measure to allow District residents to elect a nonvoting representative to Congress. The proposal finally cleared both houses of Congress in September. The District of Columbia would have a representative in Congress at last, albeit one who could not vote and had little practical power.

Meanwhile, South Carolina's Sixth District was slowly changing around Johnny Mac. The Voting Rights Act of 1965 enabled more blacks in his district to cast ballots; a new generation of younger whites with more liberal ideas about race had emerged; and even some in the older generation began to wonder why their congressman devoted so much of his time to the District of Columbia. McMillan hadn't faced a serious primary or even a general-election opponent for years. But in the summer of 1970, when a young black physician mounted a challenge, Washington's civic activists sent their money south along with Walter Fauntroy, the District's newly elected nonvoting representative, and a chartered bus of civil rights and home-rule supporters to get out the black vote. The strategy backfired when McMillan went on TV for the first time in his life and said, "This is a South Carolina election and we don't need any advice from people in Washington." Two years later, the seventy-six-year-old faced a younger, better organized, and white primary opponent. The activists stayed home but gave money to fund the defeat of the longest-serving representative in South Carolina's history. Ungraceful and mean-spirited to the end, McMillan complained that he lost because "the colored people were brought out." When they heard the news, Walter Fauntroy and the residents of Seventh Street celebrated with a parade.

At the end of his last term, John McMillan wrote his final report as chair of the District of Columbia Committee. It included a delusional epitaph of his reign: "He remains the best and most effective friend the Nation's Capital has ever had."

With McMillan out of the way as chair of the District committee, his successor immediately held hearings on various forms of government before submitting a bill for limited home rule. The usual protracted skirmish ensued as segregationists and conservative legislators raised objections, and moderates and liberals debated just how limited the bill should be; but the tone was almost entirely free of bombast, and the debates were generally civil. Even Washington's white-dominated Board of Trade, which in the past had always worked with McMillan to scuttle home-rule bills, gave its grudging assent. The compromise legislation, which Nixon signed on Christmas Eve 1973, enabled citizens to choose a mayor and a thirteen-member council, headed by an elected chairman; it also gave the new council the authority to tax, but Congress retained control of the purse. The fate of the city's budget remained in its hands. And ultimately, if a majority in Congress disagreed with legislation passed by the council, it could rescind it.

Washingtonians regarded the legislation as progress; in May 1974, they adopted the home-rule charter. Although Congress had not granted Washingtonians full citizenship, it had given them a solid start, the first since the creation of the District at the dawn of the republic. That September, 54 percent of the voters chose Walter Washington over a single primary opponent, and his victory was confirmed in the November election. For the first time since 1871, the District's citizens had been enfranchised to elect their mayor.

WALTER WASHINGTON HAD served in City Hall since Lyndon Johnson had appointed him in 1967. Although some white business leaders and members of Congress thought him soft on crime, because he had refused to order the shooting of looters during the April 1968 riots, they grudgingly, albeit silently, recognized that his leadership in the crisis and afterward had kept the city from slipping into further chaos. Richard Nixon had reappointed him in 1969 with a pledge of federal assistance on "a greater scale than has been in the past." More importantly, Washington had shown skeptical whites, especially southern conservatives, that a black man could govern the capital. The middle-class Walter Washington was the president's kind of black politician, persuasive rather than strident, restrained rather than bellicose. Others, combative personalities like Stokely Carmichael, Julius Hobson, Walter Fauntroy, and a more recent arrival, Marion Barry, seemed to be continually clamoring for change. Washington knew the city's neighborhoods, and through his work with the National Capital Housing Authority, he understood the ways of government. He would do well, Nixon believed. He could trust him.

The new mayor possessed a thick skin. He had been able to disregard the truckload of watermelons that John McMillan had sent him when Johnson had appointed him mayor, and he had proved he could work with the representative and his conservative fellow segregationists on the District of Columbia Committee in order to secure the best deals for the District. "My job," he said later, "was to get money to run the city. I didn't waste time listening to what some white bigot might say about me." To be sure, he didn't get all that he wanted, but his years in the capital had schooled him in the art of political compromise, and what he got was more than most believed possible. And, unlike many, Walter Washington understood that years of congressional abuse, incompetent and irresponsible commissioners, Vietnam War protests, the King riots, and racial division had made the capital a tinderbox; his job, especially in the Nixon years, was to keep the city from igniting.

Now mayor in his own right, he faced problems that had been building for years. The Government Accounting Office reported that the city's finances were in such chaos that they could not be audited. Promises that had been made to many groups over the years remained unfulfilled. Another event, the March 1977 terrorist attack by the Hanafi Movement, a Muslim group, on the Islamic Center of Washington, the headquarters of B'nai B'rith, and the District Building, tested his firmness of purpose. Although the terrorists murdered one person, wounded Councilman Marion Berry, and held nearly 150 people hostage for thirty-nine hours, Mayor Washington, who was in his office at the time, refused to leave. "I can't . . . turn it over to criminal elements," he said. But calm and courage were not enough.

By the spring of 1978, it was clear that Walter Washington was out of touch with many of the city's blacks. He had never cultivated the District's neighborhoods and wards as the younger, more vocal generation of leaders had. He hadn't fought on the barricades for civil rights. To them, his civility seemed more like servility, and they knew he was vulnerable. Voters agreed. In the three-way primary race, Washington came in third. So ended Walter Washington's political career. Over the years, his victories had been small and quiet, but in the aggregate they were remarkable. He had been a bridge between an older outlook and a younger one on the place of black Americans in the nation and in the District of Columbia. He shepherded the city from an "anachronism of votelessness" under three commissioners into at least a simulacrum of self-determination. Walter Washington was not a great mayor, but he was a good one, and a great man.

MARION BARRY BECAME the District of Columbia's second mayor. Born into a sharecropping family in Mississippi and raised in Memphis, Tennessee, his ambition, coupled with his first-class brain, had brought him far in forty-two years. An Eagle Scout, he had earned a bachelor's degree at LeMoyne College in Memphis and a master's in chemistry at Fisk University in Nashville. In 1963, when he was just a few credits shy of earning a doctorate at the University of Tennessee in Knoxville, he quit his studies to lead the Student Nonviolent Coordinating Committee, first in Mississippi, and in 1965 in Washington. Within months, and with elegant timing, he energized thousands in poor neighborhoods; he organized a successful bus boycott to protest a fare increase, led the "Free D.C." movement to secure home rule, and with funds from the US Department of Labor started Pride Incorporated to give black youths jobs. Elected to head the school board in 1972, he pushed salary increases for teachers and organized BANG, "Blacks Against Narcotics Genocide," to protest a "blaxploitation" film that glorified a cocaine dealer. Two years later, Washington's voters elected him as a member at large for their new city council. Black Washingtonians, especially the poor, realized that Marion Barry, through speech and action, would stand up for them and never tolerate the indignity of bigots.

And all the while, as he hustled about the capital, Marion Barry built alliances with the marginalized—gays and Asians, women and Hispanics—who were finding their voice, as well as socialites and liberal whites, real-estate developers and merchants. His prodigious memory enabled him to store vast amounts of information—names, phone numbers, addresses, and personal details—for all those whom he met in a capacious, and private, mental directory. In 1978, he used his directory to good effect. That September, as his two rivals split the middle-class black vote, Barry eked out a mayoral primary win, and he handily defeated his Republican opponent in November.

Since early 1990, many Americans have associated Washington, DC, with Mayor Marion Barry's excesses. But at the beginning of his administration in 1979, that was not the case. Today he may be chiefly remembered for his weaknesses, because they did come to dominate his actions, but Barry did not succumb to them immediately at the outset of his administration. At the start he continued his familiar frenetic pace. He created summer employment programs for youths, inaugurated a plan to reduce infant mortality, gave city contracts to black businesses, and acknowledged the rising number of Hispanics in the District by naming them to important posts. "I want to make Washington, DC," he told a Baptist church group, "the number one city, the best city, the premier city in the entire world."

When Barry took over, he inherited a deficit of $284 million and a budget in chaos. Public debt was mounting, costs were rising, unemployment was going up. The only thing coming down was the level of city services. Schools were known for poor test results and high dropout rates. Police protection was limited to the wealthier areas. Some neighborhoods had simply been abandoned by the police force. Barry made a point of publicly meeting with citizen groups regarding finances, cutting ribbons to open even the smallest business, and giving the nightly news its sound bites about his plans to restore fiscal order. He met with bankers, whom he impressed with his command of budget figures and accounting. By the end of the crisis he had balanced the budget, and for three years in the early 1980s, there was even a surplus in the city's treasury. Standard and Poor's investment service gave the District's bonds its highest rating.

Barry used the power of his administration to expand the employment opportunities for blacks to lift them into the middle class. They moved into mid- and upper-level jobs in District departments. He used his power over District contracts to break the hammerlock control that white contractors had enjoyed in the building construction industry for more than a century. Nearly half the money for a new convention center at Ninth and H streets went to black firms.

Barry breezed into his second and third terms in 1982 and 1986. But like so many other urban mayors, he had sailed against the powerful headwind of a new conservatism that was sweeping the nation. Federal budgets during Ronald Reagan's presidency slashed aid to the capital by tens of millions. In 1982 alone, the cut amounted to $107 per person; only New York and five rural states had to endure a greater hit. The recession of the early 1980s, which cost the District 42,000 jobs and stressed social services, forced Barry to increase taxes.

And then, he lost control. As early as March 1983, stories of drug abuse appeared in the press, but Barry denied them. He denied as well the allegations of a female friend claiming that he had frequented a motel with her for sex and cocaine; and again, allegations from a colleague that he had gone to the Virgin Islands to smoke crack. Barry brushed aside newspaper reports that he frequented nightclubs where prostitutes and drug dealers plied their trade, saying, "I'm a night owl." The US federal prosecutor sent Barry's top aides to jail, as well as his former wife, who had skimmed money from Pride Incorporated. At the same time, such vital city services as the fire department, housing, and sanitation began to fail.

Ever audacious and inflammatory, Barry maintained his swaggering public persona. The city was in decline, even near collapse, and yet the mayor could be seen on the newscasts in the late 1980s denying the reports, accusing all who criticized him of racism. It became clear to nearly all Washingtonians that their mayor was in free fall.

"He became uncontrollable, a child, an embarrassment," said Carol Thompson. A Washington native, Thompson had been educated in the city's public schools and at Smith College before taking a job in the city's bureaucracy. She cared deeply about her city and wanted the new home-rule government and Barry to succeed. In a succession of lower-level jobs in the administration, she gained a reputation for clear, deliberate, and independent thinking—and integrity. As his aides were shipped off to prison for corruption and a variety of other venal acts, Barry increasingly turned to Thompson; in December 1987, he appointed her city administrator.

Thwarted in every attempt to link Barry with an incriminating document, the federal attorney set up a sting to ensnare him. On the night of Thursday, January 18, 1990, detectives stormed into a seedy hotel room to arrest the mayor of Washington, who was smoking cocaine with a girlfriend. Across the nation, TV news programs played the grainy, green-hued FBI surveillance tape of Barry drawing on a crack pipe as he lurched about the room, which only served to make the entire scene even more seamy and shocking. He was convicted of drug possession and served six months in federal prison before his release in April 1992. It was a tragedy of a man who had the makings of greatness but whose weaknesses won out. Barry had become seduced by drugs, which in turn had led him to corruption and crime. His tale is one that caters to the attitudes many people have about drugs, blacks, crime, civic corruption, and the District of Columbia.

Even before his arrest, suspicion of Barry's corruption and unhappiness with his antics had sapped strength from the home-rule movement.

In 1978, Walter Fauntroy had convinced his fellow representatives and senators to propose a constitutional amendment that would give residents full voting representation in Congress. As just sixteen of the needed thirty-eight state legislatures voted to ratify the amendment by the deadline of August 1985, the proposal failed. Washingtonians remained isolated from the normal practices of American representative democracy.

TO MANY CASUAL observers, the District of Columbia continued its downward slide through the final decade of the twentieth century. The District's politics and the relationship between the city government and Congress remained as turbulent as ever. Social ills multiplied, and the population declined. Yet a community revolution that had begun even before the Nixon administration was quietly building; by the millennium it would begin to show signs of success.

On the surface the signs were as dire as ever. Barry's successor, Sharon Pratt Kelly, a light-skinned black Washington native, proved feckless in her attempts to control the budget and the many Barry loyalists who remained in the city's bureaucracy. In 1994, the federal Government Accounting Office warned that the District would run out of money if nothing drastic was done. Kelly left a $335 million deficit to her successor, Marion Barry, whom Washington's voters elected to a fourth mayoral term in November 1994.

The circumstances of Marion Barry's life resonated with many in the capital's black community. At the time, 85 percent of the black men in the District were incarcerated, or had been, or were awaiting trial, which meant that almost everyone had a family member or knew someone in prison. Congress was not so forgiving or trusting. It created a Financial Control Board that placed much of the city's government into receivership, ultimately stripping Barry of almost all but his ceremonial duties. Power was transferred to the District's new chief financial officer, Anthony Williams, who returned the city to fiscal stability. Most were relieved when Williams was elected mayor in 1998.

DRUGS, AND THE violence they created, had torn Washington's urban fabric and helped to precipitate an exodus to the suburbs. Twelve percent of whites and 18 percent of blacks who abandoned the District between 1990 and 1996 listed crime as the main reason for leaving. They abandoned a city that, among other things, had to spend more than $1 million on its police force, tend to crack babies left by drug-dependent mothers in the District hospital, care for uninsured victims of gunshot wounds, and pay for an overburdened court system and prisons. Eleanor Holmes Norton, the District's nonvoting representative in Congress since 1991, equated the violence with the Civil War. "It's brother against brother. It's domestic war." And *City Under Siege*, a half-hour program that appeared every night on Rupert Murdoch's local Fox television station, did not improve the residents' mood.

In the Barry years, the District's population declined with its fortunes, from 638,000 in 1980 to 572,000 in 2000. Between 1980 and 1990, many blacks who rose into the middle class—through jobs Marion Barry helped to create—left for the suburbs. The black population in the 1980s declined by 49,300, while the white population increased by 7,900.

Nevertheless, gradual though they were, positive changes were transforming the District of Columbia. Two important events, one above ground and one below, were catalysts for change: the scuttling of the interstate highways planned for the city, and the creation of the subway system. Transportation, the most humdrum and prosaic of subjects, brought a profound change to Washington's future.

As engineers were building the ribbon of the city's Southwest Freeway in the early 1960s, Washingtonians began to question the value of urban interstate highways. They displaced thousands of people, devastated neighborhoods, destroyed parks, increased pollution, and removed property from tax rolls. Younger city planners had misgivings as well. But members of the Federal Highway Administration were happy to build roads that engineers had drawn on city maps decades earlier. They wanted to add thirty-eight miles of highway in the District, including an "Inner Belt," a loop road that would be a smaller version of the Capital Beltway. Like the Capital Beltway, it would serve as a hub for the spokes of highways connecting the District with Maryland and Virginia. One of the principal spokes, the link with Virginia, would feature an eight-lane bridge across the Potomac at the "Three Sisters Islands," a small cluster of rocks off Georgetown. Another spoke, called the Northeast Freeway, would connect with Maryland Interstate 95.

Many in Washington's neighborhoods were determined to block the dreams of the highway planners. Where planners dreamed of an Inner Belt to enhance access to and ease travel through the capital, residents saw an eight-lane moat that would separate the city's federal and business sections from its neighborhoods. Where planners dreamed of a streamlined bridge across the Potomac, Georgetown saw the destruction of their environment and a gridlocked city. Where planners dreamed of an efficient Northeast Freeway connecting north and south, low-income residents saw an eight-lane monster calculated to destroy their homes and businesses and displace them, just as the renewal plan in the southwest had done so effectively.

Beginning in the late 1960s, the Interstate Highway System proposals proved to be important to Washington's communities because they united residents in a common cause. To fight what they deemed to be, as one critic put it, "urbacide," residents formed the Emergency Committee on the Transportation Crisis. Why, they asked, shouldn't the District have a metropolitan subway, which would be far more efficient and less expensive than a highway system? Why not upgrade the city's bus system, which in the hands of an unscrupulous private owner was falling into ruin? The level of rhetoric, especially from black residents, was such that few had heard. They had seen what happened with urban renewal in the southwest, where 88 percent of the new private houses were occupied by whites.

In testimony to a stunned congressional committee, one of the highway opponents from the Emergency Committee put the matter succinctly. His community had endured "long years of exploitation, neglect, and abuse," he said. The plan was being pushed by "freeway proponents who insist on creating more massive concrete canyons containing accelerated treadmills for rapidly dumping pollution-generating vehicles into a downtown area which is already hopelessly congested during rush hours." To him it was a "black and white issue. . . . [F]reeways solve no problems and create only additional burdens." He concluded with a stinging peroration: "It is also black and white in the sense that they are white men's roads through black men's homes. The convenience, illusory as it is, would be for white[s] . . . to speed through black communities . . . to the waiting bottleneck in the center city. Now, ironically, the black victims of this heartless property taking would have limited or no access to the freeways. The resulting anger, disgust, scorn, and distrust of government on the part of the victims should be obvious to us all by now." The tone had been struck, and the modified slogan "No more white man's roads through black bedrooms" took hold. To many the imposition of the interstates in poor urban communities was nothing less than the continued emasculation of the black man.

At the same time that protesters were working to block the District's interstate highways, others were trying to build a ninety-eight-mile subway system. The project had been in the city's consciousness since the Kennedy administration: President Johnson had signed a bill in support of a rail network in 1965; Washington's Metropolitan Area Transit Authority began its planning in 1967; and in 1968, Congress authorized the system, which, as half of it would be above ground, came to be called Metrorail, or simply the Metro.

Early in his administration Richard Nixon had supported the Metro fully. In June 1969, he and his secretary of transportation, John Volpe, toured the District and suburbs by helicopter at rush hour to view the traffic. As he looked down on the Seven Corners shopping center in Fairfax, the president had remembered that when he had lived in an apartment there, Fairfax had had "nothing more than a country store." He saw the cars backed up a mile at the bridges crossing the Potomac, and the traffic jam at Glebe Road in Arlington; he asked questions about the lack of parking facilities, and he noted that there weren't many buses; and as the helicopter landed on the South Lawn at the White House, he remarked, "I'm glad that we don't have to drive to work." The subway must be built, Nixon said, and it should be a national model.

The Metro, the first significant subway built anywhere in the United States after World War II, would become a model, but not until it endured a protracted fight in Congress that held up funding for years. It was a congressional event not unknown in the history of the District of Columbia. This time, William Huston Natcher, a small-minded, pro-highway representative from rural Kentucky, known more for his record 18,401 consecutive roll-call votes than for his intelligence, blocked the money until the District would agree to build the interstates. Although construction actually began on the piers for the Three Sisters Bridge in late 1969, highway opponents repeatedly halted it through court injunctions. Ultimately, the project, which the

Washington Evening Star came to call "The Ghost Bridge," remained tied up in the courts until 1972, when the Federal Highway Administration abandoned it along with most of the roads joining the bridge. As a consequence of the highway revolt, no four-lane concrete moat surrounds downtown Washington, no Interstate 95 cuts through the heart of the city, and no more white man's roads were built through black bedrooms. Today, cities around the country are burying their interstates, or wishing they could—or tearing them up altogether. Resistance in the capital in the 1960s and 1970s had made that unnecessary in the District of Columbia.

When it was completed at the beginning of the millennium, nearly everyone praised the Metro as a remarkable triumph of design, engineering, construction, and urban planning. Even its gigantic increase in cost—from an estimated $2 billion in 1965 to $9 billion in 2000—seemed to pale in people's minds. The first section, between the Rhode Island Avenue and Farragut North stations, opened on the last Monday in March 1976. In just two months it carried 1 million passengers, and shop owners at station stops along the route reported a substantial increase in business.

Metro passengers, especially those used to subways in New York or Boston, were in awe of the achievement. They descended underground into stations intended to make the spirit soar. Platforms stretched six hundred feet, were unobstructed by steel pillars, and featured blinking lights to announce train arrivals. Barrel-vaulted ceilings punctuated by coffered concrete rectangles rose overhead. Diffused lighting cast dramatic shadows on the walls and ceiling, suggesting quietness and calm. The bronze escalators and handrails quietly affirmed quality, while crisp lettered signs on pillars spoke with clarity. Riders realized that the Metro had become far more than an efficient means of moving people. It was a symbol of all that the federal government and the residents of the District of Columbia and the surrounding metropolitan region could achieve through democracy.

The Metro's success was due in part to the siting of its stations on the five lines that radiated from its center. Though bureaucrats, especially those in the National Park Service, thwarted the building of stations, Metro planners realized early in the process that they were changing the city in fundamental ways. Unlike the highway planners, they listened to the people whose lives would be affected by the changes that they wrought. Such participatory democracy involved seemingly endless meetings and delays, but in the end it was worth it. The Green line—each of the five lines has a color designation—is the best example. The line, which runs through Shaw, U Street, and Columbia Heights, was the last to be built. Critics charged racism on the part of Metro authorities, but participatory planning and budget cuts in the Reagan years were more to blame.

When the Shaw station opened in 1991, fifteen years after the Metro began, pedestrians came and property values rose; a city ordinance banned drive-thru restaurants, and people began restoring houses rather than replacing them. At the U Street/Cardozo metro stop at Thirteenth and U streets, residents rediscovered Duke Ellington when local businesses commissioned an artist and some students to create a large mural of the composer on the side of a building. Other murals followed in Shaw, including one with pictures of poet Langston Hughes and historian Carter Woodson. At the same time, construction projects, including an apartment complex on Seventh Street and a municipal building on Fourteenth, helped to restore the burned-out area. But it was the stops on the Green line that made it thrive. The successful highway battle and the construction of the Metro changed not just the topography of the city, but its spirit. In the decades since the riots of 1968, residents have found their voice as never before. They rediscovered the idea of community that many had forgotten.

THE 2010 CENSUS showed just how much the District of Columbia's population had changed. Reversing the steady decline that had been taking place for five decades, the Census Bureau now recorded a rise of more than 5 percent, to 601,723 people. Toward the end of the nineteenth century, the journalist and social critic Montgomery Schuyler had written that Washington was "the place to study America and all Americans. . . . [I]t is simply cosmopolitan and representative of every type from Michigan to Texas, and Maine to California." The Washington of 2010 was a very different place from Schuyler's. The demographics had changed dramatically. The black population stood close to 51 percent; the white at 38.5 percent. Just as important were the Asians and Hispanics who made up the balance. Since 2010 the population has increased 9.5 percent, reaching nearly 660,000.

This book began with a brief account of Marian Anderson's concert on the steps of the Lincoln Memorial and the tensions that led up to that Easter day in 1939. Today's Washington is a very different place. Segregation has ended and the city is more inclusive. Congress has taken halting steps to allow the citizens who live at the heart of the democracy to determine their destiny. The city has survived for more than two centuries as an outward and visible sign not only of our vices and failings, but also of our virtues and ideals. Through it all, Washington has remained the mirror of America.

ACKNOWLEDGMENTS

I t is a pleasant task to discharge some of the many debts I have incurred in writing this history. Several decades ago I began to consider a formal project on the design and character of the capital and at first imagined that it might be a documentary film. Ultimately, I decided to write this book. In the beginning, when I thought my work might result in a film, I was fortunate to meet with a number of the leading authorities about the city's past and present.

As I suggested in the Introduction, Washington is blessed with many distinguished university and independent scholars who have combined their passion and learning in a remarkable number of publications. Their works on subjects as diverse as the capital's establishment, governance, neighborhoods, subways, planning, architecture, and cartography are of the first rank. Over the years many have helped to sustain the Historical Society of Washington, DC, and its rich archival collection, now housed in the Carnegie library building at Mt. Vernon Square. (The Historical Society also produces an excellent publication, *Washington History*.)

Many of these Washington scholars—Jonetta Rose Barras, Kenneth R. Bowling, Howard Gillette, Don Hawkins, James Oliver Horton, Lois Horton, Keith Melder, Pamela Scott, and Kathryn Schneider Smith, among others—have been generous with their time. Early on in this project my colleague Larry Hott and I interviewed them, and I later followed up with numerous questions. Especially generous were the late Joseph R. Passonneau, who shared his understanding of the interrelations of Washington's physical and social culture; Phil Ogilvie, also departed, an extraordinary archivist, who freely offered his rich knowledge of the city's past, including his interpretation of Alexander

Shepherd's influence on the capital and Marion Barry's first mayoral term. My special thanks to Jane Freundel Levey, now the managing editor of *Washington History*, who early in my work put me in touch with a number of scholars and helped me to understand the nuances of the city's diverse cultural history.

The late John Hechinger and Walter Washington spoke at length and movingly about their experiences with Lyndon Johnson, Richard Nixon, the riots following the murder of Martin Luther King Jr., Resurrection City, and the various antiwar protests of the 1960s and 1970s. I am grateful to Carol Thompson for her extended conversation with me about Marion Barry, school desegregation, and race. Sam Smith, Harry Jaffe, Tom Sherwood, and Jim Gibson spent considerable time outlining the political landscape of modern Washington.

To Matthew B. Gilmore, an independent scholar and IT specialist, I offer special thanks. The DC list that he has guided for many years at the Humanities and Social Sciences Net Online (https://www.h-net .org) has been an invaluable source of information.

Countless librarians, archivists, and curators in various museums, archives, libraries, and historic houses assisted me in my research, especially in the beginning. I want to thank those at Columbia University, the New-York Historical Society, Williams College, the Historical Society of Washington, DC, the Library of Congress, the Franklin D. Roosevelt Presidential Library and Museum, the New York Public Library, the Washingtoniana Collection at the District of Columbia Public Library, the Decatur House, Washington, and the National Gallery of Art. I offer my special thanks to Andrew Krzystyniak and his staff at the Interlibrary Loan office of the Lucy Scribner Library, Skidmore College, who located scores of books and articles for me.

Paul Tucker and John Lukacs read early drafts of the complete manuscript and offered thoughtful and valuable criticism. I am also indebted to my colleague Beau Breslin for reading a draft of the James Madison section. Each of these readers has helped to make this a better book.

Over the years many others have also helped me, sometimes merely by listening patiently as I worked out my thoughts about the capital's history, and at other times by listening as I read discrete sections of my manuscript. Among them are: Robert and Peggy Boyers, Marc Woodworth, Larry Hott, Beau Breslin, Dan Nathan, Susan Kress, Tamara E. Robinson, Tappan Wilder, Mason Stokes, Linda Simon,

Pat Keane, Larry Hott, David Schuyler, Dan Schwartz, Jeff and Deane Pfeil, Michael Moore, and the late Thomas J. Condon. Early on in this project, Skidmore College supported me with a liberal sabbatical. For their special favors and interest, I also want to thank Steve Dinyer, Stephen Otrembiak, Margaret Thomas Buchholz, Muriel Poston, and Jorge Pérez-Rubio; and for their careful service as student assistants, Jacob Block, Margaret Myers, and Heather Malkani. To these good people I credit this book's virtues; any errors of fact or interpretation are mine alone.

My friend and agent Chris Calhoun encouraged me to write this book, and over the years has sustained me with his interest. My editor at Basic Books, Lara Heimert, has supported me from the beginning with her encouragement, perceptive readings of various drafts of this book, and numerous kindnesses both great and small. I am especially grateful to line editor Roger Labrie and copy editor Katherine Streckfus for their own careful reviews of the manuscript; Leah Stecher, assistant editor, and Collin Tracy, senior project editor, for helping me through the various stages of production; and Noah Throop, who took the jacket photograph.

For his sustained interest, encouragement, good humor, and invaluable help producing this book's images, I thank my son, Colin. But my foremost debt is to my wife, Jill, wise critic, discerning editor, tolerant listener, and, always, dearest companion.

Tom Lewis
Saratoga Springs, New York
May 25, 2015

NOTES

To save space and repetition in the notes that follow I have used the following abbreviations:

DCHS, *Records*: Records of the Columbia Historical Society, Washington, DC.

GWP-CS: W. W. Abbot and Dorothy Twohig, eds. *The Papers of George Washington. Confederation Series.* Charlottesville: University Press of Virginia, 1992–.

GWP-PS: Dorothy Twohig, ed. *The Papers of George Washington. Presidential Series.* Charlottesville: University Press of Virginia, 1987–.

GWP-RS: Dorothy Twohig, ed. *The Papers of George Washington. Retirement Series.* Charlottesville: University Press of Virginia, 1998–.

LOC: Library of Congress.

NYT: *New York Times.*

TJP: Julian P. Boyd, ed. *The Papers of Thomas Jefferson.* Princeton, NJ: Princeton University Press, 1950–.

TJP-RS: Jefferson Looney, ed. *The Papers of Thomas Jefferson.* Princeton, NJ: Princeton University Press, 2004–.

WP: *Washington Post.*

WS: *Washington Evening Star.*

INTRODUCTION: THE CONCERNS OF THE NATION

Sources for the Introduction include Allida M. Black, "Championing a Champion: Eleanor Roosevelt and the Marian Anderson 'Freedom Concert,'" *Presidential Studies Quarterly* 20, no. 4 (1990): 719–736; Scott Sandage, "A Marble House Divided: The Lincoln Memorial, the Civil Rights Movement, and the Politics of Memory, 1939–1963," *Journal of American History* 80, no. 1 (1993): 135–167; Walter White, *A Man Called White* (New York: Viking Press, 1948).

xv "*. . . interpretations a delight*": *WP*, May 10, 1938.

xvi *DAR's decision: WP*, February 20, 1939.

xvi *NBC radio network:* Walter White gives his account of the events in *A Man Called White*, 180–185; Alida Black, in "Championing the Champion," presents the story from Eleanor Roosevelt's perspective.

xvi "*. . . no color line*": Quoted from Allan Keiler, *Marian Anderson: A Singer's Journey* (Champaign: University of Illinois Press, 2002), 212. See also Susan Stamberg, "Denied a Stage, She Sang for a Nation," April 9, 2014, National Public Radio, www.npr.org/2014/04/09/298760473/denied-a-stage-she-sang-for-a-nation. There are numerous clips of the Ickes' speech on YouTube.

xvi *the plural pronoun, "we"*: See Sandage, "Marble House," 135–136. Sandage was the first person to note this.

xvii "*. . . step forward this was*": Joseph L. Rauh Jr., quoted in Sandage, "Marble House," 145. Rauh was at the start of a brilliant career as a civil rights lawyer.

xxii "*. . . its character and its destiny*": Quoted from *Life and Times of Frederick Douglass*, in Frederick Douglass, *Autobiographies* (New York: Library of America, 1994), 858.

PROLOGUE: THE "MUTINOUS INSULT"

Sources for the Prologue include Irving Brant, *James Madison* (Indianapolis: Bobbs-Merrill, 1941–1961); Ralph Ketcham, *James Madison* (New York: Macmillan, 1971); William T. Hutchinson and William M. E. Rachal, *The Papers of James Madison* (Chicago: University of Chicago Press, 1971), 7; Jonathan Elliot, *The Debates in the Several State Conventions on the Adoption of the Federal Constitution as Recommended by the General Convention at Philadelphia in 1787*, reprint of 2nd ed., 5 vols. (Philadelphia: J. B. Lippincott, 1941 [1888]), which compiles the debates in Philadelphia and the various state ratification debates. These volumes are also available through the American Memory project of the Library of Congress (www.memory.loc.gov). The best single source for the establishment of Washington, DC, is Kenneth R. Bowling's splendid *Creation of Washington D.C.: The Idea and Location of the American Capital* (Fairfax, VA: George Mason University Press, 1991), chaps. 1 and 2. I have also profited from conversations with Professor Beau Breslin about Madison's role in drafting Article I, Section 8, of the Constitution.

xxv "*. . . fellow slaves in Virga.*": Brant, *Madison*, 2:48; Ketcham, *Madison*, 148.

xxvi *medical student:* Brant, *Madison*, 2:283–287; Ketcham, *Madison*, 108–110. See also *TJP*, 6:333–335.

xxvi *"mutinous insult"*: Madison to Edmund Randolph, June 30, 1783, *Madison Papers*, 7:205. Madison's letter follows one he wrote on June 24 to Randolph complaining about the "revolt of Soldiery." See *Madison Papers*, 7:191–192.

xxvi *"scarcely ten feet square":* August 30, 1783, *Madison Papers,* 7:294.

xxvi *". . . accommodation for writing":* September 20, 1783, *Madison Papers,* 7:354.

xxvi *where Congress was meeting:* Ketcham, *Madison,* 31ff.

xxvii *". . . provided for at all":* September 20, 1783, *Madison Papers,* 7:352.

xxvii *demanded he remain:* September 20, 1783, *Madison Papers,* 7:352.

xxvii *"permanent seat of Congress":* Madison to Jefferson, September 20, 1783, *Madison Papers,* 7:352.

xxvii *". . . ominous prospects":* Elliot, *Debates,* 5:120.

xxvii *". . . bad use would be made of them":* Ibid., 5:558.

xxviii *". . . every part of the nation":* Ibid., 5:409.

xxviii *". . . state for protection":* Madison, *Federalist XLIII;* Bernard Bailyn, ed., *The Debate on the Constitution: Federalist and Antifederalist Speeches, Articles, and Letters During the Struggle over Ratification* (New York: Library of America, 1993), 2:71.

xxix *". . . must discover":* Elliott, *Debates,* 2:402.

CHAPTER 1: THE GENERAL'S RIVER AND THE FEDERAL CITY

Sources for Chapter 1 include Kenneth R. Bowling, *Creation of Washington D.C.: The Idea and Location of the American Capital* (Fairfax, VA: George Mason University Press, 1991); Bob Arnebeck, *Through a Fiery Trial: Building Washington, 1790–1800* (Lanham, MD: Madison Books, 1991); Saul K. Padover, ed., *Thomas Jefferson and the National Capital* (Washington, DC: US Government Printing Office, 1946); Elizabeth S. Kite, *L'Enfant and Washington, 1791–1792: Published and Unpublished Documents Now Brought Together for the First Time* (Baltimore: Johns Hopkins University Press, 1929); Kenneth R. Bowling, *Peter Charles L'Enfant and Male Friendship in the Early American Republic* (Washington, DC: Friends of the George Washington University Libraries, 2002); Les Standiford, *Washington Burning: How a Frenchman's Vision for Our Nation's Capital Survived Congress, the Founding Fathers, and the Invading British Army* (New York: Three Rivers Press, 2008); Fergus M. Bordewich, *Washington: The Making of the American Capital* (New York: HarperCollins, 2008); Scott W. Berg, *Grand Avenues: The Story of the French Visionary Who Designed Washington, D.C.* (New York: Pantheon, 2007).

1 *". . . much at heart":* TJP, 6:548.

2 *ends at the Chesapeake:* For Potomac River, see Frederick Gutheim, *The Potomac* (New York: Rinehart and Company, 1949); Richard L. Stanton, *Potomac Journey* (Washington, DC: Smithsonian Institution Press, 1993).

2 *place they inhabited, "Anacostia":* A still more fanciful etymology suggests that "Potomac" means "the place to which tribute is brought," suggesting it was the place where the Algonquins made gifts to the Iroquois to keep them from being harried. See William Wallace Tooker, "On the Meaning of the Name Anacostia," *American Anthropologist* 7, no. 4 (1894): 389–393.

2 " . . . *of women and children*": John Smith, *Works: 1608–1631*, ed. Edward Arber (Birmingham, UK: English Scholars' Library, 1884), no. 16, 63–67. Scholars have questioned Smith's conclusion as to population, as he appears to have counted able-bodied male warriors. See Maurice A. Mook, "Aboriginal Population of Tidewater Virginia," *American Anthropologist*, new ser., vol. 46, no. 2, part 1 (1944): 193–208.

2 *tokens of their presence:* I have followed the usually accepted divisions of the prehistory of the region: Paleo-Indian, 10000 to 7500 BCE; Archaic, 7500 to 1000 BCE; Woodland, 1000 BCE to AD 1600.

3 *British and Spanish control: GWP-CS*, 2:122.

3 *company's first president:* See William Smallwood, *The Laws of Maryland, with the Charter, The Bill of Rights, The Constitution of the State, and Its Alterations, The Declaration of Independence, and The Constitution of the United States, and Its Amendments* (Baltimore: Philip H. Nicklin, 1811), 1:537.

4 *Georgetown on the Potomac:* Bowling, *Creation of Washington*, 129.

5 *would profit handsomely:* See Susan Q. Stranahan, *Susquehanna, River of Dreams* (Baltimore: Johns Hopkins University Press, 1993), 44–49.

5 *Susquehanna in Pennsylvania:* Bowling, *Creation of Washington*, 153.

5 " . . . *Union at this moment*": Ibid., 142; Linda Grant De Pauw, ed., *Documentary History of the First Federal Congress of the United States of America, March 4, 1789–March 3, 1791* (Baltimore: Johns Hopkins University Press, 1972), 11:1423; Lance Banning, *The Sacred Fire of Liberty: James Madison and the Founding of the Federal Republic* (Ithaca, NY: Cornell University Press, 1995), 303–304.

5 *temporary capital in New York City:* See Hugh T. Taggart, "Old Georgetown," DCHS, *Records* 11 *(1908)*: 120–224.

6 *tear the Union asunder:* "The [bonds] of North and South Carolina were selling for no more than ten cents on the dollar [in December 1789], Virginia state certificates sold at from twenty to thirty cents." See Whitney K. Bates, "Northern Speculators and Southern State Debts: 1790," *William and Mary Quarterly*, 3rd ser., vol. 19, no. 1 (1962): 39.

7 " . . . *present fever*": *TJP*, 17:205–208.

7 *knew him by reputation:* For speculation of when Hamilton and Jefferson first met, see Dumas Malone, *Jefferson and the Rights of Man* (Boston: Little, Brown, 1951), 288.

8 *"consider the thing together":* The complete text of Jefferson's account of the bargain on the assumption of the debt and the location of the capital may be found at Founders Online, http://founders.archives.gov/documents /Jefferson/01-17-02-0018-0012.

9 *end with an agreement:* For information on this dinner, see Norman K. Risjord, "The Compromise of 1790: New Evidence on the Dinner Table Bargain," *William and Mary Quarterly*, 3rd ser., vol. 33, no. 2 (1976): 309–314.

9 *"Hamiltonopolis":* For a synopsis of the distrust of Hamilton, fear of concentrating financial power in New York, and the assumption of the debt and the location of the capital, see Ron Chernow, *Alexander Hamilton* (New York: Penguin, 2004), 325; Bowling, *Creation of Washington*, chaps. 6 and 7, esp. 178–187.

10 "... *found their graves there*": Alexander White from Virginia suffered from revulsions of stomach; Theodore Sedgwick from Massachusetts worried about going to his grave on the Potomac. Arnebeck, *Fiery Trial*, 23.

10 "... *never happen again*": Bowling, *Creation of Washington*, 189. In the House, Madison piloted his fragile bill past a Scylla and Charybdis of amendments proposed by delegates from North and South whose sole intention was to destroy it. On July 9, the day of the final vote, delegates made fifteen separate motions, including placing the capital in Baltimore or Germantown, or elsewhere on the Delaware or on the Susquehanna. The Residence Act passed 31 to 29. The final step took place on August 4, 1790, when, with Madison's help, Hamilton secured passage of his funding bill in the Congress.

10 *first Monday of December 1800:* American Memory, *Journal of the Senate of the United States of America, 1789–1793*, June 28, 1790; *Statutes at Large*, 1st Cong., 2nd sess., 130; Bowling, *Creation of Washington*, 185–195. The full name of the Residence Act was "An Act for Establishing the Temporary and Permanent Seat of the Government of the United States."

10 *to build a city: Statutes at Large*, 1st Cong., 2nd sess., 130.

11 "... *farewell for ever to the Potomac*": Arnebeck, *Fiery Trial*, 37.

11 *"Survey'd by me"*: See Donald Jackson and Dorothy Twohig, eds., *The Diaries of George Washington* (Charlottesville: University Press of Virginia, 1976), 1:17, for an image of the survey of Lawrence Washington's turnip field. Information about Washington as a surveyor may be found in Douglas Southall Freeman, *George Washington* (New York: Scribner, 1948–1957), 1:196–197, 210. Later, Washington acquired a compass from David Rittenhouse of Philadelphia, who was then the maker of the finest astronomical and surveying instruments. Most of my information about Washington comes from Freeman's biography and Rupert Hughes, *George Washington: The Human Being and the Hero, 1732–1762* (New York: William Morrow, 1926).

14 *piazza at Mount Vernon:* For an account of the Potomac's importance to Washington's conception of the future of the United States, see Joel Achenbach, *The Grand Idea: George Washington's Potomac and the Race to the West* (New York: Simon and Schuster, 2004).

14 "... *Grand Columbian Federal City*": See Allen C. Clark, "Origin of the Federal City," DCHS, *Records* 35/36 (1935): 26–27.

15 "... *Patowmac view the Federal City*": See Wilhelmus B. Bryan, *A History of the National Capital* (New York: Macmillan, 1914), 1:112.

15 "... *Seat of Empire*": TJP, 17:469–471; Bryan, *National Capital*, 1:109.

16 "... *Federal town and buildings*": March 2, 1791, *TJP*, 19:355.

16 *headstrong and fractious:* Bob Arnebeck, *Slave Labor in the Capital: Building Washington's Federal Landmarks* (Charleston, SC: History Press, 2014), 45.

17 *fought in the Maryland militia:* For information about Andrew Ellicott, see Catherine Van Cortlandt Mathews, *Andrew Ellicott: His Life and Letters* (New York: Grafteon Press, 1908); Bordewich, *Washington*, 66–79.

17 "... *art is susceptible*": Padover, ed., *Jefferson*, 40.

18 *assistant was Benjamin Banneker:* See Silvio A. Bedini, *The Life of Benjamin Banneker* (New York: Scribner, 1971); Charles A Cerami, *Benjamin Banneker: Surveyor, Astronomer, Publisher, Patriot* (New York: John Wiley and Sons, 2002); Bordewich, *Washington*, 66–71.

18 *heavens as never before:* Ellicott's zenith sector was reputedly the most accurate scientific instrument in America. The data Banneker collected would enable the surveyor to determine true north and fix the exact latitude of the new capital. To establish longitude, Banneker and Ellicott used a telescope to record the time of eclipse of one of Jupiter's satellites and compared their finding with similar measurements that had been made at the Greenwich Royal Observatory.

19 " . . . *stall-fed Ox*": Mathews, *Andrew Ellicott*, 89.

19 " . . . *unanimity of North America*": Kenton Neal Harper, *History of the Grand Lodge and of Freemasonry in the District of Columbia with Biographical Appendix* (Washington, DC: R. Beresford, 1911), 12.

19 " . . . *this day we have completed*": Ibid., 13.

20 " . . . *detested in others*": August 19, 1791, *TJP*, 22:49–52.

20 *realities of . . . political life in America:* Padover, ed., *Jefferson*, 42; Kite, *L'Enfant and Washington*, 35; Scott W. Berg, *Grand Avenues: The Story of the French Visionary Who Designed Washington, D.C.* (New York: Pantheon, 2007), chaps. 1 and 2.

21 *where the buildings should be placed:* Padover, ed., *Jefferson*, plate opposite p. 28; *TJP*, 17:462.

21 " . . . *heart of its laws and constitution*": Jefferson, *Notes of the State of Virginia*, Query XIX; Merrill D. Peterson, comp., *Thomas Jefferson, Writings* (New York: Library of America, 1984), 291.

21 " . . . *depravities of human nature*": H. A. Washington, ed., *The Writings of Thomas Jefferson* (New York: Riker, Thorne, 1854), 7:310.

21 " . . . *would be my choice*": September 23, 1800, *TJP*, 32:167.

22 " . . . *morals and happiness*": August 14, 1787, *TJP*, 12:38.

22 " . . . *preservative of morals*": Jefferson, *Notes of the State of Virginia*, 290.

23 *"bursting from a cloud":* *New-York Journal*, March 26, 1789, cited in Louis Torres, "Federal Hall Revisited," *Journal of the Society of Architectural Historians* 29, no. 4 (1970): 329. Republicans thought the building had a political dimension. It was too august, too Federalist, and its exorbitant cost made it a "Fool's Trap." Clinging to a hope that their city would become the new federal district, New Yorkers spared little expense on remodeling their City Hall for Congress.

23 *architect of the Federal Hall:* Congress had chosen L'Enfant to be part of a small group to "serve as assistants for the occasion," sit in the House chamber with the president, and walk before Washington's canary yellow carriage in the grand procession that preceded the ceremony. Surely this was a job for a hired hand, L'Enfant believed. He was an architect, no mere assistant. See the *New-York Daily Gazette*, May 1, 1789. While L'Enfant's plans for the Federal Hall were indeed extraordinary, the construction was wanting. Within a few years the building had to be demolished.

23 "*. . . permit it to pursue*": September 11, 1789, Kite, *L'Enfant and Washington*, 34.

24 "*. . . ought to be planned*": March 11, 1791, Padover, ed., *Jefferson*, 47; Kite, *L'Enfant and Washington*, 37.

24 "*. . . surrender for public purposes*": March 30, 1791, Washington, *Diaries*, 105.

24 *land that would become government property:* In some of the quotations readers will find a number of references to British currency, especially in the writings of the commissioners. In August 1792, Congress passed a Coinage Act resulting from Thomas Jefferson's proposal for a system based upon the Spanish milled dollar (a ten-dollar gold piece, a one-dollar silver piece, a tenth of a dollar in silver, and a hundredth of a dollar in copper). The British pound sterling continued to be used. The commissioners often referred to the pound (*£*) and guineas, which in the final years of the eighteenth century was set at 21 shillings (one pound, one shilling). Various reliable inflation calculators place the value of a pound in 1800 as the equivalent of $4.44, and a guinea at $4.66. In 2010, the value of a dollar in 1800 had increased to $13.75. From these figures we can extrapolate that £1 in 1800 has risen to $61.05. David Burnes and the other proprietors were to receive the equivalent of $2,775 for each acre they sold to the federal government.

24 *the men were successful:* Information about David Burnes, including his dealings with George Washington, comes from the Van Ness–Phillip Family Papers at the New-York Historical Society.

24 "*. . . barrel of corn per acre*": Arnebeck, *Fiery Trial*, 37.

25 *resist the president:* March 31, 1791, GWP-PS, 8:29.

25 "*. . . place the public buildings*": June 28, 1791, GWP, 6:164.

25 *worthy of the new republic:* The description, including quotations, comes from L'Enfant's report to Washington, printed in Kite, *L'Enfant and Washington*, 52–58.

25 *would connect the two buildings:* Arnebeck, *Fiery Trial*, 59–66.

27 *recognition for his work:* See Berg, *Grand Avenues*, 64–65.

27 "*. . . any restriction soever*": April 4, 1791, Padover, ed., *Jefferson*, 56–57; Kite, *L'Enfant and Washington*, 41–42.

27 "*. . . in such good hands*": April 10, 1791, Padover, ed., 59; Kite, *L'Enfant and Washington*, 49; Berg, *Grand Avenues*, 87. See Chapter 5 of *Grand Avenues* for Berg's thoughtful account of L'Enfant's relationship with Jefferson.

28 "*. . . credit of the property itself*": August 19, 1791, GWP-PS, 439–448.

28 "*was better qualified*": See C. M. Harris, "Washington's Gamble, L'Enfant's Dream: Politics, Design, and the Founding of the National Capital," *William and Mary Quarterly* 56 (1999): 546; Arnebeck, *Fiery Trial*, 74.

29 *have him dismissed:* See Padover, ed., *Jefferson*, 78–100, for the exchange of letters among Washington, Jefferson, the commissioners, and L'Enfant.

29 "*. . . beyond measure*": January 18, 1792, GWP-PS, 9:469.

29 "*. . . sale may commence*": January 17, 1792, GWP-PS, 9:452–467.

30 "*. . . must be at an end*": TJP, 23: 161.

30 "*. . . happiness and prosperity*": February 28, 1792, GWP-PS, 604–605.

30 *L'Enfant not at all: Universal Asylum and Columbian Magazine*, March 1792, 155–156.

31 *their map at last:* Bordewich, *Washington*, 87–88.

31 *proffered by James Monroe:* Jefferson to Commissioners, March 6, 1792, Padover, ed., *Jefferson*, 104, 116.

31 *cool rebuff: TJP*, 26:15.

31 " . . . *manner he subsists":* Benjamin Latrobe, *Journal, Travels in America* series (Carlisle, MA: Applewood Books, 2007), 178:133; Berg, *Grand Avenues*, 227.

31 " . . . *out at elboes":* Robert H. Elias and Eugene D. Finch, eds., *Letters of Thomas Attwood Digges* (Columbia: University of South Carolina Press, 1982), 588; see also William W. Warner, *At Peace with All Their Neighbors* (Georgetown, MD: Georgetown University Press, 1994), 16.

32 *mercantile North:* March 5, 1810, *TJP-RS*, 272.

32 *inducing the government to stay:* March 4, 1792, *GWP-PS*, 10:18.

32 " . . . *ensuing season":* March 6, 1792, *GWP-PS*, 10:27.

CHAPTER 2: PLANNERS, SPECULATORS, AND SLAVES

Sources for Chapter 2 include *TJP*; *GWP*; Gordon S. Brown, *Incidental Architect: William Thornton and the Cultural Life of Early Washington, D.C., 1794–1828* (Athens: Ohio University Press, 2009); William Seale, *The President's House* (Baltimore: Johns Hopkins University Press, 2008); Fergus M. Bordewich, *Washington: The Making of the American Capital* (New York: HarperCollins, 2008); Bob Arnebeck, *Through a Fiery Trial: Building Washington, 1790–1800* (Lanham, MD: Madison Books, 1991); Pamela Scott, *Temple of Liberty: Building the Capitol for a New Nation* (New York: Oxford University Press, 1995); William C. Allen, *History of the United States Capitol: A Chronicle of Design, Construction, and Politics* (Washington, DC: US Government Printing Office, 2001); Allen C. Clark, *Greenleaf and Law in the Federal City* (Washington, DC: W. F. Roberts, 1901); David McCullough, *John Adams* (New York: Simon and Schuster, 2001).

34 *few architects: GWP-PS*, 9:581.

34 *when building Mount Vernon:* For this discussion of Washington's architectural talents I have drawn from Robert F. Dalzell Jr. and Lee B. Dalzell, *George Washington's Mount Vernon* (New York: Oxford University Press, 1998). See, especially, Part I, "Landscapes of the Republic," 5–124; Allan Greenberg, *George Washington, Architect* (Newbury, UK: New Architecture Group, 1999).

34 *winning design of the President's House:* Seale, *President's House*, 1:27–37 (presents a good account of the competition, the selection of Hoban, and the laying of the cornerstone); Saul K. Padover, ed., *Thomas Jefferson and the National Capital* (Washington, DC: US Government Printing Office, 1946), 106.

35 *marked a beginning:* Seale, *President's House,* 1:36–37. The mystical Masonic ceremony, the exact place of the cornerstone and its whereabouts today, and the place of Freemasonry in the design of Washington have been the subject of numerous speculative works. Such conjectures about the purpose of Freemasonry and its codes and symbols, often connected to nefarious deeds, lie outside the author's purposes and the scope of this history.

35 *and twelve committee rooms:* See Padover, ed., *Jefferson,* 119–120; Ralph G. Giordano, *Architectural Ideology of Thomas Jefferson* (Jefferson, NC: McFarland, 2012), 128–131. In my discussion of the Capitol, I have drawn from Scott, *Temple of Liberty,* chaps. 1 and 2; Allen, *History of the United States Capitol,* 21.

36 "*. . . possessed of*": For Thornton's background, see Brown, *Incidental Architect,* 1–11.

36 "*. . . moderate in size*": February 1, 1793, *TJP,* 25:110.

36 *wondered after meeting with Thornton:* Julian Ursyn Niemcewicz, *Under Their Vine and Fig Tree,* trans. Metchie J. E. Budka (Elizabeth, NJ: Grassman, 1965), 77.

37 "*. . . expence and materials*" *of Thornton's plan:* January 31, 1793, *GWP-PS,* 12:71.

37 "*. . . too wide to support itself*": July 17, 1793, *TJP,* 26:517–520.

39 "*. . . other recreation*": For an account of the ceremony, see Charles Callahan, *Washington: The Man and the Mason* (Washington, DC: Gibson, 1998), 292.

40 *characterized it to the commissioners:* November 21, 1791, *TJP,* 23:311.

40 *urgency of a question mark:* March 21, 1792, *TJP,* 23:324.

41 "*. . . want of Cash*" *on the Charles:* April 20, 1792, *TJP,* 23:437–438; Padover, ed., *Jefferson,* 147.

41 *desperate they were for cash:* Broadside announcing the lottery in the Van Ness–Phillip Family Papers, New-York Historical Society. See also A. K. Sandoval-Strausz, *Hotel: An American History* (New Haven, CT: Yale University Press, 2007), 21. For more about Blodget, see Bordewich, *Washington,* 95–97, 153–155. At the same time Blodget created two more funding schemes: the Bank of Columbia and a tontine. He envisioned that when it was chartered by the state of Maryland, the bank would be capitalized by selling shares at $100 each, and the money would finance municipal and federal construction.

Blodget intended that those who subscribed to his tontine would be a friendly group of shareholders who would each pay $100 to purchase and improve building lots. As they died off, their shares would revert to the group until the number of those remaining equaled the number of building lots; then they would divide the spoils and dissolve the tontine.

Tontines were named for Lorenzo de Tonti, the seventeenth-century Neapolitan banker who invented the investment plan. They were far from unknown in the United States. Investors on New York City's Wall Street met daily at the Tontine Coffee House to buy and sell stocks. Blodget himself had already tried similar investment plans in Boston and Philadelphia but with indifferent results. His tontine for the capital would have the same end.

41 *large hole in the ground:* Arnebeck, *Fiery Trial*, 210.

41 *seldom seen in the city:* November 30, 1792, *GWP-PS*, 11:453.

41 "*. . . object from the beginning":* January 23, 1794, *GWP-PS*, 15:108.

43 *second scheme failed:* Arnebeck, *Fiery Trial*, 202–203.

44 *accept the terms:* August 20, 1793, *GWP-PS*, 13:508. Washington wrote: "I have reason to believe that if you can find it consistent with your duty to the public to attach Mr. Greenleaf to the Federal City, he will be a valuable acquisition." See Bordewich, *Washington*, 156–163; Clark, *Greenleaf and Law*, *passim*; Bob Arnebeck, "Tracking the Speculators," http://bobarnebeck .com/speculators.html.

44 *joining Greenleaf as partners:* The tale of Greenleaf, Nicholson, and Morris is a murky one. In *Greenleaf and Law*, Clark likens it to "a fabric so compactly and complexly woven as to be beyond finite skill to separate and sort the threads." See also Arnebeck, "Tracking the Speculators." Ryan K. Smith, *Robert Morris's Folly: The Architectural and Financial Failures of an American Founder* (New Haven, CT: Yale University Press, 2014), has valuable information on the trio. See, especially, chaps. 6, 7, and 8, 104–211. Robert Benchley's novel *Portrait of a Scoundrel* (Garden City, NY: Doubleday, 1979), presents an entertaining, though at times fanciful, account of Greenleaf's various schemes in Washington and Amsterdam.

45 *sold them on credit:* See William W. Warner, *At Peace with All Their Neighbors* (Georgetown, MD: Georgetown University Press, 1994), 172.

45 *his sister, to Washington:* William Cranch's marriage to Greenleaf's sister tells us much about the speculator's good fortune. Cranch was the nephew of John Adams, his first cousin, and Harvard classmate to John Quincy Adams. Trained in the law in Massachusetts, Cranch came to Washington as an agent for Morris, Greenleaf, and Nicholson. His activities in the capital included reporting on Supreme Court cases between 1801 and 1815; serving as commissioner of public buildings and judge on the District of Columbia Circuit Court; filling appointments he received from his uncle; and producing a draft legal code for the District in 1818, as formerly it had operated under those of Virginia and Maryland. Over time Cranch's service as a judge on the Circuit Court came to serve his brother-in-law well. See William Draper Lewis, ed., *Great American Lawyers* (Philadelphia: John C. Winston, 1907–1909), 3:87–119.

46 "*. . . he was concerned":* January 7, 1795, *GWP-PS*, 17:369–371.

46 "*. . . done to our satisfaction":* September 21, 1795. See Smith, *Robert Morris's Folly*, 134.

46 "*. . . so much money":* January 7, 1795, *GWP-PS*, 17:370.

46 *rising at the center of the nation:* For Thomas Law's background, see Clark, *Greenleaf and Law*, 233–244.

46 "*the New Jerusalem":* Arnebeck, *Fiery Trial*, 252.

46 "*. . . present of Washington City":* January 8, 1795, Clark, *Greenleaf and Law*, 101.

47 "... *vile treatment*": Arnebeck, *Fiery Trial*, 329.

47 *he knew better:* Smith, *Robert Morris's Folly*, 131.

47 *Morris lamented:* Ibid., 134.

47 *forms preprinted:* See Eleanor Young, *Forgotten Patriot, Robert Morris* (New York: Macmillan, 1950), 201.

48 "... *in every line*": Arnebeck, *Fiery Trial*, 455.

48 *filed against him:* Ibid., 242–244.

49 *agent, William Cranch:* Clark, *Greenleaf and Law*, 183–199.

49 *became the norm:* Arnebeck, *Fiery Trial*, 215.

49 "... *laborers here*": Ibid., 111; Padover, ed., *Jefferson*, 135.

49 *100 unmarried German stone masons:* Padover, ed., *Jefferson*, 142.

50 *including some stone carvers:* Arnebeck, *Fiery Trial*, 246.

50 "... *each a blanket*": Abby Gunn Baker, "The Erection of the White House," DCHS, *Records* 16 (1913): 131.

50 "... *Affairs Cool*": January 5, 1793, *TJP*, 25:25; Padover, ed., *Jefferson*, 166.

51 "... *completion of the building*": Arnebeck, *Fiery Trial*, 302–303.

51 "... *shared the earnings*": Niemcewicz, *Under Their Vine and Fig Tree*, 93.

51 *first school in the District:* Wilhelmus B. Bryan, *A History of the National Capital (New York: Macmillan, 1914)*, 1:260.

52 *tavern at Greenleaf's Point:* Arnebeck, *Fiery Trial*, 211; Clark, *Greenleaf and Law*, 277.

52 "... *work on one of them*": Thomas Twining, *Travels in America 100 Years Ago: Being Notes and Reminiscences* (New York: Harper and Brothers, 1894), 100; Bryan, *National Capital*, 1:272.

53 *largest employer in the city:* For information on Tingey, see Gordon Brown, *The Captain Who Burned His Ships: Captain Thomas Tingey, USN, 1750–1829* (Annapolis, MD: Naval Institute Press, 2011).

54 *looked down upon them:* See Washington's letter of March 19, 1798, *GWP-RS*, 2:148.

55 *Potomac in the 1790s:* Washington listed his slaves by first names—Nat, Isaac, Sambo, and Moses, among others.

55 *five shares for $250:* October 24, 1798, *GWP-RS*, 3:137, n. 2; see also 52–55.

56 "... *inveterate prejudices*": December 8, 1799, *GWP-RS*, 4:450.

56 *John Adams to the District of Columbia:* William V. Cox, comp., *Celebration of the One Hundredth Anniversary of the Establishment of the Seat of Government in the District of Columbia* (Washington, DC: US Government Printing Office, 1901), 248; A. R. Spofford, "Report of the Committee of the Columbia Historical Society upon the Removal of the Government to the District of Columbia in 1800," DCHS, *Records* 3 (1900): 257.

56 "... *protection of our country*": Address at the Union Tavern, June 4, 1800. See Hugh T. Taggart, "Presidential Journey in 1800 from the Old to the New Seat of Government," DCHS, *Records* 3 (1900): 194.

56 "... *Winter in the president's house*": John Adams to Abigail Adams, June 13, 1800, Charles Francis Adams, ed., *Letters of John Adams Addressed to His Wife* (Boston: Charles C. Little and James Brown, 1841), 2:266.

57 *"permanent seat of government":* Charles Francis Adams, ed., *The Works of John Adams, Second President of the United States* (Boston: Little, Brown, 1854), 9:233.

57 *". . . go on well":* John Adams to Abigail Adams, June 13, 1800.

57 *unfinished audience room: Letters of Mrs. Adams* (Boston: Wilkins, Carter, 1848), 282.

59 *". . . mud very deep":* John Cotton Smith, *Correspondence and Miscellanies* (New York: Harper and Brothers, 1847), 208.

60 *comfortable lodging:* Cited in Joseph B. Varnum Jr., *The Seat of Government of the United States* (Washington, DC: R. Varnum, 1854), 47.

60 *". . . without parallel":* Quoted from Wolcott's letter to wife, July 4, 1800, in Varnum, *Seat of Government,* 47.

61 *". . . self-government":* See *American Presidents: Farewell Messages to the Nation, 1796–2001* (Lanham, MD: Lexington, 2003), 32.

CHAPTER 3: "THE MOST AGREEABLE TOWN"

Sources for Chapter 3 include James Sterling Young, *The Washington Community, 1800–1828* (New York: Columbia University Press, 1966); Henry Adams, *History of the United States of America During the Administrations of Thomas Jefferson* and *History of the United States of America During the Administrations of James Madison* (New York: Library of America, 1986); Margaret Bayard Smith, *The First Forty Years of Washington Society,* ed. Galliard Hunt (New York: Charles Scribner's Sons, 1906); and the Margaret Bayard Smith Papers in the Library of Congress. See the Van Ness–Phillip Family Papers at the New-York Historical Society for background information about Washington in the War of 1812. Constance McLaughlin Green, *The Secret City: A History of Race Relations in the Nation's Capital* (Princeton, NJ: Princeton University Press, 1967), is useful for information about black life and the black codes in the capital.

63 *not to marry Samuel Harrison Smith:* Margaret's foster brother was James A. Bayard, the Delaware senator who agreed to allow the election of Thomas Jefferson, thereby blocking the election of Aaron Burr.

68 *from the turf:* See Allen C. Clark, "Doctor and Mrs. William Thornton," *DCHS, Records* 18 (1915): 144–208; Winslow Marston Watson, *In Memoriam: Benjamin Ogle Tayloe* (Washington, DC: Sherman, 1872), 100; "Dr. Mitchill's Letters from Washington: 1801–1813," *Harper's New Monthly Magazine* 58 (1879): 744; Gordon S. Brown, *Incidental Architect: William Thornton and the Cultural Life of Early Washington, D.C., 1794–1828* (Athens: Ohio University Press, 2009), 45.

69 *orderly way:* They were almost exclusively free blacks and slaves (Irish immigrants generally spurned such jobs).

70 *beneficiaries of this practice:* Jessie Carney Smith, *Notable Black American Women, Book 2* (Detroit: Gale Research, 1996), 624; Green, *Secret City,* 16, 24.

71 *building next door:* Margaret Bayard Smith to Mary Ann Smith, August 16, 1800, Margaret Bayard Smith Papers, LOC, vol. 6.

71 *"a truly good man":* Smith, *First Forty Years*, 6–8.

71 *single vote:* TJP, 33:148–152.

72 *". . . studious hours":* Smith, *First Forty Years*, 383–386.

72 *cubs from the far west:* See William Seale, *The President's House* (Baltimore: Johns Hopkins University Press, 2008), 1:92–96, for a portrait of Lewis, his explorations, and the artifacts that he shipped back to Washington.

73 *he was right:* Fawn M. Brodie, *Thomas Jefferson: An Intimate History* (New York: Norton, 1974), 413; Seale, *President's House*, 1:104–105; Adams, *Jefferson*, chap. 16, 546–566, gives a complete history of the Merry episode and a picture of Jefferson's style of entertainment.

73 *husband often received:* Smith, *First Forty Years*, 388–390.

73 *"pele-mele":* Seale, *President's House*, 1:105–106; Adams, *Jefferson*, 549.

73 *diplomatic protocol:* "Dr. Mitchill's Letters," 744. The physician, naturalist, and politician Samuel L. Mitchill served in the Congress as a representative (1801–1804) and senator (1804–1809) from New York. Jefferson called him the "Congressional Dictionary."

74 *". . . our chief magistrate":* *Baltimore American*, January 10, 1802. Jefferson accepted the cheese and several days later replied with a gift of his own for the preacher's good work, carefully recording in his account book, "Gave Rev'd Mr. Leland, bearer of the cheese of 1235 lbs weight, 200 D[ollars]." See *Edward S. Ellis, Thomas Jefferson: A Character Sketch* (Chicago, University Association, 1898), 77.

74 *". . . burr millstone":* "Dr. Mitchill's Letters," 744; see also C. A. Browne, "Elder John Leland and the Mammoth Cheshire Cheese," *Agricultural History* 18, no. 4 (1944): 145–153.

74 *". . . own nobility":* Smith, *First Forty Years*, 401.

74 *". . . show a foreign minister":* Augustus John Foster, *Jeffersonian America: Notes on the United States of Alexandria Collected in the Years 1805–6–7 and 11–12*, ed. Richard Beale Davis (Westport, CT: Greenwood, 1980), 22.

75 *his bluster:* It is a tribute to Jefferson that he and Thornton remained on good terms after the Board of Commissioners was dissolved. Thornton exchanged letters on scientific matters with the president, and he and his wife were frequent guests at Jefferson's table. See Brown, *Incidental Architect*, 30.

75 *threat of bankruptcy:* Information on Latrobe comes from Talbot Hamlin's *Benjamin Henry Latrobe* (New York: Oxford University Press, 1955), 140, 141, 174, 290.

75 *capital's public buildings:* William C. Allen, *History of the United States Capitol: A Chronicle of Design, Construction, and Politics* (Washington, DC: US Government Printing Office, 2001), 52.

76 *"personal attachment":* Seale, *President's House*, 1:113; Hamlin, *Benjamin Henry Latrobe*, 294

76 *wooden ones:* Seale, *President's House*, 1:112–114; Hamlin, *Benjamin Henry Latrobe*, 300–301.

76 *three sections of the Capitol:* For information about Jefferson, Latrobe, and the rebuilding of the Capitol see Hamlin, *Benjamin Henry Latrobe,* 258–296; Allen, *History of the United States Capitol,* chap. 2, esp. 52–53.

77 "*. . . gross inattention*": Cited in Quentin Scott King, *Henry Clay and the War of 1812* (Jefferson, NC: McFarland, 2014), 51.

77 "*. . . approbation and friendship*": February 27, 1804, Saul K. Padover, ed., *Thomas Jefferson and the National Capital* (Washington, DC: US Government Printing Office, 1946), 340–341.

77 "*. . . men of genius*": February 28, 1804, ibid., 342; *TJP.*

78 *as never before:* William Dunlap, *History of the Rise and Progress of the Arts of Design in the United States* (New York: Scott and Company, 1834), 1:336.

78 *Thornton guilty:* Allen, *History of the United States Capitol,* 95.

78 "*republicans at heart*": Ibid., 65.

80 "*. . . ought to be*": Thomas Moore, *The Complete Poetical Works* (New York: Thomas Y. Crowell, 1895), 146.

81 "*. . . civilized world*": Quoted from Frank B. Woodford, *Mr. Jefferson's Disciple: A Life of Justice Woodward* (East Lansing: Michigan State College Press, 1953), 27–28. Woodford's biography tells the life of an exceedingly strange man who stood out wherever he went. In 1805 Jefferson appointed Woodward chief justice of the Michigan Territory, where he helped to plan the city of Detroit and found the University of Michigan.

82 *rest of the country: Annals of Congress,* 6th Cong., 997–998, February 1801.

82 *ignored the affairs of the federal capital:* But not entirely. In January 1811, Representative Archibald Van Horne from Maryland, chair of the District of Columbia Committee, moved that his committee be instructed to "inquire into the expediency of establishing a government" for the District. Congress "could not or would not attend to the District," he argued, as the affairs of the nation took up their time. The motion failed.

82 *Carroll and Young families:* See James Dudley Morgan, "Robert Brent, First Mayor of Washington City," DCHS, *Records* 2 (1899): 236–251; Allen C. Clark, "The Mayoralty of Robert Brent," DCHS, *Records* 33/34 (1932): 267–305.

83 *with Alexandria, Virginia:* Owing to the scattered development, Washington did not suffer the devastating fires that consumed so many of the more densely populated cities in the nineteenth century. Information about the police comes from Kenneth G. Alfers, *Law and Order in the Capital City: A History of the Washington Police, 1800–1886, George Washington University Studies, no. 5* (Washington, DC: George Washington University Press, 1976), 5; and Richard Sylvester, *District of Columbia Police: A Retrospect of the Police Organizations of the Cities of Washington and Georgetown and the District of Columbia with Biographical Sketches, Illustrations, and Historic Cases* (Washington, DC: Gibson Brothers, 1894), 23. Unfortunately, the council's first superintendent appointment, John Willis, lasted less than a year because he failed to stop the petty thievery.

83 *first Black Codes:* Alfers, *Law and Order,* 6; Sylvester, *District of Columbia Police,* 24; Green, *Secret City,* 19.

84 " . . . *bondsmaid's arms*": "To The Lord Viscount Forbes," originally published in *Epistles, Odes, and Other Poems* (London, 1806), and in *Thomas Moore's Complete Poetical Works* (New York: Thomas Y. Crowell, 1895), 142–146. Dumas Malone recounts a story that the six-foot-two-inch Jefferson mistook the diminutive Moore for a boy, and that the poet composed these lines in revenge. But Moore, perhaps influenced by Merry and his wife, had a thorough dislike of all things democratic.

84 *New York and New England:* See *Annals of Congress*, 8th Cong., 995. Among those who voted against the resolution were Philip van Cortlandt, Killian K. Van Rensselaer, and Daniel C. Verplanck, whose families had held slaves in the Hudson River Valley.

84 *expanded Washington Navy Yard:* Much of the information about the Washington Navy Yard comes from Taylor Peck, *Round-Shot to Rockets: A History of the Washington Navy Yard and U.S. Naval Gun Factory* (Annapolis, MD: United States Naval Institute, 1949), 11–34.

85 *sure to go to Paradise:* TJP, 9:358; Kevin J. Hayes, "How Thomas Jefferson Read the Qur'ān," *Early American Literature* 39, no. 2 (2004): 256–257.

85 *thirsty men:* Constance McLaughlin Green, *Washington: Village and Capital, 1800–1878* (Princeton, NJ: Princeton University Press, 1962), 1:37.

85 *northeast of the city line:* The farm of about two hundred acres is now part of Catholic University. See Smith, *First Forty Years*, "Prefatory Note," by J. Henley Smith, ix.

85 *American State Papers:* The patronage didn't always come. William Duane, publisher of the Jeffersonian-friendly *Philadelphia Aurora*, sought and received a number of printing orders from the secretary of the treasury, Albert Gallatin. I am indebted to William E. Ames's excellent book *A History of the National Intelligencer* (Chapel Hill: University of North Carolina Press, 1972) for much of my information about the newspaper and Harrison Smith.

86 " . . . *at your feet*": Adams, *Madison*, 134. The phrase "cant of patriotism" was spoken by John Randolph.

87 *mouth of the Susquehanna:* Rear Admiral George Cockburn to Admiral J. B. Warren, April 29, 1813, in Nicholas Tracy, ed., *The Naval Chronicle: The Contemporary Record of the Royal Navy at War* (London: Chatham, 1999), 178.

87 " . . . *state of our country*": Smith, *First Forty Years*, 89.

87 *perfect target:* Adams, *Madison*, 998.

89 *national humiliation:* The story of Dolley Madison's departure from the White House on August 24, 1814, leaves us with a number of questions. As Catherine Allgor noted in *A Perfect Union: Dolly Madison and the Creation of the American Nation* (New York: Henry Holt, 2006), 1–5, there are embellishments. William Seale (*President's House*, 1:130–133) suggested there is much to question in this story of the Lansdowne portrait. It is certainly true that Dolley Madison ordered it to be cut out of the frame (which was screwed to the wall and proved difficult to remove). In "Dolley Madison Has the Last Word: The Famous Letter," *White House History* 4

(1998): 38–41, David B. Mattern wrote that "internal evidence suggests that Dolley Madison rewrote at least part of this letter—soon after the events or at a later date" (p. 39). Although she may well have revised her letter to embellish the facts, that does not alter the fundamental truth of Dolley's remarkable display of courage in the face of adversity when few around her showed any. And it is all the more remarkable because, as Seale wrote, "The British had boasted that they would exhibit her in the streets of London as a prisoner of war" (p. 131).

89 *labor of fourteen years:* See Peck, *Round-Shot to Rockets*, 47–68.

89 *medicine chest:* James Scott, *Recollections of a Naval Life* (London: Richard Bentley, 1834), 3:300–307. For information about Madison's medicine chest, see Betty C. Monkman, "Reminders of 1814," *White House History* 4 (1998): 33–34.

90 *". . . abuse my name":* See also Adams, *Madison*, 1015.

91 *flames rising from the Capitol and the White House:* Information about Ross and Cockburn comes from the *Oxford Dictionary of National Biography* online (www.oxforddnb.com).

92 *". . . followed by the Americans":* Smith, *First Forty Years*, 101, 115.

CHAPTER 4: REBUILDING AND GROWING

Sources for Chapter 4 include Henry Adams, *History of the United States of America During the Administrations of James Madison* (New York: Library of America, 1986) (for the political background); Margaret Bayard Smith, *First Forty Years of Washington Society*, ed. Galliard Hunt (New York: Charles Scribner's Sons, 1906) (for an account of everyday life among Washingtonians of means). William C. Allen, *History of the United States Capitol: A Chronicle of Design, Construction, and Politics* (Washington, DC: US Government Printing Office, 2001), and *Pamela Scott, Temple of Liberty: Building the Capitol for a New Nation* (New York: Oxford University Press, 1995), provide excellent accounts of the evolving structure of the Capitol.

93 *valiantly to secure:* General information about Lafayette's tour of the United States in 1824–1825 may be found in Auguste Levasseur's *Lafayette in America in 1824 and 1825* (Manchester, NH: Lafayette Press, 2006). Levasseur, who accompanied Lafayette on his tour, kept a lively and detailed journal of the general's thirteen months in America. In this edition it has been brilliantly translated by Alan R. Hoffman. See Levasseur's description of the city, 189–195. See also Stanley J. Idzerda, ed., *Lafayette, Hero of Two Worlds: The Art and Pageantry of His Farewell Tour of America, 1824–1825* (Hanover, NH: University Press of New England, 1989).

93 *". . . do their best":* See Edgar Ewing Brandon, *Lafayette, Guest of the Nation: A Contemporary Account of the "Triumphal Tour" of General Lafayette Through the United States in 1824–1825 as Reported by Local Newspapers* (Oxford, OH: Oxford Historical Press, 1957), 3:30. Brandon quotes the account of the *Washington Gazette*, October 15, 1824.

94 "... *emotions of gratitude*": Brandon, *Lafayette, Guest of the Nation*, 22.

94 *ashes of 1814:* The metaphor was a common one for writers of Washington history when describing the city after the War of 1812. Helen Nicolay titles the sixth chapter of *Our Capital on the Potomac* (New York: Century, 1924) "The Phoenix." Chapter 3 in Constance McLaughlin Green, *Washington: Village and Capital, 1800–1878* (Princeton, NJ: Princeton University Press, 1962), *is* titled "Phoenix on the Potomac."

95 *ready by 1815:* The Brick Capitol occupied the present site of the Supreme Court. See Harold H. Burton and Thomas E. Waggaman, "The Story of the Place: Where First and A Streets Formerly Met at What Is Now the Site of the Supreme Court Building," DCHS, *Records* 51/52 (1951/1952): 138–147.

95 *dollars to rebuild:* See Gordon S. Brown, *Incidental Architect: William Thornton and the Cultural Life of Early Washington, D.C., 1794–1828* (Athens: Ohio University Press, 2009), 80.

95 *Republicans joined them:* See Wilhelmus B. Bryan, *A History of the National Capital* (New York: Macmillan, 1914), 1:635.

95 "... *within the city*": Green, *Washington: Village and Capital*, 65; *Annals of Congress*, Senate, 13th Cong., 3rd sess., February 1815, 215–216.

95 *face other opponents:* Information about Latrobe's rebuilding of the Capitol comes largely from Talbot Hamlin, *Benjamin Henry Latrobe* (New York: Oxford University Press, 1955), chap. 18; Allen, *History of the United States Capitol*, chap. 3.

96 *churches and private houses:* The commissions weren't enough to keep Bulfinch free from debt, however. In July 1811, debts forced him to spend a month in a building of his own design, the Massachusetts State Prison.

96 *salary was reinstated:* Allen, *History of the United States Capitol*, 147.

97 "... *bear it patiently*": See ibid., 144–147 for an account of Bullfinch's experiences in the capital and the confusion about the drawings for the dome in 1842.

97 "... *for a century*": Levasseur, *Lafayette in America*, 189.

98 *ninth largest city in the United States:* Washington fell behind New York, Philadelphia, Baltimore, and Boston, but it was larger than any other southern city save New Orleans and Charleston.

98 *merited a city directory:* Quoted from a proposal that Delano circulated, available at Library of Congress, American Memory, at http://memory.loc .gov/ammem/index.html. All information that follows comes from Delano's *Washington Directory* (Washington, DC: William Duncan, 1822).

99 *Georgetown and Columbian: Washington Directory*, 130–135.

99 "... *with their companions*": See Robert Emmett Curran, *The Bicentennial History of Georgetown University: From Academy to University* (Washington, DC: Georgetown University Press, 1993), 13–15.

99 *"Prefects of Morals"*: Brandon, *Lafayette, Guest of the Nation*, 30–32.

100 "... *hand towards it*": See Washington's last will and testament, July 7, 1799. *The Papers of George Washington*, Theodore J. Crackel, ed. (Digital edition: http://rotunda.upress.virginia.edu/founders/GEWN.xqy).

101 *lobbied hard:* Law went so far as to write a treatise, "Observations on the Intended Canal in Washington City," that he had printed and distributed to Congress. See DCHS, *Records* 8 (1905): 158–167.

101 *complete construction in late 1815:* Information about the canal comes from Cornelius W. Heine, "The Washington City Canal," DCHS, *Records* 53/56 (1953/1956): 1–27.

102 *nemesis Benjamin Henry Latrobe:* Brown, *Incidental Architect,* 116–117.

103 *". . . giving to the poor":* *Daily National Intelligencer,* May 15, 1849.

103 *". . . in disposition":* George Alfred Townsend, "Thomas Law, Washington's First Rich Man," DCHS, *Records* 4 (1901): 229.

103 *died in 1802:* The slave was Oney Judge, a mulatto who attended Martha Washington. On learning that she was to be the Washingtons' wedding gift to Eliza and Thomas Law, she fled the president's house in Philadelphia and lived as a free black until her death in 1848 in New Hampshire.

103 *time to read them:* Margaret Bayard Smith to Mary Ann Smith, August 16, 1800, Margaret Bayard Smith Papers, LOC, vol. 6. Smith was not alone in her regard for Law. One story circulating the city at the time told of Law not being able to get his mail from the post office because he had forgotten his name.

103 *". . . retirement and males":* Townsend, "Thomas Law, Washington's First Rich Man," 230.

103 *steadfast supporter of the city:* Sources for John and Marcia Van Ness are the Van Ness–Phillip Family Papers at the New-York Historical Society; Allen C. Clark, "General John Peter Van Ness, a Mayor of the City of Washington, His Wife, Marcia, and Her Father, David Burnes," DCHS, *Records* 22 (1919): 125–204; Susan L. Klaus, "'Some of the Smartest Folks Here': The Van Nesses and Community Building in Early Washington," *Washington History* 3, no 2 (1991/1992): 22–45; Frances Carpenter Huntington, "The Heiress of Washington City: Marcia Burnes Van Ness, 1782–1832," DCHS, *Records* 69/70 (1969/1970): 80–101.

106 *". . . People would rule":* Smith, *First Forty Years,* 289–298.

106 *rumors continued:* H. W. Brands, *Andrew Jackson, His Life and Times* (New York: Doubleday, 2005), 423.

106 *"a noble stand":* Smith, *First Forty Years,* 288.

107 *1,400-pound cheese:* See *The Genesee Farmer and Gardener's Journal* 5, no. 42 (1835): 331.

107 *mob to eat it:* But Smith did fear the newfound democracy. In the same passage, she continued: "God grant that one day or other, the People, do not put down all rule and rulers. I fear, enlightened Freemen as they are, they will be found, as they have been found in all ages and countries where they get the Power in their hands, that of all tyrants, they are the most ferocious, cruel and despotic. The noisy and disorderly rabble in the President's House brought to my mind descriptions I had read, of the mobs in the Tuileries and at Versailles." Smith, *First Forty Years,* 296.

107 *" . . . they may be found":* Margaret Bayard Smith, *What Is Gentility? A Moral Tale* (Washington, DC: Pishey Thompson, 1828), 3.

107 *government moved to the Potomac:* See Murray H. Nelligan, "American Nationalism on Stage: The Plays of George Washington Parke Custis (1781–1857)," *Virginia Magazine of History and Biography* 58, no. 3 (1950): 299–313.

107 *" . . . cannot die in battle":* George Washington Parke Custis, *Recollections and Private Memoirs of Washington* (Washington, DC: William H. Moore, 1859), 67.

108 *Fillmore in the White House:* Robert J. Scary, *Millard Fillmore* (Jefferson, NC: McFarland, 2001), 67; Nicolay, *Our Capital on the Potomac,* 309–310.

108 *" . . . surprise his neighbors":* Frances Trollope, *Domestic Manners of the Americans* (London: Whittaker, Treacher, 1832), 189. By happy coincidence, that evening of the vomiting, the actor on stage was playing the part of a physician. He interrupted his lines to say, "I expect my services are wanted elsewhere."

109 *" . . . high historic interest":* Trollope, *Domestic Manners of the Americans,* 176.

109 *explanations of the city's government:* George Watterston, *A Picture of Washington* (Washington, DC: William M. Morrison, 1840).

110 *" . . . stomach to the sun":* Charles Dickens, *American Notes* (New York: John W. Lovell, n.d.), 30–31.

110 *" . . . and for pay":* Ibid., 698–699.

110 *his father's name:* Sources for James Smithson include Nina Burleigh, *The Stranger and the Statesman: James Smithson, John Quincy Adams, and the Making of America's Greatest Museum, The Smithsonian* (New York: William Morrow, 2003); Heather Ewing, *The Lost World of James Smithson: Science, Revolution, and the Birth of the Smithsonian* (London: Bloomsbury, 2007).

112 *Smithsonian's first secretary:* Michael I. Pupin, "Our Debt to Joseph Henry, Scientist," *American Scholar* 2, no. 2 (1933): 132–138.

113 *death in 1878:* Joseph Henry Papers Project, compilers, "Joseph Henry Quotations," Smithsonian Institution Archives, https://siarchives.si.edu/sites/default/files/pdfs/jhpp/JHP_Joseph_Henry_Quotations.pdf.

114 *his adopted city:* For Sessford's statistics, see "The Sessford Annals," DCHS, *Records* 11 (1908): 271–388.

115 *" . . . in steam coaches":* Rufus Rockwell Wilson, *Washington: The Capital City and Its Part in the History of the Nation,* vol. *1* (Philadelphia: J. B. Lippincott, 1902), 304.

116 *running feet of pavement:* "The Sessford Annals," 342–347.

CHAPTER 5: THE BIFURCATED SOUTHERN NATIONAL CITY

Sources for Chapter 5 include Helen Nicolay, *Our Capital on the Potomac* (New York: Century, 1924); Wilhelmus B. Bryan, *A History of the National Capital* (New York: Macmillan, 1914); Ada Sterling, ed., *A Belle of the Fifties: Memoirs of Mrs. Clay, of Alabama, Covering Social and Political Life in Washington and the South, 1853–1866* (New York: Doubleday, Page, 1904);

Constance McLaughlin Green, *Washington: Village and Capital, 1800–1878* (Princeton, NJ: Princeton University Press, 1962); Charles Capen McLaughlin, ed., *The Papers of Frederick Law Olmsted*, vol. 1, *The Formative Years, 1822–1852* (Baltimore: Johns Hopkins University Press, 1977); Charles Eliot Beveridge and Charles Capen McLaughlin, eds., *The Papers of Frederick Law Olmsted*, vol. 2, *Slavery and the South, 1852–1857* (Baltimore: Johns Hopkins University Press, 1977); Howard Gillette Jr., *Southern City, National Ambition: The Growth of Early Washington, D.C., 1800–1860* (Washington, DC: George Washington University Center for Washington Area Studies, 1995).

118 *impossible to attain:* Kirk Savage expresses much the same idea in "The Self-Made Monument: George Washington and the Fight to Erect a National Memorial," *Winterthur Portfolio* 22, no. 4 (1987): 226.

120 *new Treasury Building and the Patent Office:* Information for the Washington Monument comes from a variety of sources, including Savage, "The Self-Made Monument," 225–242; Rubil Morales-Vazquez, "Redeeming a Sacred Pledge: The Plans to Bury George Washington in the Nation's Capital," in Kenneth R. Bowling and Donald R. Kennon, eds., *Establishing Congress: The Removal to Washington, D.C., and the Election of 1800* (Athens: Ohio University Press, 2005), 148–189; Henry Van Brunt, "The Washington Monument," *American Art Review* 1, no. 1 (1879): 7–12; Louis Torres, *"To the Immortal Name and Memory of George Washington": The United States Army Corps of Engineers and the Construction of the Washington Monument* (Washington, DC: US Government Printing Office, c. 1984); John M. Bryan, *Robert Mills: America's First Architect* (New York: Princeton Architectural Press, 2001).

120 *enough to break ground:* "Concerning 'Martyrs' Day,'" published in *Mark Twain's Fables of Man*, John S. Tuckey, ed. (Berkeley: University of California Press, 1972), 304.

120 *". . . Egyptian architecture":* Writers have repeated the line often. See Morales-Vazquez, "Redeeming a Sacred Pledge," 182; Torres, *"To the Immortal Name,"* 13.

121 *". . . illustrious men":* Torres, *"To the Immortal Name,"* 14.

122 *appropriate Masonic ceremonies:* Ibid., 19–20.

122 *". . . Defend its Liberty":* Robert C. Winthrop, *Oration on the Occasion of Laying the Corner-Stone of the National Monument to the Memory of Washington* (Washington, DC: J. & G. S. Gideon, 1848), 23.

122 *contributed a stone:* Judith M. Jacob, *The Washington Monument: A Technical History and Catalog of the Commemorative Stones*, National Park Service, US Department of Interior, Northeast Region, Design, Construction, and Facility Management Directorate, Architectural Preservation Division, 2005, www.nps.gov/parkhistory/online_books/wamo/stones.pdf.

123 *Congress did nothing:* Torres, *"To the Immortal Name,"* 25–27.

123 *site in chaos:* See Washington Topham, "Northern Liberty Market," DCHS, *Records* 24 (1922): 49–50.

123 *hoped would become the Washington Mall:* John Muller, *Mark Twain in Washington, D.C.: The Adventures of a Capital Correspondent* (Charleston, SC: History Press, 2013), 72.

124 *architect of the Capitol extension:* For information on the competition, see William C. Allen, *History of the United States Capitol: A Chronicle of Design, Construction, and Politics* (Washington, DC: US Government Printing Office, 2001), 187–196. See chaps. 6–9 for an account of Walter's service in Washington.

127 *"... have to liberty":* Auguste Levasseur, *Lafayette in America in 1824 and 1825* (Manchester, NH: Lafayette Press, 2006), 243.

128 *"... all of Virginia":* Ibid., 264.

128 *"... hunt him up":* Robert F. Dalzell Jr. and Lee B. Dalzell, *George Washington's Mount Vernon* (New York: Oxford University Press, 1998), 134–136, and chap. 6 for information about Washington's slaves and overseers.

128 *"... fifteen, and seventeen":* Bob Arnebeck, *Through a Fiery Trial: Building Washington, 1790–1800* (Lanham, MD: Madison Books, 1991), 229.

129 *Africa's shores in 1822:* See Henry Noble Sherwood, "The Formation of the American Colonization Society," *Journal of Negro History* 2, no. 3 (1917): 209–228; Eric Burin, *Slavery and the Peculiar Solution: A History of the American Colonization Society* (Gainesville, FL: University Press of Florida, 2005); Delano's *Washington Directory* (Washington, DC: William Duncan, 1822) lists Bushrod Washington as president of the society; Henry Clay and Andrew Jackson as vice presidents; and Francis S. Key as one of the "Managers."

130 *"... any time in any place":* "Nat Turner's Insurrection," *Atlantic Monthly* 8 (1861): 186.

130 *attacked her with an axe:* For information about the attack on Anna Maria Thornton, see Bryan, *A History of the National Capital*, 2:143–146; Constance McLaughlin Green, *The Secret City: A History of Race Relations in the Nation's Capital* (Princeton, NJ: Princeton University Press, 1967), 36–37; Stephanie Cole, "Changes for Mrs. Thornton's Arthur: Patterns of Domestic Service in Washington, DC, 1800–1835," *Social Science History* 15, no. 3 (1991): 367–379; and especially Jefferson Morley, "The Snow Riot," *WP*, February 6, 2005. Morley's article, which he later expanded into a book, *Snow-Storm in August: The Struggle for American Freedom and Washington's Race Riot of 1835* (New York: Nan A. Talese, 2012), is the principal source of my account.

131 *off to Judiciary Square:* See Neil S. Kramer, "The Trial of Reuben Crandall," *DCHS, Records* 50 (1980): 123–139. Kramer points out (p. 130) that the punishment was stated in a code of laws for the District of Columbia that Congress considered in 1833 but did not approve before the end of the session. Nevertheless, Judge William Cranch employed the code.

132 *sentenced to be hanged:* As her mother passed herself off as a widow and a French schoolteacher, we cannot say for certain that Anna Thornton knew the fate of her father, who was hanged when she was a baby. Nor do we know the father of Arthur. His mother was a slave in the Thornton household, and he might well have been the son of William Thornton. We do

know that everyone, including Anna's mother, who lived with her daughter and son-in-law, spoiled the boy and treated him like a son. Arthur was educated, and judging from the letters from jail, he was a powerful writer.

133 *by the 1830s:* The background for much of this section comes from Green, *Secret City,* chap. 3.

133 *sold for profit:* Ethan Allen Andrews, *Slavery and the Domestic Slave Trade in the United States* (Boston: Light and Stearns, 1836), 148–149.

133 *east side of Lafayette Square:* Dolley Madison's finances are beyond the scope of this narrative, but they make for fascinating reading. Blinded by her love for her ne'er-do-well son, Payne Todd, she gave him thousands to invest; when he lost it all, she gave him more. Ultimately, friends like James Buchanan and Alexander H. Stephens arranged for Congress to purchase a trunk filled with Madison's papers for $25,000. They used $5,000 to pay off her debts and put what remained in a trust fund for her. John Jacob Astor picked up the $3,000 mortgage on her house and secured the return of silver and jewelry that she had pawned.

133 *"her people," as she called them:* Cited by Catherine Allgor, *A Perfect Union: Dolly Madison and the Creation of the American Nation* (New York: Henry Holt, 2006), 214.

134 *". . . sell such as are free":* Andrews, *Slavery and the Domestic Slave,* 181.

134 *". . . persons as runaways":* William Cranch, *Reports of Cases in the Circuit Court for the District of Columbia* (Boston: Little, Brown, 1852), 4:498; cited in Mary Tremain, *Slavery in the District of Columbia: The Policy of Congress and the Struggle for Abolition* (New York: G. P. Putnam's Sons, 1892), 46.

134 *free man once again:* Northup recounted his experience in *Twelve Years a Slave.*

135 *". . . droves of horses":* Abraham Lincoln, "Speech on Kansas-Nebraska Act at Peoria, Illinois," in *Speeches and Writings, 1832–1858* (New York: Library of America, 1989), 313.

135 *return on their investment:* For an account of such an arrangement, see John Hope Franklin and Loren Schweninger, *Runaway Slaves: Rebels on the Plantation* (New York: Oxford University Press, 2000), 142–143.

135 *defeated, and in this:* See Michael Burlingame, *Abraham Lincoln: A Life* (Baltimore: Johns Hopkins University Press, 2008), 1:286–289; John A. O'Brien, "Abraham Lincoln and D.C. Emancipation: Washington's Role in the American Year of Jubilee," paper presented at the 39th Annual Conference of D.C. Historical Studies, October 18–21, 2012, https://annualconferencedchistoricalstudies.files.wordpress.com/2012/10/obrien-historical-studies-conference-paper-10–12-final_abraham-lincoln-and-emancipation.pdf.

135 *". . . hunted slave is free":* William Wells Brown, *Clotel; or, The President's Daughter, A Narrative of Slave Life in the United States,* Ezra Greenspan, ed. (New York: Library of America, 2014 [1853]), 194. Lippincott published her poem under the pseudonym of Grace Greenwood.

136 *". . . capital of the Union":* Ibid., 190.

136 *". . . Congo of America":* *Letters and Speeches by Horace Mann* (Boston: B. B. Mussey, 1851), 6.

136 *". . . Potomac's tide":* "Lines Suggested by a Visit to the City of Washington in the 12th Month of 1845," *Poems of John Greenleaf Whittier* (Boston: James R. Osgood, 1878), 68.

137 *mile from Pennsylvania Avenue:* See Josephine F. Pacheco, *The Pearl: A Failed Slave Escape on the Potomac* (Chapel Hill: University of North Carolina Press, 2005); Stanley C. Harrold Jr., "The Pearl Affair: The Washington Riot of 1848," DCHS, *Records* 50 (1980): 140–160.

138 *newspaper National Era:* Harrold, "The Pearl Affair," 145.

139 *Stewart was $400:* Pacheco, *The Pearl,* 114.

139 *Washington's geography:* Much of the background information for Eastman Johnson's *Negro Life at the Old South* comes from John Davis's "Eastman Johnson's Negro Life at the Old South and Urban Slavery in Washington, D.C.," *Art Bulletin* 80, no. 1 (1998): 66–92.

141 *sold to the army:* See *Items of Interest: A Monthly Magazine of Dental Art, Science and Literature* 13 (1891): 443–444.

142 *". . . colonial general":* Elizabeth Lindsay Lomax, *Leaves from an Old Washington Diary, 1854–1863,* Lindsay Lomax Wood, ed. (New York: Dutton, 1943), 17–18.

142 *equestrian statue of the first president:* Lomax, *Leaves,* 83.

142 *". . . drawn at any moment":* Andrew Dixon White, *Autobiography* (New York: Century, 1905), 1:76. White later became the first president of Cornell University and had a distinguished career as a diplomat.

143 *upholding his honor:* See case 15,354a, reported in *The Federal Cases: Comprising Cases Argued and Determined in the Circuit and District Courts of the United States* (St. Paul, MI: West Publishing, 1896), 26:287–290.

143 *". . . no other side":* Carl Schurz, *Reminiscences: 1852–1863* (New York: McClure, 1906), 311–312. For the beating of Sumner and its aftermath, see Williamjames Hull Hoffer, *The Caning of Charles Sumner: Honor, Idealism, and the Origins of the Civil War* (Baltimore: Johns Hopkins University Press, 2010).

144 *put it delicately:* Lomax, *Leaves,* 96–97. See also Thomas Keneally, *American Scoundrel: The Life of the Notorious Civil War General Dan Sickles* (New York: Anchor Books, 2003).

144 *". . . Western and Northern abolitionists":* Lomax, *Leaves,* 108.

144 *". . . mercy on his soul":* Ibid., 111.

144 *". . . venerable as the Cross":* Ralph Waldo Emerson, *Emerson's Antislavery Writings,* ed. Len Gougeon and Joel Myerson (New Haven, CT: Yale University Press, 2002), 118–119.

144 *". . . such a disaster":* Lomax, *Leaves,* 132–133.

145 *"Perhaps . . . forever":* Ibid., 154.

CHAPTER 6: UNION NATIONAL CITY

Sources for Chapter 6 include Ulysses S. Grant, *Memoirs and Selected Letters* (New York: Library of America, 1990); Eric Foner, *Forever Free: The Story of Emancipation and Reconstruction* (New York: Knopf, 2005);

William Oliver Stevens, *Washington: The Cinderella City* (New York: Dodd, Mead, 1943); Kenneth J. Winkle, *Lincoln's Citadel: The Civil War in Washington, DC* (New York: W. W. Norton, 2013); Francine Curro Cary, *Urban Odyssey: A Multicultural History of Washington, D.C.* (Washington, DC: Smithsonian Institution Press, 1996).

147 "... *held by the National Army":* See Robert Chadwell Williams, *Horace Greeley: Champion of American Freedom* (New York: New York University Press, 2006), 221.

148 *Sixth Street and New Jersey Avenue:* William E. Baringer, *A House Dividing: Lincoln as President Elect* (Springfield, IL: Abraham Lincoln Association, 1945), 295.

148 *only when it was in session:* Wilhelmus B. Bryan, *A History of the National Capital* (New York: Macmillan, 1914), 2:295.

149 *granting any company a charter:* Congress did grant a charter for a horse-car line from the Capitol to Georgetown via Pennsylvania Avenue and Fifteenth Street, but the project failed. How different the scene in Washington must have seemed to Abraham Lincoln. Springfield, Illinois, counted 9,360 people for the 1860 census. Although it didn't have sewers, its streets were lit with gas lamps, and it was digging artesian wells for a city water supply.

149 "... *deserted Syrian city":* Henry Adams, *The Education of Henry Adams: An Autobiography* (Boston: Riverside Press, 1918), 44.

149 "... *sloughs for roads": Ibid.,* 99.

149 "... *state of incompleteness":* Henry Villard, *Memoirs* (Boston: Houghton, Mifflin, 1904), 1:289.

149 "... *indolence and sloth":* Ibid., 1:154.

151 "... *equal to the crisis":* Adams, *Education,* 106.

151 *take charge of the city's defenses:* Margaret Leech, *Reveille in Washington, 1860–1865* (New York: Harper and Brothers, 1941), 64–64.

152 "... *goodness be praised":* Burlingame, *Abraham Lincoln,* 61.

152 "... *and perpetual":* The words were spoken by Howell Cobb of Georgia, president of the Provisional Congress of the Confederate States at its convention in Montgomery, Alabama. See E. B. Long, *The Civil War Day by Day: An Almanac, 1861–1865* (Garden City, NY: Doubleday, 1971), 31.

153 "... *entire isolation":* Villard, *Memoirs,* 1:166.

153 *Confederate hands:* Leech, *Reveille,* 57–59.

153 "... *that severely":* Burlingame, *Abraham Lincoln,* 144; Lincoln, *The Collected Works of Abraham Lincoln,* ed. Marion Dolores Pratt (New Brunswick, NJ: Rutgers University Press, 1953–1955), 4:341–342.

153 "... *is a myth":* Villard, *Memoirs,* 1:170. It was John Hay who first recorded Lincoln's words, and there is some dispute about whether the president said, "I don't believe" or "I begin to believe." No matter which version is correct, it's clear Lincoln was in despair.

154 *foraged from farms:* Leech, *Reveille,* 66.

154 "... *time tomorrow":* William Howard Russell, *My Diary North and South* (New York: O. S. Felt, 1863), 448–449.

155 *". . . lined the road":* See John Howard Hinton, *History of the United States of America* (Boston: Samuel Walker, 1875), 278. Hinton's volume contains the correspondent's full report.

155 *". . . tramps and fugitives":* John G. Nicolay, *The Army in the Civil War* (New York: Charles Scribner's Sons, 1882), 207.

156 *Charles Sumner and John Brown:* Quoted from Julia Ward Howe's "Coquette et Froide" in *Passion Flowers* (Boston: Ticknor, Reed, and Fields, 1854), 117. Howe's play that so shocked Boston is *Leonora, or the World's Own.* It caused Oliver Wendell Holmes to write to his friend, "I don't know how so quiet a blend as yourself should have such tropical flashes of passion running through your veins." See also Mary H. Grant, *Private Woman, Public Person: An Account of the Life of Julia Ward Howe from 1819–1868* (New York: Carlson, 1994), 129–145; Louise Hall Tharp, *Three Saints and a Sinner* (Boston: Little, Brown, 1956), 240–245; Deborah Pickman Clifford, *Mine Eyes Have Seen the Glory: A Biography of Julia Ward Howe* (Boston: Little, Brown, 1979), 141–147; Laura E. Richards and Maud Howe Elliott, *Julia Ward Howe, 1819–1910* (Boston: Houghton Mifflin, 1916), 186–190.

156 *countenance of the first president:* Howe remembered her interview in her *Reminiscences* (Boston: Houghton Mifflin, 1899), 271–272.

156 *accompany the tune:* Ibid., 274–275.

157 *". . . mine heart":* Edmund Wilson makes this same point in his discussion of Howe in *Patriotic Gore* (New York: Oxford University Press, 1969), 91–98.

158 *election and inauguration:* Information for Corcoran comes from Holly Tank, "William Wilson Corcoran: Washington Philanthropist," *Washington History* 17, no. 1 (2005): 52–65; Henry Cohen, *Business and Politics in America from the Age of Jackson to the Civil War: The Career Biography of W. W. Corcoran* (Westport, CT: Greenwood, 1971); Mark L. Goldstein, "Washington and the Networks of W. W. Corcoran," paper presented at Business History Conference, 2007, www.thebhc.org/publications/BEHonline/2007/goldstein.pdf.

161 *". . . rights in peace":* Leech, *Reveille,* 25.

162 *". . . life in the Capital":* "An Iowa Woman in Washington, D.C., 1861–1865," *Iowa Journal of History* 52 (1954): 61.

162 *". . . houses and rooms":* Ibid., 62.

162 *commute by railroad:* See Bryan, *National Capital,* 2:544.

163 *". . . jest and dance":* "Iowa Woman in Washington," 61.

163 *". . . disloyal agitator":* Ibid., 65.

163 *"again and again":* About Mary Todd Lincoln's earrings, see *NYT,* July 24, 2011; about Lincoln's dreaming, see William Henry Herndon, *Herndon's Lincoln,* ed. Douglas L. Wilson (Urbana: University of Illinois Press, 2006), 376.

163 *". . . fair Secessionist":* "Iowa Woman in Washington," 62.

164 *". . . positive good":* Rose Greenhow, *My Imprisonment and the First Year of Abolition Rule at Washington* (London: Richard Bentley, 1863), 59.

165 *". . . more vehement than delicate":* Ibid., 169.

165 *named "Cyclops":* Ibid., 261.

166 " . . . *skillful spy*": See Ann Blackman, *Wild Rose: A Civil War Spy* (New York: Random House, 2005), 218.

167 " . . . *further delay*": Greenhow, *My Imprisonment*, 287.

167 " . . . *herself Mrs. Morris*": Ibid., 316.

168 *and a morgue*: Information about the Harewood estate (so called because William Wilson Corcoran found an abundance of hares on the land) may be found in United States Surgeon General's Office, *The Medical and Surgical History of the War of the Rebellion*, vol. 1 (Washington, DC: US Government Printing Office, 1888), part 3, 939–942.

168 " . . . *words of kindness*": "Iowa Woman in Washington," 72–74.

168 " . . . *sickness, and death*": Walt Whitman, *Specimen Days*, in *Complete Poetry and Collected Prose* (New York: Library of America, 1982), 737. Ted Genoways, *Walt Whitman and the Civil War: America's Poet During the Lost Years of 1860–1862* (Berkeley: University of California Press, 2009), is an excellent account of the poet's days in the capital.

169 " . . . *army of the wounded*": Walt Whitman first used the words "the great army of the sick" in an article for the *New York Times*, February 26, 1863. The word "sick" changed to "wounded" when R. M. Bucke, one of the poet's executors, published *The Wound Dresser* (Boston: Small, Maynard, 1897).

169 *would recover*: Whitman to Martha Whitman, January 2–4, 1863, in Edwin Haviland Miller, ed., *Walt Whitman: The Correspondence* (New York: New York University Press, 1961–1977), 1:62–64. Diarrhea affected 54 percent of the Union soldiers and 99 percent of the Confederate soldiers.

169 *needed most of all*: Whitman, *Specimen Days*, 714, 716, 726, 727.

170 " . . . *come quickly*": Whitman, *Specimen Days*, 714–715, 717–718; *Leaves of Grass, 1891–92; Drum Taps*; and "The Wound Dresser," 444, in *Complete Poetry and Collected Prose*.

170 " . . . *returned fourfold*": Whitman, *Specimen Days*, 730–731.

170 " . . . *bearded lips*": Whitman, *Leaves of Grass, 1891–92; Drum Taps*; and "The Wound Dresser," 445, in *Complete Poetry and Collected Prose*.

170 " . . . *generally supposed*": Whitman, *Specimen Days*, 727.

171 " . . . *rooms, & stables*": Ednah D. Cheney, *Louisa May Alcott: Her Life, Letters, and Journals* (Boston: Little, Brown, 1898), 143.

171 " . . . *dead house* ": Quoted from the US Sanitary Commission, *Documents of the U.S. Sanitary Commission*, 3 vols. (New York: n.p., 1866–1871), 1 Doc. No. 23. Found in John R. Brumgardt, *Civil War Nurse: The Diary and Letters of Hannah Ropes* (Knoxville: University of Tennessee Press, 1980), 40.

172 " . . . *desperately wounded*": Louisa May Alcott, *Civil War Hospital Sketches* (Mineola, NY: Dover, 2006), 20–21.

172 " . . . *sometimes a shroud*": Ibid., 32.

172 *cup of water*: Ibid., 28.

172 " . . . *on one leg*": Ibid., 17–18.

172 *"flat in the mud"*: Ibid., 52–53.

172 *model of sanitation:* Ibid., 50, 56–57.

173 *arrived to take her home:* See ibid., 70–73, for a brief account of her illness.

173 *to be fanatics:* For an account of Whitman's views on race and abolition-ism, see Roy Morris, *The Better Angel: Walt Whitman in the Civil War* (New York: Oxford University Press, 2000), 80–83.

173 *humor, and kindness:* Alcott, *Civil War,* 57–58.

173 *arrival of the Emancipation Proclamation:* Ibid., 59.

173 *abolitionists in Congress prevailed:* Constance McLaughlin Green, *The Secret City: A History of Race Relations in the Nation's Capital* (Princeton, NJ: Princeton University Press, 1967), 59.

174 *resented the proposal:* Although Congress actually appropriated $500,000 for relocation, no one said exactly where. Lincoln, who agreed with the plan, preferred a location in Chiriqui, Panama.

174 *". . . IT IS FREE":* Cited in Allen C. Guelzo, *Lincoln's Emancipation Proc-lamation: The End of Slavery in America* (New York: Simon and Schuster, 2004), 98.

174 *sell into the South:* The marshal was Abraham Lincoln's close friend and law partner, the hard-drinking, rough-mannered Ward Hill Lamon. Much to the consternation of abolitionists, whom he heartily disliked, Lamon insisted upon upholding the Fugitive Slave Law and loaded up the District Jail with escaped slaves. Some in the capital suggested that the marshal skimmed a handsome profit from the capture fees. Allen C. Guelzo dis-cusses contrabands, the Fugitive Slave Law, and Congress's Emancipation Proclamation for the District in *Lincoln's Emancipation Proclamation,* 81–89.

174 *"cobbing":* The practice entailed chaining a naked individual to a barrel face downward and striking him with a paddle "three feet long, six inches wide, and one inch thick."

175 *federal government in 1861:* Guelzo, *Lincoln's Emancipation Proclamation,* 91.

175 *". . . employ the people":* See *New York Times,* July 10, 1863; Report of D. B. Nichols, Superintendent of Freedmen. The story appeared first in the Wheeling, West Virginia, *Register* and was reprinted in the *New York Times* on April 6, 1887. Matthew Pinsker considers it in *Lincoln's Sanctu-ary: Abraham Lincoln and the Soldiers' Home* (New York: Oxford University Press, 2003), 163.

176 *". . . eight dollars per month":* Donald E. Press, "South of the Avenue: From Murder Bay to the Federal Triangle," DCHS, *Records* 51 (1984): 59.

177 *". . . ago is needed":* Whitman, *Specimen Days,* 732–734. For information about Lincoln and his trips to and from the Soldiers' Home, see Pinsker, *Lincoln's Sanctuary.*

177 *". . . welded together":* Whitman, *Leaves of Grass, 1891–92,* "Passage to India," 532, in *Complete Poetry and Collected Prose.*

178 *". . . standing upon it":* Cited by Pinsker in *Lincoln's Sanctuary,* 140; and Mark Leepson, *Desperate Engagement: How a Little-Known Civil War Battle Saved*

Washington, D.C., and Changed History (New York: St. Martin's Press, 2007), 203–204. Fort Stevens itself was a testament to the devastation war brings upon individuals. One of the many earthworks built in 1862 to protect the capital, the fort occupied the land that belonged to Elizabeth Thomas, a free black woman. By her account, one day soldiers began to tear down her house without notice as she sat under a sycamore tree watching the destruction. Then "a tall, slender man dressed in black came up and said to me, 'It is hard, but you shall reap a great reward.'" The man, of course, was Lincoln, but the great reward of financial compensation for the destruction of her house, and the return of her land, came to her family only after her death in 1917. See National Park Service, *Civil War Defenses of Washington Newsletter*, Summer 2011.

179 *no more that night:* Ward Hill Lamon, *Recollections of Abraham Lincoln, 1847–1865*, ed. Dorothy Lamon Teillard (Washington, DC: Published by the editor, 1911), 116–117; cited in Carl Sandburg, *Abraham Lincoln: The Prairie Years and the War Years* (New York: Harcourt, Brace, 1954), 698.

179 *cast-iron dome over the Capitol:* William C. Allen, *History of the United States Capitol: A Chronicle of Design, Construction, and Politics* (Washington, DC: US Government Printing Office, 2001), 314–335.

180 *march on the second:* Descriptions of the Grand Review are numerous. John McElroy has one in Marcus Benjamin, ed., *Washington During War Time: A Series of Papers Showing the Military, Political, and Social Phases During 1861 to 1865* (Washington, DC: Committee for the Thirty-sixth Annual Encampment, 1902), 97–106.

180 *all was ready:* Ward Thoron, ed., *Letters of Mrs. Henry Adams, 1858–1892* (Boston: Little, Brown, 1936), 5.

181 *Washington and Lincoln:* The number of forts protecting Washington from Confederate attack was closer to sixty-three; nevertheless, the capital was the most heavily fortified city in the world.

181 *". . . feel like crying":* Thoron, ed., *Letters of Mrs. Henry Adams*, 7.

181 *". . . decidedly the Potomac Army":* Ibid., 8.

182 *followed him still:* Ibid.

CHAPTER 7: THE MAKING OF AN UNDEMOCRATIC CITY

Sources for Chapter 7 include Eric Foner, *Forever Free: The Story of Emancipation and Reconstruction* (New York: Knopf, 2005); Kathryn Allamong Jacob, *Capital Elites: High Society in Washington, D.C., After the Civil War* (Washington, DC: Smithsonian Institution Press, 1995); Kathryn Allamong Jacob "'Like Moths to a Candle': The Nouveaux Riche Flock to Washington, 1870–1900," in Francine Curro Cary, *Urban Odyssey: A Multicultural History of Washington, D.C.* (Washington, DC: Smithsonian Institution Press, 1996); Joseph R. Passonneau, *Washington Through Two Centuries: A History in Maps and Images* (New York: Monacelli Press, 2004); American National Biography Online (www.anb.org).

183 " . . . *slope of the Atlantic*": L. U. Reavis, *A Change of National Empire; or, Arguments in Favor of the Removal of the National Capital from Washington City to the Mississippi Valley* (St. Louis: J. P. Torrey, 1869), 9.

184 " . . . *Father of Waters*": In 1866, when Reavis moved to St. Louis from Illinois to be the publisher of the *St. Louis Daily Press*, he immediately became a city booster. He continued to champion the idea long after others had abandoned it.

185 *leave the Potomac:* Some in Congress wanted to restore the original lines of the District of Columbia to include Alexandria and northern Virginia; that idea also died.

185 *connections between the city and the South:* Wilhelmus B. Bryan, *A History of the National Capital* (New York: Macmillan, 1914), 2:543–544; Constance McLaughlin Green, *Washington: Village and Capital, 1800–1878* (Princeton, NJ: Princeton University Press, 1962), 1:293.

185 *"highly improved":* John Y. Simon, ed., *The Papers of Ulysses S. Grant* (Carbondale: Southern Illinois University, 1967), 1:243.

185 *bill for removal:* Kenneth R. Bowling, "From Federal Town to National Capital: Ulysses S. Grant and the Reconstruction of Washington, D.C.," *Washington History* 14, no. 1 (2002): 8–25. Bowling's article presents an excellent discussion of Grant's interest and role.

185 " . . . *republic like ours*": Simon, *Grant Papers*, 21:95; also quoted in Bowling, "From Federal Town to National Capital," 15.

185 *went unanswered:* Simon, *Grant Papers*, 21:97.

186 *"the people's department":* Lincoln used the words in his Fourth Annual Message to Congress, December 6, 1864: "It is peculiarly the people's Department, in which they feel more directly concerned than in any other."

186 " . . . *were unsuitable*": Simon, *Grant Papers*, 21:96.

186 " . . . *it is national*": Mark Twain to Orion Clemens, March 27, 1875. See Michael B. Frank and Harriet Elinor Smith, eds., *Mark Twain's Letters* (Berkeley: University of California, 2002), 6:427.

188 " . . . *ought to wear them*": John A. Carpenter, *Sword and Olive Branch: Oliver Otis Howard* (New York: Fordham University Press, 1999), 24–25. See also Margaret S. Creighton, *The Colors of Courage: Gettysburg's Forgotten History. Immigrants, Women, and African Americans in the Civil War's Defining Battle* (New York: Basic Books, 2005), 179.

188 *blacks into American life: American National Biography Online*, anb.org, "Oliver Otis Howard."

188 *"Hercules' task":* Carpenter, *Sword and Olive Branch*, 83.

188 " . . . *government for white men*": Quoted in Hans L. Trefousse, *Andrew Johnson: A Biography* (New York: Norton, 1991), 236.

189 " . . . *Moses to the Negro*": Carpenter, *Sword and Olive Branch*, 212.

189 *33 percent:* The agent who persuaded former slaves to take jobs in the North was a remarkable abolitionist from Ohio, Josephine Griffing. For general information about the Freedmen's Bureau and living conditions for blacks in postbellum Washington, see Constance McLaughlin Green, *The Secret*

City: A History of Race Relations in the Nation's Capital (Princeton, NJ: Princeton University Press, 1967), chap. 5, esp. 81–85.

189 *making blacks landowners:* The name Anacostia is somewhat ambiguous. Strictly speaking, the name refers to a historic neighborhood east of the Anacostia River bounded by Good Hope Road, Sixteenth Street, and Mapleview.

189 *". . . refugees and freedmen":* From the Freedmen's Bureau Act, March 3, 1863. Cited in "Impeachment of the President," *Reports of Committees of the House of Representatives for the First Session of the Fortieth Congress* (Washington, DC: US Government Printing Office, 1868), 812.

190 *venture to the freedmen's schools:* Carpenter, *Sword and Olive Branch*, 113.

190 *larger community of Washington:* In all, the bureau would spend "over five million dollars for the education of the freedmen between 1865 and 1871" (Carpenter, *Sword and Olive Branch*, 159). Education for blacks proved easier to nurture in the capital than deeper in the South, where whites frequently burned freedmen's schools. Before the war, the literacy rate among free blacks in the District stood at about 42 percent. See Rayford W. Logan, *Howard University: The First Hundred Years, 1867–1967* (New York: New York University Press, 1969), 10; Walter Dyson, *The Founding of Howard University*, Howard University Studies in History, no. 1 (Washington, DC: Howard University Press, 1921).

191 *named Howard University:* The founders actually began with a goal of creating a theological seminary before refining their vision to the "Howard Normal Theological Institute for the Education of Teachers and Preachers," and later the "Howard Normal and Theological Institute," and finally settling on its present name. The change in a little more than two months represented, in the words of one historian of the institution, "one of the remarkable shifting of goals in America education." See Logan, *Howard University*, 14–18.

192 *they were encountered:* Ibid., 182–183.

192 *". . . affect the intellect":* Ibid., 181.

193 *". . . good man":* See W. E. B. Du Bois, *Black Reconstruction in America* (New York: Oxford University Press, 2007), 189.

193 *equality prevailed:* Further information for this section may be found in Alan Lessoff, *The Nation and Its City: Politics, "Corruption," and Progress in Washington, D.C., 1861–1902* (Baltimore: Johns Hopkins University Press, 1994); Green, *Secret City*, 75–81; Bryan, *National Capital*, 2:548–568.

194 *achieved little:* The mayor was Sayles J. Bowen. Opponents in the 1870 election created a rumor that Bowen had employed blacks to dig gutters with pen knives. The charge reinforced the idea that black workers had little capacity to do other work. See Lessoff, *The Nation and Its City*, 33–34, 41–42.

195 *". . . requires and demands":* Congressional Globe, Senate, 41st Cong., 3rd sess., January 24, 1871, 685; see also Lesoff, *The Nation and Its City*, 52–57.

195 *dawning for the capital:* See Green, *Washington: Village and Capital*, 338.

195 *"Justice for All":* For Alexander Robey Shepherd, see ibid., chap. 14, 339–362; William Tindall, "Sketch of Alexander Robey Shepherd," DCHS,

Records 14 (1911): 49–66; Elden E. Billings, "Alexander Robey Shepherd and His Unpublished Diaries and Correspondence," DCHS, *Records* 60/62 (1960/1962): 150–166; William M. Maury, "Alexander R. Shepherd and the Board of Public Works," DCHS, *Records* 71/72 (1971/1972): 394–410; William M. Maury, *Alexander "Boss" Shepherd and the Board of Public Works*, George Washington University Studies, no. 3 (Washington, DC: George Washington University Press, 1975); Lessoff, *The Nation and Its City*, chap. 3, "Energy and Engineering," 72–100; Henry M. Hyde, "The Man Who Made Washington," *American Mercury*, November 1931, 312–319.

197 *might cross:* See George Rothwell Brown, ed., *Reminiscences of Senator William M. Stewart of Nevada* (New York: Neale, 1908), 168. When Stewart arrived as Nevada's first senator in the winter of 1864–1865, he found "a sorry-looking city." He wrote that "the streets were cut up by great army wagons until they were nearly impassable. Hundreds of colored men carried boards around on their shoulders, and, for a consideration, assisted pedestrians to cross the 'thoroughfares,' and aided persons riding in carriages to reach the sidewalks when their vehicles mired down."

198 *soon be demolished:* See Washington Topham, "Northern Liberty Market," DCHS, *Records* 24 (1922): 54–55.

199 *". . . had to come down":* New York World, January 21, 1876.

200 *abuse of his property:* See Billings, "Alexander Robey Shepherd," 155.

200 *territory's financial problems:* See Hyde, "The Man Who Made Washington," 316–318.

200 *". . . appropriations from Congress":* Green, *Washington: Village and Capital*, 350.

202 *architect, Adolf Cluss:* See Alan Lessoff and Christof Mauch, eds., *Adolpf Cluss, Architect: From Germany to America* (Washington, DC: Historical Society of Washington, D.C., and Bergamot, 2005); Tanya Edwards Beauchamp, "Adolph Cluss: An Architect in Washington During Civil War and Reconstruction," DCHS, *Records* 71/72 (1971/1972): 338–358.

202 *taking shape:* Green, *Washington: Village and Capital*, 219–220; Francis R. Kowsky, "Gallaudet College: A High Victorian Campus," DCHS, *Records* 71/72 (1971/1972): 439–467; Brian H. Greenwald and John Vickrey Van Cleve, eds., *A Fair Chance in the Race of Life: The Role of Gallaudet University in Deaf History* (Washington, DC: Gallaudet University Press, 2002).

202 *"a disgrace to our people":* Report No. 48, *Report of Committees of the House of Representatives, Second Session of the Forty-second Congress* (Washington, DC: US Government Printing Office, 1872), 30. Information about the completion of the monument is abundant. Among the works that serve as background for this discussion are Frederick Loviad Harvey, *History of the Washington National Monument and of the Washington National Monument Society* (Washington, DC: Washington National Monument Society, 1902); Rubil Morales-Vazquez, "Redeeming a Sacred Pledge: The Plans to Bury George Washington in the Nation's Capital," in Kenneth R. Bowling and Donald R. Kennon, eds., *Establishing Congress: The Removal to Washington, D.C., and the Election of 1800* (Athens: Ohio University Press, 2005),

148–189; Richard Bing, "George Washington's Monument," *Constructor* 58 (1976): 18–25; Henry L. Abbot, "Memoir of Thomas Lincoln Casey, 1831–1896," 127–134, www.nasonline.org/publications/biographical-memoirs/memoir-pdfs/casey-thomas-l.pdf; Henry Van Brunt, "The Washington Monument," *American Art Review* 1, no. 1 (1879): 7–12; Louis Torres, *"To the Immortal Name and Memory of George Washington": The United States Army Corps of Engineers and the Construction of the Washington Monument* (Washington, DC: US Government Printing Office, c. 1984); John M. Bryan, *Robert Mills: America's First Architect* (New York: Princeton Architectural Press, 2001); Kirk Savage, *Monument Wars: Washington, D.C., the National Mall, and the Transformation of the Memorial Landscape* (Berkley: University of California Press, 2011).

203 *". . . completion of the Washington Monument":* Harvey, *History of the Washington National Monument*, 98; Torres, *"To the Immortal Name,"* 31.

203 *". . . completion without pain":* Van Brunt, "Washington Monument," 9.

203 *Washington at the top:* See ibid. for other proposed designs.

203 *monument fell to him:* For information about Casey's, see Torres, *"To the Immortal Name,"* 42ff; Abbot, "Memoir of Thomas Lincoln Casey."

204 *"the football of quacks":* Savage, *Monument Wars*, 113.

204 *rest on sand:* Torres, *"To the Immortal Name,"* 48.

204 *marble shaft:* Savage, *Monument Wars*, 116.

205 *proportions of the obelisk:* See Torres, *"To the Immortal Name,"* 55–56.

205 *"genuine chips":* WP, December 7, 1884.

207 *might become:* John Alexander Joyce, *A Checkered Life* (Chicago: S. P. Rounds, 1883), 148.

CHAPTER 8: GILDED NEIGHBORS, PROGRESSIVE CITY

Sources for Chapter 8 include Edward J. Renehan, *Dark Genius of Wall Street: The Misunderstood Life of Jay Gould, King of the Robber Barons* (New York: Basic Books, 2005); Lawrence Otis Graham, *The Senator and the Socialite: The True Story of America's First Black Dynasty* (New York: HarperCollins, 2006); Frederick Gutheim and Antoinette J. Lee, *Worthy of the Nation: Washington, DC, from L'Enfant to the National Capital Planning Commission* (Baltimore: Johns Hopkins University Press, 2006); Mona E. Dingle, *"Gemeinschaft und Gemütlichkeit:* German American Community and Culture, 1850–1920," in Francine Curro Cary, *Urban Odyssey: A Multicultural History of Washington, D.C.* (Washington, DC: Smithsonian Institution Press, 1996); David McCullough, *Mornings on Horseback: The Story of an Extraordinary Family, a Vanished Way of Life and the Unique Child Who Became Theodore Roosevelt* (New York: Simon and Schuster, 1982).

210 *". . . cities in the world":* The words from John Bunyan's *Pilgrim's Progress* were common to Washington writers of the time. See, for example, Mary S. Lockwood, *Historic Homes in Washington: Its Noted Men and Women* (New York: Belford, 1889), 254. Still others were ranking Washington with

the finest cities. See George Edward Raum, *A Tour Around the World* (New York: Ailliam S. Gottsberger, 1886), 399.

210 *newcomers of means:* WP, April 24, 1880; James M. Goode, *Best Addresses: A Century of Washington's Distinguished Apartment Houses* (Washington, DC: Smithsonian Institution Press, 1988), 8–10.

210 *arrive at Dupont Circle:* Russell R. Elliott, *The Servant of Power: A Political Biography of Senator William M. Stewart* (Reno: University of Nevada Press, 1983); William Morris Stewart, *Reminiscences* (New York: Neale, 1908); James M. Goode, *Capital Losses: A Cultural History of Washington's Destroyed Buildings* (Washington, DC: Smithsonian Institution Press, 1979), 77–79.

212 *ten cents per square foot:* See Stephen A. Hansen, *A History of Dupont Circle: Center of High Society in the Capital* (Charleston, SC: History Press, 2014), 31–34.

212 *extravagant structure:* Elliott, *Servant of Power*, 79.

212 *Massachusetts in 1882:* Hansen, *History of Dupont Circle*, 79–80.

212 *institutions and charities:* Ibid., 102–106.

213 *north of the circle:* Ibid., 114–120.

213 *vanished entirely:* Cornelius W. Heine, "The Washington City Canal," DCHS, *Records* 53/56 (1953/1956): 1–27.

213 *delivery wagons:* Information about Woodward comes from Merrill E. Gates, ed., *Men of Mark in America: Ideals of American Life Told in Biographies of Eminent Living Americans* (Washington, DC: Men of Mark Publishing, 1905), 417.

213 *on the mezzanine:* See Jan Whitaker, *Service and Style: How the American Department Store Fashioned the Middle Class* (New York: St. Martin's Press, 2006), 60, 113.

214 *summer frocks:* Martha C. Guilford, ed., *From Founders to Grandsons: The Story of Woodward and Lothrop*, Published in Commemoration of Its Seventy-Fifth Anniversary (Washington, DC: Darby Printing, 1955), 68.

214 *bargaining over every purchase:* Ibid., 43.

214 *playing cards:* Ibid., 70; Constance McLaughlin Green, *Washington: Capital City, 1879–1960* (Princeton, NJ: Princeton University Press, 1963), 33.

214 *beer annually:* See Candace Shireman, "The Rise of Christian Heurich and His Mansion," *Washington History* 5, no. 1 (1993): 4–27; Gary F. Heurich, "The Christian Heurich Brewing Company, 1872–1956," DCHS, *Records* 49 (1973/1974): 604–615; Milton Rubincam, "Mr. Christian Heurich and His Mansion," DCHS, *Records* 44 (1960/1962): 167–205.

216 " . . . *color of exterior*": See *James H. McGill's Architectural Advertiser: A Collection of Designs for Suburban Houses, Interspersed with Advertisements of Dealers in Building Supplies* (Washington, DC: n.p., 1880); "Le Droit Park: What Three Years Have Done," from the *National Republican* of September 4, 1876, reprinted at "Left for Le Droit," a blog about the neighborhood, http://leftforledroit.com/tag/james-h-mcgill/.

216 " . . . *government mapmaking*": Jerry Penry, "The Father of Government Mapmaking," *American Surveyor*, November 2007; WP, November 6, 1914.

217 *spirited it away:* WP, March 21, 1891.

217 *permanently removed:* WP, August 1, 1891.

217 *refused to sell it to them:* Mary Church Terrell, *A Colored Woman in a White World* (New York: G. K. Hall, 1996), 113–119.

218 *Sherman, the secretary of the treasury:* Goode, *Capital Losses,* 97–99.

218 *Trinidad asphalt:* Dan McNichol, *Paving the Way: Asphalt in America* (Lanham, MD: National Asphalt Pavement Association, 2005); I. B. Holley Jr., "Blacktop: How Asphalt Paving Came to the Urban United States," *Technology and Culture* 44, no. 4 (2003): 703–733; "The Roadways of the District," *WP,* October 9, 1881.

219 *distance races in Maryland and Virginia:* See David V. Herlihy, *Bicycle: The History* (New Haven, CT: Yale University Press, 2004), 182ff; *WP,* March 11, 1879, May 29, 1881, June 18, 1881, May 21, 1882, July 5, 1885, August 18, 1895, July 26, 1896.

220 "... *splendid a river":* Henry Adams, *The Education of Henry Adams: An Autobiography* (Boston: Riverside Press, 1918), 99; J. C. Levinson, ed., *Letters of Henry Adams* (Cambridge, MA: Harvard University Press, 1982–1988), 2:5.

220 "... *social organism":* Henry Adams to his brother Charles Adams, November 11, 1862, quoted in Elizabeth Stevenson, *Henry Adams: A Biography* (Livingston, NJ: Transaction, 1997), 11.

221 "... *stone age":* Adams, *Education,* 259–260.

221 "... *less than in 1868":* Stevenson, *Henry Adams,* 85.

221 *"a new Washington":* Adams, *Education,* chaps. 17 and 18, esp. 266, 268, 272.

222 "... *and botany":* Eugenia Kaledin, *The Education of Mrs. Henry Adams* (Philadelphia: Temple University Press, 1981), 39.

222 "... *quite independent":* Levinson, ed., *Letters of Henry Adams,* 2:133–134.

222 *"Lemonade Lucy":* Ibid., 2:276.

223 *American and English friends:* See Ward Thoron, ed., *First of Hearts: Selected Letters of Mrs. Henry Adams* (Boston: Atlantic Monthly Press, 2011), 26.

223 "... *capacity for more":* Levinson, ed., *Letters of Henry Adams,* 2:478.

223 *was not welcome:* Thoron, ed., *Letters of Mrs. Henry Adams,* 328, 333, 338. Clover was contemptuous of the Irishman, calling him at one point "Hosscar Wilde." Henry thought him "a tenth-rate cad."

223 *character of a national capital:* Levinson, ed., *Letters of Henry Adams,* 2:326.

224 *installed a weather station: Annual Report of the Chief Signal Officer to the Secretary of War for the Fiscal Year Ending June 30, 1881* (Washington, DC: US Government Printing Office, 1881), 186.

224 "... *work I please":* Levinson, ed., *Letters of Henry Adams,* 2:326.

224 "... *intelligent men":* Green, *Washington: Capital City,* 97–99.

224 *Committee on Admissions: The Twenty-fifth Anniversary of the Founding of the Cosmos Club* (Washington, DC: Cosmos Club, 1904), 40.

225 *Clarence King:* See Patricia O'Toole, *The Five of Hearts* (New York: C. Potter, 1990).

225 *Hay (twice):* Thoron, ed., *Letters of Mrs. Henry Adams,* 310.

226 "... *this social town":* Ibid., 278–279.

226 *author might be:* In the United States, only Clover, King, and the publisher knew; he also confided in one English friend.

226 *republic: Democracy:* For the quotations that follow, see Henry Adams, *Democracy, Esther, Mont Saint Michel and Chartres, The Education of Henry Adams* (New York: Library of America, 1983).

228 "*. . . Guiteau, and Blaine*": Levinson, ed., *Letters of Henry Adams,* 2:493.

228 *Guiteau to hang:* Thoron, ed., *Letters of Mrs. Henry Adams,* 310.

228 "*. . . idiocy, in the District Attorney*": Ernest Samuels, *Henry Adams* (Cambridge, MA: Harvard University Press, 1989), 168.

228 " *. . . I am so glad*": Charles E. Rosenberg, *The Trial of the Assassin Guiteau: Psychiatry and the Law in the Gilded Age* (Chicago: University of Chicago Press, 1968), 237.

228 "*. . . unless I must*": Levinson, ed., *Letters of Henry Adams,* 2:640.

229 "*. . . response of the observer*": Adams, *Education,* 329.

229 *sublime grace:* Over the years the holly trees that Adams planted around Saint-Gaudens's memorial filled in and grew tall, making it into a private grove, set apart from the rest of the graves. It was in the fall of 1918, the year Henry Adams died quietly in his bedroom on Lafayette Square, that Eleanor Roosevelt, who had often taken tea at his house, made frequent visits to Rock Creek. Invariably Eleanor drove herself in the Roosevelts' Stutz, from her house at 2131 R Street NW, to sit upon the angled bench while she considered the shattering revelation that her husband, Franklin, then assistant secretary of the navy, was having an affair with the woman who served as her social secretary. Sitting on the bench, she contemplated the mysterious figure and her own life. Eleanor Roosevelt's trips to the Adams monument continued after the shock of Franklin's infidelity passed. At 7:45 on the bleak morning of Saturday, March 4, 1933, the day of her husband's presidential inauguration, she and her companion Lorena Hickok took a cab from the Mayflower Hotel to Rock Creek Cemetery to sit before the figure that had so assuaged her pain fifteen years earlier. "In the old days," she told Hickok, "I was much younger and not so very wise, sometimes I would feel very sorry for myself. . . . [I]f I could manage, I'd come here alone, and sit and look at that woman. And I'd always come away somehow feeling better. And stronger. I've been here many, many times." See Lorena A. Hickok, *Eleanor Roosevelt: Reluctant First Lady* (New York: Dodd, Mead, 1962), 92.

230 *wilderness of the Rock Creek Valley:* Cornelius W. Heine, "The Contributions of Charles Carroll Glover and Other Citizens to the Development of the National Capital," DCHS, *Records* 53/56 (1953/1956): 229–248. Glover's Late Victorian three-story brick house with a hexagonal bay, now 734 Jackson Place NW, is still there. From 1911 to 1948, it served as the headquarters of the American Peace Society, and now as offices for the White House Council on Environmental Quality. It was declared a National Historic Landmark in 1974.

231 *shipped from California:* Green, *Washington: Capital City,* 20–21; *WP,* June 19, 1889.

232 *"miasma" in the air: WP,* September 16, 1881.

232 *poisoning him:* Garfield stayed at the White House until early September, when he was moved to the seaside resort of Elberon, New Jersey. He died there on September 19.

232 *painfully slow:* Green, *Washington: Capital City*, 44.

233 *signed the bill:* Heine, "Contributions of Charles Carroll Glover," 242.

234 ". . . *combined into one":* See Washington Board of Trade, *Second Annual Report* (Washington, DC: 1891), n.p. See Jessica I. Elfenbein, Howard Gillette Jr., and William H. Becker, *Civics, Commerce, and Community: The History of the Greater Washington Board of Trade* (Washington, DC: Center for Washington Area Studies, George Washington University, 1989), for valuable background information about the board.

234 ". . . *taxes upon it":* Green, *Washington: Capital City*, 25.

235 *"A Full Dinner Pail":* Margaret Leech, *In the Days of McKinley* (New York: Harper and Brothers, 1959), 544.

235 *"divine mission":* Congressional Record, Senate, 56th Cong., 1st sess., January 9, 1900, 712.

236 *shouted out the latest news:* WP, November 6, 1900.

236 *Edgewood in the northeast:* WP, December 23, 1900.

237 ". . . *heights of eloquence":* WP, December 19, 1900, December 3, 1900, December 6, 1900, December 15, 1900.

237 *anniversary as the capital of the United States:* William V. Cox, compiler, *Celebration of the One Hundredth Anniversary of the Establishment of the Seat of Government in the District of Columbia* (Washington, DC: US Government Printing Office, 1901); WP, February 22, 1900, December 5, 1900, December 8, 1900, December 13, 1900.

238 *water and sewers:* Green, *Washington: Capital City*, 45.

239 *yellow fever:* Green, *Secret City, 130.*

239 . . . *capacity for development":* See Benjamin R. Justesen, ed., *In His Own Words: The Writings, Speeches, and Letters of George Henry White* (Lincoln, NE: iUniverse, 2004), 113.

239 *Congress until 1972:* See Benjamin R. Justesen, "George Henry White and the End of an Era," *Washington History* 15, no. 2 (2003/2004): 34–51. Among North Carolinians who attacked the representative was Josepheus Daniels, editor of the *Raleigh News and Observer.* Daniels often used his editorial pages to describe White as a "nigger Congressman." The editor later became secretary of the navy in the Wilson administration.

239 ". . . *reelection of the President":* WP, December 3, 1900, December 24, 1900.

240 ". . . *madman and the Presidency":* Leech, *In the Days of McKinley*, 537.

241 *earned its place as the capital of the nation:* Quotations for this paragraph come from *Washington: Its Desirability as a Place of Residence and the Opportunities It Affords for Profitable Investment* (Washington, DC: Washington Board of Trade, 1899), n.p.

CHAPTER 9: L'ENFANT REDIVIVUS

Sources for Chapter 9 include Stacy A. Cordery, *Alice: Alice Roosevelt Longworth, from White House Princess to Washington Power Broker* (New York: Penguin, 2008); Edmund Morris, *Theodore Rex* (New York: Random House, 2001); Mark Sullivan, *Our Times*, vol. 1, *The Turn of the Century*

(New York: Scribners, 1926); Harold Evans, *The American Century* (New York: Knopf, 1998); American National Biography Online (www.anb.org); Frank Oppel and Tony Meisel, eds., *Washington, D.C.: A Turn-of-the-Century Treasury* (Secacus, NJ: Castle, 1987).

244 "... *worthily adorned*": *Scribner's Magazine* 21 (1897): 727. Spofford said of his library: "Not until I stand before the seat of God, do I ever expect this building transcended." Quoted from John Y. Cole and Henry Hope Reed, eds., *The Library of Congress: The Art and Architecture of the Thomas Jefferson Building* (New York: Norton, 1997), 66.

244 *monumental proportions:* John L. Smithmeyer and Paul J. Pelz, the building's architects, insisted that it be sited in such a way as to block off Pennsylvania Avenue and the view it afforded of the Capitol. Like so many other architects in the capital, Smithmeyer and Pelz had an unhappy experience with those who employed them, and the press portrayed them as incompetent. Soon they were eclipsed by Thomas L. Casey and his son Edward. Another builder, Bernard Green, oversaw the construction. See Cole and Reed, eds., *Library of Congress,* 49–51.

244 *Capitol and the White House:* Laura Wood Roper, *FLO: A Biography of Frederick Law Olmsted* (Baltimore: Johns Hopkins University Press, 1973), 348, 373–378.

245 "... *federal bond*": Charles E. Beveridge, Carolyn F. Hoffman, and Kenneth Hawkins, eds., *The Papers of Frederick Law Olmsted* (Baltimore: Johns Hopkins University Press, 2007), 7:36.

246 "... *boldly forward*": Ibid., 7:37–43.

247 *gardener's shed:* James M. Goode, *Capital Losses: A Cultural History of Washington's Destroyed Buildings* (Washington, DC: Smithsonian Institution Press, 1979), 325–326; *WP,* July 1, 1979. The treehouse was removed to Arlington in 1932, and later burned. As Goode noted, the structure was named to honor John Willcock Noble, who "pushed for passage of a law to preserve millions of acres of western forests owned by the federal government. . . . [A] giant sequoia tree named in his honor for this act of preservation of natural resources was cut down and publicly exhibited for forty years, and later burned as refuse."

248 *bridge to Arlington:* Bingham had a tempestuous career. See John W. Reps, *Monumental Washington: The Planning and Development of the Capital City* (Princeton, NJ: Princeton University Press, 1967), 76–78, and William Seale, *The President's House* (Baltimore: Johns Hopkins University Press, 2008), 1:609–620, 674–675. Bingham was a West Point graduate, an engineer, and from 1897–1901, superintendent of the Office of Buildings and Grounds in the capital. He later became police commissioner in New York City, where he ruled with an iron hand until his dismissal in 1909.

248 *arbiter of aesthetics:* For James McMillan and the plan for Washington, see Charles Moore, *Daniel H. Burnham: Architect, Planner of Cities* (Boston: Houghton Mifflin, 1921); John W. Reps, *Monumental Washington;* Thomas S. Hines, *Burnham of Chicago: Architect and Planner* (New York:

Oxford University Press, 1974); Geoffrey G. Drutchas, "Gray Eminence in a Gilded Age: The Forgotten Career of Senator James McMillan of Michigan," *Michigan Historical Review* 28 (2002): 78–113; Alan Lessoff, *The Nation and Its City: Politics, "Corruption," and Progress in Washington, D.C., 1861–1902* (Baltimore: Johns Hopkins University Press, 1994), 253–260; John A Peterson, "The Senate Park Commission Plan for Washington, D.C.," in Sue Kohler and Pamela Scott, eds., *Designing the Nation's Capital: The 1901 Plan for Washington, D.C.* (Washington, DC: US Commission of Fine Arts, 2006), electronic edition, www.nps.gov/parkhistory/online _books/ncr/designing-capital/index.html.

249 *stature to Charles Moore:* See Thomas E. Luebke, ed., *A Centennial History of the U.S. Commission of Fine Arts* (Washington, DC: US Commission on Fine Arts, 2013); Alan Lessoff, "The Early Career of Charles Moore," *Washington History* 6 (1994–1995): 64–80.

250 *executive secretary, Glenn Brown:* See William Bushong, *The Centennial History of the Washington Chapter AIA, 1887–1987* (Washington, DC: Architectural Foundation Press, 1987); Tony P. Wrenn, "The American Institute of Architects Convention of 1900: Its Influence on the Senate Park Commission Plan," in Kohler and Scott, *Designing the Nation's Capital*, 49–73.

250 "... *and Statuary":* Wrenn, "American Institute of Architects Convention, 57.

251 "... *Park system of the District of Columbia":* Charles Moore, ed., *The Improvement of the Park System of the District of Columbia: Report of the District of Columbia* (Washington, DC: US Government Printing Office, 1902), 7.

252 "... *minds could conceive":* Quoted by Hines, *Burnham of Chicago*, 143.

252 *served without pay:* The total expenditures that the commissioners incurred was likely far more.

252 "... *best we can give":* Moore, *Daniel H. Burnham*, 1:143.

254 *tunnel under Capitol Hill:* See Reps, *Monumental Washington*, 98–99. Reps speculates that Cassatt perhaps shared the artistic sensibilities of his sister, the artist Mary Cassatt, and "realized the potential beauty of the Mall if once freed from the baneful effects of the railroad." There can be no doubt that Cassatt often combined his capitalist instincts with his highly developed aesthetic taste. He employed some of the leading architects to design his stations: Burnham for Pittsburgh and Washington; Kenneth Murchison for Baltimore; and McKim for New York.

255 *bursting into official meetings:* Seale, *President's House*, 1:622.

255 "... *president is about six":* David Henry Burton, *Cecil Spring Rice: A Diplomat's Life* (Carnbury, NJ: Associated University Presses, 1990), 56.

255 *official name: WP*, October 11, 1901.

255 "... *highly appreciative":* Moore, *Daniel H. Burnham*, 1:167.

256 *swings for children:* Moore, *Improvement of the Park System*, 49.

256 *"great memorial":* Ibid., 50.

256 *Riverside Drive to Rock Creek Park:* Ibid., 51.

257 *". . . pride in the Capital":* In "The Art of City Making," *Architectural Record* 12 (1902): 25.

258 PARTING GUEST: Charles William Eliot, *Inscriptions over Pavilion Union Station, Washington, D.C.* (pamphlet issued by the Washington Terminal Company, n.d.).

259 *present location:* See Glenn Brown, *Memories: A Winning Crusade to Revive George Washington's Vision of a Capital City* (Washington, DC: W. F. Roberts, 1931), 150; *WP,* March 19, 1905.

259 *". . . still predominant":* "The New Washington," *Scribner's Magazine* 51, no. 2 (1912): 129.

260 *Daughters of 1812: WP,* October 19, 1910.

261 *". . . modern improvements":* WP, January 30, 1903.

262 *took it seriously:* Constance McLaughlin Green, *Washington: Capital City, 1879–1960* (Princeton, NJ: Princeton University Press, 1963), 175.

262 *Washington's civic life:* For Shad: *WP,* May 17, 1903; May 22, 1904; May 14, 1905; May 13, 1906; May 21, 1910; May 26, 1912; April 6, 1913, among others. For Board of Trade, see Jessica I. Elfenbein, Howard Gillette Jr., and William H. Becker, *Civics, Commerce, and Community: The History of the Greater Washington Board of Trade* (Washington, DC: Center for Washington Area Studies, George Washington University, 1989).

263 *rival his in Cambridge: Boston Daily Advertiser,* August 9, 1873; Charles W. Eliot, *A National University,* Report to the National Education Association, August 5, 1873 (Cambridge, MA: Charles W. Sever, 1874); David L. Madsen, "The University of the United States: A Durable Dream," *Journal of Higher Education* 33, no. 7 (1962): 353–360.

263 *ballot for president of the United States:* See Jill Norgren and Belva Lockwood, *The Woman Who Would Be President* (New York: New York University Press, 2007).

263 *into the twentieth:* See Elmer Louis Kayser, *Bricks Without Straw: The Evolution of George Washington University* (New York: Appleton-Century-Crofts, 1970).

264 *into insolvency: WP,* April 28, 1910.

264 *place as the national university:* Karin M. E. Alexis, "The American University: Classical Visions of the National University," DCHS, *Records* 52 (1989): 163–182.

265 *closing years of the century:* See Robert Emmett Curran, *The Bicentennial History of Georgetown University: From Academy to University* (Washington, DC: Georgetown University Press, 1993), chaps. 10 and 11; George Hardy, "Georgetown University's Healy Building," *Journal of the Society of Architectural Historians* 31, no. 3 (1972): 208–216.

265 *"equal to any in the country":* Curran, *Bicentennial History,* 281.

266 *undergraduate curriculum:* See ibid., 332–333.

266 *design of a century earlier:* Michael R Harrison, "The 'Evil of Misfit Subdivisions': Creating the Permanent System of Highways of the District of Columbia," *Washington History* 14, no. 1 (2002): 26–55 (Part 1); Green, *Washington: Capital City,* 134.

267 *suburban transformation:* See Michael R. Harrison, "Above the Boundary: The Development of Kalorama and Washington Heights, 1872–1900," *Washington History* 14, no. 2 (2002/2003): 56–69 (Part 2); Mary Mitchell, "Kalorama: Country Estate to Washington Mayfair," DCHS, *Records* 71/72 (1971/1972): 164–189.

267 *definition of the land:* Donald Beekman Myer, *Bridges and the City of Washington* (Washington, DC: Commission of Fine Arts, 1974), 68–69.

268 *dining room:* James M. Goode, *Best Addresses: A Century of Washington's Distinguished Apartment Houses* (Washington, DC: Smithsonian Institution Press, 1988), 43–46.

268 *and at Fifteenth and L, among other locations:* WP, February 19, 1901, May 2, 1901, October 13, 1901.

269 *across the landscape:* NYT, March 26, 1909, May 23, 1911; WP, March 26, 1909, April 23, 1909, April 27, 1911; *Los Angeles Times*, April 29, 1909.

CHAPTER 10: WASHINGTON APARTHEID AND THE END OF INNOCENCE

Sources for Chapter 10 include Frederick Lewis Allen, *The Big Change: America Transforms Itself, 1900–1950* (New York: Harper and Brothers, 1952); Louis Auchincloss, *Woodrow Wilson* (New York: Penguin, 2000); August Heckscher, *Woodrow Wilson* (New York: Schibner, 1991); John M. Barry, *The Great Influenza: The Epic Story of the Deadliest Plague in History* (New York: Viking, 2004); Melvin I Urofsky, *Louis D. Brandeis and the Progressive Tradition* (Boston: Little, Brown, 1981); Harold Evans, *The American Century* (New York: Knopf, 1998); American National Biography Online (www.anb.org).

271 "*. . . put out of school*": *Atlantic Monthly* 87, no. 6 (1901).

272 *even today:* See John Milton Cooper, *Woodrow Wilson: A Biography* (New York: Knopf, 2009); John Lukacs, *A New Republic* (New Haven, CT: Yale University Press, 2004), 221–225. Lukacs makes the case that a number of twentieth-century presidents—Hoover, Roosevelt, Nixon, and Reagan—were Wilsonian.

272 *interests of their race:* Cooper, *Woodrow Wilson*, 171.

272 *room at the Post Office Department:* Constance McLaughlin Green, *The Secret City: A History of Race Relations in the Nation's Capital* (Princeton, NJ: Princeton University Press, 1967), 171–178. Wilson had invited Booker T. Washington to his inauguration at Princeton in 1902, but over the objections of Ellen Wilson's family. Ellen's aunt declared that "if she had known he was to be there she wouldn't have gone." Cooper, *Woodrow Wilson*, 80.

272 "*. . . best for the service*": E. David Cronon, ed., *The Cabinet Diaries of Josephus Daniels, 1913–1921* (Lincoln: University of Nebraska Press, 1963), 32–33. The postmaster general was Albert S. Burleson.

273 *more intimidating:* See Kathleen L. Wolgemuth, "Wilson's Appointment

Policy and the Negro," *Journal of Southern History* 24, no. 4 (1958): 457–471; Kathleen L. Wolgemuth, "Woodrow Wilson and Federal Segregation," *Journal of Negro History* 44, no. 2 (1959): 158–173; Nancy J. Weiss, "The Negro and the New Freedom: Fighting Wilsonian Segregation," *Political Science Quarterly* 84, no. 1 (1969): 61–79.

274 *professors from Howard:* See Elizabeth McHenry, *Forgotten Readers: Recovering the Lost History of African American Literary Societies* (Durham, NC: Duke University Press, 2002), chap. 3.

274 *would have none of it:* Chester A. Arthur appointed Blanche Kelso Bruce in 1881; he served until 1885, when Grover Cleveland appointed a white man. In 1897, William McKinley reappointed Bruce, and Roosevelt and Taft followed.

275 "*. . . further consideration*": Patterson's letter is dated July 30, 1913. See *The Papers of Woodrow Wilson*, 28:97–98.

275 *Jim Crowism: NYT,* May 4, 1913; *The Crisis,* August 1914, 198; *Washington Bee,* December 20, 1913.

276 "*. . . terribly true*": According to John Hope Franklin, "Wilson vigorously denied that he had ever expressed an opinion about the film. He asked his secretary to convey this fact to Mrs. Walter Damrosch who had inquired of the President's views (Wilson to Joseph Tumulty, March 29, 1915)." See "*Birth of a Nation:* Propaganda as History," *Massachusetts Review* 20, no. 3 (1979): 417–434, n. 12.

276 *Pierce Arrow automobile:* Louis Brownlow, *A Passion for Anonymity* (Chicago: University of Chicago Press, 1958), 27.

276 *reporter for United Press:* Oliver P. Newman covered Wilson's 1912 campaign for United Press and after the election vacationed with him in Bermuda. Newman is generally given credit for suggesting that Wilson create the press conference. Siddons's law degrees were from Columbian College.

277 *behind in the twentieth:* Brownlow, *Passion for Anonymity,* 3–4, 39–40.

278 *embassy on Connecticut Avenue and N Street:* Ibid., 44–55.

278 *smuggled into the Capitol: WP,* July 5, 1915. The bomber, Eric Muenter, who also attempted to murder J. P. Morgan, was captured; later he committed suicide.

278 "*. . . colored people of Washington*": *WP,* January 1, 1916; January 4, 1916; April 28, 1916; May 22, 1916.

278 *Selective Service Act:* Brownlow, *Passion for Anonymity.*

279 *sale of alcohol:* See Daniel Okrent, *Last Call: The Rise and Fall of Prohibition* (New York: Scribner, 2011); Garrett Peck, *Prohibition in Washington, D.C.: How Dry We Weren't* (Charleston, SC: History Press, 2011).

279 *German Americans, without work: WP,* March 1, 1917; October 29, 1917; November 1, 1917. The *Washington Post* also reported "1,000 Negroes Out of Jobs Through New Dry Law," October 31, 1917.

280 *Anglicized their surnames:* Frank H. Pierce III, *The Washington Saengerbund: A History of German Song and German Culture in the Nation's Capital* (Washington, DC: Washington Saengerbund, 1981), 64–70.

280 *Wilson's future wife:* Gary F. Heurich, "The Christian Heurich Brewing Company, 1872–1956," DCHS, *Records* 49 (1973/1974): 609.

281 *run the auction: WP,* April 30, 1918, May 12, 1918, May 25, 1918; *Christian Science Monitor,* April 30, 1918, May 20, 1918.

281 "... *all reckoning":* J. C. Levinson, ed., *Letters of Henry Adams* (Cambridge, MA: Harvard University Press, 1982–1988), 6:779–779.

282 *office tenement:* See *Main Navy Building: Its Construction and Original Occupants,* n.d., Navy Department Library, www.history.navy.mil/library /online/main_navy_bldg.htm.

283 *pumps operating:* Brownlow, *Passion for Anonymity,* 68–69.

283 *new government workers: WP,* January 17, 1918.

283 "*to the utmost":* Harriot Stanton Blatch, *Mobilizing Woman-power* (New York: Women's Press, 1918), 5, 7.

284 "... *for a profession":* Levinson, ed., *Letters of Henry Adams,* 6:780.

284 "... *men patients":* Lettie Gavin, *American Women in World War 1: They Also Served* (Niwot: University Press of Colorado, 1997), 110. Gavin quotes an unpublished memoir, "The Great Adventure," of occupational therapist Lena Hitchcock.

284 *sanitary home care:* Gavin, *American Women in World War 1,* 202.

284 *new life in Washington:* See Margaret Thomas Bucholz, *Josephine: From Washington Working Girl to Fisherman's Wife* (West Creek, NJ: Down the Shore Publishing, 2012).

284 "*flying colors":* Ibid., 15.

284 "... *double pay for overtime":* Ibid., 21.

284 "... *just about anything":* Ibid., 25.

284 *seemed like a dorm mother:* Ibid., 20.

285 *glad to be in Washington:* Ibid., 22, 25, 37–40.

286 *brakeman on the Pennsylvania Railroad: WP,* September 22, 1918; *WS,* September 21, 1918.

286 *incubator for the virus:* See Brownlow, *Passion for Anonymity,* 69–73.

286 "... *victims died": WP,* October 24, 1965.

286 *stricken, had died:* Brownlow, *Passion for Anonymity,* 73.

287 *hearth with her family:* There were actually two groups: the Democratic National Committee created the Women's National Democratic League, and Wilson created the Women's National Wilson and Marshall Organization (Thomas Marshall was Wilson's running mate). See Jo Freeman, *We Will Be Heard: Women's Struggles for Political Power in the United States* (Lanham, MD: Rowman and Littlefield, 2008), 60–65.

287 "... *mothers of our country": NYT,* May 10, 1914.

287 *Alice Paul come to Washington:* See Sidney R. Bland, "New Life in an Old Movement: Alice Paul and the Great Suffrage Parade of 1913 in Washington, D.C.," DCHS, *Records* 71/72 (1971/1972): 657–678; Sally Hunter Graham, "Woodrow Wilson, Alice Paul, and the Women Suffrage Movement," *Political Science Quarterly* 98, no. 4 (1983–1984), 665–679; Christine A. Lunardini, *From Equal Suffrage to Equal Rights: Alice Paul and the*

National Woman's Party, 1910–1928 (New York: New York University Press, 1986).

287 *Charity, and Hope:* Bland, "New Life in an Old Movement," 663; *WP,* January 20, 1913. The parade was to be led by Inez Milholland, a Vassar graduate whom the *Washington Post* called "the most beautiful girl in the suffrage movement." The idea of beauty was never far from the minds of the reporters, who repeatedly described the women as "the fair sex." Louis Brownlow presents a very different view of the suffragettes. See Brownlow, *Passion for Anonymity,* 74–82.

288 "... *with the rioters*": *NYT,* March 5, 1913.

288 *returning to the picket lines: NYT,* July 19, 1917.

289 "... *to the lockup*": Bucholz, *Josephine,* 31.

289 *stories of ill treatment:* "Photograph of Suffragist with 'Kaiser Wilson' Poster," Record Group 165, Records of the War Department General and Special Staff, National Archives and Records Administration, www.archives.gov/global-pages/larger-image.html?i=/education/lessons /woman-suffrage/images/kaiser-wilson-1.gif&c=/education/lessons/woman -suffrage/images/kaiser-wilson.caption.html.

290 *question of suffrage:* Graham, "Woodrow Wilson, Alice Paul," 677.

290 *Nineteenth Amendment before state legislatures:* See ibid., 678, for an outline of these events.

290 "... *learn the lesson*": See Wilson's message dated September 30, 1918, in *Supplement to the Messages and Papers of the Presidents: Covering the Second Term of Woodrow Wilson,* March 4, 1917, to March 4, 1921 (Washington, DC: Bureau of National Literature, 1921), 8601.

291 *fair treatment:* Green, *Secret City,* 184–188.

292 *"Red Summer":* See ibid., 189–199; David F. Krugler, "A Mob in Uniform: Soldiers and Civilians in Washington's Red Summer, 1919," *Washington History* 21 (2009): 48–77; *WP,* July 20, 22, 23, 1918, among others. Several of the stories describe assaults and discuss citizens purchasing guns. George E. Haynes, "The Darkest Cloud," *Survey,* August 2, 1919, 675–676; George E. Haynes, "Race Riots in Relation to Democracy," *Survey,* August 9, 1919, 697–699. Among the most perceptive observers at the time, Haynes reported that a prominent Washington black was overheard to say in Brownlow's office, "I am beginning to realize that the prize of manhood for the American Negro requires the sacrifice of life."

294 *amendment granting suffrage: WP,* February 22, 1918.

295 *leaders deflected:* For Wilson's flirtation, see Cooper, *Woodrow Wilson,* 565–569.

CHAPTER 11: NORMALCY AND NEGLECT

Sources for Chapter 11 include Frederick Lewis Allen, *Only Yesterday: An Informal History of the 1920s* (New York: John Wiley, 1997); John W. Dean, *Warren G. Harding* (New York: Times Books, 2004); Phillip G. Payne,

Dead Last: The Public Memory of Warren G. Harding's Scandalous Legacy (Athens: Ohio University Press, 2009); Robert K. Murray, *The Harding Era: Warren G. Harding and His Administration* (Minneapolis: University of Minnesota Press, 1969); Francis Russell, *The Shadow of Blooming Grove: Warren G. Harding in His Times* (New York: McGraw-Hill, 1968); David Greenberg, *Calvin Coolidge* (New York: Times Books, 2006); Faith Berry, *Langston Hughes: Before and Beyond Harlem* (Westport, CT: L. Hill, 1983); Harvey G. Cohen, *Duke Ellington's America* (Chicago: University of Chicago Press, 2010); Hedrick Smith and Stanley Nelson, *Duke Ellington's Washington* [videorecording] (Princeton, NJ: Films for the Humanities and Sciences, 2004); Barbara Foley, "Jean Toomer's Washington and the Politics of Class: From 'Blue Veins' to Seventh-Street Rebels," *Modern Fiction Studies* 42 (1996): 289–321.

297 *himself, understood:* The word's meaning was confined to mathematics until Harding said, on May 14, 1920, "America's present need is not heroics but healing; not nostrums but normalcy; not revolution but restoration."

297 *passing in August 1923:* Alice Roosevelt Longworth, *Crowded Hours* (New York: C. Scribner's Sons, 1935), 325.

298 "*. . . Mr. Harding came in*": Edward G. Lowry, *Washington Close Ups: Intimate Views of Some Public Figures* (Boston: Houghton Mifflin, 1921), 11, 14; *WP*, March 11, 1921, May 14, 1921, May 19, 1921, January 31, 1922.

298 *dedication of the Lincoln Memorial:* See Christopher A. Thomas, *The Lincoln Memorial and American Life* (Princeton, NJ: Princeton University Press, 2002); Kirk Savage, *Monument Wars: Washington, D.C., the National Mall, and the Transformation of the Memorial Landscape* (Berkley: University of California Press, 2011).

298 *suppliant slave:* Melissa Dabakis, "Sculpting Lincoln: Vinnie Ream, Sarah Fisher Ames, and the Equal Rights Movement," *American Art* 22, no. 1 (2008): 78–101.

299 *pantheon of America:* See Scott Sandage, "A Marble House Divided: The Lincoln Memorial, the Civil Rights Movement, and the Politics of Memory, 1939–1963," *Journal of American History* 80, no. 1 (1993): 135–167.

299 *even with Richmond:* In *The Lincoln Memorial*, 31–32, 52–54, Thomas discusses the connections between the good roads movement, which was trying to construct the coast-to-coast Lincoln Highway, and the effort to build the memorial.

299 "*. . . damned swamp*": Howard Gillette, *Between Justice and Beauty: Race, Planning, and the Failure of Urban Policy in Washington, D.C.* (Philadelphia: University of Pennsylvania Press, 2006), 106.

299 *supporters of the McMillan Plan to the commission:* Quoted from Sue A. Kohler, *The Commission of Fine Arts: A Brief History, 1910–1995* (Washington, DC: The Commission, 1996), 4.

300 "*. . . brain of the citizen*": Thomas, *Lincoln Memorial*, 59, 62–63.

301 "*the Nation's savior*," *NYT*, May 31, 1922; Thomas, *Lincoln Memorial*, 155–157.

301 "*union and security*": *NYT*, May 31, 1922; *WP*, May 31, 1922.

302 *enclosure for blacks:* Constance McLaughlin Green, *The Secret City: A History of Race Relations in the Nation's Capital* (Princeton, NJ: Princeton University Press, 1967), 199.

302 " . . . *become victorious":* For a text of Moton's speech, see Harold Holzer, ed., *The Lincoln Anthology: Great Writers on His Legacy from 1860 to Now* (New York: Library of America, 2009), 428–434; *Chicago Defended,* June 10, 1922.

303 *Harding's side:* Longworth, *Crowded Hours,* 324.

303 *sybaritic Evalyn and Ned McLean:* For Harding and the McLeans, see Evalyn Walsh McLean, *Father Struck It Rich* (Boston: Little, Brown, 1936); Carl Sferrazza Anthony, *Florence Harding: The First Lady, the Jazz Age, and the Death of America's Most Scandalous President* (New York: William Morrow, 1998).

303 *tray of martinis:* Shirley Povich's reminiscence is in *WP,* May 11, 1948. Povich served as McLean's caddie in Bar Harbor, Maine.

304 *characterize his presidency:* Anthony, *Florence Harding,* 487–489.

304 *Plymouth Notch, Vermont:* See Donald R. McCoy, *Calvin Coolidge: The Quiet President* (New York: Macmillan, 1967).

304 *"assassins of character":* Allen, *Only Yesterday,* 116.

305 *master to the office:* Calvin Coolidge, *Autobiography* (New York: Cosmopolitan Book Corporation, 1929), 221. More information about the president's menagerie may be found on the website of the Calvin Coolidge Presidential Foundation, http://coolidgefoundation.org.

307 *District's commissioners carefully:* The reappointment of two commissioners, Cuno Hugo Rudolph and James Frederick Oyster, met with some controversy in the Senate over Rudolph's ownership of stock in his hardware and brick company. *WP,* March 9, 1924; March 26, 1924; April 9, 1924; April 10, 1924.

308 " . . . *justice demands":* Frank Hendrick, ed., *Republicanism of Nineteen-twenty* (Albany, NY: Albany Evening Journal, 1920), 164.

309 " . . . *opportunity for both": Address of the President of the United States at the Celebration of the Semicentennial of the Founding of the City of Birmingham, Alabama,* October 26, 1921 (Washington, DC: US Government Printing Office, 1921), 7–8. But Harding also said in his best foggy rhetoric: "It would be helpful to have the word 'equality' eliminated from this consideration; to have it accepted on both sides that this is not a question of social equality, but a question of recognizing a fundamental, eternal, and inescapable difference."

309 " . . . *hideous crime of lynching":* "Annual Message to Congress," December 6, 1923, in The American Presidency Project, University of California at Santa Barbara. www.presidency.ucsb.edu/ws/?pid=29564.

309 *across the Mall from the White House:* Only by the efforts of a courageous representative from Illinois were the barriers at Rock Creek Park and the Potomac removed. See Green, *Secret City,* 201.

310 " . . . *great Lord of Hosts": WP,* December 21, 1922.

310 *crypt beneath the Capitol . . . and Navy Building: New-York Tribune,* November 25, 1922, 6 (from Library of Congress, Chronicling America: Historic

American Newspapers, p. 6, image 6, http://chroniclingamerica.loc.gov/lccn /sn83030214/1922-11-25/ed-1/seq-6/).

310 *permission . . . could not be denied:* For accounts of the Klan march, see Constance McLaughlin Green, *Washington: Capital City, 1879–1960* (Princeton, NJ: Princeton University Press, 1963), 327. Green observed, "No white newspaper suggested any impropriety in permitting a formal gathering of the Klan in the capital." See also *NYT,* June 22, 27, 28, 1925, July 8, 1925, August 6, 7, 8, 10, 1925; *WP,* July 28, 31, 1925, August 4, 5, 6, 7, 8, 9, 10, 1925; *Chicago Defender,* January 3, 1925, July 25, 1925.

313 *evening in August 1925:* See Blair A. Ruble, *Washington's U Street: A Biography* (Washington, DC: Woodrow Wilson Center Press; Baltimore: Johns Hopkins University Press, 2010); Green, *Secret City,* 205–214.

314 *apart and silent:* Green, *Secret City,* 202–203.

315 *campus in the 1920s:* See Richard I. McKinney, "Mordecai Johnson: An Early Pillar of African-American Higher Education," *Journal of Blacks in Higher Education* 27 (2000): 99–104.

315 *". . . admiration of the world":* Rayford W. Logan, *Howard University: The First Hundred Years, 1867–1967* (New York: New York University Press, 1969), 218.

315 *Native America Drama:* Durkee forced Gregory's resignation in 1924.

316 *"honor to be associated:"* The Musolit Club met at 1327 R Street. See Ronald M. Johnson, "Those Who Stayed: Washington Black Writers of the 1920's," DCHS, *Records* 50 (1980): 484–499.

316 *professionals from around the country:* One member of Musolit was Robert R. Taylor, the MIT-trained architect who designed most of the buildings on the Tuskegee campus.

317 *Harlem Renaissance:* Gloria T. Hull, *Color, Sex and Poetry: Three Women Writers of the Harlem Renaissance* (Bloomington: Indiana University Press, 1987), 6–8.

317 *". . . people strolled":* Pearl Bailey, *The Raw Pearl* (New York: Harcourt Brace, 1968), 5.

317 *". . . dependent on him":* *WP,* July 16, 1903. Roosevelt wrote: "No one can watch with more interest than I do the progress of the colored race; and with the colored man as with the white man, the first step must be to show his ability to take care of himself and those dependent on him."

318 *complete the building in 1912:* Green, *Secret City,* 170, 179; *WP,* December 14, 1953.

318 *design for the Twelfth Street Y:* For information about Pittman, see Ruth Ann Stewart, *Portia: The Life of Portia Washington Pittman, the Daughter of Booker T. Washington* (Garden City, NY: Doubleday, 1977), 72–80.

318 *successful entrepreneurs: Washington Tribune,* May 21, 1921, 1.

319 *weren't married:* See Jane Freundel Levey, "The Scurlock Studio," *Washington History* 1, no. 1 (1989), 40–57.

320 *occasionally at the White House:* Ellington also absorbed his father's great capacity for flattery. He addressed his wife as "queen," his daughter as

"princess," and was known for remarks like, "The millions of beautiful snowflakes are a celebration in honor of your beauty." Mark Tucker, *Ellington: The Early Years* (Urbana: University of Illinois Press, 1991), 24.

321 *". . . incipient gangs":* William H. Jones, *Recreation and Amusement Among Negroes in Washington* (Washington, DC: Howard University Press, 1927), 136.

321 *". . . lascivious orgies":* Ibid., 122.

321 *". . . behavior intensified":* Ibid., 131.

322 *". . . street-car tracks":* Jean Toomer, *Cane* (New York: Harper and Row, 1969), 71.

323 *office at the Journal of Negro History:* The *Journal* was the creation of the redoubtable Carter Woodson, doctor of philosophy in American history from Harvard who had been dean of the College of Arts and Sciences at Howard until James Stanley Durkee forced his resignation.

323 *". . . too white Truth":* Arnold Rampersad and David Roessel, eds., *The Collected Poems of Langston Hughes* (New York: Knopf, 1995), 44.

CHAPTER 12: NEW DEAL CITY

Sources for Chapter 12 include Gene Smith, *The Shattered Dream: Herbert Hoover and the Great Depression* (New York: Morrow, 1970); Richard Norton Smith, *An Uncommon Man: The Triumph of Herbert Hoover* (New York: Simon and Schuster, 1984); Albert U. Romasco, *The Poverty of Abundance: Hoover, the Nation, the Depression* (New York: Oxford University Press, 1965); Geoffrey Ward, *A First-Class Temperament: The Emergence of Franklin Roosevelt* (New York: Harper and Row, 1989); Arthur M. Schlesinger Jr., *The Crisis of the Old Order, 1919–1933* (Boston: Houghton Mifflin, 1957); H. W. Brands, *Traitor to His Class: The Privileged Life and Radical Presidency of Franklin Delano Roosevelt* (New York: Doubleday, 2008); Gore Vidal, *Washington, D.C.* (Boston: Little, Brown, 1967); Robert Caro, *The Years of Lyndon Johnson*, vol. 1, *Path to Power* (New York: Knopf, 1982).

325 *all its guises:* See William E. Leuchtenburg, *Herbert Hoover* (New York: Times Books, 2009); George H. Nash, *The Life of Herbert Hoover* (New York: W. W. Norton, 1983–2010).

325 *"Hooveria":* The astronomer was Johan Palisa, who discovered 120 asteroids between 1874 and his death in 1925.

326 *fire . . . Oval Office:* William Seale, *The President's House* (Baltimore: Johns Hopkins University Press, 2008), 2:147–149.

326 *". . . comforts of life":* Herbert Hoover, *Memoirs of Herbert Hoover, vol. 1, Years of Adventure, 1874–1920* (New York: Macmillan, 1951), 132–133.

327 *". . . spend enough":* Edmund William Starling, *Starling of the White House: The Story of the Man Whose Secret Service Detail Guarded Five Presidents from Woodrow Wilson to Franklin D. Roosevelt* (New York: Simon and Schuster, 1946), 263.

327 *antiquated morgue: WP*, November 7, 1932.

327 *". . . their dependents": WP*, March 2, 1932.

328 *plight of the nation:* See Donald J. Lisio, *The President and Protest: Hoover, Conspiracy, and the Bonus Riot* (Columbia: University of Missouri Press, 1974); Schlesinger, *Crisis of the Old Order*, 257–265.

328 *would be dead:* Called by congressional legislation the "Adjusted Service Certificate," the bonus promised to pay each veteran $1 for each day's service in the United States and $1.25 for each day in Europe. Lisio, *President and Protest*, 7.

329 *". . . city dump":* John Dos Passos, *Travel Books and Other Writings* (New York: Library of America, 2003), 401.

329 *words to "America": WP*, June 18, 1932.

330 *1,000 packs of cigarettes:* Evalyn Walsh McLean, *Father Struck It Rich* (Boston: Little, Brown, 1936), 302–303.

330 *worsened by malnutrition: WP*, June 5, 1932; July 5, 10, 14, 15, 28, 1932.

331 *to go forth: WP*, July 27, 1932.

332 *federal military might:* Douglas MacArthur, *Reminiscences* (Annapolis, MD: Naval Institute Press, 1964), 92.

332 *forth on his crusade:* Lisio, *President and Protest*, 193.

332 *disobey his commander in chief:* See ibid., 288.

332 *". . . give orders":* Dwight D. Eisenhower, *At Ease: Stories I Tell to Friends* (Garden City, NY: Doubleday, 1967), 217.

333 *smoke-filled sky:* See James F. Vivian and Jean H. Vivian, "The Bonus March of 1932: The Role of General George Van Horn Moseley," *Wisconsin Magazine of History* 51, no. 1 (1967): 26–36. The authors make the point that "the police and fleeing veterans themselves [rather than the army] put Anacostia to the torch" (32).

334 *". . . service to the Nation":* Franklin Delano Roosevelt, *The Public Papers and Addresses of Franklin D. Roosevelt* (New York: Random House, 1938), 1:17–18.

334 *good cheer:* See William E. Leuchtenburg, *Franklin D. Roosevelt and the New Deal* (New York: Harper and Row, 1963); Arthur M. Schlesinger Jr., *The Coming of the New Deal* (Boston: Houghton Mifflin, 1959).

335 *February ever recorded: WP*, November 18, 23, 26, 1933; December 4, 16, 31, 1933; March 1, 1934.

335 *auction on Thanksgiving Day:* Constance McLaughlin Green, *Washington: Capital City, 1879–1960* (Princeton, NJ: Princeton University Press, 1963), 391.

336 *preached the gospel:* John W. Robinson, "A Song a Shout, and Prayer," in C. Eric Lincoln, ed., *The Black Experience in Religion* (Garden City, NY: Doubleday, 1974), 212ff; Arthur Huff Fauset, *Black Gods of the Metropolis: Negro Religious Cults of the Urban North* (Philadelphia: University of Pennsylvania Press, 1971 [1944]), 22–40.

336 *house at Logan Circle:* Later he moved the church to 1721½ Seventh Street in Shaw.

337 *eroticism in Daddy's services:* Fauset, *Black Gods*, 24, 29. The son of an American Methodist Episcopal minister, Fauset was particularly harsh about

all that he witnessed in Grace's United House of Prayer, including "the definite money emphasis" (24) of the cult and its frequent allusions to sex ("Daddy, you feel so good").

337 *opposite of Daddy Grace:* See Constance McLaughlin Green, *The Secret City: A History of Race Relations in the Nation's Capital* (Princeton, NJ: Princeton University Press, 1967), 238–240; Lillian Ashcraft Webb, *About My Father's Business: The Life of Elder Michaux* (Westport, CT: Greenwood, 1911); *WP*, January 29, 1933, July 17, 1933, September 4, 1933.

338 *spread across the country: Chicago Defender,* April 28, 1934, October 31, 1936. Michaux met with Franklin Roosevelt on two occasions (March 31, 1937, and May 26, 1939), and Eleanor Roosevelt appeared with Michaux on Gene Autry's *Melody Ranch* program. See *Chicago Defender,* January 27, 1940.

338 *apartments opened 1946:* Green, *Secret City,* 239; Pamela Scott and Antoinette J. Lee, *The Buildings of the District of Columbia* (New York: Oxford University Press, 1993), 279; Beth L. Savage, African American Historic Places (Hoboken, NJ: John Wiley, 1994), 143.

339 *"... worthy families":* WP, August 5, 1933.

339 *76 hotels:* George E. Allen, "Washington: A Capital That Went Boom," *Nation's Business* 25, no. 9 (1937): 33.

340 *"... kept out of heaven":* Press conference, August 19, 1941; Franklin Delano Roosevelt, *The Public Papers and Addresses of Franklin D. Roosevelt* (New York: Random House, 1938), 12:77.

340 *"... always have it":* "Radio Address on the Election of Liberals," November 4, 1938, Franklin D. Roosevelt Presidential Library and Museum.

341 *particular aversion:* Franklin D. Roosevelt, Campaign speech at Forbes Field, Pittsburgh, Pennsylvania, October 19, 1932, Franklin D. Roosevelt Presidential Library and Museum.

342 *"... classes of people":* Quoted by Geoffrey Ward, *Before the Trumpet: Young Franklin Roosevelt, 1882–1905* (New York: Harper and Row, 1985).

342 *cash-strapped Soviet Leningrad:* See David Cannadine, *Mellon: An American Life* (New York: Vintage, 2008), 415ff, for an account of Mellon's acquisitions.

343 *"brings out a picture":* Ibid., 532.

343 *would be the "National Gallery":* Ibid., 560.

344 *"give and take":* Ibid., 562.

344 *"... valid gift":* Ibid., 584.

344 *"... modesty of his spirit":* Ibid., 590; *WP*, March 18, 1941.

345 *bound for Great Britain: WP*, March 17, 1941.

345 *"... created it": WP*, March 18, 1941.

CHAPTER 13: WAR CITY

Sources for Chapter 13 include Joseph P. Lash, *Eleanor and Franklin: The Story of Their Relationship, Based on Eleanor Roosevelt's Private Papers* (New York: Norton, 1971); John Q. Barrett, ed., *That Man: An Insider's Portrait of*

Franklin D. Roosevelt (New York: Oxford University Press, 2003); Geoffrey Ward, ed., *Closest Companion: The Unknown Story of the Intimate Friendship Between Franklin Roosevelt and Margaret Suckley* (Boston: Houghton Mifflin, 1995); Robert Caro, *The Years of Lyndon Johnson*, vol. 2, *Means of Ascent* (New York: Knopf, 1990); Robert Caro, *The Years of Lyndon Johnson*, vol. 3, *Master of the Senate* (New York: Knopf, 2002).

347 *June 8, 1939:* See *WP, WS,* and *NYT,* June 8, 9, 10, and 11, 1939.

347 *complete with a naval sword: WP,* June 9, 1939.

348 *capital as well as New York:* Quoted by Stephen M. Leahy, "Even the Irish Kept Quiet: The British Foreign Office and the 1939 Royal Visit to the United States," *New York History* 71, no. 4 (1990): 437.

348 *recital by Marian Anderson: WP,* June 9, 1939. On the afternoon of their arrival, the Roosevelts took the king and queen on a swift thirty-one-mile tour of the capital's sights, including the Lincoln Memorial, the Tidal Basin and cherry trees, the National Cathedral, Rock Creek Park, and Georgetown. The *Post* titled the story "Sovereigns See Washington in a Hurry."

348 *". . . blue-bonneted girls of Texas": WP,* June 10, 1939. The folksy greeter was "Cousin Nat" Patton from Crockett, Texas.

350 *entered World War I: WP,* February 2, 1937; April 4, 1937; October 10, 1937. George Gallup published a regular column in the *Washington Post* reporting on his polls of American public opinion on political and international questions.

350 *by the end of the year: WP,* January 29, 1939.

350 *". . . regular American citizen": WP,* June 9, 1939; June 10, 1939.

350 *approved of his presidency: WP,* October 27, 1939. The headline for Gallup's column: "Roosevelt's Popularity Rises Sharply Since Outbreak of War, More Popular Than Ever."

351 *duration of the war:* See Robert E. Sherwood, *Roosevelt and Hopkins: An Intimate History* (New York: Harper and Brothers, 1948), 228–229; Susan Dunn, *1940: FDR, Wilkie, Lindbergh, Hitler—The Election amid the Storm* (New Haven, CT: Yale University Press, 2013), 277–289.

351 *isolationist fervor:* Dunn, *1940,* 65.

351 *"Roosevelt War": NYT,* May 14, 1941.

351 *forties by noon:* Sources for this description come from *WP,* November 7, 8, 1941.

353 *offices immediately:* See Shirley Povich, in *WP,* December 8, 1941. Povich reported that "as early as the first eight minutes of the opening quarter, the public address system began a field day of its own. Important persons were being paged, too many important persons to make it a coincidence." Although rumors created a "buzzing" through the stands, the general manager of the Washington Redskins refused to allow an announcement of the attack, saying, "We don't want to contribute to any hysteria."

353 *August 1942: Atlanta Constitution,* December 8, 1941; *NYT,* December 8, 1941.

353 *"Oriental flowering trees":* *NYT,* December 11, 1941; *WP,* December 11, 1941.

354 *capitulated in 1945:* *NYT,* December 10, 1941.

355 *refused to visit it:* Doris Kearns Goodwin, *No Ordinary Time* (New York: Simon and Schuster, 1994), 298–299; William Seale, *The President's House* (Baltimore: Johns Hopkins University Press, 2008), 2:224–227.

355 *" . . . decent world":* Goodwin, *No Ordinary Time,* 305–306; Seale, *President's House,* 2:224.

356 *" . . . targets of the Nation":* *WP,* January 3, 1942; November 15, 1941.

356 *Harper's Magazine:* Stevens reprinted his article in *Arms and the People* (New York: Harper and Brothers, 1942), chap. 8, 116–136.

357 *200 conventions:* Figures can be manipulated, of course, and it seems likely that Stevens was reporting the total number of civilians and military personnel. In "Dimensions of Regional Change in the District of Columbia," Carl Abbot reports that in the decade ending in 1940 the number of *civilian* federal workers had jumped from 73,032 to 139,770. See *American Historical Review* 95 no. 5 (1990): 1376. The number of new workers arriving each day might have been higher than 5,000. Jerry Kluttz reported in his "Federal Diary" column in the *Washington Post* that the number was "200 new employees a day or about 6,000 a month" (*WP,* February 14, 1942).

357 *surprised few in the District:* See Constance McLaughlin Green, *Washington: Capital City, 1879–1960* (Princeton, NJ: Princeton University Press, 1963), 40–87; David Brinkley, *Washington Goes to War* (New York: Knopf, 1988); Scott Hart, *Washington at War, 1941–1945* (Englewood Cliffs, NJ: Prentice-Hall, 1970).

357 *shortage of nurses:* *WP,* September 18, 1941; September 23, 1941.

358 *chaotic as the capital:* *WP,* October 4, 1942; May 15, 1943.

358 *train to Cincinnati:* *WP,* January 11, 1942.

359 *National Cemetery in Arlington:* *WP,* December 2, 1941.

360 *after construction began:* Hart, *Washington at War,* 133–135; *WP,* March 7, 8, 10, 14, 30, 1942; April 7, 9, 12, 1942; October 20, 1942; June 14, 1943.

360 *aircraft and rockets:* Hart, *Washington at War,* 38–39; *WP,* July 4, 1941; Brinkley, *Washington Goes to War,* 119. Brinkley reported that the government took over "358 buildings that had previously served other purposes."

360 *male schools:* An exception: American University lost some of its land to the navy. But the military never took the entire campus of a men's institution.

360 *sea duty:* Nina Mikalevsky, *Dear Daughters: A History of Mount Vernon Seminary and College* (Washington, DC: Mount Vernon Seminary and College Alumni Association, 2001), 121–125; *WP,* August 27, 1942; Brinkley, *Washington Goes to War,* 116–117.

361 *" . . . accommodations for colored persons":* *WP,* March 23, 1941; Brinkley, *Washington Goes to War,* 231–235; *Christian Science Monitor,* September 8, 1941.

361 *5,000 by others:* Hart, *Washington at War,* 88–89.

361 *antiquated furnace:* Brinkley, *Washington Goes to War,* 244.

362 *group of four brownstones:* Roselyn Dreshold Silverman, "World War II in Washington: Life at Dissins," *The Record* 22 (1996–1997): 41–48; Leslie T.

Davol, "Shifting Mores: Esther Bubley's World War II Boarding House Photos," *Washington History* 10, no. 2 (1998–1999): 44–62.

362 *". . . marriages, too"*: Silverman, "World War II in Washington," 43.

363 *stylish Scott's Club: WP*, November 30, 1941; March 16, 1960.

364 *entire project: WP*, January 1, 1942; February 5, 1942; March 7, 1943.

364 *capital's major landlord: WP*, October 25, 1942.

365 *"government girls"*: See Cynthia Gueli, *"Girls on the Loose"? Women's Wartime Adventures in the Nation's Capital, 1941–1945* (dissertation, American University, 2006). Gueli provides an excellent perspective on women in Washington during the war.

365 *wedding ring than munitions: NYT*, December 6, 1942. Titled "Uncle Sam's Seminary for Girls," the article is typical of newspaper reports that were circulating around the country.

365 *". . . practically unknown"*: *WP*, October 6, 1944.

366 *". . . search of diversion"*: *WP*, October 14, 1944.

366 *took a job with the Navy Department*: See Mary Herring Wright, *Far from Home: Memories of World War II, and Afterward* (Washington, DC: Gallaudet University Press, 2002).

366 *". . . pig has with a Bible"*: Ibid., 18.

367 *". . . across the river"*: Ibid., 41.

367 *". . . parade for destruction"*: *WP*, May 9, 1940.

367 *"No Third Term Parade"*: *WP*, October 23, 1940.

368 *"Back the Attack"*: *WP*, September 7, 1941.

368 *march in protest up Pennsylvania Avenue*: Goodwin, *No Ordinary Time*, 246–253; Constance McLaughlin Green, *The Secret City: A History of Race Relations in the Nation's Capital* (Princeton, NJ: Princeton University Press, 1967), 254–255; Herbert Garfinkel, *When Negroes March: The March on Washington Movement in the Organizational Politics for FEPC* (New York: Atheneum, 1969); Paula F. Pfeffer, *A. Philip Randolph: Pioneer of the Civil Rights Movement* (Baton Rouge: Louisiana State University Press, 1990).

368 *pass an antilynching bill*: William E. Leuctenburg, *Franklin D. Roosevelt and the New Deal* (New York: Harper and Row, 1963), 103.

369 *". . . two other negroes"*: See "The White House Jim Crow Plan," *The Crisis*, November 1940, 350–351.

369 *". . . in the past"*: Goodwin, *No Ordinary Time*, 250.

370 *". . . no other alternative"*: Ibid., 251.

370 *". . . or national origin"*: *WP*, June 26, 1941; *Chicago Defender*, July 5, 1941.

370 *". . . go on to others"*: Goodwin, *No Ordinary Time*, 253.

371 *benign image . . . to the world*: See Roy Emerson Stryker and Nancy Wood, eds., *In This Proud Land: America, 1935–1943, as Seen in the FSA Photographs* (Greenwich, NY: New York Graphic Society, 1973); "Oral History Interview with John Collier," January 18, 1965, Smithsonian Archives of American Art, www.aaa.si.edu/collections/interviews/oral-history-interview-john-collier-12715#transcript; "Oral History Interview with Roy Emerson Stryker," 1963–1965, Smithsonian Archives of American Art, www.aaa.si.edu/collections/interviews/oral-history-interview-roy-emerson

-stryker-12480#transcript; Gordon Parks, *Voices in the Mirror* (New York: Doubleday, 1990), 80–91.

374 "... *city is very different* ... ": *WP*, November 11, 1944.

CHAPTER 14: WORLD CAPITAL, CONGRESSIONAL TOWN

Sources for Chapter 14 include Ward Just, *City of Fear* (New York: W. W. Norton, 1990); Ward Just, *The Congressman Who Loved Flaubert, and Other Washington Stories* (Boston: Little, Brown, 1973); Michael Nelson, "Ward Just's Washington," *Virginia Quarterly Review* 74 (1998): 205–220; Stephen E. Ambrose, *Eisenhower*, vol. 2, *The President* (New York: Simon and Schuster, 1984); Robert Caro, *The Years of Lyndon Johnson*, vol. 3, *Master of the Senate* (New York: Knopf, 2002); Robert Caro, *The Years of Lyndon Johnson*, vol. 4, *Passage of Power* (New York: Knopf, 2012); Robert Dallek, *An Unfinished Life: John F. Kennedy, 1917–1963* (Boston: Little, Brown, 2003); Arthur M. Schlesinger Jr., *Thousand Days: John F. Kennedy in the White House* (Boston: Houghton Mifflin, 1965); Stephen E. Ambrose, *Nixon*, vol. 2, *The Triumph of a Politician, 1962–1972* (New York: Simon and Schuster, 1989); William P. Jones, *The March on Washington: Jobs, Freedom, and the Forgotten History of Civil Rights* (New York: W. W. Norton, 2013); Sam Smith, *Captive Capital: Colonial Life in Modern Washington* (Bloomington: Indiana University Press, 1974); Robert Parker, *Capitol Hill in Black and White* (New York: Dodd, Mead, 1986).

377 *prosecuted the war:* See *WP*, May 7, 8, 1945; August 14, 15, 1945.

380 *demand for space:* See *WP*, August 16, 1945; August 13, 1948; December 4, 1953; February 26, 1954; March 30, 1954; April 15, 1955; October 5, 1955; April 25, 26, 27, 1958; May 5, 1958; July 24, 1960; September 18, 1960; January 8, 1961; December 16, 1962; May 4, 1963; January 3, 11, 1964; October 4, 1964.

381 *accommodated the wealthy:* See Richard Conn, *Foxhall Community at Half Century: A Fond Look Backwards* (Washington, DC: Foxhall Community Citizens Association, 1979); Kathryn S. Smith, ed., *Washington at Home: An Illustrated History of Neighborhoods in the Nation's Capital* (Baltimore: Johns Hopkins University Press, 2010), chaps. 17, 24.

382 "... *shaped for speed":* Cathy D. Knepper, *Greenbelt, Maryland: A Living Legacy of the New Deal* (Baltimore: Johns Hopkins University Press, 2001); Ralph Steiner and Willard Van Dyke, directors, *The City* (New York World's Fair, 1939), text: Pare Lorentz; narration: Lewis Mumford; music: Aaron Copland.

383 "... *distinct importance":* *The Community Builders Handbook* (Washington, DC: Community Builders' Council of the Urban Land Institute, 1947), 7.

383 *within the District boundaries:* Constance McLaughlin Green, *Washington: Capital City, 1879–1960* (Princeton, NJ: Princeton University Press), chap. 23.

383 "... *within the city walls":* *WP*, August 23, 1949.

384 *". . . beyond the District line":* See *WP*, January 13, 17, 1954; July 14, 1954; January 7, 1955.

384 *"Our Eroding City":* **WP*, April 5, 1955.

386 *"shy away from responsibilities":* Green, *Washington: Capital City*, 429.

387 *wanted the job:* *WP*, January 23, 1941.

387 *". . . white electorate":* J. Douglas Smith, *Managing White Supremacy: Race, Politics, and Citizenship in Jim Crow Virginia* (Chapel Hill: University of North Carolina Press, 2002), 24; John Dinan, *The Virginia State Constitution* (New York: Oxford University Press, 2014), 24, n. 100. Glass's views were well known to blacks. See Francis Saylor, "The Poll Tax Kills Democracy," *The Crisis*, May 1942, 162.

387 *". . . after the war is over":* Antero Pietila, *Not in My Neighborhood: How Bigotry Shaped a Great American City* (Chicago: Ivan R. Dee, 2010), 80.

388 *defeated for reelection in 1938:* Julian M. Pleasants and Buncombe Bob, *The Life and Times of Robert Rice Reynolds* (Chapel Hill: University of North Carolina Press, 2000), 80.

388 *countries in West Africa:* Chester M. Morgan, *Redneck Liberal: Theodore G. Bilbo and the New Deal* (Baton Rouge: Louisiana State University Press, 1985).

388 *". . . control the avenues":* *WP*, March 17, 1944; March 23, 1944.

388 *distillation of his credo:* See Theodore G. Bilbo, *Take Your Choice—Separation or Mongrelization* (Poplarville, MS: Dream House, 1947).

388 *famous citizens:* See "Theodore W. Noyes, 1858–1946," DCHS, *Records* 48/49 (1946/1947): 321–326; Theodore Noyes, *Our National Capital and Its Un-Americanized Americans* (Washington, DC: Washington Loan and Trust, 1951); Arthur John Keeffe, "Neocolonialism in the District of Columbia," *American Bar Association Journal* 57, no. 8 (1971): 793–796.

390 *". . . access to the federal courts":* Noyes, *Our National Capital*, 132.

390 *". . . sends them to war":* Ibid., 90.

390 *"the last plantation":* McMillan chaired the House Committee on the District of Columbia for over twenty years, 1945–1946, 1949–1952, and 1955–1972. See Michael K. Fauntroy, *Home Rule or House Rule? Congress and the Erosion of Local Governance in the District of Columbia* (Dallas: University Press of America, 2003), 40–44; Ronald Walters and Toni-Michelle C. Travis, eds., *Democratic Destiny and the District of Columbia: Federal Politics and Public Policy* (New York: Lexington Books, Rowman and Littlefield, 2010), chaps. 2 and 3.

391 *"a model for the nation":* See David A. Nichols, *A Matter of Justice: Eisenhower and the Beginning of the Civil Rights Revolution* (New York: Simon and Schuster, 2007), 66; Matthew N. Green, Julie Yarwood, Laura Daughtery, and Maria Mazzenga, *Washington 101* (New York: Palgrave Macmillan, 2014), 132–136.

392 *vote in an election for their president:* *WP*, May 2, 1959; January 19, 1960; February 11, 1960; May 11, 1960; June 11, 1960; July 9, 1960; November 8, 1960; January 4, 1961; March 14, 1961; May 21, 1961; March 22, 1963.

393 *influence over the decades:* For information about Justement, see Jennifer Murck's overview to his career at Washington, DC: History Matters website, "Louis Justement's Washington: Overview," http://dc historymatters.org/introduction.php?mod=44. The site contains relevant documents and images of some of his designs. The Library of Congress has images of his plans for Washington at http://cdn.loc.gov/service/pnp /thc/5a44000/5a44200/5a44246r.jpg. Justement's papers are housed at the Gelman Library, George Washington University.

393 *green space:* Justement to Commissioner of Patents, October 7, 1926 (Washington, DC, History Matters).

393 *male enclave:* For information about Smith, see Sarah Booth Conroy, "Sketches of a Designing Woman: Architect Chloethiel Woodard Smith, Leaving Her Mark on Washington," *WP*, November 4, 1989; *Christian Science Monitor*, July 8, 1967. Smith once said, "I'm an architect with a capital A. Being a woman has nothing to do with it." See biography on University of Oregon's School of Architecture and Applied Arts, http://aaa.uoregon .edu/100stories/alumni/chloethiel-woodard-smith. See as well the appreciation by Benjamin Forgey, "On Chloethiel's Corner, *WP*, January 1, 1993.

394 *healthier environment:* Louis Justement, *New Cities for Old* (New York: McGraw-Hill, 1946), plate 24.

395 *". . . waterfront drive":* Ibid., 101.

397 *"stately government buildings":* WP, February 17, 1954.

398 *". . . going to be Washington, DC":* Richard Reeves, *President Kennedy: Profile in Power* (New York: Simon and Schuster, 1994), 504.

398 *". . . show on the Capitol":* Peter J. Ling, *John F. Kennedy* (New York: Routledge, 2013), 164.

400 *". . . freedom of the human spirit":* WP, August 28, 1963. The *Post's* coverage of the march is curious. The newspaper made no mention of Martin Luther King's words "I have a dream."

402 *". . . enjoyed to the nation's capital":* John Hechinger, interview with the author, July 7, 1999.

402 *truckload of watermelons:* Harry S. Jaffe and Tom Sherwood, *Dream City: Race, Power, and the Decline of Washington, D.C.* (New York: Simon and Schuster, 1994), 62.

402 *". . . Washington did not":* Walter Washington, interview with the author, July 7, 1999.

CHAPTER 15: FREE FALL AND AFTER

Sources for Chapter 15 include Matthew N. Green, Julie Yarwood, Laura Daughtery, and Maria Mazzenga, *Washington 101* (New York: Palgrave Macmillan, 2014); Kim Roberts, *Full Moon on K Street: Poems About Washington, DC* (Alexandria, VA: Plan B Press, 2010); Ronald Waters and Toni-Michelle C. Travis, eds., *Democratic Destiny and the District of Columbia: Federal Politics and Public Policy* (Lanham, MD: Lexington Books,

2010); Eric J. Sundquist, *King's Dream* (New Haven, CT: Yale University Press, 2009); Jonetta Rose Barras, *The Last of the Black Emperors: The Hollow Comeback of Marion Barry in the New Age of Black Leaders* (Baltimore: Bancroft Press, 1998); Sam Smith, *Captive Capital: Colonial Life in Modern Washington* (Bloomington: Indiana University Press, 1974). See also Sam Smith's other writings in the Progressive Review Online, especially his "Short History of Black Washington, http://prorev.com/dcblackhist.htm.

406 *"strangled": NYT,* April 12, 1963.
406 *". . . great revolution": WP,* April 1, 1968.
407 *". . . going to be shooting":* Peniel E. Joseph, *Waiting 'Til the Midnight Hour: A Narrative History of Black Power in America* (New York: Henry Holt, 2006), 228.
407 *". . . let them escape": WP,* April 10, 1968.
407 *"I'd resign": WP,* April 26, 1968.
408 *citizen in poverty: WP,* April 1, 1968.
408 *promised later in the year:* See, for example, *WP,* March 5, 1968.
408 *". . . additional civil disorder":* Gordon Keith Mantler, *Power to the Poor: Black-Brown Coalition and the Fight for Economic Justice* (Chapel Hill: University of North Carolina Press, 2013), 122.
408 *". . . poor to come to them": WP,* April 29, 1968.
409 *"to Dr. King": WP,* May 17, 1968.
409 *tempo buildings that had been on the Mall: WP,* May 19, 1968.
409 *black entertainers: WP,* May 18, 1968.
410 *disorder, and chaos: WP,* May 29, 1968.
411 *". . . stack of plywood":* Walter Washington, interview with the author, July 7, 1999.
411 *failure of leadership at the city: WP,* June 9, 1968.
411 *for a sauna: WP,* June 11, 1968.
411 *". . . whether they be black":* Evan Thomas, *Robert Kennedy: His Life* (New York: Simon and Schuster, 2000), 367.
412 *"just a song": WP,* June 21, 1968.
412 *lowest of any major US city:* Walter Washington replied to Nixon's attack by citing the fact that "the District is 19th in serious crime per 1,000 population in metropolitan areas." See *CQ Weekly Report* 26, part 4, October 4, 1968, p. 2639. In Nixon's defense, however, President Johnson's Commission on Crime issued a report in 1967 that said the capital's increase in serious crimes between 1959 and 1965 was double that of cities of comparable size and that the number of homicides had doubled. See *Chicago Tribune,* January 1, 1967.
413 *". . . D.C. crime now":* Stephen E. Ambrose, *Nixon, vol. 2, The Triumph of a Politician, 1962–1972* (New York: Simon and Schuster, 1989), 235.
414 *". . . full of fleas": WP,* March 24, 1970.
417 *". . . Washington in the spring":* Charles DeBenedetti and Charles Chatfield, *An American Ordeal: The Antiwar Movement of the Vietnam Era* (Syracuse: Syracuse University Press, 1990), 305.

417 *government in 1974:* Ibid., 456.

418 " . . . *with a plan":* The agencies included the National Capital Planning Commission, the Redevelopment Land Agency, the Model Cities Commission, the City Council, and the city's Reconstruction and Development Corporation.

422 " . . . *say about me":* Walter Washington, interview with the author, July 7, 1999.

422 *calm and courage were not enough:* Even though the Muslims murdered a reporter in the District Building, and wounded councilman Marion Barry near his heart, Walter Washington declared, "I can't . . . turn it over to criminal elements."

425 *appointed her city administrator:* Thompson understood the gap in their backgrounds and between her Washington and Barry's Memphis. The light-skinned woman came from established Washington; her grandparents had worked in Hoover's White House. The dark-skinned Barry was a "Bama," the name those in the capital's black community gave to their brothers and sisters who moved to the capital from the Deep South. Despite his obvious talents, his electoral victories, and the adulation he received from thousands, Barry felt he did not fit in. As he was spiraling downward, Thompson confronted him, later reporting: "'We work together,' I said, 'but we don't relate as two people. You don't know me and I don't understand you.' I'll never forget his reply: 'You're going to be ok. You're one of the black people who's going to be successful. But I was never meant to succeed. I'm from a poor background. I'll never make it in some people's eyes.' I argued with him: 'You've made it,' I said. 'You're the mayor.' He said, 'You're acceptable. But white people will never accept me.'" Author's interview with Carol Thompson, June 1999.

425 *civic corruption, and the District of Columbia:* See *WP*, January 19 and 20, 1990, for accounts of Barry's arrest and its repurcussions, especially the January 20 article headlined "When Bad Things Happen in a City . . . National Reputation, Residents' Pride Often Take a Beating in the Public Eye."

428 *Emergency Committee on the Transportation Crisis: WP*, September 26, 1967; January 8, 1968.

428 *falling into ruin: WP*, April 24, 1969; June 7, 1969.

429 " . . . *obvious to us all by now": The Interstate System in the District of Columbia: Hearings,* on H.R. 16000, 19th Cong., 2nd sess., April 2, 3, 4, 1968: 6.

429 " . . . *drive to work": WP*, June 4, 1969; June 28, 1969.

430 *construction, and urban planning:* For information on the Metro, see Zachary M. Scharg, *The Great Society Subway: A History of the Washington Metro* (Baltimore: Johns Hopkins University Press, 2006).

INDEX

Noah Throop

TOM LEWIS IS professor emeritus of English at Skidmore College. The author of four books, including *The Hudson*, he lives in Saratoga Springs, New York.